Modern Real Estate Practice
in Pennsylvania

Modern Real Estate Practice
in Pennsylvania

Herbert J. Bellairs
James L. Helsel
Thomas D. Caldwell, Jr.

Fifth Edition

**Real Estate
Education Company**
a division of Dearborn Financial Publishing, Inc.

While a great deal of care has been taken to provide accurate and current information, the ideas, suggestions, general principles and conclusions presented in this text are subject to local, state and federal laws and regulations, court cases and any revisions of same. The reader is thus urged to consult legal counsel regarding any points of law—this publication should not be used as a substitute for competent legal advice.

Library of Congress Cataloging-in-Publication Data

Bellairs, Herbert J.
  Modern real estate practice in Pennsylvania.

  "Developed and endorsed by the Pennsylvania
Association of Realtors."
  Includes index.
  1. Real property—Pennsylvania.   2. Real estate
business—Law and legislation—Pennsylvania.
I. Helsel, James L.   II. Caldwell, Thomas D.
III. Pennsylvania Association of Realtors.   IV. Title.
KFP112.B4   1989   346.74804'37   88-32372
ISBN 0-88462-817-5   347.4806437

Executive Editor: Richard A. Hagle
Sponsoring Editor: Cheryl D. Wilson
Project Editor: Jack L. Kiburz

Real Estate Education Company Series

Anderson & Otto	California Real Estate Practice
Coit	Introduction to Real Estate Law, 3rd Edition
Cyr & Sobeck	Real Estate Brokerage: A Success Guide, 2nd Edition
Deickler	New York Real Estate Exam Guide
Floyd	Real Estate Principles, 2nd Edition, Revised
Friedman & Henszey	Protecting Your Sales Commission: Professional Liability in Real Estate
Fournier	How to Use the HP-18C in Real Estate
Gaddy & Hart	Real Estate Fundamentals, 3rd Edition
Gaines & Coleman	Basic Real Estate Math, 3rd Edition
Gaines & Coleman	Florida Real Estate Principles, Practices & Law
Gaines & Coleman	Salesman Review Outline & Exam Guide for Florida Real Estate Principles, Practices & Law
Gaines & Coleman	Continuing Education for Real Estate Brokers & Salespersons

Galaty, Allaway & Kyle	Modern Real Estate Practice, 11th Edition
	 Study Guide for Modern Real Estate Practice
	 State Supplements to Modern Real Estate Practice
	     Alabama Supplement, 2nd Edition
	     Arizona Supplement, 5th Edition
	     Arkansas Supplement, 3rd Edition
	     Modern Real Estate Principles in California, 2nd Edition (integrated text)
	     Connecticut Supplement, 4th Edition
	     Idaho Supplement, 5th Edition
	     Illinois Supplement, 9th Edition
	     Indiana Supplement
	     Iowa Supplement
	     Kansas Supplement, 2nd Edition
	     Kentucky Supplement, 2nd Edition
	     Louisiana Supplement
	     Maryland Supplement, 5th Edition
	     Massachusetts Supplement, 3rd Edition
	     Michigan Supplement, 2nd Edition

Minnesota Supplement, 5th Edition
Missouri Supplement
New Hampshire Supplement, 3rd Edition
New Jersey Supplement, 5th Edition
Modern Real Estate Practice in New York: For Salespersons and Brokers, 2nd Edition (integrated text)
North Dakota Supplement
Ohio Supplement, 7th Edition
Oklahoma Supplement
Modern Real Estate Practice in Pennsylvania, 5th Edition (integrated text)
South Carolina Supplement
Tennessee Supplement
Modern Real Estate Practice in Texas, 5th Edition (integrated text)
Washington Supplement
Wisconsin Supplement, 5th Edition

Gibson, Karp & Klayman	Real Estate Law, 2nd Edition
Greynolds & Aronofsky	Practical Real Estate Financial Analysis: Using the HP-12C Calculator
Johnson & Irby	Texas Real Estate Law
Kadosh & Beckner	California Real Estate Escrow
Kyle	Property Management, 3rd Edition
Lush & Sirota	California Real Estate Finance
Lush, Reilly & Vitousek	California Real Estate Exam Guide
Lyon & Rosenauer	How to Prepare for the Texas Real Estate Exam, 4th Edition
Mettling	Modern Residential Financing Methods: Tools of the Trade
Pivar	California Real Estate Law
Pivar	Classified Secrets, 2nd Edition
Pivar	Power Real Estate Listing, 2nd Edition
Pivar	Power Real Estate Selling, 2nd Edition
Pivar	Real Estate Ethics, 2nd Edition

Pivar	Real Estate Guide for the Licensing Exam (ASI), 2nd Edition
Developed by Real Estate Education Company	Professional Real Estate Selling Skills
Developed by Real Estate Education Company in Conjunction with Grubb & Ellis Company	Successful Industrial Real Estate Brokerage, 3rd Edition
Developed by Real Estate Education Company in Conjunction with Grubb & Ellis Company	Successful Leasing & Selling of Office Property, 3rd Edition
Developed by Real Estate Education Company in Conjunction with Grubb & Ellis Company	Successful Leasing & Selling of Retail Property, 3rd Edition
Reilly	Agency Relationships in Real Estate
Reilly	Language of Real Estate, 3rd Edition
Reilly & Vitousek	Questions and Answers to Help You Pass the Real Estate Exam, 3rd Edition
Rosenauer	Effective Real Estate Sales and Marketing, 2nd Edition
Sager	Guide to Passing the Real Estate Exam, 3rd Edition (ACT)
Sirota	Essentials of Real Estate Investment, 3rd Edition
Sirota	Essentials of Real Estate Finance, 5th Edition
Sirota & Eubanks	Texas Real Estate Finance
Smith & Gibbons	The Real Estate Education Company Real Estate Exam Manual, 4th Edition (ETS)

Stapleton, Moran & Williams	California Real Estate Principles
Stone	New Home Sales
Ventolo	Residential Construction
Ventolo, Allaway & Irby	Mastering Real Estate Mathematics, 5th Edition
Ventolo & Williams	Fundamentals of Real Estate Appraisal, 4th Edition
Williams	California Real Estate Appraisal
Williams & Reilly	Agency Relationships in California Real Estate

Contents

21   **Closing the Real Estate Transaction**   **322**

About the Authors

Herbert J. Bellairs, GRI, CRS, Reading, Pennsylvania, is a graduate of the Wharton School, University of Pennsylvania, where he majored in Real Estate. He has taught real estate courses at Penn State, Albright College and the Graduate REALTORS® Institute. Mr. Bellairs has operated his own realty firm since 1953. He is past president of the Greater Reading Board of REALTORS®, Pennsylvania Association of REALTORS® and the Pennsylvania REALTORS® Education Foundation. In 1983, he was named Pennsylvania REALTOR-of-the-Year. He also served as Regional Vice President for the National Association in 1983 and Treasurer in 1987 and 1988.

James L. Helsel, MAI, SRPA, CCIM, SIR, of Middletown, Pennsylvania, is a graduate of Harrisburg Academy and attended Franklin and Marshall and Gettysburg Colleges. Mr. Helsel is president of Helsel, Incorporated, REALTORS®, specialists in commercial and industrial property. He is past president of the Greater Harrisburg Board of REALTORS® and the Pennsylvania Association of REALTORS® and was Pennsylvania REALTOR-of-the-Year in 1973. He also served as treasurer for the national association in 1979 and 1980. He is a trustee of the Pennsylvania REALTORS® Education Foundation and is on the faculty of the REALTORS® Institute.

Thomas D. Caldwell, Jr., of Harrisburg, Pennsylvania, is a graduate of Dickinson College and Dickinson Law School. He is a partner in Caldwell, Clouser and Kearns and is the counsel for the Pennsylvania Association of REALTORS®. He has been admitted to the Pennsylvania Supreme and Superior Courts, Dauphin County Court, Federal District Court, Middle District of Pennsylvania and District of Columbia. Attorney Caldwell was a member of the House of Representatives from 1965 to 1966, is past president of the Dauphin County Bar Association and served as a member of the Board of Governors of the Pennsylvania Bar Association.

The authors wish to express their deepest appreciation to Laurel McAdams, GRI, who served as Development Writer on this latest edition. Ms. McAdams is the real estate program coordinator and an instructor at Robert Morris College in Pittsburgh. She serves on the board of directors of the Pennsylvania Association of REALTORS® and is chairman of the Voluntary Education Advisory Committee to the Pennsylvania Real Estate Commission.

For their assistance in the development of the Fifth Edition of *Modern Real Estate Practice in Pennsylvania,* the authors would like to thank the following people:

Barbara Korns, Real Estate Institute of Temple University
Andrew V. Olock, Olock Realty Company
R. Dennis McClelland, Director, Realtors Educational Institute
William G. Rech, Bucks County Community College
John W. Fielding, III, GRI, Delaware County Board of REALTORS®
Thomas E. LoDolce, Director of Real Estate Studies, Financial Estate Institute
Ben Simon, Berks Real Estate Institute

Michael B. Dunphy, CRB, CRS, GRI, American Real Estate Academy, Inc.
Terry Romanik, Penn State University

Val Pasquarella, Jr., Greater Philadelphia Realty Board
Holbrook M. Bunting, Jr., Delaware County Community College
Barbara G. Samet, CRS, CRB, DREI, Pocono Real Estate Academy
James J. Skindzier, Career Growth Enterprises, Inc.
Joseph G. Kandala, CRB, GRI, Associate Instructor
John Paul Weber, Century 21—Weber Realty, Inc.
Nicholas A. Sabatine, Patt, White Co., Realtors, *Better Homes and Gardens*

Thanks are also extended to John C. Becker, James H. Koch, John E. Isselmann, Robert Freeman, Michael Frolove, Brian Gross, Ken Lusht and Edward Pauksta for their contributions to earlier editions of the book.

Special credit is extended to the following for permission to use forms: All-State Legal Supply Company, American Land Title Association, Chicago Title Insurance Company, George E. Cole and Co., P. O. Naly Company, Alfred B. Patton Company, Professional Publishing Corporation and Pennsylvania Association of REALTORS®. These sample forms may not be applicable to all jurisdictions and are subject to pertinent changes in the law.

For their support and guidance, the authors wish to thank the staff of the Pennsylvania Association of REALTORS®, in particular Mike Bernardo, Executive Vice President, and Tana Waitkavicz, Director of Education.

Finally, the authors would like to extend their appreciation to Cheryl Wilson, Rich Hagle, Margaret Maloney and Jack Kiburz of Real Estate Education Company for their assistance in the production of this Fifth Edition.

Preface

Thousands of professional men and women have studied *Modern Real Estate Practice in Pennsylvania* since its first printing in 1975. Although its primary use as a text has been to prepare candidates for state broker and salesperson licensing examinations, many others have studied the book as part of college and university degree programs in real estate and related fields. Still others have read it because of an interest in personal investment or because they hold positions close to the real estate profession in banks, savings and loan associations, mortgage firms, insurance companies, property management firms or corporate real estate departments.

Through the years, the real estate industry has placed a growing emphasis on education and professionalism. State licensing examinations and educational requirements for prospective brokers and salespeople have become more sophisticated since the first edition of this book, requiring the student to demonstrate knowledge and understanding of increasingly technical information. In preparing the Fifth Edition of *Modern Real Estate Practice in Pennsylvania,* the authors have revised and updated the text to meet these requirements and to keep pace with recent trends and developments, particularly in the areas of real estate finance, appraising and taxation.

Modern Real Estate Practice in Pennsylvania consists of 24 chapters that cover the broad subject of real estate in general, together with specific real estate laws and operating procedures applicable to the state of Pennsylvania. Opinions were solicited from real estate educators throughout the state regarding the order of chapter presentation. Their suggestions confirmed that the Fifth Edition would be enhanced by reordering the chapters to present a more logical development of real estate concepts. In addition the finance chapter has been divided: "Real Estate Financing" includes the principles and instruments of finance; "Financing the Real Estate Transaction" discusses costs of credit and specific loan programs. As in previous editions, the chapters may be taught or studied in the order presented or may be adapted to any class outline or lesson plan.

Modern Real Estate Practice in Pennsylvania can easily be adapted to the outlines prescribed by the Pennsylvania Real Estate Commission for Real Estate Fundamentals and Real Estate Practice. The suggested topics and corresponding chapters are listed below.

Real Estate Fundamentals is designed to acquaint the student with the language, principles and laws that govern real estate; the concepts of land, property, rights in realty and title; and the laws and methods of evidencing and conveying ownership.

Basic Concepts	Chapters 1, 2
Property Development	Chapters 3, 4
Property Description	Chapter 5
Interests and Holdings	Chapters 6, 7, 8
Contracts	Chapter 9

Real Estate Practice is designed to acquaint the student with all facets of the real estate business, including fields of specialization; the activities, ethics and legal responsibilities of a real estate licensee, with emphasis on residential brokerage; the sequence of events in a transaction; and the documents and math involved.

Included in the Fifth Edition are an appendix explaining the state real estate licensing exam; a Mathematics Review, designed to help math-shy students with basic real estate computations; a Residential Construction Appendix, containing many illustrations that will assist the student in identifying important building-component terminology; the Pennsylvania Real Estate Licensing and Registration Act; and a Glossary of Real Estate Terms, providing definitions of hundreds of real estate terms for easy review.

A *Study Guide for Modern Real Estate Practice* contains additional review questions and study problems to further assist the student in his or her real estate education. In addition, a comprehensive Instructor's Manual and many helpful in-class transparencies are available to instructors as companions to this text. Contact Real Estate Education Company for further details about these materials.

Any comments on this text should be directed to Anita Constant, Senior Vice President, Real Estate Education Company, 500 North Dearborn, Chicago, IL 60610.

1

Introduction to Modern Real Estate Practice

Key Terms

Attorney
Broker
Bundle of legal rights
Common law
Judicial precedent
Pennsylvania Real Estate Licensing and Registration Act
Realtist
REALTOR®
REALTOR-Associate®
Salesperson
Seven sources of law

Overview

The real estate business is "big" business. Hundreds of thousands of men and women in the United States and Canada work in some aspect of the industry as brokers, salespeople, appraisers or property managers, as well as in other areas of specialization. They aid buyers, sellers and investors in making decisions that involve billions of dollars in property each year. In addition to people and money, real estate is a big business in terms of laws and regulations. Because real estate is one of the most heavily regulated markets, the real estate practitioner must be familiar with many sources of law on the federal, state and local levels. This chapter will introduce you to the industry in general, as well as to the many legal considerations affecting today's real estate practitioner.

Real Estate Transactions

The purchase of real estate involves an entirely different type of transaction from the purchase of personal property, such as groceries, clothing, fuel, automobiles or television sets. Although every type of sales transaction creates a change of ownership involving certain relatively simple legal problems, *even the simplest of real estate transactions brings into play a body of complex laws.*

Real property (which we commonly refer to as real estate) has often been described as a **bundle of legal rights.** In other words, a purchaser of real estate is actually buying the rights of ownership previously held by the seller. These *rights of ownership* (see Figure 1.1) include the right of *possession,* the right to *control the property* within the framework of the law, the right of *enjoyment* (to use the property in any legal manner), the right of *exclusion* (to keep others from entering or occupying the property), and the right of *disposition* (to be able to sell or otherwise convey the property). Within these ownership rights are included further rights to will, devise, mortgage, encumber, cultivate, explore, lease, license, dedicate, give away, share, trade or exchange.

**Figure 1.1
Bundle of Legal Rights**

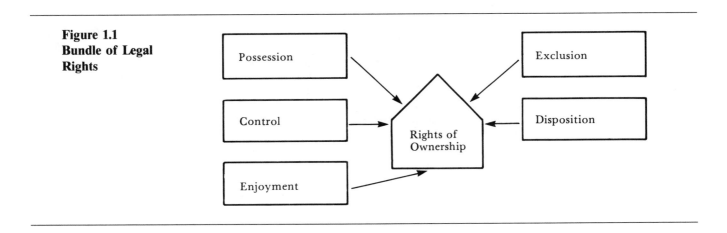

Although ownership under these rights is extensive, it is diminished by limitations on the use of these rights through public and private restrictions. When a person acquires ownership of real estate, this ownership is subject to any rights that *others* may have in the property or rights that the prior *owner* may have reserved for himself or herself. For example, the lending institution that holds a seller's mortgage has the right to force a sale of the property if the loan is not repaid. Likewise, a person may sell real estate while retaining the rights to certain minerals or natural resources located on or beneath the surface of the land. The various rights in real estate will be discussed in chapters 3 and 6.

Buying real estate is usually the biggest financial transaction of a person's life. The buyer pays more cash, undertakes more debt and has a deeper personal interest in this transaction than in any other purchase made during his or her lifetime.

When a person sells real estate, the situation is similar. The real estate is likely to have been that person's biggest single investment, not only in terms of money but also of work. Of course, there are people to whom the sale or purchase of real estate is a routine matter; but for most people, it can be a very important, complicated and perhaps confusing affair.

At the center of this important and sensitive transaction, generally there is a middleman—the real estate **broker.** A real estate **salesperson** works on behalf of the broker. The broker and the salesperson generally represent the seller and seek a buyer for the property. Once they have found a prospective buyer, they bring the parties together. Then both seller and buyer look to the broker and their respective lawyers to guide and facilitate the transfer of the real estate from one party to the other.

Real Estate Law

The average citizen has very little notion of the nature of law. People usually think of laws as nothing more than rules laid down by the state to govern their conduct. *However, real estate brokers and salespeople must have a broader and better understanding of law and how various laws affect real estate.*

Sources of Real Estate Law

There are generally **seven sources of law** in the United States, all of which affect the ownership and transfer of real estate (see Figure 1.2). These are: the *Constitution of the United States; laws passed by Congress; federal regulations adopted by the various agencies and commissions created by Congress; state constitutions; laws passed by state legislatures; ordinances passed by cities, towns and other local governments; and court decisions.*

**Figure 1.2
Sources of Real
Estate Law**

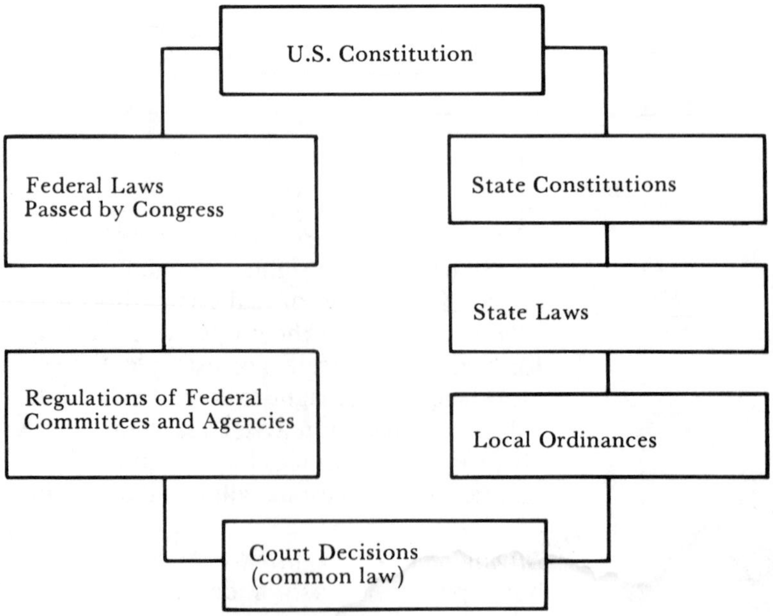

The primary purpose of the *U.S. Constitution and the individual state constitutions* is to establish the rights of citizens and delineate the limits of governmental authority. In a few areas of the country, municipalities also are empowered to set up local constitutions or charters with similar effects. Because they set down only broad provisions, such constitutions have only an indirect influence on the real estate business.

Laws passed by Congress and by state and local legislative bodies may establish specific provisions on any issue or they may simply set broad standards of conduct and establish administrative and enforcement agencies. Generally, these agencies have the authority to adopt regulations and procedures to expand on the law and to carry out the established standards. These regulations have the effect of law.

Governmental agencies that enact rules and regulations range from the Federal Housing Administration through state real estate commissions to local zoning boards. These regulations are a means of implementing and enforcing legislative acts; they provide detailed information on legal and illegal actions and practices and they designate penalties and violations.

Court decisions of federal, state and municipal courts serve to clarify and interpret laws, regulations and constitutional provisions. By applying and interpreting the laws in relation to a specific event, a court decision expands the meaning of the law. For example, an attorney draws up what appears to be a valid contract under the provisions of state law. If the court disallows the contract, it will render an opinion as to why the contract does not fulfill the legal requirements for such a document. Future contracts in that state will then be based on the **judicial precedent** of the requirements established by prior court decisions as well as on the statutes governing contracts.

The courts are not always bound by the established precedent, however. Courts in one jurisdiction (area of authority) may not be bound by the decisions of courts in other jurisdictions. In addition, a court with superior authority in its jurisdiction may, at its discretion, reverse the ruling of a lower court.

The **common law** is the body of rules and principles founded on custom, usage and the decisions and opinions of the courts. It is derived mainly from practices developed in England and, as it applies to the United States, dates back to the practices that were in effect at the time of the American Revolution. Today the common law includes not only custom but the decisions of courts.

Laws Affecting Real Estate Practice

The general sources of law encompass a number of specific areas that are important to the real estate practitioner. These include the *law of contracts,* the *general property law,* the *law of agency* (which covers the obligations of a broker to the person who engages his or her services) and the *real estate license law,* all of which will be discussed in this text.

A person engaged in the real estate business need not be an expert on real estate law, but should have a knowledge and understanding of the basic principles of the law under which he or she operates. A real estate professional must be able to recognize the technical legal problems involved in transactions to be negotiated and should appreciate the necessity of referring such problems to a competent attorney. *An* **attorney** *is a person trained and licensed to represent another person in court, to prepare documents defining or transferring rights in property, or to* *give advice or counsel on matters of law.* Brokers and salespeople must be aware of their limitations in such areas.

Extreme care should be taken in handling all phases of a real estate transaction. Carelessness in handling the documents connected with a real estate sale can result in expensive legal actions. In many cases, costly court actions could have been avoided if the parties handling negotiations had exercised greater care and employed competent legal counsel.

Real estate license laws. Because real estate brokers and salespeople are engaged in the business of handling other people's real estate and money, the need for regulation of their activities has long been recognized. In an effort to protect the public from fraud, dishonesty or incompetence in the buying and selling of real estate, all 50 states, the District of Columbia and all Canadian provinces have passed laws that require real estate brokers and salespeople to be licensed. The first *real estate license law* was passed in California in 1917. Pennsylvania's first license law was enacted in 1929. More recently, the **Pennsylvania Real Estate Licensing Act** was passed in 1980. In 1984, the name of the act was amended to **Pennsylvania Real Estate Licensing and Registration Act.** The license laws of the various states are similar in many respects but differ in the details of their requirements.

Under these laws, a person must obtain a license in order to engage in the real estate business. In most cases, the applicant must possess certain stated personal and educational qualifications and must pass an examination to prove an adequate knowledge of the business. In addition, to qualify for license renewal and continue in business, the licensee must follow certain prescribed standards of conduct in the operation of his or her business. Certain states also require licensees to complete continuing education courses. Chapter 14 describes more fully the specific provisions of the Pennsylvania Real Estate Licensing and Registration Act and the required standards. See Appendix D for the current license law.

| The Real Estate Business Is "Big" Business | Billions of dollars' worth of real estate is sold each year in the United States. In addition to this great volume of annual sales, there are rental collections by real estate management firms, appraisals of properties ranging from vacant land to modern office and apartment buildings, and the lending of money through mortgage loans on real estate. |

Hundreds of thousands of people are professionally engaged in the real estate business. Full-time real estate practitioners include not only brokers, salespeople, appraisers, managers and mortgage lenders; they also include building managers and superintendents who handle real estate belonging to industrial firms, banks, trust companies, insurance firms and other businesses, as well as state, local and federal governments.

The need for trained real estate specialists is increasing. As the technical aspects of real estate activities become more complex, real estate offices require an increasing number of people properly trained to handle and solve real estate problems. Many professional and business people and organizations, such as attorneys, banks, trust companies, abstract and title insurance companies, architects, surveyors, accountants and tax specialists, are also highly dependent on the real estate specialist.

Professional Organizations

The real estate business has many active, well-organized trade organizations, the largest being the NATIONAL ASSOCIATION OF REALTORS® (NAR). Founded in 1908 as the National Association of Real Estate Boards, this national organization sponsors many specialized institutes offering professional designations upon completion of required courses for brokers, salespeople, appraisers, managers and other real estate professionals. (Such institutes and designations are listed in Table 1.1.) The majority of local real estate associations throughout the U.S. and Canada are affiliated with the NAR. Active members of these affiliated state associations and local boards subscribe to the Association's strict Code of Ethics and are entitled to be known as **REALTORS®**. The term REALTOR® is a registered mark. Through its many specialized institutes, the NAR serves the interests of its members by keeping them informed of developments in their field, publicizing the services of members, improving standards and practices and recommending or taking positions on public legislation or regulations affecting the operations of members and member firms. Some boards offer a separate category of membership, **REALTOR-Associate®**, to salespeople affiliated with an active REALTOR® and actively engaged in the real estate business as employees or independent contractors.

Table 1.1
NATIONAL ASSOCIATION OF REALTORS® Institutes and Professional Designations

Institute	Designation(s)
NAR—NATIONAL ASSOCIATION OF REALTORS®	GRI—Graduate, REALTORS® Institute
AIREA—American Institute of Real Estate Appraisers	MAI—Member, Appraisal Institute
ASREC—American Society of Real Estate Counselors	RM—Residential Member
	CRE—Counselor in Real Estate
RLI—REALTORS® Land Institute	AFLM—Accredited Farm and Land Member
IREF—International Real Estate Federation	CIPS—Certified International Property Specialist
IREM—Institute of Real Estate Management	CPM®—Certified Property Manager
	AMO®—Accredited Management Organization
	ARM®—Accredited Resident Manager
RESSI—Real Estate Securities and Syndication Institute	SRS—Specialist in Real Estate Securities
RNMI—REALTORS National Marketing Institute®	CCIM—Certified Commercial-Investment Member
	CRB—Certified Residential Broker
	CRS—Certified Residential Specialist
SIOR—Society of Industrial and Office REALTORS®	SIOR—full member
WCR—Women's Council of REALTORS®	LTG—Leadership Training Graduate

National Association of Real Estate Brokers. In addition to the NAR, there are also many independent real estate boards and other professional associations that were organized to set high standards for their members, promote their members' best interests and educate the public about the real estate profession. Among them is the National Association of Real Estate Brokers, founded in 1947. Its membership includes individual members, as well as brokers who belong to state and local real estate boards that are affiliated with the organization. The members are known as **Realtists** and subscribe to a code of ethics that sets professional standards for all Realtists.

Summary   Even the simplest real estate transactions involve a complex body of laws. A purchase of real estate involves not only the purchase of the land itself but also the *legal rights* to use the land in certain ways that were formerly held by the seller.

The *seven sources of law* in the United States are the U.S. Constitution, laws passed by Congress, federal regulations, state constitutions, laws passed by state legislatures, local ordinances and court decisions.

Common law in the United States evolved predominantly from custom and usage in early England. Gradually the basis of common law expanded to include prior court decisions as well. Much of real property law is founded in common law.

The real estate business is a dynamic industry employing hundreds of thousands of professional men and women. Every state and Canadian province has some type of *licensing requirement* for local real estate brokers and salespeople.

Questions

1. Rules and regulations adopted by government agencies:
   I. are used to implement and enforce legislative acts.
   II. usually outline specific illegal acts and set down penalties for violations.
   a. I only   c. both I and II
   b. II only   d. neither I nor II

2. Professional associations of specialists in various fields of real estate activity were organized to serve the interests of their members. Which of the following is (are) generally a service expected of such organizations?
   a. keeping members informed of developments in their field
   b. improving standards and practices
   c. providing a clearinghouse of information
   d. all of the above

3. There are seven sources of law. Which of the following is (are) among them?
   I. court decisions
   II. local ordinances
   a. I only   c. both I and II
   b. II only   d. neither I nor II

4. Laws passed by the Congress and various state legislatures may:
   a. establish specific provisions on an issue.
   b. set precedents for future laws.
   c. empower administrative agencies to carry out the provisions of the law.
   d. a and c

5. Court decisions:
   a. clarify and interpret laws.
   b. apply the law to the facts of a specific case.
   c. establish judicial precedents.
   d. all of the above

6. Areas of law that are of particular importance to the real estate broker include:
   a. the law of contracts.
   b. the law of agency.
   c. the general property law.
   d. all of the above

7. The legal concept of precedent:
   I. grew out of the common law.
   II. must always be followed by judges when formulating court decisions.
   a. I only   c. both I and II
   b. II only   d. neither I nor II

8. Constitutional provisions:
   I. establish the rights of citizens and delineate government authority.
   II. may have a direct influence on real estate activities.
   a. I only   c. both I and II
   b. II only   d. neither I nor II

9. Real estate is often referred to as a *bundle of legal rights*. Which of the following is *not* among these rights?
   a. right of exclusion
   b. right to use the property for illegal purposes
   c. right of enjoyment
   d. right to sell or otherwise convey the property

10. When a person purchases real estate from a seller:
    I. that person is actually buying the legal rights to the property that were previously held by the seller.
    II. the seller may legally retain one or more of his or her rights of ownership.
    a. I only   c. both I and II
    b. II only   d. neither I nor II

11. The purchase of real estate:
    a. is generally the largest financial investment in a person's lifetime.
    b. involves a complex body of laws.
    c. is usually facilitated by a real estate broker.
    d. all of the above

12. Real estate license laws:
    I. are in effect in all states.
    II. were passed to protect the public from the possible fraud, dishonesty and incompetence of unscrupulous brokers and salespeople.
        a. I only   c. both I and II
        b. II only   d. neither I nor II

13. Common law:
    I. is derived from practices developed in the Spanish Empire.
    II. as it applies today, includes both customs and court decisions.
        a. I only   c. both I and II
        b. II only   d. neither I nor II

14. The designation REALTOR® refers to:
    a. a registered mark.
    b. any licensed real estate broker.
    c. an active member of a local board of the NATIONAL ASSOCIATION OF REALTORS® who subscribes to the Association's Code of Ethics.
    d. a and c

15. Government agencies issue rules and regulations in order to:
    a. create control activity.
    b. implement legislative acts.
    c. expedite adherence to the laws.
    d. confuse the public action.

16. As a real estate professional, a real estate licensee should:
    I. be able to recognize the technical legal problems involved in transactions.
    II. appreciate the necessity of referring such problems to a competent attorney.
        a. I only   c. both I and II
        b. II only   d. neither I nor II

2

Real Property

Key Terms
Air rights
Chattel
Fixture
Improvement
Land
Parcel
Personal property
Real estate
Real property
Severance
Subsurface rights
Surface rights
Trade fixture (chattel fixture)
Uniqueness (Nonhomogeneity)

Overview
Will Rogers is often quoted as saying, "Buy land—they ain't making any more of the stuff!" The preamble to the NATIONAL ASSOCIATION OF REALTORS® Code of Ethics begins with the words, "Under all is the land...." We see it, touch it and refer to it every day, but what exactly is land? When we own it, do we own just the ground beneath our feet, and if so, how deep does this ownership go? What about the trees we sit under and the air we breathe—are these part of the land also? This chapter will discuss the nature and characteristics of real estate, as well as the similarities and distinctions among land, real estate, and real property. In addition, this chapter will illustrate the distinctions between real estate and personal property and will show how an item of personal property can be converted into real estate and vice versa.

Land, Real Estate and Real Property

You have probably heard the words *land, real estate* and *real property* used synonymously to describe the same commodity. While the terms are often used interchangeably, there are subtle but important differences in their technical meanings.

Land

Land is defined as *the earth's surface extending downward to the center of the earth and upward to infinity, including things permanently attached by nature, such as trees and water* (see Figure 2.1).

The term *land* thus refers to more than just the surface of the earth. It includes the underlying soil and things that are naturally attached to the land, such as boulders and growing things. Land also includes the minerals and substances below the earth's surface together with the airspace above the land up to infinity. The surface, subsurface and airspace can be owned by different individuals as surface rights, subsurface rights and air rights.

A specific tract of land is commonly referred to as a **parcel.**

Figure 2.1
Land/Real Estate

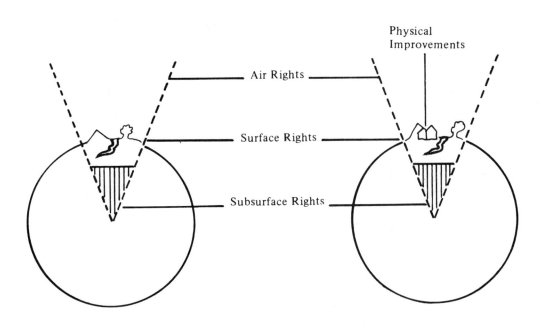

Air Rights

Physical Improvements

Surface Rights

Subsurface Rights

Earth's surface to the center of the earth and the airspace above the land, including the trees and water.

Real Estate
Land plus permanent man-made additions

Real Estate

Real estate is defined as *the earth's surface extending downward to the center of the earth and upward into space, including all things permanently attached to it by nature or by people* (see Figure 2.1).

The term *real estate* is somewhat broader than the term *land* and includes not only the physical components of the land as provided by nature but also all man-made permanent improvements on and to the land. An **improvement** applies to the buildings erected on the land as well as to streets, utilities, sewers and other man-made additions to the property.

Real Property

Real property is defined as *the earth's surface extending downward to the center of the earth and upward into space, including all things permanently attached to it by nature or by man, as well as the interests, benefits and rights inherent in the ownership of real estate* (see Figure 2.2).

**Figure 2.2
Real Property**

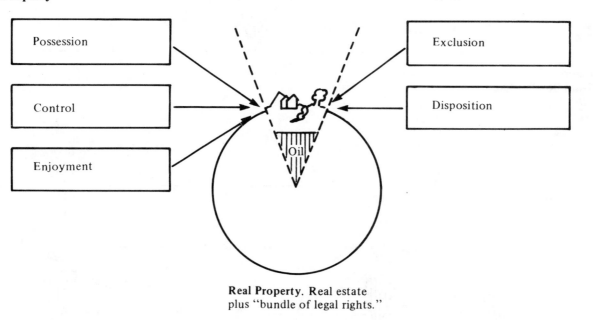

Real Property. Real estate
plus "bundle of legal rights."

The term *real property* is broader than land or real estate: it refers to the physical surface of the land, what lies below it, what lies above it and what is permanently attached to it, as well as to the *legal rights of real estate ownership*. As discussed in Chapter 1, this *bundle of legal rights* includes the rights of possession, control, enjoyment, exclusion and disposition, among others.

In Practice...

When people talk about buying or selling homes, office buildings, land and the like, they usually call these things real estate. *For all practical purposes, the term is synonymous with* real property, *as defined here. Thus, in everyday usage,* real estate *includes the legal rights of ownership specified in the definition of real property. Sometimes the term* realty *is used instead.*

Subsurface and air rights. As you can see, the concept of real estate ownership involves more than **surface rights**—the rights to use the surface of the earth—it also includes subsurface rights and air rights.

Subsurface rights are the rights to the natural resources lying below the earth's surface. A transfer of surface rights may be accomplished without transfer of subsurface rights.

For example, a landowner may sell to an oil company rights to any oil and gas found in the land. Later the same landowner can sell the remaining interest to a purchaser and reserve the rights to all coal that may be found in the land. After these sales, three parties have ownership interests in this real estate: (1) the oil company owns all oil and gas, (2) the seller owns all coal and (3) the purchaser owns the rights to the remainder of the real estate.

Figure 2.3
Air Rights

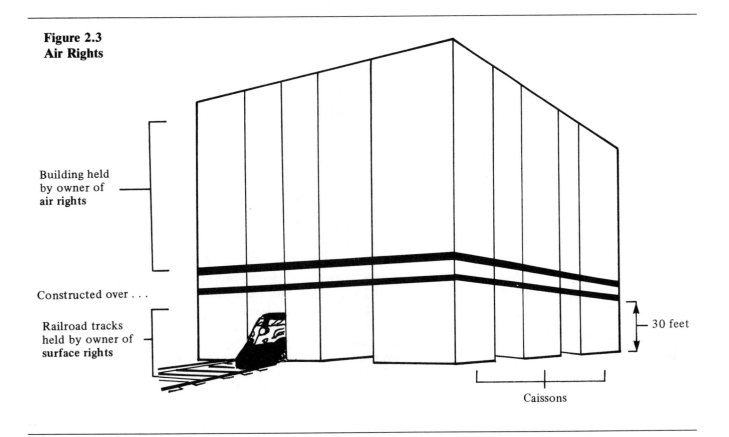

Building held by owner of **air rights**

Constructed over . . .

Railroad tracks held by owner of **surface rights**

30 feet

Caissons

As with the rights to minerals that lie below the surface of the land, the rights to use the air above the land may be sold or leased independently of the land itself. Such **air rights** are an increasingly important part of real estate, particularly in large cities, where air rights over railroads have been purchased to construct huge office buildings like the Pan-Am Building in New York City and the Merchandise Mart in Chicago. For the construction of such a building, the developer must purchase not only the air rights above the land but also numerous small portions of the actual land in order to construct the building's foundation supports, called *caissons*. The caisson locations are regularly spaced, and the caisson portions usually are planned to meet the lower limit of the airspace about 30 feet or so above the land so that the finished foundation supports do not interfere with the operation of trains over the surface of the railroad's remaining land ownership (see Figure 2.3).

Until the development of airplanes, a property's air rights were considered to be unlimited. Today, however, the ownership of air rights is generally considered to extend upward only so far as is reasonably necessary for the enjoyment of the property. This is a subjective standard, primarily dependent on the location of the property. Governments and airport authorities often purchase air rights adjacent to an airport to provide glide patterns for air traffic. Pennsylvania law provides that local government authorities can obtain aviation easements (air rights) over land surrounding airports in order to prevent interference with takeoffs and landings.

With the continuing development of solar electric power, air rights—more specifically, *sun rights*—may be redefined by the courts. They may consider tall buildings that block sunlight from smaller solar-powered buildings to be interfering with the smaller buildings' sun rights.

In summary, one parcel of real property may be owned by many people, each holding a separate right to a different part of the real estate. There may be: (1) an owner of the surface rights, (2) an owner of the subsurface mineral rights, (3) an owner of the subsurface gas and oil rights and (4) an owner of the air rights.

In Practice...

When any subsurface rights are transferred or leased to others, the surface owner retains ownership to the remaining subsurface and surface ownership. The surface owner cannot interfere with the enjoyment of rights by the subsurface owner. Likewise, the subsurface owner cannot interfere with the rights of enjoyment of the surface owner. The rights of each must be equally respected. The purchaser should be aware of the status of subsurface ownership.

Many parts of Pennsylvania are rich in minerals, particularly coal. The possibility of mine subsidence should be considered by a purchaser. In areas where bituminous coal has been found, Pennsylvania law requires a seller to certify to a purchaser whether a structure on the land is entitled to support from the underlying coal. If the seller cannot certify to this right of support, then the purchaser must be informed that there is no protection to the structure against subsidence due to mining operations. A structure may be protected from damage due to subsidence by the owner obtaining mine subsidence insurance. This insurance is separate from the normal coverage in a homeowner's insurance policy.

Real Estate versus Personal Property

Property may be classified as either real estate or personal property. As you know, real estate is defined as a part of the earth, including the permanent additions or growing things attached to it, the airspace above it and the minerals below it.

Personal property, on the other hand, sometimes referred to as "personalty," is considered to be *all property that does not fit the definition of real estate.* Thus, personal property has the unique characteristic of being *movable.* Items of personal property, also referred to as **chattels,** include such tangibles as chairs, tables, clothing, money, bonds and bank accounts (see Figure 2.4).

It is possible to change an item of real estate to personal property by **severance.** For example, a growing tree is real estate; but if the owner cuts down the tree and thereby severs it from being permanently attached to the earth, it becomes personal property. Similarly, an owner can pick an apple from a tree or cut the wheat in a field on his or her property.

Trees and crops are generally considered in two classes: (1) trees, perennial bushes, and grasses that do not require annual cultivation are considered real estate (fructus naturales, fruits of nature); and (2) seasonal crops of wheat, corn, vegetables, and fruit, known as _emblements_ (fructus industriales, fruits of industry), are generally considered personal property.

As previously noted, ownership of real estate usually includes not only rights to the surface of the ground but also rights to the minerals and substances below the surface of the ground. When an owner drills into the land, discovers oil and stores the oil in tanks ready for transport, the oil is converted from real estate to personal property.

Figure 2.4
Real versus Personal Property

Real Property (Real Estate)
Land and anything permanently attached to it.

Personal Property
Movable items not attached to real estate; items severed from real estate.

Fixture
Item of personal property converted to real property by permanent attachment to the real property; may not be removed by tenant.

Trade Fixture
Item of personal property owned by a tenant and used in a business, but attached to real estate; legally removable by tenant.

The reverse situation, changing personal property into real estate, is also possible. If an owner buys cement, stones and sand and constructs a concrete walk on the parcel of real estate, the component parts of the concrete, which were originally personal property, are converted into real estate because they have become a permanent improvement on the land.

In Pennsylvania, mobile homes are included within the definition of motor vehicles and are therefore considered to be _personal property;_ as such, they may be sold by licensed motor vehicle salespeople. A mobile home may, however, be considered part of the real estate if (1) it is transferred in conjunction with and as a part of an assignment of a land lease or the transfer of an interest in land on which the mobile home is situated, (2) the mobile home is permanently attached to a foundation and (3) the registration is canceled by the owner with the Pennsylvania Bureau of Motor Vehicles. In this instance it may be sold by a licensed real estate salesperson, broker or associate broker.

Classification of Fixtures

In considering the differences between real estate and personal property, it is important to be able to distinguish between the term *fixture* and the term *trade (or chattel) fixture.*

Fixtures. *An article that was once personal property but has been so affixed to land or to a building that the law construes it to be a part of the real estate is a* **fixture.** Examples of fixtures are heating plants, elevator equipment in highrise buildings, radiators, kitchen cabinets, light fixtures and plumbing fixtures. Almost any item that has been added with the intention that it be permanently affixed to a building is considered a fixture.

Trade fixtures. An article owned by a tenant and attached to a rented space or building for use in conducting a business is a **trade fixture,** also called a **chattel fixture.** Examples of trade fixtures are bowling alleys, store shelves, bars and restaurant equipment. Agricultural fixtures such as chicken coops and tool sheds are also included in this definition (see Figure 2.4). Trade fixtures must be removed on or before the last day of the lease. Trade fixtures that are not removed become the real property of the landlord. Acquiring the property in this way is known as *accession.*

Trade fixtures, or chattel fixtures, differ from other fixtures in the following ways:

1. Fixtures belong to the owner of the real estate, but trade fixtures are usually owned and installed by a tenant for his or her use.

2. Fixtures are considered a permanent part of a building, but trade fixtures are removable. Trade fixtures may be affixed to a building so as to appear to be fixtures (real estate); however, due to the relationship of the parties (landlord and tenant), the law gives a tenant the right to remove his or her trade fixtures if the removal is completed before the term of the lease expires and the rented space is restored to approximately its original condition. Remember that leases usually require that at the expiration of a lease the tenant return the premises to the landlord in as good a condition as they were at the beginning of the lease, except for reasonable wear and tear and damage by the elements.

3. Fixtures are legally construed to be real estate, but trade fixtures are legally construed to be personal property. Trade fixtures (chattel fixtures) are not included in the sale or mortgage of real estate except by special agreement.

Legal tests of a fixture. Courts apply four basic tests to determine whether an article is a fixture (and therefore a part of the real estate) or a trade fixture (removable personal property). These tests are based on: (1) the intention and relationship of the parties, (2) the adaptation of the article to the real estate, (3) the method of annexation of the item and (4) the existence of an agreement.

The *intent of the parties* at the time an article was attached is generally considered the most important factor in deciding whether an article is a fixture. For example, a tenant who opens a jewelry store may bolt the display cases to the floor. If the tenant wishes to remove them later, it can usually be done. Because these items are an integral part of the business property and the tenant never intended to make them a permanent part of the structure, they would be considered trade fixtures.

The *adaptation of an article* to use in a particular building is another test of the nature of the article. For example, air conditioners installed into wall slots specifically constructed for that purpose would be considered fixtures even though they could be readily removed.

The *permanence of the matter of annexation*, or attachment, often provides a third basis for court decisions relating to fixtures. For instance, a furnace, although removable, is usually attached in such a way that it cannot be taken out without causing extensive damage to the property. Moreover, the furnace is considered an essential part of the complete property and as such is a fixture.

Although these three tests seem simple, there is no uniformity in court decisions regarding what constitutes a fixture. Articles that appear permanently affixed have sometimes been held by the courts to be personal property, while items that do not appear permanently attached have been held to be fixtures.

In the sale of property, the one certain way to avoid confusion over the nature of an article is to make a *written agreement* between the parties establishing which items are considered part of the real estate. The real estate broker or salesperson should ensure that a sales contract includes a list of all articles that are being included in the sale, particularly if there is any doubt as to whether they are permanently attached fixtures. Articles that might cause confusion include television antennas, built-in appliances, built-in bookcases, wall-to-wall carpeting, wood stoves and chandeliers. In a commercial lease, where trade fixtures are involved, the contract usually lists the items and provides for restoring the property to the condition at the time of possession.

Characteristics of Real Estate

Real estate possesses seven basic characteristics that affect its use both directly and indirectly. These characteristics fall into two broad categories—economic characteristics and physical characteristics (see Figure 2.5).

Economic Characteristics

The basic economic characteristics of land are: (1) scarcity, (2) improvements, (3) permanence of investment and (4) area preferences.

Scarcity. Although land as such is not rare, scarcity in an economic sense means that the total supply of land is fixed. While a considerable amount of land is still not in use, land in a given location or of a particular quality is in short supply in some areas.

Improvements. The building of an improvement on one parcel of land affects the value and utilization of other neighboring tracts. Not only does an improvement affect adjoining tracts, but it often has a direct bearing on whole communities. For example, the improvement of a parcel of real estate by the construction of a steel plant or the selection of a site for the building of an atomic reactor can directly influence a large area. Such land improvements can influence other parcels and other communities favorably or unfavorably and may affect not only the land use itself but also the value and price of land.

Permanence of investment. Once land has been improved, the capital and labor used to build the improvement represent a large fixed investment. Although an older building can be razed to make way for a newer building or other use of the land, improvements such as drainage, electricity, water and sewerage remain because they generally cannot be dismantled or removed economically. The return on such investments is generally long-term and relatively stable. This permanence generally makes improved real estate unsuitable for short, rapid-turnover investing.

Figure 2.5 Characteristics of Real Estate

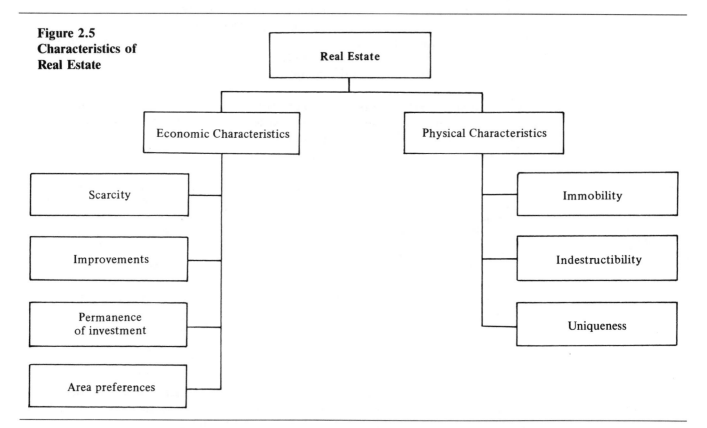

Area preferences. This economic characteristic, sometimes called situs, does not refer to a geographical location per se but rather to people's choices and preferences for a given area. It is the unique quality of people's preferences that results in different valuations being attributed to similar units.

Examples of likes and dislikes are numerous. Social preferences influenced the rapid movement of people to suburban areas. Some are now returning to the urban areas, however, preferring the environments and amenities offered by city living to those offered by suburbia. *Area preference is the most important economic characteristic of land.*

Physical Characteristics

The basic physical characteristics of land are: (1) immobility, (2) indestructibility and (3) uniqueness.

Immobility. Land, a part of the earth's surface, is considered to be immobile. It is true that some of the substances of land are removable and that topography can be changed, yet that part of the earth's surface always remains. *The geographic location of any given parcel of land can never be changed.* It is rigid; it is fixed.

Because land is immobile, the rights to use land are regulated more easily than other forms of property. For example, local governments are supported largely by property taxes on real estate. These taxes become a lien on the land. Consequently, if the owner does not pay the taxes, the land is readily available to be sold to satisfy the lien. The fixed amount of land in a given area enables the local government to rely on a certain amount of annual revenue from property taxes, which in turn allows the government to make long-range plans based on the projected income.

Indestructibility. Just as land is immobile, it is *durable* and *indestructible*. This permanence, not only of land but also of the improvements (including the buildings) that are placed on it, has tended to stabilize investments in land.

The fact that land is indestructible does not, of course, change the fact that the improvements on land do depreciate and can become obsolete, thereby reducing values—perhaps drastically. This gradual depreciation should not be confused with the fact that the *economic desirability* of a given location can change, thus creating "ghost towns."

Uniqueness. The characteristic of **uniqueness** stems from the fact that no two parcels of land are ever exactly the same. Although there may be substantial similarity, *all parcels differ geographically,* as each parcel has its own location. This may also be referred to as *heterogeneity* or **nonhomogeneity.**

Characteristics Define Land Use

The various characteristics of a parcel of real estate affect its desirability for a specific use. Some specific physical and economic factors that would affect land use include: (1) contour and elevation of the parcel, (2) prevailing winds, (3) transportation, (4) public improvements and (5) availability of natural resources, such as water. For example, hilly, heavily wooded land would need considerable work before it could be used for industrial purposes, but would be ideally suited for residential use. Likewise, flat land located along a major highway network would be undesirable for residential use, but would be a desirable location for industrial or commercial usage.

Summary

Although most people think of *land* as the surface of the earth, the definition applies not only to the *earth's surface* but also to the *mineral deposits under the earth* and the *air above it.* The term *real estate* further expands this definition to include *all natural and man-made improvements attached to the land.* Real property is the term used to describe real estate plus the "bundle of legal rights" associated with its ownership.

The same parcel of real estate may be owned and controlled by different parties, one owning the *surface rights,* one owning the *air rights,* and another owning the *subsurface rights.*

All property that does not fit the definition of real estate is classified as *personal property,* or *chattels*. When articles of personal property are affixed to land, with the intention that they be permanent, they may become *fixtures* and as such are considered a part of the real estate. However, personal property attached to real estate by a tenant for business purposes is classified as a *trade,* or *chattel, fixture* and remains personal property.

The unique nature of land is apparent in both its economic and physical characteristics. The economic characteristics consist of *scarcity, improvements, permanence of investment,* and *area preferences.* The physical characteristics are *immobility, uniqueness* and *indestructibility.*

Questions

1. Which of the following is *not* a physical characteristic of land?
   a. indestructibility
   c. immobility
   b. scarcity
   d. uniqueness

2. A construction firm builds an office center over a railroad right-of-way. This means:
   I. trains can no longer operate on the tracks under the building during business hours if the noise disturbs the occupants of the office center.
   II. the construction firm has built the office center using the subsurface rights to the property.
   a. I only
   c. both I and II
   b. II only
   d. neither I nor II

3. The term *fructus naturales* refers to which of the following?
   a. annual crops
   b. real estate
   c. personal property
   d. a and c

4. John Sexton purchases a parcel of land and sells the rights to any minerals located in the ground to an exploration company. This means that Sexton now owns all but which of the following with regard to this property?
   a. air rights
   d. right to drill
   b. surface rights
      a water well
   c. rights to coal

5. A store tenant firmly attaches appropriate appliances for his restaurant business on the leased premises. These appliances are:
   I. trade fixtures.
   II. part of the real estate once they are installed.
   a. I only
   c. both I and II
   b. II only
   d. neither I nor II

6. The definition of real estate includes many elements. Which of the following items would *not* be a part of real estate?
   a. fences
   b. permanent buildings
   c. farm equipment
   d. growing trees

7. Emblements are:
   a. fructus naturales.
   b. fructus industriales.
   c. fixtures.
   d. improvements.

8. Which of the following best defines real estate?
   a. land and the air above it
   b. land and all that there is above or below the surface, including all things permanently attached to it
   c. land and buildings permanently affixed to it
   d. land and the mineral rights in the land

9. A fixture:
   I. is considered to be real estate.
   II. is an item that at one time was personal property.
   a. I only
   c. both I and II
   b. II only
   d. neither I nor II

10. The definition of *land* includes all but which of the following?
    a. minerals in the earth
    b. the air above the ground
    c. trees
    d. buildings

11. Fred and Celia Evers are building a new enclosed front porch to their home. The lumber dealer with whom they are contracting has just unloaded in front of their house a truckload of lumber that will be used to build the porch. At this point, the lumber is considered to be:

  I. personal property.
  II. real estate.

    a. I only   c. both I and II
    b. II only   d. neither I nor II

12. When the Evers' new front porch, as described in question 11, is completed, the lumber that the dealer originally delivered will be considered to be:

  I. personal property.
  II. real estate.

    a. I only   c. both I and II
    b. II only   d. neither I nor II

13. Suppose that halfway through the construction of the Evers' new front porch, as described in question 11, work is delayed indefinitely because of unforeseen difficulties. At this point, the lumber the dealer originally delivered would be considered as:

  I. personal property if it has not been used in construction.
  II. real estate if it has been used in construction.

    a. I only   c. both I and II
    b. II only   d. neither I nor II

14. The definition of the term *real property* includes all but which of the following?

    a. items of personal property permanently affixed to the real estate
    b. legal ownership rights
    c. air and subsurface rights
    d. chattels

15. Man-made, permanent additions to land are called:

    a. chattels.   c. improvements.
    b. parcels.   d. trade fixtures.

16. Real estate may be converted into personal property:

  I. by severance.
  II. by accession.

    a. I only   c. both I and II
    b. II only   d. neither I nor II

17. Steve Jackson rents a detached, single-family home under a one-year lease. Two months into the rental period, Jackson installs awnings over the building's front windows because the house is uncomfortable in the summer. Which of the following is true?

    a. Jackson must remove the awnings before the rental period is over.
    b. Because of their permanent nature, the awnings are considered to be real property.
    c. The awnings are considered to be fixtures.
    d. b and c

18. *Area preference* refers to:

  I. scarcity.
  II. a physical characteristic of land.

    a. I only   c. both I and II
    b. II only   d. neither I nor II

19. Which of the following physical and economic factors would a land developer take into consideration when determining the optimum use for a parcel of land?

    a. transportation
    b. natural resources available
    c. contour and elevation
    d. all of the above

20. Which of the following would be an example of a chattel?

  I. cattle
  II. trade fixtures

    a. I only   c. both I and II
    b. II only   d. neither I nor II

21. The term *uniqueness* refers to:

    a. a particular choice in neighborhoods.
    b. land's durability and indestructibility.
    c. capital expenditures represented by a fixed investment.
    d. the fact that no two parcels of land are exactly alike.

3

Control of Land Use

Key Terms
Buffer zone
Building codes
Building permit
Conditional-use permit
Covenant
Deed restriction
Direct public ownership
Enabling acts
Laches
Master plan
Nonconforming use
Spot zoning
Subdivision regulations
Variance
Zoning board of appeal
Zoning ordinances

Overview
The various ownership rights a person possesses in a parcel of real estate are subject to certain public and private land-use controls, such as zoning ordinances, building codes and deed restrictions. The purpose of these controls is to insure that our limited supply of land is being put to its most beneficial use, considering the needs of the general public as well as private owners. This chapter will discuss the three types of land-use controls and how they help shape and preserve the physical surface of our nation.

Land-Use Controls	The control and regulation of land use is accomplished through: (1) public land-use controls, (2) private land-use controls through deed restrictions and (3) public ownership of land—including parks, schools and expressways—by federal, state and local governments.

| **Public Controls** | What is referred to as the "police power" of the states is their inherent authority to adopt regulations necessary to protect the public health, safety and general welfare. The states, in turn, allow counties, cities and towns to make regulations in keeping with general laws. Our largely urban population and the increasing demands placed on our limited natural resources have made it necessary for cities, towns and villages to increase their limitations on the private use of real estate. We now have controls over noise, air and water pollution, as well as population density. |

Regulations on privately owned real estate include the following:

1. planning
2. zoning
3. subdivision regulations
4. codes that regulate building construction, safety and public health
5. environmental protection legislation

| **The Master Plan** | The primary method by which local governments recognize development goals is through the formulation of a comprehensive **master plan**, also commonly referred to as a *general plan*. Municipalities, cities and counties develop master plans to insure that social and economic needs are balanced against environmental and aesthetic concerns. |

The master plan is both a statement of policies and a presentation of how those policies can be realized. As created by the city, county or regional *planning commission*, a typical master plan provides for:

- *land use*, including standards of population density and economic development;
- *public facilities*, including utilities, schools and civic centers;
- *circulation*, including public transportation and highways;
- *conservation* of natural resources and energy conservation; and
- *noise problems*.

Economic and physical surveys both are essential in preparing a master plan. County-wide plans must also include the coordination of numerous civic plans and developments to insure orderly city growth with stabilized property values.

City plans are put into effect by enactment and enforcement of zoning ordinances, our next topic.

Zoning

Zoning ordinances are laws of local government authorities (such as municipalities, cities and counties) that regulate and control the use of land and structures within designated districts or zones. Zoning regulates and affects such things as use of the land, lot sizes, types of structures permitted, building heights, setbacks (the minimum distance away from streets or sidewalks that structures may be built) and density (the ratio of land area to structure area or population). The purpose of zoning is to implement a local master plan.

Zoning powers are conferred on municipal governments by state **enabling acts**. There are no nationwide zoning ordinances; with the exception of Hawaii, no states have statewide zoning ordinances. (State and federal governments may, however, regulate land use through special legislation, such as scenic easement and coastal management laws.)

Zoning ordinances generally divide land use into use classifications: (1) residential, (2) commercial, (3) industrial and (4) agricultural. A fifth use now included by many communities is *cluster zoning*, or *multiple-use zoning*, which permits planned unit developments.

To insure adequate control, land-use areas are further divided into subclasses. For example, residential areas may be subdivided to provide for detached single-family dwellings, semidetached structures containing not more than four dwelling units, walk-up apartments, high-rise apartments and so forth. In addition, some communities require the use of **buffer zones**—such as landscaped parks and playgrounds—to separate and screen residential areas from nonresidential areas.

Adoption of zoning ordinances. Today, almost all cities with populations in excess of 10,000 have enacted comprehensive zoning ordinances governing the utilization of land located *within corporate limits*. Many states have enacted legislation that provides that the use of land located *within one to three miles* of an incorporated area must receive the approval and consent of the incorporated area, even if the property is not contiguous to the village, town or city.

Zoning ordinances must not violate the rights of individuals and property holders (as provided under the due process provisions of the Fourteenth Amendment of the U.S. Constitution) or the various provisions of the state constitution of the state in which the real estate is located. If the means used to regulate the use of property are destructive, unreasonable, arbitrary or confiscatory, the legislation is usually considered void. Tests commonly applied in determining the validity of ordinances require that:

1. The power must be exercised in a reasonable manner.

2. The provisions must be clear and specific.

3. The ordinance must be free from discrimination.

4. The ordinance must promote public health, safety and general welfare under the police power concept.

5. The ordinance must apply to all property in a similar manner.

When *downzoning* occurs in an area—for instance, when land zoned for residential construction is rezoned for conservation or recreational purposes—the government ordinarily is not responsible to the property owner for any resulting loss of value. Rezoning in this manner is considered an appropriate use of the police powers, provided it meets the tests for valid ordinances. However, certain cases of downzoning have been challenged by property owners as an action of taking private property for public use under the government's right of eminent domain, for which fair compensation is due the property owner. If downzoning is construed to be an action of "taking" without compensation, it is an unconstitutional attempt to use the right of eminent domain.

Zoning laws are generally enforced through local requirements that building permits must be obtained before property owners can build on their land. A permit will not be issued unless a proposed structure conforms to the permitted zoning, among other requirements.

Nonconforming use. In the enforcement of a zoning ordinance, a frequent problem is the situation in which an improvement does not conform to the zoning use because it was erected prior to the enactment of the zoning law. Such **nonconforming uses** legally may be allowed to continue for a specific number of years or until: (1) the improvements are destroyed or torn down or (2) the current use is abandoned. If the nonconforming use is allowed to continue indefinitely, it is considered to be "grandfathered in" to the new zoning.

Zoning boards of appeal. **Zoning boards of appeal** have been established in most communities for the specific purpose of hearing complaints about the effects of zoning ordinances on specific parcels of property. Petitions may be presented to the appeal board for variances or exceptions in the zoning law.

Zoning variations. Each time a plan is created or a zoning ordinance enacted, some owners are inconvenienced and want to change the use of a property. Generally, such owners may appeal for either a conditional-use permit or a variance to allow a use that does not meet zoning requirements.

A **conditional-use permit** is usually granted a property owner to allow a special use of property if that is in the public interest—such as a church in a residential district. A **variance** may be sought to provide a deviation from an ordinance. For example, if an owner's lot is level next to a road, but slopes steeply 30 feet away from the road, the zoning board may be willing to allow a variance so the owner can build closer to the road than would normally be allowed.

In addition, a property owner can change the zoning classification of a parcel of real estate by obtaining an *amendment* to the official *zoning map*, which is part of the original zoning ordinance for the area. The proposed amendment must be brought before a public hearing on the matter and approved by the governing body of the community.

If proposed zoning variations result in small areas that differ significantly from adjoining parcels in a way that is not in harmony with the general plan for the area, such variations might be considered to be **spot zoning**. An example would be a store being given a different zoning status than the surrounding area in a residential area. In such cases, and when spot zoning appears to be arbitrary and unreasonable, spot zoning is usually not permitted by the courts.

When local officials fail to grant the desired relief from zoning regulations, the unhappy property owner can appeal to the courts.

Subdivision Regulations

Most communities have adopted **subdivision regulations,** often as part of a master plan. These will be covered in detail in Chapter 4, "Subdividing and Property Development." Subdivision regulations usually provide for:

1. location, grading, alignment, surfacing and widths of streets, highways and other rights of way.

2. installation of sewers and water mains.

3. minimum dimensions of lots and length of blocks.

4. environmental protection and energy conservation building design.

5. building and setback lines.

6. areas to be reserved or dedicated for public use, such as parks or schools.

7. easements for public utilities.

Subdivision regulations, like all other forms of zoning or building regulations, cannot be static. They must remain flexible to meet the ever-changing needs of society.

Building Codes

Most cities and towns have enacted ordinances to *specify construction standards* that must be met when repairing or erecting buildings. These are called **building codes,** and they set the requirements for kinds of materials, sanitary equipment, electrical wiring, fire prevention standards and the like.

Most communities require the issuance of a **building permit** by the city clerk or other official before a person can build a structure or alter or repair an existing building on property within the corporate limits of the municipality. Through the permit requirement, city officials are made aware of new construction or alterations and can verify compliance with building codes and zoning ordinances by examining the plans and inspecting the work. Once the completed structure has been inspected and found satisfactory, the city inspector issues a *certificate of occupancy.*

If the construction of a building or an alteration violates a deed restriction (discussed later in this chapter), the issuance of a building permit will *not* cure this violation. A building permit is merely evidence of the applicant's compliance with municipal regulations.

In Practice...

The subject of city planning, zoning and restriction of the use of real estate is extremely technical, and the interpretation of the law is not altogether clear. Questions concerning any of these subjects in relation to real estate transactions should be referred to legal counsel.

Environmental Protection Legislation

Federal and state legislators have passed a number of environmental protection laws in an attempt to respond to the growing public concern over the improvement and preservation of America's natural resources.

The various states have responded to the environmental issue by passing a variety of localized environmental protection laws regarding all forms of pollution—air, water, noise and solid waste disposal. For example, many states have enacted laws that prevent builders or private individuals from constructing septic tanks or other effluence-disposal systems in certain areas, particularly where public bodies of water—streams, lakes and rivers—are affected.

In addition to the states and federal government, cities and counties also frequently pass environmental legislation.

Private Land-Use Controls

A real estate owner can include in the deed, when property is conveyed, a **deed restriction** limiting the use of the property.

There is a distinction between restrictions on the right to *sell* and restrictions on the right to *use.* In general, provisions in a deed conveying a fee simple estate with restrictions that the subsequent owners will not sell, mortgage or convey it are void. Such restrictions attempt to limit the basic principle of the *free alienation (transfer) of property;* the courts consider them against public policy and therefore unenforceable.

A subdivider may establish restrictions on the right to *use* land through a **covenant** in a deed or by reference to a separate recorded declaration. When a lot in that subdivision is conveyed by an owner's deed, the deed refers to the plat or declaration of restrictions and incorporates these restrictions as limitations on the title conveyed by the deed. In this manner, the restrictive covenants are included in the deed by reference and become binding on all grantees. Such covenants or restrictions usually relate to: (1) type of building; (2) use to which the land may be put; and (3) type of construction, height, setbacks and square footage.

These use restrictions are usually considered valid if they are reasonable restraints and are for the benefit of all property owners in the subdivision. If, however, such restrictions are too broad in their terms, they prevent the free transfer of property. If they are "repugnant" to the estate granted, such restrictions will probably not be enforceable. If any restrictive covenant or condition is considered ineffective by a court, the estate will then stand free from the invalid covenant or condition.

Deed restrictions may be more restrictive of an owner's use than a zoning ordinance. The more restrictive of the two takes precedence.

Restrictions may have a *time limitation,* for example, "effective for a period of 25 years from this date." After that time, the restrictions become inoperative or may be extended by majority agreement of the people who own the property at that time.

Subdivision restrictions give each lot owner the right to apply to the court for an *injunction* to prevent a neighboring lot owner from violating the recorded restrictions. If granted, the court injunction will direct the violator to stop or remove the violation upon penalty of being in contempt of court. The court retains the power to punish the violator for failure to obey the court order. If adjoining lot owners stand idly by while a violation is being committed, they can *lose the right* to the court's injunction by their inaction; the court might claim their right was lost through **laches**, that is, loss of a right through undue delay or failure to assert it.

| **Direct Public Ownership** | Over the years, the government's general policy has been to encourage private ownership of land. It is necessary, however, for a certain amount of land to be owned by the government for such uses as municipal buildings, state legislative houses, schools and military stations. Such **direct public ownership** is a means of land control. |

Over the years, the government's general policy has been to encourage private ownership of land. It is necessary, however, for a certain amount of land to be owned by the government for such uses as municipal buildings, state legislative houses, schools and military stations. Such **direct public ownership** is a means of land control.

There are other examples of necessary public ownership. Urban renewal efforts, especially government-owned housing, are one way that public ownership serves the public interest. Publicly owned streets and highways serve a necessary function for the entire population. In addition, public land is often used for such recreational purposes as parks. National and state parks and forest preserves create areas for public use and recreation, and at the same time help to conserve our natural resources.

At present, the federal government owns approximately 775 million acres of land, nearly one-third of the total area of the United States. At times the federal government has held title to as much as 80 percent of the nation's total land area.

Summary

The control of land use is exercised in two ways: through public controls and private (or nongovernment) controls.

Public controls are ordinances based upon the states' *police powers* to protect the public health, safety and welfare. Through power conferred by state enabling acts, local governments enact comprehensive *master plans*.

Zoning ordinances carrying out the provisions of the master plan segregate residential areas from business and industrial zones and control not only land use but also height and bulk of buildings and density of populations. Zoning enforcement problems involve boards of appeal, conditional-use permits, variances and exceptions, as well as nonconforming uses. *Subdivision regulations* are required to maintain control of the development of expanding community areas so that growth will be harmonious with community standards.

Building codes specify standards for construction, plumbing, sewers, electrical wiring and equipment.

In addition to land-use control on the local level, the state and federal governments have occasionally intervened when necessary to preserve natural resources through *environmental legislation*.

Private controls are exercised by owners, generally subdividers, who control use of subdivision lots by carefully planned *deed restrictions* that are made to apply to all lot owners. The usual recorded restrictions may be enforced by adjoining lot owners obtaining a court *injunction* to stop a violator.

Public ownership is a means of land-use control that provides land for such public benefits as parks, highways, schools and municipal buildings.

Questions

1. A provision in a subdivision declaration used as a means of forcing the grantee to live up to the terms under which he or she holds title to the land is a:
   a. restriction.
   b. reverter.
   c. laches.
   d. conditional-use clause.

2. For a zoning ordinance to be valid, the courts have decided that the ordinance must:
   I. not violate the due process provisions of the Fourteenth Amendment of the U.S. Constitution.
   II. be free from discrimination.
   III. not result in a loss of property values.

   a. I and II   c. I and III
   b. II and III   d. I, II and III

3. If a land owner wants to use property in a manner that is prohibited by a local zoning ordinance but would be of benefit to the community, the property owner can ask for which of the following?
   a. variance
   b. downzoning
   c. conditional-use permit
   d. dezoning

4. A new building is erected; it does not conform to local zoning ordinances and the builder did not seek prior permission to construct the building in this manner. This building is an example of a:
   I. nonconforming use.
   II. variance.

   a. I only   c. both I and II
   b. II only   d. neither I nor II

5. Public land-use controls include all but which of the following?
   a. subdivision regulations
   b. deed restrictions
   c. environmental protection laws
   d. master plan specifications

6. The police power allows regulation of:
   a. the number of buildings.
   b. building sizes.
   c. building ownership.
   d. a and b

7. To determine whether or not a location can be used for a retail store, one would examine:
   I. the city building code.
   II. the city's list of permitted nonconforming uses.

   a. I only   c. both I and II
   b. II only   d. neither I nor II

8. The purpose of a building permit is:
   a. to override a deed restriction.
   b. to maintain municipal control over the volume of building.
   c. to provide evidence of compliance with municipal regulations.
   d. all of the above

9. Which of the following could be included in a list of deed restrictions?
   I. types of buildings that may be constructed on the property
   II. minimum requirements for setbacks and square footage

   a. I only   c. both I and II
   b. II only   d. neither I nor II

10. The goals of a city planning commission include:
    a. formulation of policy.
    b. determination of land uses.
    c. conservation of natural resources.
    d. all of the above

11. The grantor of a deed may place effective restrictions on:
    a. the right to sell the land.
    b. use of the land.
    c. who the next purchaser will be.
    d. a and b

12. Zoning powers are conferred on municipal governments:

   a. by state enabling acts.
   b. through police power.
   c. by eminent domain.
   d. a and b

13. A restriction in a seller's deed may be enforced by which of the following?

   I. court injunction
   II. zoning board of appeal

      a. I only   c. both I and II
      b. II only   d. neither I nor II

14. Zoning laws are generally enforced by:

   a. zoning boards of appeal.
   b. ordinances stipulating that building permits will not be issued unless the proposed structure conforms to the zoning ordinance.
   c. deed restrictions.
   d. a and b

15. Zoning boards of appeal are established to hear complaints about:

   a. restrictive covenants.
   b. the effects of a zoning ordinance.
   c. building codes.
   d. a and c

4

Subdividing and Property Development

Key Terms

Clustering
Cul-de-sac
Curvilinear system
Dedicated
Density zoning
Developer
Gridiron pattern
Interstate Land Sales Full Disclosure Act
Pennsylvania Municipalities Planning Code
Pennsylvania Real Estate Licensing and Registration Act
Minimum standards
Plat of subdivision
Property report
Subdivider
Subdivision

Overview

As our country's population grows and shifts to new locations, the demand for housing grows and shifts. To meet demand, subdividers and property developers convert raw land or property that is no longer serving its highest and best use into subdivisions for residential and other uses. These subdividers and developers, working with local officials, are largely responsible for the orderly growth of such communities. This chapter will deal with the process of developing and subdividing property and will also discuss some of the legal aspects of selling subdivided land.

**Land
Development**

Land in large tracts must receive special attention before it can be converted into sites for homes, stores or other uses. As our cities and towns grow in size, additional land is required for their expansion. In order for such new areas to develop soundly, the services of competent subdividers and land developers working closely with city planners are required. A **subdivider** buys undeveloped acreage and divides it into smaller lots for sale to individuals or developers or for the subdivider's own use. A **developer** (who may also be a subdivider) builds homes or other buildings on the lots and sells them. Developing is generally a much more extensive activity than is subdividing. A developer may have a sales staff or may use the services of local real estate brokerage firms.

**Regulation of Land
Development**

As discussed in Chapter 3, "Control of Land Use," *no uniform city planning and land development legislation exists that affects the entire country.* Laws governing subdividing and land planning are controlled by the state and local governmental bodies where the land is located. However, rules and regulations developed by governmental agencies such as the Federal Housing Administration, have provided certain **minimum standards** as usable guides. These minimum standards are not mandatory except for those developers who are seeking FHA approval in anticipation of making FHA mortgage financing available to purchasers. These regulations are not uniform throughout the entire country. They are flexible and subject to review by regional officers, who have the authority to modify the regulations to meet customs and local climate, health and hazard conditions. Some of the major FHA minimum standards will be discussed later in this chapter. Although many governmental agencies have adopted some of these FHA minimum standards, a large number have established higher standards for subdividers of land under their jurisdiction.

In Pennsylvania, the Municipalities Planning Code—Act 247—contains laws governing the subdivision and use of land within the state. These regulations authorize local municipalities to establish ordinances regulating subdivision and land use within their jurisdictions.

Although the recording of a plat of subdivision of land prior to public sale for residential or commercial use is usually required, land planning precedes the actual subdividing process. The land development plan must comply with the overall *master plan* adopted by the county, city, village or town. The basic city plan and zoning requirements are not inflexible, but long, expensive and frequently complicated hearings are usually required before alterations can be authorized. Approval of the subdivision plat is, however, a necessary step before recording.

As discussed in Chapter 3, most villages, cities and other areas that are incorporated under state laws have *planning commissions.* Depending upon how the particular group was organized, such committees or commissions may have only an advisory status to the aldermen or trustees of the community. In other instances, the commission can have authority to approve or disapprove plans. Communities establish strict criteria before approving new subdivisions. The following are frequently included: (1) *dedication*, a transfer of private land to the public for such purposes as streets, schools and parks; (2) assurance by *bonding* that sewer and street costs will be paid, or completion of such improvements before construction begins; and (3) *compliance with zoning ordinances* governing use and lot size, along with fire and safety ordinances.

Because they may pollute streams, rivers, lakes and underground water sources, septic systems are no longer authorized in many areas, and an approved sewage-disposal arrangement must be included in a land development plan. The possible shortage of water has caused great concern, and local authorities usually require land planners to submit information on how they intend to satisfy sewage-disposal and water-supply requirements. Development and/or septic tank installation may first require a *percolation test* of the soil's absorption and drainage capacities. Frequently a planner will also have to submit an *environmental impact report*.

In Pennsylvania, the Department of Environmental Resources is authorized to adopt and administer rules, regulations, standards and procedures regarding the planning of community and individual sewage systems. Also, disclosure statements in certain land sale contracts are required by Pennsylvania law. Such land sale contracts must clearly state that a buyer should contact the local agency charged with administering this act before signing the contract to determine the procedure and requirements for obtaining a permit for an individual sewage system if one has not already been obtained.

When property to be subdivided is located outside the limits of cities, villages and incorporated towns, most state laws require that the proposed land plan be submitted to county authorities for approval, and also to all incorporated communities (cities, towns or villages) located within a radius of one to three miles. If there is more than one such incorporated area, each must review and approve the plan.

Subdividing

The process of **subdivision** normally involves three distinct stages of development: (1) the initial planning stage, (2) the final planning stage and (3) the disposition, or start-up.

During the *initial planning stage,* the subdivider seeks out raw land in a suitable area. Once the land is located, the property is analyzed for its highest and best use, the possible use of a property that would produce the greatest net income, and therefore the highest land value. Preliminary subdivision plans are drawn up accordingly. As previously discussed, close contact is initiated between the subdivider and local planning and zoning officials. If the project requires zoning variances, negotiations begin along these lines. The subdivider also locates financial backers and initiates marketing strategies.

The *final planning stage* is basically a follow-up of the initial stage. Final plans are prepared, approval is sought from local officials, permanent financing is obtained, the land is purchased, final budgets are prepared and marketing programs are designed.

The *disposition,* or *start-up,* carries the subdividing process to a conclusion. Subdivision plans are recorded with local officials, and streets, sewers and utilities are installed. Buildings, open parks and recreational areas are constructed and landscaped if they are part of the subdivision plan. Marketing programs are then initiated, and title to the individual parcels of subdivided land is transferred as the lots are sold.

Subdivision Plans   In plotting out a subdivision according to local planning and zoning controls, a subdivider usually determines the size as well as the location of the individual lots. The size of the lots, both in front footage and in depth, together with the total amount of square footage, is generally regulated by local ordinances and must be given careful consideration. Frequently ordinances regulate both the minimum and the maximum size of a lot.

The land itself must be studied, usually in cooperation with a surveyor, so that the subdivision can be laid out with consideration of natural drainage and land contours.

In laying out a subdivision, a subdivider should provide for *utility easements* as well as easements for water and sewer mains. Usually the water and sewer mains will be laid in the street, with connecting junction boxes available for each building site. When the city, town or village installs the water or sewer mains connecting a new building with the junction box in the street, a tie-in, or connection, fee is frequently charged to help the authority defray the cost of such installation.

Most subdivisions are laid out by use of *lots and blocks*. An area of land is designated as a block and the area making up this block is divided into lots. Usually, lots and blocks are both numbered consecutively. However, if a developer does not intend to subdivide an entire tract of land at one time, some variation from consecutive numbering may be granted.

Although subdividers customarily designate areas reserved for schools, parks and future church sites, this is not usually considered good subdividing. Once a subdivision has been recorded, the purchasers of the lots have a vested interest in those areas reserved for schools, parks and churches. If for any reason in the future, any such purpose is not appropriate, it will become difficult for the developer to abandon the original plan and use that property for residential purposes. To get around this situation, many developers designate such areas as *out-lot A, out-lot B* and so forth. Such a designation does not vest any rights in these out-lots in the purchasers of the homesites. Then, for example, if one of these areas is to be used for church purposes, it can be so conveyed and so used. If, on the other hand, the out-lot is not used for such a purpose, it can be resubdivided into residential properties without the burden of securing the consent of the lot owners in the area.

Plat of subdivision. The subdivider's completed **plat of subdivision,** a map of the development indicating the location and boundaries of individual properties, must contain all necessary approvals of public officials and must be recorded in the county where the land is located.

Once the plat has been filed for record, all areas that have been accepted by the municipality for street purposes are considered to be **dedicated.** This usually means that the land shown as streets now belongs to the city or town. If this is not the subdivider's intention, the plat should specify that the streets are private.

Because the plat will be the basis for future conveyances, the subdivided land should be carefully measured, with all lot sizes noted by the surveyor and accurately entered on the document. Survey monuments should be established and measurements should be made from these monuments, with the location of all lots carefully marked. (See Chapter 5, "Legal Description," for further discussion.)

Covenants and restrictions. Deed restrictions, discussed in Chapters 3 and 6, are usually originated and recorded by a subdivider as a means of *controlling and maintaining the desirable quality and character of the subdivision.* These restrictions can be included in the subdivision plat, or they may be set forth in a separate recorded instrument, commonly referred to as a *declaration of restrictions.*

FHA standards. FHA **minimum standards** have been established for residential area subdivisions that are to be submitted for approval for FHA loan insurance. The primary minimum standards established by the FHA are the following:

1. Streets must comply with approved widths and must be paved.

2. The area must be free from hazards, such as airplane landing fields, heavy through traffic and excessive noise or air pollution.

3. Each lot must have access to all utilities.

4. Provisions for shopping, schools, churches, recreation and transportation must be available.

5. Lots must comply with minimum, and in some cases maximum, size requirements.

6. Plans for construction must be approved and must meet minimum standards.

7. Uniform building setbacks and lot lines are usually required.

8. Minimum landscaping is usually required.

There are also FHA standards applicable to building construction. Since 1986, in recognition of the more stringent local codes in effect, FHA has allowed local building codes (where pre-approved by HUD—the Department of Housing and Urban Development) to serve as the standards. Exceptions generally include site conditions, thermal (insulation) standards and certain other material standards.

Development costs. In the subdivision of a typical parcel of raw land, a lot's sales price will generally reflect such expenses as cost of land; installation of sewers, water mains, storm drains, landscaping and street lights; earthworks (mass dirt removal, site grading and similar operations); paving; engineering and surveying fees; broker's commissions; inspections; bonding costs; filing and legal fees; sales costs; and overhead. In certain areas, a subdivider may also be required to give financial assistance to school districts, park districts and the like, either in the form of donated school or park sites or in the form of a fixed subsidy per subdivision lot. Should such further costs be incurred, they must, of course, be added proportionately to the sales price of each building site.

Subdivision Density

Zoning ordinances control land use. Such controls often include minimum lot sizes and population density requirements for subdivisions and land developments. For example, a typical zoning restriction may set the minimum lot area on which a subdivider can build a single-family housing unit at 10,000 square feet. This means that the subdivider will be able to build four houses per acre. Many zoning authorities now establish special density zoning standards for certain subdivisions. **Density zoning** ordinances restrict the *average maximum number of houses per acre* that may be built within a particular subdivision. If the area is density zoned at an average maximum of four houses per acre, for example, by *clustering* building lots, the developer is free to achieve an open effect. Regardless of lot size or the number of units, the subdivider will be consistent with the ordinance as long as the average number of units in the development remains at or below the maximum density. This average is called *gross density.*

Street patterns. By varying street patterns and clustering housing units, a subdivider can dramatically increase the amount of open and/or recreational space in a development. Some of these patterns are illustrated in Figure 4.1.

The **gridiron pattern** evolved out of the government rectangular survey system. Featuring large lots, wide streets and limited-use service alleys, the system works reasonably well up to a point. An overabundance of grid-patterned streets often results in monotonous neighborhoods, with all lots facing busy streets. In addition, sidewalks are usually located adjacent to the streets, and the system provides for little or no open, park or recreational space.

The **curvilinear system** integrates major arteries of travel with smaller secondary and **cul-de-sac** streets carrying minor traffic. In addition, small open parks are often provided at intersections.

Clustering for open space. By slightly reducing lot sizes and **clustering** them around varying street patterns, a developer can house as many people in the same area as could be done using traditional subdividing plans, but with substantially increased tracts of open space.

**Figure 4.1
Street Patterns**

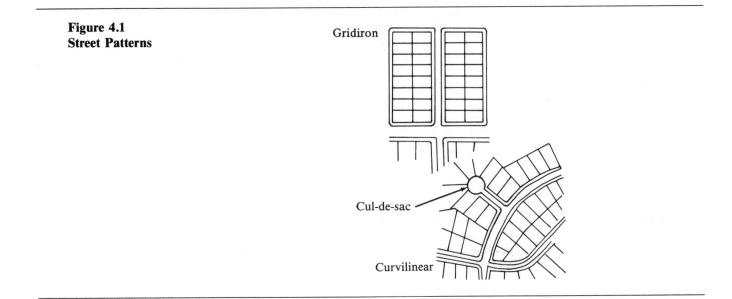

For example, compare the two illustrations in Figure 4.2. The first is a plan for a conventionally designed subdivision containing 368 housing units. It uses 23,200 linear feet of street and leaves only 1.6 acres open for park areas. Contrast this with the second subdivision pictured. Both subdivisions are equal in size and

Figure 4.2
Clustered Subdivision
Plan

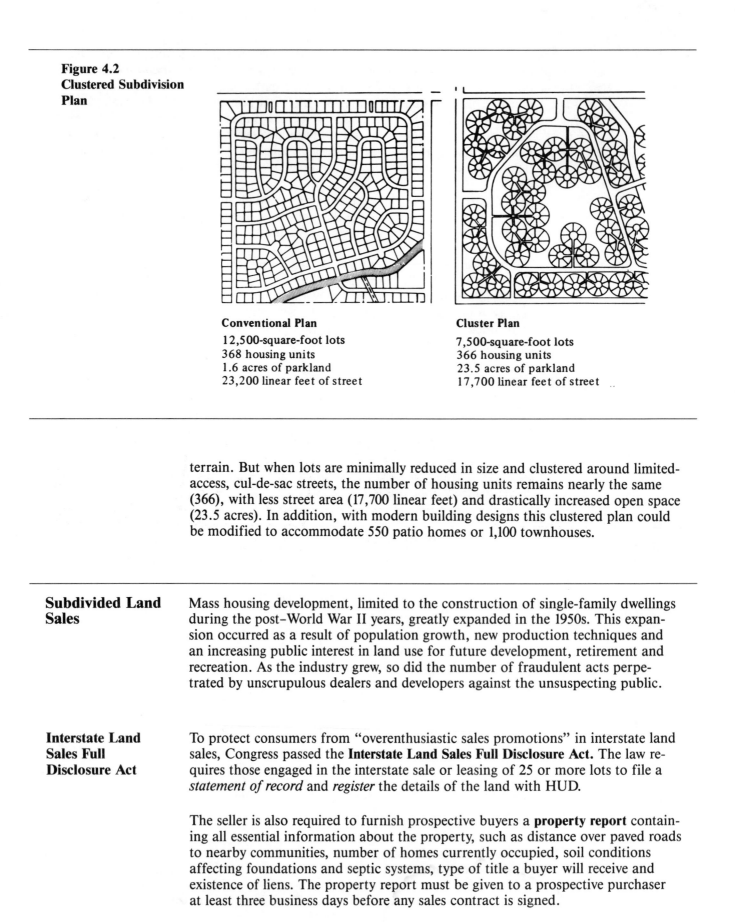

Conventional Plan
12,500-square-foot lots
368 housing units
1.6 acres of parkland
23,200 linear feet of street

Cluster Plan
7,500-square-foot lots
366 housing units
23.5 acres of parkland
17,700 linear feet of street

terrain. But when lots are minimally reduced in size and clustered around limited-access, cul-de-sac streets, the number of housing units remains nearly the same (366), with less street area (17,700 linear feet) and drastically increased open space (23.5 acres). In addition, with modern building designs this clustered plan could be modified to accommodate 550 patio homes or 1,100 townhouses.

**Subdivided Land
Sales**

Mass housing development, limited to the construction of single-family dwellings during the post–World War II years, greatly expanded in the 1950s. This expansion occurred as a result of population growth, new production techniques and an increasing public interest in land use for future development, retirement and recreation. As the industry grew, so did the number of fraudulent acts perpetrated by unscrupulous dealers and developers against the unsuspecting public.

**Interstate Land
Sales Full
Disclosure Act**

To protect consumers from "overenthusiastic sales promotions" in interstate land sales, Congress passed the **Interstate Land Sales Full Disclosure Act.** The law requires those engaged in the interstate sale or leasing of 25 or more lots to file a *statement of record* and *register* the details of the land with HUD.

The seller is also required to furnish prospective buyers a **property report** containing all essential information about the property, such as distance over paved roads to nearby communities, number of homes currently occupied, soil conditions affecting foundations and septic systems, type of title a buyer will receive and existence of liens. The property report must be given to a prospective purchaser at least three business days before any sales contract is signed.

Any contract to purchase a lot covered by this act may be revoked at the purchaser's option until midnight of the seventh business day following the signing of the contract. If a contract is signed for the purchase of a lot covered by the act and a property report is not given to the purchaser, an action to revoke the contract may be brought by the purchaser within two years.

If the seller misrepresents the property in any sales promotion, a buyer induced by such a promotion is entitled to sue the seller for civil damages under federal law. Failure to comply with the law may also subject a seller to criminal penalties of up to five years' imprisonment and a $10,000 fine for each violation.

Pennsylvania Laws **Sale of subdivided land within the state (Municipalities Planning Code).** The **Pennsylvania Municipalities Planning Code** authorizes each county, city or town to institute ordinances to regulate subdivisions and land development within its jurisdiction according to the provisions set forth in the state code. These local ordinances may include but are not limited to the following general provisions for:

1. submission, processing and specification of plats;

2. conformity with local comprehensive plans of layout and arrangement of subdivisions;

3. coordination according to local standards of streets within and bordering subdivisions, and regulation of street width, grading, location and improvements;

4. assurance of effective easements and rights-of-way for drainage, utilities and public grounds;

5. supervision of the adequacy of safety provisions and environmental hazards;

6. establishment of water and sewage regulations;

7. regulations governing the erection of buildings, gutters, curbs, walkways, street lights, fire hydrants and the like; and

8. encouragement of flexibility and ingenuity of planning in accordance with modern site development.

The governing bodies of Pennsylvania municipalities may set up their own procedures for plat approval, but they are subject to the state planning code with respect to time limits on approval decision. A local governing body or planning committee must make its decision and communicate it to an applicant within *90 days* after an application is filed. The decision must be communicated to the applicant within *15 days* after the decision is made. If the governing body does not act on a subdivision plat application within the time limits specified in the planning code, the plat will automatically be considered approved.

Before reaching a decision on a subdivision plat a local governing body may hold a public hearing. The decision must *be in writing* and must *specify any defects* found in an application that is not approved.

After a plat is approved, it must be registered with the office of the recorder of deeds in the county in which the municipality is located. A plat may not be recorded unless the plat officially notes the approval of the governing body.

Until a plat of subdivision has been approved and recorded, no buildings can be erected on subdivided land and no sales agreements or transfers can be entered into. Violations of the planning code in this respect are misdemeanors and any persons, partnerships or corporations responsible for such violations will be fined up to $1,000 per lot, parcel or dwelling within each lot or parcel. Fines are paid to the municipality whose ordinance is violated.

Promotional land sales and approval. The **Pennsylvania Licensing and Registration Act** (see Appendix D, Sec. 605) requires that persons who propose to engage in real estate transactions of a promotional nature must first register with the Real Estate Commission for its approval and also comply with rules and regulations stipulated by the Commission. Registration shall not be required for property subject to exemption under the Federal Interstate Land Sales Full Disclosure Act or real estate interest involving less than 50 lots or shares, cemetery lots and land involving less than 25 acres. The information submitted for the registration shall include the following:

1. Identity of the persons having interests in the property (including corporation documents if owner is a corporation).

2. Legal description; topography; maps and dimensions of property, including relation to existing roads and streets.

3. Conditions of the title, including liens and restrictions.

4. Terms and conditions of transactions, including selling price.

5. Improvements to the property and estimated schedule of completion.

6. Copies of forms to be used for conveyance in the sales.

7. Evidence of the developer's ownership and the developer's financial statements.

8. Irrevocable consent form agreeing to submit to the jurisdiction of Commonwealth Court for any action that might occur.

The licensing act requires this registration for the purposes of verifying the nature of the development and promotional methods to protect consumers in Pennsylvania from unscrupulous land sales promotions. This is only a *registration,* which must be renewed annually, and is not a Commission endorsement of the project and cannot be advertised as such. The Commission currently has no authority under the licensing act to physically inspect the development, so is seeking additional legislation and approval of revised rules and regulations to further monitor these activities.

Similar to the federal legislation, the Pennsylvania Real Estate Commission requires that a prospective purchaser be given a property report about the real estate development.

Summary

A *subdivider* buys undeveloped acreage, divides it into smaller parcels and develops it or sells it. A *land developer* builds homes on the lots and sells them, through the developer's own sales organization or through local real estate brokerage firms. City planners and land developers, working together, plan whole communities that are later incorporated into cities, towns or villages.

Land development must comply with the master plans adopted by counties, cities, villages or towns. This may entail approval of land-use plans by local *planning committees* or *commissioners.*

The process of subdivision includes dividing the tract of land into *lots and blocks* and providing for *utility easements,* as well as laying out street patterns and widths. A subdivider must generally record a completed *plat of subdivision,* with all necessary approvals of public officials, in the county where the land is located. Subdividers usually place *restrictions* upon the use of all lots in a subdivision as a general plan for the benefit of all lot owners.

Subdivisions that are to be submitted for approval for FHA loan insurance must meet certain *FHA minimum standards.*

By *varying street patterns and housing density* and *clustering housing units,* a subdivider can dramatically increase the amount of open and recreational space within a development.

Subdivided land sales are regulated on the federal level by the *Interstate Land Sales Full Disclosure Act.* This law requires developers engaged in interstate land sales or the leasing of 25 or more units to register the details of the land with HUD. At least three business days before any sales contract is signed, such developers must also provide prospective purchasers with a property report containing all essential information about the property. Subdivided land sales are also regulated in Pennsylvania by the Municipalities Planning Code (sale of subdivided land within the state) and the Real Estate Licensing and Registration Act of Pennsylvania (sale of subdivided land outside the state).

Questions

1. To control and maintain the quality and character of a subdivision, a developer will establish which of the following?
   a. easements
   b. deed restrictions
   c. buffer zones
   d. b and c

2. An owner of a large tract of land who, after adequate study of all facts, legally divides the land into lots of suitable size and location for the construction of residences, is known as a:
   a. subdivider.
   b. land developer.
   c. land planning commissioner.
   d. all of the above

3. A map illustrating the sizes and locations of streets and lots in a subdivision is called a:
   a. gridiron pattern.
   b. survey.
   c. plat of subdivision.
   d. property report.

4. Which of the following is *not* included in the FHA minimum standards for subdivisions?
   a. provisions for shopping must be available
   b. lots must be of uniform size
   c. streets must be of approved width and be paved
   d. the area must be free from hazards

5. *Gross density* refers to which of the following?
   a. the maximum number of residents that may, by law, occupy a subdivision
   b. the average maximum number of houses per acre that may, by law, be built in a subdivision
   c. the maximum size lot that may, by law, be built in a subdivision
   d. the minimum number of houses that may, by law, be built in a subdivision

6. The type of street pattern that is based on the rectangular survey system is called the:
   a. block plan.
   b. gridiron system.
   c. rectangular streets plan.
   d. cul-de-sac system.

7. FHA minimum standards for land development:
   I. must be complied with by all subdividers.
   II. concern only the design and construction of buildings.
   a. I only   c. both I and II
   b. II only   d. neither I nor II

8. Which of the following is true regarding the Pennsylvania Licensing Act requirements for out-of-state land sales promotion?
   a. Registration of the development is for the purpose of obtaining Real Estate Commission endorsement.
   b. Prospective purchasers are entitled to a property report about the development.
   c. A Real Estate Commission representative will personally inspect the development.
   d. The promotion methods of the developer are not considered by the Commission in the registration process.

9. Soil absorption and drainage are measured by a:
   a. land survey.
   b. plat of subdivision.
   c. density test.
   d. percolation test.

10. Which of the following items are *not* usually designated on the plat for a new subdivision?
    a. easements for sewer and water mains
    b. land to be used for streets, schools and civic facilities
    c. numbered lots and blocks
    d. prices of residential and commercial lots

11. The possibility of pollution has led to:
   I. elimination of the general use of the septic system as a means of sewage disposal.
   II. strict compliance with local zoning laws in drawing up a plan for sewage disposal.
      a. I only
      b. II only
      c. both I and II
      d. neither I nor II

12. A street pattern featuring housing units grouped into cul-de-sac blocks is generally called a:
   a. cluster plan.
   b. curvilinear system.
   c. rectangular street system.
   d. gridiron system.

13. In compliance with the Interstate Land Sales Full Disclosure Act, which of the following kinds of information need *not* be included in a property report given to a land buyer?
   a. soil conditions affecting foundations
   b. financial conditions of the seller
   c. number of homes currently occupied
   d. existence of liens

14. Many real estate brokers serve as agents for developers in:
   I. instructing the developers in their legal responsibilities.
   II. finding property buyers.
      a. I only
      b. II only
      c. both I and II
      d. neither I nor II

15. To protect the public from fraudulent interstate land sales, the Pennsylvania Real Estate Licensing and Registration Act requires developers to:
   I. submit for the commission's approval all promotional materials used for the sale of out-of-state land.
   II. pay the prospective buyer's expenses to see the property involved.
      a. I only
      b. II only
      c. both I and II
      d. neither I nor II

16. A subdivider can increase the amount of open and/or recreational space in a development by:
   a. varying street patterns.
   b. meeting FHA standards.
   c. clustering housing units.
   d. a and c

5

Legal Descriptions

Key Terms

Air lot
Base line
Benchmark
Datum
Legal description
Lot and block system
Metes and bounds
Monument
Plat of subdivision
Point of beginning
Principal meridian
Rectangular (government) survey system
Section

Overview

In everyday life, we often describe real estate casually, perhaps as "the lot on 1546 East Main Street," or "the big house on the corner of Main and Oak." In real estate practice, however, parcels of land cannot always be referred to in such an imprecise manner. Deeds, sales contracts and other documents must state the exact size and location of real estate according to an established system of land description. This chapter will explain how land is identified and measured and will include discussions of each of the forms of legal description used in Pennsylvania.

Describing Land

One of the essential elements of a valid deed is an accurate description of the land being conveyed. The real estate involved must be identifiable from the wording of the deed and with reference to only the documents named in the deed. The courts have usually held that a description of land is legally sufficient if a competent surveyor can locate the real estate in question.

The courts of most states have accepted a street address as being sufficient to locate or identify a parcel of real estate, but not to serve as a legal description. However, the legal description in a deed or mortgage may be followed by the words "commonly known as" and the street address. A **legal description** is an *exact way of describing real estate in a contract, deed, mortgage or other document that will be accepted by a court of law.*

The average parcel of land has been conveyed and transferred many times in the past. The description of the land in a deed, mortgage or other instrument should be the same as that used in the previous instrument of conveyance. Discrepancies, errors and legal problems can be avoided or reduced if this practice is followed in drawing subsequent conveyances.

Methods of Describing Real Estate

There are three basic methods of describing real estate: (1) metes and bounds, (2) rectangular survey and (3) recorded lot and block system. Figure 5.1 depicts the methods of land description as used throughout the country. Note that Pennsylvania, as well as the other states in the east, describes land by metes and bounds and lot and block, not by rectangular survey.

Metes and Bounds

A **metes-and-bounds** description makes use of the boundaries and measurements of the land in question. Such a description starts at a definitely designated point called the **point of beginning** (abbreviated POB) and proceeds around the boundaries of the tract by reference to linear measurements and directions. A metes-and-bounds description always ends at the point where it began (the POB), so that the tract being described is fully enclosed.

In a metes-and-bounds description, the actual distance between monuments takes precedence over linear measurements set forth in the description if the two measurements differ. **Monuments** are fixed objects used to establish real estate boundaries. Natural objects such as stones, large trees, lakes, streams and intersections of major streets or highways, as well as man-made markers placed by surveyors, are commonly used as monuments. (Under the rectangular survey system, as discussed later, section lines, quarter-section lines, township lines and similar points of reference are used in the same way as monuments in the description and location of property.) Measurements often include the words "more or less"; the location of the monuments is more important than the distance stated in the wording.

An example of a metes-and-bounds description of a parcel of land (pictured in Figure 5.2) follows.

Figure 5.1
Public Land Survey
Systems of the
United States

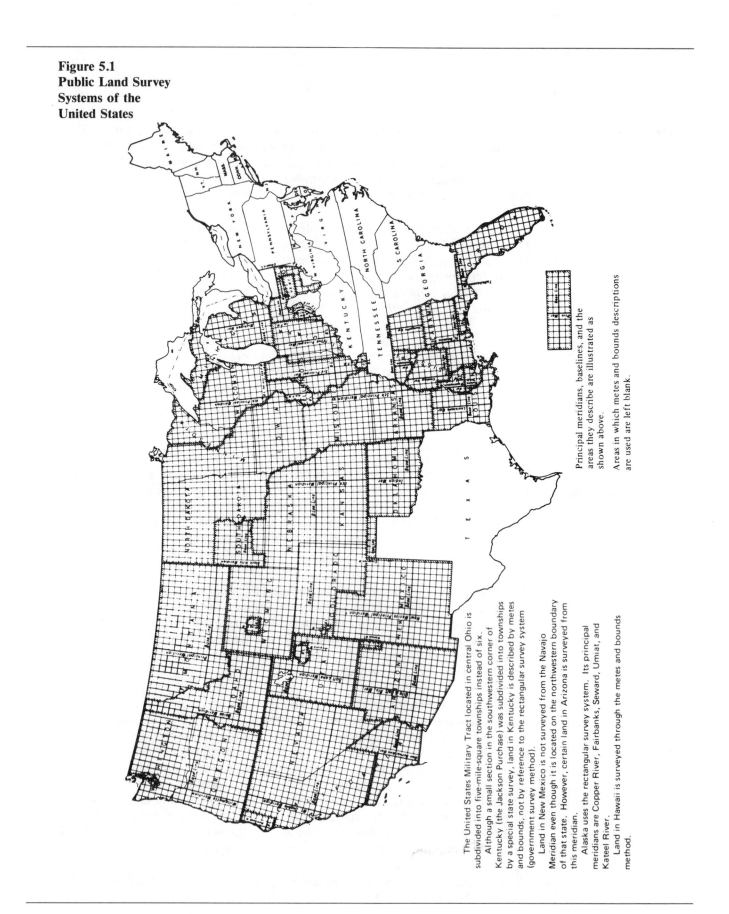

The United States Military Tract located in central Ohio is subdivided into five-mile-square townships instead of six.

Although a small section in the southwestern corner of Kentucky (the Jackson Purchase) was subdivided into townships by a special state survey, land in Kentucky is described by metes and bounds, not by reference to the rectangular survey system (government survey method).

Land in New Mexico is not surveyed from the Navajo Meridian even though it is located on the northwestern boundary of that state. However, certain land in Arizona is surveyed from this meridian.

Alaska uses the rectangular survey system. Its principal meridians are Copper River, Fairbanks, Seward, Umiat, and Kateel River.

Land in Hawaii is surveyed through the metes and bounds method.

Principal meridians, baselines, and the areas they describe are illustrated as shown above.

Areas in which metes and bounds descriptions are used are left blank.

Figure 5.2
Metes-and-Bounds
Tract

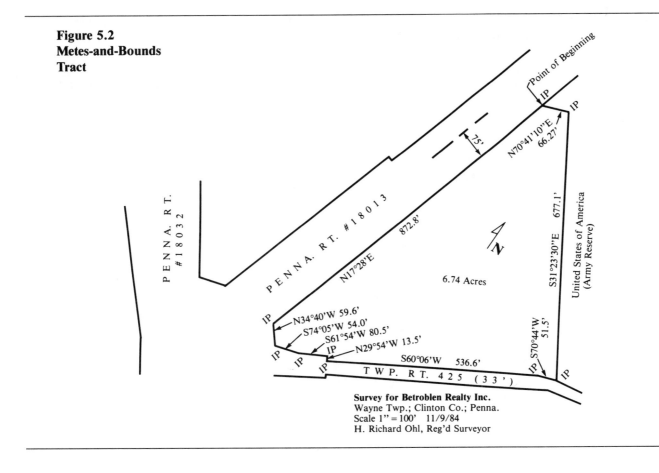

Survey for Betroblen Realty Inc.
Wayne Twp.; Clinton Co.; Penna.
Scale 1" = 100'   11/9/84
H. Richard Ohl, Reg'd Surveyor

"ALL THAT CERTAIN piece of parcel of land situate in Wayne Township, Clinton County, Pennsylvania, bounded and described in accordance with a survey made by H. Richard Ohl, Registered Surveyor, dated November 9, 1984, as follows:

BEGINNING at an iron pin on the Easterly line of Pennsylvania Route 18013, which iron pin is on the Boundary line between the parcel to be conveyed and land of the United States of America (United States Army Reserve Center of Lock Haven); thence along the land of the said United States of America, North 70 degrees 41 minutes 10 seconds East a distance of sixty-six and 27/100 (66.27) feet to an iron pin; thence continuing along the same, South 31 degrees 23 minutes 30 seconds East a distance of six hundred seventy-seven and 1/10 (677.1) feet to an iron pin on the Northerly line of Township Route 425, thence along the Northerly line of said Township Route 425, the following five (5) courses and distances: (1) South 70 degrees 44 minutes West a distance of fifty-one and 5/10 (51.5) feet to an iron pin, (2) South 60 degrees 06 minutes West a distance of five hundred thirty-six and 6/10 (536.6) feet to an iron pin, (3) North 29 degrees 54 minutes West a distance of thirteen and 5/10 (13.5) feet to an iron pin, (4) South 61 degrees 54 minutes West a distance of eighty and 5/10 (80.5) feet to an iron pin; (5) South 74 degrees 05 minutes West a distance of 54.0 feet to an iron pin; thence along Pennsylvania Route 18013 North 34 degrees 40 minutes West a distance of fifty-nine and 6/10 (59.6) feet to an iron pin; thence continuing along Pennsylvania Route 18013 North 17 degrees 28 minutes East a distance of eight hundred seventy-two and 8/10 (872.8) feet to an iron pin, the place of beginning, containing an area of 6.74 acres.

BEING a portion of Tract No. 12 of the premises granted and conveyed to the Grantors herein by Deed of Betroblen Realty, Inc., dated January 6, 1986, and recorded in Clinton County Deed Book 295, Page 191."

The description must close by returning to the POB.

Metes-and-bounds descriptions may be very complex and should be handled with extreme care. When they include compass directions of the various lines and concave or convex curved lines, they can be difficult to understand. In such cases, the advice of a surveyor should be sought.

Rectangular (Government) Survey System	The **rectangular survey system,** sometimes called the *government survey method,* was established by Congress in 1785, soon after the federal government was organized. The system was developed as a standard method of describing all lands conveyed to or acquired by the federal government, including the extensive area of the Northwest Territory.
	The rectangular survey system is based on sets of two intersecting lines: principal meridians and base lines. The **principal meridians** are north and south lines and the **base lines** are east and west lines. Both are exactly located by reference to degrees of longitude and latitude. Each principal meridian has a name or number and is crossed by its own base line. Each principal meridian and its corresponding base line are used to survey a definite area of land within prescribed boundary lines. Land parallel to meridians and base lines is divided into ranges and townships, respectively, forming imaginary squares, known as townships, that are further divided into **sections,** then into fractions of sections. These descriptions are frequently combined with metes-and-bounds or lots and blocks descriptions to define smaller or irregularly shaped parcels of land.
Lot and Block System	The third method of land description is by **lot and block system** using a **plat of subdivision** filed in the recorder of deeds office in the county where the land is located.
	The first step in subdividing land is the preparation of a *plat of survey* by a licensed surveyor or engineer, as illustrated in Figure 5.3. On this plat the land is divided into blocks and lots, and streets or access roads for public use are indicated. The blocks and lots are assigned numbers or letters. Lot sizes and street details must be indicated completely and must comply with all local ordinances and requirements. When properly signed and approved, the subdivision plat may be recorded in the county in which the land is located; it thereby becomes part of the legal description. In describing a lot from a recorded subdivision plat, the lot and block number, name or number of the subdivision plat and name of the county and state are used. For example:
	Lots 2, 3 and 4 in Block 5 of L. Robinson's Subdivision of the property beginning at a point on the North side of Main Road, 175 feet east from the corner formed

Figure 5.3
Subdivision Plat
Map

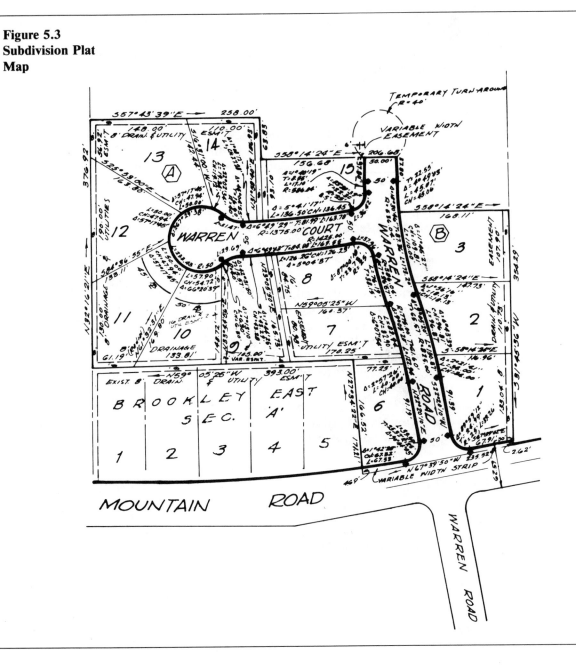

by the intersection of the south side of Main Road and the east side of State Route 54; thence...

Some subdivided lands are further divided by a later resubdivision. For example, if Alan Roswell bought two full blocks of John Welch's subdivision and resubdivided this land into different-sized lots, then Roswell might convey:

Lot 1 in Block A of Roswell's resubdivision of Blocks 2 and 3 and John Welch's Hometown Subdivision of the property beginning at a point on the east side of State Route 33...

This method of land description is used, at least in part, in all states. Some states have passed *plat acts* that specify the smallest tract that may be conveyed without a subdivision plat being prepared, approved and recorded. In some states, for example, the minimum size is five acres.

Preparation and Use of a Survey

Legal descriptions should not be changed, altered or combined without adequate information from a competent authority, such as a surveyor or title attorney. Legal descriptions should *always* include the name of the county in which the land is located. Meridians often relate to more than one state and occasionally relate to two base lines, so a description cannot be certain unless the county and state are given when the rectangular survey system is used. For example, the description "the southwest quarter of Section 10, Township 4 North, Range 1 West of the Fourth Principal Meridian" could refer to land in either Illinois or Wisconsin. The county and state must be specified in order to clarify the ambiguity.

A licensed surveyor is trained and authorized to locate a given parcel of land and to determine its legal description. The surveyor does this by preparing a *survey,* which sets forth the legal description of the property, and a *survey sketch,* which shows the location and dimensions of the parcel. When a survey also shows the location, size and shape of buildings located on the lot, it is referred to as a *spot survey.* Surveys are required in many real estate transactions, such as when: (1) conveying a portion of a given tract of land, (2) conveying real estate as security for a mortgage loan, (3) showing the location of new construction, (4) locating roads and highways and (5) determining the legal description of the land on which a particular building is located.

In Practice . . .

Because legal descriptions, once recorded, affect title to real estate, they should be prepared only by a surveyor or attorney. Real estate licensees who attempt to draft legal descriptions create potential risks for themselves and their clients and customers. Further, when entered on a document of conveyance, legal descriptions should be copied with care. For example, an incorrectly worded legal description in a sales contract may obligate the seller to convey or the buyer to purchase more or less land than intended. Title problems can arise for the buyer when he or she seeks to convey the property at a future date. Even if the contract can be corrected by the parties involved before the sale is closed, the licensee runs the risk of losing a commission. In addition, he or she may be held liable for damages suffered by an injured party because of an improperly worded legal description.

Measuring Elevations

The owner of a parcel of land may subdivide the air above his or her land into **air lots.** Air lots are composed of airspace within specific boundaries located over a parcel of land. This type of description is found in titles to tall buildings located on air rights, generally over railroad tracks. (See the discussion of air rights in Chapter 2, "Real Property.") Similarly a surveyor, in preparing a subdivision plat for condominium use, describes each condominium unit by reference to the elevation of the floors and ceilings on a vertical plane above the city datum.

Datum

A point, line, or surface from which elevations are measured or indicated is a **datum.** For the purposes of the United States Geological Survey, datum is defined

**Figure 5.4
Benchmark**

as the mean sea level at New York harbor. It is of special significance to surveyors in determining the height of structures, establishing the grade of streets and similar situations.

Virtually all large cities have established a local official datum that is used in place of the U.S. Geological Survey datum. For instance, the official datum for Chicago is known as the *Chicago City Datum* and is a horizontal plane below the surface of the city. This plane was established in 1847 as corresponding to the low water level of Lake Michigan in that year and is considered to be zero elevation.

Benchmarks. To aid surveyors, permanent reference points called **benchmarks** have been established throughout the United States (see Figure 5.4). Cities with local datums also have designated local benchmarks, which are given official status when assigned a permanent identifying number. Local benchmarks simplify surveyors' work, for measurements may be based on them rather than on the basic benchmark, which may be miles away.

A surveyor's measurement of elevation based on the USGS datum will differ from one computed according to a local datum. A surveyor can always translate an elevation based on a local datum to the elevation based on the USGS.

Legal Description of a Condominium Interest

The *condominium property acts* passed in all states (see Chapter 7) require that a registered land surveyor prepare a plat of survey showing the elevations of floor and ceiling surfaces and the boundaries of a condominium apartment with reference to an official datum. Typically, a separate plat will be prepared for each floor in the condominium building.

The following is an example of the legal description of a condominium apartment unit that includes a fractional share of the common elements of the building and land:

"THAT certain Unit in the property known, named and identified in the Declaration Plan referred to below as King's Arms Condominium, situate in the Village of Westover, Hampden Township, Cumberland County, Pennsylvania, which has been submitted to the provisions of the Unit Property Act of Pennsylvania, Act of July 3, 1963, P.L. 196 (68P.S. §700.101, *et. seq.*), by recording in the Office of the Recorder of Deeds of Cumberland County, Pennsylvania, of a Declaration dated May 20, 1975, recorded in Miscellaneous Book 215, Page 836, and a Declaration Plan dated May 21, 1975, recorded in the Office of the Recorder of Deeds of Cumberland County in Plan Book 26, Page 70 and a Code of Regulations, being Exhibit "B" of said Declaration, described as follows:

BEING and designated on the Declaration Plan as Unit A-3, detached garage, said garage designated on the Declaration Plan as Unit A-3-G, together with an undivided interest appurtenant to the Unit in all Common Elements (as defined in the Declaration) of 5.26%.

THE Unit is municipally known and numbered as Three King's Arms, Village of Westover, Mechanicsburg, Pennsylvania.

BEING the same premises which Pennsboro Homes, Inc., by Deed dated August 1st, 1975, recorded in the Office of the Recorder of Deeds of Cumberland County in Deed Book E, Volume 26, Page 359, granted and conveyed unto Thomas D. Caldwell, Seller herein."

Land Units and Measurements

It is important to know and understand land units and measurements—they are an integral part of legal descriptions. Some commonly used measurements follow:

1. A *rod* is 16½ feet.

2. A *chain* is 66 feet, or 100 links.

3. A *mile* is 5,280 feet.

4. An *acre* contains 43,560 square feet, or 160 square rods.

5. A *section* of land is one square mile and contains 640 acres; a *quarter section* contains 160 acres; a *quarter of a quarter section* contains 40 acres.

6. A *circle* contains 360 degrees; a *quarter segment* of a circle contains 90 degrees; a *half segment* of a circle contains 180 degrees. One *degree* (1°) can be subdivided into 60 minutes (60′), each of which contains 60 seconds (60″). One-and-a-half degrees would be written 1°30′0″.

Table 5.1 lists further land measurement units and their metric equivalents.

Table 5.1 Units of Land Measurement

Unit	Measurement	Metric Equivalent
mile	5,280 feet; 320 rods; 1,760 yards	1.609 kilometers
rod	5.50 yards; 16.50 feet	5.029 meters
sq. mile	640 acres	2.590 sq. kilometers
acre	4,840 sq. yards; 160 sq. rods; 43,560 sq. feet	4,047 sq. meters
sq. yard	9 sq. feet	0.836 sq. meters
sq. foot	144 sq. inches	0.093 sq. meters
chain	66 feet or 100 links	20.117 meters
kilometer	0.62 mile	1,000 meter
hectare	2.47 acres	10,000 sq. meters

Summary

Documents affecting or conveying interests in real estate must contain an accurate description of the property involved. There are three methods of legal description of land in the United States: (1) metes and bounds, (2) rectangular (government) survey and (3) lot and block system. Pennsylvania, however, does not use the rectangular survey system. A legal description is a precise method of identifying a parcel of land. A property's description should always be the same as the one used in previous documents.

Pennsylvania, as well as 19 states (and parts of Ohio), has always used only metes-and-bounds descriptions of land and continues to do so. In a *metes-and-bounds description,* the actual location of monuments takes precedence over the written linear measurement in a document. When property is being described by metes and bounds, the description must always enclose a tract of land; that is, the boundary line must end at the point at which it started.

The *rectangular survey system* is used in 30 states. It involves surveys based on 35 principal meridians. Under this government survey system, each principal meridian and its corresponding base line are specifically located.

Land in every state can be subdivided into *lots and blocks* by means of a recorded plat of subdivision. An approved plat of survey showing the division into blocks, giving the size, location and designation of lots, and specifying the location and size of streets to be dedicated for public use is filed for record in the recorder's office of the county in which the land is located. *It is possible to resubdivide portions of a previously recorded subdivision.* By referring to a subdivision plat, the legal description of a building site in a town or city can be given by lot, block and subdivision in a county and state.

A plat of survey prepared by a surveyor is the usual method of certifying the legal description of a certain parcel of land. When a survey also shows the location, size and shape of the buildings located on the lot, it is referred to as a *spot survey.* Spot surveys are customarily required in purchases of real estate when a mortgage or new construction is involved.

Air lots, condominium descriptions and other measurements of vertical elevations may be computed from the United States Geological Survey *datum,* which is the mean sea level in New York harbor. Most large cities have established local survey datums for surveying within the area. The elevations from these datums are further supplemented by reference points, called *benchmarks,* placed at fixed intervals from the datums.

Figure 5.5

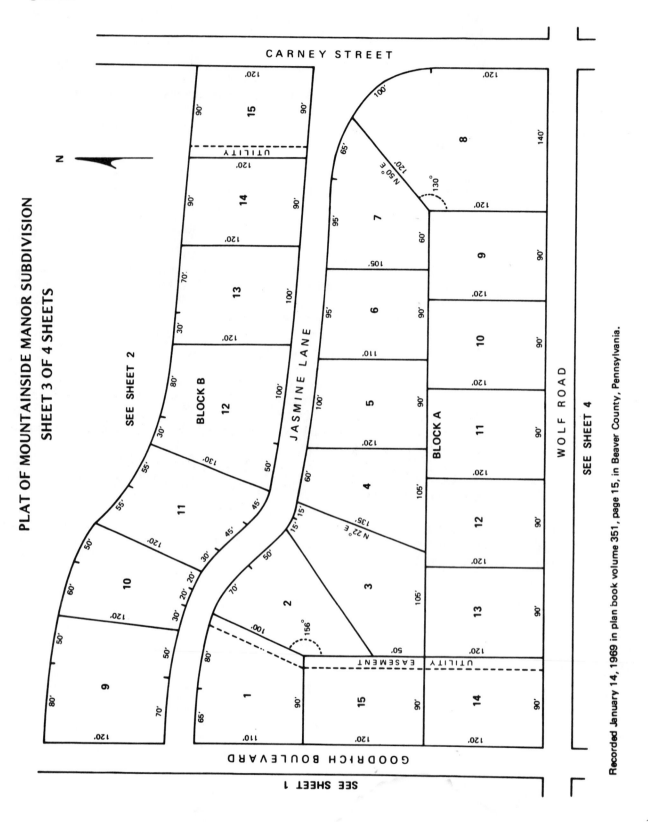

PLAT OF MOUNTAINSIDE MANOR SUBDIVISION
SHEET 3 OF 4 SHEETS

Recorded January 14, 1969 in plan book volume 351, page 15, in Beaver County, Pennsylvania.

Questions

1. A *monument* is used in which of the following types of legal descriptions?
   a. lot and block
   b. metes and bounds
   c. rectangular survey
   d. all of the above

2. The N½ of the SW¼ of a section contains:
   a. 40 acres.   c. 160 acres.
   b. 20 acres.   d. 80 acres.

3. A street address identifying a parcel of real estate:
   a. may be used in conjunction with a metes-and-bounds legal description.
   b. is generally by itself an adequate legal description.
   c. is never necessary.
   d. all of the above

4. An acre contains:
   a. 160 sq. ft.   c. 640 sq. ft.
   b. 43,560 sq. ft.   d. 360 degrees.

5. A *datum* is:
   a. used in the description of an air lot.
   b. measured in New York only.
   c. a calendar method of measurement.
   d. all of the above

6. In describing real estate a system that uses feet, degrees and monuments is:
   a. rectangular survey.
   b. metes and bounds.
   c. government survey.
   d. lot and block.

7. Plats of subdivision:
   I. are prepared by licensed surveyors.
   II. are filed for record in the counties where the lands are located.
   a. I only   c. both I and II
   b. II only   d. neither I nor II

8. A metes-and-bounds legal description:
   I. must completely enclose the tract of land being described.
   II. must end at the POB.
   a. I only   c. both I and II
   b. II only   d. neither I nor II

9. At $800 per acre, a lot that is 264 feet wide and 660 feet long would cost:
   a. $1,320.   c. $3,200.
   b. $1,584.   d. $4,356.

10. A survey that shows the location, size and shape of buildings located on a lot is called:
    a. a survey sketch.
    b. a legal description.
    c. an angular course.
    d. a spot survey.

Answer questions 11 through 14 according to the information given on the plat of Mountainside Manor in Figure 5.5.

11. Which of the following statements is (are) true?
    I. Lot 9, Block A is larger than Lot 12 in the same block.
    II. The plat for the lots on the southerly side of Wolf Road between Goodrich Boulevard and Carney Street is found on Sheet 3.
    a. I only   c. both I and II
    b. II only   d. neither I nor II

12. Which of the following lots has the most frontage on Jasmine Lane?
    a. Lot 10, Block B
    b. Lot 11, Block B
    c. Lot 1, Block A
    d. Lot 2, Block A

13. "Beginning at the intersection of the east line of Goodrich Boulevard and the south line of Jasmine Lane and running south along the east line of Goodrich Boulevard a distance of 230 feet; thence east parallel to the north line of Wolf Road a distance of 195 feet; thence northeasterly on a course N 22° E a distance of 135 feet; and thence northwesterly along the south line of Jasmine Lane to the point of beginning." Which lots are described here?

a. Lots 13, 14, and 15, Block A
b. Lots 9, 10, and 11, Block B
c. Lots 1, 2, 3, and 15, Block A
d. Lots 7, 8, and 9, Block A

14. On the plat, how many lots have easements?

a. one   c. three
b. two   d. four

6

Interests in Real Estate

Overview

Ownership of a parcel of real estate is not necessarily absolute; this ownership is dependent upon the type of interest a person holds in the property. For example, a person may own real property forever and be able to pass it on to heirs, or this ownership may exist only as long as the person lives. Real estate ownership may be restricted to exist as long as the owner uses it for one specific purpose; likewise, it may be restricted to exist as long as the owner refrains from using it for a specific purpose. In addition, the interest in real estate a person possesses may be reduced by the interests others possess in the property. This chapter will discuss the various interests in real estate and how they affect real estate ownership and use.

| **Historical Background** | According to old English common law, the government or king held title to all lands under what was known as the **feudal system** of ownership. Under this system, the individual was merely a tenant whose rights of use and occupancy of real property were held at the sufferance of an overlord. Through a series of social reforms in the seventeenth century, however, the feudal system evolved into the **allodial system** of ownership. Under the allodial system, the individual was entitled to property rights without proprietary control being held by the king. |

Land in the United States is held under the allodial system. The Bill of Rights of the U.S. Constitution firmly establishes the private ownership of land.

| **Government Powers** | Although an individual in the United States has maximum rights in the land he or she owns, these ownership rights are subject to certain powers, or rights, held by federal, state and local governments. Because these limitations on the ownership of real estate are for the general welfare of the community, they supersede the rights of the individual. Such government rights include the following: |

1. **Taxation: Taxation** is a charge on real estate to raise funds to meet the public needs of a government (see Chapter 11, "Real Estate Taxes and Other Liens").

2. **Police power:** This is the power vested in a state to establish legislation to preserve order, to protect the public health and safety and to promote the general welfare. There is no federal police power as such—it exists in this manner on a state level only. As discussed in Chapter 3, a state's **police power** is passed on to municipalities and counties through legislation called *enabling acts.* The use and enjoyment of property is subject to restrictions authorized by such legislation, including both environmental protection laws and zoning and building ordinances regulating the use, occupancy, size, location, construction and rents of real estate.

3. **Eminent domain:** Through the *process of condemnation,* a government may exercise the right of **eminent domain** to acquire privately owned real estate for public use. Three conditions must be met: (a) the proposed use must be declared by the court to be a public use, (b) just compensation must be paid to the owner and (c) the rights of the property owner must be protected by due process of law.

   The exercise of decision making under the right of eminent domain is generally granted by state laws to quasi-public bodies such as public housing or redevelopment authorities, as well as to publicly held companies such as railroads, public utilities and mining companies.

   Public agencies begin by trying to acquire real property through direct negotiation and purchase from the owner. Condemnation is instituted only when the owner's consent cannot be obtained. Condemnations are presumed to be a proper use of the government's right of eminent domain unless the landowner objects. A property owner has the right to object if the owner feels the "taking" is improper and may file suit for the court to decide the matter.

4. **Escheat:** Although **escheat** is not actually a limitation on ownership, state laws provide for ownership of real estate to revert, or escheat, to the state when an owner dies and leaves no heirs and no will disposing of the real estate. In some states, real property will escheat to the county where the land is located, rather than to the state. Escheat occurs only when a property becomes ownerless and is not unique to real estate.

Estates in Land

The degree, quantity, nature, and extent of interest that a person has in real property is an **estate in land.** Estates in land are divided into two major classifications: (1) freehold estates and (2) leasehold estates (those involving tenants). These two classifications exist for historical reasons. Under the common law, freehold estates were classified as real estate, while leasehold estates were considered contracts and construed to be personal property. This classification of estates was based primarily on the duration of the estate or interest. Note that there are various lesser interests or rights to real estate that are not estates in land.

Freehold estates are *estates of indeterminable length,* such as those existing for a lifetime or forever. These include (1) fee simple (indefeasible fee), (2) defeasible fee and (3) life estates.

The first two of these estates continue for an indefinite period and are inheritable by the heirs of the owner. The third terminates upon the death of the person on whose life it is based.

Leasehold estates are *estates for a fixed term of years.* These include estate for years and estate from period to period. Estate at will and estate at sufferance are also leaseholds, though by their operation they are not generally viewed as for fixed terms. Leaseholds are discussed in Chapter 8, "Leases."

The various estates and interests in real estate are illustrated in Figure 6.1.

Fee Simple Estate

An estate in **fee simple** is the *highest type of interest in real estate recognized by law.* A fee simple estate is one in which the holder is entitled to all rights incident to the property. There is no time limit on its existence—it is said to run forever. It is complete ownership. Because this estate is of unlimited duration, upon the death of its owner it passes to the owner's heirs or as provided by will. A fee simple estate is thus an *estate of inheritance.* It is, however, subject to the governmental powers previously explained.

Fee simple absolute. If there are no limitations on fee simple ownership (other than the governmental powers), it is a **fee simple absolute.** In common usage, the terms *fee* and *fee simple* are used interchangeably with *fee simple absolute.*

Fee simple defeasible. A fee simple defeasible (or **defeasible fee estate**) is qualified and may be lost on the occurrence or nonoccurrence of a specified event.

A fee simple may be qualified by a **condition subsequent,** which dictates some action or activity that the new owner must not perform. The former owner retains a *right of reentry,* so that, if the condition is broken, the former owner can retake possession of the property. A grant of land "on the condition that" there

Figure 6.1
Estates and Interests
in Real Estate

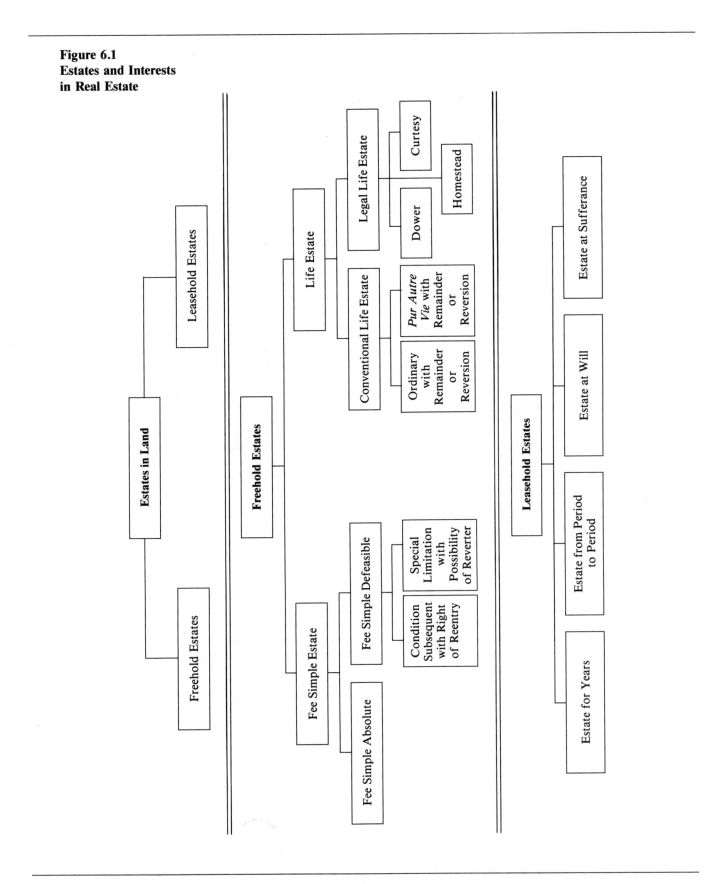

**Figure 6.2
Conventional Life
Estate**

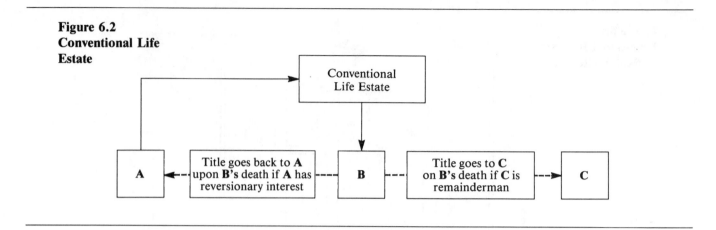

be no consumption of alcohol on the premises is a fee simple on condition subsequent. If alcohol is consumed on the property, the former owner has the right to reacquire full ownership, but it will be necessary for the grantor (or the grantor's heirs or successors) to go to court to assert that right. Conditions in a deed are different from restrictions or covenants because of the grantor's right to reclaim ownership, which does not exist under private restrictions.

If a fee simple estate has a *special limitation,* the estate ends *automatically* upon failure to comply with the limitation. The former owner (or the former owner's heirs or successors) retains a *possibility of reverter* and reacquires full ownership, with no need to reenter the land. A fee simple with a special limitation is also called a **fee simple determinable** since it may end automatically. The language used to distinguish a special limitation—the words "so long as" or "while" or "during"—is the key to the creation of this estate. For example, a grant of land from Aunt Fran to her church "so long as" the land is used only for religious purposes is a fee simple with a special limitation. If the church uses the land for a non-religious purpose, title reverts back to Aunt Fran (or her heirs or successors).

Because they will take effect, if at all, only at some time in the future, the *right of entry* and *possibility of reverter* are termed **future interests.**

Life Estate

A **life estate** is an estate in land that is *limited in duration to the life of the owner or to the life or lives of some other designated person or persons.*

Conventional life estate. A *conventional life estate* is created by grant from the owner of the fee simple estate. The owner retains a reversionary interest in the property or names a remainderman.

A *conventional life estate* is limited to the lifetime of the owner of the life estate (the life tenant); that is, it *ends with the death of the person to whom it was granted* (see Figure 6.2). A life estate created for the life of another person is known as an *estate pur autre vie* (for the life of another). For example, A, who owns fee simple title to Blackacre, can convey a life estate in Blackacre to C for the life of D. C is the life tenant, but the measuring life is D's. While a life estate is *not* considered an estate of inheritance, a life estate pur autre vie provides a qualified right in that it can be inherited by the life tenant's heirs, but only until the death of the person against whose life the estate is measured.

Remainder and reversion. A fee simple owner who creates a life estate must also consider the future ownership of the property after the termination of the life estate. The future interest may take one of two forms:

1. **Remainder interest:** If the deed or will that creates a life estate names someone to whom title will pass upon the termination of the life estate, the person named (the *remainderman)* is said to own a remainder interest or estate. The remainder interest is a nonpossessory estate—a *future interest.*

2. **Reversionary interest:** If the creator of a life estate does not convey a remainder interest, then upon the termination of the life estate, full ownership returns to the original fee simple owner (if deceased, to the heirs or devisees set forth in the fee simple owner's will). This interest or estate is called a *reversion,* and is also a *future interest.*

Thus, upon the death of the life estate owner or other designated person, the holder of the future interest, whether remainder or reversion, will be the owner of a fee simple estate.

A life tenant's interest in real property is a true ownership interest. In general, the life tenant is not answerable to the holder of the future interest. A life tenant's rights are not absolute, however. A life tenant can enjoy the rights of the land but cannot encroach upon those of the remainderman or reversioner. In other words, the life tenant cannot perform any acts that would permanently injure the land or property. Such injury to real estate is known in legal terms as *waste.* In such a case, those having a future interest in the property would be able to seek an injunction or bring legal action against the life tenant for the damages.

The life tenant enjoys all of the "bundle of rights" for life and is entitled to all income and profits arising from the property during his or her term of ownership. A life interest may be sold, leased or mortgaged, but such interest will always terminate upon the death of the person against whose life the estate is measured.

Legal life estate. A *legal life estate* is one created by statute in some states. A legal life estate becomes effective automatically by operation of law upon the occurrence of certain events. Curtesy, dower and homestead are the forms of legal life estate currently used in some states.

Most states have abolished the common-law concepts of dower and curtesy. **Dower** is the life estate that a wife has in the real estate of her deceased husband. A husband's life estate in the real estate of his deceased wife is called **curtesy.**

Generally, the right of dower (or curtesy) becomes effective only upon the death of a spouse. During the lifetimes of the parties, the dower right is *inchoate,* or incomplete—merely the possibility of an interest. For this reason, the right of dower cannot be assigned or transferred to another party and the owning spouse cannot cancel the right by selling the property. *Curtesy and dower rights no longer exist in Pennsylvania.* Such rights have been repealed in favor of the provisions of the Pennsylvania Law of Descent and Distribution. This law, which will be discussed in detail in Chapter 10, "Transfer of Title," allows the surviving spouse to take a specific portion of the estate owned by the deceased spouse at the time of death. The interest taken by a surviving spouse in this instance is an absolute fee estate. In addition, the law provides that the surviving spouse can choose to take the interest given by the deceased's will (if one was properly executed during his or her lifetime) or the share provided by statute.

In Practice...

The right of dower (or curtesy) can usually be released to a purchaser of property by both spouses signing the deed of conveyance. One spouse can also release his or her interest by executing a separate quitclaim deed to the other spouse. If the dower right is not so released when property is conveyed, it can create a cloud, or imperfection, on the title to the property. It is therefore essential that both spouses sign any conveyance of one spouse's real estate. It is also a good idea for the nonowning spouse to sign any sales contract or other document involved in the transaction as well.

Even in states where dower and curtesy have been abolished in favor of descent laws, and, therefore legally, spousal signatures are not necessary, in practice it is best to get both spouses to sign all instruments of conveyance. A nonowning spouse's signature on a conveyance releases any such statutory interests in the real estate being sold.

Homestead. *A tract of land that is owned and occupied as the family home is a* **homestead.** In those states that have homestead exemption laws, a portion of the area or value of such land is protected, or exempt, from judgments for unsecured debts. The purpose of state homestead laws is to protect the family against eviction by general creditors and to protect the spouses by requiring that both husband and wife join in executing any deed conveying the homestead property. The homestead value that is exempt from creditors' claims is specifically defined by state law. *Pennsylvania does not grant homestead exemptions.*

Encumbrances

A claim, charge, or liability that attaches to and is binding on real estate is an **encumbrance.** In plain words, an encumbrance is *anything* that affects title to real estate. It is a right or interest held by a party who is not the fee owner of the property. An encumbrance may lessen the value or obstruct the use of the property, but it does not necessarily prevent a transfer of title.

Encumbrances may be divided into two general classifications: (1) liens (usually monetary) that affect the title, and (2) encumbrances that affect the physical condition of the property, such as restrictions, easements, and encroachments.

Liens

A charge against property that provides security for a debt or obligation of the property owner is a **lien.** If the obligation is not repaid, the lienholder, or creditor, has the right to have it paid out of the property on which the lien is imposed, usually from the proceeds of a court sale. Real estate taxes, mortgages and trust deeds, judgments and mechanics' liens (for people who have furnished labor or materials in the construction or repair of real estate) all represent possible liens against an owner's real estate. Liens will be discussed in detail in Chapter 11.

Restrictions

Private agreements placed in the public record that affect the use of land are **deed restrictions** *and covenants.* They usually are imposed by an owner of real estate when the property is sold and are included in the seller's deed to the buyer. Deed restrictions that would typically be imposed by a developer or subdivider to main-

Figure 6.3
Easements

The owner of Lot A has an **easement by necessity** across Lot B to gain access to his property from the paved road. The owner of Lot B has an **easement appurtenant** across Lot A so that she may reach the lake. Lot A is the servient tenement; Lot B is the dominant tenement as it relates to Lot A under appurtenant easement. The utility company has an **easement in gross** across both parcels of land for its electric power lines.

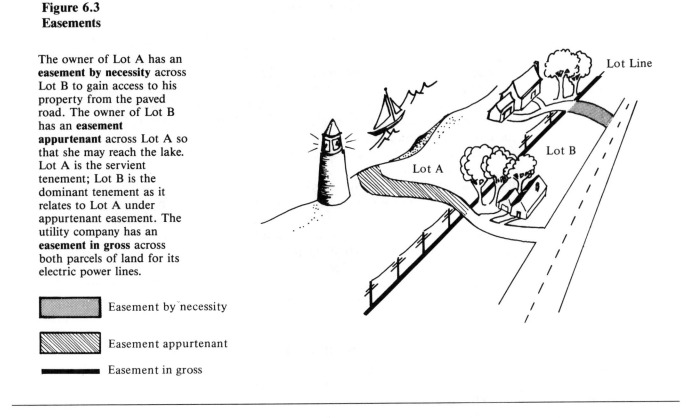

☐ Easement by necessity

☐ Easement appurtenant

▬ Easement in gross

tain specific standards in a subdivision are *restrictive covenants* and would be listed in the original development plans for the subdivision filed in the public record. Deed restrictions were discussed in Chapter 3, "Control of Land Use."

Easements

A right to use the land of another party for a special purpose is an **easement.** An easement right may be in any portion of land, including the airspace above a parcel.

Because *an easement is a right to use land* it is classified as an interest in real estate, but it is not an estate in land. The holder of an easement has only a right, not an estate or ownership interest, in the land over which the easement exists. An easement is sometimes referred to as an *incorporeal right* in land (a nonpossessory interest).

Easement appurtenant. An easement that is *annexed to the ownership and used for the benefit of another's parcel of land* is an **easement appurtenant.** For an easement appurtenant to exist, there must be two adjacent tracts of land owned by different parties. The tract over which the easement runs is known as the *servient tenement;* the tract that is to benefit from the easement is known as the *dominant tenement.* For example (see Figure 6.3), if *A* and *B* own adjacent properties in a resort community and only *A*'s property borders the lake, *A* may grant *B* an easement across *A*'s property to the beach. An easement appurtenant is considered part of the dominant tenement, and if the dominant tenement is conveyed to another party, the easement passes with the title. In legal terms it is said that *the* *easement runs with the land.* However, title to the land over which an easement actually runs is still retained by the servient tenement.

A **party wall** is an exterior wall of a building that straddles the boundary line between two owners' lots, with half of the wall on each lot. Each lot owner owns the half of the wall on his or her lot, and each has an easement appurtenant in the other half of the wall for support of his or her building. A written party-wall agreement should be used to create the easement rights. Expenses to build and maintain the wall are usually shared. A **party driveway** shared by and partly on the land of adjoining owners should also be created by written agreement, specifying responsibility for expenses.

Easement in gross. An *individual interest* in or right to use the land of another is an **easement in gross** and is not appurtenant to any ownership estate in land. Examples of easements in gross are the easement right a railroad has in its right-of-way or the right-of-way for a pipeline or high-tension power line (utility easements). Commercial easements in gross may be assigned or conveyed and may be inherited. However, personal easements in gross usually are not assignable and terminate upon the death of the easement owner. Easements in gross are often confused with the similar personal right of license, discussed later in this chapter.

Easement by necessity. An appurtenant easement that arises when an owner sells part of his or her land that has no access to a street or public way except over the seller's remaining land is an **easement by necessity.** An easement by necessity arises because all owners have rights of ingress to and egress from their land—they cannot be landlocked. (See Figure 6.3.)

Easement by prescription. When the claimant has made use of another's land for a certain period of time as defined by state law, an **easement by prescription** is acquired. This *prescriptive period* in Pennsylvania is *21 years.* The claimant's use must have been continuous, exclusive and without the owner's approval. Additionally, the use must be visible, open and notorious, so that the owner could readily learn of it.

Through the concept of *tacking,* a party not in possession of real property for the entire required statutory period may successfully establish a claim of an easement by prescription. Successive periods of continuous, uninterrupted occupation by different parties may be tacked on, or combined, to reach the prescriptive period. In order to tack on one person's possession to that of another, the parties must have been *successors in interest,* such as an ancestor and his or her heir, landlord and tenant, or seller and buyer.

An **easement by condemnation** is acquired for a public purpose, such as a power line or sewage treatment facility, through the right of eminent domain. The owner of the servient tenement must be compensated for any loss in property value.

Creating an easement. Today, easements are commonly created by written agreement between the parties establishing the easement right. They may also be created in a number of other ways: (1) by express grant from the owner of the property over which the easement will run; (2) by the grantor in a deed of conveyance either *reserving* an easement over the sold land or *granting* the new owner an easement over the grantor's remaining land; (3) by longtime usage, as in an easement by prescription; (4) by necessity; and (5) by *implication*—that is, the situation or the parties' actions may imply that they intend to create an easement.

To create an easement there must be *two separate parties,* one of whom is the owner of the land over which the easement runs. It is impossible for the owner of a parcel of property to have an easement over his or her own land. Thus, where a valid easement exists and the dominant tenement is acquired by the owner of the servient tenement, the easement becomes dormant. The easement will not be considered terminated unless it is either the express or the implied intention of the user to terminate it.

Terminating an easement. Easements may be terminated:

1. when the purpose for which the easement was created no longer exists.
2. when the owner of either the dominant or the servient tenement becomes the owner of the other (a situation called a *merger*).
3. by release of the right of easement to the owner of the servient tenement.
4. by abandonment of the easement (the intention of the parties is the determining factor).
5. by nonuse of a prescriptive easement.
6. by adverse possession by the owner of the servient tenement.
7. by destruction of the servient tenement, as in the demolition of a party wall.
8. by lawsuit (an *action to quiet title*) against someone claiming an easement.
9. by excessive use, as when a residential use is converted to commercial purposes.

Note that an easement may not *automatically* terminate for these reasons. Certain legal steps may be required.

License

A personal privilege to enter the land of another for a specific purpose is a **license.** It is *not* an estate in land; it is a personal right of the party to whom it is given. A license differs from an easement in that *it can be terminated or canceled by the licensor* (the person who granted the license). If a right to use another's property is given orally or informally, it will generally be considered to be a license rather than a personal easement in gross. A license ceases upon the death of either party and is revoked by the sale of the land by the licensor. Examples of license would include permission to park in a neighbor's driveway and the privileges that are granted by the purchase of a ticket for the theater or a sporting event.

Encroachments

When a building (or some portion of it) or a fence or driveway illegally *extends beyond the land of its owner* and covers some land of an adjoining owner or a street or alley, an **encroachment** arises. Encroachments are usually disclosed by either a physical inspection of the property or a spot survey. A spot survey shows the location of all improvements located on a property and whether any improvements extend over the lot lines.

Figure 6.4
Riparian Rights

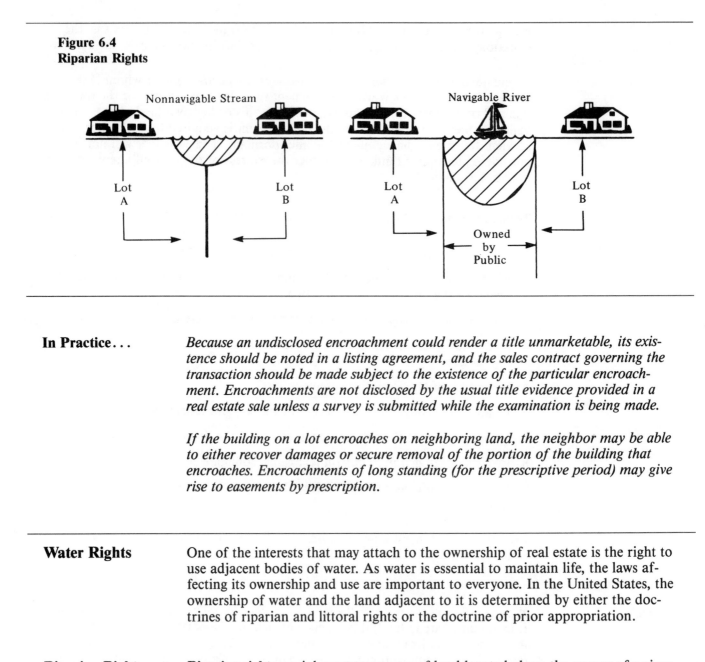

In Practice... *Because an undisclosed encroachment could render a title unmarketable, its existence should be noted in a listing agreement, and the sales contract governing the transaction should be made subject to the existence of the particular encroachment. Encroachments are not disclosed by the usual title evidence provided in a real estate sale unless a survey is submitted while the examination is being made.*

If the building on a lot encroaches on neighboring land, the neighbor may be able to either recover damages or secure removal of the portion of the building that encroaches. Encroachments of long standing (for the prescriptive period) may give rise to easements by prescription.

Water Rights One of the interests that may attach to the ownership of real estate is the right to use adjacent bodies of water. As water is essential to maintain life, the laws affecting its ownership and use are important to everyone. In the United States, the ownership of water and the land adjacent to it is determined by either the doctrines of riparian and littoral rights or the doctrine of prior appropriation.

Riparian Rights **Riparian rights** are inherent to owners of land located along the course of a river, stream or lake. Such an owner has the unrestricted right to use the water, provided such use does not contaminate the water or interrupt or alter its flow. In addition, an owner of land that borders a nonnavigable waterway owns the land under the water to the exact center of the waterway. Land adjoining navigable rivers is usually owned to the water's edge, with the state holding title to the submerged land (see Figure 6.4). Navigable waters are considered public highways in which the public has an easement or right to travel. The laws governing and defining riparian rights differ from state to state.

Littoral Rights Closely related to riparian rights are the **littoral rights** of owners whose land borders on large, navigable lakes and oceans. Owners with littoral rights may enjoy unrestricted use of available waters, but own the land adjacent to the water only

Figure 6.5
Littoral Rights

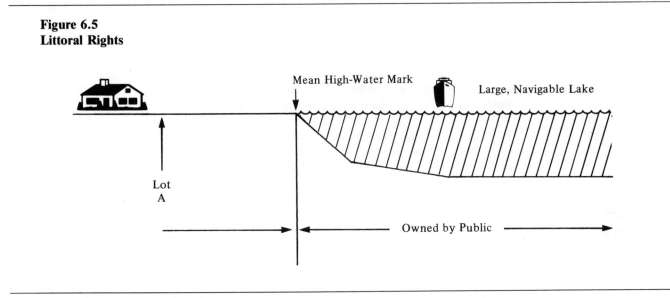

Mean High-Water Mark

Large, Navigable Lake

Lot A

Owned by Public

up to the mean high-water mark (see Figure 6.5). All land below this point is owned by the government.

Riparian and littoral rights are appurtenant (attached) to the land and cannot be retained when the property is sold. This means that the right to use the water belongs to whoever owns the bordering land and cannot be retained by a former owner after the land is sold.

Where land adjoins streams or rivers, an owner is entitled to all land created through *accretion,* increases in the land resulting from the deposit of soil by the natural action of the water. (Such deposits are called *alluvion.)*

Likewise, an owner may lose land through *erosion,* the gradual and imperceptible wearing away of the land caused by flowing water (or other natural forces). This is contrasted to *avulsion,* the sudden removal of soil by an act of nature. A riparian owner generally does not lose title to land lost by avulsion—the boundary lines stay the same no matter how much soil is lost. In contrast, a riparian owner loses title to any land washed away by erosion.

Doctrine of Prior Appropriation

In states where water is scarce, the ownership and use of water are often determined by the **doctrine of prior appropriation.** Under this doctrine, *the right to use any water, with the exception of limited domestic use, is controlled by the state rather than by the adjacent landowner.* Ownership of the land bordering bodies of water in prior appropriation states is generally determined in the same way as riparian and littoral ownership.

To secure water rights, a person must show a beneficial use for the water, such as crop irrigation, and file for and obtain a permit from the proper state department. Although statutes governing prior appropriation vary from state to state, the priority of the water right is usually determined by the oldest recorded permit date.

Once granted, water rights may be perfected through the legal processes prescribed by the individual state. When the water right is perfected, it generally becomes attached to the land of the person holding the permit. The permit holder may, if he or she chooses, sell such a water right to another party.

Issuance of a water permit does not grant access to the water source. All access rights-of-way over the land of another (easements) must be obtained from the property owner.

Summary

An *estate* is the degree, quantity, nature and extent of interest a person holds in land. There are several types of estates, distinguished according to the degree of interest held. *Freehold estates* are estates of indeterminate length. Less than freehold estates are called *leasehold estates;* they concern tenants. Freehold estates are further divided into estates of inheritance and life estates. Estates of inheritance include *fee simple* and *defeasible fee* estates. There are two types of life estates: (1) conventional life estates, which are created by acts of the parties; and (2) legal life estates, which are created by law. Pennsylvania law does not, however, recognize *curtesy, dower* or *homestead.*

Encumbrances against real estate may be in the form of liens, deed restrictions, easements, licenses and encroachments.

An *easement* is the right acquired by one person to use another's real estate. Easements are classified as interests in real estate, but are not estates in land. *Easements appurtenant* involve two separately owned tracts. The tract benefited is known as the *dominant tenement;* the tract that is subject to the easement is called the *servient tenement.* An *easement in gross* is an individual right, such as that granted to utility companies to maintain poles, wires and pipelines.

Easements may be created by agreement, express grant, grant or reservation in a deed, implication, necessity, prescription or party-wall agreement. They can be terminated when the purpose of the easement no longer exists, by merger of both interests with an express intention to extinguish the easement, by release, or by an intention to abandon the easement.

A *license* is permission to enter another's property for a specific purpose. A license is usually created orally, is of a temporary nature, and can be revoked.

An *encroachment* is an unauthorized use of another's real estate.

Ownership of land encompasses not only the land itself but also the right to use the water on or adjacent to it. Many states subscribe to the common-law doctrine of *riparian rights,* which gives the owner of land adjacent to a non-navigable stream ownership of the stream to its midpoint. *Littoral rights* are held by owners of land bordering large lakes and oceans and include rights to the water and ownership of the land up to the high-water mark. In states where water is scarce, water use is often decided by the doctrine of prior appropriation. Under prior appropriation, water belongs to the state and is allocated to users who have obtained permits.

Questions

1. The term *dower* refers to which of the following?
   a. a conventional life estate in real property
   b. ownership of a homestead
   c. a type of encumbrance
   d. a life estate not recognized in Pennsylvania

2. The right of a governmental body to take ownership of real estate for public use is called:
   a. escheat.
   b. eminent domain.
   c. littoral rights.
   d. police power.

3. Peter Kelly's apple tree has been growing in the backyard. It is a big tree and several of its branches extend across Kelly's lot line into the backyard of a neighbor, Alice Manley. These branches are an example of an:
   a. easement.
   b. encroachment.
   c. avulsion.
   d. a and b

4. In Pennsylvania, the prescriptive period for an easement by prescription is which of the following?
   a. 20 years
   b. 30 years
   c. 21 years
   d. 31 years

5. A purchaser of real estate learned that his ownership rights will continue forever and that no other person claims to be the owner or has any ownership control over the property. This person owns a:
   a. fee simple interest.
   b. life estate.
   c. determinable fee estate.
   d. fee simple estate subject to a condition subsequent.

6. Ed Roberts has the legal right to pass over the land owned by his neighbor. This is an:
   a. estate in land.
   b. easement.
   c. emblement.
   d. a and b

7. A husband's interest in property owned by his deceased wife is determined by Pennsylvania state laws regarding:
   I. curtesy.
   II. descent.
   a. I only
   b. II only
   c. both I and II
   d. neither I nor II

8. Janet Auden owned the fee simple title to a vacant lot adjacent to a hospital and was persuaded to make a gift of the lot. She wanted to have some control over its use, so her attorney prepared her deed to convey ownership of the lot to the hospital "as long as it is used for hospital purposes." After completion of the gift, the hospital will own a:
   a. fee simple estate.
   b. license.
   c. determinable fee estate.
   d. leasehold estate.

9. After Peter Desmond had purchased his house and moved in, he discovered that his neighbor regularly used Desmond's driveway to reach a garage located on the neighbor's property. Desmond's attorney explained that ownership of the neighbor's real estate includes an easement appurtenant that gives him the driveway right. Desmond's property is properly called:
   a. the dominant tenement.
   b. a tenement.
   c. a leasehold.
   d. the servient tenement.

10. A father conveys ownership of his residence to his son but reserves for himself a life estate in the residence. The interest the son owns during the father's lifetime is:
    a. pur autre vie.
    b. a remainder.
    c. a reversion.
    d. a and b

11. If the owner of real estate does not take action to evict an encroacher before the prescriptive period has passed, then the encroacher may acquire:

    I. an easement by necessity.
    II. a license.

    a. I only
    b. II only
    c. both I and II
    d. neither I nor II

12. Which one of the following best describes a life estate?

    a. an estate conveyed to *A* for the life of *Z* and upon *Z*'s death to *B*
    b. an estate held by *A* and *B* in joint tenancy with right of survivorship
    c. an estate without condition
    d. a fee simple estate

13. Encumbrances on real estate:

    I. may include liens, easements and deed restrictions.
    II. make it impossible to sell the encumbered property.

    a. I only
    b. II only
    c. both I and II
    d. neither I nor II

14. An estate in land that will automatically extinguish upon the occurrence of a specified event is called a:

    a. determinable fee.
    b. fee simple subject to a condition subsequent.
    c. fee simple.
    d. a and b

15. A *license* is an example of a(n):

    a. easement.
    b. encroachment.
    c. personal privilege.
    d. restriction.

16. A tenant in an apartment building holds a:

    I. less-than-freehold estate.
    II. license.

    a. I only
    b. II only
    c. both I and II
    d. neither I nor II

17. Many states determine water use by allocating water to users who hold recorded beneficial-use permits. This type of water-use privilege is called:

    a. the doctrine of riparian rights.
    b. the doctrine of highest and best use.
    c. the doctrine of prior appropriation.
    d. none of the above

18. Under the allodial system, individual landowners have maximum rights, subject to certain government powers such as:

    I. police power.
    II. eminent domain.

    a. I only
    b. II only
    c. both I and II
    d. neither I nor II

7

How Ownership Is Held

Key Terms
Beneficiary
Common elements
Community property
Condominium
Cooperative
Co-ownership
Corporation
General partnership
Joint tenancy
Limited partnership
Partition
Partnership

Pennsylvania Uniform Condominium Act
Right of survivorship
Separate property
Severalty
Syndicate
Tenancy by the entirety
Tenancy in common
Time-sharing
Trust
Trustee
Trustor
Undivided interest

Overview
There are many different forms of ownership that purchasers must consider before taking title to a parcel of real estate. The choice of ownership form will affect such matters as the owner's legal right to sell the real estate without the consent of others, the owner's right to choose who will own the property after his or her death and the rights of creditors in the future. The choice will also in many cases have tax implications, both in terms of a possible gift tax resulting from a present transfer and in terms of future income and estate taxes. This chapter will discuss the many basic forms of real estate ownership available to individuals as well as to business entities, and will also include a discussion of the increasingly popular cooperative and condominium forms of ownership.

Forms of Ownership	A fee simple estate in land may be held (1) in **severalty,** which means that title is held by one owner; (2) in **co-ownership,** where title is held by two or more persons; or (3) in **trust,** where title is held by a third person for the benefit of another or others, called the beneficiary or beneficiaries.
	The form by which property is owned is important to the real estate broker's work for two reasons: (1) *the form of ownership existing when a property is sold determines who must sign the various documents involved* (listing contract, acceptance of offer to purchase, sales contract and deed); and (2) *the purchaser must determine in what form to take title.* For example, if there is one purchaser taking title in his or her name alone, it is tenancy in severalty; if there are two or more purchasers, they may take title as tenants in common or as joint tenants. Married purchasers' choices are governed by state laws. Pennsylvania provides for married couples to own real estate as tenants by the entireties, unless the deed creating the estate identifies a different form of ownership.
	The forms of ownership available are controlled by the laws of the state in which the land is located. When questions about these forms are raised by the parties to a transaction, the real estate broker should recommend that the parties seek legal advice.
Ownership in Severalty	When title to real estate is *vested in* (presently owned by) one person or one organization, that person or organization is said to own the property *in severalty.* This person is also referred to as the *sole owner.* The various states have special laws that affect title held in severalty by either a husband or a wife. In some states, when either the husband or wife owns property in severalty (alone), it is still necessary for the spouse to join in signing documents: (1) to release dower or curtesy in states that have such rights, (2) to release homestead rights in states that provide a homestead exemption for homeowners, (3) when the spouse is a minor or (4) to release any other spousal claims or question of claim that might exist.
Co-Ownership	When title to one parcel of real estate is vested in (owned by) two or more persons or organizations, those parties are said to be *co-owners,* or *concurrent owners,* of the property. Concurrent ownership means that two or more owners are vested in the property at the same time, each sharing in the rights of ownership, possession and so forth. There are several forms of co-ownership, each having unique legal characteristics. The forms most commonly recognized by the various states are: (1) tenancy in common, (2) joint tenancy, (3) tenancy by the entirety, (4) community property and (5) partnership property. Each of these forms of co-ownership will be discussed separately.
Tenancy in Common	A parcel of real estate may be owned by two or more people as **tenants in common,** each of the owners holding an undivided interest in severalty; that is, *each*

owner's fractional interest is held just as though he or she were a sole owner. There are two important characteristics of a tenancy in common.

First, the ownership interest of a tenant in common is an **undivided interest;** there is a *unity of possession* between the co-owners. This means that although a tenant in common may hold, say, a one-half or one-third interest in a property, this does not distinguish a physical half or third of the property the tenant in common owns. The deed creating a tenancy in common may or may not state the fractional interest held by each co-owner: if no fractions are stated and two people hold title to the property as co-owners, each has an undivided one-half interest. Likewise, if five people held title, each would own an undivided one-fifth interest.

The second important characteristic of a tenancy in common is that *each owner holds his or her undivided interest in severalty* and can sell, convey, mortgage or transfer that interest *without consent* of the other co-owners. Upon the death of a co-owner, that tenant's undivided interest passes to any heirs or devisees according to the will. The interest of a deceased tenant in common does not pass to another tenant in common unless the surviving co-owner is an heir, devisee or purchaser (see Figure 7.1). In many states, the spouse of a married tenant in common must sign a deed to a purchaser in order to release his or her dower or homestead rights.

When two or more people acquire title to a parcel of real estate and the deed of conveyance does not stipulate the character of the tenancy created, then by operation of law, the grantees will acquire title as tenants in common. In Pennsylvania, if the conveyance is made to a husband and wife with no further explanation (as will be detailed later in the chapter), a tenancy by the entirety will be created.

Joint Tenancy

Most states recognize some form of **joint tenancy,** which is an estate or unit of interest in land owned by two or more people. The basis of joint tenancy is *unity of ownership.* Only one title exists and it is vested in a unit made up of two or more people. Traditionally, the death of one of the joint tenants does not destroy the unit; it only reduces by one the number of people who make up the owning unit. The remaining joint tenants would then receive the interest of the deceased tenant by **right of survivorship** (see Figure 7.2).

Right of survivorship is an alternative to ownership passing through a will or inheritance upon death. As such, it has come to be known as the "poor man's will," though it can be a dangerous substitute for a will.

Historically, under common law, the creation of a joint tenancy carried with it the right of survivorship. A Pennsylvania statute passed in 1812, however, provides that the interest of a joint tenant who dies shall not accrue automatically to the survivor. Although this statute does not prevent the creation of the right of survivorship, it does make it necessary for the conveyance to include language that specifies such survivorship if it is desired as a feature of the joint tenancy. For example, the conveyance might be made "to *A* and *B* and to the survivor of them, his or her heirs and assigns, as joint tenants and not tenants in common."

In the absence of this language, a joint tenancy would not have the characteristic of survivorship. A joint tenancy without the right of survivorship is similar to a tenancy in common in effect; however, the co-owners are known as joint tenants.

Figure 7.1
Tenancy in Common

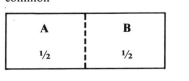

The distinction between such a joint tenancy, and a tenancy in common is more technical than actual.

Creating joint tenancies. A joint tenancy can be created only through a deed of conveyance or by devise (giving the property by will). It cannot be implied or created by operation of law. The conveyance must specifically state the intention to create a joint tenancy, and the grantees or devisees must be explicitly identified as joint tenants. For example, typical wording in a conveyance creating a joint tenancy would be "to *A* and *B* as joint tenants and not as tenants in common." In order to create a joint tenancy with the right of survivorship in Pennsylvania, the conveyance must also explicitly indicate the intention to create the right of survivorship in order for that right to exist. In such cases, appropriate wording might be "to *A* and *B* and to the survivor of them, his or her heirs and assigns, as joint tenants."

Four unities are required to create a joint tenancy:

1. unity of *time*—all joint tenants acquire their interest at the same time;

2. unity of *title*—all joint tenants acquire their interest by the same instrument of conveyance;

3. unity of *interest*—all joint tenants hold equal ownership interests; and

4. unity of *possession*—all joint tenants hold an undivided right to possession.

These four unities are present when title is acquired by *one deed, executed and delivered at one time, and conveying equal interests to all the grantees, who hold undivided possession of the property as joint tenants.*

In many states, if real estate is owned in severalty by a person who wishes to create a joint tenancy between himself or herself and others, the owner will have to convey the property to an intermediary (usually called a *nominee*) and the nominee must convey it back, naming all the parties as joint tenants in the conveyance. Some states, including Pennsylvania, have eliminated this "legal fiction" by allowing an owner in severalty to execute a deed to himself or herself and others "as joint tenants and not as tenants in common" and thereby create a valid joint tenancy without the actual presence of the four unities. Intermediaries in Pennsylvania are seldom used.

Terminating joint tenancies. A joint tenancy is destroyed when any one of the essential unities of joint tenancy is terminated. Thus, although a joint tenant is free to convey his or her interest in the jointly held property, doing so will destroy the unity of interest and, in turn, the joint tenancy. For example, if *A*, *B* and *C*

**Figure 7.2
Joint Tenancy with
Right of Survivorship**

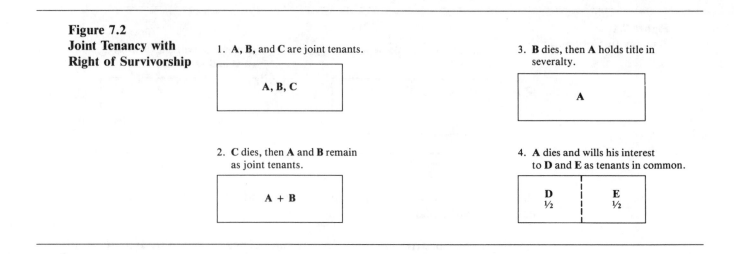

1. **A, B,** and **C** are joint tenants.

> **A, B, C**

2. **C** dies, then **A** and **B** remain as joint tenants.

> **A + B**

3. **B** dies, then **A** holds title in severalty.

> **A**

4. **A** dies and wills his interest to **D** and **E** as tenants in common.

> **D** **E**
> ½ ½

hold title as joint tenants and *A* conveys her interest to *D,* then *D* will own an undivided one-third interest in severalty as a tenant in common with *B* and *C,* who will continue to own their undivided two-thirds interest as joint tenants (see Figure 7.3).

Joint tenancies may also be terminated by operation of law, such as in bankruptcy or foreclosure sale proceedings. In addition, in states where a mortgage on real property is held to be a conveyance of land, a joint tenant who mortgages his or her property without the other tenants joining in the mortgage will also destroy the joint tenancy.

Termination of Co-Ownership by Partition Suit

Tenants in common or joint tenants who wish to terminate their co-ownership of real estate may file in court a suit to **partition** the land. The right of partition is a legal way to dissolve a co-ownership when the parties do not voluntarily agree to its termination. If the court determines that the land cannot actually be divided into parts, it will order the real estate sold and divide the proceeds of the sale among the co-owners according to their fractional interests.

Tenancy by the Entirety

A **tenancy by the entirety** is a *special joint tenancy between husband and wife in Pennsylvania.* Each spouse has an equal, undivided interest in the property; each, in essence, owns the entire estate. Upon the death of one spouse, the tenancy operates such that the surviving spouse automatically becomes sole owner. The distinguishing characteristics of this tenancy are: (1) the owners must be husband and wife; (2) the surviving owner becomes owner in severalty; (3) during the owners' lives, title can be conveyed *only by a deed signed by both parties* (one party cannot convey a one-half interest); and (4) there is generally no right to partition. Under early common law, a husband and wife were held to be one person in the eyes of the law—the wife's legal personality was merged with that of her husband's. As a result, real estate owned by a husband and wife as tenants by the entireties is considered to be held by one indivisible legal unit. Married couples often take title to property as tenants by the entirety so that the surviving spouse, who automatically becomes sole owner of the property, can enjoy the benefits of ownership without waiting for the conclusion of probate proceedings.

**Figure 7.3
Combination of
Tenancies**

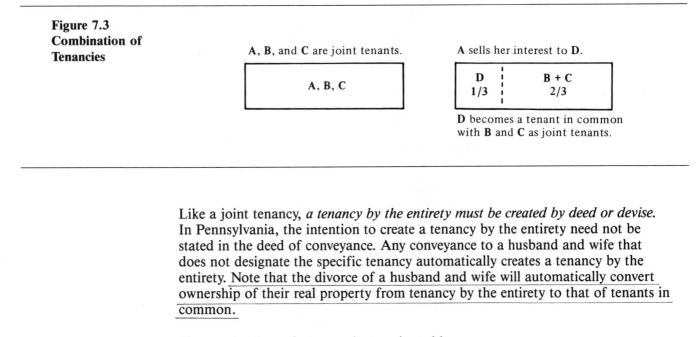

A, B, and C are joint tenants.

A, B, C

A sells her interest to D.

D 1/3	B + C 2/3

D becomes a tenant in common
with **B** and **C** as joint tenants.

Like a joint tenancy, *a tenancy by the entirety must be created by deed or devise.* In Pennsylvania, the intention to create a tenancy by the entirety need not be stated in the deed of conveyance. Any conveyance to a husband and wife that does not designate the specific tenancy automatically creates a tenancy by the entirety. Note that the divorce of a husband and wife will automatically convert ownership of their real property from tenancy by the entirety to that of tenants in common.

Tenancy by the entirety may be terminated by:

1. the death of either spouse;

2. divorce (leaving the parties as tenants in common);

3. mutual agreement of the spouses; or

4. execution proceedings in favor of a *joint* creditor of husband and wife.

**Community
Property Rights**

The concept of community property originated in Spanish law rather than English common law and was adopted by eight of the western and southwestern states (Arizona, California, Idaho, Louisiana, Nevada, New Mexico, Texas and Washington). There are many variations among the community property laws of these states.

Community property laws are based on the concept that a husband and wife, rather than merging into one entity, are equal partners. Thus, any property acquired during a marriage is considered to be obtained by mutual effort. Community property states recognize two kinds of property. **Separate property** is that owned solely by either spouse before the marriage or is acquired by gift or inheritance after the marriage. Such separate, or exempted, property also includes any property purchased with separate funds after the marriage. Any income earned from a person's separate property generally remains part of his or her separate property. Property classified as sole and separate can be mortgaged or conveyed by the owning spouse without the signature of the nonowning spouse.

Community property consists of all other property, real and personal, acquired by either spouse during the marriage. Any conveyance or encumbrance of community property requires the signatures of both spouses. Upon the death of one spouse, the survivor automatically owns one-half of the community property. The other half is distributed according to the deceased's will. If the deceased died without a will, the other half is inherited by the surviving spouse or by the deceased's other heirs, depending upon state law. Pennsylvania is not a community property state. Legal counsel is recommended for proper planning of one's affairs.

Examples of Co-Ownership

To clarify the concepts of co-ownership further, note the following four examples of co-ownership arrangements:

1. A deed conveys title to *A* and *B*. The intention of the parties is not stated, so generally ownership as tenants in common is created. If *A* dies, her one-half interest will pass to her heirs or according to her will.

2. A deed conveying title one-third to *C* and two-thirds to *D* creates a tenancy in common, with each owner having the fractional interest specified.

3. A deed to *H* and *W* as husband and wife creates a tenancy by the entirety.

4. A conveyance of real estate to two people (not husband and wife) by such wordings as "to *Y* and *Z,* as joint tenants and to the survivor and his or her heirs and assigns," creates a joint tenancy ownership with the right of survivorship. Upon the death of *Y,* his share of the title to the property will pass to *Z* automatically. In Pennsylvania, if this right of survivorship is not specifically stated in the deed of conveyance, that portion of the title will pass to *Y*'s heirs, rather than to *Z*.

Note also that *a combination of interests can exist in one parcel of real estate.* For example, when *M* and spouse hold title to an undivided one-half as joint tenants, and *S* and spouse hold title to the other undivided one-half as joint tenants, the relationship among the owners of the two half interests is that of tenants in common.

Trusts

In Pennsylvania, title to real estate can be held in a trust. In order for a trust to be created, the title to the real estate involved must be conveyed by the **trustor** (also known as a *settlor)*, the person originating the trust, to a **trustee,** who will own the property for one or more people or legal entities, called **beneficiaries.** The trustee is a *fiduciary,* one who acts in confidence or trust, and has a special legal relationship with the beneficiary or beneficiaries. The trustee can be either an individual or a corporation, such as a trust company. The trustee has only as much power and authority as is given by the instrument that created the trust. Such an instrument may be a trust agreement, will, trust deed or deed in trust (see Figure 7.4). Real estate ownership can generally be held under either: (1) living and testamentary trusts or (2) land trusts. In addition, real estate may be held by a number of people in a *real estate investment trust,* which will be discussed in Chapter 23, "Real Estate Investment."

Living and Testamentary Trusts

Property owners may provide for their own financial care and/or that of their families by establishing a trust. Such trusts may be created by agreement during a property owner's lifetime (living) or established by will after his or her death (testamentary).

Figure 7.4
Trust Ownership

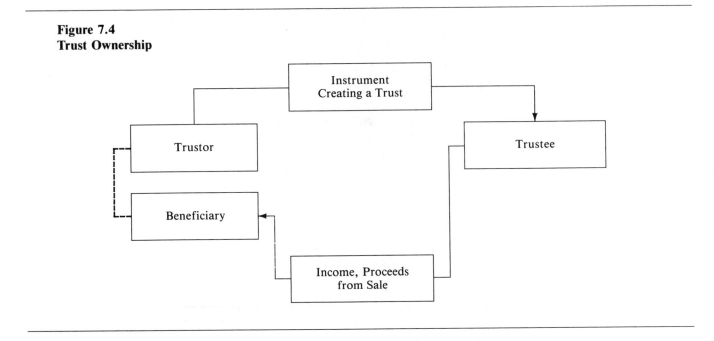

The individual creating a trust makes an agreement with a trustee (usually a corporate trustee) by which the individual conveys assets (real and/or personal), to the trustee with the understanding that the trustee will assume certain duties. These duties include the care and investment of the trust assets to produce an income. After payment of operating expenses and trustee's fees, this income is paid to or used for the benefit of the beneficiaries. These trusts may continue for the lifetimes of the beneficiaries or the assets can be distributed when the property owner's children reach certain predetermined ages.

Land Trusts

A few states, including Pennsylvania, permit the establishment of land trusts in which real estate is the only asset. As in all trusts, the legal title to the property is conveyed to a trustee, and the beneficial interest is in the beneficiary, who, in the case of land trusts, is usually the trustor.

One of the distinguishing characteristics of a land trust is that the *public records do not indicate the beneficiary's identity.* A land trust agreement is executed by the trustor and the trustee. Under this agreement, the trustee has a *real property* interest, yet deals with the property only upon the beneficiary's written direction. Although the beneficial interest in the trust real estate is considered to be *personal property,* the beneficiary retains management and control of the property and has the right of possession as well as the right to any income or proceeds from its sale.

Usually only individuals create land trusts, but corporations as well as individuals can be beneficiaries. A land trust generally continues for a definite term (such as 20 years). If the beneficiaries do not extend the trust term when it expires, the trustee is usually obligated to sell the real estate and distribute the net proceeds to the beneficiaries.

Ownership of Real Estate by Business Organizations

A business entity is an organization that exists independently of the people who are members of the organization—for example, a corporation. Ownership by a business organization makes it possible for many people to hold an interest in the same parcel of real estate. There are various ways in which investors may be organized to finance a real estate project. Some provide for the real estate to be owned by the entity itself; others provide for direct ownership of the real estate by the investors. Business organizations may be categorized as: (1) partnerships, (2) corporations or (3) syndicates. The purchase or sale of real estate by any business organization involves complex legal questions, and legal counsel is usually required.

Partnerships

An association of two or more people to carry on a business as co-owners and share in the business's profits and losses is a **partnership.** There are two kinds of partnerships, general and limited. In a **general partnership,** all partners participate to some extent in the operation and management of the business and may be held personally liable for business losses and obligations. A **limited partnership** includes general partners as well as limited, or silent, partners. The business is run by the general partner or partners. The limited partners do not participate and each can be held liable for the business's losses *only* to the extent of his or her investment. The limited partnership is a popular method of organizing investors in a real estate project.

A partnership is not usually a legal entity, and technically, under common law, a partnership cannot own real estate. Title must be vested in the partners as individuals in a tenancy in common or joint tenancy, not in the partnership. However, Pennsylvania has adopted the *Uniform Partnership Act,* under which realty may be held in the partnership name, and the *Uniform Limited Partnership Act,* which establishes the legality of the limited partnership form and also provides that realty may be held in the partnership name.

General partnerships are dissolved and must be reorganized if one partner dies, withdraws or goes bankrupt. In a limited partnership, the agreement creating the partnership may provide for the continuation of the organization upon the death or withdrawal of one of the partners.

Corporations

A **corporation** is a non-natural person, or legal entity, created under the authority of the laws of the state from which it receives its charter. Because the corporation is a legal entity, real estate ownership by a corporation is an *ownership in severalty.* A corporation is managed and operated by its *board of directors.* A corporation's charter sets forth the powers of the corporation, including its right to buy and sell real estate after passage of a resolution to that effect by its board of directors. Some charters permit a corporation to purchase real estate for any purpose; others limit such purchases to land that is needed to fulfill the entity's corporate purpose.

As a legal entity, a corporation exists in perpetuity until it is formally dissolved. The death of one of the officers or directors does not affect title to property that is owned by the corporation.

Individuals participate, or invest, in a corporation by purchasing stock. Because stock is *personal property,* stockholders do not have a direct ownership interest in real estate owned by a corporation. Each stockholder's liability for the corporation's losses is usually limited to the amount of the investment.

One of the main disadvantages of corporate ownership of income property is that the profits are subject to double taxation. As a legal entity, a corporation must file an income tax return and pay tax on its profits. In addition, the portions of the remaining profits distributed to stockholders as dividends are taxed again as part of the stockholders' individual incomes. An alternative that provides the benefit of a corporation as a legal entity but avoids the double taxation is known as a *Chapter S Corporation.* Only stockholder dividends are taxed and not the profits of the corporation.

Syndicates

Generally speaking, a **syndicate** is a *joining together of two or more people or firms in order to make and operate a real estate investment.* A syndicate is not in itself a legal entity; however, it may be organized into a number of ownership forms, including co-ownership (tenancy in common, joint tenancy), partnership (general or limited), trust or corporation. A *joint venture* is a form of partnership in which two or more people or firms carry out a *single business project.* Joint ventures are characterized by a time limitation resulting from the fact that the joint venturers do not intend to establish a permanent relationship. More will be said about these organizations in Chapter 23, "Real Estate Investment."

Condominium and Cooperative Ownership

As the nation's population grew, the population concentrated in large urban areas. This led to multiple-unit housing. Initially these buildings were occupied by "tenants" under the traditional rental system. But the urge to "own a part of the land," together with certain tax advantages that accrue to such ownership, gave rise to the condominium and cooperative forms of ownership.

Condominium Ownership

The **condominium** form of ownership has gained increasing popularity in recent years. Condominium laws have been enacted in every state. In Pennsylvania the law governing condominiums is known as the **Pennsylvania Uniform Condominium Act.** Under these laws, the owner of each apartment holds a *fee simple estate* to the unit and a specified share of the indivisible parts of the building and land, known as the **common elements** (see Figure 7.5). The individual unit owners in a condominium own these common elements together as tenants in common. State law usually limits this relationship among unit owners in that there is *no right to partition,* as was previously discussed in tenancy in common.

Architectural style. The condominium form of ownership can exist in a variety of *architectural styles.* These range from single free-standing units and townhouse arrangements to highrise buildings. The common elements include such items as the land, walls, hallways, elevators, stairways and roof. In some instances lawns and recreational facilities such as swimming pools, clubhouses, tennis courts and golf courses may also be considered common elements. In addition, the condominium form of ownership is used for other types of properties such as commercial property, office buildings or multi-use buildings that contain offices and shops as well as residential units.

**Figure 7.5
Condominium
Ownership**

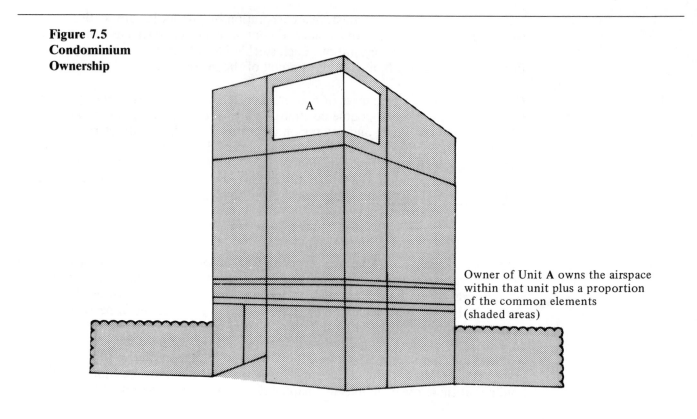

Owner of Unit **A** owns the airspace
within that unit plus a proportion
of the common elements
(shaded areas)

Creation of a condominium. According to the provisions of the state Uniform
Condominium Act, a condominium is created and established when the owner of
an existing building or the developer of unimproved land executes and records a
Declaration of Condominium, which is a declaration of its creation in the county
where the property is located. The declaration must include: (1) a legal description of the condominium units and the common elements (including *limited* common elements—those that serve only one particular unit); (2) a copy of the
condominium's bylaws, drafted to govern the operation of the owners' association; (3) a survey of the property; and (4) an architect's drawings of the buildings,
illustrating both the vertical and horizontal boundaries of each unit. It may also
include restrictive covenants controlling the use of the rights of ownership.

If the development is to be a *flexible* condominium—one in which the owner or
developer leaves open the right to add or subtract units or convert units to common elements or vice versa—this must be spelled out in the declaration. In addition, the owner or developer must record a *certificate of completion* from an
independent surveyor, architect or engineer, assuring that all structural components and mechanical systems have been substantially completed.

Ownership. Once the property is established as a condominium, each unit becomes a separate parcel of real estate that may be dealt with like any other parcel
of real property. A condominium unit is *owned in fee simple, including rights inherent to real estate as may be restricted publicly and privately, and may be held by
one or more people in any type of ownership or tenancy that is recognized by state
law. Because it is real estate, it can be mortgaged.*

Real estate taxes are assessed and collected on each unit as an individual property. Default in the payment of taxes or a mortgage loan by one unit owner may result in a foreclosure sale of that owner's unit, but does not affect the ownership of the other unit owners.

Operation and administration. The condominium property generally is administered by an association of unit owners according to the bylaws set forth in the declaration. The association may be governed by a board of directors or other official entity, it may manage the property on its own or it may engage a professional property manager to perform this function.

Acting through its board of directors or other officers, the association functions to enforce restrictive covenants and any rules it adopts regarding the operation and use of the property. The association is responsible for the maintenance, repair, cleaning and sanitation of the common elements and structural portions of the property. It must also maintain fire and extended-coverage insurance as well as liability insurance for these portions of the property.

Expenses incurred in fulfilling these responsibilities are paid for by the unit owners in the form of monthly *assessments,* collected by the owners' association. Such fees are assessed each unit owner. They are due monthly, quarterly, semiannually or annually, depending on the provisions of the bylaws. If such assessments are not paid, the association has the right to lien the property and to seek a court-ordered judgment to have the property sold to cover the outstanding amount.

A unit owner may sue the owners' association for damages and may be liable for any losses or judgments incurred by the association. The association may, at its discretion, terminate any contracts or leases originally entered into by the owner or developer if the association determines that they are unfair to the unit owners.

Condominium conversions. Pennsylvania law requires an owner or developer converting an existing rental property to condominium ownership to give the building's tenants *one year's prior notice* that such conversion will occur. Tenants cannot be evicted from their rental units unless they have received one year's prior notice (unless, of course, they violate the terms of the original lease or rental agreement). This notice must inform the tenants of their rights under state law and include a copy of the owner's or developer's public offering statement (described later in this section), detailing the proposed conversion and sale.

Tenants must be given a six-month option to purchase their units; if a tenant chooses not to exercise this option, the owner or developer *may not sell the unit to any other person for a higher price within one year* from the date the original notice of conversion was issued.

After receiving a notice of conversion, a tenant may, without penalty, choose to terminate the original lease within a 90-day period. The owner or developer is prohibited by law from coercing the tenant in any way to terminate his or her lease.

At least 30 days prior to issuing a conversion notice, the owner or developer is required to hold a tenant meeting, open to the public, to discuss the conversion.

Tenants who are 62 or older, or who are blind or otherwise disabled, and who have lived in the building for at least two years are entitled by law to remain in possession of their units for at least *two years* after the conversion notice is issued, even if their lease is set to expire within the two-year period. In addition, the owner or developer cannot raise rents for such persons during this period, except to cover the costs of increased real estate taxes and/or utilities.

Note that if an existing rental building was rehabilitated using federal community development funds, the building cannot be converted to condominium ownership for a period of *ten years* after such rehabilitation has taken place.

Unit sales—newly created condominiums. An owner or developer of a new or existing condominium conversion must, by law, provide each prospective unit purchaser with a *public offering statement* at least 15 days before a sales contract is signed. This document, similar to a stock prospectus, must detail 22 separate categories of information, including such items as bylaws, rules and regulations, projected operating budgets for the building, liens or encumbrances on the property and so forth. If the purchaser is not provided with a copy of the statement within the prescribed period, he or she may cancel the contract without penalty within 15 days after receiving the material. In addition, the prospective buyer may recover an amount equal to five percent of the unit's sale price—up to a maximum of $2,000—or actual damages, whichever is greater.

Owners or developers of newly converted units must, by law, give purchasers a two-year warranty against structural defects in both the building's units and the common elements; this takes effect on the day the units are conveyed. In addition, such purchasers must be furnished with a report prepared by an independent architect or engineer, describing the age and condition of all structural components and mechanical/electrical systems.

Unit sales—existing condominiums. When a unit owner wants to sell his or her unit, the owner must, by law, provide the prospective purchaser with a *resale certificate,* prepared by the building owners' association, along with a complete set of documents for review prior to the closing. In addition, the seller must furnish the buyer with: (1) a copy of the condominium declaration, (2) the bylaws, (3) the rules and regulations of the owners' association and (4) a certificate containing pertinent information such as monthly assessments, capital expenditures, insurance coverage and so forth. The owners' association is permitted to charge the seller for the expense of providing this information. Note that if the buyer receives this information after a sales agreement has been signed, he or she has the right to void the agreement within five days after receiving it, if the buyer so chooses.

Cooperative Ownership

In the typical **cooperative**, a corporation, which owns title to the land and building, offers shares of stock to a prospective tenant. The price set by the corporation for each apartment becomes the price of the stock. The purchaser becomes a shareholder in the corporation by virtue of stock ownership and receives a proprietary lease to the apartment for the life of the corporation. The shareholder does not own real estate, per se, as is the case in a condominium.

Operation and management. Although the cooperative tenant-owners do not own real estate (stock is personal property), they do control the property and its operation as shareholders. Shareholders elect officers and directors as provided for in the corporation bylaws. These individuals are then responsible for directing the affairs of the corporation and its real estate operation. They may engage the services of a professional property manager to assist them. The corporation establishes bylaws that provide for such matters as the tenant use of the property (similar to the matters addressed in the restrictive covenants in a condominium) and the method of transfer of the shares in the corporation, including approval of prospective shareholders by the board of directors as the corporation deems appropriate. Some cooperatives provide that a tenant-owner must sell the stock back to the corporation at the original purchase price, resulting in the corporation realizing any profits as the shares are resold. Ownership in the cooperative corporation is accompanied by the individual shareholder's commitment to abide by these bylaws.

The corporation incurs costs in the operation and maintenance of the entire parcel, including the common property as well as the individual apartments. These costs include real estate taxes and any mortgage payments that the corporation may have. In addition to these obligations, the corporation budgets for such expenses as insurance, utilities, repairs and maintenance, janitorial and other services, replacement of equipment and reserves for capital expenditures. Funds for the budget are assessed to the individual shareholders, generally in the form of monthly fees, similar to those charged by a homeowners' association in a condominium.

Unlike a condominium association, which has the authority to lien the ownership in the event of defaulted maintenance payments, the burden of any defaulted payment in a cooperative falls on the remaining shareholders. Each shareholder is affected by the financial ability of the others whereas, in a condominium, the other owners are unaffected. For this reason approval of prospective tenant-owners by the board of directors frequently involves financial evaluation. If the corporation is unable to make mortgage and tax payments, such defaults could result in the property being sold by court order in a foreclosure suit. This would destroy the interests of all tenant-shareholders, including those who have paid their assessments. Such nonpayment in a condominium would result in foreclosure against only the property of the defaulted owner.

Advantages. Cooperative ownership, despite its risks, has become more desirable in recent years in several ways. Lending institutions view the shares of stock, although personal property, as acceptable collateral for financing, which was not always the case. The availability of financing expands the transferability of shares beyond "cash buyers." As a tenant-owner, rather than a tenant who pays rent to a landlord, the shareholder has some control over the property and realizes some income tax advantage from the payment of property tax. Owners also enjoy freedom from maintenance.

Time-shared Ownership

Time-sharing permits multiple purchasers to buy interests in real estate—usually a unit of a resort development—with each purchaser having a right to use the facility for a fixed or variable time period. A *time-share estate* is condominium ownership as a fee simple estate. A *time-share use* is a right by contract, such as a long-term lease, a license or membership, wherein the developer owns the real estate.

Some time-sharing programs allow for a rotation system in which the tenant in common can occupy the unit at different times of the year in different years. Other programs sell only specific months or weeks of the year. For example, 12 individuals could own equal, undivided interests in one condominium unit, with each owner entitled to use the premises for a specified month in each year. Maintenance and other common expenses are prorated among the unit owners.

The laws regarding the origination and sale of time-shared units are generally complex and vary from state to state. Time-shares may be subject to subdivision requirements, for instance. You should be familiar with the provisions of the relevant statutes before dealing with such properties.

Summary

Sole ownership, or *ownership in severalty,* indicates that title is held by one person or entity. There are several ways in which title to real estate can be held concurrently by more than one person, called *co-ownership.*

Under *tenancy in common,* each party holds an undivided interest in severalty. An individual owner may sell his or her interest. Upon the death of an owner, the interest passes to the heirs or according to the will. There are no special requirements to create this interest. When two or more parties hold title to real estate, they will hold title as tenants in common unless there is an expressed intention otherwise. *Joint tenancy* indicates two or more owners with the right of survivorship, if the intention of the parties to establish a joint tenancy with right of survivorship is clearly stated.

Tenancy by the entirety, in those states where it is recognized, resembles a joint tenancy but is between husband and wife. It gives the surviving spouse sole ownership upon the death of the other owner. During their lives, both must sign the deed for any title to pass to a purchaser. *Community property* rights exist only in certain states and pertain only to land owned by husband and wife.

Real estate ownership may also be held in *trust.* In creating a trust, title to the property involved is conveyed to a *trustee* under a living or testamentary trust or a land trust.

Various types of business organizations may own real estate. A *corporation* is a legal entity and holds title to real estate in severalty. Although a *partnership* is technically not a legal entity, the *Uniform Partnership Act* and the *Uniform Limited Partnership Act,* adopted in Pennsylvania, enable a partnership to own property in the partnership's name. A *syndicate* is an association of two or more people or firms to make an investment in real estate. Many syndicates are *joint ventures* and are organized for only a single project. A syndicate may be organized as a co-ownership, trust, corporation or partnership.

Cooperative ownership of apartment buildings indicates title to real estate held by a corporation that must pay taxes, mortgage interest and principal and all operating expenses. Reimbursement comes from shareholders through monthly assessments. Shareholders have proprietary, long-term leases entitling them to occupy their apartments. Under *condominium ownership,* each occupant/owner holds fee simple estate to the unit plus a share of the common elements. Each owner receives an individual tax bill and may mortgage the unit as desired. Expenses for operating the common elements are collected by an owners' association through monthly assessments. The Uniform Condominium Act is the Pennsylvania law governing condominiums. *Time-sharing* enables multiple purchasers to own an estate or use interest in real estate with the right to use a unit of a resort development for a part of each year.

Questions

1. The *unities* necessary to create a joint tenancy include which of the following?
   a. interest
   b. time
   c. possession
   d. all of the above

2. A parcel of real estate was purchased by Howard Evers and Tinker Chance. The seller's deed received at the closing conveyed the property "to Howard Evers and Tinker Chance," without further explanation. Thus:
   a. Evers and Chance are joint tenants.
   b. Evers and Chance are tenants in common.
   c. Evers and Chance each own an undivided one-half interest in the property.
   d. b and c

3. Martin, Barton and Fargo are joint tenants owning a tract of land. Fargo conveys her interest to Vonder. This means that:
   I. Martin and Barton still are joint tenants.
   II. Vonder is a tenant in common with Martin and Barton.
   a. I only
   b. II only
   c. both I and II
   d. neither I nor II

4. In Pennsylvania a conveyance made "to Arnold and Julia Haber, Husband and Wife," without further elaboration, creates a:
   a. joint tenancy.
   b. tenancy in common.
   c. tenancy by the entirety.
   d. partnership.

5. A purchaser under the cooperative form of ownership receives:
   I. a deed to his or her unit.
   II. a proprietary lease and the right to use the common facilities.
   a. I only
   b. II only
   c. both I and II
   d. neither I nor II

6. Ownership of real property by one person without the ownership participation of others is called:
   a. trust.
   b. severalty.
   c. solety.
   d. condominium.

7. The *right of survivorship* is closely associated with a:
   a. corporation.
   b. cooperative.
   c. trust.
   d. joint tenancy.

8. An owner or developer of a newly built condominium building must provide each prospective unit purchaser with which of the following?
   I. a public offering statement
   II. a two-year warranty against structural defects
   a. I only
   b. II only
   c. both I and II
   d. neither I nor II

9. In a trust, the person in whom title is vested is called the:
   a. trustee.
   b. trustor.
   c. beneficiary.
   d. nominee.

10. Which of the following forms of ownership may be created by operation of law?
    a. joint tenancy
    b. tenancy by the entirety
    c. joint tenancy with right of survivorship
    d. none of the above

11. If property is held by two or more owners as tenants in common, upon the death of one owner the ownership interest will pass:
    a. to the remaining owner or owners.
    b. to the heirs or whoever is designated under the deceased owner's will.
    c. to the surviving owner and/or his or her heirs.
    d. to the deceased owner's surviving spouse.

12. Joan Smith has organized a group of investors to finance the development of a shopping center. This group of investors:
    a. may be called a syndicate.
    b. may be organized as a limited partnership.
    c. may be a joint venture.
    d. all of the above

13. Real estate owned by a corporation:

I. may be sold upon a stockholder's request.
II. is held in severalty.

    a. I only   c. both I and II
    (b.) II only   d. neither I nor II

14. Alma Johnson bought an apartment in a large building for her personal use and received a deed conveying to her fee simple estate. Each year Johnson receives a tax bill on her apartment. Her form of apartment ownership is called a:

a. real estate investment trust.
b. cooperative.
c. corporation.
(d.) condominium.

15. Peter Scolari is married and jointly owns an apartment building located in Pennsylvania with James Adam. The deed to the apartment building specifies the form of ownership as being "to Peter Scolari and James Adam as joint tenants," without further elaboration. Should Scolari die, his ownership interest in the apartment building will pass:

a. to James Adam, as the surviving joint tenant.
b. to his wife as a tenant by the entirety.
c. half to his wife and half to James Adam.
(d.) to his heirs as specified in his will.

16. Harold Albertson owns a fee simple title to unit 12 and 4.5 percent of the common elements. Albertson:

I. owns a life estate.
II. may mortgage unit 12 without placing a lien on the title of the other unit owners.

    a. I only   c. both I and II
    (b.) II only   d. neither I nor II

17. A legal arrangement whereby title to property is held for the benefit of a beneficiary is a:

I. trust.
II. limited partnership.

    (a.) I only   c. both I and II
    b. II only   d. neither I nor II

18. A, B and C were co-owners of a parcel of real estate. B died and his interest passed, according to his will, to become part of his estate. B was a:

a. tenant by the entirety.
b. joint tenant.
(c.) tenant in common.
d. corporate officer.

19. In a tenancy by the entirety:

I. the co-owners are husband and wife.
II. the co-owners have the right to partition.

    (a.) I only   c. both I and II
    b. II only   d. neither I nor II

20. A condominium is created:

a. when construction is completed on the structure.
(b.) when the owner or developer files a declaration of condominium and other documents in the public record.
c. when a condominium owners' association is established.
d. when all unit owners file documents in the public records asserting their decision.

21. A married couple is selling their home, owned under a tenancy by the entirety. In order for the deed conveying the property to be valid, who must sign it?

I. the husband
II. the wife

    a. I only   (c.) both I and II
    b. II only   d. neither I nor II

22. Generally, a condominium building:

I. is managed under the supervision of an association of unit owners.
II. may only be a residential structure.

    (a.) I only   c. both I and II
    b. II only   d. neither I nor II

23. Which of the following best describes ownership of a cooperative?

(a.) The purchaser is a stockholder.
b. The purchaser holds a fee simple title.
c. The purchaser holds a reverter.
d. a and c

8

Leases

Overview

An owner of real property who does not wish to use the property personally or wants to derive some measure of income from its ownership can allow it to be used by another person in exchange for consideration. The person who makes periodic payments for the use of the property *leases* it from the owner. Generally, any type of real property may be leased. The apartment dweller as well as the commercial or industrial tenant may find it advantageous to lease real estate for a given period of time rather than purchase it. This chapter will examine the various leasehold estates a landlord and a tenant may enter into and the types and specific provisions of lease agreements commonly used in the real estate business.

Leasing Real Estate	A **lease** is a contract between an owner of real estate (known as the *lessor*) and a tenant (the *lessee*) that transfers the right to exclusive possession and use of the owner's property to the tenant for a specified period of time. This agreement generally sets forth the length of time the contract is to run, the amount to be paid by the lessee for the right to use the property and other rights and obligations of the parties.

In effect, the lease agreement is a combination of a conveyance (of an interest in the real estate) and a contract (to pay rent and assume other obligations). The landlord (lessor) grants the tenant (lessee) the right to occupy the premises and use them for purposes stated in the lease. In return, the landlord retains the right to receive payment for the use of the premises as well as a **reversionary right** to retake possession after the lease term has expired. The lessor's interest in leased property is called a *leased fee estate plus reversionary right.*

The statute of frauds in Pennsylvania requires that an agreement to lease real estate be in writing to be enforceable if it will not be performed within three years of the date of making. In other words, a *lease for a term of more than three years must be written.* It should also be signed by both lessor and lessee. An oral lease for three years or less is usually enforceable.

In Practice. . .	*While the statute of frauds requires leases of more than three years to be in writing to be enforceable, the rules and regulations of the Pennsylvania Real Estate Commission require that all contracts used by licensees shall be in writing. References to the use of oral leases are relevant when no licensee is involved in the transaction. Further, written contracts that are specific and all-inclusive will help avoid controversies between the parties.*

Leasehold Estates	When a landowner leases his or her real estate to a tenant, the tenant's right to occupy the land for the duration of the lease is called a **leasehold estate.** A leasehold estate is an estate in land that is considered personal property.

In the discussion of interests and estates in Chapter 6, "Interests in Real Estate," freehold estates were differentiated from leasehold estates. Just as there are several types of freehold (ownership) estates, there are also various leasehold estates. The four most important are: (1) estate for years, (2) periodic estate, or estate from period to period (year to year), (3) estate at will and (4) estate at sufferance (see Table 8.1).

Estate or Tenancy for Years	A leasehold estate that continues for a *definite period of time,* whether for years, months, weeks or days, is an **estate for years.** An estate for years always has a specific starting and ending time and does not automatically renew itself at the end of the lease period. When that period of time expires, the lessee is required to vacate the premises and surrender possession to the lessor. No notice is required

Table 8.1 Leasehold Estates	Type of Estate	Distinguishing Characteristics
	Estate for years	For definite period of time
	Estate from period to period (year to year)	Automatically renews, if not terminated with notice by either party
	Tenancy at will	For indefinite period of time
	Tenancy at sufferance	Without landlord's consent

to terminate such a lease at the end of the lease period. A lease for years may be terminated prior to the expiration date by the mutual consent of both parties, but otherwise neither party may terminate without showing that the lease agreement has been breached. As is characteristic of all leases, a tenancy or estate for years gives the lessee the right to occupy and use the leased property—subject, of course, to the terms and covenants contained in the lease agreement. Any continuity in tenancy requires the negotiation of a new contract unless the original agreement provides for the conversion to a periodic tenancy.

Periodic Estate or Tenancy

Periodic estates, sometimes called **estates from period to period** or from **year to year,** are created when the landlord and tenant enter into an agreement that continues for an *indefinite length of time without a specific expiration date;* rent, however, is payable at definite intervals. These tenancies are usually created to run for a certain amount of time, for instance, month to month, week to week or year to year. The agreement is automatically renewed with no change in terms for similar succeeding periods until one of the parties gives notice to terminate. In effect, the payment and acceptance of rent extends the lease for another period. A **month-to-month tenancy** is, for example, created when a tenant takes possession with no definite termination date and pays rent on a monthly basis. Periodic tenancy is commonly used in residential leases.

A tenancy from period to period can be created when a tenant with an estate for years remains in possession, or holds over, after the expiration of the lease term. If no new lease agreement has been made, a **holdover tenancy** is created, and the landlord may evict the tenant or treat the holdover tenant as a periodic tenancy. Acceptance of rent is usually considered conclusive proof of the landlord's acquiescence. The courts customarily hold that a tenant who holds over can do so for a term equal to the term of the original lease, providing the period is for one year or less. Thus, if the original lease were for six months and the tenancy were held over, the courts would usually consider the holdover to be for a like period, that is, six months. However, if the original lease were for five years, the holdover tenancy could not exceed one year. Some leases stipulate that in the absence of a renewal agreement, a tenant who holds over does so as a month-to-month tenant. This is usually a valid agreement.

In order to *terminate* a periodic estate, either the landlord or the tenant must give *proper notice.* In Pennsylvania, to terminate an estate from week to week, one week's notice is required; to terminate an estate from month to month, one month's notice is required. In order to terminate an estate from year to year, a minimum of three months' notice is required. To avoid controversy most written lease agreements stipulate the period of notice required to terminate a periodic tenancy. These interpretations of notice are most applicable in the event of an oral lease or when no provisions are stipulated in the contract.

Estate or Tenancy at Will

An estate that gives the tenant the right to possess with the *consent of the landlord* for a term of unspecified or uncertain duration is a **tenancy at will.** It may be created by express agreement or by operation of law, and during its existence the tenant has all the rights and obligations of a lessor-lessee relationship, including the payment of rent at regular intervals. Tenancy at will is rarely used in a written agreement in recent years and is viewed skeptically by the courts. It could be viewed as a periodic tenancy — the period being interpreted by the interval of rental payment.

For example, at the end of a lease period, a landlord informs a tenant that in a few months the city is going to demolish the apartment building to make way for an expressway. The landlord gives the tenant the option to occupy the premises until demolition begins. If the tenant agrees to stay, a tenancy at will is created.

The term of an estate at will is indefinite, but the estate may be terminated by giving 30 days' notice. An estate at will is automatically terminated by the death of either the landlord or the tenant.

Estate or Tenancy at Sufferance

A **tenancy at sufferance** arises when a tenant who lawfully came into possession of real property continues, after the rights have expired, to hold possession of the premises *without the consent of the landlord*. Two examples of estates at sufferance are: (1) when a tenant for years *fails to surrender* possession at the expiration of the lease and (2) when a mortgagor, without consent of the purchaser, continues in possession after the foreclosure sale and expiration of the redemption period. The latter example is a tenancy at sufferance *by operation of law.*

Standard Lease Provisions

In determining the validity of a lease, the courts apply the rules governing contracts (see Chapter 9, "Real Estate Contracts"). If the intention to convey temporary possession of a certain parcel of real estate from one person to another is expressed, the courts generally hold that a lease has been created. Most states require no special wording to establish the landlord-tenant relationship. The lease may be written, oral or implied, depending on the circumstances. The practice in recent years is the use of a written lease. However, the provisions of the statutes of the state where the real estate is located must be followed to assure the validity of the lease. An example of a typical residential lease is Figure 8.1.

Once a valid lease has been executed, the lessor, as the owner of the real estate, is usually bound by the implied *covenant of quiet possession.* Under this covenant, the lessor guarantees that the lessee may take possession of the leased premises and that the landlord will not interfere in the tenant's possession or use of the property.

The requirements for a valid lease are essentially the same as those for any other contract. Generally, the essentials of a valid lease are:

1. *Offer and acceptance:* The parties must reach a mutual agreement on all the terms of the contract.

Figure 8.1
Residential Lease
Agreement

There are 4 copies
of this agreement.
1
1. White ....Lessor
2. Yellow ...Agent
3. Pink ......Lessee
4. Blue ....

LEASE FOR REAL ESTATE
PART ONE OF A TWO PART AGREEMENT
This form recommended and approved for, but not restricted to
use by members of the Pennsylvania Association of Realtors when
used with an approved addendum attached hereto.
————— Agent For The Lessor —————

L-1969
REV. 1/78

PRINCIPALS
(1-78)

This Agreement, made this...........................day of .........................A.D. 19........

Between ....
....hereinafter called Lessor, and
....
....hereinafter called Lessee,

PROPERTY
(11-74)

1. (a) WITNESSETH: Lessor agrees to let unto the Lessee premises being known as.........................
....
.... in the
.... of .... , County of .... , State of Penna.
with improvements consisting of ....

upon the following terms and conditions to wit:

(b)　Total rental for entire term payable to Lessor　　　　　　　　　$ ....

(c)　Payments in advance ☐ Monthly ☐ .... in the amount of:　$ ....

(d)　Cash or check to be paid before possession by Lessee which is to be applied on account as follows:

Advance rent..... .... 19....to............19.... Paid $ .... Due $ ....

On account of final payment of rent........................... Paid $ .... Due $ ....

Security deposit (see par.1 (f)........................... Paid $ .... Due $ ....

Credit report... Paid $ .... Due $ ....

.... Paid $ _____ Due $ _____

Totals – Paid to date .... Paid $...................

Balance due before possession........................... Due $ ....

(e)　Adjusted payment of rent until regular due date, if any　　　　　$ ....

(f)　Security deposit　　　　　　　　　　　　　　　　　　　　$ ....

(g)　Late charge if rent not paid within grace period　　　　　　　$ ....

(h)　Due date for each payment...

(i)　Term of this lease...

(j)　Commencement date of lease........................... day of ...........................A.D. 19.....

(k)　Expiration date of lease........................... day of ...........................A.D. 19.....

(l)　Required written notice to terminate this lease...

(m)　Renewal term if not terminated by either party...

(n)　Lessee will occupy premises ONLY as...

(o)　Maximum number of occupants under this lease...

(p)　Payments to be made promptly when due in lawful money of the United States of America to: ☐ Lessor　☐ Agent

(q)　Utilities & services to be supplied as follows:

Lessor will supply: ☐ cold water, 　☐ hot water , 　☐ gas, 　☐ heat, 　☐ electric, 　☐ lawn care,
☐ snow removal, 　☐ janitor service, 　☐ yearly oil burner cleaning, 　☐ cesspool cleaning, 　☐ ....
☐ Lawn & Shrubbery care. 　　☐ ....

Lessee will supply: ☐ cold water, 　☐ hot water 　☐ gas, 　☐ heat, 　☐ electric, 　☐ lawn care,
☐ snow removal, 　☐ water in excess of yearly minimum charge, 　☐ yearly oil burner cleaning,
☐ cesspool cleaning, 　☐ Lawn & Shrubbery care. 　☐ ....

(r)　Notwithstanding anything herein to the contrary, Lessee will pay cost of any or all repairs of any kind whatsoever,
occurring after commencement of this lease where the individual cost of each repair is less than $ ....

(s)　No pets or animals of any kind whatsoever will be permitted on or within the herein described premises excepting
....

SPECIAL
CLAUSES

2.

ADDENDUM

3. The Lessor and Lessee agree for themselves, their respective heirs and successors and assigns to the herein described terms and also to those set forth in the addendum attached hereto entitled "TERMS AND CONDITIONS," (PART TWO) all of which are to be regarded as binding and as strict legal conditions.

LESSEE.............. 　LESSEE.............. 　LESSEE.............. 　LESSOR.............. 　LESSOR.............. 　AGENT..............

INITIALS

**Figure 8.1
(cont.)**

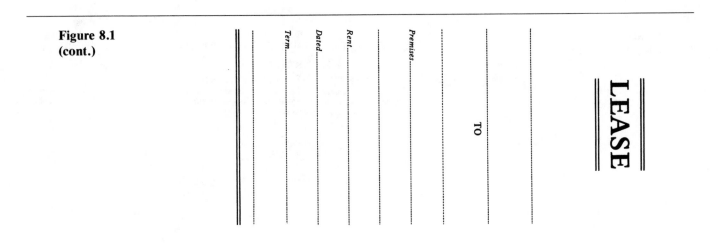

FOR VALUE RECEIVED, the undersigned hereby assign, transfer and set over unto ....

....

Executors, Administrators and assigns all Lessor's rights, title and interest in the within described premises and all benefit and advantages to be derived therefrom.

WITNESS .... hand and seal this .... day of .... A.D. 19 ....

WITNESS .... }   LESSOR .... (SEAL)

WITNESS .... }   LESSOR .... (SEAL)

Figure 8.1 (cont.)

PART TWO OF A TWO PART AGREEMENT
GENERAL LEASE
TERMS AND CONDITIONS

This form recommended and approved for, but not restricted to,
use by members of the Pennsylvania Association of REALTORS®
Copyright Pennsylvania Association of REALTORS® 1973

Special Clauses

Taxes
(5-72)

4. (a) Lessee agrees to pay as rent in addition to the minimum rental herein received, all taxes, sewer rent, garbage and/or trash collection charges assessed or imposed upon the demised premises and/or the building of which the demised premises is a part during the term of this lease, in excess of and over and above those assessed or imposed at the time of making this lease. The amount due hereunder on account of such taxes shall be apportioned for that part of the first tax year, as assessed, and each subsequent tax year, as assessed thereafter during the term of this lease including extensions or renewals hereof. The same shall be paid by the Lessee to the Lessor as additional rent on or before sixty days from the Agent's of the Lessor's notice to the Lessee having been delivered as notice of any such tax increase.
(b) Unless specified herein to the contrary, the percentage of any such tax increases to be paid by the Lessee hereunder shall be apportioned in accordance with that percentage which the Lessee's rent represents to the total income that the building would yield if fully leased.

Fire Insurance Premiums Sewer Rent

(c) Lessee further agrees to pay to Lessor as additional rent all increase or increases in fire insurance premiums upon the demised premises and/or the building of which the demised premises is a part, due to an increase in the rate of fire insurance in excess of the rate on the demised premises at the time of making this lease, if said increase is caused by any act or neglect of the Lessee or the nature of the Lessee's business.
(d) Lessee further agrees to pay as additional rent, if there is a metered water connection to said premises, all sewer rental or charges for use of sewers, sewer system, and sewage treatment works servicing the demised premises in excess of the yearly minimum of such sewer charges, immediately when the same become due.

Condition of Pavement

(e) Lessee shall be responsible for the condition of the pavement, curb, cellar doors, awnings and other erections in the pavement during the term of this lease; shall keep the pavement free from snow and ice, and shall be, and hereby agrees that Lessee is solely liable for any aacidents, due or alleged to be due to their defective condition, or to any accumulations of snow or ice.

Security Deposit
(12-85)

5. The "security deposit" specified in Par. #1. (f) shall be held by Agent as security for the performance of all the terms, covenants and conditions of this lease and for the cost of any trash removal, housecleaning and the cost of repairs and/or the correction of damage (which is, in the opinion of the Lessor and/or Agent, in excess of normal wear and tear); otherwise, the "security deposit" or any balance thereof shall be returned after the Lessee has vacated and left the premises in an acceptable condition (following a personal inspection by Lessor and/or Agent) and surrendered all keys to Agent. If the Lessor determines that any loss, damage or injury chargeable to the Lessee hereunder, exceeds the security deposit, may retain the said sum as liquidated damages or may apply the sum against any actual loss, damage or injury and the balance thereof will be the responsibility of the Lessee. Lessor's determination of the amount, if any, to be returned to the Lessee shall be final. It is further understood and agreed that the said security deposit is not to be considered as the last payment under the lease, however the rights of the Lessor shall not be hindered to retain the security deposit, or a portion thereof as payment on account of uncollected rents, if any.
The aforementioned "security deposit" shall be paid to the Agent who will deposit same in a separate custodial type account. Agent shall keep records of all funds so deposited as required in accordance with the Act of February 19, 1980, P.L. 15, No. 9, Section 604 (63 P.S. 455.604). Said account will be clearly identified as required indicating the date and from whom he received money, the date deposited, the date of withdrawals and other pertinent information concerning this transaction. It is understood and agreed that should the property herein mentioned be sold, exchanged, transferred or conveyed to a new owner, that at the time of settlement, any money held as a security deposit shall be transferred to the new owner or his agent, to be continued to be held as a security deposit.

Affirmative Covenants of Lessor

6. (a) If the Lessee so desires, Lessor, if possible, may make available to Lessee, without charge, a space in the building for the storage of goods and effects of Lessee. In consideration of the fact that no extra charge is made for the furnishing of such space by the Lessor, it is understood that Lessor shall not be liable for loss or damage to any stored goods through fire or theft or any cause whatever, and Lessee expressly releases Lessor as bailee or otherwise from all claims for any such loss or damage. It is further understood that the use of storage space by the Lessee shall be limited to the time of the Lessee's occupancy, and that goods left over thirty days after the expiration of Lessee's occupancy may be sold for storage charges at public or private sale without further notice to Lessee.
(b) The Lessor may furnish additional service not herein provided for but any such service shall be gratuitous unless otherwise agreed and shall not be an obligation of the Lessor or part of the consideration for the rent.

Place of Payment

7. All rent shall be payable without prior notice or demand at the office of Lessor or Agent as specified in paragraph #1. (p).

Affirmative Covenants of Lessee
(11-74)
Payment of Rent
Late Charges
(11-74)

8. Lessee covenants and agrees that he will without demand:
(a) Pay the rent and all other charges herein reserved as rent on the days and times and at the place that the same are made payable, without fail, and if Lessor shall at any time or times accept said rent or rent charges after the same shall have become due and payable, such acceptance shall not excuse delay upon subsequent occasions, or constitute or be construed as a waiver of any of Lessor's rights. Lessee agrees that any charge or payment herein reserved, included, or agreed to be treated or collected as rent and/or any charges, expenses, or costs herein agreed to be paid by the Lessee may be proceeded for and recovered by the Lessor by legal process in the same manner as rent due and in arrears.
(b) All rental payments are due and payable on the date as specified in paragraph #1.(h) of this agreement or within five days thereafter (grace period) without penalty. However, after 5:00 P.M. on the fifth day after due date as aforementioned, any rental payment not paid in full will be subject to a late charge. Payments not made on or before 5:00 P.M. on the tenth day after due date, together with late charge, may be referred to Magistrate or Justice of the Peace for the collection and/or ejectment.

Cleaning, Repairing, etc.

(c) Keep the demised premises clean and free from all ashes, dirt and other refuse matter; replace all broken glass windows, doors, etc.; keep all waste and drain pipes open; repair all damages to plumbing and to the demised premises; in general, keep the same in as good order and repair as they are at the beginning of the term of this lease, reasonable wear and tear and damage by accidental fire or other causalty not occuring through negligence of Lessee or those employed by or acting for Lessee alone excepted. The Lessee agrees to surrender the demised premises in the same condition in which Lessee has herein agreed to keep the same during the continuance of this lease.

Requirements of Public Authorities
Fire

(d) Comply with any requirements of any of the constituted public authorities, and with the terms of any State or Federal statute or local ordinance or regulation applicable to Lessee or his use of the demised premises, and save Lessor harmless from penalties, fines, costs or damages resulting from failure to do so.
(e) Use every reasonable precaution against fire.

Surrender of Possession
(11-74)
Notice of Fire, etc.
Pay for Gas and Electricity

(f) Peaceably deliver up and surrender possession of the demised premises to the Lessor at the expiration or sooner termination of this lease, promptly delivering to Lessor at his office, all keys for the demised premises, with all trash and personal belongings removed and building(s) broom-swept clean.
(g) Give to Lessor prompt written notice of any accident, fire or damage occuring on or to the demised premises.
(h) Promptly pay for all gas and electricity, water, heat, lawn care and services consumed in the herein demised premises during the continuance of this lease if so specified in paragraph #1.(q); and should Lessee fail to make these payments when due, Lessor shall have the right to settle therefor, such sums to be considered additional rent and collectable from Lessee, as such, by distress or other process and to have all the priorities given by law to claims for rent.

Indemnification

(i) Indemnify and save Lessor harmless from any and all loss occasioned by Lessee's breach of any of the covenants, terms and conditions of this lease, or caused by his family, guests, visitors, agents and employees.

Negative Covenants of Lessee
Use of Premises
Assignment and Subletting

9. Lessee covenants and agrees that he will do none of the following things without the consent in writing of Lessor:
(a) Occupy the demised premises in any other manner or for any other purpose than as above set forth in paragraph #1. (n).
(b) Assign, mortgage or pledge this lease or under-let or sub-lease the demised premises, or any part thereof, or permit any other person, firm or corporation to occupy the demised premises, or any part thereof; nor shall any assignee or sub-lessee assign, mortgage or pledge this lease or such sub-lease, without an additional written consent by the Lessor, and without such consent no such assignment, mortgage or pledge shall be valid. If the Lessee becomes embarrassed or insolvent, or makes an assignment for the benefit of creditors, or if a petition in bankruptcy is filed or against the Lessee or a bill in equity or other proceeding for the appointment of a receiver for the Lessee is filed, or if the real or personal property of the Lessee shall be sold or levied upon by any Sheriff, Marshal or Constable, the same shall be a violation of this covenant.

Signs

(c) Place or allow to be placed any stand, booth, sign or show case upon the doorsteps, vestibules or outside walls or pavements of said premises, or paint, place, erect or cause to be painted, placed or erected any sign, projection or device on or in any part of the premises. Lessee shall remove any sign, projection or device painted, placed or erected, if permission has been granted and restore the walls, etc., to their former conditions, at or prior to the expiration of this lease. In case of the breach of this covenant (in addition to all other remedies given to Lessor in case of breach of any conditions or covenants of this lease) Lessor shall have the privilege of removing said stand, booth, sign, show case,

Figure 8.1 (cont.)

projection or devise, and restoring said walls, etc., to their former condition, and Lessee, at Lessor's option, shall be liable to Lessor for any and all expenses so incurred by Lessor.

Alterations Improvements (d) Make any alterations, improvements, or additions to the demised premises. All alterations, improvements, additions or fixtures, whether installed before or after the execution of this lease, shall remain upon the premises at the expiration or sooner determination of this lease and become the property of Lessor, unless Lessor shall, prior to the determination of this lease, have given written notice to Lessee to remove the same, in which event Lessee will remove such alterations, improvements and additions and restore the premises to the same good order and condition in which they now are. Should Lessee fail to do so, Lessor may do so, collecting, at Lessor's option, the cost and expense thereof from Lessee as additional rent.

Machinery (e) Use or operate any machinery that, in Lessor's opinion, is harmful to the building or disturbing to other tenants occupying other parts thereof.

Weights (f) Place any weights in any portion of the demised premises beyond the safe carring capacity of the structure.

Fire Insurance (g) Do or suffer to be done, any act, matter or thing objectionable to the fire insurance companies, whereby the fire insurance or any other insurance now in force or hereafter to be placed on the demised premises, or any part thereof, or on the building of which the demised premises may be a part, shall become void or suspended, or whereby the same shall be rated as a more hazardous risk than at the date of execution of this lease, or employ any person or persons objectionable to the fire insurance companies or carry or have been benzine or explosive matter of any kind in and about the demised premises. In case of a breach of this covenant (in addition to all other remedies given to Lessor in case of the breach of any of the conditions of covenants of this lease) Lessee agrees to pay to Lessor as additional rent any and all increase or increases of premiums on insurance carried by Lessor on the demised premises, or any part thereof, or on the building of which the demised premises may be a part, caused in any way by the occupancy of Lessee.

Removal of Goods (h) Remove, attempt to remove or manifest an intention to remove Lessee's goods or property from or out of the demised premises otherwise than in the ordinary and usual course of business, without having first paid and satisfied Lessor for all rent which may become due during the entire term of this lease.

Vacate Premises (i) Vacate or desert said premises during the term of this lease, or permit the same to be empty and unoccupied.

Agency on Removal 10. The Lessee agrees that if, with the permission in writing of Lessor, Lessee shall vacate or decide at any time during the term of this lease, or any renewal thereof, to vacate the herein demised premises, prior to the expiration of this lease, or any renewal hereof, Lessee will not cause or allow any agent to represent Lessee in any sub-letting or reletting of the demised premises other than an agent approved by the Lessor, and that should Lessee do so, or attempt to do so, that Lessor may remove any signs that may be placed on or about the demised premises by such other agent without any liability to Lessee or to said agent, the Lessee assuming all responsibility for such action.

Lessor's Rights 11. Lessee covenants and agrees that Lessor shall have the right to do the following things and matters in and about the demised premises:

Inspection of Premises (a) At all reasonable times by himself or his duly authorized agents to go upon and inspect the demised premises and every part thereof, and/or at his option to make repairs, alterations and additions to the demised premises or the building of which the demised premises is a part.

Rules and Regulations (b) At any time or times and from time to time make such rules and regulations as in his judgement may from time to time be necessary for the safety, care and cleanliness of the premises, and for the preservation of good order therein. Such rules and regulations shall, when notice thereof is given to Lessee, from a part of this lease.

Sale, Rent, Signs and Prospects (11-74) (c) To display a "For Sale" sign at any time, and also, after notice from either party of intention to determine this lease, or at any time within six months prior to the expiration of this lease, a "For Rent" sign, or both "For Rent" and "For Sale" signs; and all of said signs shall be placed upon such part of the premises as Lessor may elect and may contain such matter as Lessor shall require. Prospective purchasers or tenants authorized by Lessor may inspect the premises Monday thru Saturday between the hours of 11:00 A.M. and 8:00 P.M.

Discontinue Service, etc. 12. (a) In the event that the demised premises is totally destroyed or so damaged by fire or other casualty not occuring through fault or negligence of the Lessee or those employed by or acting for him, that the same cannot be repaired or restored within a reasonable time, this lease shall absolutely cease and determine, and the rent shall abate for the balance of the term.

(b) If the damage caused as above be only partial and such that the premises can be restored to their former condition within a reasonable time, the Lessor may, at his option, restore the same with reasonable promptness, reserving the right to enter upon the demised premises for that purpose. The Lessor also reserves the right to enter upon the demised premises whenever necessary to repair damage caused by fire or other casualty to the building of which the demised premises is a part, even though the effect of such entry be to render the demised premises or a part thereof untenantable. In either event the rent shall be apportioned and suspended during the time the Lessor is in possession, taking into account the proportion of the demised premises rendered untenantable and the duration of the Lessor's possession. If a dispute arises as to the amount of rent due under this clause, Lessee agrees to pay the full amount claimed by Lessor. Lessee shall, however, have the right to proceed by law to recover the excess payment, if any.

Damage for Interrupted Use (c) Lessor shall not be liable for any damage, compensation or claim by reason of inconvenience or annoyance from the necessity of repairing any portion of the building, the interruption in the use of the premises, or the termination of this lease by reason of the destruction of the premises.

Representation of Condition 13. The Lessor has let the demised premises in their present condition and without any representation on the part of the Lessor, his officers, employees, servants and/or agents. It is understood and agreed that the Lessor is under no duty to make alterations at the time of letting or at any time thereafter.

Miscellaneous Agreements and Conditions 14. (a) No contract entered into or that may be subsequently entered into by Lessor with Lessee, relative to any alterations, additions, improvements or repairs, nor the failure of Lessor to make such alterations, additions, improvements or repairs as required by any such contract, nor the making by Lessor or his agents or contracts of such alterations, additions, improvements or repairs shall in any way affect the payment of the rent or said other charges at the time specified in this lease.

Effect of Repairs or Rentals Waiver of Custom (b) It is hereby covenanted and agreed, any law, usage or custom to the contrary notwithstanding, that Lessor shall have the right at all times to enforce the covenants and provisions of this lease in strict accordance with the terms hereof, notwithstanding any conduct or custom on the part of the Lessor in refraining from so doing at any time or times; and further, that the failure of Lessor at any time or times to enforce its rights under said covenants and provisions strictly in accordance with the same not be construed as having created a custom in any way or manner contrary to the specific terms, provisions and covenants of this lease or as having in any way or manner modified the same.

Failure of Lessee to Repair (c) In the event of the failure of Lessee promptly to perform the covenants of Par. #8. (c) hereof, Lessor may go upon the demised premises and perform such covenants, the cost thereof, at the sole option of Lessor, to be charged to Lessee as additional and delinquent rent.

Remedies of Lessor (11-74) 15. If the Lessee

(a) Does not pay in full when due any and all installments of rent and/or any other charge or payment herein reserved, included, or agreed to be treated or collected as rent and/or any other charge, expense, or cost herein agreed to be paid by the Lessee; or

(b) Violates or fails to perform or otherwise breaks any covenant or agreement herein contained; or

(c) Vacates the demised premises or removes or attempts to remove or manifests an intention to remove any goods or property therefrom otherwise than in the ordinary and usual course of business without having first paid and satisfied the Lessor in full for all rent and other charges then due or that may thereafter become due until the expiration of the than current term, above mentioned; or

(d) Becomes embarrassed or insolvent, or makes an assignment for the benefit of creditors, or if a petition in bankruptcy is filed by or against the Lessee or a bill in equity or other proceeding for the appointment of a reciever for the Lessee is filed, or if proceedings for reorganization or for composition with creditors under any State or Federal law be instituted by or against Lessee, or if the real or personal property of the Lessee shall be sold or levied upon by any due process of law, then and in any or either of said events, there shall be deemed to be a breach of this lease, and thereupon ipso facto and without entry or other action by Lessor;

(d1) The rent for the entire unexpired balance of the term of this lease, as well as all other charges, payments, costs and expenses herein agreed to be paid by the Lessee, or at the option of Lessor any part thereof, and also all costs and officers' commissions including watchmen's wages and further including the five percent chargeable by Act of Assembly to the Lessor, shall, in addition to any and all instruments of rent already due and payable and in arrears and/or any other charge or payment herein reserved, included or agreed to be treated or collected as rent, and/or any other charge, expense or cost herein agreed to be paid by the Lessee which may be due and payable and in arrears, be taken to be due and payable and in arrears as if by the terms and provisions of this lease, the whole balance of unpaid rent and other charges, payments, taxes, costs and expenses were on that date payable in advance; and if this lease or any part thereof is assigned, or if the premises or any part thereof is sub-let, Lessee hereby irrevocably constitutes and appoints Lessor Lessee's agent to collect the rents due by such assignee or sub-leasee and apply the same to the rent due hereunder without in any way affecting Lessee's obligation to pay unpaid balance of rent due hereunder; or in the event of any of the foregoing at any time at the option of Lessor;

(d2) This lease and the term hereby created shall determine and become absolutely void without any right on the part of the Lessee to save the forfeiture by payment of any sum due or by other performance of any condition; term or covenant broken; whereupon, Lessor shall be entitled to recover damages for such breach in an amount equal to the amount of rent reserved for the balance of the term of this lease, less the fair rental value of the said demised premises, for the residue of said term.

Further Remedies of Lessor 16. In the event of any default as aforesaid, the Lessor, or anyone acting on Lessor's behalf, at Lessor's option:

(a) May lease said premises or any part or parts thereof to such person or persons as may in Lessor's discretion seem best and the Lessee shall be liable for any loss of rent for the balance of the then current term.

(b) Any re-entry or re-letting by Lessee under the terms hereof shall be without prejudice to Lessor's claim for damages and shall under no circumstances release Lessee from liability for such damages arising out of the breach of any of the covenants, terms and conditions of this lease.

Zoning 17. It is understood and agreed that the Lessor hereof does not warrant or undertake that the Lessee shall be able to obtain a permit under any Zoning Ordinance or Regulation for such use as Lessee intends to make of the said premises, and nothing in this lease contained shall obligate the Lessor to assist Lessee in obtaining said permit; the Lessee further agrees that in the event a permit cannot be obtained by Lessee under any Zoning Ordinance, or Regulation, this lease shall not terminate without Lessor's consent, and the Lessee shall use the premises only in a manner permitted under such Zoning Ordinance or Regulation.

Confession of Judgement 18. If rent and/or charges hereby reserved as rent shall remain unpaid on any day when the same should be paid Lessee hereby empowers any Prothonotary or attorney of any Court of Record to appear for Lessee in any and all actions which may be brought for rent and/or the charges, payments, costs and expenses reserved as rent, or agreed to be paid by the Lessee and/or to sign for Lessee an agreement for entering in any competent Court an amicable action or actions for the recovery of rent or other charges or expenses, and in said suits or in said amicable action or actions to confess judgment against Lessee for all or any part of the rent specified in this lease and then unpaid including, at Lessor's option, the rent for the entire unexpired balance of the term of this lease, and/or other charges, payments, costs and expenses reserved as rent or agreed to be paid by the Lessee, and for interest and costs together with an attorney's commission of 15%. Such authority shall not be exhausted by one exercise thereof, but judgment may be confessed as aforesaid from time to time as often as any of said rent and/or other charges reserved as rent shall fall due or be in arrears, and such powers may be exercised as well after the expiration of the original term and/or during any extension or renewal of this lease.

Ejectment 19. When this lease shall be determined by condition broken, either during the original term of this lease or any renewal or extension thereof, and also when and as soon as the term hereby created or any extension thereof shall have expired, it shall be lawful for any attorney as attorney for Lessee to file an agreement for entering in any competent Court an amicable action and judgment in ejection against Lessee and all persons claiming under Lessee for the recovery of possession of the herein demised premises, for which this lease shall be his sufficient warrant,

Figure 8.1
(cont.)

whereupon, if Lessor so desires, a writ of habere facias possessionem may issue forthwith, without any prior writ or proceedings whatsoever, and provided that if for any reason after such action shall have been commenced the same shall be determined and the possession of the premises hereby demised remain in or be restored to Lessee.   Lessor shall have the right upon any subsequent default or defaults, or upon the termination of this lease as hereinbefore set forth, to bring one or more amicable action or actions as hereinbefore set forth to recover possession of the said premises.

Affidavit of Default

20. In any amicable action of ejectment and/or for rent in arrears, Lessor shall first cause to be filed in such action an affidavit made by him or someone acting for him setting forth the facts necessary to authorize the entry of judgment, of which facts such affidavit shall be conclusive evidence, and if a true copy of this lease (and of the truth of the copy such affidavit shall be sufficient evidence) be filed in such action, it shall not be necessary to file the original as a warrant of attorney, any rule of Court, custom or practice to the contrary notwithstanding.

Remedies Cumulative

21. All of the remedies hereinbefore given to Lessor and all rights and remedies given to it by law and equity shall be cumulative and concurrent.   No determination of this lease or the taking or recovering of the premises shall deprive Lessor of any of its remedies or action against the Lessee for rent due at the time or which, under the terms hereof, would in the future become due as if there has been no determination, or for sums due at the time or which, under the terms hereof, would in the future become due as if there had been no determination, nor shall the bringing of any action for rent or breach of covenant, or the resort to any other remedy herein provided for the recovery of rent be construed as a waiver of the right to obtain possession of the premises.

Subordination

22. This Agreement of Lease and all of its terms, covenants, and provisions are and each of them is subject and subordinate to any lease or other arrangement or right to possession, under which the Lessor is in control of the demised premises, to the rights of the owner or owners of the demised premises and of the land or buildings of which the demised premises are a part to all rights of the Lessor's landlord and to any and all mortgages and other encumbrances now or hereafter placed upon the demised premises or upon the land and/or buildings containing the same; and Lessee expressly agrees that if Lessor's tenancy, control, or right to possession shall terminate either by expiration, forfeiture or otherwise, then this lease shall thereupon immediately terminate and the Lessee shall, thereupon, give immediate possession and Lessee hereby waives any and all claims for damages or otherwise by reason of such termination as aforesaid.

Condemnation

23. In the event that the premises demised or any part thereof is taken or condemned for a public or quasi-public use, this lease shall, as to the part so taken, terminate as of the date title shall vest in the condemnor, and rent shall abate in proportion to the square feet of leased space taken or condemned or shall cease if the entire premises be so taken.   In either event the Lessee waives all claims against the Lessor by reason of the complete or partial taking of the demised premises, and it is agreed that the Lessee shall not be entitled to any notice whatsoever of the partial or complete termination of this lease by reason of the aforesaid.

Termination of Lease

24. It is hereby mutually agreed that either party hereto may determine this lease at the end of the said term by giving to the other party prior written notice thereof in accordance with paragraph #1.(l), but in default of such notice, this lease shall continue upon the same terms and conditions in force immediately prior to the expiration or the term hereof as are herein contained for a further period as specified in paragraph #1.(m), and so on from renewal to renewal unless or until termination by either party hereto, giving the other the aforementioned written notice for renewal previous to expiration of the then current term; PROVIDED, however, that should this lease be continued for a further period under the terms hereinabove mentioned, any allowance given Lessee on the rent during the original term should not exceed beyond such original term, and further provided, however, that if Lessor shall have given such written notice prior to the expiration of any term hereby created, of its intention to change the terms and conditions of this lease, and Lessee shall not within thirty days from such notice notify Lessor of Lessee's intention to vacate the demised premises at the end of the then current term, Lessee shall be considered as Lessee under the terms and conditions mentioned in such notice for a further term as above provided, or for such further term as may be stated in such notice.   In the event that Lessee shall give notice, as stipulated in this lease, of intention to vacate the demised premises at the end of the present term, or any renewal or extension thereof, and shall fail or refuse so to vacate the same on the date designated by such notice, then it is expressly agreed that Lessor shall have the option either (a) to disregard the notice so given as having no effect, in which case all the terms and conditions of this lease shall continue thereafter with full force precisely as if such notice had not been given, or (b) Lessor may, at any time within thirty days after the present term or any renewal or extension thereof, as aforesaid, give the said Lessee ten days written notice of his intention to terminate the said lease; whereupon the Lessee expressly agrees to vacate said premises at the expiration of the said period of ten days specified in said notice.   All powers granted to Lessor by this lease may be exercised and all obligations imposed upon Lessee by this lease shall be performed by Lessee as well during any extension of the original term of this lease as during the original term itself.

Inability to give Possession

25. If Lessor is unable to give Lessee possession of the demised premises, as herein provided, by reason of the holding over of a previous occupant, or by reason of any cause beyond the control of the Lessor, the Lessor shall not be liable in damages to the Lessee therefore, and during the period that the Lessor is unable to give possession, all rights and remedies of both parties hereunder shall be suspended.

Additional Rent

26. Lessee agrees to pay as additional rent any and all sums which may become due by reason of the failure of Lessee to comply with any of the covenants of this lease and any and all damages, costs and expenses which the Lessor may suffer or incur by reason of any default of the Lessee or failure on his part to comply with the covenants of this lease, and also any and all damages to the demised premises caused by any act or neglect of the Lessee, his guests, agents, employees or other occupants of the demised premises.

Notices

27. All notices required to be given by Lessor to Lessee shall be sufficiently given by leaving the same upon the demised premises, but notices given by Lessee to Lessor must be given by certified mail, and as against Lessor the only admissable evidence that notice has been given by Lessee shall be a certified return receipt signed by Lessor or his agent.

Right to Enforce

28. The Lessor shall have the right, at all times, to enforce any or all the convenants and provisions of this lease, notwithstanding the failure of Lessor at any previous time, or times, to enforce his rights under any of the convenants and provisions of this lease.

Definition of Lessor and Lessee

29. The word "Lessor" as used herein, shall include the Owner and the Landlord, whether Person, Firm or Corporation, as well as the Heirs, Executors, Administrators, Successors and Assigns each of whom shall have the same rights, remedies, powers, privileges and obligations as though he, she, it or they had originally signed this lease as Lessor, including the right to proceed in his, her, its, or their own name to enter judgment by confession, or otherwise.   The word "Lessee" as used herein, shall include Tenant, whether Person, Firm or Corporation, as well as the Heirs, Executors, Administrators, Successors and Assigns, each of whom shall have the same rights, remedies, powers, privileges, and shall have no other liabilities, rights, privileges or powers than he, she, it or they would have been under or possessed had he, she, it or they originally signed this lease as Lessee.

Agent

30. It is expressly understood and agreed between the parties hereto that the herein named agent, his salesmen and employees or any officer or partner of agent and any cooperating broker and his salesmen and employees and any officer or partner of the cooperating broker are acting as agent only and will in no case whatsoever be held liable either jointly or severally to either party for the performance of any term of covenant of this agreement or for damages for the nonperformance thereof.

Heirs and Assignees

31. All rights and liabilities herein given to, or imposed upon, or waivers of the respective parties hereto shall extend to and bind the several and respective heirs, executors, administrators, successors and assigns of said parties; and if there shall be more than one Lessee, they shall all be bound jointly and severally by the terms, covenants and agreements herein, and the word "Lessee" shall then be deemed taken to mean each and every person or party mentioned as a Lessee herein, be the same one or more; and if there shall be more one Lessee, any notice required or permitted by the terms of this lease may be given by or to any one thereof, and shall have the same force and effect as if given by or to all thereof.   No rights, however, shall inure to the benefit of any assignee of Lessee unless the assignment of such assignee has been approved by Lessor in writing as aforesaid.

Lease Contains Entire Agreement

32. The Lessor and Lessee hereby agree that this lease sets forth all the promises, agreements, conditions and understandings between the Lessor, or his Agent, and the Lessee relative to the demised premises, and that there are no promises, agreements, conditions or understandings, either oral or written, between them other than as are herein set forth, and any subsequent alteration, amendment, change or addition to this lease shall not be binding upon the Lessor or Lessee unless reduced to writing and signed by them.

Severability
(11-74)

33. If any section, subsection, sentence, clause phrase or requirement of this lease is contrary to law or laws subsequently enacted, or should be found contrary to laws during the term or any renewal or extension thereof, the validity of the remaining portions shall not be affected thereby.   The parties hereby agree that they would have agreed to each section, subsection, clause sentence, phrase or requirement herein irrespective of the fact that one or more section, subsection sentence, clause, phrase or requirement was contrary to law or during the term or any renewal or extension thereof or are found to be contrary to the law.

Descriptive Heading

34. The descriptive headings used herein are for convenience only and they are not intended to indicate all of the matter in the sections which follow them.   Accordingly, they shall have no effect whatsoever in determining the rights or obligations of the parties.

**Figure 8.1
(cont.)**

**Approval
(7-86)**

IN WITNESS WHEREOF, the parties hereto, including to be legally bound hereby, have hereunder set their hands and seals the day and year first above written.

WITNESS AS
TO LESSEE ....

LESSEE ....(SEAL)

WITNESS AS
TO LESSEE ....

LESSEE ....(SEAL)

LESSEE ....(SEAL)

The Lessor hereby approves this contract on this .... day of........................... 19...... and in consideration of the services rendered in procuring the herein named Lessee and/or collection of rents as agreed and specified in part one of this lease, the Lessor agrees to pay the herein named agent a fee in the amount of .... for obtaining Lessee together with a fee of .... for the collection of rents during the term, renewal or extension of this lease or additional lease with the herein named Lessee. Should the Lessee purchase the demised premises from the Lessor during the term of this lease, or during a renewal, extension or any additional lease between said parties for the demised premises, or within a reasonable period of time after the expiration of any such lease, the Lessor agrees to pay the agent, at the time of settlement, a sales fee of/from the specified sale price.

WITNESS AS
TO LESSOR ....

LESSOR ....(SEAL)

WITNESS AS
TO LESSOR ....

LESSOR ....(SEAL)

AGENT BY ....

2. *Consideration:* All leases, being contracts, must be supported by a valid consideration. *Rent* is the normal consideration granted for the right to occupy the leased premises; however, the payment of rent is not essential as long as consideration was granted in creation of the lease itself. The courts consider a lease to be a contract and not subject to subsequent changes in the rent or other terms unless these changes are in writing and executed in the same manner as the original lease.

3. *Capacity to contract:* The parties must have the legal capacity to contract.

4. *Legal objectives:* The objectives of the lease must be legal.

When the statute of frauds applies an oral lease is considered to be *unenforceable.* In addition, a description of the leased premises should be clearly stated. If the lease covers land, such as a ground lease, the legal description of the real estate should be used. If the lease is for a part of the building, such as office space or an apartment, the space itself or the apartment designation should be clearly and carefully described. If supplemental space is to be included, the lease should clearly identify it.

Use of Premises

A lessor may restrict a lessee's use of the premises through provisions included in the lease. This is most important in leases for stores or commercial space. For example, a lease may provide that the leased premises are to be used *only* for the purpose of a real estate office *and for no other.* In the absence of such limitations, the lease should state a lessee may use the premises for any lawful purpose.

Term of Lease

The term of a lease is the period for which the lease will run, and it should be set out precisely. The date of the beginning of the term and the date of its ending should be stated together with a statement of the total period of the lease; for example, "for a term of 30 years beginning June 1, 1986 and ending May 31, 2016." Courts do not favor leases with an indefinite term and will hold that such perpetual leases are not valid unless the language of the lease and the surrounding circumstances clearly indicate that such is the intention of the parties. Leases are controlled by the statutes of the various states and must be in accordance with those provisions. In some states, terms of agricultural leases are limited by statute. Also, the laws of some states prohibit leases that run for 100 years or more. Act 77 of 1986 in Pennsylvania requires the payment of transfer taxes on leases for more than 30 years.

Security Deposits

Most leases require the tenant to provide some form of **security deposit** to be held by the landlord during the lease term and kept, wholly or partially, in the event of the tenant's default in payment of rent or destruction of the premises. The landlord's entitlement to recover damages from the security deposit has been subjected to various interpretations. Some assert that damage to the premises, not including damage from defaulted rent, is the intent of the security deposit and, therefore, is the only recovery the landlord can claim through this vehicle. Because of varied interpretations the lease agreement should clearly state the purpose of the security deposit and the recovery that may be claimed by the landlord. Other safeguards against nonpayment of rent may include an advance rental payment, contracting for a lien on the tenant's property and/or requiring the tenant to have a third person guarantee payment.

In Practice...   *A lease should specify whether a payment is a security deposit or an advance rental. If it is a security deposit, the tenant is usually not entitled to apply it to the final month's rent. If it is an advance rental, the landlord must treat it as income for tax purposes.*

Pennsylvania law limits the amount that landlords may require residential tenants to pay as security deposits, or funds to be deposited in escrow for the payment of damages to the leasehold premises and/or default in rent payments. During the first year of the lease, a maximum of two months' rent may be required, with one month's security returned to the tenant after the first year. Note that after a lease has run five years, the landlord cannot raise the amount of security deposit in escrow to reflect increased rents.

All such funds deposited with a landlord by a tenant in excess of $100 must be deposited in an escrow account (interest-bearing or noninterest-bearing) in a federal or state regulated banking or savings and loan institution. The tenant must be notified of the name and address of the institution where the deposits are held and the amount. Interest on deposited funds is generally required to be paid to the tenant commencing on the second anniversary of the lease. In such cases, the interest earned on the tenant's deposit must be paid each year on the anniversary of the tenant's lease. The landlord may retain one percent of such monies as administrative expenses.

The landlord must return the security deposit including any interest owed to the tenant within 30 days of the termination of the tenancy. If any of the money is withheld for damages, the landlord must provide the tenant with a list of such damages. At the same time, the landlord must pay the tenant the difference between the funds deposited in escrow (including any unpaid interest) and the damages. A landlord who fails to provide a written list within 30 days of the termination of the tenancy forfeits all rights to any portion of the security deposit. Any landlord who fails to return to the tenant the difference between the deposit and the damages within the same time period is liable for double the amount of the security deposit. Note that a tenant must provide a forwarding address, in writing, to the landlord or agent or forfeit any claim to a security deposit that might otherwise be returned.

Bond in lieu of escrowing. Instead of depositing such funds in a financial institution, a Pennsylvania landlord has the option of purchasing a guarantee bond, or surety bond, which guarantees that the security deposit (including any required interest) less the cost of any necessary repairs will be returned to the tenant at the termination of the tenancy.

Confession of Judgment Clauses   **Confession of judgment clauses** are included in many leases to assist the landlord in forcing *collection of rent*. The tenant authorizes any attorney of record to appear in court in the tenant's name and to confess judgment, or to agree that a judgment be entered against the tenant in favor of the landlord for the delinquent rent, court costs and attorney's fees. Such a clause may be called a *cognovit*. Many states have now declared confession of judgment clauses illegal when used in residential leases.

Because of a federal court ruling regarding the use of confession of judgment clauses, a practice has developed in Pennsylvania for tenants who sign a confession of judgment to sign an *explanation of rights* as well. This is a document that explains to the signer the terms of the confession of judgment.

Legal Principles of Leases

Most states provide that leases can be filed for record in the county in which the property is located. But unless the lease is for a relatively long term, it *usually is not recorded*. Possession of the property by the lessee is notice to the world of his or her rights, and an inspection of the property will result in *actual notice* of the lessee's leasehold interest.

When a lease runs for a period of *three years* or longer, recordation is more common. The recording of a *long-term lease* places the world on notice of the long-term rights of the lessee. The recordation of such a lease is usually required if the lessee intends to mortgage the leasehold interest.

In Pennsylvania, only a *memorandum of lease* is filed for record. The terms of the lease are not disclosed to the public by the filing of a memorandum of lease; however, the objective of giving public notice of the rights of the lessee is still accomplished. The memorandum of lease must set forth the names of the parties and a description of the property being leased.

Possession of Leased Premises

As noted earlier, leases carry the implied covenant that the landlord will give the tenant possession of the premises. In Pennsylvania, the landlord must give the tenant *actual* occupancy, or possession, of the leased premises. Thus, if the premises are occupied by a holdover tenant, or adverse claimant, at the beginning of the new lease period, it is the landlord's duty to bring whatever action is necessary to recover possession and to bear the expense of this action.

Improvements

Neither the landlord nor the tenant is required to make any improvements to the leased property. In the absence of an agreement to the contrary, the tenant may make improvements with the landlord's permission. Any such alterations generally become the property of the landlord; that is, they become fixtures. However, as discussed in Chapter 2, "Real Property," a tenant may be given the right to install trade fixtures or chattel fixtures by the terms of the lease. It is customary to provide that such trade fixtures may be removed by the tenant before the lease expires, provided the tenant restores the premises to the previous condition.

Maintenance of Premises

Many states, including Pennsylvania, now require a residential lessor to maintain dwelling units in a habitable condition and to make any necessary repairs to common elements, such as hallways, stairs or elevators. The tenant does not have to make any repairs, but must return the premises in the same condition they were received, with allowances for ordinary use.

Assignment and Subleasing

The lessee may assign the lease or may sublease if the lease terms do not prohibit it. A tenant who transfers all of the leasehold interests *assigns* the lease. One who transfers less than all of the leasehold interests by leasing them to a new tenant **subleases** (see Figure 8.2). In most cases, the sublease or assignment of a lease does not relieve the original lessee of the obligation to make rental payments unless the landlord agrees to waive such liability. Most leases prohibit the lessee

**Figure 8.2
Assignment versus
Subletting**

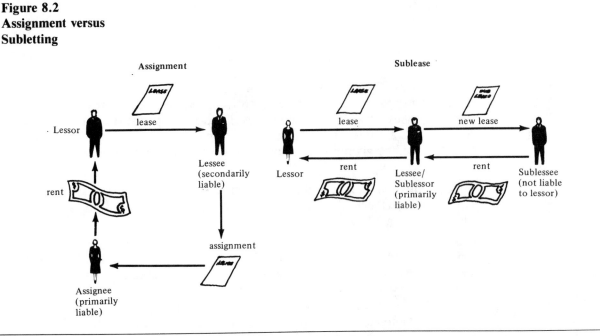

from assigning or subletting without the lessor's consent. The lessor thus retains control over the occupancy of the leased premises, but must not unreasonably withhold consent. The sublessor's (original lessee's) interest in the real estate is known as a *sandwich lease.*

Options

Many leases contain an *option* that grants the lessee the privilege of *renewing* the lease but requires that the lessee give *notice* before a specific date of the intention to exercise the option. An *option to purchase* grants to the lessee the option to purchase the leased premises; the provisions for the option to purchase vary widely. Options to purchase are becoming more common (see Chapter 9, "Real Estate Contracts").

Destruction of Premises

In land leases involving *agricultural land,* the courts have held that damage to or destruction of the improvements, even if it is not the tenant's fault, does not relieve the tenant from the obligation to pay rent to the end of the term. This ruling has been extended in most states to include *ground leases* upon which the tenant has constructed a building and, in many instances, leases that give possession of an entire building to the tenant. When the tenant leases an entire building, the courts have held that the tenant is also leasing the land upon which it is located.

In cases where the leased premises are only a part of the building (such as office or commercial space or an apartment in an apartment building), the tenant is *not* required to continue to pay rent upon destruction of the leased premises. In some states, if the property was destroyed as a result of the landlord's negligence, the tenant can recover damages from the landlord.

In Practice...

All of these general statements concerning destruction of leased premises are controlled largely by the terms of the lease. Printed lease forms and all carefully pre-

pared leases generally include a provision covering the subject of destruction of the premises. Great care must be exercised in reading the entire lease document before signing it.

Termination of Lease

A written lease for a definite period of time, an estate for years, expires at the end of that time period; no separate notice is required to terminate the lease when it expires. Oral and written leases that do not specify a definite expiration date (such as a month-to-month or year-to-year tenancy or a tenancy at will) may be terminated by giving proper notice in advance as required by state law.

Under Pennsylvania law, oral and written leases that do not specify a definite expiration date (such as a month-to-month or a tenancy at will) may be terminated by giving 30 days' notice in advance.

When the conditions of a lease are *breached*, or *broken*, a landlord may give the tenant proper notice to quit and eject the tenant. If the term of the lease is for less than one year or for an indeterminate time, the landlord must give the tenant 30 days' notice; if the term is for one year or more, three months' notice is required. If the tenant has defaulted in rent payments, the required notice is 15 or 30 days, depending upon the time of year (winter or summer).

It is possible that the parties to a lease will mutually agree to cancel the lease. The tenant may offer to surrender the lease, and acceptance by the landlord will result in termination. A tenant who abandons leased property, however, remains liable for the terms of the lease—including the rent. The terms of the specific lease will usually dictate whether or not the landlord is obligated to try to rerent the space.

When the owner of leased property dies or the property is sold, *the lease does not terminate*. There are two exceptions: (1) a lease from the owner of a life estate terminates on the death of that person and (2) the death of either party terminates a tenancy at will. The heirs of a deceased landlord are bound by the terms of existing valid leases. In addition, if a landlord conveys leased real estate, the new landlord takes the property subject to the rights of the tenants. If a tenant under an estate for years or from year to year dies, the lease will remain in effect; the deceased lessee's heirs will be bound by the terms of his or her lease agreement. Note that a tenancy may be terminated by operation of law, as in a bankruptcy or condemnation proceeding.

A lease agreement may provide for a new landlord, after taking title, to give some period of notice to the tenant to terminate an existing lease. Since the new owner has taken title subject to the rights of the tenant, this affords the landlord the ability to claim possession and/or negotiate new leases under the new owner's terms and conditions. This is commonly known as a *sale clause*.

Breach of Lease

When a tenant breaches any lease provision, the landlord may sue the tenant to obtain a judgment to cover past due rent, damages to the premises or other defaults. Likewise, when a landlord breaches any lease provision, the tenant is entitled to similar remedies.

Suit for possession—actual eviction. When a tenant breaches a lease or improperly retains possession of the leased premises, possession can be obtained by the landlord through a suit for possession, known as a **summary proceedings.** Pennsylvania law requires the landlord to serve *notice* on the tenant before commencing the suit. As discussed earlier, when the tenant breaks the terms of the lease, the landlord must give the tenant proper notice to quit (15 days' to three months' notice, depending on the circumstances). When a court issues a judgment for possession to the landlord, the tenant must peaceably remove himself or herself and all belongings, or the landlord can have the judgment enforced by a constable who *will forcibly remove* the tenant and his or her possessions.

Tenants' remedies—constructive eviction. If a landlord breaches any clause of a lease agreement, the tenant has the right to sue, claiming a judgment for damages against the landlord. If an action or omission on the landlord's part results in the leased premises becoming uninhabitable for the purpose intended in the lease, the tenant may have the right to abandon the premises. This action, called **constructive eviction,** terminates the lease agreement if the tenant can prove that the premises have become uninhabitable because of the conscious neglect of the landlord. In order to claim constructive eviction, the tenant must actually remove himself or herself from the premises while the uninhabitable condition exists.

For example, a lease requires the landlord to furnish steam heat; because of the landlord's failure to repair a defective heating plant, the heat is not provided. If this results in the leased premises becoming uninhabitable, the tenant may abandon them. It should be noted that some leases provide that if the failure to furnish heat is accidental and not the landlord's fault, it is not grounds for constructive eviction.

Warranty of habitability. Pennsylvania courts recognize a doctrine known as **warranty of habitability.** The doctrine applies only to residential leases. The theory of the warranty of habitability is that the lessor leasing residential premises warrants that the premises shall be fit for habitation. If the lessee can prove that the premises are not fit for habitation, the court can order a reduction in or cessation of rent.

Pro-Tenant Legislation

For the most part, leases are drawn up primarily for the benefit of the landlord. Recent consumer awareness, however, has fostered the belief that a valid lease is dependent on both parties' fulfillment of certain obligations. To provide laws outlining such obligations, several states have adopted some variation of the *Uniform Residential Landlord and Tenant Act.* This model law addresses such issues as the landlord's right of entry, maintenance of premises, the tenant's protection against retaliation by the landlord for complaints and the disclosure of the property owners' names and addresses to the tenants. The act further sets down specific remedies available to both the landlord and the tenant if a breach of the lease agreement occurs.

The Pennsylvania Landlord and Tenant Act of 1951 contains the remedies available to the landlord in the event of a lease default. The leasing of residential property in Pennsylvania is subject to the Pennsylvania Consumer Protection law, which prohibits unfair practices in the conduct of commerce. Tenants' remedies are outlined in this law.

The federal government also took steps to increase tenants' protection with the implementation of the Tenants' Eviction Procedures Act in 1976. This act establishes standardized eviction procedures for people living in *government-subsidized housing.* It requires that the landlord have a valid reason for evicting the tenant and that the landlord give the tenant proper notice of eviction. This act does not supersede state laws in this area; however, it does provide recourse for tenants in states that have no such laws. The act applies only to multiunit residential buildings that are owned or subsidized by the Department of Housing and Urban Development and to buildings that have government-insured mortgages.

Types of Leases

The manner in which rent is determined indicates the type of lease that is in force. The three primary types of leases are based upon rentals. They are: (1) the gross lease, (2) the net lease and (3) the percentage lease (see Table 8.2).

**Table 8.2
Types of Leases**

Type of Lease	Lessee Pays	Lessor Pays
Gross lease Residential (also small commercial)	Basic rent	Property charges (taxes, repairs, insurance, etc.)
Net lease Commercial/industrial	Basic rent plus most or all property charges	May pay some property charges
Percentage lease Commercial/industrial	Basic rent plus percent of gross sales (may pay property costs)	May pay some or all property charges

Gross Lease

In a **gross lease,** the tenant's obligation is to pay a *fixed rental,* and the landlord pays all taxes, insurance, mortgage payments, repairs and the like connected with the property (usually called *property charges*).

Net Lease

The **net lease** provides that in addition to the rent, the *tenant pays property charges* as defined in the lease agreement. The monthly rental paid to the landlord is in addition to these charges and so is net income for the landlord after operating costs have been paid. Leases for entire commercial or industrial buildings and the land on which they are located, ground leases and long-term leases are usually net leases. In a *triple net lease,* or *net-net-net lease,* the tenant pays all operating and other expenses, such as taxes, insurance, assessments, maintenance and other charges.

Percentage Lease

Either a gross lease or a net lease may be a **percentage lease.** A percentage lease provides that the rental is based on a *percentage of the gross or net income* received by the tenant doing business on the leased property. This type of lease is usually used in the rental of retail business locations.

The percentage lease usually provides for a minimum fixed rental fee plus a percentage of that portion of the tenant's business income that exceeds a stated minimum. For example, a lease might provide for a minimum monthly rental of $1,200, with the further agreement that the tenant pay an additional amount each month equivalent to four percent of all gross sales in excess of $30,000. (Note that while the $1,200 rental represents four percent of $30,000 gross, the percentage feature of this lease will not actually begin to apply until after the tenant has grossed in excess of $30,000.) The percentage charged in such leases varies widely with the nature of the business and is negotiable between landlord and tenant. A tenant's bargaining power is determined by the volume of the business. Percentages vary with the location of the property and with economic conditions.

Other Lease Types

Variable leases. There are several types of leases that allow for increases in the fixed rental charge during the lease period. Two of the more common ones are the *graduated lease,* which provides for increases in rent at set future dates, and the *index lease,* which allows rent to be increased or decreased periodically based on changes in the government cost-of-living or consumer price index or some other index.

Ground leases. When a landowner leases the land to a tenant who agrees to *erect a building* on it, the lease is usually referred to as a **ground lease,** involving separate ownership of the land and building. Such a lease must be for a long enough term to make the transaction desirable to the tenant making the investment in the building. These leases are generally *net leases* that require the lessee to pay rent as well as real estate taxes, insurance, upkeep and repairs. Such leases often run for terms of 50 years or longer, and a lease for 999 years is not impossible. Although such leases are considered to be personal property, certain states' laws may give leaseholders some of the rights and obligations of real property owners.

Oil and gas leases. When oil companies lease land to explore for oil and gas, a special lease agreement must be negotiated. Usually, the landowner receives a cash payment for executing the lease. If no well is drilled within a year or other period stated in the lease, the lease expires; however, most oil and gas leases provide that the oil company may continue its rights for another year by paying another flat rental fee. Such rentals may be paid annually until a well is produced. If oil and/or gas is found, the landowner usually receives one-eighth of its value as a royalty. In this case, the lease will continue for as long as oil or gas is obtained in significant quantities.

Summary

A *lease* is an agreement that grants one person the right to use the property of another for a certain period in return for consideration. The lease agreement is a combination of a conveyance creating a leasehold interest in the property and a contract outlining the rights and obligations of the landlord and the tenant.

A leasehold estate that runs for a specific length of time creates a *tenancy for years,* while one that runs for an indefinite period creates a *periodic tenancy* (year to year, month to month) or a *tenancy at will.* A leasehold estate is generally classified as personal property. A tenancy at sufferance arises when a tenant continues to hold possession without consent of the landlord.

The requirements of a valid lease include offer and acceptance, consideration, capacity to contract and legal objectives. In addition, the state statute of frauds requires that any lease that will not be executed within three years must be in writing to be enforceable. Leases also generally include clauses relating to such rights and obligations of the landlord and tenant as the use of the premises, subletting, judgments, maintenance of the premises and termination of the lease period.

Leases may be terminated by the expiration of the lease period, the mutual agreement of the parties or a breach of the lease by either landlord or tenant. It is important to note that neither the death of the tenant nor the landlord's sale of the rental property terminates a lease.

Upon a tenant's default on any of the lease provisions, a landlord may sue for a money judgment or for *actual eviction* through *summary proceedings* in a case where a tenant has improperly retained possession of the premises. If the premises have become uninhabitable as a result of the landlord's negligence, the tenant may have the right of *constructive eviction,* that is, the right to abandon the premises and refuse to pay rent until the premises are repaired.

There are several basic types of leases, including *net leases, gross leases* and *percentage leases.* These leases are classified according to the method used in determining the rental rate of the property.

Questions

1. Alvin Yates's lease will expire in two weeks. At that time, he will move to larger quarters on the other side of town. In order to terminate this lease agreement:

   I. Yates must give the landlord prior notice.
   II. the landlord must give Yates prior notice.

   a. I only
   b. II only
   c. both I and II
   d. neither I nor II

2. A tenant's right to occupy, or take possession of, leased premises is:

   a. a reversionary interest.
   b. an estate in land.
   c. a leasehold interest.
   d. b and c

3. A ground lease is usually:

   a. short-term.
   b. for 100 years or longer.
   c. long-term.
   d. a gross lease.

4. A percentage lease is a lease that provides for:

   a. a rental of a percentage of the value of a building.
   b. a definite periodic rent not exceeding a stated percentage.
   c. a definite monthly rent plus a percentage of the tenant's gross receipts in excess of a certain amount.
   d. a graduated amount due monthly and not exceeding a stated percentage.

5. If several renting tenants moved out of a store building because the building collapsed:

   a. this would be an actual eviction.
   b. the tenants would be liable for the rent until the expiration date of their leases.
   c. the landlord would have to provide substitute space.
   d. this would be a constructive eviction.

6. Under the terms of a net lease:

   I. the tenant is usually responsible for paying the real estate taxes for the leased property.
   II. the tenant has an option to buy the leased property within a specified length of time.

   a. I only
   b. II only
   c. both I and II
   d. neither I nor II

7. A lease for more than three years must be in writing to be enforceable because:

   a. the landlord or tenant may forget the terms.
   b. the tenant must sign the agreement to pay rent.
   c. the statute of frauds requires it.
   d. it is the customary procedure to protect the tenant.

8. A lease calls for a minimum rent of $1,200 per month plus four percent of the annual gross business over $150,000. If the total rent paid at the end of the year was $19,200, how much business did the tenant do during the year?

   a. $159,800
   b. $25,200
   c. $270,000
   d. $169,200

9. Paul Robinson occupies a building under a written lease for a five-year term with monthly rental payments. The lease expired last month but Robinson has remained in possession and the landlord has accepted his most recent rent payment without comment. At this point:

   a. Robinson is a holdover tenant.
   b. Robinson's lease has been renewed for another five years.
   c. Robinson's lease has been renewed for another month.
   d. Robinson is a tenant at sufferance.

10. Albert Franzen rented a studio apartment to Wilbur Post under a one-year written lease. Three and one-half months into the lease term, Franzen died. With regard to the written lease between Post and his late landlord:

  I. Post continues to be bound by its terms.

  II. Franzen's heirs are now bound by its terms.

    a. I only   c. both I and II
    b. II only   d. neither I nor II

11. Which of the following terms refers to a tenant's legal right to possession of leased property against the ownership claims of third parties?

    a. tenancy at will
    b. cognovit
    c. covenant of quiet possession
    d. constructive eviction

12. A tenant's lease has expired, the tenant has neither vacated nor negotiated a renewal lease and the landlord has declared that she does not want the tenant to remain in the building. The tenancy is called:

    a. estate for years.
    b. periodic estate.
    c. tenancy at will.
    d. tenancy at sufferance.

13. The requirements of a valid lease include:

    a. offer and acceptance.
    b. consideration.
    c. capacity to contract.
    d. all of the above

14. When a tenant holds possession of a landlord's property without a current lease agreement and without the landlord's approval:

    a. the tenant is maintaining a gross lease.
    b. the landlord may file suit for possession.
    c. the tenant has no obligation to pay rent.
    d. b and c

15. Which of the following best describes a *net lease?*

    a. an agreement in which the tenant pays a fixed rent and the landlord pays all taxes, insurance and so forth on the property
    b. a lease in which the tenant pays rent in addition to some or all property charges
    c. a lease in which the tenant pays the landlord a percentage of the monthly income derived from the property
    d. an agreement granting an individual a leasehold interest in fishing rights to shoreline properties

16. In Pennsylvania, a tenant may cancel a tenancy at will by:

    a. giving the landlord 30 days' notice.
    b. giving the landlord one week's notice.
    c. giving the landlord two months' notice.
    d. removing his or her possessions from the premises—no notice is necessary.

17. If a residential tenant is unable to receive hot water because of a faulty hot-water heater, which of the following remedies may the tenant take if the landlord is obliged by the lease terms to fix the equipment?

    a. The tenant may sue the landlord for damages.
    b. The tenant may abandon the premises.
    c. The tenant may terminate the lease agreement.
    d. all of the above

18. Actual eviction occurs when:

    a. a tenant peaceably vacates a property upon termination of a lease.
    b. a landlord regains possession through a legal action.
    c. a court officer removes a tenant from the premises.
    d. b and c

19. A tenant who transfers all of his or her leasehold interests is:

   a. a sublettor.
   b. assigning the lease.
   c. automatically relieved of any further obligation under it.
   d. giving the third party a sandwich lease.

20. Which of the following leases would probably be recorded?

   I. a two-year residential lease
   II. a five-year net lease for commercial property with provisions for yearly rental increases and an option to purchase the property at the end of the lease term

   a. I only
   b. II only
   c. both I and II
   d. neither I nor II

9

Real Estate Contracts

Key Terms

Agreement in writing
Assignment
Bilateral contract
Breach
Consideration
Contract
Counteroffer
Earnest money
Equitable title
Escrow agreement
Executed contract
Executory contract
Express contract
Implied contract
Installment contract

Legality of object
Legally competent parties
Novation
Offer and acceptance
Option
Real estate sales contract
Statute of frauds
Statute of limitations
Suit for specific performance
Unenforceable contract
Unilateral contract
Valid contract
Void contract
Voidable contract

Overview

"Get it in writing" is a phrase commonly used to warn one party to an agreement to protect his or her interests by entering into a written *contract* with the other party, outlining the rights and obligations of both. The real estate business makes use of many different types of contracts, including listing agreements, leases and sales contracts. Brokers and salespeople must understand the content and uses of such agreements and must be able to explain them to buyers and sellers. This chapter will first deal with the legal principles governing contracts in general, and will then examine the types of contracts used in the real estate business in particular.

| **Contracts** | Brokers and salespeople use many types of contracts and agreements in the course of their business to carry out their responsibilities to sellers, buyers and the general public. Among these are listing agreements, sales contracts, option agreements, installment contracts, leases and escrow agreements. |

Before studying these specific types of contracts, you first must understand the general body of law that governs the operation of such agreements. This area of law is known as *contract law.*

Contract Law

A **contract** is a legally enforceable promise or set of promises that must be performed and for which, if a breach of promise occurs, the law provides a remedy. Depending on the situation and the nature or language of the agreement, a contract may be: (1) express or implied, (2) unilateral or bilateral, (3) executory or executed and (4) valid, unenforceable, voidable or void. These terms are used to describe the type, status and legal effect of a contract and are discussed in the sections that follow.

Express and Implied Contracts

Depending upon how a contract is created, it may be express or implied. In an **express contract,** the parties state the terms and show their intentions in words. An express contract may be either oral or written. In an **implied contract,** the agreement of the parties is demonstrated by their acts and conduct.

In Practice...

In the usual agency relationship, a listing agreement is an express contract between the seller and the broker that names the broker as the agent of the seller. The courts have held that a broker may, under certain situations, also have created an implied contract to represent a buyer. For example, a broker took a listing for a residence and showed it to several potential purchasers, one of whom requested that a physical inspection of the property be made. The broker complied but mistakenly hired an unqualified person to make the inspection. The interested party bought the property, discovered a serious physical defect and sued the broker. The court ruled that, although the broker was the agent of the seller, in complying with the buyer's request he had by implication accepted an agency agreement to represent the purchaser. By hiring an inspector who was not competent to do the job, the broker violated his duty to the purchaser under this implied agreement.

Bilateral and Unilateral Contracts

Contracts may be classified as either bilateral or unilateral. In a **bilateral contract,** both parties promise to do something; one promise is given in exchange for another. A real estate sales contract is a bilateral contract because the seller promises to sell a parcel of real estate and deliver title to the property to the buyer, who promises to pay a certain sum of money for the property.

A **unilateral contract** is a one-sided agreement whereby one party makes a promise in order to induce a second party to do something. The second party is not legally obligated to act; however, if the second party does comply, the first party is obligated to keep the promise. An offer of a reward would be an example of a unilateral contract. For example, if a person runs a newspaper ad offering a reward for the return of a lost pet, that person is promising to pay if the act of returning the pet is fulfilled.

Executed and Executory Contracts

A contract may be classified as either executed or executory, depending on whether or not the agreement is completely performed. A fully **executed contract** is one in which both parties have fulfilled their promises and thus performed the contract. An **executory contract** exists when something remains to be done by one or both parties.

Validity of Contracts

A contract can be described as either valid, void, voidable or unenforceable (see Table 9.1), depending on the circumstances.

A **valid contract** complies with all the essential elements (which will be discussed later in this chapter) and is binding and enforceable on both parties.

A **void contract** is one that has no legal force or effect because it does not meet the essential elements of a contract. For example, one of the essential conditions for a contract to be considered valid is that it be for a legal purpose; thus, a contract to commit a crime is void.

A **voidable contract** is one that may be rescinded or disaffirmed by the party who might be injured if the contract were to be enforced. (In some cases, this may be both parties.) For example, a contract entered into with a minor is usually voidable; a minor is generally permitted to disaffirm a real estate contract at any time while under age and for a period of time into majority age. A voidable contract will be considered by the courts to be a valid contract if the party who has the option to disaffirm the agreement does not do so within a prescribed period of time.

An **unenforceable contract** has all the elements of a valid contract; however, neither party can sue the other to force performance. For example, an oral agreement for the sale of a parcel of real estate is unenforceable. This means that, if either the buyer or the seller does not comply with the terms of an oral sales agreement, the other party will be unable to sue to force the defaulting party to

Table 9.1 Legal Effects of Contracts	Type of Contract	Legal Effect	Example
	Valid	Binding and Enforceable on all Parties	Agreement Complying with Essentials of a Valid Contract
	Void	No Legal Effect	Contract for an Illegal Purpose
	Voidable	One or Both Parties May Disaffirm	Contract with a Minor (Minor May Disaffirm)
	Unenforceable	Neither Party May Sue to Force Performance	Certain Oral Agreements

perform. Unenforceable contracts are said to be "valid as between the parties," because once the agreement is fully executed and both parties are satisfied, neither has reason to initiate a lawsuit to force performance.

Elements Essential to a Valid Contract

In general, the essentials of a valid contract include the following:

1. **Offer and acceptance:** There must be an offer by one party, the offeror, that is accepted by the other, the offeree. This requirement, also called *mutual assent,* means that there must be a "meeting of the minds." Courts look to the objective intent of the parties to determine if they intended to enter into a binding agreement. The terms of the agreement must be fairly definite and understood by both parties.

   Revocation of an offer. An offer may be *revoked* by the offeror at any time prior to acceptance, if the revocation is communicated directly to the offeree by the offeror. It also is revoked if the offeree learns of the revocation and observes the offeror act in a manner that indicates that the offer no longer exists.

2. **Consideration:** Courts will not enforce gratuitous (free) promises. A promise will not be legally enforced unless something is exchanged for the promise. Consideration is something of legal value bargained for and given in exchange for a promise or an act. The phrase "good and valuable consideration" is sometimes used in contracts. Any return promise to perform that has been bargained for and exchanged is legally sufficient to satisfy the consideration element.

3. **Legally competent parties:** Both parties to the contract must be of legal age and have sufficient mental capacity. In most states, 18 is the age of contractual capacity. A party has sufficient mental capacity if he or she understands the nature and effect of the contract. Mental capacity is not the same as medical sanity.

4. **Legality of object:** To be valid, a contract must not contemplate a purpose that is illegal or against public policy.

* **No misrepresentation, fraud, undue influence or duress.** To be valid, a contract must be entered into as the free and voluntary act of each party. Misrepresentation, fraud, undue influence or duress would deprive a person of the ability to enter into a contract freely using reasonable judgment and caution. If these detriments are present, the contract is voidable by the injured party. If the uninjured party were to sue for breach, the injured party could use lack of voluntary assent, the ability to make a prudent and knowledgeable decision without undue influence, as a defense.

Agreement in writing and signed. Every state, including Pennsylvania, has passed a **statute of frauds** that requires certain types of contracts to be in writing to be enforceable in a court of law. The Pennsylvania law provides that all contracts for the sale of real estate must be in writing and signed by the seller in order to be enforceable. A contract that is properly written and signed prevents the acceptance of fraudulent proof of a fictitious oral contract. The Pennsylvania Real Estate Commission's rules and regulations require that a real estate broker representing a party to a transaction ensure that all such contracts are in writing.

Signatures. A real estate sales contract requires the signatures of the buyer and seller. The seller's spouse may also be required to sign, to release potential marital rights. When sellers are co-owners, all co-owners must sign if the entire ownership is being transferred. An individual holding a properly executed power of attorney may execute signature in behalf of an owner. However, Pennsylvania license law prohibits licensees from having a power of attorney for a principal. Corporate seals are required, accompanied by the signature of the authorized corporate representative, when a corporation is a party to a contract.

Accurate description of the property. A real estate sales contract must contain an accurate description of the property being conveyed. The test that most courts use is whether the subject property can be identified with reasonable certainty. This may require a legal description, but in some cases a street address is sufficient.

Performance of Contract

Under any contract, each party has certain rights and duties to fulfill. The question of when a contract must be performed is an important factor. Many contracts call for a specific time at or by which the agreed-upon acts must be completely performed. In addition, many contracts provide that "time is of the essence." This means that the contract should be performed within the time limit specified and any party who has not performed on time will be liable for breach of contract.

When a contract does not specify a date for performance, the acts it requires should be performed within a reasonable time. The interpretation of what constitutes a reasonable time will depend upon the situation. Generally, if the act can be done immediately—such as a payment of money—it should be performed immediately, unless the parties agree otherwise. Some courts have declared contracts invalid because they did not contain a time or date for performance.

Assignment and Novation

Often after a contract has been entered into, one party may want to withdraw without actually terminating the agreement. This may be accomplished through either assignment or novation.

Assignment refers to a transfer of rights and/or duties under a contract. Generally speaking, rights may be assigned to a third party, assignee, unless the agreement forbids such an assignment. Duties may also be assigned (delegated), but the original obligor, the assignor, remains primarily liable for them (after the new obligor), unless specifically released from this responsibility. A party to a contract might elect to assign the contract obligations in lieu of defaulting or performing on a contract that is no longer in the party's best interest. Many contracts include a clause that either permits or forbids assignment.

A contract may also be performed by **novation,** or the substitution of a new contract for an existing agreement with the intent of extinguishing the old contract. The new agreement may be between the same parties, or a new party may be substituted for either (this is *novation of the parties).* The parties' intent must be to discharge the old obligation. The new agreement must be supported by consideration and must conform with all the essential elements of a valid contract. For example, when a real estate purchaser assumes the seller's existing mortgage loan (see Chapter 13, "Real Estate Financing"), the lender may choose to release the seller and substitute the buyer as the party primarily liable for the mortgage debt.

Default—Breach of Contract

A contract may be completely performed, with all terms carried out, or it may be breached (broken) if one of the parties defaults. A **breach** of contract is a violation of any of the terms or conditions of a contract without legal excuse, such as when a seller breaches a sales contract by not delivering title to the buyer under the conditions stated in the agreement. The breaching or defaulting party assumes certain burdens and the nondefaulting party has certain rights.

With real estate contracts, if the *seller defaults,* the buyer has three alternatives:

1. The buyer may *rescind, or cancel, the contract* and recover earnest money.

2. The buyer may file a court suit, known as a **suit for specific performance,** to force the seller to perform the contract.

3. The buyer may *sue the seller for compensatory damages* (a personal judgment).

If the *buyer defaults,* the seller may pursue one of the following courses:

1. The seller may *declare the contract forfeited.* The right to forfeit is usually provided in the terms of the contract and the seller is usually entitled to retain the earnest money and all payments received from the buyer as *liquidated damages.*

2. The seller may *rescind the contract,* that is, may cancel, or terminate, the contract as if it never had been made. This requires the seller to return all payments the buyer has made.

3. The seller may *sue for compensatory damages.*

4. In Pennsylvania, a seller of real estate may also sue the buyer for the purchase money.

Statute of limitations. State law allows a specific time limit during which parties to a contract may bring legal suit to enforce their rights. In Pennsylvania, the **statute of limitations** for written contracts is six years and for oral contracts is four years from the date the contract is breached. Any party who does not take steps to enforce his or her rights within this statute of limitations may lose them. (Compare this with the principle of *laches,* discussed in Chapter 3, "Control of Land Use.")

Contracts Used in the Real Estate Business

As mentioned earlier, the types of written agreements most commonly used by brokers and salespeople are listing agreements, real estate sales contracts, option agreements, contracts for deed, leases and escrow agreements.

Broker's Authority to Prepare Documents

In many areas, specific guidelines have been drawn, either by agreement between lawyer and broker associations, by court decision or by statute, regarding the authority of real estate licensees to prepare contracts for their clients and customers. As a rule, a licensed real estate broker is not authorized to practice law—that is, to prepare legal documents such as deeds and mortgages. A broker or salesperson is, however, permitted to fill in the blanks on certain preprinted documents (such as sales contracts and leases) approved by the state bar association and/or real estate commission or association, provided the licensee does not charge a separate fee for completing such forms. A broker is permitted to draft deeds in Pennsylvania. However, the licensee is liable for injury resulting from errors in the drafting of documents.

Contract forms. *Printed forms* are used for all kinds of contracts because most transactions are basically similar in nature. The use of printed forms raises three problems: (1) what to *fill in the blanks,* (2) what printed matter is not applicable to a particular sale and is to be *ruled out* by drawing lines through the unwanted words and (3) what additional clauses or agreements (called *riders* or *addenda*) are to be *added.* All changes and additions are usually initialed in the margin or on the rider by both parties when the contract is executed. The newer forms provide more alternate provisions, which may be used or ruled out depending upon what the parties wish to express in their agreement.

In Practice...

It is essential that both parties to a contract understand exactly what they are agreeing to. Poorly drafted documents, especially those containing extensive legal language, may be subject to various interpretations and lead to litigation. The parties to a real estate transaction should be advised to have sales contracts and other legal documents examined by their attorneys before signing to ensure that such agreements accurately reflect their intentions. Where preprinted forms do not sufficiently cover special provisions in a transaction, the parties should be encouraged to have an attorney draft a contract that properly covers such provisions.

Listing Agreements

Listing agreements are *instruments used by the real estate broker in order to legally represent a principal.* They are contracts that establish the rights of the broker as agent and of the seller as principal. There are many forms of listing agreements: (1) open listing, (2) net listing, (3) exclusive-agency listing and (4) exclusive-right-to-sell listing. Review the explanations of the types of listing agreements presented in Chapter 18, "Listing Agreements."

Sales Contracts

A **real estate sales contract** sets forth all details of the agreement between a buyer and a seller for the purchase and sale of a parcel of real estate. In Pennsylvania, this agreement is usually referred to as an *agreement of sale* or as a real estate sales contract. But whatever the contract is called, when it has been prepared and signed by the purchaser it is an offer to purchase the subject real estate. If the document is accepted and signed by the seller, it then becomes, or ripens into, a contract of sale. A real estate sales contract is shown in Figure 9.1. Various addenda to Pennsylvania real estate sales contracts are shown in Figure 9.1 through Figure 9.5.

In a few localities, it is customary to prepare a shorter document, known as a *binder,* for the purchaser to sign. This document states the essential terms of the purchaser's offer and acknowledges receipt of the deposit. It also provides that the parties agree to have a more formal and complete contract of sale drawn up by an attorney upon the seller's acceptance and signing of the binder. Throughout the country, a binder receipt might be used in any situation where the details of the transaction are too complex for the standard sales contract form.

Every sales contract requires at least two parties, a seller and a buyer. The same person cannot be both the buyer and seller, as a person cannot legally contract with himself or herself. The contract of sale is the most important document in the sale of real estate, for it sets out in detail the agreement between the buyer and the seller and establishes their legal rights and obligations. It is more important than the deed itself, because *the contract, in effect, dictates the contents of the deed.*

As previously discussed, the statute of frauds provides that no action may be brought for the performance on any contract for the sale of real estate unless the contract is in writing and signed by the conveyor. A written agreement establishes the interest of the purchaser and the purchaser's rights to enforce that interest by court action. It thus prevents the seller from selling the property to another person who might offer a higher price. The signed contract agreement also obligates the buyer to complete the transaction according to the terms agreed upon in the contract.

Details to be included in a real estate sales contract are the price, terms, accurate description of the real estate, kind and condition of the title, form of deed the seller will deliver, kind of title evidence required, who will provide title evidence and how defects in the title, if any, are to be eliminated. The contract must state all the terms and conditions of the agreement and spell out all contingencies. In situations where a contract is vague in its terms and one party sues the other based on one of these terms, the courts may refuse to make a contract for the parties. The real estate broker must be aware of the responsibilities and legal rights of the parties to a sale and must see that an adequate contract is prepared.

Offer and acceptance. A broker lists an owner's real estate for sale at the price and conditions set by the owner. This is considered to be an invitation for prospective buyers to make purchase offers. A prospective buyer is found who wants to purchase the property at those terms or some other terms. A contract of sale is drawn up, signed by the prospective buyer, and presented by the broker to the seller. This is an *offer to purchase.* If the seller agrees to the offer *exactly as it was made* and signs the contract, the offer has been *accepted* and the contract is *valid.* The broker must then communicate the seller's acceptance, preferably by delivering a signed copy of the contract to the buyer.

Any attempt by the seller to change the terms proposed by the buyer creates a **counteroffer.** The buyer is relieved of the original offer because the seller has, in effect, rejected it. The buyer can accept the seller's counteroffer or can reject it and, if desired, make another counteroffer. Any change in the last offer made results in a counteroffer, until one party finally agrees to the other party's last offer and both parties sign the final contract (see Figure 9.6).

An offer or counteroffer *may be withdrawn at any time before it has been accepted* (even if the person making the offer or counteroffer agreed to keep the offer open for a set period of time). In addition, an offer is not considered to be accepted until the person making the offer has been *notified of the other party's acceptance.*

Negotiation of an agreement of sale creates certain responsibilities for the salesperson whose duty it is to present *all* offers and counteroffers and communicate acceptances *as soon as possible.* Simple as this sounds, the process can be complicated by multiple offers being generated at the same time, during negotiations involving a counteroffer or after the seller has accepted an offer. A great deal of

**Figure 9.1
Real Estate Sales
Contract**

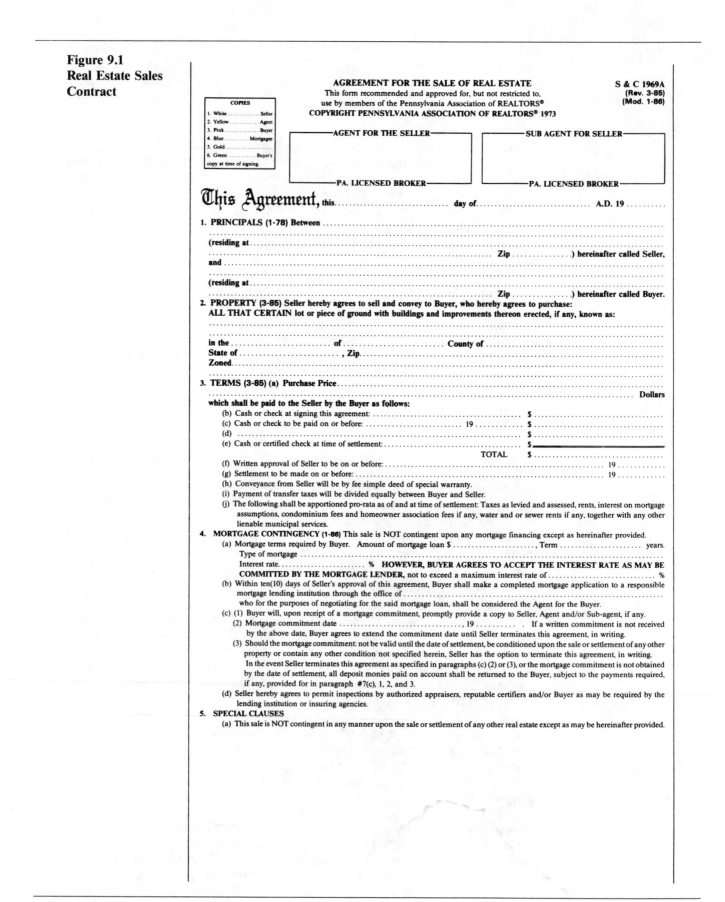

AGREEMENT FOR THE SALE OF REAL ESTATE
This form recommended and approved for, but not restricted to,
use by members of the Pennsylvania Association of REALTORS®
COPYRIGHT PENNSYLVANIA ASSOCIATION OF REALTORS® 1973

S & C 1969A
(Rev. 3-85)
(Mod. 1-86)

COPIES
1. White . . . . Seller
2. Yellow . . . . Agent
3. Pink . . . . Buyer
4. Blue . . . . Mortgagee
5. Gold . . . .
6. Green . . . . Buyer's
copy at time of signing.

┌─── **AGENT FOR THE SELLER** ───┐   ┌─── **SUB AGENT FOR SELLER** ───┐

└─── **PA. LICENSED BROKER** ───┘   └─── **PA. LICENSED BROKER** ───┘

This Agreement, this. . . . . day of . . . . A.D. 19 . . . .

1. **PRINCIPALS (1-78)** Between . . . .
. . . .
(residing at . . . .
. . . . **Zip** . . . .**) hereinafter called Seller,**
and . . . .
. . . .
(residing at . . . .
. . . . **Zip** . . . .**) hereinafter called Buyer.**

2. **PROPERTY (3-85)** Seller hereby agrees to sell and convey to Buyer, who hereby agrees to purchase:
ALL THAT CERTAIN lot or piece of ground with buildings and improvements thereon erected, if any, known as:
. . . .
in the . . . . **of** . . . . **County of** . . . .
State of . . . . , **Zip**. . . . .
Zoned. . . . .

3. **TERMS (3-85) (a)** Purchase Price. . . . .
. . . . **Dollars**
which shall be paid to the Seller by the Buyer as follows:
(b) Cash or check at signing this agreement: . . . . $ . . . .
(c) Cash or check to be paid on or before: . . . . 19 . . . . $ . . . .
(d) . . . . $ . . . .
(e) Cash or certified check at time of settlement: . . . . $. . . . .
                                                                            TOTAL $ . . . .
(f) Written approval of Seller to be on or before: . . . . 19 . . . .
(g) Settlement to be made on or before: . . . . 19 . . . .
(h) Conveyance from Seller will be by fee simple deed of special warranty.
(i) Payment of transfer taxes will be divided equally between Buyer and Seller.
(j) The following shall be apportioned pro-rata as of and at time of settlement: Taxes as levied and assessed, rents, interest on mortgage
assumptions, condominium fees and homeowner association fees if any, water and or sewer rents if any, together with any other
lienable municipal services.

4. **MORTGAGE CONTINGENCY (1-86)** This sale is NOT contingent upon any mortgage financing except as hereinafter provided.
(a) Mortgage terms required by Buyer. Amount of mortgage loan $ . . . . , Term . . . . years.
Type of mortgage . . . .
Interest rate. **% HOWEVER, BUYER AGREES TO ACCEPT THE INTEREST RATE AS MAY BE
COMMITTED BY THE MORTGAGE LENDER,** not to exceed a maximum interest rate of . . . . %
(b) Within ten(10) days of Seller's approval of this agreement, Buyer shall make a completed mortgage application to a responsible
mortgage lending institution through the office of . . . .
who for the purposes of negotiating for the said mortgage loan, shall be considered the Agent for the Buyer.
(c) (1) Buyer will, upon receipt of a mortgage commitment, promptly provide a copy to Seller, Agent and/or Sub-agent, if any.
(2) Mortgage commitment date . . . . , 19 . . . . If a written commitment is not received
by the above date, Buyer agrees to extend the commitment date until Seller terminates this agreement, in writing.
(3) Should the mortgage commitment not be valid until the date of settlement, be conditioned upon the sale or settlement of any other
property or contain any other condition not specified herein, Seller has the option to terminate this agreement, in writing.
In the event Seller terminates this agreement as specified in paragraphs (c) (2) or (3), or the mortgage commitment is not obtained
by the date of settlement, all deposit monies paid on account shall be returned to the Buyer, subject to the payments required,
if any, provided for in paragraph #7(c), 1, 2, and 3.
(d) Seller hereby agrees to permit inspections by authorized appraisers, reputable certifiers and/or Buyer as may be required by the
lending institution or insuring agencies.

5. **SPECIAL CLAUSES**
(a) This sale is NOT contingent in any manner upon the sale or settlement of any other real estate except as may be hereinafter provided.

Figure 9.1 (cont.)

6. NOTICES & ASSESSMENTS (3-85)

(a) Seller represents as of the approval date of this agreement, that no public improvement, condominium or homeowner association assessments have been made against the premises which remain unpaid and that no notice by any government or public authority has been served upon the Seller or anyone on the Seller's behalf, including notices relating to violations of zoning, housing, building, safety or fire ordinances which remain uncorrected unless otherwise specified herein.

(b) If required by law, Seller shall deliver to Buyer on or before settlement, a certification from the appropriate municipal department or departments disclosing notice of any uncorrected violation of zoning, housing, building, safety or fire ordinances.

(c) Seller will be responsible for any notice of improvements or assessments received on or before the date of Sellers approval of this agreement, unless improvements consist of sewer or water lines not in use.

(d) Buyer will be responsible for any notice served upon Seller after the approval date of this agreement and for the payment thereafter of any public improvement, condominium or homeowner association assessments.

7. TITLE AND COSTS (1-86)

(a) The premises are to be conveyed free and clear of all liens, encumbrances, and easements, EXCEPTING HOWEVER, the following: existing building restrictions, ordinances, easements of roads, easements visible upon the ground, privileges or rights of public service companies, if any; otherwise the title to the above described real estate shall be good and marketable and such as will be insured by a reputable Title Insurance Company at the regular rates.

(b) In the event the Seller is unable to give a good and marketable title and such as will be insured by a reputable Title Company, subject to aforesaid, Buyer shall have the option of taking such title as the Seller can give without abatement of price or of being repaid all monies paid by Buyer to the Seller on account of the purchase price and the Seller will reimburse the Buyer for any costs incurred by the Buyer for those items specified in paragraph 7(c) items (1), (2), (3), and in paragraph 7(d); and in the latter event there shall be no further liability or obligation on either of the parties hereto and this agreement shall become NULL AND VOID and all copies will be returned to Seller's agent for cancellation.

(c) The Buyer will pay for the following:

(1) The premium for mechanics lien insurance and/or title search, or fee for cancellation of same, if any.
(2) The premiums for flood insurance and/or fire insurance with extended coverage, insurance binder charges or cancellation fee, if any.
(3) Appraisal fees and charges paid in advance to mortgagee if any.
(4) Buyer's normal settlement costs and accruals.

(d) Any survey or surveys which may be required by the Title Insurance Company or the abstracting attorney, for the preparation of an adequate legal description of the premises (or the correction thereof), shall be secured and paid for by the Seller. However, any survey or surveys desired by the Buyer or required by his/her mortgagee shall be secured and paid for by the Buyer.

8. FIXTURES, TREES, SHRUBBERY, ETC. (1-81) All existing plumbing, heating and lighting fixtures (including chandeliers) and systems appurtenant thereto and forming a part thereof, and other permanent fixtures, as well as all ranges, laundry tubs, T.V. antennas, masts and rotor systems, together with wall to wall carpeting, screens, storm sash and/or doors,shades, awnings, venetian blinds, couplings for automatic washers and dryers, etc., radiator covers, cornices, kitchen cabinets, drapery rods, drapery rod hardware, curtain rods, curtain rod hardware, all trees, shrubbery, plantings now in or on property, if any, unless specifically excepted in this agreement, are included in the sale and purchase price. None of the above mentioned items shall be removed by the Seller from the premises after the date of this agreement.; Any remaining heating and/or cooking fuels stored on the premises at time of settlement are also included under this agreement. Seller hereby warrants that he will deliver good title to all of the articles described in this paragraph, and any other fixtures or items of personalty specifically scheduled and to be included in this sale.

9. DEPOSIT AND RECOVERY FUND (5-85) Deposits or hand monies shall be paid to agent for Seller, who shall retain the same until consummation or termination of this agreement in conformity with all applicable laws and regulations. Agent for the Seller may, at his/her sole option, hold any uncashed check tendered as deposit or hand monies, pending the acceptance of this offer.

A real estate recovery fund exists to reimburse persons who have suffered monetary loss and have obtained an uncollectable judgment due to fraud, misrepresentation or deceit in a real estate transaction by a Pennsylvania licensee. For complete details, call 717-783-3658.

10. POSSESSION AND TENDER (3-85)

(a) Possession is to be delivered by deed, keys and physical possession to a vacant building (if any) broom clean, free of debris at day and time of settlement, or by deed and assignment of existing lease(s) at time of settlement if premises is tenant occupied at the signing of this agreement, unless otherwise specified herein. Buyer will acknowledge existing lease(s) by initialing said lease(s) at time of signing of this agreement of sale if tenant occupied.

(b) Seller will not enter into any new leases, written extension of existing leases, if any, or additional leases for the premises without expressed written consent of the Buyer.

(c) Formal tender of an executed deed and purchase money is hereby waived.

(d) Buyer reserves the right to make a pre-settlement inspection of the subject premises.

11. MAINTENANCE AND RISK OF LOSS (3-85)

(a) Seller shall maintain the property (including all items mentioned in paragraph #8 herein) and any personal property specifically scheduled herein in its present condition, normal wear and tear excepted.

(b) Seller shall bear risk of loss from fire or other casualties until time of settlement. In the event of damage to any property included in this sale by fire or other casualties, not repaired or replaced prior to settlement, Buyer shall have the option of rescinding this agreement and receiving all monies paid on account or of accepting the property in its then condition together with the proceeds of any insurance recovery obtainable by Seller. Buyer is hereby notified that he may insure his equitable interest in this property as of the time of the acceptance of this agreement.

12. RECORDING (3-85) This agreement shall not be recorded in the Office for the Recording of Deeds or in any other office or place of public record and if Buyer causes or permits this agreement to be recorded, Seller may elect to treat such act as a breach of this agreement.

13. ASSIGNMENT (3-85) This agreement shall be binding upon the parties, their respective heirs, personal representatives, guardians and successors, and to the extent assignable, on the assigns of the parties hereto, it being expressly understood, however, that the Buyer shall not transfer or assign this agreement without the written consent of the Seller.

14. DEFAULT-TIME OF THE ESSENCE (1-79) The said time for settlement and all other times referred to for the performance of any of the obligations of this agreement are hereby agreed to be of the essence of this agreement. Should the Buyer:

(a) Fail to make any additional payments as specified in paragraph #3, or

(b) Furnish false or incomplete information to the Seller, the Seller's agent, or the mortgage lender, concerning the Buyer's legal or financial status, or fail to cooperate in the processing of the mortgage loan application, which acts would result in the failure to obtain the approval of a mortgage loan commitment, or

(c) Violate or fail to fulfill and perform any other terms or conditions of this agreement,

then in such case, all deposit money and other sums paid by the Buyer on account of the purchase price, whether required by this agreement or not, may be retained by the Seller:

(1) On account of the purchase, or
(2) As monies to be applied to the Seller's damages, or
(3) As liquidated damages for such breach,

as the Seller may elect, and in the event that the Seller elects to retain the monies as liquidated damages in accordance with paragraph #14(3), the Seller shall be released from all liability or obligations and this agreement shall be NULL AND VOID and all copies will be returned to the Seller's agent for cancellation.

15. AGENT(S) (3-85) It is expressly understood and agreed between the parties that the named Agent, Broker, and any Sub Agent, Broker and their salespeople, employees, officers and or partners, are Agent(s) for the Seller, not the Buyer, however, the Agent(s) may perform services for the Buyer in connection with financing, insurance and document preparation.

16. REPRESENTATIONS (3-85) It is understood that Buyer has inspected the property, or hereby waives the right to do so and has agreed to purchase it as a result of such inspection and not because of or in reliance upon any representation made by the Seller or any other officer, partner or employee of Seller, or by the Agent, Sub Agent, if any, of the Seller, their salespeople and employees, officers and or partners.

The Buyer has agreed to purchase it in its present condition unless otherwise specified herein. It is further understood that this agreement contains the whole agreement between the Seller and the Buyer and there are no other terms, obligations, covenants, representations, statements or conditions, oral or otherwise of any kind whatsoever concerning this sale. Furthermore, this agreement shall not be altered, amended, changed or modified except in writing executed by the parties.

APPROVAL BY BUYER

BUYER...(SEAL)

WITNESS AS TO BUYER.. BUYER...(SEAL)

WITNESS AS TO BUYER.. BUYER...(SEAL)

APPROVAL BY SELLER

Seller hereby approves the above contract this .... day of .... A.D. 19 ....

and in consideration of the services rendered in procuring the Buyer, Seller agrees to pay the named Agent a fee of...............................

of/from the herein specified sale price. In the event Buyer defaults hereunder, any monies paid on account shall be divided ...., Seller, ..., Agent, but in no event will the sum paid to the Agent be in excess of the above specified Agent's fee.

WITNESS AS TO SELLER.. SELLER...(SEAL)

WITNESS AS TO SELLER.. SELLER...(SEAL)

AGENT BY:.. SELLER...(SEAL)

TO:.. (Agent) Date.. 19 ....

In conjunction with the purchase of the premises described in this agreement of sale attached hereto, I/We hereby authorize your firm to perform the services as indicated below by my/our initials.

A. Order Title insurance in any reputable title insurance company ....(INITIALS)

B. Order insurance in the amount of $ .... ☐ Homeowners ☐ Fire & Extended Coverage ☐ Flood ....(INITIALS)

C. ....(INITIALS)

**Figure 9.2
Wood
Infestation
Endorsement**

WOOD INFESTATION - ADDENDUM TO AGREEMENT OF SALE

_____ 19____

RE PROPERTY: _____

SELLERS _____

BUYERS _____

DATE OF AGREEMENT_____19____ , SETTLEMENT DATE_____ 19____ , SALE PRICE $_____

1. Within fifteen days of the execution of this agreement, Seller shall, at Seller's expense, order from a reputable Pest Control Operator certified by the Pennsylvania Department of Agriculture, a written "Wood Destroying Insect Infestation and Resultant Damage Report" and shall present said report to the Buyer on or before settlement. Such report is to provide that an inspection of the readily visible and accessible areas of all structures within the property limits has been made satisfactory to and in compliance with: applicable laws, mortgage and lending institutions, and/or Federal Insuring and Guaranteeing Agency requirements, if any.

2. If the inspection reveals evidence of active infestation(s), previous infestation(s) and/or resultant damage, which has not been corrected, Seller agrees, at Seller's expense to have the structure(s) treated for such infestation excepting: _____

   Seller shall upon receipt of said report, promptly advise Buyer in writing of such condition(s) and make available to Buyer all documents and drawings received from the Pest Control Operator, showing the location of visible evidence of infestation(s) and/or damage.

3. At the time of notice to the Buyer as specified above in par. #2., Seller shall also advise whether or not the resultant damage will be repaired, at Seller's expense, prior to settlement. If Seller elects not to repair the said damage, if any, Buyer shall have the option of accepting the property with the defects revealed by the inspection, without abatement of price, or being repaid all monies paid by the Buyer on account of the purchase price, together with Buyer's expenses, if any, as may be incurred or provided for under the terms of the Agreement of Sale, including but not limited to the following:
   A. Cancellation fee for title insurance or abstract fee for searching title.
   B. Cancellation fee or binder charge for fire insurance with extended coverage and/or flood insurance if any.
   C. Appraisal fees, credit report charges, and/or survey costs.

   In the latter event, there shall be no further liability or obligation on either of the parties hereto, and this agreement of sale shall become NULL AND VOID. Buyer shall notify Seller in writing of his election within five (5) days after Buyer receives Seller's notice of refusal to correct the condition(s).

All other terms and conditions of the said agreement shall remain unchanged and in full force and effect.

WITNESS_____ BUYER _____(S)

WITNESS_____ BUYER _____(S)

WITNESS_____ SELLER _____(S)

AGENT_____ SELLER _____(S)

COPIES: White; Seller,   Yellow; Agent,   Pink; Buyer,   Blue;_____ ,   Gold;_____ ,   Green;_____   12-79

**Figure 9.3
Radon
Disclosure**

RADON DISCLOSURE ADDENDUM TO AGREEMENT OF SALE

_____ 19_____

RE: PROPERTY _____

SELLERS: _____

BUYERS: _____

DATE OF AGREEMENT _____ 19____, SETTLEMENT DATE _____ 19____, SALE PRICE $_____

1. BUYER acknowledges receipt of notice as set forth on reverse side hereof.

2. SELLER hereby acknowledges receipt of notice as set forth on the reverse side hereof, and certifies that:

   ( ) The property was tested and Radon was found to be at or below 0.02 working levels (4 picocuries/liter).

   ( ) The property was tested and Radon was found to be above 0.02 working levels (4 picocuries/liter).

      ( ) The property was modified after which it was retested and Radon was found to be at or below 0.02 working levels (4 picocuries/liter).

   Seller does not warrant either the method or result of the test.

   ( ) I have no knowledge concerning the presence or absence of Radon.

3. BUYER'S OPTION (Check only one)

   ( ) Buyer acknowledges he has the right to have the buildings inspected to determine if Radon gas/daughters is present. BUYER waives this right and agrees to accept the property on the basis of SELLER'S certification and agrees to the release as set forth in paragraph 4 below.

   ( ) BUYER, at BUYER'S expense, shall within _____ days upon approval of this agreement, arrange a Radon test of the residential buildings on the property.

   If the inspection reveals the presence of Radon which exceeds 0.02 working levels (4 picocuries/liter), the Buyer, within five (5) days of the receipt of the report, shall notify the SELLER, in writing, of the BUYER'S option to:

   a. Declare this agreement NULL and VOID, at which time all deposit monies paid on account shall be returned to the BUYER.

   b. Accept the property, which action shall constitute a release as set forth in paragraph 4 below.

   NOTE: There are various firms in Pennsylvania through which a Radon test can be arranged.

4. RELEASE

   The BUYER hereby releases, quit claims and forever discharges SELLER, SELLER'S AGENTS, SUBAGENTS, EMPLOYEES and any OFFICER or PARTNER or any one of them and any other PERSON, FIRM or CORPORATION, who may be liable by or through them, from any and all claims, losses or demands, including personal injuries, and all of the consequences thereof, where now known or not, which may arise from the presence of Radon in any building on the property.

WITNESS _____ BUYER _____(s)

WITNESS _____ BUYER _____(s)

WITNESS _____ SELLER _____(s)

AGENT _____ SELLER _____(s)

COPIES: WHITE; SELLER,   YELLOW; AGENT,   PINK; BUYER,   BLUE;_____ ,   GOLD;_____ ,   GREEN;_____   8/87

**Figure 9.4
U.F.F.I.
Disclosure**

U.F.F.I. DISCLOSURE ADDENDUM TO AGREEMENT OF SALE

RE PROPERTY: _____
SELLERS _____
BUYERS _____
DATE OF AGREEMENT _____19___, SETTLEMENT DATE _____19___, SALE PRICE $_____

1. BUYER hereby acknowledges receipt of notice as set forth on the reverse side hereof.

2. SELLER hereby acknowledges receipt of notice as set forth on the reverse side hereof, and certifies that (check one only)

    ( ) urea-formaldehyde foam insulation was installed in _____
                       (date)

    ( ) urea-formaldehyde foam insulation was installed in _____ but removed in _____
                       (date)   (date)

    ( ) urea-formaldehyde foam insulation has not been installed.

    ( ) I have no knowledge concerning the presence or absence of urea-formaldehyde foam insulation, but it has not been installed
        since _____
               (date)

3. BUYERS OPTIONS (check one only)
    ( ) BUYER acknowledges his right to have the buildings inspected to determine if urea-formaldehyde foam insulation (UFFI) is
        present.   BUYER waives this right and agrees to accept the property on the basis of SELLER'S certification and agrees to the
        release as set forth in paragraph 4 below.
    ( ) BUYER at BUYERS expense shall within 15 days from the approval date of this agreement order a written inspection report of the
        residential buildings on the property.

        If the inspection reveals the presence of U.F.F.I. the buyer, within five (5) days of receipt of the report, shall notify the seller in
        writing of Buyers option to:
        a. Declare this agreement NULL and VOID, at which time all deposit monies paid on account shall be returned to the
            BUYER.
        b. Accept the property with the UFFI, which action shall constitute a release as set forth in paragraph 4 below.
        c. Order an air sampling with an analysis by a state certified laboratory.   The BUYER shall, within 10 days of receipt of the
           laboratory analysis, exercise option (a) or (b) above.

4. RELEASE
    The BUYER hereby releases, quit claims and forever discharges SELLER, SELLER'S AGENTS, SUB AGENT'S, EMPLOYEES and any
    OFFICER or PARTNER of any one of them and any other PERSON, FIRM or CORPORATION who may be liable by or through them,
    from any and all claims, losses or demands, including personal injuries, and all of the consequences thereof, where now known or not, which
    may arise from the presence of UFFI in any building on the property.

WITNESS _____   BUYER _____
WITNESS _____   BUYER _____
WITNESS _____   SELLER _____
AGENT _____   SELLER _____

COPIES: White: SELLER,   YELLOW: AGENT,   PINK: BUYER,   BLUE: _____ ,   GOLD: _____ ,   GREEN: _____   6/84

111-8

**Figure 9.5
FHA-VA
Addendum**

F.H.A./V.A. ADDENDUM TO AGREEMENT OF SALE

_____ 19___

RE PROPERTY: _____
SELLERS _____
BUYERS _____
DATE OF AGREEMENT _____19___, SETTLEMENT DATE _____19___, SALE PRICE $_____
It is understood and agreed that the above agreement of sale shall be endorsed as follows:

4. MORTGAGE CONTINGENCY *(1-79)* (continued)   F.H.A. ☐   V.A. ☐
    (h) Maximum mortgage placement fee, if any, to be paid by Seller: $_____
    (i) Minimum amount of appraisal required if FHA financing (exclusive of closing costs) $_____
    (j) **FHA/VA** If the mortgage above referred to is an FHA or VA type mortgage loan, it is expressly agreed that, not withstanding any
        other provisions of this contract, the Buyer shall not be obligated to complete the purchase of the property described herein or to
        incur any penalty by forfeiture of earnest money deposits or otherwise:
        (1) in case of an FHA loan, unless Seller has delivered to the Buyer a written statement issued by the Federal Housing
            Commissioner setting forth the appraised value of the property, exclusive of closing costs, for mortgage loan insurance
            purposes of not less than the amount specified in paragraph #4(i), which statement the Seller hereby agrees to deliver to the
            Buyer promptly after such statement is made available to the Seller, or
        (2) in the case of a VA loan, if the contract purchase price or cost exceeds the reasonable value of the property established by the
            Veterans Administration.
        provided the Buyer, within five days of his/her receipt of notice of the FHA appraised value or the VA reasonable value, delivers
        written notice to the herein named agent, of the Buyer's intention to terminate the contract. The Buyer shall however, have the
        privilege and option of proceeding with the consummation of this contract without regard to the amount of the VA reasonable
        value or the appraised valuation made by the Federal Housing Commissioner. The appraised valuation is arrived at to determine the
        maximum mortgage the Department of Housing and Urban Development will insure. HUD does not warrant the value or the
        condition of the property. The Buyer should satisfy himself/herself that the price and the condition of the property are acceptable.

    (k) We, the undersigned, the seller(s), the purchaser(s) and the broker(s) involved in this transaction each certify that the terms of this
        contract for purchase are true to their best knowledge and belief, and that any other agreement entered into by any of these parties
        in connection with this transaction, is attached to this Agreement of Sale.

PENNSYLVANIA ASSOCIATION OF REALTORS

108-6

All other terms and conditions of the said agreement shall remain unchanged and in full force and effect.

WITNESS _____   BUYER _____ (S)
SELLING AGENT_____   BUYER _____ (S)
WITNESS _____   SELLER _____ (S)
LISTING AGENT _____   SELLER _____ (S)

COPIES: White: Seller,   Yellow: Agent,   Pink: Buyer,   Blue: _____ ,   Gold: _____ ,   Green: _____

Figure 9.6
Offer and Acceptance

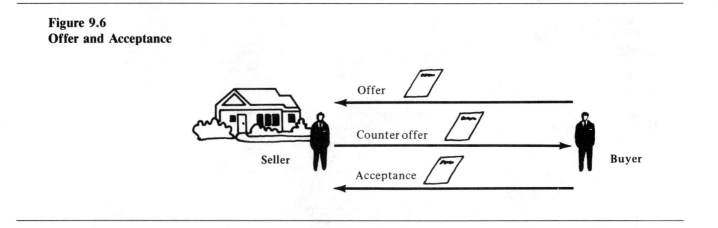

care and counsel is required to assure that the seller's interests are protected. The salesperson has no authority, in behalf of the seller, to decide the merits of an offer; thus, all offers are presented. The seller must be cautioned about the liability of signing multiple agreements while only being able to perform on one. It is also important for the salesperson to communicate with buyers, sellers and any cooperating brokers involved during the negotiations to avoid any question of whether an acceptance, rejection or counteroffer has taken place.

Equitable title. When signing a contract to purchase real estate, a buyer does not receive title to the land; only a deed can actually convey title. However, after both buyer and seller have executed a sales contract, the buyer acquires an interest in the land known as **equitable title.** Equitable title is the right to obtain absolute ownership to property when legal title is held in another's name. Acquisition of equitable title may give the buyer an insurable interest in the property.

Destruction of premises. In Pennsylvania, once the sales contract is signed by both parties and *unless the contract provides otherwise,* the buyer must bear the loss of any damage to or *destruction of the property* by fire or other casualty. Through laws and court decisions, however, a growing number of states have placed the risk of any loss that occurs before the deed is delivered on the seller. In any case, the seller may be made to assume the risk of loss when he or she has been negligent, is unable to deliver good title or has delayed the closing of the transaction. In practice, the agreement of sale usually provides explanation of risk of loss to avoid confusion. Regardless of the risk of loss, the seller should maintain adequate insurance through the date of closing; the buyer commonly insures the equitable interest.

Earnest money deposits. It is customary for a purchaser to give a cash deposit when making an offer to purchase real estate. This cash deposit, commonly referred to as **earnest money,** *generally gives evidence of the purchaser's intention to carry out the terms of the contract.* The sales contract typically provides that, upon acceptance of the offer, all monies are to be deposited in a trust account (under the control of the broker or a neutral escrow depository) until the closing.

The amount of the deposit is a matter to be agreed upon by the parties. A real estate broker is obliged to accept a reasonable amount as earnest money. Generally, the deposit should be sufficient to discourage the buyer from defaulting, to compensate the seller for taking the property off the market and to cover any expenses the seller and the broker might incur if the buyer defaults. The broker must accurately represent to the seller the form of the earnest money—for example, cash, check or note. The seller must be aware that a note is held because of the potential difficulty in collecting the funds. While the note is made payable to the broker (as is a check), it should be a negotiable instrument, containing confession of judgment that, in the event of default on the note, it may be endorsed to the seller to pursue collection. The broker is also at considerable risk in misrepresenting the existence of earnest money in the event the buyer defaults on the agreement of sale and the broker has not collected the funds that the seller expects are being held on his or her behalf. The deposit (less any previously agreed-upon commission that may be owed the broker) becomes the seller's property if the buyer defaults and the seller elects this alternative.

Under state law, earnest money must be held by a broker in a special *trust,* or *escrow, account.* This money cannot be *commingled,* or mixed, with a broker's personal funds. (However, in many states a broker is permitted to place a minimal amount of his or her own money into the trust account in order to keep it open.) Likewise, a broker may not use such funds for a purpose not intended, such as for his or her own personal use. This illegal act is known as *conversion.* A broker need not open a special escrow account for each earnest money deposit received; one such account into which all such funds are deposited is sufficient. A broker should maintain full, complete and accurate records of all earnest money deposits. The escrow account is not normally interest-bearing unless funds are to be held for a prolonged period of time. The agreement of sale should stipulate the ownership of the interest. The state license law has strict provisions covering these deposits (these will be discussed in Chapter 14, "Pennsylvania Real Estate Licensing and Registration Act").

There is some uncertainty as to exactly who owns the earnest money once it is put on deposit. Until the offer is officially accepted, the money is, in a sense, the buyer's. Once the seller accepts the offer, however, the buyer may not secure the return of the money, even though the seller is not entitled to it until the transaction has been completed. Under no circumstances does the money belong to the broker. This uncertain nature of earnest money deposits makes it absolutely necessary that such funds be properly protected pending a final decision on their disbursement.

Parts of a sales contract. All real estate sales contracts can be divided into a number of general parts. Although each form of contract will contain these divisions, their location in the contract may vary. Study the sample contract in Figure 9.1 to determine the exact terms of agreement. This contract is divided into the following main sections:

1. Identification of the seller and buyer.

2. Legal or adequate description of the real estate involved.

3. Statement of the type of deed the seller agrees to give, including the conditions and provisions (interests of others) to which the deed will be made subject; this is sometimes known as the "subject to" section of the contract.

4. Consideration statement of the purchase price and how the purchaser intends to pay for the property, including provision for an earnest money deposit and the conditions of any mortgage financing the purchaser intends to obtain.

5. Provisions for the closing and the purchaser's possession of the property, including dates.

6. Provisions for title evidence.

7. Provisions for prorations, which are adjustments for taxes, insurance, fuel and the like.

8. Provisions in the event of destruction or damage to premises.

9. Provisions for default.

10. Provisions for contingencies.

11. Miscellaneous provisions.

12. Dates and signatures.

Provisions for notices and contingencies. An agreement of sale may include addenda (Figures 9.2, 9.3, 9.4) for *inspections.* Examples are wood-boring insects, structural and mechanical systems, sewage facilities and radon or other toxic materials. Experts in these fields are used to assure that the purchaser is informed about these conditions. *Contingencies* create additional conditions which must be satisfied before an agreement is fully enforceable. The most common is a mortgage contingency, which protects the buyer's earnest money until a lender has committed to the mortgage funds (Figure 9.6). (See Chapter 20, "Financing the Real Estate Transaction.") The common practice in some areas is to make the agreement of sale contingent on the inspections referred to above.

Disclosures required by the Pennsylvania Licensing and Registration Act, Sec. 607. A broker who has taken a listing agreement from a seller is required to disclose to the prospective buyer that the broker is the agent (represents) of the seller, not of the buyer. The agreement of sale must also contain a statement describing the purpose of the Real Estate Recovery Fund established by the Act and the telephone number of the Commission at which the purchaser can receive further information about the fund. (This disclosure was already made to a seller in the listing contract.) The zoning classification of a property must be disclosed unless it is a single-family dwelling. Failure of the sales agreement to contain the zoning statement shall render the agreement null and void and deposits shall be returned to the buyer.

Estimated statements of closing costs. Pennsylvania license laws require real estate licensees to prepare *estimated statements of closing costs* for buyers and sellers prior to the parties signing an agreement of sale. Closing costs are discussed in Chapter 21, "Closing the Real Estate Transaction."

Option Agreements

An **option** is a *contract by which an* optionor *(generally an owner) gives an* optionee *(a prospective purchaser or lessee) the right to buy or lease the owner's property at a fixed price within a stated period of time.* The optionee pays a fee (the agreed-upon consideration) for this option right and assumes no obligation to make any other payment until deciding, within the specified time, either to:

(1) exercise the option right (to buy or lease the property) or (2) allow the option right to expire. An option is enforceable by only one party—the optionee.

For example, for a consideration of a specified amount of money, a present owner (optionor) agrees to give an optionee an irrevocable right to buy real estate at a certain price for a limited period of time. At the time the option is signed by the parties, the owner does not sell nor does the optionee buy. They merely agree that the optionee will have the right to buy and the owner will be obligated to sell *if* the optionee decides to exercise his or her right of option.

The option agreement, which is a unilateral contract, requires the optionor to act only after the optionee gives notice that he or she elects to execute the option and buy. If the option is not exercised within the time specified, then the optionor's obligation and the optionee's right will expire unless the contract provides for a renewal. The optionee cannot recover the consideration paid for the option right. The contract may state whether the money paid for the option is to be applied to the purchase price of the real estate if the option is exercised.

A common application of an option is a lease that includes an option for the tenant to purchase the property. Options on commercial real estate are frequently made dependent upon the fulfillment of specific conditions, such as the obtaining of a zoning change or a building permit. The optionee is usually obligated to exercise the option if the conditions are met. Similar terms could also be included in a sales contract.

Installment Contracts (Contracts for Deed)

A real estate sale can be made under an **installment contract,** sometimes called a *contract for deed, land contract of sale* or *articles of agreement for warranty deed.* In other words, the real estate is sold under contract. An installment contract is a means of financing a buyer's purchase of land whereby *the seller receives a nominal down payment and regular periodic payments (usually monthly) over a number of years,* in accordance with the contract terms.

Under an installment contract, the seller, also known as the *vendor,* retains fee ownership while the buyer, known as the *vendee,* secures possession and an equitable interest in the property. The buyer agrees to give the seller a down payment and pay regular monthly installments of principal and interest over a number of years. The buyer also agrees to pay real estate taxes, insurance premiums, repairs and upkeep on the property. Although the buyer obtains possession when the contract is signed by both parties, *the seller is not obligated to execute and deliver a deed to the buyer until the terms of the contract have been satisfied.* Under most installment contracts, the buyer is entitled to a deed as soon as he or she is able to complete the terms of the contract.

Real estate is occasionally sold with the new buyer assuming an existing installment contract from the original buyer/vendee. Generally, when a buyer assumes an existing contract, the original buyer/vendee must assign or convey his or her interest to the new buyer, and the original seller/vendor must approve the new purchaser.

Default—termination of contract. Installment contracts usually include a provision that a *default* by the buyer permits the seller to forfeit the contract, retain all payments already made and evict the buyer. In some states, however, laws have been enacted that require the seller to refund to the buyer, any payments received in excess of a reasonable rental or use value of the property. In other states, a defaulted installment contract must be foreclosed in the same manner as would be a mortgage.

In Practice...   *Legislatures and courts have not looked favorably on the harsh provisions of some real estate installment contracts. A seller and buyer contemplating such a sale should first consult an attorney to make sure that the agreement meets all legal requirements and addresses the individual concerns of the parties.*

Leases   A lease is a contract in which the owner agrees to give possession of all or a part of the real estate to another person in exchange for a rental fee. Leases were discussed in detail in Chapter 8.

Escrow Agreements   An escrow is *a means by which the parties to a contract carry out the terms of their agreement.* The parties appoint a disinterested third party to act as the *escrowee,* or *escrow agent.* This escrow agent must be someone who is not a party to the contract and will not benefit in any way from the contract. In Pennsylvania, few transactions are closed in escrow.

An **escrow agreement** (usually a separate agreement from the contract) sets forth the duties of the escrow agent and the obligations and requirements of the parties to the transaction. An escrow agreement may be used in closing such real estate transactions as a sale, mortgage loan, exchange of property, installment contract (contract for deed) or lease.

***

Summary   A *contract* is defined as a legally enforceable promise or set of promises that must be performed, and, if a breach occurs, the law provides a remedy.

Contracts may be classified according to whether the parties' intentions are *express* or are *implied* by their actions. They may also be classified as *bilateral,* when both parties have obligated themselves to act, or *unilateral,* when one party is obligated to perform only if the other party acts. In addition, contracts may be classified according to their legal enforceability as either *valid, void, voidable* or *unenforceable.*

Many contracts specify a time for performance. In any case, all contracts must be performed within a reasonable time. An *executed* contract is one that has been fully performed. An *executory* contract is one in which some act remains to be performed.

The *essentials of a valid real estate contract* are: (1) offer and acceptance, (2) consideration, (3) legally competent parties and (4) legality of object. A valid *real estate contract* must include a description of the property and should be in writing and signed by both parties.

In a number of circumstances, a contract may be canceled before it is fully performed. Furthermore, in many types of contracts, either of the parties may transfer his or her rights and obligations under the agreement by *assignment* of the contract or *novation* (substitution of a new contract).

If either party to a real estate sales contract defaults, several alternative actions are available. Contracts usually provide that the seller has the right to declare a sale canceled through forfeiture if the buyer defaults. In general, if either party has suffered a loss because of the other's default, he or she may sue for damages to cover the loss. If one party insists on completing the transaction, he or she may sue the defaulter for *specific performance* of the terms of the contract; in this way, a court can order the other parties to comply with the agreement.

Contracts frequently used in the real estate business include listings, sales contracts, options, installment contracts (contracts for deed), leases and escrow agreements.

A *real estate sales contract* binds a buyer and a seller to a definite transaction, as described in detail in the contract. The buyer is bound to purchase the property for the amount stated in the agreement. The seller is bound to deliver a good and marketable title, free from liens and encumbrances (except those allowed by the "subject to" clause of the contract).

Under an *option* agreement, the optionee purchases from the optionor for a limited time period the exclusive right to purchase or lease the optionor's property. For a potential purchaser or lessee, an option is a means of buying time to consider or complete arrangements for a transaction. An *installment contract,* or contract for deed, is a sales/financing agreement under which a buyer purchases a seller's real estate on time. The buyer may take possession of and responsibility for the property but does not receive the deed until the terms of the contract are complete.

Any real estate transaction may be completed through an *escrow,* a means by which the parties to a contract carry out the terms of their agreement. The parties appoint a third party to act as the *escrowee,* or *escrow agent.*

Questions

1. A contract is said to be *bilateral* if:
   a. one of the parties is a minor.
   b. the contract has yet to be fully performed.
   c. only one party to the agreement is bound to act.
   d. all parties to the contract are bound to act.

2. Timothy Smith makes an offer to purchase certain property listed with Olaf Real Estate and leaves a deposit with broker Janice Olaf. Regarding this deposit, Olaf should:
   a. divide it evenly between her employer and the seller.
   b. deposit it in a trust account.
   c. give it to the seller along with the offer.
   d. deposit it in her checking account.

3. A contract for the sale of real estate that does not state the consideration to be paid for the property and is not signed by the parties is considered to be:
   a. voidable.
   b. executory.
   c. void.
   d. enforceable.

4. A real estate purchaser is said to have *equitable title:*
   a. when the sales contract is signed by both buyer and seller.
   b. when the transaction is closed.
   c. when escrow is opened.
   d. when a contract for deed is paid off.

5. A seller gave an open listing to several brokers, specifically promising that if one of the brokers found a buyer for the seller's real estate, the seller would then be obligated to pay a commission to that broker. This offer by the seller is a(n):
   a. executed agreement.
   b. discharged agreement.
   c. implied agreement.
   d. unilateral agreement.

6. In the completion of a printed form of sales contract, several words were crossed out and others inserted. In order to eliminate future controversy as to whether the changes were made before or after the contract was signed, the broker should:
   a. write a letter to each party listing the changes.
   b. have each party write a letter to the other approving the changes.
   c. redraw the entire contract.
   d. have both parties initial or sign on the margin near each change.

7. For a real estate sales contract to be valid in Pennsylvania:
   I. the seller must be at least 18 years of age.
   II. the document must contain the signatures of both buyer and seller.
   a. I only   **c. both I and II**
   b. II only   d. neither I nor II

8. If, after the sales contract is signed, the seller decides not to sell:
   a. the seller may cancel the contract and retain the buyer's earnest money deposit.
   b. the buyer may institute a suit for specific performance of the contract or for money damages.
   c. the seller may revoke the original offer.
   d. all of the above

9. Under the state statute of frauds all contracts for the sale of real estate must be in writing to be enforceable. The principal reason for this statute is to:
   a. prevent the buyer from defrauding the seller.
   b. protect the broker.
   c. prevent fraudulent proof of a fictitious oral contract.
   d. protect the buyer from the broker.

10. During the period of time after a real estate sales contract is signed but before the title actually passes, the status of the contract is:
    a. voidable.   c. executed.
    b. executory.   d. implied.

11. Which of the following is *not* one of the elements essential to a valid contract?
    a. offer and acceptance
    b. earnest money
    c. legality of object
    d. consideration

12. A party may transfer obligations to the terms of a contract through which of the following legal concepts?
    I. assignment
    II. novation
      a. I only   c. both I and II
      b. II only   d. neither I nor II

13. The earnest money deposit:
    I. is made by the buyer upon signing the sales contract and evidences his or her intention to carry out the contract terms.
    II. is generally held by the seller under the terms of the typical real estate sales contract.
      a. I only   c. both I and II
      b. II only   d. neither I nor II

14. Which of the following best describes a land installment contract, or contract for deed?
    a. a contract to buy land only
    b. a mortgage on land
    c. a means of conveying title immediately while the purchaser pays for the property in installments
    d. a method of selling real estate whereby the purchaser pays for the property in regular installments while the seller retains title to the property

15. A seller breached a written contract for sale. Some years later, the buyer sued for specific performance but was unsuccessful because of the:
    a. parol evidence rule.
    b. statute of frauds.
    c. statute of limitations.
    d. rule against perpetuities.

16. Which of the following provisions covers the kind and condition of the seller's title and may be found under the "subject to" part of the sales contract?
    I. "...agree to buy at the price of sixty-five thousand dollars..."
    II. "General taxes for the current year are to be prorated from January 1 to the date of closing."
      a. I only   c. both I and II
      b. II only   d. neither I nor II

17. A real estate broker or salesperson helping to complete a real estate sales contract should be careful to include all pertinent information in the document because:
    I. it establishes the legal rights and obligations of buyer and seller.
    II. it establishes what the contents of the deed of conveyance will be.
      a. I only   c. both I and II
      b. II only   d. neither I nor II

18. Broker Sam Manella has found a buyer for Joe Taylor's home. The buyer has entered into a real estate sales contract for the property for $3,000 less than the asking price and has deposited $2,000 earnest money with broker Manella. Taylor is out of town for the weekend and Manella has been unable to inform him of the signed agreement. At this point, the real estate sales contract is a(n):
    a. voidable contract.
    b. offer.
    c. executory agreement.
    d. implied contract.

19. If, in Question 19, seller Taylor does not agree to the terms of the real estate sales contract as presented to him by broker Manella, he may:

    a. refuse to sign it and ask that Manella return the buyer's earnest money.
    b. present the buyer with a counteroffer.
    c. sign it provisionally.
    d. a and b

20. When a broker uses a client's earnest money deposit for his or her own personal use, the broker is guilty of:

    a. commingling.
    b. conversion.
    c. violating the parol evidence rule.
    d. a and b

21. An option agreement:

    I. is generally limited to a specified time period.
    II. must recite a set amount of consideration for purchase of the property.

    a. I only   c. both I and II
    b. II only   d. neither I nor II

22. The purchaser of real estate under an installment contract:

    a. generally pays no interest charge.
    b. is called a vendor.
    c. is not required to pay property taxes for the duration of the contract.
    d. is called a vendee.

23. By local law or court decision, who is usually authorized to draft deeds and other legal contracts?

    I. a licensed real estate salesperson
    II. an attorney licensed to practice law

    a. I only   c. both I and II
    b. II only   d. neither I nor II

10

Transfer of Title

Key Terms

Acknowledgment
Adverse possession
Bargain and sale deed
Consideration
Deed
Delivery and acceptance
Descent
Devise
Escheat
General warranty deed
Grantee
Granting clause
Grantor
Habendum clause
Heir

Intestate
Involuntary alienation
Judicial deed
Last will and testament
Pennsylvania Realty Transfer Tax
Probate
Quitclaim deed
Special warranty deed
"Subject to" clause
Testate
Testator
Title
Trust deed
Trustee's deed
Voluntary alienation

Overview

A parcel of real estate may be transferred from one owner to another in a number of different ways. It may be given *voluntarily*, such as by sale or gift, or it may be taken *involuntarily*, by operation of law. In addition, it may be transferred by the living or it may be transferred by will or descent after death. In every instance, however, a transfer of title to a parcel of real estate is a complex legal procedure involving a number of laws and documents. This chapter will discuss the four methods of title transfer, as well as the various legal documents of conveyance that the real estate broker or salesperson must be familiar with.

Title

✳ **Title** to real estate means the right to or ownership of the land. It represents the *evidence* of ownership. The term *title* has two functions: It represents the "bundle of rights" the owner possesses in the real estate, and it also denotes the facts that, if proved, would enable a person to recover or retain ownership or possession of a parcel of real estate.

The laws of each state govern real estate transactions for land located within its boundaries. Each state has the authority to pass legislative acts that affect the methods of transferring title or other interests in real estate. Title to real estate may be transferred by the following methods: (1) voluntary alienation, (2) involuntary alienation, (3) will and (4) descent.

Voluntary Alienation

Voluntary alienation (transfer) of title may be made by gift or sale. To transfer title by voluntary alienation during one's lifetime, an owner must use some form of deed of conveyance.

A **deed** is a *written instrument by which an owner of real estate intentionally conveys to a purchaser the owner's right, title or interest in a parcel of real estate.* All deeds must be in writing in accordance with the requirements of the statute of frauds. The owner is referred to as the **grantor,** and the one who acquires the title is the **grantee.** A deed is executed (signed) by the grantor.

Requirements for a Valid Deed

The basic requirements for a valid deed in Pennsylvania are illustrated in Figure 10.1 and are as follows:

1. a *grantor* having the legal capacity to execute (sign) the deed;

2. a *grantee* named with reasonable certainty, so that he or she can be identified;

3. a recital of *consideration;*

4. a *granting clause* (words of conveyance);

5. *a habendum clause* (to define ownership taken by the grantee);

6. designation of any *limitations* on the conveyance of a full fee simple estate;

7. an *accurate legal description* of the property conveyed;

8. *exceptions and reservations,* if any, affecting the title ("subject to" clause);

9. the *signature of the grantor,* sometimes with a seal;

10. *delivery* of the deed and *acceptance* by the grantee to pass title.

Grantor. A grantor must have a legal existence, be of lawful age, and be legally competent in order to convey title to real estate. The laws of the state where the real estate is located will control the precise legal requirements to convey title.

Figure 10.1
Elements of a
Valid Conveyance

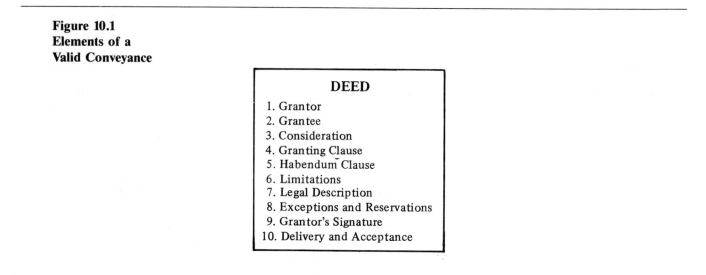

```
                        DEED
         1. Grantor
         2. Grantee
         3. Consideration
         4. Granting Clause
         5. Habendum Clause
         6. Limitations
         7. Legal Description
         8. Exceptions and Reservations
         9. Grantor's Signature
        10. Delivery and Acceptance
```

However, rules governing contracts (discussed in Chapter 9, "Real Estate Contracts") usually apply to determine if a grantor is competent to convey real property.

A grantor must be of sound mind and of lawful age, generally at least 18 years old. As is the case with most documents, a deed executed by an *infant* or minor (one who has not reached majority) is considered to be *voidable,* not void. The general rule is that an infant can disaffirm, or repudiate, the conveyance of real estate during minor age and within a reasonable period after reaching majority. What constitutes a reasonable time varies with the particular case.

A grantor generally is held to have sufficient mental capacity to execute a deed if he or she is capable of understanding the action. A deed executed by a person considered to be *mentally* incompetent is only *voidable*—it is not void. In some states, a deed executed by a person who has been judged *legally* incompetent is considered to be void. In such instances, court authority must be secured before real estate owned by a legally incompetent person can be conveyed.

It is important that a grantor's name be spelled correctly and that there be no variation in its spelling throughout the deed. If for any reason a grantor's name has been changed from that by which title was originally acquired, he or she must show both names. It is customary for such a grantor to be described as, for example, "John Smith, now known as John White." It is best for a grantor to first state the name under which the title was acquired and then indicate the current name.

When title to property has been acquired under a woman's unmarried name and she subsequently marries, the conveyance must show both names.

Grantee. To be valid, a deed must name a grantee and do so in such a way that the person is readily identifiable. A deed naming as the grantee a wholly fictitious person, a company that does not legally exist or a society or club that is not properly incorporated is considered void.

Consideration. In order to be valid, all deeds must contain a clause acknowledging the grantor's receipt of a **consideration.** Generally, the amount of consideration must be stated in dollars. When a deed conveys real estate as a gift to a relative, "love and affection" may be sufficient consideration, but it is customary in most states to recite a *nominal* consideration, such as "$10.00 and other good and valuable consideration."

Granting clause (words of conveyance). A deed of conveyance transfers a present interest in real estate. It must contain words of grant that state the grantor's intention to convey the property at this time. An expression of intent to convey at some future time is inadequate. Such words of grant, or conveyance, are contained in the **granting clause.** Depending on the type of deed and the obligations agreed to by the grantor, the wording is generally either "convey and warrant," "grant," "grant, bargain and sell" or "remise, release and quitclaim."

If more than one grantee is involved, the granting clause should cover the creation of their specific rights in the property. The clause might state, for example, that the grantees will take title as joint tenants or tenants in common. The wording is especially important in states where specific wording is necessary to create a joint tenancy.

The granting clause should also indicate what interest in the property is being conveyed by the grantor. Deeds that convey the entire fee simple interest of the grantor usually contain such wording as "to Jacqueline Smith and to her heirs and assigns forever." If the grantor is conveying less than complete interest, such as a life estate to property, the wording must indicate this limitation on the grantee's interest. For example, a deed creating a life estate would convey property "to Jacqueline Smith for the duration of her natural life."

Habendum clause. When it is necessary to define or explain the ownership to be enjoyed by the grantee, a **habendum clause** follows the granting clause. The habendum clause begins with the words "to have and to hold." Its provisions must agree with those set down in the granting clause. When there is a discrepancy between the two clauses, the provisions in the granting clause are usually followed.

Description of real estate. For a deed to be valid, it must contain an accurate description of the real estate conveyed. Land is considered adequately described if a competent surveyor can locate the property from the description used. The rules relative to describing real estate were discussed in Chapter 5, "Legal Descriptions."

Exceptions and reservations ("subject to" clauses). A deed should specifically note any encumbrances, reservations, or limitations that affect the title being conveyed. Such exceptions to clear title may include mortgage liens, taxes, restrictions and easements that run with the land. For example, a deed may grant title to a grantee "subject to general real estate taxes for the year 1982 and subsequent years."

In addition to existing encumbrances, a grantor may reserve some right in the land for his or her own use (an easement, for instance). A grantor may also place certain restrictions on a grantee's use of the property. For example, a developer may restrict the number of houses that may be built on a one-acre lot in a subdivision. A deed must clearly indicate such private restrictions. They may be stated in the deed or contained in a previously recorded document (such as the subdivider's master deed) that is expressly cited in the deed. Many of these deed restrictions have time limits, often including renewal clauses.

Who signs the deed?

Signature of grantor. To be valid, a deed must be signed by *all grantors* named in the deed. As discussed previously, a grantor's spouse with marital or other rights, may also be required to sign the deed. This requirement will vary according to state law and the manner in which title is held by the conveying parties. In some states there must be witnesses to the grantor's signature.

Most states, including Pennsylvania, permit a grantor's signature to be signed by an attorney-in-fact acting under a power of attorney. An *attorney-in-fact* is any person who has been given power of attorney (specific written authority) to execute and sign legal instruments for a grantor. In such cases, it is usually necessary for an authorizing document known as a *power of attorney* to be recorded in the county where the property is located. As the power of attorney terminates upon the death of the person granting such authority, adequate evidence must be submitted that the grantor was alive at the time the attorney-in-fact signed the deed.

A grantor who is unable to write is permitted to sign his or her name by *mark* in Pennsylvania. With this type of signature, two persons other than the notary public taking the acknowledgment usually must witness the grantor's execution of the deed and sign as witnesses.

In Pennsylvania, unlike some states, it is not necessary for a seal or the word *seal* to be written or printed after an individual grantor's signature. The use of a corporate seal by corporations, however, is always required.

Acknowledgment. An **acknowledgment** is a form of declaration made voluntarily by a person who is signing a formal, written document before a *notary public* or authorized public officer (judge, justice of the peace, or recorder of deeds). This acknowledgment usually states that the person signing the deed or other document is known to the officer or has produced sufficient identification and that the person signing is doing so as his or her own *free and voluntary act*. The acknowledgment provides evidence that the signature is genuine.

While an acknowledgment is not essential to the *validity* of a deed, one that is not acknowledged is not a satisfactory instrument. In Pennsylvania, an unacknowledged deed is not eligible for recording. And although an unrecorded deed is valid between the grantor and the grantee, it is often not a valid conveyance against subsequent innocent purchasers. For this reason a grantee would not, in effect, secure good title to the property. To help assure good title, a grantee should always require acknowledgment of the grantor's signature on a deed. Recording is discussed in Chapter 12, "Title Records."

Delivery and acceptance. Before a transfer of title by conveyance can take effect, there must be an actual **delivery** of the deed by the grantor and either actual or implied **acceptance** by the grantee. Delivery may be made by the grantor to the grantee personally or to a third party, commonly known as an *escrowee,* for ultimate delivery to the grantee upon the completion of certain requirements. *Title is said to pass when a valid deed is delivered.* The effective date of the transfer of title from the grantor and to the grantee is the date of delivery of the deed itself. When a deed is delivered in escrow, the date of delivery of the conveyance is generally ("relates back" to) the date that it was deposited with the escrow agent.

Delivery is a very technical aspect of the validity of a deed and is usually strictly construed by the courts. Brokers should consult legal counsel with questions regarding delivery.

Execution of Corporate Deeds

A corporation is considered to be a legal entity. The laws affecting corporations' rights to convey real estate are complex. Some basic rules must be followed:

1. A corporation can convey real estate only by authority granted in its *bylaws* or upon a proper resolution passed by its *board of directors.* If all or a substantial portion of a corporation's real estate is being conveyed, it is usually required that a resolution authorizing the sale can be secured from the *stockholders.*

2. Deeds to real estate can be *signed only by an authorized officer.*

3. The corporate *seal* must be affixed to the conveyance.

Rules pertaining to religious corporations and not-for-profit corporations vary widely. Because the legal requirements must be followed explicitly, it is advisable to consult an attorney for all corporate conveyances.

Types of Deeds

The deed, being a contract between the grantor and the grantee, can take several forms, depending on the extent of the representations and obligations the grantor pledges to the grantee. It should be noted, that despite the promises made in the deed by the grantor, the grantee is best protected by further evidence that the grantor's representations of ownership are valid. For this reason the grantee seeks assurance with a certificate of title or title insurance (see Chapter 12, "Title Records"). The most common deed forms are:

1. general warranty deed

2. special warranty deed

3. quitclaim deed

4. deed of bargain and sale

5. deed in trust

6. trustee's deed

7. deed executed pursuant to a court order

General warranty deeds. For a purchaser of real estate, a **general warranty deed** (shown in Figure 10.2) provides the *greatest protection* of any deed. It is referred to as a general warranty deed because the grantor is legally bound by certain covenants or warranties. In most states, the warranties are usually implied by the use of certain words specified in the state statutes. In Pennsylvania, however, the grantor's warranties are expressly written into the deed itself. The basic warranties are:

1. *Covenant of seisin:* The grantor warrants that he or she is the owner of the property and has the right to convey title to it. The grantee may recover damages up to the full purchase price if this covenant is broken.

2. *Covenant against encumbrances:* The grantor warrants that the property is free from any liens or encumbrances except those specifically stated in the deed. Encumbrances would generally include such items as mortgages, mechanics' liens and easements. If this covenant is breached, the grantee may sue for expenses to remove the encumbrance.

3. *Covenant of quiet enjoyment:* The grantor guarantees that the grantee's title is good against third parties who might bring court actions to establish superior title to the property. If the grantee's title is found to be inferior, the grantor is liable for damages.

4. *Covenant of further assurance:* The grantor promises to obtain and deliver any instrument needed in order to make the title good. For example, if the grantor's spouse has failed to sign away dower rights, the grantor must deliver a quitclaim deed executed by the spouse to clear the title.

5. *Covenant of warranty forever:* The grantor guarantees that if at any time in the future the title fails, he or she will compensate the grantee for the loss sustained.

These covenants in a general warranty deed are not limited to matters that occurred during the time the grantor owned the property; they extend back to its origins. The grantor defends the title against himself *and against all others as predecessors in title.*

Special warranty deeds. A conveyance that carries only one covenant is a **special warranty deed.** The grantor warrants that the grantor received title and *only* that the property was not encumbered during the time the grantor held title except as noted in the deed. Special warranty deeds generally contain the words "remise, release, alienate and convey" in the granting clause. The grantor defends the title against himself. Any additional warranties to be included must be specifically stated in the deed.

A special warranty deed is usually used by fiduciaries, such as trustees, executors and corporations, and sometimes by grantors who have acquired title at tax sales. It is based on the theory that a fiduciary or corporation has no authority to warrant against acts of its predecessors in title. Such unauthorized warranties by a corporation are considered to be beyond the scope and authority of the corporate powers and are referred to as *ultra vires.* Fiduciaries may hold title for a limited time without having a personal interest in the proceeds.

Bargain and sale deeds. Deeds using the words "grant and release" or "grant, bargain and sell" in the granting clause are usually **bargain and sale deeds.** A bargain and sale deed contains no real warranties against encumbrances; however, it does *imply* that the grantor holds title and possession of the property. Because the warranty is not specifically stated, the grantee has little legal recourse if defects later appear in the title. In some areas, a covenant against encumbrances initiated by the grantor may be added to a standard bargain and sale deed to create a *bargain and sale deed with covenant against the grantor's acts.* This deed is roughly equivalent to a special warranty deed. In other areas, warranties used in general warranty deeds may be inserted into a bargain and sale deed to give the grantee similar protection.

Figure 10.2
Warranty Deed

P102—DEED—WARRANTY   A D G R   COPYRIGHT 1976 © by ALL-STATE LEGAL SUPPLY CORP.
   IND. OR CORP.   1316 Arch St. Philadelphia. Pa. 19107

This Deed, *made the*   *day of*   19   ;

Between

herein designated as the Grantors,

And

herein designated as the Grantees;

Witnesseth, *that the Grantors, for and in consideration of*

lawful money of the United States of America, to the Grantors in hand well and truly paid by the Grantees, at or before the sealing and delivery of these presents, the receipt whereof is hereby acknowledged and the Grantors being therewith fully satisfied, do by these presents grant, bargain, sell and convey unto the Grantees forever,

All   *tract*   *or parcel*   *of land and premises, situate, lying and being in the*
                        of   *in the County of*
and Commonwealth of Pennsylvania, more particularly described as follows:

Reprinted by permission of All-State Legal Supply Co.

Figure 10.2
(cont.)

Together *with all and singular the buildings, improvements, ways, woods, waters, watercourses, rights, liberties, privileges, hereditaments and appurtenances to the same belonging or in anywise appertaining; and the reversion and reversions, remainder and remainders, rents, issues and profits thereof, and of every part and parcel thereof;* **And also** *all the estate, right, title, interest, use, possession, property, claim and demand whatsoever of the Grantors both in law and in equity, of, in and to the premises herein described and every part and parcel thereof with the appurtenances.* **To have and to hold** *all and singular the premises herein described together with the hereditaments and appurtenances unto the Grantees and to Grantees' proper use and benefit forever.*

And *the Grantors covenant that, except as may be herein set forth, they do and will* **forever warrant** *and* **defend** *the lands and premises, hereditaments and appurtenances hereby conveyed, against the Grantors and all other persons lawfully claiming the same or to claim the same.*

In all references herein to any parties, persons, entities or corporations, the use of any particular gender or the plural or singular number is intended to include the appropriate gender or number as the text of the within instrument may require.
Wherever in this instrument any party shall be designated or referred to by name or general reference, such designation is intended to and shall have the same effect as if the words "heirs, executors, administrators, personal or legal representatives, successors and assigns" had been inserted after each and every such designation.

In Witness Whereof, *the Grantors have hereunto set their hands and seals, or if a corporation, it has caused these presents to be signed by its proper corporate officers and its corporate seal to be affixed hereto, the day and year first above written.*

Signed, Sealed and Delivered
in the presence of
or Attested by   ....

....

Commonwealth of Pennsylvania, County of   **ss.:**

Be it Remembered, *that on*   *19*   *, before me the subscriber*

personally appeared

known to me (or satisfactorily proven) to be the person   whose name   subscribed to the within deed and acknowledged that   he   executed the same for the purposes therein contained.

Witness *my hand and seal the day and year aforesaid.*

....

**Figure 10.2
(cont.)**

Commonwealth of Pennsylvania, County of   **§ ss.:**

Be it Remembered, *that on*   *19*   *, before me the subscriber,*

personally appeared

who acknowledged   self to be the   of

*a Corporation, and that being authorized to do so as such corporate officer executed the foregoing instrument
for the purposes therein contained on behalf of the corporation.*

Witness *my hand and seal the day and year aforesaid.*

....

Deed

TO

19

Dated

*The Undersigned certifies that the precise
residence and complete post office address of the
Grantee is:*

STREET

ZIP CODE

CITY

STATE

✳ **Quitclaim deeds.** A **quitclaim deed** provides the grantee with the least protection of any deed. It carries no covenant or warranties and generally conveys only such interest, if any, that the grantor may have when the deed is delivered. By a quitclaim deed, the grantor only "remises, releases and quitclaims" his or her interest in the property to the grantee. Usually, a quitclaim deed is the only type of deed that may be used to convey less than a fee simple title. For example, it might convey an easement or it might reconvey equitable title back to a seller.

In Pennsylvania, a quitclaim deed does not necessarily convey property; rather, it conveys only the grantor's right, title or interest, whatever that may be. Thus, if the grantor has no interest in the property, the grantee will acquire nothing by virtue of the quitclaim deed, nor will the grantee acquire any right of warranty claim against the grantor. A quitclaim deed can convey title as effectively as a warranty deed if the grantor has good title when he or she delivers the deed, but it provides none of the guarantees that a warranty deed does.

A quitclaim deed is frequently used to cure a defect, called a "cloud on the title," in the recorded history of a real estate title. For example, if the name of the grantee is misspelled on a warranty deed placed in the public record, a quitclaim deed with the correct spelling may be executed to the grantee in order to perfect the title. When a deed is to be used for the special purpose of clearing a cloud on the title or releasing an interest in property of which the grantor never had possession, caution should be used in selecting the form of the deed. A grantor who "grants and releases" will probably be bound by a covenant of possession, but if the grantor "releases and quitclaims all interest, if any," then the quitclaim deed will pass, without warranty, any title the grantor may have.

A quitclaim deed is also used when a grantor allegedly has *inherited* property but is not certain of the validity of the title of the decedent from whom the property was inherited. The use of a warranty deed in such an instance could carry with it obligations of warranty, while a quitclaim deed would convey only the grantor's interest.

Trust deed. A **trust deed** is the means by which a *trustor* conveys real estate to a *trustee* for the benefit of a *beneficiary*. The real estate is held by the trustee in order to fulfill the purpose of the trust. In a few states, what is called a *deed in trust* is used to convey full power to sell, mortgage, subdivide and the like, to the trustee under a land trust, which is controlled by the beneficiary under the provisions of the trust agreement. In many states, a *deed of trust* enables the trustor to pledge real estate as security for a loan, and thus serves the same purpose as a mortgage. The deed of trust is discussed in detail in Chapter 13, "Real Estate Financing."

Trustee's deed. A deed of conveyance executed by a trustee is a **trustee's deed.** It is usually used when a trustee named in a will, agreement or deed in trust sells or conveys the trust real estate's title out of the trust. The trustee's deed sets forth the fact that the trustee executes the instrument in accordance with the powers and authority granted to him or her by the trust instrument or the deed in trust.

Deeds executed pursuant to court order (judicial deeds). This classification covers such deed forms as executors' deeds, masters' deeds, administrators' deeds, sheriffs' deeds and many others. These statutory deed forms are used to convey title to property that is transferred by court order or by will. The forms of such deeds must conform to the laws of the state where the property is located.

One characteristic of such instruments is that the *full consideration* is usually stated in the deed. This is done because the deed is executed pursuant to a court order, and as the court has authorized the sale of the property for a given amount of consideration, this amount should be stated *exactly* in the document.

✳ Pennsylvania Realty Transfer Tax

Most states have enacted laws providing for a tax on conveyances of real estate, usually referred to as the state *transfer tax*. There are no state revenue stamps used for the Pennsylvania Realty Transfer Tax. A notation is made on the document itself as to the amount of tax paid.

The **Pennsylvania Realty Transfer Tax** is imposed at the rate of one percent of the full consideration paid for the real estate. In addition, Pennsylvania law permits the local taxing districts (city, borough, township and school district) to impose an additional transfer tax of one percent of the full consideration. Municipalities with a "Home Rule Charter Government" may exceed the one percent state-imposed limitation. Some, including the city of Pittsburgh, have a 1.5 percent Local Deed Transfer Tax.

In Pennsylvania, the real estate transaction itself is taxed, not the buyer or seller. For this reason, the tax is usually divided equally between the buyer and seller, as provided in the agreement of sale.

Certain deeds normally are *exempted* from the tax. These include: transfers of real estate between parent and child or between siblings; deeds not made in connection with a sale, such as changing joint tenants; conveyances to or from or between governmental bodies; deeds between charitable, religious or educational institutions; deeds securing debts; deeds releasing property as security for a debt; partitions; tax deeds; deeds pursuant to mergers of corporations; and deeds from subsidiary to parent corporations for cancellations of stock.

Note that in certain areas of Pennsylvania, 99-year ground leases are common. Transfer of such property is accomplished by lease assignment. Transfer taxes are charged on leases in excess of 30 years (see Chapter 8, "Leases").

Involuntary Alienation

Title to property can be transferred by **involuntary alienation,** that is, without the owner's consent (see Figure 10.3). Such transfers are usually carried out by operations of law ranging from government condemnation of land for public use to the sale of property to satisfy delinquent tax or mortgage liens. When a person dies intestate and leaves no heirs, the title to the estate passes to the state by operation of law based on the principle of **escheat.**

Federal, state and local governments, school boards, some governmental agencies, and certain public and quasi-public corporations and utilities (railroads and gas and electric companies) have the right of *eminent domain*. Under this right, private property may be taken for public use through *condemnation*. The exercise of eminent domain is subject to three necessary conditions: (1) that the use is for the benefit of the public; (2) that an equitable amount of compensation will be paid to the owner; and (3) that the rights of the property owner will be protected by due process of law. Pennsylvania's Eminent Domain Code provides that the owner is entitled to just compensation, or the difference between the fair market value of the entire property interest immediately before condemnation and its fair

**Figure 10.3
Involuntary
Alienation**

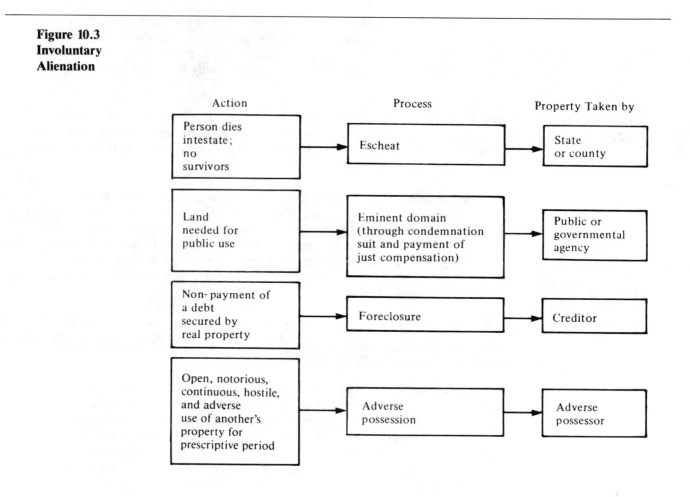

Action	Process	Property Taken by
Person dies intestate; no survivors	Escheat	State or county
Land needed for public use	Eminent domain (through condemnation suit and payment of just compensation)	Public or governmental agency
Non-payment of a debt secured by real property	Foreclosure	Creditor
Open, notorious, continuous, hostile, and adverse use of another's property for prescriptive period	Adverse possession	Adverse possessor

market value after condemnation. (See discussion of eminent domain—Chapter 6, "Interests in Real Estate.")

Land may also be transferred without an owner's consent in order to satisfy debts contracted by the owner. In such cases the debt is foreclosed, the property is sold, and the proceeds of the sale are applied to pay off the debt. Debts that could be foreclosed include mortgage loans, real estate taxes, mechanics' liens or general judgments against the property owner (see Chapters 11 and 13).

In addition to the involuntary transfer of land by legal processes, land may be transferred by natural forces. As discussed in Chapter 6, "Interests in Real Estate," owners of land bordering on rivers, lakes and other bodies of water may acquire additional land through the process of *accretion,* the slow accumulation of soil, rock or other matter deposited by the movement of water on an owner's property. The opposite of accretion is *erosion,* the gradual wearing away of land by the action of water and wind. In addition, property may be lost through *avulsion,* the sudden tearing away of land by such natural means as earthquakes or tidal waves.

Adverse possession is another means of involuntary transfer. An owner who does not use the land or does not inspect it for a number of years may lose title to another person who has some claim to the land, takes possession and, most importantly, uses the land. Usually the possession of the claimant must be open, notorious, hostile and uninterrupted for the number of years set by state law (21 years in Pennsylvania). Through the principle of *tacking,* successive periods of adverse possession can be combined by successive adverse possessors, thus enabling a person who is not in possession for the entire required time to establish a claim of adverse possession.

Through adverse possession, the law recognizes that the use of land is an important function of its ownership. In many cases, an adverse user's rights may supersede those of a fee owner. In Pennsylvania, a person claiming title to land by adverse possession can secure undisputed title by filing an action in court to quiet title. A claimant who does not receive title may acquire an easement by prescription (see Chapter 6). When a transaction involves the possibility of title by adverse possession, the parties should seek legal counsel.

Transfer of a Deceased Person's Property

Every state has a law known as the *statute of descent and distribution*. When a person dies **intestate** (without having left a will), the decedent's real estate and personal property pass to the decedent's heirs according to this statute. In effect, the state makes a will for such decedents. In contrast, a person who dies **testate** has prepared a will indicating the way the property will be disposed of after death.

Legally, when a person dies, title to the real estate immediately passes either to the heirs by descent or to the persons named in the will by **devise.** However, before the heirs can take possession of the property, the estate must be probated and all claims against it must be satisfied.

Transfer of Title by Will

A **last will and testament** is an instrument made by an owner to voluntarily convey title to property after the owner's death. A will takes effect only after the death of the decedent; until that time, any property covered by the will can be conveyed by the owner and thus be removed from the owner's estate.

A person who has died and left a will is said to have died *testate*. A party who makes a will is known as a **testator,** or *devisor;* the gift of real property by will is known as a *devise;* and a person who receives property by will is known as a *devisee*. Technically, an *heir* is one who takes property by the law of descent, but the term is commonly used to include devisees, as well. In addition, a gift of personal property is known as a *legacy* or *bequest;* the person receiving the personal property is known as a *legatee*.

The privilege of disposing of property by will is statutory; so to be effective, a will must conform to all the statutory requirements of the state in which the real estate is located. In a case where a will does not provide the minimum statutory inheritance, the surviving spouse has the option of informing the court that he or she will take the minimum statutory share rather than the lesser share provided in the will. This practice, called *renouncing (or taking against) the will,* is a right reserved only to a surviving spouse.

A will differs from a deed in that a deed conveys a present interest in real estate during the lifetime of the grantor, while a will conveys no interest in the property until after the death of the testator. To be valid, a deed *must* be delivered during the lifetime of the grantor. The parties named in a will have no rights or interests so long as the party who has made the will is still alive; they acquire interest or title only after the owner's death. Upon the death of a testator the will must be filed and *probated* in order for title to pass to the devisees.

Legal requirements for making a will. The legal capacity to make a will varies widely from state to state (see Figure 10.4). In Pennsylvania, a person must be of *legal age* (18) and *sound mind* when he or she executes the will. There are no rigid tests to determine the capacity to make a will. Usually, the courts hold that to make a valid will the testator must have sufficient mental capacity to understand the nature and extent of the property owned, the identity of natural heirs, and that execution of the will means that at the testator's death property goes to those named in the will. The drawing of a will must be a voluntary act, free of any undue influence by other people. A will may be modified or amended by a *codicil*. Every will in Pennsylvania must be signed by the testator.

In Pennsylvania, a handwritten will or *holographic will* must be signed by the testator and need not be further witnessed or acknowledged. If the testator is unable to sign the will for some reason, he or she may make his or her mark (usually an "x") on the document, with the name subscribed. This mark, however, must be signed by two witnesses in order to be valid. Note that Pennsylvania also recognizes the use of *nuncupative wills,* those that are given orally and put into writing by witnesses.

Transfer of Title by Descent

By law, the title to real estate and personal property of a person who dies intestate passes to the decedent's heirs. Under the **descent** statutes, the primary **heirs** of the deceased are the spouse and close blood relatives, such as children, parents, brothers, sisters, aunts, uncles and, in some cases, first cousins. The closeness of the relationship to the decedent determines the specific rights of the heirs.

Rights under such laws of descent vary from state to state. In Pennsylvania, when a person dies leaving a spouse and one child, the spouse and child usually take the entire estate, divided equally between them. If, however, a spouse and two or more children survive, the spouse takes one-third and the children divide the remaining two-thirds equally among them. If a spouse but no children or descendants of deceased children exist, Pennsylvania law gives the spouse up to $20,000 in real and personal property and one-half of the remainder of the estate; the rest is divided among those in the next existing class of heirs, such as parents or brothers and sisters of the decedent. The surviving children of a deceased heir will usually divide their parent's share. If there are no other heirs or children of deceased heirs, the spouse takes the entire estate.

In Pennsylvania, illegitimate children may inherit from both the father and the mother, provided parentage has been established legally.

When children have been legally adopted, most states, including Pennsylvania, consider them to be heirs of the adopting parents, but not heirs of ancestors of the adopting parents.

**Figure 10.4
Requirements for a
Valid Will**

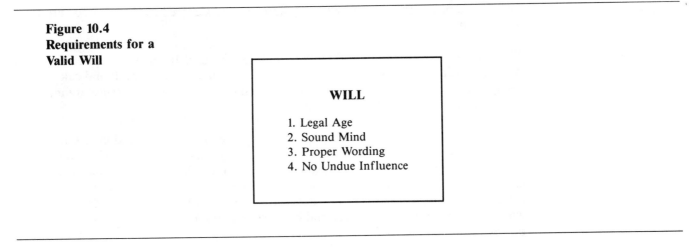

WILL

1. Legal Age
2. Sound Mind
3. Proper Wording
4. No Undue Influence

**Probate
Proceedings**

Probate is a legal process by which a court determines the assets of the deceased person and who will inherit the property. Probate court proceedings must take place in the county where the real estate in question is located. In Pennsylvania, a will is probated by filing with the registrar of wills in the county in which the testator last resided. The Pennsylvania statute known as the Intestate Act determines who will inherit the estate of a person who dies intestate. There are statutory requirements for the form and execution of a will. A will is assumed to be valid unless it is challenged. The court rules on a challenge to the validity of the will. If the will is upheld, the property is distributed according to its provisions.

In Practice...

A broker entering into a listing agreement with the executor or administrator of an estate in probate should be aware that the amount of commission may be fixed by the court. An amount of commission could be challenged and if deemed unreasonable, the court could reduce it. Such commission is payable only from the proceeds of the sale. The broker will not be able to collect a commission unless the court approves the sale.

Summary

Title to real estate is the right to and evidence of ownership of the land. It may be transferred in four ways: (1) voluntary alienation, (2) involuntary alienation, (3) will and (4) descent.

The voluntary transfer of an owner's title is made by a *deed,* executed (signed) by the owner as *grantor* to the purchaser or donee as *grantee.* The form and execution of a deed must comply with the statutory requirements of the state in which the land is located.

Among the most common of these requirements are: a grantor with legal capacity to contract; a readily identifiable grantee; a granting clause; a legal description of the property; a recital of consideration, exceptions and reservations on the title ("subject to" clause); and the signature of the grantor, properly witnessed if necessary. In addition, the deed should be acknowledged before a notary public or other officer in order to provide evidence that the signature is genuine and to allow recording. Deeds are subject to state transfer taxes when they are recorded.

Title to the property passes when the grantor delivers a deed to the grantee and it is accepted.

The obligation of a grantor is determined by the form of the deed, that is, whether it is a general warranty deed, special warranty deed, bargain and sale deed, or quitclaim deed. The words of conveyance in the granting clause are important in determining the form of deed.

A *general warranty deed* provides the greatest protection of any deed by binding the grantor to certain covenants or warranties. A *special warranty deed* warrants only that the grantor received title and that the real estate is not encumbered except as stated in the deed. A *bargain and sale deed* carries with it no warranties but implies that the grantor holds title to the property. A *quitclaim deed* carries with it no warranties whatsoever and conveys only the interest, *if any,* the grantor possesses in the property.

An owner's title may be transferred without his or her permission by a court action, such as a *foreclosure* or judgment sale, a tax sale, *condemnation* under the right of eminent domain, *adverse possession* or *escheat*. Land also may be transferred by the natural forces of water and wind, which either increase property by *accretion* or decrease it through *erosion* or *avulsion*.

The real estate of an owner who makes a valid *will* (who dies testate) passes to the devisees through the probating of the will. The title of an owner who dies without a will (intestate) passes according to the provisions of the state *law of descent*.

Questions

1. Title to real estate may be transferred during a person's lifetime by which of the following means?
   a. voluntary alienation
   b. descent
   c. involuntary alienation
   d. a and c

2. Who is required to sign a deed in order to make it valid?
   I. grantor
   II. grantee
      a. I only   c. both I and II
      b. II only   d. neither I nor II

3. Harry Hughes, 15, recently inherited many parcels of real estate from his late father and has decided to sell one of them in order to pay inheritance taxes. If Hughes entered into a deed conveying his interest in the property to a purchaser without the signature of his legal guardian, such a conveyance would be:
   a. valid.   c. invalid.
   b. void.   d. voidable.

4. A deed that an owner of real estate may use to voluntarily transfer a right, title or interest in real estate may be a:
   a. sheriff's deed.
   b. warranty deed.
   c. foreclosure deed.
   d. all of the above

5. Title to an owner's real estate can be transferred at the death of owner by which one of the following documents?
   a. warranty deed
   b. special warranty deed
   c. trustee's deed
   d. last will and testament

6. The determination of the type of deed used in conveying title can be made by examining:
   a. the grantor's name.
   b. the grantee's name.
   c. the granting clause.
   d. the acknowledgment.

7. Matilda Fairbanks bought acreage in a distant county, never went to see the acreage and did not use the ground. Harold Sampson moved his mobile home onto the land, had a water well drilled and lived there for many years. Sampson may become the owner of the land if he has complied with the state law regarding:
   I. requirements for a voluntary valid conveyance.
   II. adverse possession.
      a. I only   c. both I and II
      b. II only   d. neither I nor II

8. All deeds should be:
   a. recorded.
   b. signed by the grantee.
   c. surveyed.
   d. all of the above

9. Alvin Rosewell executes a deed to Sylvia Plat as grantee, has it acknowledged and receives payment from the buyer. Rosewell holds the deed, however, and arranges to meet Plat the next morning at the county recorder's office to deliver the deed to her. In this situation at this time:
   a. Plat owns the property because she has paid for it.
   b. title to the property will not officially pass until Plat has been given the deed the next morning.
   c. title to the property will not pass until Plat has received the deed and recorded it the next morning.
   d. Plat will own the property when she has signed the deed the next morning.

10. Claude Johnson, a bachelor, died owning real estate that he devised by his will to his niece, Annette. Legally, at what point does title pass to his niece?

   a. immediately upon Johnson's death
   b. after his will has been probated
   c. after Annette has paid all inheritance taxes
   d. when Annette executes a new deed to the property

11. A person who pays for and receives a quitclaim deed:

   I. will receive whatever title the grantor possessed in the property.
   II. can force the grantor to make the title good by a suit in court.

   a. I only   c. both I and II
   b. II only   d. neither I nor II

12. Which of the following types of deeds most usually recites the full, actual consideration paid for the property?

   a. gift deed
   b. trustee's deed
   c. deed in trust
   d. deed executed pursuant to court order

13. A grantor in a special warranty deed is bound by which of the following warranties?

   a. warranty of quiet enjoyment
   b. warranty against encumbrances
   c. warranty against encumbrances by the grantor
   d. a and b

14. In order for a will to be valid in Pennsylvania, it must be:

   I. signed by the testator, if he or she is physically able to do so.
   II. recorded in the county where the testator resides.

   a. I only   c. both I and II
   b. II only   d. neither I nor II

15. An owner of real estate who was adjudged legally incompetent made a will during his stay at a nursing home. He later died and was survived by a wife and three children. His real estate will pass:

   a. to his wife.
   b. to the heirs mentioned in his will.
   c. according to the state law of descent.
   d. to the state.

16. In Pennsylvania, a warranty deed automatically carries with it which of the following warranties?

   a. seisin
   b. quiet enjoyment
   c. further assurance
   d. only those expressly written in the deed

17. Which of the following types of deeds merely implies but does not specifically warrant that the grantor holds good title to the property?

   a. special warranty deed
   b. bargain and sale deed
   c. quitclaim deed
   d. trustee's deed

18. A house is selling for $89,500; the buyer is paying $50,000 cash and is giving the seller a mortgage for the balance. What is the amount of state transfer tax that must be paid on this transaction?

   a. $895   c. $8,950
   b. $3,950   d. $17,900

19. In Pennsylvania, who usually pays the transfer tax?

   I. the buyer
   II. the seller

   a. I only   c. both I and II
   b. II only   d. neither I nor II

20. Which of the following is *not* one of the manners in which title to real estate may be transferred by involuntary alienation?

   a. eminent domain   c. erosion
   b. escheat   d. seisin

21. A person who has died leaving a valid will is called a(n):

   a. devisee.   c. legatee.
   b. testator.   d. intestate.

22. Jim Gorzelany dies intestate and is survived by a wife and two children. According to the Pennsylvania law of descent, what share of Gorzelany's estate will pass to his surviving spouse?

    a. one-fourth   c. one-half
    b. one-third   d. the entire estate

23. Which of the following best describes the covenant of quiet enjoyment?

    a. The grantor promises to obtain and deliver any instrument needed to make the title good.
    b. The grantor guarantees that if the title fails in the future, he or she will compensate the grantee.
    c. The grantor warrants that he or she is the owner and has the right to convey title to it.
    d. The grantor assures that the title is good against the title claims of third parties.

24. Which of the following instruments would be given to a purchaser of real estate?

    I. executor's deed
    II. trustee's deed

    a. I only   c. both I and II
    b. II only   d. neither I nor II

25. An instrument authorizing one person to act for another is called a(n):

    a. power of attorney.
    b. release deed.
    c. deed in trust.
    d. acknowledgment.

11

Real Estate Taxes and Other Liens

Key Terms

Ad valorem tax
Assessment
Attachment
Confession of judgment
Corporation franchise tax
Equalization factor
Estate taxes
General contractor
General lien
Inheritance taxes
Internal Revenue Service tax lien
Involuntary lien
Judgment
Lien
Lis pendens

Mechanic's lien
Mill
Mortgage lien
Municipal utility lien
Priority of liens
Redemption
Special assessment
Specific lien
Subcontractor
Subordination agreement
Surety bail bond
Tax bill
Tax lien
Tax sale
Voluntary lien

Overview

As discussed in previous chapters, the ownership interest a person has in real estate can be diminished by the interests of others. Specifically, taxing bodies, creditors and courts can lessen an ownership interest by making a claim—called a *lien*—against a person's property to secure payment of taxes, debts and other obligations. This chapter will discuss the nature of liens, specifically focusing on real estate tax liens, which affect every owner of real estate. In addition, the chapter will describe liens other than taxes that involve real and personal property.

Figure 11.1
General Liens

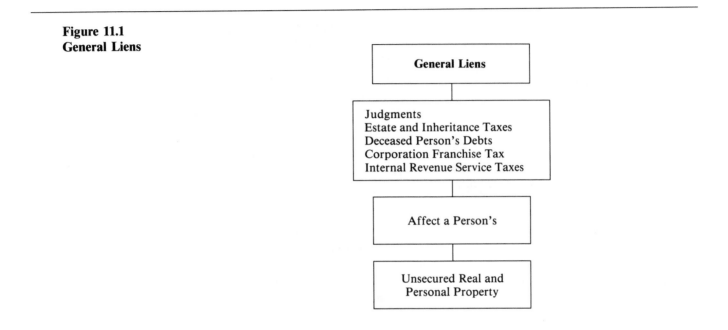

General Liens

Judgments
Estate and Inheritance Taxes
Deceased Person's Debts
Corporation Franchise Tax
Internal Revenue Service Taxes

Affect a Person's

Unsecured Real and
Personal Property

Liens

A **lien** is defined as a charge against property that provides security for a debt or obligation of the property owner. A lien allows a creditor (lienor) to force the sale of property that has been given as security by the debtor (lienee) to satisfy the lienee's debt in case of default. A lien does not constitute ownership; it is a type of *encumbrance*—a charge or burden on a property. Note, however, that although all liens are encumbrances, not all encumbrances are necessarily liens. As discussed in Chapter 6, "Interests in Real Estate," encumbrances that are not liens (such as easements and deed restrictions) are *incorporeal rights* in real estate and give the parties in question certain rights, or interests, in the real estate.

Generally, liens are enforced by court order. A creditor must institute a legal action for the court to sell the real estate in question for full or partial satisfaction of the debt.

A lien may be voluntary or involuntary. A **voluntary lien** is created by the lienee's action, such as taking out a mortgage loan. An **involuntary lien** is created by law. A real estate tax lien, for example, is involuntary, created by law without any action by the property owner. A court-ordered judgment requiring payment of the balance on a delinquent charge account would be an involuntary lien on the debtor's property.

Liens may be classified further into two other categories: general and specific. As illustrated in Figure 11.1, **general liens** usually affect all the property of a debtor, both real and personal, and include judgments, estate and inheritance taxes, debts of a deceased person, corporation franchise taxes and Internal Revenue Service taxes. There is a difference, however, between a lien on real and personal property in that the lien attaches to real property when it is entered but does not attach to personal property until the personal property is seized. **Specific liens,** on the other hand, are usually secured by a specific parcel of real estate and affect only that

Figure 11.2
Specific Liens

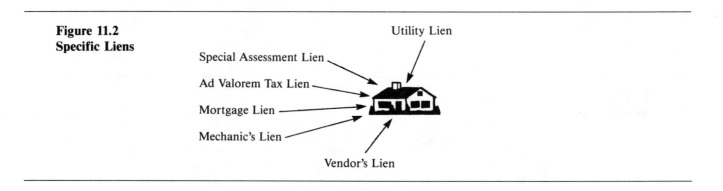

particular property. As illustrated in Figure 11.2, these include mechanics' liens, mortgages, taxes, special assessments, liens for public utilities, surety bail bond liens and attachments.

Effects of Liens on Title

Although the fee simple estate held by a typical real estate owner can be reduced in value by the lien and encumbrance rights of others, the owner is still free to convey title to a willing purchaser. This purchaser will, however, buy the property subject to any liens and encumbrances of the seller. Once properly established, liens will *run with the land;* that is, they will bind successive owners if steps are not taken to clear the lien.

Remember, liens attach to property, not to the property owner. Thus, although a purchaser who buys real estate under a delinquent lien is not responsible for payment of the debt secured by the lien, he or she faces a possible loss of the property if the creditors take court action to enforce payment of their liens.

Priority of liens. **Priority of liens** establishes the order of claim against the property. Liens other than general real estate taxes and special assessments take priority from the date of recording in the public records of the county where the property is located (see Figure 11.3). Exceptions to this rule include mechanics' liens (discussed later in this chapter), which take priority as provided by state law but never take priority over tax and special assessment liens.

Real estate taxes and special assessments generally take *priority* over all other liens. This means that if the property goes through a court sale to satisfy unpaid debts or obligations, outstanding real estate taxes and special assessments will be paid from the proceeds *first*. The remainder of the proceeds will be used to pay other outstanding liens in the order of their priority.

Subordination agreements are written agreements between lienholders to change the priority of mortgage, judgment and other liens under certain circumstances. Priority and recording of liens will be discussed in detail in Chapter 12, "Title Records."

Tax Liens

As discussed in Chapter 6, the ownership of real estate is subject to certain government powers. One of these powers is the right of state and local governments to impose **tax liens** for the support of their governmental functions. Because the location of real estate is permanently fixed, the government can levy taxes with a

**Figure 11.3
Priority of Liens**

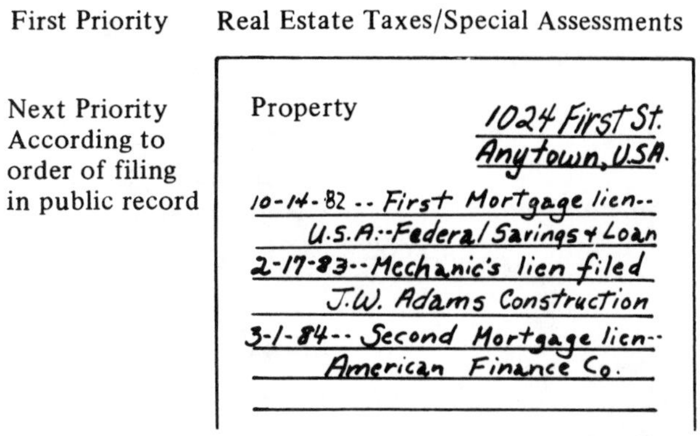

First Priority   Real Estate Taxes/Special Assessments

Next Priority
According to
order of filing
in public record

Property   *1024 First St.
Anytown, USA.*

*10-14-82 -- First Mortgage lien --
U.S.A. -- Federal Savings & Loan
2-17-83 -- Mechanic's lien filed
J.W. Adams Construction
3-1-84 -- Second Mortgage lien --
American Finance Co.*

rather high degree of certainty that the taxes will be collected. As the annual taxes levied on real estate usually have priority over other previously recorded liens, they may be enforced by the court sale of the real estate free of such other liens.

Real estate taxes can be divided into two types: (1) *general real estate tax,* or **ad valorem tax,** and (2) **special assessment,** or *improvement tax.* Both of these taxes are specific, involuntary liens.

General Tax (Ad Valorem Tax)

The general real estate tax is made up of the taxes levied on real estate by various governmental agencies and municipalities. These include cities, towns, villages and counties. Other taxing bodies are school districts or boards (including local elementary and high schools, junior colleges and community colleges), drainage districts, water districts and sanitary districts. Municipal authorities operating recreational preserves such as forest preserves and parks are also authorized by the legislatures of the various states to levy real estate taxes.

General real estate taxes are levied for the *general support or operation* of the governmental agency authorized to impose the levy. These taxes are known as *ad valorem* taxes because the amount of the tax varies in accordance with the *value of the property being taxed.*

Exemptions from general taxes. Under Pennsylvania and most other state laws, certain real estate is exempt from real estate taxation. For example, property owned by cities, various municipal organizations, the state and federal governments, religious corporations, hospitals or educational institutions is tax exempt. Usually the property must be used for tax-exempt purposes by the exempted group or organization. If it is not so used, it will be subject to tax. (For example, a parking lot owned by a church and adjacent to the church building is not exempt from taxation because the purpose of the parking lot is to park cars, not to conduct religious activities.)

Many state laws also allow special exemptions to reduce real estate tax bills for certain property owners or land users. Some states offer real estate tax reductions to attract industries, for agricultural land and temporary reductions for rehabilitation of property.

Assessment. Real estate is valued, or assessed, for tax purposes by county or township assessors. The land is usually assessed separately from the building. **Assessments** are frequently a certain percentage of fair market value.

Property owners who claim that errors were made in determining the assessed value of their property may appeal the assessment, usually to a local board of appeal or board of review. Protests or appeals regarding tax assessments may ultimately be taken to court.

Equalization. In some jurisdictions, when it is necessary to correct general equalities in statewide tax assessments, uniformity may be achieved by use of an **equalization factor.** Such a factor may be provided for use in counties or districts where the assessments are to be raised or lowered. The assessed value of each property is multiplied by the equalization factor, and the tax rate is then applied to the equalized assessment. For example, the assessments in one county are determined to be 20 percent lower than the average assessments throughout the rest of the state. This underassessment can be corrected by decreeing the application of an equalization factor of 120 percent to each assessment in that county. Thus, a parcel of land assessed for tax purposes at $98,000 would be taxed on an equalized value of $117,600 ($98,000 × 1.20 = $117,600).

Tax rates. The process of arriving at a real estate tax rate begins with the *adoption of a budget* by each county, city, school board or other taxing district (see Figure 11.4). Each budget covers the financial requirements of the taxing body for the coming fiscal year, which may be the January to December calendar year or some other 12-month period designated by statute. The budget must include an estimate of all expenditures for the year and indicate the amount of income expected from all fees, revenue sharing and other sources. The net amount remaining to be raised from real estate taxes is then determined from these figures.

The next step is *appropriation,* the action taken by each taxing body that authorizes the expenditure of funds and provides for the sources of such monies. Appropriation generally involves the adoption of an ordinance or the passage of a law setting forth the specifics of the proposed taxation.

The amount to be raised from the general real estate tax is then imposed on property owners through a *tax levy,* the formal action taken to impose the tax, by a vote of the taxing district's governing body.

The *tax rate* for each individual taxing body is computed separately. To arrive at a tax rate, the total monies needed for the coming fiscal year are divided by the total assessments of all real estate located within the jurisdiction of the taxing body. For example, a taxing district's budget indicates that $300,000 must be raised from real estate tax revenues, and the assessment roll (assessor's record) of all taxable real estate within this district equals $10,000,000. The tax rate is computed thus:

$$\$300,000 \div \$10,000,000 = .03, \text{ or } 3\%$$

The tax rate may be expressed in a number of different ways. In many areas it is expressed in mills. A **mill** is *1/1,000 of a dollar, or $.001.* The tax rate computed in the foregoing example could be expressed as follows:

**Figure 11.4
Determining a Real
Estate Tax Rate**

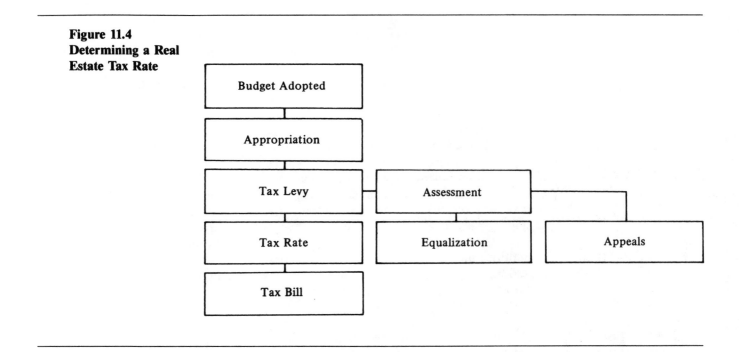

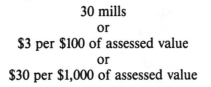

30 mills
or
$3 per $100 of assessed value
or
$30 per $1,000 of assessed value

Tax bills. A property owner's **tax bill** is computed by applying the tax rate to the assessed valuation of the property. For example, on a property assessed for tax purposes at $90,000 at a tax rate of three percent, or 30 mills, the tax will be $2,700 ($90,000 × .030 = $2,700). If an equalization factor is used, the computation on a property with an assessed value of $120,000 and a tax rate of four percent with an equalization factor of 120 percent would be as follows:

$$\$120,000 \times 1.20 = \$144,000; \$144,000 \times .040 = \$5,760 \text{ tax}$$

Generally, one tax bill that incorporates all real estate taxes levied by the various taxing districts is prepared for each property. In some areas, however, separate bills are prepared for select taxing bodies. Sometimes the real estate taxing bodies may operate on different budget years, so that the taxpayer receives separate bills for various taxes at different times during the year.

Due dates for payment of taxes are usually set by statute. In many areas, taxes are payable in two installments. Collection procedures vary: In some areas, taxes become due during the current tax year; in others, they are payable in arrears during the year after the taxes are levied; and in still others, a partial payment is due in the year of the tax, with the balance due the following year. Knowledge of local tax-payment schedules is especially important in computing the proration of current taxes when a property is sold.

Some states offer discounts to encourage prompt payment of real estate taxes. Penalties in the form of monthly interest charges are added to all taxes that are not paid when due. The due date is also called the *penalty date.*

Enforcement of tax liens. To be enforceable, real estate taxes must be valid, which means they must be: (1) properly levied, (2) used for a legal purpose and (3) applied equitably to all affected property. Tax liens are generally given priority over all other liens against a property. Real estate taxes that have remained delinquent for the period of time specified by state law can be collected by the tax-collecting officer through a tax foreclosure or a **tax sale.**

A 1947 statute provides that the individual counties may set up tax claim bureaus. Under this system, which most Pennsylvania counties have adopted, the names of real estate owners who have not paid their taxes after one year are turned over to the tax claim bureau. Such property may be sold after the second week in September of the following year. Once the property is sold, the owner usually does not have the right to redeem the interest, that is, buy back the real estate by settling all back taxes and other costs. Note, however, there are still some counties in which the county treasurer holds tax sales and a **redemption** period is granted. In addition, the cities of Pittsburgh and Scranton are governed by special acts regarding the sale of property to satisfy delinquent real estate taxes. Ask local authorities which system is used in your county.

Special Assessments (Improvement Taxes)

Special assessments are *special taxes levied on real estate that require property owners to pay for improvements that benefit the real estate they own.* These taxes are often levied to pay for such improvements as streets, sewers, street lighting, curbs and similar items, and are enforced in the same manner as general real estate taxes.

The authority to recommend or initiate the *specific improvement* is vested in either the property owners, who may petition for an improvement, or in a proper legislative authority, such as the city council or board of trustees, who may initiate the proposal for an improvement. Hearings are held and notices are given to the owners of the property affected.

After the preliminary legal steps have been taken, the government body authorized by statute to act in such cases adopts an *ordinance* that sets out the nature of the improvement, its cost and a description of the area to be assessed.

The proper authority spreads the assessment (called the *assessment roll*) over the various parcels of real estate that will benefit. The amount of the assessment for each parcel is usually determined by one of the following criteria: (1) estimated benefit each tract will receive by reason of the assessment and (2) front footage. Regardless of the basis used, the assessment will usually vary from parcel to parcel, as all will not benefit equally from the improvement.

After hearing the benefits and nature of improvements to be made, and after hearing any objections from members of the local community affected by the improvements, the local authority, usually a court of record, will either approve or reject the proposal. This is usually referred to as *confirming the assessment roll.*

After all of these steps have been taken, the assessment becomes a lien on the land assessed. When the improvement has been completed, a *warrant* is issued by the proper authority, often the clerk of the court that approved the roll. This warrant gives the local collector the authority to issue special assessment bills and begin collection.

In most states, an assessment becomes a *lien* following the confirmation of the roll. In Pennsylvania, if the assessment is determined by the front footage method, it becomes a lien from the date the lien is filed. If it is determined by the benefit method (described above), the assessment becomes a lien from the date the taxing authority determines its assessment of benefits. Special assessments are usually due and payable in equal annual installments over a period of five to ten years. Interest is also charged each property owner on the total amount of the assessment. The first installment generally becomes due during the year following confirmation. The bill will include yearly interest on the entire assessment. As subsequent installments are billed in following years, each bill will include a year's interest on the unpaid balance. Property owners usually have the right to prepay any or all installments and thereby stop the interest charges.

In Practice...   *Although real property taxes are deductible items for income-tax purposes, note that special assessment taxes are not. Annual interest charged in connection with special assessments is deductible, however.*

At the time of sale the agreement should disclose special assessments and responsibility for payment.

Liens Other than Taxes

In addition to real estate tax and special assessment liens, the following types of liens may be charged against real property either voluntarily or involuntarily: mortgage liens, mechanics' liens, judgments, estate and inheritance tax liens, liens for municipal utilities, surety bail bond liens, corporation franchise tax liens and Internal Revenue Service tax liens.

Mortgage Liens

A **mortgage lien** is a specific, voluntary lien on real estate given to a lender by a borrower as security for a mortgage loan. It becomes a lien on real property when the lender files or records the mortgage in the recorder of deeds office in the county where the property is located. Mortgage lenders generally require a first lien, referred to as a *first mortgage lien;* this means that (aside from real estate taxes) there are no other major liens against the property that would take priority over the mortgage lien. Mortgage and mortgage liens will be discussed in detail in Chapter 13, "Real Estate Financing."

Mechanics' Liens

The purpose of the **mechanic's lien** is to *give security to those who perform labor or furnish material in the improvement of real property.* The mechanic's lien right is based on the *enhancement of value theory.* The labor performed and material furnished have enhanced the value of the real estate. Therefore, the parties who performed the work or supplied materials are given a right of lien on the real estate on which they worked as security for the payment of their proper charges. A mechanic's lien is a specific, involuntary lien.

In order for a person to be entitled to a mechanic's lien, the work that was done must have been by contract (express or implied consent) with the owner or owner's authorized representative. Such a lien is relied on to cover situations in which the owner has not fully paid for the work or when the general contractor has been paid but has not paid the subcontractors or suppliers of materials.

Under the Pennsylvania Mechanic's Lien Law of 1963, a contractor or subcontractor can file a claim with the court of common pleas in the county in which the property is located within four months after the work is completed. (This requirement is subject to certain exceptions and requirements regarding notice to be served on the owner of the property.) If the claim is successful, the lien takes priority:

1. in the case of the erection or construction of an improvement, as of the date of the first "visible construction";

2. in the case of the alteration or repair of an improvement, as of the date the claim is filed.

A claimant must take steps to enforce a lien within two years of the date the claim is filed. Enforcement usually requires a court action to foreclose the lien through the sale of the real estate to produce money to pay the lien.

A property owner can avoid mechanic's lien problems by including a *waiver of liens* in the master contract. The purpose of the waiver is to insulate the title from the filing of liens by the **general contractor**. It is this person to whom all monies are paid. The general contractor, in turn, may hire **subcontractors** who actually furnish labor and materials. The general contractor is liable to them for payment. A waiver of liens in a master contract is insufficient protection against liens by subcontractors unless they receive notice. In Pennsylvania, notice is accomplished by filing a "stipulation against liens" in the prothonotary's office.

Another way to protect against mechanics' liens is the *release of liens.* This is signed by all who have delivered material or labor to the property after work is completed. However, this is not foolproof as there is no way to show that all subcontractors have signed it.

The possibility of unrecorded mechanics' liens (because they can be filed within four months after completion of the work) can cause problems for the purchaser of a property recently constructed, altered or repaired. The mortgage lender may require evidence that no work has been done or a release of liens as evidence that there are no lien claims. Because of the failings inherent in a release the lender may require *mechanic's lien insurance.* This accompanies a title insurance policy (discussed in Chapter 12, "Title Records").

If improvements have been ordered by a third party, such as a tenant, a property owner should execute a document called a *notice of nonresponsibility* to be relieved from possible mechanics' liens. By posting this notice in a conspicuous place on the property and recording a verified copy of it in the public record, the owner gives notice that he or she will not be responsible for the work done.

Judgments

A **judgment** is a *decree issued by a court.* When the decree provides for the awarding of money and sets forth the amount of money owed by the debtor to the creditor, the judgment is referred to as a *money judgment.*

A judgment becomes a *general, involuntary lien on both real and personal property* owned by the debtor. Usually, a lien covers only property located within the county in which the judgment is issued. Notices of the lien must be filed in other counties when a creditor wishes to extend the lien coverage. To enforce a judgment, the creditor must obtain a *writ of execution* directing the sheriff to seize and sell as much of the debtor's property as is necessary to pay the debt and the expenses of the sale. A judgment differs from a mortgage in that a *specific* parcel of real estate was not given as security at the time that the debtor-creditor relationship was created.

In Pennsylvania, a judgment does not become a lien against the personal property of a debtor until the creditor orders the sheriff to levy on the property and the levy is actually made.

In Pennsylvania, judgments obtained as a result of a *court suit* take priority from the time they are filed in the prothonotary's office. Amicable judgments, however, are those resulting from **confessions of judgments.** These are clauses included in notes, bonds and leases that authorize any attorney to confess a judgment against the borrower or lessee for nonpayment of the debt. Because of recent federal court rulings regarding confession of judgment clauses in notes, a practice has developed in some states, including Pennsylvania, where persons who sign a confession of judgment also sign an explanation of rights. This document explains the rights that are waived when a party agrees to a confession of judgment and is recorded along with the judgment. The judgment takes priority from the date of that recording.

Judgments are enforced through the issuance of an *execution* and the ultimate sale of the debtor's real or personal property by a sheriff. When the property is sold to satisfy the debt, the debtor should receive a *satisfaction of judgment,* unless there are insufficient funds from the sale, which should be filed with the *prothonotary,* so that the record will be cleared of the judgment.

Attachments. To prevent a debtor from conveying title to unsecured real estate (realty that is not mortgaged or is similarly unencumbered) while a court suit is being decided, a creditor may seek a writ of **attachment.** By this writ, the court retains custody of the property until the suit is concluded. In order to obtain an attachment, a creditor must first post with the court a surety bond or deposit sufficient to cover any possible loss or damage the debtor may sustain during the period the court has custody of the property, in case the judgment is not awarded to the creditor.

Lis pendens. A judgment or other decree affecting real estate is rendered at the conclusion of a lawsuit. Generally, there is a considerable time lag between the filing of a lawsuit and the rendering of a judgment. When any suit is filed that affects title to a specific parcel of real estate (such as a foreclosure suit), a notice known as a **lis pendens** (Latin for "litigation pending") is recorded, or registered. A lis pendens is not a lien, but rather a *notice of a possible future lien.* Recording of the lis pendens gives notice to all interested parties, such as prospective purchasers and lenders, and establishes a priority for the later lien, which is the date when the lis pendens was filed for record.

Estate and Inheritance Tax Liens

Federal **estate taxes** and state **inheritance taxes** (as well as the debts of deceased persons) are *general, involuntary liens* that encumber a deceased person's real and personal property. These are normally paid or cleared in probate court proceedings. Probate and issues of inheritance were discussed in Chapter 10, "Transfer of Title."

Liens for Municipal Utilities

Municipalities are generally given the right to a *specific, involuntary* **municipal utility lien** on the property of an owner who refuses to pay bills for water or any other municipal utility services.

Surety Bail Bond Lien

A real estate owner charged with a crime for which he or she must face trial may choose to put up real estate instead of cash as surety for bail. The execution and recording of such a **surety bail bond** creates a *specific, voluntary lien* against the owner's real estate. This lien is enforceable by the sheriff or other court officer if the accused person does not appear in court as required.

Corporation Franchise Tax Lien

State governments generally levy a **corporation franchise tax** on corporations as a condition of allowing them to do business in the state. Such a tax is a *general, involuntary* lien on all property, real and personal, owned by the corporation.

IRS Tax Lien

An **Internal Revenue Service (IRS) tax lien** results from a person's failure to pay any portion of federal IRS taxes, such as income and withholding taxes. A federal tax lien is a *general, involuntary lien* on all real and personal property held by the delinquent taxpayer.

Summary

Liens are claims, or charges, of creditors or tax officials against the real and personal property of a debtor. A lien is a type of encumbrance. All liens are encumbrances, but not all encumbrances are necessarily liens. Liens are either *general,* covering all real and personal property of a debtor-owner, or *specific,* covering only the specific parcel of real estate described in the mortgage, tax bill or building or repair contract or other document.

With the exception of real estate tax liens and mechanics' liens, the priority of liens generally is determined by the order in which they are filed in the prothonotary's office of the county in which the debtor's property is located.

Real estate taxes are levied annually by local taxing authorities. Tax liens are normally given priority over other liens. Payments are required before stated dates, after which penalties accrue. An owner may lose title to the property for nonpayment of taxes, because such tax-delinquent property can be sold at a tax sale. Some states allow a time period during which a defaulted owner can redeem the real estate from a tax sale.

Special assessments are levied to allocate the cost of improvements such as new sidewalks, curbs or paving to the real estate that benefits from them. Assessments are usually payable annually over a five- or ten-year period, together with interest due on the balance of the assessment.

Mortgage liens are voluntary, specific liens given to lenders to secure payment for mortgage loans.

Mechanics' liens protect general contractors, subcontractors and material suppliers whose work enhances the value of real estate.

A *judgment* is a court decree obtained by a creditor, usually for a money award from a debtor. The lien of a judgment can be enforced by issuance of a *writ of execution* and sale by the sheriff to pay the judgment amount and costs.

Attachment is a means of preventing a defendant from conveying real estate before completion of a suit in which a judgment is sought.

Lis pendens is a recorded notice of a lawsuit that is awaiting trial in court and may result in a judgment that will affect title to a parcel of real estate.

Federal estate taxes and *state inheritance taxes* are general liens against a deceased owner's property.

Liens for *water charges or other municipal utilities* and *surety bail bond liens* are specific liens, while *corporation franchise tax liens* are general liens against a corporation's assets.

Internal Revenue Service tax liens are general liens against the property of a person who is delinquent in payment of IRS taxes.

Questions

1. Which of the following best refers to the type of lien that affects all real and personal property of a debtor?
   a. specific lien
   b. voluntary lien
   c. involuntary lien
   d. general lien

2. General contractor Ralph Hammond was hired to build a room addition to Thom and Harriet Elkins' home. Hammond completed the work several weeks ago, but still has not been paid. Hammond is entitled to a mechanic's lien. Which of the following is correct concerning his lien?
   a. It is a general lien.
   b. It is a specific lien.
   c. Hammond must file a notice of his lien in the public records.
   d. b and c

3. In the above question regarding Ralph Hammond's mechanic's lien, the lien will take priority over later claims against the Elkins' property:
   a. as of the date the work is completed.
   b. as of the date the lien claim is filed.
   c. as of the date the work is begun.
   d. two years after the date the claim is filed.

4. *Priority of liens* refers to which of the following?
   a. the order in which a debtor assumes responsibility for payment of obligations
   b. the order in which liens will be paid if property is sold by court order to satisfy a debt
   c. the dates liens are filed for record; the lien with the earliest recording date will always take priority over other liens
   d. the fact that specific liens have greater priority than general liens

5. A lien on real estate made to secure payment for specific municipal improvements made to a parcel of real estate is which of the following?
   a. mechanic's lien
   b. special assessment
   c. ad valorem
   d. utility lien

6. When real estate is assessed for tax purposes:
   I. the homeowner usually may appeal the assessment.
   II. the homeowner must sign a confession of judgment.
   a. I only
   b. II only
   c. both I and II
   d. neither I nor II

7. Which of the following municipalities or agencies usually make levies for general real estate taxes?
   I. school districts
   II. counties
   a. I only
   b. II only
   c. both I and II
   d. neither I nor II

8. A specific parcel of real estate has a market value of $80,000 and is assessed for tax purposes at 25 percent of market value. The tax rate for the county in which the property is located is 30 mills. The tax bill will be:
   a. $500.
   b. $550.
   c. $600.
   d. $700.

   mil = 1/10 cent

9. Which of the following taxes is (are) used to distribute the cost of public services among real estate owners?
   a. personal property tax
   b. sales tax
   c. real property tax
   d. all of the above

10. A mechanic's lien claim arises when a general contractor has performed work or provided material to improve a parcel of real estate on the owner's order and the work has not been paid for. Such a contractor has a right to:
    a. tear out his or her work.
    b. record a notice of the lien.
    c. record a notice of the lien and file a court suit within the time required by state law.
    d. have personal property of the owner sold to satisfy the lien.

11. Which of the following is a lien on real estate?

    a. an easement running with the land
    b. an unpaid mortgage loan
    c. an encroachment
    d. a license

12. A mortgage lien and a judgment lien have which of the following characteristics in common?

    I. Both may involve a debtor-creditor relationship.
    II. Both are general liens.

    a. I only   c. both I and II
    b. II only   d. neither I nor II

13. Which of the following is classified as a general lien?

    a. mechanic's lien
    b. surety bail bond lien
    c. debts of a deceased person
    d. general real estate taxes

14. Which of the following liens would usually be given higher priority?

    a. a mortgage dated last year
    b. real estate tax
    c. a mechanic's lien for work started before the mortgage was made
    d. a judgment rendered yesterday

15. Which of the following steps is usually required *before* a special assessment becomes a lien against a specific parcel of real estate?

    a. an ordinance is passed
    b. the improvement is completed
    c. work on the improvement is begun
    d. a new tax year begins

16. Special assessment liens:

    a. take priority over mechanics' liens.
    b. are voluntary liens.
    c. are general liens.
    d. a and c

17. What is the annual real estate tax on a property that is valued at $135,000 and assessed for tax purposes at $47,250 with an equalization factor of 125 percent, when the tax rate is 25 mills?

    a. $1,417.50   c. $4,050.00
    b. $1,476.56   d. none of the above

18. Which of the following is a voluntary, specific lien?

    a. IRS tax lien   c. mortgage lien
    b. mechanic's lien   d. vendor's lien

19. A lis pendens:

    a. is filed to record a final judgment or decree in a lawsuit.
    b. serves as a notice of possible future liens during a lawsuit.
    c. establishes a priority for later liens.
    d. b and c

20. A judgment:

    a. is a general, involuntary lien on real and personal property.
    b. involves the giving of a specific parcel of real estate as security.
    c. covers property located within several counties.
    d. allows the creditor to issue and enforce a personal writ of execution.

12

Title Records

Key Terms
Abstract of title
Actual notice
Attorney's opinion of title
Bulk transfer
Certificate of title
Chain of title
Constructive notice
Evidence of title
Financing statement
Marketable title
Priority
Recorder of deeds
Recording
Security agreement
Subrogation
Suit to quiet title
Title insurance
Title search
Uniform Commercial Code

Overview
For the protection of real estate owners, taxing bodies, creditors and the general public, public records are maintained in every city, county, parish or borough in the United States. Such records help to establish official ownership, give notice of encumbrances and establish priority of liens. The placing of documents in the public record is known as **recording**. This chapter will discuss the necessity for recording and the various types of title evidence that may be determined by an examination of the public records.

Public Records and Recording

In all states, public records are maintained by designated officials as required by state laws. These include records maintained by the recorder of deeds, the prothonotary, county clerk, county treasurer, city clerk and clerks of various courts of record. Records involving titles, taxes, special assessments, ordinances and zoning and building records also fall into this category. In Pennsylvania, most records affecting title to a parcel of real estate are kept in the office of the **recorder of deeds.**

In addition to the statute of frauds, which requires that instruments affecting interests in real estate must be in writing to be enforceable, Pennsylvania law also requires owners or parties interested in real estate to record, or file, in the public records all documents affecting their interest in real estate in order to give *legal, public and constructive notice* to the world of their interest. These statutory enactments are commonly referred to as *recording acts.*

Necessity for Recording

An individual planning to purchase a fee simple estate to a parcel of real estate wants to be sure that the seller will be able to convey a good title to the property. The question of *kind and condition* of title has been inquired into many times in the past—as often as the property has changed hands. As long as taxes are paid and liens do not become delinquent, it is expected that a fee simple title will remain a marketable title (discussed later in this chapter).

Pennsylvania law provides that a *deed or mortgage may not be effective so far as later purchasers* are concerned unless such documents have been *recorded.* Thus the condition of the title should be apparent from a search of such public records. However, an unrecorded deed or mortgage should not be considered void.

Recording Acts

Under the recording acts, in order to give constructive notice (discussed in the next section of this chapter) all instruments in writing affecting any estate, right, title or interest in land *must be recorded in the county where the land is located.* Everyone interested in the title to a parcel of property can thus obtain notice of the various interests of all other parties. From a practical point of view the recording acts give legal priority to those interests that are recorded first.

In Pennsylvania, in order to be *eligible for recording,* a document must be in writing, signed by the person executing it and acknowledged. Individuals who cannot sign by placing their signature on a document may sign "by mark," complying with statutory requirements.

Notice

The courts charge a prospective real estate buyer or mortgagee (lender) with the responsibility of inspecting the property and searching the public records to ascertain the interests, if any, of other parties. **Constructive notice** is a presumption of law that charges a buyer with knowledge that could be obtained from such an inspection and search. The information is available; therefore the buyer or lender is responsible for learning it. Failure to do so is no defense for not knowing of a right or interest, for the recording of that interest in the public records or the

Figure 12.1
Notice

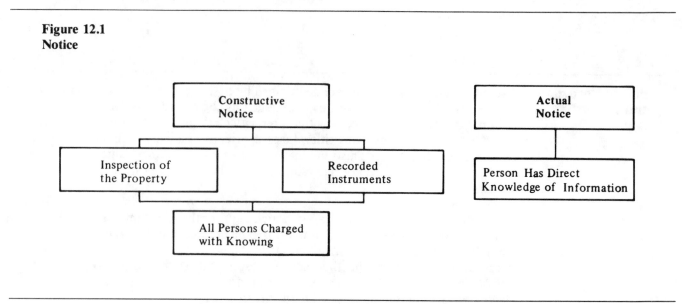

possession of the real estate gives notice to the world, or constructive notice, of an individual's rights in the property.

Constructive notice, or what a buyer is charged with knowing, is distinguished from **actual notice,** or what the person actually knows (see Figure 12.1). An individual who has searched the public records and inspected the property has actual notice, *direct knowledge*, of the information learned. If it can be proved an individual has *actual knowledge* of information concerning a parcel of real estate, he or she cannot rely on a lack of *constructive notice*, such as an unrecorded deed or an owner who is not in possession. For example, Bill Wilson mortgaged his land to Jane Fry, who failed to record the mortgage. Wilson later mortgaged the same land to Edgar Morse, who *knew* of the existence of the earlier mortgage. In this case, Morse is charged with actual knowledge of the existing mortgage, so his mortgage is a second mortgage, Fry's mortgage having a prior claim on the property.

In Practice...

Frequently, lenders prohibit borrowing any portion of the down payment for a purchase of real estate as a condition of granting the mortgage. The existence of a prior claim on the property is a concern to the lender who intended to be first recorded lien.

Real estate taxes and special assessments are direct liens on specific parcels of real estate and need not be recorded in the recorder's office. Other liens, such as inheritance taxes and franchise taxes, are placed by statutory authority against all real estate owned either by a decedent at the time of death or by a corporation at the time the franchise tax became a lien; these liens are not recorded either. Notice of these liens must be detected from sources other than the recorder's office. Evidence of the payment of real estate taxes, special assessments, municipal utilities and other taxes is gathered from paid tax receipts and letters from municipalities to provide information about the likelihood of a title being encumbered by these "silent" liens.

Priorities. Many complicated situations can arise that affect the *priority* of rights in a parcel of real estate. For example, a purchaser may receive a deed and take possession of the property but not record the deed. By taking possession, a purchaser gives constructive notice of an interest in the land. Such a purchaser's rights would be considered superior to the rights of a subsequent purchaser who acquired a deed from the original owner at a later date and recorded the deed but did not inspect the property to determine who was in possession. How the courts rule in any situation depends on the specific facts of the case. They are strictly legal questions that should be referred by the parties to their lawyers.

Chain of Title

The **chain of title** is the record of ownership of the property. An **abstract of title** is a condensed history of all the instruments affecting a particular parcel of land, depending on the length of the title search. In the United States, chains of title in colonial states frequently date back to a grant from the king of England. In those states admitted to the Union after the formation of the United States, the deeds of conveyance in the chain of title generally stem from the *patent* issued by the U. S. government.

Through the chain of title, the ownership of the property can be traced backward from its present owner to its source. If there is a period for which ownership is unaccounted, there is a *gap* in the chain. In such cases, it is usually necessary to establish ownership by a court action called a **suit to quiet title**. The court's judgment, following a proceeding in which all possible claimants are allowed to present evidence, can then be filed. A suit to quiet title may be required when, for instance, a grantor acquired title under one name and conveyed title under a different name. Title acquired by adverse possession can also be established of record by a quiet title action.

Title Search and Abstract of Title

The examination undertaken by an abstractor or title insurance company to determine what, if any, defects there are in a property's chain of title is called a **title search,** beginning with the present owner and tracing to its origin. Depending on local custom, the search may trace records back 40–60 years. After examining the title records in the recorder of deeds and prothonotary's offices, the abstractor searches the records in other governmental offices such as the tax offices and assessment offices (for sewer or special assessment liens that may be in effect).

An abstract of title is a brief history (in abstract, or brief, form) of the instruments appearing in the county record that affect title to the parcel in question. After the abstractor has completed the abstract it is submitted to an attorney, who *examines the entire abstract.* This means that the lawyer must examine each section from the origin of that title to evaluate all the facts and material in order to prepare a written report on the condition of the ownership; this report is called an **attorney's opinion of title.**

Marketable Title

Under the terms of the usual real estate sales contract, the seller is required to deliver **marketable title** to the buyer at the closing. In order for title to be marketable it must: (1) be free from any significant liens and encumbrances; (2) disclose no serious defects and not be dependent on doubtful questions of law or fact to prove its validity; (3) not expose a purchaser to the hazard of litigation or threaten the quiet enjoyment of the property; and (4) convince a reasonably well-informed and prudent person, acting upon business principles and willful knowledge of the facts and their legal significance, that he or she could, in turn, sell or mortgage the property at a fair market value.

Although an unmarketable title (one that does not meet these requirements) does not mean that the property cannot be transferred under any circumstances, it does mean that there are *certain defects in the title that may limit or restrict its ownership.* A buyer cannot be forced to accept a conveyance that is materially different from the one bargained for in the sales contract; the buyer cannot be forced to buy a lawsuit. Note that questions of marketable title must be raised by a buyer (or the buyer's broker or attorney) prior to acceptance of the deed. Once a buyer has accepted a deed with unmarketable title, the only available legal recourse is to sue the seller under the covenants of warranty (if any) contained in the deed.

In Practice...   *A title search is not normally ordered until major contingencies in the sales contract, such as financing, have been cleared (for example, after a loan commitment has been secured from a lender). Before a lender will forward money on a loan secured by real estate, it will generally order a title search at the expense of a borrower to assure itself that there are no liens superior in priority to its mortgage on the property.*

In addition, in some states a preliminary title report is ordered upon acceptance of an offer to purchase, and copies are given to the buyers, agents, and sellers. In fact, the entire contract may depend upon the buyers' written approval of this document within a given number of days after receiving it. Sellers usually are given a copy first, to ensure that the correct property has been researched.

Evidence of Title   There are two forms of title evidence in common use in Pennsylvania: certificate of title and title insurance.

Sometimes the question is raised as to whether a recorded warranty deed or other form of conveyance is **evidence of title**. A deed is not considered sufficient evidence of title. Although it conveys the interest of the grantor, even a warranty deed contains no proof of the kind or condition of the grantor's title. The only effective proof must be one of the evidences of title, based upon an adequate search of the public records to *ascertain the ownership interests and condition of the title.*

Certificate of Title   In some Pennsylvania localities, a **certificate of title** *prepared by an attorney* is used as title evidence. The attorney examines the public records, prepares an abstract and issues a certificate of title that expresses an opinion of the status of the title. The certificate will state the title owner and give the details of all liens and encumbrances against the title. It is an opinion of the validity of the grantor's or mortgagor's title and the existence of liens and encumbrances. However, it is not a title insurance policy and does not carry the full protection of such a policy.

In many ways the use of a certificate of title is imperfect and open to objection. For example, it is difficult to detect forged deeds or other documents or false statements, including incorrect marital status and transfers involving incompetent parties or minors. An honest mistake could be made against which the owner of

Table 12.1 Owner's Title Insurance Policy	Standard Coverage	Extended Coverage	Not Covered by Either Policy
	1. Defects found in public records 2. Forged documents 3. Incompetent grantors 4. Incorrect marital statements 5. Improperly delivered deeds	Standard coverage plus defects discoverable through: 1. Property inspection 2. Inquiries of persons in possession 3. Examination of survey 4. Unrecorded liens not known of by policy-holder	1. Defects and liens listed in policy 2. Unrecorded defects 3. Rights of parties in possession 4. Questions of survey

real estate has no recourse. To provide for protection against this type of problem, title insurance became available.

Title Insurance

A **title insurance** policy is a contract by which a title insurance company agrees, subject to the terms of its policy, to indemnify (that is, to compensate or reimburse) the insured (the owner, mortgagee or other interest holder) against any losses sustained as a result of defects in the title other than those exceptions listed in the policy. The title company agrees to defend, at its own expense, any lawsuit attacking the title if the lawsuit is based on a defect in title against which the policy insures. Title insurance is the best defense of title and should be considered by all purchasers.

A property owner seeking to obtain a title insurance policy as evidence of ownership makes an application to the title insurance company and agrees to pay a fee; the title company examines the title records and agrees to insure against certain undiscovered defects. Exactly which defects the title company will insure against depends on the type of policy it issues (see Table 12.1). A *standard coverage* policy usually insures against defects that may be found in the public records plus such items as forged documents, documents of incompetent grantors, incorrect marital statements and improperly delivered deeds. *Extended coverage* provided by an *American Land Title Association* policy generally includes all the protection of a standard policy plus additional protection to cover risks that may be discovered only through inspection of the property, inquiries of persons in actual possession of the land or examination of an accurate survey. The company does not agree to insure against any defects in or liens against the title that are found by the title examination and listed in the policy.

Upon completion of the examination, the title company usually issues a report of title, or a commitment to issue a title policy. This describes the policy that will be issued and includes the following: (1) the name of the insured party, (2) the legal description of the real estate, (3) the estate or interest covered, (4) a schedule of all exceptions, consisting of encumbrances and defects found in the public records and (5) conditions and stipulations under which the policy is issued. An *owner's policy will usually exclude coverage* against the following exceptions: unrecorded documents, unrecorded defects of which the policyholder has knowledge, rights of parties in possession and questions of survey. Under the contract, the title insurance company promises to defend the title at its own expense as well as to pay any claims against the property if the title proves to be defective. This is subject, of course, to the conditions and stipulations of the policy itself.

The consideration for the policy (the premium) is paid once for the life of the policy. The maximum loss for which the company may be liable cannot exceed the face amount of the policy (unless the amount of coverage has been extended by use of what is called an *inflation rider*). When a title company makes a payment to settle a claim covered by a policy, the company acquires by the right of **subrogation** all the remedies and rights of the insured party against anyone responsible for the settled claim.

Title companies issue various forms of title insurance policies, the most common of which are the *owner's* title insurance policy, the *mortgage* title insurance policy, the *leasehold* title insurance policy and the *certificate of sale* title insurance policy. As the names indicate, each of these policies is issued to insure specific interests. For example, a mortgage title insurance policy insures a mortgage company or lender that it has a valid first lien against the property. A leasehold title insurance policy insures a lessee that he or she has a valid lease. A certificate of sale policy is issued to a purchaser in a court sale and insures the purchaser's interest in property sold under a court order.

Uniform Commercial Code	The **Uniform Commercial Code** (UCC) is a codification of commercial law that has been adopted, wholly or in part, in all states. While this code generally does not apply directly to real estate, it has replaced state laws relating to chattel mortgages, conditional sales agreements and liens on chattels, crops or items that are to become fixtures. In many areas, UCC filings have replaced chattel mortgages as financing instruments for personal property.

To create a security interest in a chattel, including chattels that will become fixtures, Article 9 of the UCC requires the use of a **security agreement,** which must contain a complete description of the items against which the lien applies. A short notice of this agreement, called a **financing statement** (which includes the legal description of the real estate involved), must be filed in the recorder's office where mortgages are recorded. The recording of the financing statement constitutes notice to subsequent purchasers and mortgagees of the security interest in chattels and fixtures on the real estate. Many mortgagees require the signing and recording of a financing statement when the mortgaged premises include chattels or readily removable fixtures (washers, dryers and the like) as part of the security for the mortgage debt. If the financing statement has been properly recorded, upon the borrower's default the creditor can repossess the chattels and remove them from the property.

Article 6 of the UCC covers **bulk transfers,** which are defined as the sale of the major part of the materials, supplies, merchandise or other inventory of an enterprise *not* made in the ordinary course of the transferor's business. The purpose of this article is to outlaw the fraud perpetrated when a business person who is in debt sells all stock in trade (personal property) and disappears without having paid his or her creditors. Under Article 6, a bulk sale does not give the purchaser of such goods a clear title unless the purchaser complies with the article's requirements, which include giving notice of the sale to the seller's creditors. Some sales of business property involve the sale of the business and all of the owner's stock in trade, which may constitute a bulk sale.

Summary   The purpose of the recording acts is to give legal, public and *constructive notice* to the world of parties' interests in real estate. The recording provisions have been adopted to create system and order in the transfer of real estate. Without them, it would be virtually impossible to transfer real estate from one party to another. The interests and rights of the various parties in a particular parcel of land must be recorded so that such rights will be legally effective against third parties who do not have knowledge or notice of the rights.

Possession of real estate is generally interpreted as notice of the rights of the person in possession. *Actual notice* is knowledge acquired directly and personally.

There are two forms of *title evidence* commonly in use throughout Pennsylvania: (1) certificate of title and (2) owner's title insurance policy.

A deed of conveyance is evidence that a grantor has conveyed his or her interest in land, but it is not evidence of the kind or condition of the title. The purpose of a deed is to transfer a grantor's interest in real estate to a grantee. It does not *prove* that the grantor has any interest at all, even if he or she conveys the interest by means of a warranty deed that carries with it the implied covenants of warranty.

Each of the forms of title evidence bears a date and is evidence up to and including that date. All forms of title evidence show the previous actions that affect the title. Each must be *later dated,* or continued or reissued, to cover a more recent date.

Title evidence shows whether or not a seller is conveying *marketable title.* Marketable title is generally one that is so free from significant defects that the purchaser can be assured against having to defend the title.

Under the Uniform Commercial Code (UCC), security interests in chattels must be recorded using a *security agreement* and *financing statement.* The recording of a financing statement gives notice to purchasers and mortgagees of the security interests in chattels and fixtures on the specific parcel of real estate.

Questions

1. Jim Anderson bought Ward Cleaver's home and Cleaver delivered his deed to Anderson. Because it was a general warranty deed, Anderson can assume which of the following?

   I. He has evidence of title.
   II. There are no outstanding mortgages or liens on the property.

   a. I only   c. both I and II
   b. II only   d. neither I nor II

2. An owner's title insurance policy with standard coverage generally covers all but which of the following?

   a. forged documents
   b. incorrect marital statements
   c. rights of parties in possession
   d. incompetent grantors

3. Actual notice refers to:

   a. the facts a person may ascertain by examining the public records.
   b. what a person has actual knowledge of.
   c. what could be found by a property inspection.
   d. all of the above

4. Phil Simpson bought Larry Fine's house, received a deed, moved into the residence, but neglected to record the document. One week later, Fine died, and his heirs in another city conveyed title to Melvin Howard, who knew of the previous conveyance but recorded the deed. Who owns the property?

   a. Phil Simpson
   b. Melvin Howard
   c. Larry Fine's heirs
   d. both Simpson and Howard

5. Marketable title refers to:

   a. a property that can command a fair market value.
   b. a property that is free from significant title defects.
   c. the title being sold.
   d. a and b

6. Acceptable title evidence in Pennsylvania includes:

   I. certificate of title.
   II. an attorney's opinion.

   a. I only   c. both I and II
   b. II only   d. neither I nor II

7. A purchaser went to the county building to check the recorder's records. She found that the seller was the grantee in the last recorded deed and that no mortgage was on record against the property. Thus, the purchaser may assume which of the following?

   a. All taxes are paid and no judgments are outstanding.
   b. The seller has good title.
   c. The seller did not mortgage the property.
   d. all of the above

8. When a title insurance policy is being issued, the public records are searched and the title company's record of title is continued to date. When the title examination is completed, the title company notifies the parties in writing of the condition of the title. This notification is referred to as:

   a. a chain of title.
   b. a report of title or commitment for title insurance.
   c. a certificate of title.
   d. an abstract.

9. In order to be eligible for recording in Pennsylvania, a document must be:

   I. signed and acknowledged.
   II. in writing.

   a. I only   c. both I and II
   b. II only   d. neither I nor II

10. In Pennsylvania, a certificate of title:

    I. is prepared by an attorney.
    II. may not reveal forged deeds or incorrect marital status.

    a. I only   c. both I and II
    b. II only   d. neither I nor II

11. A purchaser of real estate is charged with knowledge of all recorded documents, so he or she must have current title evidence to indicate the rights and interests revealed by public records. The purchaser is also charged with the responsibility to:

I. make improvements on the property.
II. learn the rights of the parties in possession.

a. I only
b. II only
c. both I and II
d. neither I nor II

12. Which *one* of the following statements *best* explains why instruments affecting real estate are recorded with the recorder of deeds of the county where the property is located?

a. Recording gives constructive notice to the world of the rights and interests in a particular parcel of real estate.
b. The law requires that such instruments be recorded.
c. The instruments must be recorded to comply with the terms of the statute of frauds.
d. Recording proves the execution of the instrument.

13. When a claim is settled by a title insurance company, the company acquires all rights and claims of the insured against any other person who is responsible for the loss. This is called:

a. escrow.
b. abstract of title.
c. subordination.
d. subrogation.

14. The documents referred to as title evidence include:

a. title insurance.
b. warranty deeds.
c. security agreements.
d. all of the above

15. Evidence of the kind of estate and all liens against an interest in a parcel of real estate can usually be proved by:

a. a recorded deed.
b. a court suit for specific performance.
c. one of the two evidences of title.
d. a foreclosure suit.

16. Written instruments affecting real estate should be recorded:

a. in the county where the real estate is located.
b. to give actual notice of the owner's interest in the property.
c. to give constructive notice of the owner's interest in the property.
d. a and c

17. A title insurance policy usually includes:

I. a legal description of the insured parcel of real estate.
II. the exceptions that are not covered by the policy.

a. I only
b. II only
c. both I and II
d. neither I nor II

18. To give notice of a security interest in personal property items, a lienholder must record which of the following?

a. security agreement
b. financing statement
c. bulk transfer
d. quitclaim deed

19. *Chain of title* refers to which of the following?

a. a summary or history of all instruments and legal proceedings affecting a specific parcel of land
b. a series of links measuring 7.92 inches each
c. an instrument or document that protects the insured parties (subject to specific exceptions) against defects in the examination of the record and hidden risks such as forgeries, undisclosed heirs, errors in the public records, and so forth
d. the succession of conveyances from some starting point whereby the present owner derives his or her title

20. The date and time a document was recorded establish which of the following?

    a. priority
    b. chain of title
    c. subrogation
    d. marketable title

21. The person who prepares an abstract of title for a parcel of real estate:

    a. writes a brief history of the title after inspecting the county records for documents affecting the title.
    b. insures the condition of the title.
    c. inspects the property.
    d. all of the above

13

Real Estate Financing

Key Terms

Acceleration clause
Alienation clause
Amortized loan
Deed in lieu of foreclosure
Defeasance clause
Deficiency judgment
Discount rate
Fannie Mae (FNMA)
Foreclosure
Freddie Mac (FHLMC)
Ginnie Mae (GNMA)
Hypothecation
Interest
Lien theory
Loan fee
Mortgage

Mortgagor/Mortgagee
Negotiable instrument
Note (Bond)
Points
Prepayment penalty
Primary mortgage market
Right of redemption
Satisfaction
Secondary mortgage market
Straight (term) loan
Title theory
Trust deed
Usury
Warehousing agency

Overview

Since almost every real estate transaction involves some type of financing, an understanding of real estate financing is of prime importance to the real estate licensee. Usually the buyer finances the major portion of the purchase price by securing a loan and pledging the real property involved as security (collateral) for the loan. This chapter will discuss the types of financing instruments used, as well as the sources of mortgage money and the role of the federal government in real estate financing.

Mortgage Theory

The earliest form of lending using real estate as collateral was the mortgage used in England under Anglo-Saxon law. A borrower who needed to finance the purchase of land (the **mortgagor)** was forced to convey title to the property to the lender (the **mortgagee)**, to ensure payment of the debt. If the obligation was not paid, the mortgagor automatically forfeited the land to the creditor, who was already the legal owner of the property.

Through the years, English courts began to acknowledge that a mortgage was only a *security device* and the mortgagor was the true owner of the mortgaged real estate. Under this concept, real estate was merely given as *security* for the payment of a debt, which was represented by a *note*.

United States Mortgage Law

Upon gaining independence from England, the original 13 colonies adopted the English laws as their own basic body of law. From their inception, American courts of equity considered a mortgage as a voluntary lien on real estate given to secure the payment of a debt or the performance of an obligation.

Even so, some of the states recognized a lender as the owner of mortgaged land. This ownership is defeated upon full payment of the debt. These states are called **title theory** states. Under title theory, a mortgagee has the right to possession of and rents from the mortgaged property upon default by the mortgagor.

Those states that interpret a mortgage purely as a lien on real property are called **lien theory** states. In such states, if a mortgagor defaults, the lender is required to foreclose the lien (generally through a court action), offer the property for sale and apply the funds received from the sale to reduce or extinguish the obligation. As protection to the borrower, these states generally allow a statutory redemption period during which a defaulted mortgagor can redeem the property. Failure to redeem within this time period will result in the borrower's loss of the property.

Today, a number of states, including Pennsylvania, have modified the strict interpretation of title and lien theories, known as *intermediary* theories. Pennsylvania, historically, is a title theory state but has become a hybrid of philosophy. Title theory in Pennsylvania does not mean that the property owner automatically forfeits the real estate upon default of payment. The borrower is entitled to "notice of intention to foreclose" prior to the lender filing suit and proceeding with foreclosure (discussed later in this chapter).

Regardless of whether a state follows the title or lien theory of mortgages, the security interest that the mortgagee has in the real estate is legally considered *personal property*. This interest can be transferred *only* with a transfer of the debt that the mortgage secures. In reality, *the differences between the rights of the parties to a mortgage loan in a lien theory state and a title theory state are more technical than actual.*

Security and Debt   Generally, any interest in real estate that may be sold may be pledged as security for a debt. The basic principle of the property law, that a person cannot convey greater rights in property than he or she actually has, applies equally to the right to mortgage. So the owner of a fee simple estate can mortgage the fee, and the owner of a leasehold or subleasehold can mortgage that leasehold interest. For example, a large retail corporation renting space in a shopping center may mortgage its leasehold interest in order to finance some remodeling work.

As discussed in Chapter 7, "How Ownership Is Held," the owner of a cooperative interest holds a personal property interest, which is becoming more acceptable to lenders as collateral. The owner of a condominium unit can mortgage the fee interest in the condominium apartment.

Mortgage Loan Instruments   There are two parts to a *mortgage loan*—the debt itself and the security for the debt. When a property is to be mortgaged, the owner must execute, or sign, two separate instruments:

1. The **note (bond),** or *financing instrument,* is the personal promise or general obligation of the debtor. It is an agreement to repay a debt according to agreed upon terms. The note exposes all assets to the claim by creditors. The mortgagor executes one or more promissory notes to total the amount of the debt.

2. The **mortgage,** or *security instrument,* is the document that creates the lien on the property. The mortgage exposes the real estate to claim by the creditor and is the document on which the lender would sue for foreclosure.

Hypothecation is the term used to describe the pledging of property as security for payment of a loan. A pledge of security—a mortgage—cannot be legally effective unless there is a debt to secure. *Both note and mortgage must be excuted in order to create an enforceable mortgage loan.*

Trust deeds. In some areas of the country, and in certain situations, lenders prefer to use a three-party instrument known as a **trust deed,** or *deed of trust,* rather than a mortgage document. In Pennsylvania, however, they are rarely used. A trust deed conveys the real estate as security for the loan to a third party, called the *trustee.* The trustee then holds title on behalf of the lender, known as the *beneficiary,* who is the legal owner and holder of the note. The wording of the conveyance sets forth actions that the trustee may take if the borrower, usually known as the *trustor,* defaults under any of the trust deed terms. (See Figure 13.1 for a comparison of mortgages and trust deeds.) In states where trust deeds are generally preferred, foreclosure procedures for defaulted trust deeds are usually simpler and faster than those for mortgage loans.

Provisions of the Note   In general, the promissory note (or notes) executed by a borrower (known as the *maker* or *payor*) states the amount of the debt, the time and method of payment and the rate of interest. If the note is used with a mortgage, it names the mortgagee as the payee; if it is used with a trust deed, the note may be made payable to the bearer. It may also refer to or repeat several of the clauses that appear in the mortgage document. The note, like the mortgage, should be signed by all

**Figure 13.1
Mortgage and Trust
Deed**

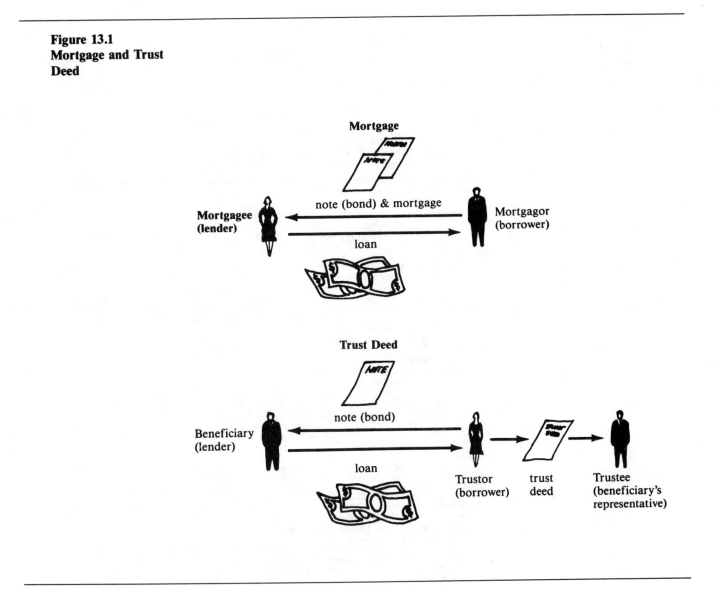

parties who have an interest in the property. Figure 13.2 is an example of a note commonly used with a mortgage.

A note is a written promise to pay a specific sum of money. A note is said to be a **negotiable instrument** if it contains language permitting its holder, the *payee,* to transfer the right to receive payment to a third party. This may be accomplished by signing the instrument over to the third party or, in some cases, by merely delivering the instrument to that person. Other examples of negotiable instruments include checks and bank drafts.

To be negotiable, or freely transferable, an instrument must meet certain requirements of Article 3 of the Uniform Commercial Code. The instrument must be in writing, made by one person to another and signed by the maker. It must contain an unconditional promise to pay a sum of money on demand or at a set date in the future. In addition, the instrument must be payable to the order of a person

Figure 13.2
Note (Used with
Mortgage)

NOTE

...., 19.........   ...., ...
                                                                              [City]   [State]

....
                                                  [Property Address]

1. BORROWER'S PROMISE TO PAY

In return for a loan that I have received, I promise to pay U.S. $... (this amount is called
"principal"), plus interest, to the order of the Lender. The Lender is ....
.... I understand
that the Lender may transfer this Note. The Lender or anyone who takes this Note by transfer and who is entitled to
receive payments under this Note is called the "Note Holder."

2. INTEREST

Interest will be charged on unpaid principal until the full amount of principal has been paid. I will pay interest at a
yearly rate of ....%.

The interest rate required by this Section 2 is the rate I will pay both before and after any default described in
Section 6(B) of this Note.

3. PAYMENTS

(A) Time and Place of Payments

I will pay principal and interest by making payments every month.

I will make my monthly payments on the .... day of each month beginning on ....,
19......... I will make these payments every month until I have paid all of the principal and interest and any other charges
described below that I may owe under this Note. My monthly payments will be applied to interest before principal. If, on
...., ..., I still owe amounts under this Note, I will pay those amounts in full on that date,
which is called the "maturity date."

I will make my monthly payments at ....
.... or at a different place if required by the Note Holder.

(B) Amount of Monthly Payments

My monthly payment will be in the amount of U.S. $...

4. BORROWER'S RIGHT TO PREPAY

I have the right to make payments of principal at any time before they are due. A payment of principal only is
known as a "prepayment." When I make a prepayment, I will tell the Note Holder in writing that I am doing so.

I may make a full prepayment or partial prepayments without paying any prepayment charge. The Note Holder
will use all of my prepayments to reduce the amount of principal that I owe under this Note. If I make a partial
prepayment, there will be no changes in the due date or in the amount of my monthly payment unless the Note Holder
agrees in writing to those changes.

5. LOAN CHARGES

If a law, which applies to this loan and which sets maximum loan charges, is finally interpreted so that the interest
or other loan charges collected or to be collected in connection with this loan exceed the permitted limits, then: (i) any
such loan charge shall be reduced by the amount necessary to reduce the charge to the permitted limit; and (ii) any sums
already collected from me which exceeded permitted limits will be refunded to me. The Note Holder may choose to make
this refund by reducing the principal I owe under this Note or by making a direct payment to me. If a refund reduces
principal, the reduction will be treated as a partial prepayment.

6. BORROWER'S FAILURE TO PAY AS REQUIRED

(A) Late Charge for Overdue Payments

If the Note Holder has not received the full amount of any monthly payment by the end of .... calendar
days after the date it is due, I will pay a late charge to the Note Holder. The amount of the charge will be ....% of my
overdue payment of principal and interest. I will pay this late charge promptly but only once on each late payment.

(B) Default

If I do not pay the full amount of each monthly payment on the date it is due, I will be in default.

(C) Notice of Default

If I am in default, the Note Holder may send me a written notice telling me that if I do not pay the overdue amount
by a certain date, the Note Holder may require me to pay immediately the full amount of principal which has not been paid
and all the interest that I owe on that amount. That date must be at least 30 days after the date on which the notice is
delivered or mailed to me.

(D) No Waiver By Note Holder

Even if, at a time when I am in default, the Note Holder does not require me to pay immediately in full as described
above, the Note Holder will still have the right to do so if I am in default at a later time.

(E) Payment of Note Holder's Costs and Expenses

If the Note Holder has required me to pay immediately in full as described above, the Note Holder will have the
right to be paid back by me for all of its costs and expenses in enforcing this Note to the extent not prohibited by applicable
law. Those expenses include, for example, reasonable attorneys' fees.

7. GIVING OF NOTICES

Unless applicable law requires a different method, any notice that must be given to me under this Note will be given
by delivering it or by mailing it by first class mail to me at the Property Address above or at a different address if I give the
Note Holder a notice of my different address.

Any notice that must be given to the Note Holder under this Note will be given by mailing it by first class mail to the
Note Holder at the address stated in Section 3(A) above or at a different address if I am given a notice of that different
address.

MULTISTATE FIXED RATE NOTE—Single Family—**FNMA/FHLMC UNIFORM INSTRUMENT**   Form 3200 12/83

**Figure 13.2
(cont.)**

8. OBLIGATIONS OF PERSONS UNDER THIS NOTE

If more than one person signs this Note, each person is fully and personally obligated to keep all of the promises made in this Note, including the promise to pay the full amount owed. Any person who is a guarantor, surety or endorser of this Note is also obligated to do these things. Any person who takes over these obligations, including the obligations of a guarantor. surety or endorser of this Note, is also obligated to keep all of the promises made in this Note. The Note Holder may enforce its rights under this Note against each person individually or against all of us together. This means that any one of us may be required to pay all of the amounts owed under this Note.

9. WAIVERS

I and any other person who has obligations under this Note waive the rights of presentment and notice of dishonor. "Presentment" means the right to require the Note Holder to demand payment of amounts due. "Notice of dishonor" means the right to require the Note Holder to give notice to other persons that amounts due have not been paid.

10. UNIFORM SECURED NOTE

This Note is a uniform instrument with limited variations in some jurisdictions. In addition to the protections given to the Note Holder under this Note, a Mortgage, Deed of Trust or Security Deed (the "Security Instrument"), dated the same date as this Note, protects the Note Holder from possible losses which might result if I do not keep the promises which I make in this Note. That Security Instrument describes how and under what conditions I may be required to make immediate payment in full of all amounts I owe under this Note. Some of those conditions are described as follows:

Transfer of the Property or a Beneficial Interest in Borrower. If all or any part of the Property or any interest in it is sold or transferred (or if a beneficial interest in Borrower is sold or transferred and Borrower is not a natural person) without Lender's prior written consent, Lender may, at its option, require immediate payment in full of all sums secured by this Security Instrument. However, this option shall not be exercised by Lender if exercise is prohibited by federal law as of the date of this Security Instrument.

If Lender exercises this option, Lender shall give Borrower notice of acceleration. The notice shall provide a period of not less than 30 days from the date the notice is delivered or mailed within which Borrower must pay all sums secured by this Security Instrument. If Borrower fails to pay these sums prior to the expiration of this period, Lender may invoke any remedies permitted by this Security Instrument without further notice or demand on Borrower.

WITNESS THE HAND(S) AND SEAL(S) OF THE UNDERSIGNED.

....(Seal)
-Borrower

....(Seal)
-Borrower

....(Seal)
-Borrower

[Sign Original Only]

specifically named or to *the bearer* (whoever has possession of the note). Instruments that are payable *to order* must be transferred by endorsement; those payable *to bearer* may be transferred by delivery.

Interest

A charge for the use of money is called **interest**. Interest may be due either at the end of each payment period (known as payment *in arrears*) or at the beginning of each payment period (payment *in advance*). Whether interest is charged in arrears or in advance is specified in the note. In practice, the distinction becomes important if the property is sold before the debt is repaid in full, as will become evident in Chapter 21, "Closing the Real Estate Transaction."

Usury. The maximum rate of interest that may be charged on loans may be set by state law (with the exception we will note later in this discussion). Charging interest in excess of this rate is called **usury**, and lenders are penalized for making usurious loans. In some states, a lender who makes a usurious loan will be permitted to collect the borrowed money, but only at the legal rate of interest. In other states, a usurious lender may lose the right to collect any interest or may lose the entire amount of the loan in addition to the interest. Loans made to corporations are generally exempt from usury laws.

Usury laws were enacted primarily to protect consumers from unscrupulous lenders who would charge unreasonably high interest rates. Some states specifically limit the legal maximum interest rate to a fixed amount, while other states have what is known as a *floating interest rate*. In such states, the maximum rate that may be charged is adjusted up or down at specific intervals based on a certain economic standard, such as the prime lending rate or the rate of return on government bonds. *The rate of interest charged on any one loan, however, remains constant throughout the term of the loan* (except for variable interest loans).

Usury laws are state laws, but federal law preempts state law, and the Depository Institutions Deregulation and Monetary Control Act of 1980 specifically exempts from state interest limitations *all* federally related residential first mortgage loans made after March 31, 1980. Federally related loans are those made by federally chartered institutions or insured or guaranteed by a federal agency. The exemption includes loans used to finance manufactured housing (the federal term for mobile homes) and the acquisition of stock in a cooperative housing corporation. The federal act effectively limits state usury laws to private lenders.

Points. When a mortgage is originated, a mortgage placement fee or service charge is computed as a percentage of the loan amount. This **loan fee**, or *loan origination fee,* is commonly referred to as **points**; one point equals approximately one percent (1%) of the loan amount. For example, a service charge of two points on an $80,000 mortgage loan would be two percent of $80,000, or $1,600. (See Chapter 20, "Financing the Real Estate Transaction," for further discussion on points.)

Note that, in some areas, a service charge based on a percentage of the loan amount and included in the loan origination fee is termed *prepaid interest,* rather than points.

Prepayment

When a loan is paid in installments over a long term, the total interest paid by the borrower can be a larger amount of money than the principal of the loan. If such a loan is paid off ahead of its full term, the lender will collect less interest from the borrower. For this reason, some mortgage and trust deed notes contain a *prepayment clause* requiring the borrower to pay a **prepayment penalty,** against the unearned portion of the interest for any payments made ahead of schedule.

Pennsylvania law, however, does not permit such penalties to be charged on residential mortgage loan prepayments when the principal amount is $50,000 or less. In addition, as will be discussed in Chapter 20, "Financing the Real Estate Transaction," lenders are prohibited from charging prepayment penalties on mortgage loans insured or guaranteed by the federal government.

Payment Plans

Most mortgage loans are **amortized loans.** That is, regular payments are made—each payment being applied first to the interest owed and the balance to the principal amount—over a term of perhaps 15 to 30 years. At the end of the term, the full amount of the principal and all interest due will be reduced to zero. Such loans are also called *direct reduction loans.*

Most amortized mortgage loans are paid in monthly installments; some, however, are payable quarterly or semiannually. These payments may be computed based on a number of payment plans, which tend alternately to gain and lose favor with lenders and borrowers as the cost and availability of mortgage money fluctuate. These will be discussed in additional detail in Chapter 20. Note that, while these are commonly referred to as "mortgages," they are *loans* that may be secured by a mortgage.

Fully amortized mortgage. The most frequently used plan, the *fully amortized mortgage,* requires the mortgagor to pay a *constant amount,* usually monthly. This may be referred to as a *level payment* loan. The mortgagee credits each payment first to the interest due and then applies the balance to reduce the principal of the loan. Thus, while each payment is the same, the portion applied toward repayment of the principal grows and the interest due declines as the unpaid balance of the loan is reduced. Note that the loan can be amortized more rapidly, unless prohibited by the note (lock-in clause), by paying additional amounts that would be applied directly to the principal. The result is that less interest is paid because the loan is paid off before the end of its term.

The constant payment is determined from a prepared mortgage payment book or a mortgage factor chart (Table 13.1). The mortgage factor chart indicates the amount of monthly payment per $1,000 of loan depending on the term and interest rate. The factor is multiplied by the number of thousands (and fractions thereof) of the amount being borrowed.

A lender charges a borrower a certain percentage of the principal as interest for each year the debt is outstanding. The amount of interest due on any one installment payment date is calculated by computing the total yearly interest, based on the unpaid balance, and dividing that figure by the number of payments made each year. For example, if the current outstanding loan balance is $50,000 with interest at the rate of 10 percent per annum and constant monthly payments of $439.00, the interest and principal due on the next payment would be computed as shown on page 195.

Table 13.1
Mortgage Factor
Chart

Monthly Payment Factors to Amortize a Loan of $1,000

TERM RATE	10 yrs.	15 yrs.	20 yrs.	25 yrs.	30 yrs.	TERM RATE	10 yrs.	15 yrs.	20 yrs.	25 yrs.	30 yrs.
7 %	11.62	8.99	7.76	7.07	6.66	11.0	13.78	11.37	10.33	9.81	9.53
7.1	11.66	9.05	7.82	7.14	6.73	11.1	13.83	11.43	10.39	9.87	9.60
7.2	11.71	9.11	7.88	7.20	6.79	11.2	13.89	11.49	10.46	9.95	9.67
7.25	11.75	9.13	7.91	7.23	6.83	11.25	13.92	11.53	10.50	9.99	9.72
7.3	11.77	9.16	7.94	7.27	6.86	11.3	13.95	11.56	10.53	10.02	9.75
7.4	11.81	9.22	8.00	7.33	6.93	11.4	14.00	11.62	10.60	10.09	9.83
7.5	11.88	9.28	8.06	7.39	7.00	11.5	14.06	11.69	10.67	10.17	9.91
7.6	11.92	9.33	8.12	7.46	7.07	11.6	14.12	11.75	10.73	10.24	9.98
7.7	11.97	9.39	8.18	7.53	7.13	11.7	14.17	11.81	10.80	10.31	10.06
7.75	12.01	9.42	8.21	7.56	7.17	11.75	14.21	11.85	10.84	10.35	10.10
7.8	12.02	9.45	8.25	7.59	7.20	11.8	14.23	11.87	10.87	10.38	10.13
7.9	12.08	9.50	8.31	7.65	7.27	11.9	14.29	11.94	10.94	10.46	10.21
8.0	12.14	9.56	8.37	7.72	7.34	12.0	14.35	12.01	11.02	10.54	10.29
8.1	12.19	9.62	8.43	7.79	7.41	12.1	14.40	12.07	11.08	10.61	10.36
8.2	12.24	9.68	8.49	7.86	7.48	12.2	14.46	12.13	11.15	10.68	10.44
8.25	12.27	9.71	8.53	7.89	7.52	12.25	14.50	12.17	11.19	10.72	10.48
8.3	12.29	9.74	8.56	7.92	7.55	12.3	14.52	12.20	11.22	10.75	10.52
8.4	12.35	9.79	8.62	7.99	7.62	12.4	14.58	12.26	11.29	10.83	10.60
8.5	12.40	9.85	8.68	8.06	7.69	12.5	14.64	12.33	11.37	10.91	10.68
8.6	12.45	9.91	8.75	8.12	7.77	12.6	14.70	12.39	11.43	10.98	10.75
8.7	12.51	9.97	8.81	8.19	7.84	12.7	14.75	12.46	11.50	11.05	10.83
8.75	12.54	10.00	8.84	8.23	7.87	12.75	14.79	12.49	11.54	11.10	10.87
8.8	12.56	10.03	8.87	8.26	7.91	12.8	14.81	12.52	11.57	11.13	10.91
8.9	12.61	10.09	8.94	8.33	7.98	12.9	14.87	12.59	11.64	11.20	10.98
9.0	12.67	10.15	9.00	8.40	8.05	13.0	14.94	12.66	11.72	11.28	11.07
9.1	12.72	10.21	9.07	8.47	8.12	13.1	14.99	12.72	11.79	11.35	11.14
9.2	12.78	10.27	9.13	8.53	8.20	13.2	15.05	12.78	11.86	11.43	11.22
9.25	12.81	10.30	9.16	8.57	8.23	13.25	15.08	12.82	11.90	11.47	11.26
9.3	12.83	10.33	9.20	8.60	8.27	13.3	15.11	12.85	11.93	11.50	11.30
9.4	12.89	10.39	9.26	8.67	8.34	13.4	15.17	12.92	12.00	11.58	11.38
9.5	12.94	10.45	9.33	8.74	8.41	13.5	15.23	12.99	12.08	11.66	11.46
9.6	12.99	10.51	9.39	8.81	8.49	13.6	15.29	13.05	12.15	11.73	11.53
9.7	13.05	10.57	9.46	8.88	8.56	13.7	15.35	13.12	12.22	11.81	11.61
9.75	13.08	10.60	9.49	8.92	8.60	13.75	15.38	13.15	12.26	11.85	11.66
9.8	13.10	10.63	9.52	8.95	8.63	13.8	15.41	13.18	12.29	11.88	11.69
9.9	13.16	10.69	9.59	9.02	8.71	13.9	15.47	13.25	12.36	11.96	11.77
10.0	13.22	10.75	9.66	9.09	8.78	14.0	15.53	13.32	12.44	12.04	11.85
10.1	13.27	10.81	9.72	9.16	8.85	14.1	15.59	13.38	12.51	12.11	11.93
10.2	13.33	10.87	9.78	9.23	8.92	14.2	15.65	13.45	12.58	12.19	12.01
10.25	13.36	10.90	9.82	9.27	8.97	14.25	15.68	13.49	12.62	12.23	12.05
10.3	13.38	10.93	9.85	9.30	9.00	14.3	15.71	13.52	12.65	12.27	12.09
10.4	13.44	10.99	9.92	9.37	9.07	14.4	15.77	13.59	12.73	12.34	12.17
10.5	13.50	11.06	9.99	9.45	9.15	14.5	15.83	13.66	12.80	12.43	12.25
10.6	13.55	11.12	10.05	9.51	9.22	14.6	15.89	13.72	12.87	12.50	12.33
10.7	13.61	11.18	10.12	9.59	9.30	14.7	15.95	13.79	12.95	12.58	12.40
10.75	13.64	11.21	10.16	9.63	9.34	14.75	15.99	13.83	12.99	12.62	12.45
10.8	13.66	11.24	10.19	9.66	9.37	14.8	16.01	13.86	13.02	12.65	12.48
10.9	13.72	11.30	10.25	9.73	9.45	14.9	16.07	13.93	13.09	12.73	12.56

$50,000.00
×   .10
$ 5,000.00   annual interest
$ 439.00
−   416.67
$ 22.33   month's principal

$\underline{\quad\$416.666\quad}$ (rounded to $416.67)
12)$5,000.00   month's interest

Straight-line amortized mortgage. With *straight-line amortization,* the mortgagor may pay a *different amount for each installment,* with each payment consisting of a fixed amount credited toward the principal plus an additional amount for the interest due on the balance of the principal outstanding since the last payment was made.

Straight payment mortgage. A mortgagor may choose a *straight payment plan* that calls for periodic payments of interest, with the principal to be *paid in full at the end of the loan term.* This is known as a **straight,** or **term, loan.** Such plans are generally used for home-improvement loans and second mortgages rather than for residential first mortgage loans. Prior to the 1930s, the only form of mortgage loan available was the straight payment loan, payable after a relatively short term, such as three to five years. The high rate of foreclosure of such loans in the Depression years prompted the use of the more manageable amortized loans that are now the norm.

Provisions of the Mortgage Document

The mortgage document refers to the terms of the note and clearly establishes that the conveyance of land is security for the debt. It identifies the lender as well as the borrower, and it includes an accurate legal description of the property. It should be signed by all parties who have an interest in the real estate. (Figure 13.3 is a sample mortgage.)

Duties of the Mortgagor

The borrower is required to fulfill many obligations. These usually include the following:

1. payment of the debt in accordance with the terms of the note.

2. payment of all real estate taxes on the property given as security.

3. maintenance of adequate insurance to protect the lender if the property is destroyed or damaged by fire, windstorm or other hazard.

4. maintenance of the property in good repair at all times.

5. lender authorization before making any major alterations on the property.

Failure to meet any of these obligations can result in a borrower's default. When this happens, the loan documents may provide for a grace period (30 days, for example) during which the borrower can meet the obligation and cure the default. If the borrower does not do so, the lender has the right to foreclose the mortgage and collect on the note. The most frequent cause of default is the borrower's failure to meet monthly installments.

Figure 13.3
Mortgage

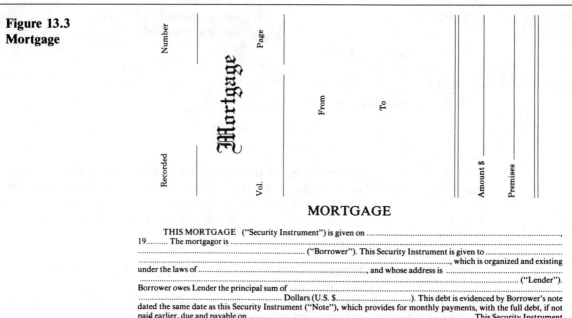

MORTGAGE

THIS MORTGAGE ("Security Instrument") is given on ....,
19......... The mortgagor is ....
.... ("Borrower"). This Security Instrument is given to ....
...., which is organized and existing
under the laws of ...., and whose address is ....
.... ("Lender").
Borrower owes Lender the principal sum of ....
.... Dollars (U.S. $..................................). This debt is evidenced by Borrower's note
dated the same date as this Security Instrument ("Note"), which provides for monthly payments, with the full debt, if not
paid earlier, due and payable on .... This Security Instrument
secures to Lender: (a) the repayment of the debt evidenced by the Note, with interest, and all renewals, extensions and
modifications; (b) the payment of all other sums, with interest, advanced under paragraph 7 to protect the security of this
Security Instrument; and (c) the performance of Borrower's covenants and agreements under this Security Instrument and
the Note. For this purpose, Borrower does hereby mortgage, grant and convey to Lender the following described property
located in .... County, Pennsylvania:

which has the address of ...., ...,
                                                        [Street]   [City]
Pennsylvania .... ("Property Address");
                        [Zip Code]

   TOGETHER WITH all the improvements now or hereafter erected on the property, and all easements, rights,
appurtenances, rents, royalties, mineral, oil and gas rights and profits, water rights and stock and all fixtures now or
hereafter a part of the property. All replacements and additions shall also be covered by this Security Instrument. All of the
foregoing is referred to in this Security Instrument as the "Property."

   BORROWER COVENANTS that Borrower is lawfully seised of the estate hereby conveyed and has the right to
mortgage, grant and convey the Property and that the Property is unencumbered, except for encumbrances of record.
Borrower warrants and will defend generally the title to the Property against all claims and demands, subject to any
encumbrances of record.

   THIS SECURITY INSTRUMENT combines uniform covenants for national use and non-uniform covenants with
limited variations by jurisdiction to constitute a uniform security instrument covering real property.

PENNSYLVANIA—Single Family—**FNMA/FHLMC UNIFORM INSTRUMENT**   Form 3039 12/83

Figure 13.3
Mortgage (cont.)

UNIFORM COVENANTS.   Borrower and Lender covenant and agree as follows:

1.   Payment of Principal and Interest; Prepayment and Late Charges.   Borrower shall promptly pay when due the principal of and interest on the debt evidenced by the Note and any prepayment and late charges due under the Note.

2.   Funds for Taxes and Insurance.   Subject to applicable law or to a written waiver by Lender, Borrower shall pay to Lender on the day monthly payments are due under the Note, until the Note is paid in full, a sum ("Funds") equal to one-twelfth of: (a) yearly taxes and assessments which may attain priority over this Security Instrument; (b) yearly leasehold payments or ground rents on the Property, if any; (c) yearly hazard insurance premiums; and (d) yearly mortgage insurance premiums, if any. These items are called "escrow items." Lender may estimate the Funds due on the basis of current data and reasonable estimates of future escrow items.

The Funds shall be held in an institution the deposits or accounts of which are insured or guaranteed by a federal or state agency (including Lender if Lender is such an institution). Lender shall apply the Funds to pay the escrow items Lender may not charge for holding and applying the Funds, analyzing the account or verifying the escrow items, unless Lender pays Borrower interest on the Funds and applicable law permits Lender to make such a charge. Borrower and Lender may agree in writing that interest shall be paid on the Funds. Unless an agreement is made or applicable law requires interest to be paid, Lender shall not be required to pay Borrower any interest or earnings on the Funds. Lender shall give to Borrower, without charge, an annual accounting of the Funds showing credits and debits to the Funds and the purpose for which each debit to the Funds was made. The Funds are pledged as additional security for the sums secured by this Security Instrument.

If the amount of the Funds held by Lender, together with the future monthly payments of Funds payable prior to the due dates of the escrow items, shall exceed the amount required to pay the escrow items when due, the excess shall be, at Borrower's option, either promptly repaid to Borrower or credited to Borrower on monthly payments of Funds. If the amount of the Funds held by Lender is not sufficient to pay the escrow items when due, Borrower shall pay to Lender any amount necessary to make up the deficiency in one or more payments as required by Lender.

Upon payment in full of all sums secured by this Security Instrument, Lender shall promptly refund to Borrower any Funds held by Lender. If under paragraph 19 the Property is sold or acquired by Lender, Lender shall apply, no later than immediately prior to the sale of the Property or its acquisition by Lender, any Funds held by Lender at the time of application as a credit against the sums secured by this Security Instrument.

3.   Application of Payments.   Unless applicable law provides otherwise, all payments received by Lender under paragraphs 1 and 2 shall be applied: first, to late charges due under the Note; second, to prepayment charges due under the Note; third, to amounts payable under paragraph 2; fourth, to interest due; and last, to principal due.

4.   Charges; Liens.   Borrower shall pay all taxes, assessments, charges, fines and impositions attributable to the Property which may attain priority over this Security Instrument, and leasehold payments or ground rents, if any. Borrower shall pay these obligations in the manner provided in paragraph 2, or if not paid in that manner, Borrower shall pay them on time directly to the person owed payment. Borrower shall promptly furnish to Lender all notices of amounts to be paid under this paragraph. If Borrower makes these payments directly, Borrower shall promptly furnish to Lender receipts evidencing the payments.

Borrower shall promptly discharge any lien which has priority over this Security Instrument unless Borrower: (a) agrees in writing to the payment of the obligation secured by the lien in a manner acceptable to Lender; (b) contests in good faith the lien by, or defends against enforcement of the lien in, legal proceedings which in the Lender's opinion operate to prevent the enforcement of the lien or forfeiture of any part of the Property; or (c) secures from the holder of the lien an agreement satisfactory to Lender subordinating the lien to this Security Instrument. If Lender determines that any part of the Property is subject to a lien which may attain priority over this Security Instrument, Lender may give Borrower a notice identifying the lien. Borrower shall satisfy the lien or take one or more of the actions set forth above within 10 days of the giving of notice.

5.   Hazard Insurance.   Borrower shall keep the improvements now existing or hereafter erected on the Property insured against loss by fire, hazards included within the term "extended coverage" and any other hazards for which Lender requires insurance. This insurance shall be maintained in the amounts and for the periods that Lender requires. The insurance carrier providing the insurance shall be chosen by Borrower subject to Lender's approval which shall not be unreasonably withheld.

All insurance policies and renewals shall be acceptable to Lender and shall include a standard mortgage clause. Lender shall have the right to hold the policies and renewals. If Lender requires, Borrower shall promptly give to Lender all receipts of paid premiums and renewal notices. In the event of loss, Borrower shall give prompt notice to the insurance carrier and Lender. Lender may make proof of loss if not made promptly by Borrower.

Unless Lender and Borrower otherwise agree in writing, insurance proceeds shall be applied to restoration or repair of the Property damaged, if the restoration or repair is economically feasible and Lender's security is not lessened. If the restoration or repair is not economically feasible or Lender's security would be lessened, the insurance proceeds shall be applied to the sums secured by this Security Instrument, whether or not then due, with any excess paid to Borrower. If Borrower abandons the Property, or does not answer within 30 days a notice from Lender that the insurance carrier has offered to settle a claim, then Lender may collect the insurance proceeds. Lender may use the proceeds to repair or restore the Property or to pay sums secured by this Security Instrument, whether or not then due. The 30-day period will begin when the notice is given.

Unless Lender and Borrower otherwise agree in writing, any application of proceeds to principal shall not extend or postpone the due date of the monthly payments referred to in paragraphs 1 and 2 or change the amount of the payments. If under paragraph 19 the Property is acquired by Lender, Borrower's right to any insurance policies and proceeds resulting from damage to the Property prior to the acquisition shall pass to Lender to the extent of the sums secured by this Security Instrument immediately prior to the acquisition.

6.   Preservation and Maintenance of Property; Leaseholds.   Borrower shall not destroy, damage or substantially change the Property, allow the Property to deteriorate or commit waste. If this Security Instrument is on a leasehold, Borrower shall comply with the provisions of the lease, and if Borrower acquires fee title to the Property, the leasehold and fee title shall not merge unless Lender agrees to the merger in writing.

7.   Protection of Lender's Rights in the Property; Mortgage Insurance.   If Borrower fails to perform the covenants and agreements contained in this Security Instrument, or there is a legal proceeding that may significantly affect Lender's rights in the Property (such as a proceeding in bankruptcy, probate, for condemnation or to enforce laws or regulations), then Lender may do and pay for whatever is necessary to protect the value of the Property and Lender's rights in the Property. Lender's actions may include paying any sums secured by a lien which has priority over this Security Instrument, appearing in court, paying reasonable attorneys' fees and entering on the Property to make repairs. Although Lender may take action under this paragraph 7, Lender does not have to do so.

Any amounts disbursed by Lender under this paragraph 7 shall become additional debt of Borrower secured by this Security Instrument. Unless Borrower and Lender agree to other terms of payment, these amounts shall bear interest from the date of disbursement at the Note rate and shall be payable, with interest, upon notice from Lender to Borrower requesting payment.

Figure 13.3
Mortgage (cont.)

If Lender required mortgage insurance as a condition of making the loan secured by this Security Instrument, Borrower shall pay the premiums required to maintain the insurance in effect until such time as the requirement for the insurance terminates in accordance with Borrower's and Lender's written agreement or applicable law.

8. Inspection. Lender or its agent may make reasonable entries upon and inspections of the Property. Lender shall give Borrower notice at the time of or prior to an inspection specifying reasonable cause for the inspection.

9. Condemnation. The proceeds of any award or claim for damages, direct or consequential, in connection with any condemnation or other taking of any part of the Property, or for conveyance in lieu of condemnation, are hereby assigned and shall be paid to Lender.

In the event of a total taking of the Property, the proceeds shall be applied to the sums secured by this Security Instrument, whether or not then due, with any excess paid to Borrower. In the event of a partial taking of the Property, unless Borrower and Lender otherwise agree in writing, the sums secured by this Security Instrument shall be reduced by the amount of the proceeds multiplied by the following fraction: (a) the total amount of the sums secured immediately before the taking, divided by (b) the fair market value of the Property immediately before the taking. Any balance shall be paid to Borrower.

If the Property is abandoned by Borrower, or if, after notice by Lender to Borrower that the condemnor offers to make an award or settle a claim for damages, Borrower fails to respond to Lender within 30 days after the date the notice is given, Lender is authorized to collect and apply the proceeds, at its option, either to restoration or repair of the Property or to the sums secured by this Security Instrument, whether or not then due.

Unless Lender and Borrower otherwise agree in writing, any application of proceeds to principal shall not extend or postpone the due date of the monthly payments referred to in paragraphs 1 and 2 or change the amount of such payments.

10. Borrower Not Released; Forbearance By Lender Not a Waiver. Extension of the time for payment or modification of amortization of the sums secured by this Security Instrument granted by Lender to any successor in interest of Borrower shall not operate to release the liability of the original Borrower or Borrower's successors in interest. Lender shall not be required to commence proceedings against any successor in interest or refuse to extend time for payment or otherwise modify amortization of the sums secured by this Security Instrument by reason of any demand made by the original Borrower or Borrower's successors in interest. Any forbearance by Lender in exercising any right or remedy shall not be a waiver of or preclude the exercise of any right or remedy.

11. Successors and Assigns Bound; Joint and Several Liability; Co-signers. The covenants and agreements of this Security Instrument shall bind and benefit the successors and assigns of Lender and Borrower, subject to the provisions of paragraph 17. Borrower's covenants and agreements shall be joint and several. Any Borrower who co-signs this Security Instrument but does not execute the Note: (a) is co-signing this Security Instrument only to mortgage, grant and convey that Borrower's interest in the Property under the terms of this Security Instrument; (b) is not personally obligated to pay the sums secured by this Security Instrument; and (c) agrees that Lender and any other Borrower may agree to extend, modify, forbear or make any accommodations with regard to the terms of this Security Instrument or the Note without that Borrower's consent.

12. Loan Charges. If the loan secured by this Security Instrument is subject to a law which sets maximum loan charges, and that law is finally interpreted so that the interest or other loan charges collected or to be collected in connection with the loan exceed the permitted limits, then: (a) any such loan charge shall be reduced by the amount necessary to reduce the charge to the permitted limit; and (b) any sums already collected from Borrower which exceeded permitted limits will be refunded to Borrower. Lender may choose to make this refund by reducing the principal owed under the Note or by making a direct payment to Borrower. If a refund reduces principal, the reduction will be treated as a partial prepayment without any prepayment charge under the Note.

13. Legislation Affecting Lender's Rights. If enactment or expiration of applicable laws has the effect of rendering any provision of the Note or this Security Instrument unenforceable according to its terms, Lender, at its option, may require immediate payment in full of all sums secured by this Security Instrument and may invoke any remedies permitted by paragraph 19. If Lender exercises this option, Lender shall take the steps specified in the second paragraph of paragraph 17.

14. Notices. Any notice to Borrower provided for in this Security Instrument shall be given by delivering it or by mailing it by first class mail unless applicable law requires use of another method. The notice shall be directed to the Property Address or any other address Borrower designates by notice to Lender. Any notice to Lender shall be given by first class mail to Lender's address stated herein or any other address Lender designates by notice to Borrower. Any notice provided for in this Security Instrument shall be deemed to have been given to Borrower or Lender when given as provided in this paragraph.

15. Governing Law; Severability. This Security Instrument shall be governed by federal law and the law of the jurisdiction in which the Property is located. In the event that any provision or clause of this Security Instrument or the Note conflicts with applicable law, such conflict shall not affect other provisions of this Security Instrument or the Note which can be given effect without the conflicting provision. To this end the provisions of this Security Instrument and the Note are declared to be severable.

16. Borrower's Copy. Borrower shall be given one conformed copy of the Note and of this Security Instrument.

17. Transfer of the Property or a Beneficial Interest in Borrower. If all or any part of the Property or any interest in it is sold or transferred (or if a beneficial interest in Borrower is sold or transferred and Borrower is not a natural person) without Lender's prior written consent, Lender may, at its option, require immediate payment in full of all sums secured by this Security Instrument. However, this option shall not be exercised by Lender if exercise is prohibited by federal law as of the date of this Security Instrument.

If Lender exercises this option, Lender shall give Borrower notice of acceleration. The notice shall provide a period of not less than 30 days from the date the notice is delivered or mailed within which Borrower must pay all sums secured by this Security Instrument. If Borrower fails to pay these sums prior to the expiration of this period, Lender may invoke any remedies permitted by this Security Instrument without further notice or demand on Borrower.

18. Borrower's Right to Reinstate. If Borrower meets certain conditions, Borrower shall have the right to have enforcement of this Security Instrument discontinued at any time prior to the earlier of: (a) 5 days (or such other period as applicable law may specify for reinstatement) before sale of the Property pursuant to any power of sale contained in this Security Instrument; or (b) entry of a judgment enforcing this Security Instrument. Those conditions are that Borrower: (a) pays Lender all sums which then would be due under this Security Instrument and the Note had no acceleration occurred; (b) cures any default of any other covenants or agreements; (c) pays all expenses incurred in enforcing this Security Instrument, including, but not limited to, reasonable attorneys' fees; and (d) takes such action as Lender may reasonably require to assure that the lien of this Security Instrument, Lender's rights in the Property and Borrower's obligation to pay the sums secured by this Security Instrument shall continue unchanged. Upon reinstatement by Borrower, this Security Instrument and the obligations secured hereby shall remain fully effective as if no acceleration had occurred. However, this right to reinstate shall not apply in the case of acceleration under paragraphs 13 or 17.

**Figure 13.3
Mortgage (cont.)**

NON-UNIFORM COVENANTS. Borrower and Lender further covenant and agree as follows:

19. Acceleration; Remedies. Lender shall give notice to Borrower prior to acceleration following Borrower's breach of any covenant or agreement in this Security Instrument (but not prior to acceleration under paragraphs 13 and 17 unless applicable law provides otherwise). Lender shall notify Borrower of, among other things: (a) the default; (b) the action required to cure the default; (c) when the default must be cured; and (d) that failure to cure the default as specified may result in acceleration of the sums secured by this Security Instrument, foreclosure by judicial proceeding and sale of the Property. Lender shall further inform Borrower of the right to reinstate after acceleration and the right to assert in the foreclosure proceeding the non-existence of a default or any other defense of Borrower to acceleration and foreclosure. If the default is not cured as specified, Lender at its option may require immediate payment in full of all sums secured by this Security Instrument without further demand and may foreclose this Security Instrument by judicial proceeding. Lender shall be entitled to collect all expenses incurred in pursuing the remedies provided in this paragraph 19, including, but not limited to, attorneys' fees and costs of title evidence to the extent permitted by applicable law.

20. Lender in Possession. Upon acceleration under paragraph 19 or abandonment of the Property, Lender (in person, by agent or by judicially appointed receiver) shall be entitled to enter upon, take possession of and manage the Property and to collect the rents of the Property including those past due. Any rents collected by Lender or the receiver shall be applied first to payment of the costs of management of the Property and collection of rents, including, but not limited to, receiver's fees, premiums on receiver's bonds and reasonable attorneys' fees, and then to the sums secured by this Security Instrument.

21. Release. Upon payment of all sums secured by this Security Instrument, Lender shall discharge this Security Instrument without charge to Borrower. Borrower shall pay any recordation costs.

22. Reinstatement Period. Borrower's time to reinstate provided in paragraph 18 shall extend to one hour prior to the commencement of bidding at a sheriff's sale or other sale pursuant to this Security Instrument.

23. Purchase Money Mortgage. If any of the debt secured by this Security Instrument is lent to Borrower to acquire title to the Property, this Security Instrument shall be a purchase money mortgage.

24. Interest Rate After Judgment. Borrower agrees that the interest rate payable after a judgment is entered on the Note or in an action of mortgage foreclosure shall be the rate payable from time to time under the Note.

25. Riders to this Security Instrument. If one or more riders are executed by Borrower and recorded together with this Security Instrument, the covenants and agreements of each such rider shall be incorporated into and shall amend and supplement the covenants and agreements of this Security Instrument as if the rider(s) were a part of this Security Instrument. [Check applicable box(es)]

☐ Adjustable Rate Rider   ☐ Condominium Rider   ☐ 2–4 Family Rider

☐ Graduated Payment Rider   ☐ Planned Unit Development Rider

☐ Other(s) [specify]

BY SIGNING BELOW, Borrower accepts and agrees to the terms and covenants contained in this Security Instrument and in any rider(s) executed by Borrower and recorded with it.

Witnesses:

.... (Seal)
                                                                                                              —Borrower

.... (Seal)
                                                                                                              —Borrower

COMMONWEALTH OF PENNSYLVANIA, ... County ss:

On this, the .... day of .... , 19 ...., before me, ...
.... the undersigned officer, personally appeared ....
.... known to me (or satisfactorily proven) to be the person .... whose name .... subscribed to the within instrument and acknowledged that .... executed the same for the purposes herein contained.

IN WITNESS WHEREOF, I hereunto set my hand and official seal.

My Commission expires:

....

....
                        Title of Officer

I certify that the precise place of business of the within named Mortgagee is ....

....

RECORDED in the Office for Recording of Deeds in and for ....
in Mortgage Book .... No. .... Page .... &c.
Date ....   Recorder ....

Provisions for Default

The provisions of a mortgage include an **acceleration clause** to assist the lender in foreclosure. If a borrower defaults, the lender has the right to accelerate the maturity of the debt—to declare the *entire* debt due and payable *immediately*—even though the terms of the mortgage allow the borrower to amortize the debt in regular payments over a period of years. Without the acceleration clause, the lender would have to sue the borrower every time a payment became due and in default.

Other clauses in a mortgage enable the lender to take care of the property in the event of the borrower's negligence or default. If the borrower does not pay taxes or insurance premiums or make necessary repairs on the property, the lender may step in and do so to protect the security (the real estate). Any money advanced by the lender to cure such defaults is either added to the unpaid debt or declared immediately due and owing from the borrower.

Assignment of the Mortgage

As mentioned earlier, a note that is a negotiable instrument may be sold to a third party. If the holder of the note wishes to sell and the third party also wishes to have the real estate as security, the mortgagee must execute an *assignment of mortgage document*. Under its terms, the present owner of the mortgage note (the mortgagee) becomes the assignor and executes the assignment to the assignee, who becomes the new owner of the mortgage and the debt. This assignment must be recorded. Upon payment in full, or satisfaction of the debt, the assignee is required to execute the satisfaction, or release, of mortgage as discussed in the following section. In the event of a foreclosure, the assignee (not the original mortgagee) is required to file the suit.

Release of the Mortgage Lien

When all mortgage loan payments have been made and the note paid in full, the mortgagor wants the public record to show that the debt has been paid and the mortgage has been satisfied. By the provisions of the **defeasance clause** in the usual mortgage, when the note has been fully paid the mortgagee is required to execute a **satisfaction** of mortgage or *release of mortgage*. This document reconveys to the mortgagor all interest in the real estate that was conveyed to the mortgagee by the original recorded mortgage document. By having this release entered in the public record, the owner shows that the mortgage lien has been removed from the property. If a mortgage has been assigned by a recorded assignment, the release must be executed by the assignee-mortgagee.

Tax and Insurance Reserves

Many lenders require borrowers to provide a reserve fund, called an escrow account, to meet future real estate taxes and insurance premiums. When the mortgage loan is made, the borrower starts the reserve by depositing funds to cover the amount of unpaid real estate taxes prorated from the lien date to the end of the current month. If a new insurance policy has just been purchased, the insurance premium reserve will be started with the deposit of one-twelfth of the annual tax and insurance premium liability. Thereafter, the monthly loan payments required of the borrower will include principal, interest and tax and insurance reserves (PITI—Principal, Interest, Taxes and Insurance). RESPA, the federal Real Estate Settlement Procedures Act (discussed in Chapter 21, "Closing the Real Estate Transaction"), limits the amount of tax and insurance reserves that a lender may require.

Federal flood insurance program. As will be discussed in Chapter 16, "Concepts of Home Ownership," this subsidized plan authorized by Congress requires property owners in certain areas to obtain flood-damage insurance on properties financed by mortgages or other loans, grants, or guarantees obtained from federal agencies and federally insured or regulated lending institutions. The program seeks to improve future management and planning of flood-plain areas through land-use and control measures.

Assignment of Rents

The borrower may make an assignment of rents to the lender, to be effective upon the borrower's default. The rent assignment may be included in the mortgage or it may be made as a separate document. In either case, the rent assignment should be drafted in language that clearly indicates that the parties intend to assign the rents, not merely pledge them as security for the loan.

Buying Subject to or Assuming a Seller's Mortgage

A person who purchases real estate that has an outstanding mortgage on it may take the property subject to the mortgage or may assume it and agree to pay the debt. This technical distinction becomes important if the buyer defaults and the mortgage is foreclosed.

When the property is sold *subject to* the mortgage, the purchaser is not personally obligated to pay the debt in full. The purchaser has bought the real estate knowing that he or she must make the loan payments and that, upon default, the lender will foreclose and the property will be sold by court order to pay the debt. If the sale does not pay off the entire debt, the purchaser is not liable for the difference. However, the original seller might still have some liability for that difference. In contrast, when the grantee not only purchases the property subject to the mortgage but *assumes and agrees to pay* the debt, the grantee becomes personally obligated for the payment of the *entire debt*. If the mortgage is foreclosed in such a case and the court sale does not bring enough money to pay the debt in full, a deficiency judgment against both the assumer and the original borrower, unless the borrower has been released, may be obtained for the unpaid balance of the note. When a mortgage is assumed, most lending institutions charge a transfer fee to cover the costs of changing their records; this charge is customarily borne by the purchaser.

Before a conventional mortgage may be assumed, most lending institutions require the assumer to qualify financially. A desirable feature of FHA-insured and VA-guaranteed loans is their easy assumability. These types of loans are discussed in Chapter 20, "Financing the Real Estate Transaction."

Alienation clause. Frequently, when a real estate loan is made, the lender wishes to prevent some future purchaser of the property from being able to assume that loan, particularly at its old rate of interest. For this reason, some lenders include an **alienation clause** (also known as a *resale clause* or *due-on-sale clause*) in the note. An alienation clause provides that upon the sale of the property by the borrower to a buyer who wants to assume the loan, the lender has the choice of either declaring the entire debt to be immediately due and owing or permitting the buyer to assume the loan at current market interest rates. Government-backed loans generally prohibit use of alienation clauses.

| **Recording Mortgages** | The mortgage document must be recorded in the recorder's office of the county in which the real estate is located. The recordation gives constructive notice to the world of the borrower's obligations and establishes the lien's priority. |

| **First and Second Mortgages** | Mortgages and other liens normally have priority in the order in which they have been recorded. A mortgage on land that has no prior mortgage lien on it is a *first mortgage.* When the owner of this land later executes another loan for additional funds, the new loan becomes a *second mortgage,* or *junior lien,* when recorded. The second lien is subject to the first lien; the first has prior claim to the value of the land pledged as security. Because second loans represent a greater risk to the lender, they are usually issued at higher interest rates. The priority of mortgage liens may be changed by the execution of a *subordination agreement,* in which the first lender subordinates the lien to that of the second lender. To be valid, such an agreement must be signed by both lenders. |

| **Foreclosure** | When a borrower defaults in making payments or fulfilling any of the obligations set forth in the mortgage, the lender's rights can be enforced through a foreclosure. A **foreclosure** is a legal procedure whereby the property that is pledged as security in the mortgage document is sold to satisfy the debt. The foreclosure procedure brings the rights of all parties to a conclusion and passes title in the subject property to either the person holding the mortgage document or a third party who purchases the realty at a *foreclosure sale.* Property thus sold is *free of the mortgage and all junior liens.* |

| **Methods of Foreclosure** | There are three general types of foreclosure proceedings—judicial, nonjudicial and strict foreclosure. The specific provisions of these vary from state to state.

Judicial foreclosure. A judicial foreclosure proceeding provides that the property pledged as security may be sold by court order after the mortgagee gives sufficient public notice. Upon a borrower's default, the lender may *accelerate* the due date of all remaining monthly payments. The lender's attorney can then file a suit to foreclose the lien after the borrower has been informed of the lender's intention. A public sale is advertised and held, and the real estate is sold to the highest bidder. This is the prevalent form of mortgage foreclosure in Pennsylvania.

Nonjudicial foreclosure. Other states allow nonjudicial foreclosure procedures to be used when a *power-of-sale clause* is contained in the loan document. In states that recognize trust deed loans, the trustee is generally given the power of sale. Some states allow a similar power of sale to be used with a mortgage loan.

To institute a nonjudicial foreclosure, the mortgagee must record a notice of default at the county recorder's office within a designated time period in order to give notice to the public of the intended auction. This official notice is generally accompanied by advertisements published in local newspapers that state the total amount due and the date of the public sale. The purpose of this notice is not to notify the defaulting debtor but to publicize the sale. After selling the property, the mortgagee may be required to file a copy of a notice of sale or affidavit of foreclosure. |

Strict foreclosure. Although the judicial foreclosure procedure is prevalent in Pennsylvania, in some states it is still possible for a lender to acquire the mortgaged property by a strict foreclosure process. After appropriate notice has been given to the delinquent borrower and the proper papers have been prepared and filed, the court establishes a specific time period during which the balance of the defaulted debt must be paid in full. If this is not done, the court usually awards full legal title to the lender.

Deed in Lieu of Foreclosure

An alternative to foreclosure would be for the lender to accept, or "buy," a **deed in lieu of foreclosure** from the borrower. This is sometimes known as a *friendly foreclosure,* for it is by agreement rather than by civil action. The major disadvantage to this manner of default settlement is that the mortgagee takes the real estate subject to all junior liens, while foreclosure eliminates all such liens.

Redemption

Most states give a defaulting borrower a chance to redeem the property. Redemption generally takes one of two forms—equitable redemption and statutory redemption.

Historically, the **right of redemption** is inherited from the old common-law proceedings in which the court sale ended the *equitable right of redemption.* Carried over to statutory law, this concept provides that if, during the course of a foreclosure proceeding but *before the foreclosure sale,* the borrower or any other person who has an interest in the real estate (such as another creditor) pays the lender the amount currently due, plus costs, the debt will be reinstated as before. In Pennsylvania, a borrower may cure a default in a residential mortgage loan with an outstanding balance of $50,000 or less by merely bringing the payments up to date. If some person other than the mortgagor redeems the real estate, the borrower will be responsible to that person for the amount of the mortgage redemption.

As discussed earlier, many states also allow a defaulted borrower a period in which to redeem the real estate after the sale. During this *statutory redemption* period (which may be as long as one year) the court may appoint a receiver to take charge of the property, collect rents, pay operating expenses and so forth. The mortgagor raises the necessary funds to redeem the property within the statutory period and pays the redemption money to the court. Because the debt was paid from the proceeds of the sale, the borrower can take possession free and clear of the former defaulted loan.

Deed to Purchaser at Sale

If redemption is not made or if no redemption period is allowed by state law, then the successful bidder at the sale receives a deed to the real estate. This is a statutory form of deed that may be executed by a sheriff or master-in-chancery to *convey such title as the borrower had* to the purchaser at the sale. There are no warranties with such a deed; the title passes as is, but free of the former defaulted debt.

Deficiency Judgment

If the foreclosure sale of the real estate secured by a mortgage does not produce a sales price sufficient to pay the loan balance in full after deducting expenses and accrued unpaid interest, the mortgagee may be entitled to a *personal judgment* against the maker of the note for the unpaid balance. Such a judgment is called a

deficiency judgment. It may also be obtained against any endorsers or guarantors of the note and any owners of the mortgaged property who may have assumed the debt by written agreement. If there are any surplus proceeds from the foreclosure sale after the debt and all junior liens are paid off and expenses and interest are deducted, these proceeds are paid to the borrower.

Sources of Real Estate Financing—The Primary Mortgage Market

The funds used to finance the purchase of real estate come from a variety of sources that comprise the **primary mortgage market**—lenders who supply funds to borrowers as an investment. Lenders may originate loans for the purpose of selling them to other investors as part of what is termed the *secondary mortgage market*. We will take a look at the secondary mortgage market later in this chapter.

Savings and Loan Associations

Savings and loan associations are traditionally the most active participants in the home-loan mortgage market, specializing in long-term residential loans. The principal function of a savings and loan is to promote thrift and home ownership. Generally, real estate mortgages are the main source of investment for savings and loan associations—more than 85 percent of their assets are annually fed into the mortgage market. Traditionally, they are the most flexible of all the lending institutions with regard to their mortgage lending procedures, and they are generally local in nature. In addition, savings and loans participate in government-insured and government-guaranteed loans, though only to a limited extent.

All savings and loan associations must be chartered, either by the federal government or by the state in which they are located. Savings and loans are regulated on a national level by the Federal Home Loan Bank system (FHLB). The FHLB sets up mandatory guidelines for member associations and provides depositors with savings insurance through the Federal Savings and Loan Insurance Corporation (FSLIC).

Commercial Banks

Commercial banks are an important source of real estate financing. While commercial banks historically were interested primarily in such short-term loans as construction, home-improvement and mobile-home loans, these institutions are increasingly more active in conventional mortgage lending. Commercial banks usually issue a larger portion of government-insured and government-guaranteed loans than do savings and loan associations. Like the savings and loans, banks must be chartered by the state or federal government. Bank deposits are insured by the Federal Deposit Insurance Corporation (FDIC).

Mutual Savings Banks

These institutions, which operate like savings and loan associations, are located primarily in the northeastern section of the United States. They issue no stock and are mutually owned by their investors. Although mutual savings banks do offer checking account privileges, they are primarily savings institutions and are highly active in the mortgage market, investing in loans secured by income property as well as residential real estate. In addition, because mutual savings banks usually seek low-risk loan investments, they often prefer to originate government-insured or government-guaranteed loans.

Life Insurance Companies

Insurance companies amass large sums of money from the premiums paid by their policyholders. While a certain portion of this money is held in reserve to satisfy claims and cover operating expenses, much of it is invested in profit-earning enterprises, such as long-term real estate loans.

Most insurance companies like to invest their money in large, long-term loans that finance commercial and industrial properties. They also invest in residential mortgage loans by purchasing large blocks of government-backed loans (FHA-insured and VA-guaranteed loans) from the Federal National Mortgage Association and other agencies that warehouse such loans for resale in the secondary mortgage market (as discussed later in this chapter).

In addition, many life insurance companies seek to further ensure the safety of their investments by insisting on equity positions (known as *equity kickers*) in many projects they finance. This means that the company requires a partnership arrangement with, for example, a project developer or subdivider as a condition of making a loan. This is called *participation financing*.

Mortgage Banking Companies

Mortgage banking companies originate mortgage loans with money belonging to such other institutions as insurance companies and pension funds or to individuals and funds of their own to make real estate loans that may later be sold to investors (with the mortgage company receiving a fee for servicing the loans). Mortgage banking companies are often involved in all types of real estate loan activities and often serve as middlemen between investors and borrowers, but they are not mortgage brokers.

Mortgage banking companies are generally organized as stock companies. As a source of real estate financing, they are subject to considerably fewer lending restrictions than commercial banks or savings and loans.

Credit Unions

Credit unions are cooperative organizations in which members place money in savings accounts, usually at higher interest rates than other savings institutions offer. In the past, most credit unions made only short-term consumer and home-improvement loans, but in recent years they have been branching out to originating longer-term first and second mortgage loans.

Mortgage Brokers

This discussion ends with a group who are not lenders, but are often instrumental in obtaining financing. Mortgage brokers are individuals who are licensed to act as intermediaries in bringing borrowers and lenders together. They locate potential borrowers, process preliminary loan applications and submit the applications to lenders for final approval. Frequently, they work with or for mortgage banking companies in these activities. They are not involved in servicing a loan once it is made. Many mortgage brokers are also real estate brokers who offer these financing services in addition to their regular brokerage activities.

Government Influence in Mortgage Lending

Aside from FHA-insured and VA-guaranteed loan programs, the federal government influences mortgage lending through the Federal Reserve System as well as through various federal agencies, such as the Farmer's Home Administration. It also deals in the secondary mortgage market through the Government National

Mortgage Association, the Federal Home Loan Mortgage Corporation and the Federal National Mortgage Association.

Federal Reserve System

Established in 1913 under President Woodrow Wilson, the Federal Reserve System (also known as "the Fed") operates to maintain sound credit conditions, help counteract inflationary and deflationary trends and create a favorable economic climate. The Federal Reserve System divides the country into 12 federal reserve districts, each served by a federal reserve bank. All nationally chartered banks must join the Federal Reserve and purchase stock in its district reserve banks.

The Federal Reserve regulates the flow of money and interest rates in the marketplace indirectly, through its member banks, by controlling their *reserve requirements* and *discount rates*.

Reserve controls. The Federal Reserve requires each member bank to keep a certain amount of its assets on hand as reserve funds unavailable for loans or any other use. This requirement was designed primarily to protect customer deposits, but more importantly, it provides a means of manipulating the flow of cash in the money market. By increasing its reserve requirements, the Federal Reserve, in effect, limits the amount of money that member banks can use to make loans, causing interest rates to increase.

In this manner, the government can slow down an overactive economy by limiting the number of loans that would have been directed toward major purchases of goods and services. The opposite is also true—by decreasing the reserve requirements, the Federal Reserve can allow more loans to be made, thus increasing the amount of money circulated in the marketplace and causing interest rates to decline.

Discount rates. Federal Reserve member banks are permitted to borrow money from the district reserve banks to expand their lending operations. The interest rate that the district banks charge for the use of this money is called the **discount rate**. This rate is the basis on which the banks determine the percentage rate of interest that they, in turn, charge their loan customers. Theoretically, when the Federal Reserve discount rate is high, bank interest rates are high; therefore, fewer loans will be made and less money will circulate in the marketplace. Conversely, a lower discount rate results in lower interest rates, more bank loans and more money in circulation.

Government Influence in the Secondary Market

Mortgage lending takes place in both the primary and secondary mortgage markets. The primary market, which this chapter has principally dealt with thus far, includes: (1) lenders who supply funds to borrowers as an investment and (2) lenders who also originate loans for the purpose of selling them to investors. Loans are bought and sold in the **secondary mortgage market** after they have been originated. For example, a lender may wish to sell a number of loans in order to raise immediate funds when it needs more money to meet the mortgage demands in its area. Secondary market activity is especially desirable when money is in short supply because it provides a great stimulant to the housing construction market as well as to the mortgage market.

Generally, when a loan has been sold, the original lender continues to collect the payments from the borrower. The lender then passes the payments along to the investor who has purchased the loan, charging the investor a fee for servicing the loan.

A major source of secondary mortgage market activity is a **warehousing agency,** which purchases a number of mortgage loans and assembles them into one or more packages of loans for resale to investors. The major warehousing agencies are the Federal National Mortgage Association (FNMA), the Government National Mortgage Association (GNMA) and the Federal Home Loan Mortgage Corporation (FHLMC).

Federal National Mortgage Association. The Federal National Mortgage Association (FNMA), often referred to as **Fannie Mae,** is a quasi-governmental agency, organized as a privately owned corporation, that provides a secondary market for mortgage loans—primarily FHA and VA loans. The corporation raises funds to purchase loans by selling government-guaranteed FNMA bonds at market interest rates. These bonds are secured by blocks, or pools, of mortgages acquired through FNMA's loan commitment program.

Mortgage banking firms are generally actively involved with FNMA, originating loans and selling them to FNMA while retaining the servicing functions.

Government National Mortgage Association. The common name for the Government National Mortgage Association (GNMA) is **Ginnie Mae.** It exists as a corporation without capital stock and is a division of the Department of Housing and Urban Development (HUD). GNMA is designed to administer special assistance programs and work with FNMA in secondary market activities. Fannie Mae and Ginnie Mae can join forces in times of tight money and high interest rates through their tandem plan. Basically, the *tandem plan* provides that FNMA can purchase high-risk, low-yield (usually FHA) loans at full market rates, with GNMA guaranteeing payment and absorbing the difference between the low yield and current market prices.

Ginnie Mae also guarantees investment securities issued by private offerors, such as banks, mortgage companies and savings and loan associations, that are backed by pools of FHA and VA mortgage loans. The *Ginnie Mae pass-through certificate* is a security interest in a pool of mortgages that provides for a monthly "pass-through" of principal and interest payments directly to the certificate holder. Such certificates are guaranteed by Ginnie Mae.

Federal Home Loan Mortgage Corporation. The Federal Home Loan Mortgage Corporation (FHLMC), or **Freddie Mac,** provides a secondary market for mortgage loans, primarily conventional loans. Freddie Mac has the authority to purchase mortgages, pool them and sell bonds in the open market with the mortgages as security. Note, however, that FHLMC does not guarantee payment of Freddie Mac mortgages.

Many lenders use the standardized forms and follow the guidelines issued by Fannie Mae and Freddie Mac, as use of FNMA/FHLMC forms is mandatory for lenders who wish to sell mortgages in these agencies' secondary mortgage market. The standardized documents include loan applications, credit reports and appraisal forms.

Farmer's Home Administration

The Farmer's Home Administration (FmHA) is a federal agency of the Department of Agriculture that was originally designed to handle emergency farm financing and that channels credit to farmers and rural residents, as well as to certain small communities. FmHA loan programs fall into two categories: (1) guaranteed loans made and serviced by a private lender and guaranteed for a specific percentage by the FmHA and (2) insured loans that are originated, made and serviced by the agency.

Summary

Mortgage loans provide the principal sources of financing for real estate operations. Mortgage loans involve a borrower, called the *mortgagor,* and a lender, the *mortgagee.*

Some states recognize the lender as the owner of mortgaged property; these are known as *title theory states.* Others recognize the borrower as the owner of mortgaged property and are known as *lien theory states. Intermediary states*, such as Pennsylvania, recognize modified versions of these theories.

After a lending institution has received, investigated and approved a loan application, it issues a commitment to make the mortgage loan. The borrower is required to execute a *note,* agreeing to repay the debt, and a *mortgage,* placing a lien on the real estate to secure the note. This is recorded in the public record in order to give notice to the world of the lender's interest.

The note for the amount of the loan usually provides for *amortization* of the loan. The note also sets the rate of *interest* at which the loan is made and that the mortgagor must pay as a charge for borrowing the money.

If a state has a "Usury Act" for mortgages, charging more than the maximum interest rate allowed by state statute is called *usury* and is illegal. The mortgage document secures the debt and sets forth the obligations of the borrower and the rights of the lender. Payment in full of the note by its terms entitles the borrower to a satisfaction, or *release,* which is recorded to clear the lien from the public records. Default by the borrower may result in *acceleration* of payments, a *foreclosure* sale and *loss of title*.

The *primary mortgage market* consists of lenders who originate the loans. Savings and loan associations, commercial banks, mutual savings banks, life insurance companies, mortgage banking companies and credit unions are participants in the primary mortgage market. Mortgage brokers, who are instrumental in bringing borrowers and lenders together, are not, themselves, lenders.

The federal government affects real estate financing money and interest rates through the Federal Reserve Board's *discount rate* and *reserve requirements;* it also participates in the *secondary mortgage market*. The secondary market is generally composed of the investors who ultimately purchase and hold the loans as investments. These include insurance companies, investment funds and pension plans. *Fannie Mae* (Federal National Mortgage Association), *Ginnie Mae* (Government National Mortgage Association) and *Freddie Mac* (Federal Home Loan Mortgage Corporation) take an active role in creating a secondary market by regularly purchasing mortgage loans from originators and retaining, or *warehousing,* them until investment purchasers are available.

Questions

1. In general, a promissory note:
   - I. may be a negotiable instrument.
   - II. may be sold by the lender to a third party.
     - a. I only
     - b. II only
     - c. both I and II
     - d. neither I nor II

2. With a fully amortized mortgage loan:
   - a. interest may be charged in arrears, meaning at the end of each period for which interest is due.
   - b. the interest portion of each payment remains the same throughout the entire term of the loan.
   - c. interest only is paid each period.
   - d. a and b

3. Freddie Mac:
   - a. mortgages are guaranteed by the full faith and credit of the federal government.
   - b. buys and pools blocks of conventional mortgages, selling bonds with such mortgages as security.
   - c. can tandem with GNMA to provide special assistance in times of tight money.
   - d. buys and sells VA and FHA mortgages.

4. In theory, when the Federal Reserve Board raises its discount rate, which of the following should happen?
   - I. Interest rates will rise.
   - II. Interest rates will fall.
   - III. Mortgage money will become scarce.
     - a. I only
     - b. II only
     - c. I and III
     - d. II and III

5. Which of the following best defines the *secondary market?*
   - a. lenders who exclusively deal in second mortgages
   - b. where loans are bought and sold after they have been originated
   - c. the major lender of residential mortgages and trust deeds
   - d. the major lender of FHA and VA loans

6. Generally, the most active participant in the residential-loan market is which of the following?
   - a. commercial bank
   - b. credit union
   - c. savings and loan association
   - d. mortgage banker

7 Which of the following is a participant in the secondary market?
   - a. FNMA
   - b. GNMA
   - c. RESPA
   - d. a and b

8. The person who obtains a real estate loan by signing a note and a mortgage is called the:
   - a. mortgagor.
   - b. beneficiary.
   - c. mortgagee.
   - d. vendor.

9. A loan charge of three points on a $120,000 loan is:
   - a. $450.
   - b. $116,400.
   - c. $4,500.
   - d. $3,600.

10. In Pennsylvania, a borrower in default on a mortgage loan may retain title to the property by redeeming the loan:
    - I. at any time before a foreclosure sale.
    - II. within one year after the property is sold to satisfy the debt.
      - a. I only
      - b. II only
      - c. both I and II
      - d. neither I nor II

11. A borrower obtains a $76,000 mortgage loan at 10½ percent interest. If the monthly payments of $695.21 are credited first on interest and then on principal, what will the balance of the principal be after the borrower makes the first payment?
    - a. $75,335.00
    - b. $75,943.33
    - c. $75,969.79
    - d. $75,304.79

12. Which of the following is true of a second
    mortgage?
    a. It has priority over a first mortgage.
    b. It cannot be used as a security
       instrument.
    c. It is not negotiable.
    d. It is usually issued at a higher rate of
       interest than a first mortgage.

14

Pennsylvania Real Estate Licensing and Registration Act

Key Terms

Associate broker
Broker of record
Builder-owner salesperson
Business name
Commingling
Commissioner of Professional and Occupational Affairs
Conflict of interest
Escrow account
Estimated cost and return statement
Guilty knowledge
Limited broker
Limited salesperson
Panic selling
Pennsylvania Human Relations Act
Pennsylvania Real Estate Licensing and Registration Act
Real estate broker
Real Estate Recovery Fund
Real estate salesperson
Rental listing referral agent
State Real Estate Commission

Overview

All states, the District of Columbia and the Canadian provinces have adopted real estate license laws. These laws provide the states with authority to license and regulate the activities of real estate brokers and salespeople. Although a fee is charged for real estate licenses, the purpose of the license laws generally is not to raise revenue. Rather, the laws have been enacted to: (1) protect the public from dishonest or incompetent brokers and salespeople, (2) prescribe certain standards and qualifications for licensing brokers and salespeople, (3) raise the standards of the real estate profession and (4) protect licensed brokers and salespeople from unfair or improper competition. This chapter will focus on the *Pennsylvania Real Estate Licensing and Registration Act* and the *Rules and Regulations of the Real Estate Commission*. As a prospective licensee you must be thoroughly familiar with their provisions; many of the questions that appear on the state portion of the Pennsylvania Real Estate Licensing Examination are taken specifically from the license law and rules and regulations.

Pennsylvania Real Estate Licensing and Registration Act

The state's first legislation written to regulate the real estate business was the Pennsylvania Real Estate Brokers License Act, passed by the General Assembly on May 1, 1929. The law has subsequently been replaced and amended. The **Pennsylvania Real Estate Licensing and Registration Act,** as it is currently named, was passed February 19, 1980, and has been amended most recently in 1984. It exists to protect the public by defining licensed activities, licensure requirements and standards of conduct and practice, and by regulating real estate schools and promotional land sales.

In addition to the statute itself, the **State Real Estate Commission** has developed *Rules and Regulations* that elaborate on the basic law and provide additional guidelines for real estate licensees. These rules and regulations have the same force and effect as the law.

This chapter contains the major provisions of the licensing act that are in effect and revised rules and regulations as they are expected to be adopted by the date of publication of this text. Be advised that the licensing act and rules and regulations could be amended at any time by legislative action. The language has been simplified and the material reorganized to help the student better understand this important information. The complete text of the licensing act is in Appendix D; the Commission's rules and regulations may be obtained without cost from the State Real Estate Commission, P.O. Box 2649, Harrisburg, PA 17105-2649.

Who Must Be Licensed

The Pennsylvania license law requires that any person or foreign or domestic corporation, association or partnership acting as a real estate broker or a salesperson in Pennsylvania must hold a license issued by the Department of State.

Definitions

Real estate broker. Section 201 of the licensing act and Regulation 35.201 define a **real estate broker** as a person or corporation, association or partnership who performs, offers to perform, or holds himself or herself out as performing any of the following actions for another's real estate in return for a fee, commission or other valuable consideration:

1. negotiates with or aids a person in locating or obtaining for purchase, lease or acquisition of interest in any real estate;

2. negotiates the listing, sale, purchase, exchange, lease, time share, financing or option for any real estate;

3. manages or appraises any real estate;

4. represents himself or herself as a real estate consultant, counselor or house finder;

5. undertakes to promote the sale, exchange, purchase or rental of real estate (with the exception of any person or entity whose main business is that of advertising, promotions or public relations);

6. attempts to perform any of the above acts.

Cemetery plots and mausoleums are considered real estate. Persons selling cemetery plots and mausoleums are required to obtain special licenses, which will be discussed later in the chapter.

Real estate salesperson. Section 201 of the licensing act and Regulation 35.201 define a **real estate salesperson** as one who is employed by a licensed real estate broker to perform any of the following acts:

1. Sell, offer to sell or list real estate for sale;

2. Buy or offer to buy real estate;

3. Negotiate the purchase, sale or exchange of real estate;

4. Negotiate a loan on real estate;

5. Lease, rent or offer to lease or rent real estate;

6. Collect, offer or attempt to collect rent.

The license law prohibits salespeople from appraising or managing real estate. The salesperson may *assist* under the direct supervision, control and total responsibility of the person's broker of record.

Associate broker. Section 201 defines an **associate broker** as a person licensed as a real estate broker who chooses to work under another broker rather than establish his or her own place of business. A licensed broker wishing to become an associate broker must return the broker license and be issued an associate broker license. Associate brokers may perform all of the activities reserved for brokers except employ salespeople and engage in the real estate business in their own name or from their own place of business.

Broker of record. Regulation 35.201 defines a **broker of record** or *designated broker* as the individual broker who is responsible for the real estate transactions of a partnership, association or corporation licensed to engage in real estate. This individual assumes responsibility for all business conducted by the firm.

Exceptions (Section 304 and Regulation 35.202). The provisions of the license law do not apply to any person, corporation, association or partnership acting as:

1. a property owner performing the previously listed actions for his or her own property;

2. a person acting under a duly recorded power of attorney;

3. an attorney-at-law performing any of the previously listed actions within the scope of the attorney–client relationship;

4. a trustee in bankruptcy, administrator or executor acting under court order;

5. a trustee acting under the authority of a will or deed;

6. an elected officer of a federal or state banking institution or trust company performing any of the previously listed acts for property belonging to the institution or company;

7. an officer or employee of a cemetery company who, as incidental to principal duties, shows cemetery lots without compensation;

8. a cemetery or cemetery company owned by a church, religious congregation or fraternal organization;

9. an employee of a public utility who performs duties with respect to the purchase, sale or lease of property held by the utility;

10. an auctioneer at a bona fide auction who is licensed under current Pennsylvania auctioneer licensing laws.

The State Real Estate Commission

In 1963 the State Real Estate Commission was placed under the direction of the **Commissioner of Professional and Occupational Affairs,** Department of State. The Pennsylvania license act gives the Commission the power to supervise and investigate the actions of any individual or firm engaged in the real estate business in the state. The act also grants the commission the power to create any rules and regulations it considers necessary for the effective enforcement of the state license act.

The State Real Estate Commission is composed of 11 people: the Commissioner of Professional and Occupational Affairs, the Director of the Bureau of Consumer Protection or his or her designee and nine representatives from the public and the real estate industry. Five members must be licensed real estate brokers who have been active in the real estate business in Pennsylvania for *at least ten years immediately prior to appointment.* One member must have been engaged in the sale of cemetery lots for ten years and have been licensed to do so for at least five years prior to the appointment. Three people—called *public members*—are appointed from outside the real estate industry. All members of the Commission are appointed by the governor for staggered five-year terms. A Commission chairperson may be chosen. In addition, the Commission may appoint a secretary, who need not be a Commission member, to carry out the resolutions of the Commission.

Licensing Procedures (Section 501)

Licenses shall be granted to and renewed only for persons who bear a good reputation for honesty, trustworthiness, integrity and competence to transact business. Applications are made on forms provided by the Real Estate Commission. The Commission has the authority to verify the accuracy of papers filed. This includes evidence of satisfaction of qualifications for licensure and the statements made on applications. Untruthful and inaccurate statements would be grounds for denial of the application or disciplinary action against a licensee who participated in untruthful representations.

License renewal. All real estate licenses expire the last day of February every two years. Consequently, when a license is first issued, it expires at the end of the current license period. An individual who chooses not to renew the license may escrow it and be inactive. The maximum inactive period is five years before retesting is required for the license to be reissued. Any person who continues in business after the renewal date without renewing the license may be subject to disciplinary action.

Fees (Section 407)

The Real Estate Commission has the authority under the license law to set fees. These are reviewed in accordance with the "Regulatory Review Act" and may be revised from time to time as necessary to match expenditures to meet minimum enforcement efforts of the Bureau of Professional and Occupational Affairs. Fees are collected for such items as license applications and renewal, reissuing of licenses, recovery fund, branch offices and fees relating to the conduct of private real estate schools. Current fees are listed on the forms that they accompany.

Application and Requirements

Broker requirements (Sections 511 and 512 and Regulations 35.221, .222 and .271). A person applying for a real estate broker's license must:

1. be at least 21 years of age;

2. be a high school graduate or equivalent;

3. be actively engaged as a licensed salesperson for three years prior to application (or equivalent experience) and serve proof of the activities;

4. have acquired 16 credits or 240 hours of instruction in professional real estate education as determined by the Commission within 10 years of the date of passing the license examination;

5. pass a written examination prescribed by the Commission within three years of license application;

6. state the name and address where the applicant will do business after licensure. This place of business must meet the requirements set forth by the Commission, as discussed later in this chapter;

7. submit recommendations attesting to good reputation for honesty, trustworthiness, integrity and competence from one licensed real estate broker and two unrelated property owners from the county where the applicant resides or does business.

Salesperson requirements (Sections 521 and 522 and Regulations 35.223 and .272). A person applying for a real estate salesperson license must:

1. be at least 18 years of age;

2. have completed four credits or 60 hours of instruction in basic real estate courses as determined by the Commission within 10 years of the date of passing the examination;

3. pass a written examination prescribed by the Commission within three years of license application;

4. submit a sworn statement from the broker with whom the applicant desires to be affiliated attesting to the applicant's reputation for honesty, trustworthiness, integrity and competence and that the broker will actively supervise and train the applicant.

Examinations (Section 403 and Regulations 35.271–.275)

Applicants for broker or salesperson licenses must pass an examination prescribed by the Real Estate Commission. These examinations are prepared and administered by Educational Testing Service (ETS) of Princeton, New Jersey, an independent testing service. See Appendix A for a description of the examination.

Applicants are admitted to the examination on the date requested in the application provided this application is received by ETS by the filing deadline. Late registrants are admitted to the examination on-site as "walk-in" candidates. Fees and admission procedures are described in the "Candidate Bulletin" provided by ETS.

Licensing Corporations (Sections 513 and 533 and Regulation 53.222)

Corporations, partnerships and associations may be licensed as real estate brokers by meeting all the requirements for regular licensure. In addition, the corporate application must name the *broker of record* or *designated broker* to be responsible for all business conducted by the firm. The designated broker must be licensed as a broker. Although the designated broker has the responsibility for overseeing all real estate transactions, every officer or partner who will actively engage in the practice of real estate must be individually licensed. Corporations, partnerships and associations may be licensed as brokers or limited brokers (see the following discussion).

Limited Licenses (Sections 531, 532, 541 and 542 and Regulations 35.224, .225 and .273)

Limited licenses are issued to persons engaged in the specialized practice of the sale of cemetery lots, plots and mausoleum spaces. A **limited broker** license permits the licensee to engage only in this area of specialization. The limited broker must comply with the requirements for an office and be responsible for the business activities of the firm in the same manner as a licensed broker. The requirements for this license are essentially the same as for a broker except that the educational requirement is reduced to four credits or 60 hours of instruction as determined by the Commission.

A **limited salesperson** license is issued to any person employed by a broker or limited broker to engage in the specialized field of cemetery lot sales as previously described. The applicant is required to be at least 18 years of age and submit a sworn affidavit from the employing broker attesting to the applicant's good reputation and that the broker will actively supervise and train the applicant. There is no education or examination requirement.

Builder-Owner Salesperson License (Sections 201, 551 and 552 and Regulations 35.226 and .274)

The **builder-owner salesperson** license is issued to a person who is a full-time employee of a builder-owner of single-family and multifamily dwellings and who is authorized, on behalf of the builder-owner, to perform certain activities relative *only to properties owned by the employer*. The licensee may list, sell, negotiate the sale or exchange, lease or rent real estate and collect rent. The license procedures are similar to those of a salesperson except that there is no education requirement. The builder-owner, who is unlicensed, functions in place of the broker/ employer.

Rental Listing Referral Agent (Sections 201 and 561 and Regulations 35.227 and .275)

The **rental listing referral agent** license is issued to the owner or manager whose business collects rental information for the purpose of referring prospective tenants to rental units. The licensee is responsible for verifying the availability of rental units no more than four days prior to the day the list is given to a prospective tenant and a fee is collected for this service. The qualifications are the same as for the salesperson license. This licensee is not affiliated with a broker.

Licensing Nonresidents (Section 602)

Any person who is not a Pennsylvania resident but who wishes to engage in real estate business within the state must fulfill certain licensure requirements:

1. Within the five years prior to application for a Pennsylvania license, the applicant must have held a similar type of license in another state.

2. The applicant must present proof of having taken a written licensing examination.

3. The applicant must meet Pennsylvania minimum real estate education requirements. The commission will not accept work done to meet continuing education requirements of a licensing jurisdiction. It will accept real estate courses taken at colleges, universities and private real estate schools approved by the state in which the individual is currently licensed.

4. The applicant must provide certification of licensure status, any past disciplinary action and the name and address of employer.

5. The applicant must submit a written consent to service of jurisdiction (not applicable if business address is located within Pennsylvania).

6. The applicant must pay a licensing fee.

7. The applicant must furnish proof of passing the Pennsylvania state portion of the license examination.

Applicants for salesperson or associate broker licensure must have an employer who is a Pennsylvania-licensed real estate broker. If that broker's office is not located within the state, applicants must present a certification of state licensure indicating the commission's licensing authority. All applicants for nonresident licensure must submit an irrevocable consent notice that all actions brought against the licensee within Pennsylvania may be served on the Secretary of the Commonwealth.

Real Estate Recovery Fund (Sections 801, 802 and 803)

Pennsylvania's **Real Estate Recovery Fund** was created in 1980 to provide a fund to which aggrieved persons may apply for the payment of uncollected judgments against real estate licensees in connection with fraud, deceit or misrepresentation in a real estate transaction.

Every licensee must pay an initial $10 fee to the fund upon application for licensure. Individuals who were licensed prior to the initiation of the fund paid the $10 fee at the time of their next license renewal. An additional fee not to exceed $10 may be charged an applicant for renewal in any year the fund drops below $300,000. This is to yield revenues sufficient to bring the balance of the fund to $500,000.

The maximum amount that may be paid out of the fund for any one claim is $20,000 and the maximum per licensee is $100,000. If this amount is insufficient to settle the claims of all aggrieved parties to a particular transaction, it is distributed among them accordingly in proportion to the amount of their original claims.

In order to collect from the fund, an aggrieved person must first obtain a final judgment against the defendant licensee. After all appeals, the aggrieved person may file an application with the court, asking the court to direct payment of the judgment from the fund.

In order to collect, the aggrieved person must prove to the court that:

1. he or she is not the licensee's spouse or the spouse's personal representative;

2. he or she has obtained a final judgment as mentioned above;

3. he or she has taken all other legal steps to collect the amount from the licensee; and

4. application was made within one year after termination of proceedings.

The real estate commission may defend the fund before the court and may negotiate a compromise between the parties.

If at any time the monies deposited in the fund should be insufficient to settle a claim, the commission will later satisfy the claim when funds are available, including accumulated interest at the rate of *six* percent per year.

When recovery is granted from the fund as a result of a licensee's actions, the license is automatically suspended. It is not reinstated until the licensee repays in full the amount recovered from the fund, plus *ten* percent annual interest.

General Operation of a Real Estate Business

Place of Business (Section 601 and Regulations 35.241–.245)

Every licensed broker or limited broker (with the exception of nonresident licensees) must maintain a place of business within the Commonwealth of Pennsylvania, the address of which must appear on the broker application and license.

The Commission regulations require that the office be devoted to the transaction of real estate and that transactions be conducted in privacy. If the office is located in a private home, the office must have a separate entrance. The **business name** shall be prominently displayed on the outside of the office exactly as it appears on the license.

Branch office. A broker may have responsibility for supervising more than one office. The broker must obtain a license issued in the name under which the broker does business in the main office and indicate the address of the branch office. The office must meet the same requirements as listed above. A branch office license terminates automatically with the termination, for whatever reason, of the license of the broker. A person designated as manager to assist the broker in supervision of the branch office must be an *associate broker.*

Change of address. If the broker changes the place of business, all licensees registered at that location must notify the Commission in writing within ten days of the move and submit a fee for the issuance of a license at the new address. Failure to notify the Commission of a change of address is grounds for disciplinary action.

Business name. The name under which the broker conducts business must always be the name that is designated on the license. This must be the name displayed on a sign at the place of business and any other place the business name is represented. It would be the full name of the broker as it appears on the license or the name of the firm as in a corporation.

Display of Licenses   The current license of every licensee must be prominently displayed at the office out of which the licensee works. The broker shall maintain at the main office a list of licensed employees and the branch out of which each licensee works. The authority to transact business under any real estate license is restricted to the person named on the license. The license cannot be transferred to another individual.

Termination of Employment   A salesperson or associate broker must notify the commission of a change of employer within ten days of the change. A license showing the name and address of the new employing broker will be issued. Failure to notify the Commission of a change in employment may result in disciplinary action by the Commission.

Real Estate Documents

Listing Agreements (Regulations 35.331–.332)   *The rules and regulations require that all documents involved with a real estate transaction must be in writing.* Brokers are required to retain copies of all such documents for three years following the consummation or termination of the transactions.

Listings. In Pennsylvania every exclusive agency or exclusive-right-to-sell listing must contain certain provisions:

1. sales price;

2. commission expected on such price;

3. duration of the contract;

4. a statement that the broker's commission is negotiable;

5. a statement that the time period of the listing is negotiable;

6. a statement describing the purpose of the Real Estate Recovery Fund established under the Licensing Act and specifying the phone number at the Commission where the seller can get more information; and

7. a statement that monies received by the broker will be placed in an escrow account.

The license law prohibits an exclusive agency or exclusive-right-to-sell listing contract from:

1. extending for longer than one year;

2. containing an automatic renewal clause;

3. requiring a cancellation notice to terminate the contract at the end of the period set by the contract;

4. granting the broker power to execute a signed agreement of sale on behalf of the owner;

5. granting the broker an option to purchase the property covered by the contract;

6. authorizing the broker to confess judgment against the owner for the commission if the property is sold.

In addition, if the principal signs an exclusive-right-to-sell listing, the listing must have the following phrase in bold type: *"The broker earns a commission on the sale, during the listing period by whomsoever made, including the owner."*

When the principal signs an open-listing contract, the broker is required to give the party a written memorandum stating all the terms of the listing.

Estimated cost and return statements (Regulation 35.334). The Pennsylvania Rules and Regulations require a broker to provide each party with a written **estimated cost and return statement** *before the agreement of sale is signed*. The statement must give the estimated cost of each closing expense and designate the party responsible for that expense. Items that must be included on this statement are:

1. the broker's commission;

2. all settlement expenses;

3. all taxes, assessments, water bills and other such charges;

4. the financing costs, charges and any other expense for which there is a reasonable possibility that the party may be liable or responsible as a result of the transaction; and

5. the amount of the mortgage payments the purchaser shall pay as a result of this transaction.

Agreements of Sale (Regulation 35.333)

Every agreement of sale in Pennsylvania must include:

1. the date of the agreement;

2. the names of the buyer and seller;

3. the description of the real estate and interest therein to be conveyed;

4. the sales price;

5. the date for conveyance and payment;

6. a statement that the broker who has taken a listing agreement from a seller is the agent of the seller, not the buyer;

7. a reference to the real estate recovery fund (same as listing agreement);

8. the zoning classification, except for single-family dwelling, including a statement that the absence of this disclosure shall render the agreement null and void and any deposit tendered by the buyer shall be returned; and

9. a statement that monies received by the broker will be placed in an escrow account.

In addition, certain Pennsylvania municipalities may require other types of information be included with the agreement of sale.

If the agreement of sale is conditional upon the buyer's obtaining a mortgage, the agreement must indicate:

1. the type and principal amount of mortgage;

2. the maximum interest rate and minimum term;

3. the deadline for obtaining the mortgage; and

4. the nature and extent of assistance to be rendered to a buyer by a broker.

Regulations prohibit a sales agreement from containing provisions that relieve the seller from responsibility for defects in the premises, require the buyer to sign a release for such defects, or, if the house is still under construction, relieve the builder of the obligation to produce a house as originally described in the contract, *unless such provisions are emphasized in the contract by bold type.*

Finally, the broker is responsible for delivering a copy of the executed agreement of sale to all parties to the transaction.

Escrow Requirements (Regulations 35.321–.328)

Pennsylvania brokers are required to deposit all earnest monies received in a separate **escrow account** in a federally or state-insured bank or depository, pending consummation or termination of the transaction. The broker's duty to escrow cannot be waived or altered by agreement between the parties to the transaction. The account may be noninterest bearing or interest bearing; it is expected that if monies are to be held for more than six months, the account should be interest bearing. The interest follows the principal amount of escrow funds unless the parties state otherwise in the agreement.

The account is established in the name of the broker as it appears on the license. The broker may give written authority to associate brokers or salespeople to make deposits and/or withdrawals from the account. Brokers must maintain records of all deposits and withdrawals for the account; these records must be open to inspection by the commission.

A broker is required to deposit all monies by the end of the next business day of receipt. When the money tendered is in the form of a check the broker may withhold an uncashed check pending acceptance of the offer with the written permission of both the buyer and the seller. The seller must be informed of the nature of the funds. A salesperson must immediately turn over all deposits to the supervising broker.

A broker must retain all deposits in the escrow account until the transaction is completed or until it is terminated by agreement of the parties. If a dispute arises, the broker shall retain all escrow monies until the dispute is settled or until the monies are turned over to the court. If the sale is not consummated, the broker must look to the seller for a commission and may not appropriate any part of the earnest money as compensation.

Escrow in cobrokerage transactions (Regulation 35.323). If the buyer tenders the earnest money to the selling broker, the selling broker is responsible for depositing the money into an escrow account. Likewise, if the money is tendered to the listing broker, it is that broker's responsibility to deposit the money. However, if the selling broker has given the buyer prior notice of intention to pay the money to the listing broker, the listing broker is responsible for depositing the earnest money.

Escrow of security deposits for rental property (Regulation 35.321). When a broker acts as a rental agent for property, the broker is responsible for depositing all monies received as security deposits into an escrow account. This responsibility should be stated in the lease and in the broker's employment agreement with the property owner. Rents received are deposited into a rental management account, which is separate from the escrow and general business accounts.

Commissions (Section 604 [12])

Salespersons and associate brokers are prohibited from receiving compensation from any person other than the broker with whom they are affiliated. The license law does not control amounts of commissions or fees, nor does the Real Estate Commission have any jurisdiction over commission disputes between licensees.

Advertising (Regulations 35.301, .304 and .305)

A broker may not place any advertisement to sell or lease property without the authority of the owner or the owner's agent. When placing the ad, the broker must include the business name of the broker's firm as it appears on the license. "Blind ads" are therefore prohibited. A broker who sells or leases real estate owned by the broker must disclose in the advertising that he or she is licensed.

Salespeople are forbidden to advertise exclusively under their own names. The salesperson's name and phone number, however, may appear in the ad provided that the name and phone number of the employing broker are given greater prominence.

"For sale" or "for rent" signs (Section 604 [8]). The law requires written consent from the owner before these signs may be placed on the property.

Other Ethical Considerations

Conflicts of interest and disclosures (Regulations 35.283, .284 and .288). Licensees are prohibited from:

1. participating in a real estate transaction where the licensee has an ownership interest in the real estate without first disclosing in writing the interest to all parties;

2. selling or renting the licensee's own real estate without first disclosing the licensed status to the prospective buyer or tenant. A licensee is required to comply with the license law and regulations in personal transactions in the same manner as in business transactions;

3. representing more than one party to a real estate transaction without the parties expressly agreeing in writing to such multiple representation;

4. accepting any commission, rebate or profit on expenditures made for an owner in the management of property without knowledge and written consent of the owner.

Section 607 of the license law requires disclosure of who the broker represents, i.e., a broker who has taken a listing agreement from a seller must disclose to the buyer that the *broker represents the seller and not the buyer*. Additional disclosures at an initial interview with a seller and buyer (*Section 608*) shall be prescribed by the Real Estate Commission. Such disclosures will include the representation of the broker, information about the recovery fund, the negotiability of commissions and term of listings, and statement of the zoning classification of the property.

Harassment (Section 604 [22] and Regulation 35.302). Licensees are prohibited from soliciting by personal contact, telephone, mail or advertising with such frequency as to amount to clear harassment of the property owner.

Panic selling (Regulation 35.303). Licensees are prohibited from using any techniques designed to result in **panic selling** or blockbusting. Panic selling is frequent efforts to sell residential real estate in a particular neighborhood because of fear of declining values when the fear is not based on facts relating to the intrinsic value of the real estate.

Out-of-State Land Sales (Section 605)

Pennsylvania regulates the conduct of brokers, subdividers, and developers seeking to sell, within the state, subdivided land located outside Pennsylvania. This section of the act was discussed in Chapter 4, "Subdividing and Property Development."

Fines, Suspension and Revocation of License (Section 604)

The State Real Estate Commission has the right to investigate the actions or business transactions of any licensee on receipt of a written complaint. The Commission may levy a fine up to $1,000, or suspend, deny or revoke a real estate license for any of the following activities:

1. making any substantial misrepresentation;

2. making any false promise to influence, persuade or induce any person to enter into a contract or agreement;

3. making misrepresentations or false promises through salespeople, associate brokers, other persons, any advertising medium or otherwise;

4. using misleading or untruthful advertising, or using a trade name or insignia of or claiming membership in a real estate association or organization of which the licensee is not a member;

5. failing to comply with the following requirements:

   a. All deposits or other monies accepted by every person, partnership or association holding a real estate broker's license under the provisions of this act must be retained by the real estate broker pending consummation or termination of the transaction involved and shall be accounted for in the full amount at the time of the consummation or termination.

   b. Every real estate salesperson shall pay over promptly to the real estate broker any deposit or other monies on any transaction in which he or she is engaged on behalf of his or her broker-employer.

   c. A real estate broker shall not **commingle** the money or other property of principal with his or her own.

   d. Every real estate broker shall immediately deposit monies belonging to others in a separate custodial or trust fund account maintained with some bank or recognized depository until the transaction involved is consummated or terminated; at that time the real estate broker shall account for the full amount received. Under no circumstances shall a real estate broker permit any funds belonging to others to be deposited in his or her business or personal account or to be commingled with any funds he or she may have on deposit.

e. Every real estate broker shall keep records of all funds deposited, clearly indicating from whom and the date on which he or she received money, the date deposited, the dates of withdrawals and other pertinent information concerning the transaction. The broker shall show clearly for whom the money was deposited and to whom the money belongs. The account must provide for withdrawal of funds without previous notice and designate the broker as trustee. All records of deposits and withdrawals and all funds are subject to inspection by the commission;

6. failing to keep all records relating to real estate transactions for at least three years following the consummation of the transaction;

7. acting for more than one party to a transaction without the knowledge and written consent of all parties;

8. placing a "for sale" or "for rent" sign on any property without the written consent of the owner or the owner's authorized agent;

9. failing to furnish copies of any listing, sales contract or lease or other contract to all parties signing the agreement at the time of its execution;

10. failing to include a termination date, which is not subject to prior notice in any listing agreement;

11. inducing any party to a contract to break an existing contract in order to replace it with a new agreement, when this action is motivated by the licensee's personal gain;

12. accepting a commission as a salesperson or associate broker from any broker other than the one with whom he or she is affiliated;

13. failing to disclose to a seller in writing his or her intention to purchase, option or obtain any interest in property listed with his or her firm;

14. being convicted of forgery, embezzlement, obtaining money under false pretenses, bribery, larceny, extortion, conspiracy to defraud or other similar offenses, or pleading guilty or *nolo contendere* (no contest) to any such offense;

15. violating any of the Real Estate Commission's Rules and Regulations;

16. failing as a broker to exercise adequate supervision over the activities of all salespeople and associate brokers licensed under the broker;

17. failing within reasonable time to provide information to the Real Estate Commission when requested to do so as a result of a formal or informal complaint;

18. soliciting, selling or offering for sale real property by offering "free lots," conducting lotteries or contests, or offering prizes with the intent to deceive a prospective purchaser;

19. paying, accepting, giving or charging any undisclosed commission, rebate, compensation or profit;

20. demonstrating bad faith, dishonesty, untrustworthiness or incompetency in a real estate transaction;

21. performing any act for which a real estate license is required when such license is not in effect.

In addition to the above activities, a licensee may be fined or have the license suspended or revoked if found in violation of the **Pennsylvania Human Relations**

Act. Such violations include, but are not limited to, the following discriminatory acts in regard to a person's race, color, religious creed, sex, ancestry, national origin, physical handicap, disability, use of a guide animal because of blindness and deafness; users of support animals by the handicapped and trainers of same.

1. accepting listings based on the understanding that discrimination is to be practiced in the rental or sale of listed properties;

2. giving false information for the purpose of discrimination in the rental or sale of real estate;

3. making distinctions in the locations of property for different persons based on discrimination.

The Pennsylvania Human Relations Act will be discussed further in Chapter 24, "Fair Housing Laws and Ethical Practices."

Guilty Knowledge (Section 702)

A broker's license may not be suspended or revoked because of the actions of a salesperson or associate broker in the broker's employ unless it can be shown that the broker had prior **guilty knowledge** of the violation. An established course of business that constitutes a violation of the license law is considered evidence of guilty knowledge (*prima facie* evidence).

Reporting of Crimes and Disciplinary Actions (Regulation 35.290)

A licensee shall notify the Commission of being convicted of, or pleading guilty or nolo contendere to, a felony or misdemeanor, within 30 days of the verdict or plea. A licensee shall also notify the Commission of any disciplinary action taken against the licensee by the licensing authority of another jurisdiction within 30 days of that action. The Real Estate Commission may take its own disciplinary action against a licensee in these cases.

Revocation of Corporate License

If the license of a partner or officer of a corporation is suspended or revoked, the license issued to the partnership or corporation will not be revoked if the organization immediately severs all ties with the guilty person.

Procedures (Section 701)

Prior to taking any action to fine, suspend, deny or revoke a license, the Commission must notify the licensee or applicant in writing of the charges against him or her. If the investigation is the result of a complaint, the Commission must also give the licensee a copy of the complaint.

Before the Commission rules on the charges, the licensee or applicant has the right to defend himself or herself (either personally or through counsel) at a hearing before the Commission. The Commission may appoint one of its members to conduct the hearing, or the entire Commission may be present. In either case, the Commission must notify the licensee at least ten days before the hearing date.

After the hearing, the Commission must issue a report of its findings. If a single member of the Commission has conducted the hearing, that person will file a report to the Commission. The Commission may either adopt that report or undertake further investigation. Once the Commission has reached a final decision, it must immediately notify the licensee or applicant in writing of its findings and publish notice of the action in one or more newspapers of general circulation in the county where the licensee or applicant does business.

The licensee or applicant has the right to appeal the Commission's ruling to a Commonwealth Court. Notice of this appeal must be filed with the Commission.

Posting of Suspension Notice (Regulation 35.291)

A broker or limited broker whose license is suspended by the Commission shall return the license and post a notice of the suspension provided by the Commission, at the main office and any branch offices. It shall be posted prominently on or near the public entrance to each office. Failure to post this notice constitutes grounds for further disciplinary action.

Civil Suits (Section 302)

Any person, partnership, corporation or association that engages in any business regulated by the act without obtaining a license or after having had a license revoked or suspended is guilty under Pennsylvania law as follows:

Persons found guilty of a summary offense may be fined a maximum of $500 and/or sentenced to imprisonment for not more than three months for a first offense. Persons found guilty for second and subsequent offenses shall be guilty of a third-degree felony and the sentence would be a fine of not less than $2,000 and not more than $5,000 and/or imprisonment for not less than one year and not more than two years.

Reissue of Revoked Licenses

No person whose license has been revoked by the Commission will be reinstated for at least five years from the date of revocation. After that period, the license will be issued at the discretion of the commission.

Summary

Real estate licenses are granted to qualified individuals, corporations and partnerships under the provisions of the state *Real Estate Licensing and Registration Act.* The law is administered by the *State Real Estate Commission* under the direction of the Commissioner of Professional and Occupational Affairs, Department of State. The Real Estate Commission has adopted a set of *Rules and Regulations,* which elaborate on the license law and provide additional legal guidelines for Pennsylvania licensees.

In Pennsylvania, a real estate license is required to legally perform for others and for a fee such activities as real estate brokerage, appraisal, mortgaging, exchanging, and property management.

Licenses are issued for two-year terms; each license is a personal right and terminates upon either its expiration, death of the individual, or the dissolution of partnership or corporation. Certain persons are exempt from the license law, such as owners dealing with their own property, trustees, executors, receivers and others operating under court orders. Certain practices, such as selling cemetery plots, require issuance of special licenses called limited real estate licenses.

The license law regulates such matters as the general operation of a real estate business, real estate documents, earnest money deposits, advertising and ethical considerations. The law establishes a *recovery fund* from which aggrieved persons may collect unpaid judgments resulting from a civil court suit for damages resulting from actions of a licensee for such acts as fraud, misrepresentation or deceit. In addition, the license law establishes procedures by which the Real Estate Commission may investigate a licensee and subsequently fine, suspend or revoke that person's license.

Questions

1. A salesperson who is an employee or associate of a licensed broker may legally accept a commission from:
   I. his or her supervising broker.
   II. an associate broker with the firm.
   a. I only
   b. II only
   c. both I and II
   d. neither I nor II

2. If a salesperson violates the provisions of the state license law without the consent or knowledge of his or her supervising broker:
   a. the salesperson may lose his or her license for this violation.
   b. the broker may lose his or her license for this violation.
   c. both the salesperson and the broker may lose their licenses for this violation.
   d. neither the broker nor the salesperson may lose their licenses for this violation.

3. A broker's office must, by law, prominently display which of the following?
   a. the broker's license
   b. licenses of salespeople working on behalf of the broker
   c. licenses of associate brokers working on behalf of the broker
   d. all of the above

4. A real estate broker must keep in his or her files records of all real estate transactions:
   a. for at least one year following the closing date.
   b. for at least three years following the listing date.
   c. for at least three years following the consummation date.
   d. indefinitely.

5. A licensee may be fined or have the license suspended or revoked for violating which of the following Pennsylvania laws?
   I. Real Estate Licensing and Registration Act
   II. Human Relations Act
   a. I only
   b. II only
   c. both I and II
   d. neither I nor II

6. When advertising a property, a broker must, by law, include which of the following?
   I. address of the property
   II. broker's business name
   a. I only
   b. II only
   c. both I and II
   d. neither I nor II

7. If a salesperson's license is revoked by the State Real Estate Commission, he or she may appeal directly to:
   a. the Real Estate Commission.
   b. the state commonwealth court.
   c. the federal court.
   d. the state supreme court.

8. Which of the following persons would require a limited real estate license?
   I. real estate appraiser
   II. seller of cemetery plots
   a. I only
   b. II only
   c. both I and II
   d. neither I nor II

9. To qualify for a real estate broker's license, an applicant must:
   I. serve a three-year apprenticeship as a real estate salesperson.
   II. hold a bachelor's degree from a college or university.
   a. I only
   b. II only
   c. both I and II
   d. neither I nor II

10. When recovery is granted an aggrieved person from the state Real Estate Recovery Fund because of a licensee's actions:
    a. the maximum amount that may be paid the aggrieved person is $30,000.
    b. the licensee's license is automatically revoked.
    c. the aggrieved person may sue the licensee for further damages if the amount paid from the fund was not sufficient.
    d. the licensee's license is suspended until he or she pays in full the amount recovered from the fund, plus interest.

11. To provide evidence that he or she is qualified, Pennsylvania law requires that a broker applicant:

   I. furnish statements from two persons residing in the county where the applicant lives or does business attesting to his or her good character.
   II. complete 240 hours of real estate courses.

   a. I only   c. both I and II
   b. II only   d. neither I nor II

12. To meet the requirements of the Pennsylvania license law, all agreements of sale must include:

   a. the names of the parties.
   b. a description of the real estate to be conveyed.
   c. the date the conveyance will take place.
   d. all of the above

13. Which of the following is *not* cause for suspension or revocation of a Pennsylvania real estate license?

   a. accepting a listing with the understanding that illegal discrimination is to be exercised in the sale or rental of the property
   b. failure to provide the client with a copy of the exclusive-listing contract at the time it is signed
   c. the display of a "for rent" or "for sale" sign without either an exclusive-listing contract or the permission of the property owner
   d. payment of a commission by a licensed Pennsylvania broker to a person licensed as a nonresident broker in Pennsylvania

14. Provided he or she is licensed, a salesperson may:

   I. leave the employment of one broker and become associated with another without reporting the change.
   II. place an advertisement using only his or her name and phone number.

   a. I only   c. both I and II
   b. II only   d. neither I nor II

15. Persons who must obtain a real estate license in order to sell real estate include:

   I. homeowners who are selling their own homes.
   II. a trustee selling trust property.

   a. I only   c. both I and II
   b. II only   d. neither I nor II

16. A broker of record:

   a. is employed by another broker.
   b. is the officer in charge of a corporate, partnership, or sole proprietorship real estate agency.
   c. is a broker who is only permitted to sell dwelling units for a builder-owner.
   d. none of the above

17. The State Real Estate Commission:

   I. is composed of the Commissioner of Professional and Occupational Affairs, six licensed Pennsylvania real estate brokers, three members of the public at large, and the Director of the Bureau of Consumer Protection.
   II. is responsible for conducting investigations into the actions of licensees.

   a. I only   c. both I and II
   b. II only   d. neither I nor II

18. All applications for real estate salespersons' licenses:

   I. must be by citizens of the United States.
   II. must state that the applicant is at least 18 years old.

   a. I only   c. both I and II
   b. II only   d. neither I nor II

19. Persons selling single- or multiunit residences for an owner-builder:

   I. must obtain a builder-owner salesperson license from the Department of State.
   II. may work for more than one owner-builder at the same time.

   a. I only   c. both I and II
   b. II only   d. neither I nor II

20. A licensed Pennsylvania real estate broker's place of business does *not* have to:
    a. be the same as that appearing on his or her license.
    b. be located in a commercial building.
    c. constitute at least one room used for the transaction of real estate.
    d. display licenses.

21. A licensee must renew his or her license:
    I. every other year.
    II. on or before May 1.
       a. I only   c. both I and II
       b. II only   d. neither I nor II

22. To receive a limited broker's license to sell mausoleums, the applicant must:
    I. complete four semester hours in real estate.
    II. meet all the requirements except education for a regular broker's license.
       a. I only   c. both I and II
       b. II only   d. neither I nor II

23. Who of the following persons is *not* exempt from the provisions of the Pennsylvania license law?
    a. Sam Landon, a homeowner who decides to sell his home without a real estate agent
    b. the executor of a will selling property to divide the estate
    c. a neighbor who finds a prospective buyer for his friend's home
    d. a niece acting under power of attorney to sell her aunt's house

24. Every broker must maintain:
    I. a definite place of business.
    II. a special escrow account for monies belonging to clients.
       a. I only   c. both I and II
       b. II only   d. neither I nor II

25. A broker may lose his or her license for:
    I. violating any provision of the Pennsylvania Consumer Housing Act.
    II. failing to furnish a copy of the agreement of sale to the buyer.
       a. I only   c. both I and II
       b. II only   d. neither I nor II

15

The Real Estate Business

Key Terms
Agricultural real estate
Business cycle
Commercial real estate
Demand
Industrial real estate
Market
Residential real estate
Special-purpose real estate
Supply

Overview
The real estate business is more than just the neighborhood storefront with the sign "Realty" hanging in the window; likewise, it employs not only brokers and salespeople. The real estate industry is composed of a variety of people specializing in many different fields and dealing with many different types of real estate. Whether sales, management or appraisal, this business deals primarily with the real estate market. This chapter will discuss the many facets of the real estate industry and in particular how it is shaped by the influences of supply and demand in the real estate market.

Real Estate—A Business of Many Specializations	Some people think of the real estate business as made up only of brokers and salespeople. Today's real estate industry, however, employs scores of well-trained, knowledgeable individuals in areas other than real estate brokerage. Modern real estate practice provides many specializations for people who want to serve the community while earning their livelihoods.
Real Estate Professions	The specializations that make up the real estate business include brokerage, appraisal, property management, real estate financing, property development, counseling and education. Each of these is a business unto itself. To be truly competent, a real estate practitioner must possess at least a basic knowledge of all of these specializations.

Brokerage. The bringing together of people interested in making a real estate transaction is *brokerage.* Typically, the broker acts as an *agent;* that is, a broker negotiates the sale, purchase or rental of property on behalf of others for a fee or commission. The agent's commission is generally a percentage of the amount involved in the transaction, and is negotiated between the agent and the principal. Fees are *not* fixed but vary in the marketplace. The commission is usually paid by the seller or, in a rental transaction, by the owner of the property. Brokerage is discussed further in Chapter 17, "Real Estate Brokerage."

Appraisal. The process of estimating the value of a parcel of real estate is *appraisal.* Although brokers must have some understanding of valuation as part of their training, qualified appraisers are ordinarily employed when property is financed, sold by court order, condemned, partitioned, or appraised for tax appeal or a decedent's estate. The appraiser must have sound judgment, experience and a detailed knowledge of the methods of valuation. Appraisal is covered in Chapter 19, "Real Estate Appraisal."

Property management. Anyone who operates a property for its owner is involved in *property management.* The property manager may be responsible for soliciting tenants, collecting rents, altering or constructing new space for tenants, ordering repairs and generally maintaining the property. The scope of work of a property manager varies according to the terms of the individual employment contract. The manager's basic responsibility is to protect the owner's investment and maximize the owner's return on the investment. Property management is discussed in Chapter 22, "Property Management and Insurance."

Financing. The business of providing the funds necessary to complete real estate transactions is *financing.* Most transactions are financed by means of a mortgage loan, in which the property is pledged as security for the eventual payment of the loan. However, there are other forms and methods of financing real estate in addition to mortgages. Real estate financing is examined in Chapter 13, "Real Estate Financing" and Chapter 20, "Financing the Real Estate Purchase."

**Figure 15.1
Uses of Real
Property**

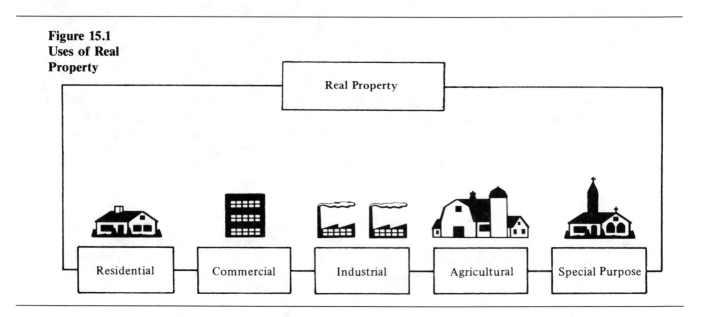

Residential   Commercial   Industrial   Agricultural   Special Purpose

Property development. The profession of *property development* includes the work of subdividers who purchase raw land, divide it into lots, build roads and install sewers; the skills of land developers who improve the building lots with houses and other buildings and who sell the improved real estate, either themselves or through brokerage firms; and the work of builders and architects who plan and construct the houses and other buildings. Property development is covered in Chapter 4, "Subdividing and Property Development."

Counseling. Providing competent, independent advice, sound guidance, and informed judgment on a variety of real estate problems, including the purchase, use and investment of property, is *counseling*. A counselor attempts to furnish the client with direction in choosing among alternate courses of action. Increasing knowledge is fundamental to every counselor's ability to render his or her services. Fees are typically a set dollar amount or on a per diem basis.

Education. Both the real estate practitioner and the consumer can learn more about the complexities of the real estate business through *education*. Colleges, schools, real estate organizations and continuing education programs conduct courses and seminars in all areas of the business. These courses are often taught by experienced real estate personnel.

**Uses of Real
Property**

Just as there are many areas of specialization within the real estate industry, there are many different types of property in which to specialize (see Figure 15.1). Real estate can generally be classified into one of the following categories according to its use.

1. **Residential**—all property used for housing, from acreage to small city lots, both single- and multifamily, in urban, suburban and rural areas.

2. **Commercial**—business property, including offices, shopping centers, stores, executive offices, theaters, hotels and parking facilities.

3. **Industrial**—warehouses, factories, land in industrial districts, and research facilities.

4. **Agricultural**—farms, timberland, pastureland, ranches and orchards.

5. **Special-purpose**—churches, schools, cemeteries and government-held lands.

The market for each of these types of properties can be subdivided further into: (1) the sale market, which involves the transfer of title, and (2) the rental market, which involves the transfer of space on a rental basis.

In Practice... *Although a real estate person or firm can, in theory, perform all the aforementioned services and handle all five classes of property, this is rarely done, except in small towns. Most real estate firms tend to specialize to some degree, especially in urban areas. In some cases, a real estate person may perform only one service for one type of property. Farm brokers and appraisers of industrial property are two examples of such specialization. The vast majority of real estate firms perform two or more services for two or more types of property. One firm may provide brokerage and management services for residential property only; another firm may perform all services but specialize in industrial or commercial property.*

Since the greatest number of individuals in the real estate field are involved in residential brokerage, most people tend to think of the marketing of real estate as the primary activity in the field. But many other people are also a part of the real estate business. For example, people associated with mortgage banking firms and those who negotiate mortgages for banks and savings and loan associations, people in property management firms and real estate departments of corporations, title insurance companies and officials and employees of government agencies such as zoning boards and assessing offices are all involved in the real estate business.

The Real Estate Market

In literal terms a **market** is a place where goods can be bought and sold, where a price can be established and where it becomes advantageous for buyers and sellers to trade. The function of the market is to facilitate this exchange by providing a setting in which the *supply and demand forces* of the economy can establish market value.

Supply and Demand

The economic forces of **supply** and **demand** continually interact in the market to establish and maintain price levels. Essentially, *when supply goes up, prices will drop as more producers compete for buyers; when demand increases, prices will rise as more buyers compete for the product.*

Production will slow or stop during a period of oversupply, since market prices must at least equal the cost of production. When there is more demand than the market can meet, production will increase to take advantage of demand. Supply and demand are balanced at what is called the point of equilibrium.

Supply and demand in the real estate market. The characteristics of the goods in the marketplace determine how quickly the forces of supply and demand will be able to establish their price. Such characteristics are:

1. the degree of standardization of the product;

2. the mobility of the product; and

3. the mobility of the parties (buyer and seller).

Real estate is not a standardized product; no two parcels can ever be exactly alike. The apparent exceptions to this are in some developments where a number of units may be built to the same specification. But even where this condition exists, each parcel of real estate is unique because it has its own geographic location.

Since real estate is fixed in nature (immobile), it cannot be moved from area to area to satisfy the pressures of supply and demand. Property buyers are also generally limited in their mobility. For these reasons the real estate business has local markets where offices can maintain detailed familiarity with the market conditions and available units. However, increasing mobility of the population and the growing impact of new technologies in communication and data handling have resulted in growing interest in geographic expansion of real estate firms. Computer-based market data networks have led to joint undertakings by widely dispersed real estate organizations.

Where standardization and mobility are relatively great, the supply and demand forces will balance relatively quickly. But because of its characteristics of nonhomogeneity and immobility, the real estate market is generally relatively slow to adjust. As the product cannot be removed from the market or transferred to another market, an oversupply usually results in a lowering of price levels. Because development and construction of real estate take a considerable period of time from conception to completion, increases in demand may not be met immediately. Building and housing construction may occur in uneven spurts of activity due to such factors.

Factors Affecting Supply

Factors that tend to affect supply in the real estate market include the labor supply, construction costs, and government controls and financial policies (see Figure 15.2).

Labor supply and construction costs. A shortage of labor in the skilled building trades, an increase in the cost of building materials or a scarcity of materials will tend to lower the amount of housing that will be built. The impact of the labor supply and price levels depends on the extent to which higher costs can be passed on to the buyer or renter in the form of higher purchase prices or rents. Technological advances that result in cheaper materials and more efficient means of construction may tend to counteract some price increases. The labor supply may be slow to adjust in an advancing market due to the skill mix inherent in construction.

Government controls and financial policies. Government monetary policy can have a substantial impact on the real estate market. The Federal Reserve Board, as well as such government agencies as the Federal Housing Administration (FHA), the Government National Mortgage Association (GNMA) and the

**Figure 15.2
Factors Affecting
Supply and Demand**

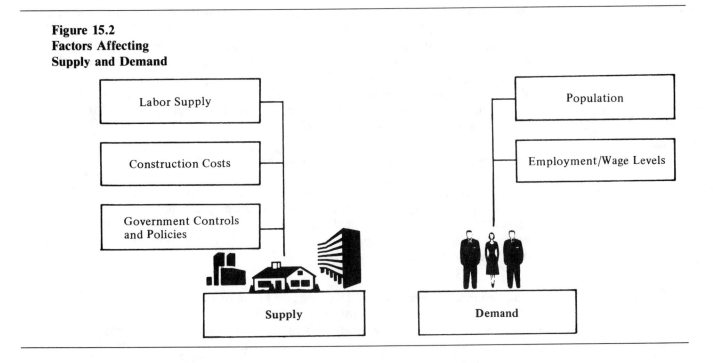

Federal Home Loan Mortgage Corporation (FHLMC), can affect the amount of money available to lenders for mortgage loans (see Chapter 13).

In addition to acting through these agencies, the government can influence the amount of money available for real estate investment and interest on mortgage loans through its fiscal and/or monetary policies. For these reasons, persons working in real estate watch carefully all government policies affecting real estate. Such policies include the amount of money taken out of circulation through interest on the federal debt, taxation and other methods and the amount of money the government puts into circulation through spending programs ranging from welfare to farm subsidies.

At the local level, real estate taxation is one of the primary sources of revenue for government. Policies on taxation of real estate can have either positive or negative effects. Tax incentives have been one way for communities to attract new businesses and industries to their areas. And, of course, along with these enterprises come increased employment and expanded residential real estate markets. Where land is not being used to its maximum potential, some urban areas adjust the assessment to stimulate a more productive use of the real estate.

Local governments can also affect market operations and the development and construction of real estate by applying land-use controls. Health, zoning and building ordinances are used by communities to control and stimulate the highest potential use of land. Real estate values and markets are thereby stabilized. Community amenities (such as churches, schools and parks) and efficient governmental policies are influential factors affecting the real estate market.

**Factors Affecting
Demand**

Factors that tend to affect demand in the real estate market include population and employment and wage levels (Figure 15.2).

Population. Since shelter (whether in the form of owned or rented property) is a basic human and family need, it is obvious that the general need for housing will grow as the population grows. However, although the total population of the country may continue to increase, this trend is not uniform in all localities in the country. Some areas are growing faster than others. Some are not growing at all. We have modern-day examples of the old western ghost towns, where the exhaustion of natural resources or the termination of an industrial operation have resulted in a mass exodus of population.

In studies of the impact of population on the real estate market, the makeup of the population, or demographics, and any shift in those demographics must also be taken into account. Because residential real estate is usually for family occupancy, family size and the ratio of adults to children are important. Marriage rates affect the population mix. Doubling up—two or more families using one housing unit—is generally on the increase, an indication of an increasing shortage of affordable housing.

Employment and wage levels. Decisions on home ownership or rental are closely related to ability to pay. Employment opportunities and wage levels in a small community can be affected drastically by decisions made by major employers in the area. Individuals involved in the real estate market in such communities must keep themselves well informed of the business plans of local employers.

In order to estimate how changes in wage levels will generally affect people's decisions concerning real estate, it is also important to look for trends in how individual income is likely to be used. Trends in the economy (availability of credit, the impact of inflation and the like) will influence an individual's decision as to how income will be spent and if it will be put into savings or some other investment. *A tightening of mortgage credit may result in income being channeled into other investment areas, with a resultant lessening of real estate activity.*

Business Cycles

Over the years, business has had its ups and downs. These upward and downward fluctuations in business activity are called **business cycles.** Although business cycles often seem to recur within a certain number of years, they are actually caused primarily by internal forces (such as population growth) and external forces (such as wars and oil embargoes) rather than by the passage of time.

The business cycle can be characterized by four stages: *expansion, recession, depression* and *revival.* The movements of the cycle are gradual and not clearly defined.

In analyzing the patterns of business cycles, it is possible to consider a number of trends simultaneously. The long-term trend (referred to as the *secular trend*) tends to be smooth and continuous. It is most affected by such basic influences as population growth, technological advances, capital accumulation and so on. Within this overall pattern are business cycles of varying lengths. Various segments or industries within the economy (including real estate) may have shorter cycles with different timing and different characteristics. Seasonal cycles also reflect characteristics in particular industries. Some relate to climatic conditions, consumer buying habits, vacation patterns and the like. Some industries (such as real estate) are much more subject to seasonal fluctuations than others.

The real estate cycle. As stated earlier, the real estate market is slow in adjusting to variations in supply and demand. Because one factor of the real estate cycle is building activity, the time lag between the demand for units and the completion of those units causes real estate cycles to peak after the rest of the economy does and to take longer to recover from depressed periods than other economic sectors. It is also important to remember that the local character of the real estate market creates many local conditions that may not correspond to the general movement of the real estate cycle.

Governmental anticyclical efforts. Since the Great Depression of the 1930s, the federal government has attempted to establish fiscal and monetary policies to prevent extreme fluctuations in the business cycle. By increasing government spending during times of recession and taking money out of circulation through taxation and control of lending institutions during times of inflation/expansion, the government attempts to promote steady, gradual economic growth. The goal of a completely stable economy often seems elusive, nonetheless.

Summary

Although selling is the most widely recognized activity of the real estate business, the industry also involves many other services, such as *appraisal, property management, property development, counseling, property financing* and *education*. Most real estate firms specialize in only one or two of these areas. However, the highly complex and competitive nature of our society requires that a real estate person be an expert in a number of fields.

A *market* is a place where goods and services can be bought and sold and price levels established. The ideal market allows for a continual balancing of the forces of supply and demand. Because of its unique characteristics, real estate is relatively slow to adjust to the forces of supply and demand.

Supply can be defined as the amount of goods available in the market for a given price. *Demand* is defined as the amount of goods people are willing to buy at a given price. The supply of and demand for real estate are affected by many factors, including *population changes, wage and employment levels, percentage of unoccupied space, construction costs and availability of labor* and *governmental monetary policy and controls*.

Fluctuations of business activity in this country are observed in *cycles*. Business cycles occur in four stages: *expansion, recession, depression* and *revival*. The real estate cycle involves similar stages, but it tends to peak after the rest of the economy peaks and takes longer to recover than do other parts of the business community.

Questions

1. Which of the following is a specialized service of the real estate business?

   a. building and development
   b. estimating value
   c. brokerage
   d. all of the above

2. The factors that influence the demand for real estate include:

   I. wage levels and employment opportunities.
   II. the number of real estate brokers.

      a. I only   c. both I and II
      b. II only   d. neither I nor II

3. Property that is part of the commercial market includes:

   a. office buildings for lease.
   b. single-family homes.
   c. churches.
   d. factories.

4. Business cycles:

   I. involve periods of expansion, recession, depression and revival.
   II. can be regulated somewhat by government fiscal and monetary policy.

      a. I only   c. both I and II
      b. II only   d. neither I nor II

5. The forces that influence and affect supply in the real estate market include:

   a. construction costs.
   b. labor force.
   c. government controls.
   d. all of the above

6. The real estate market is considered local in character because:

   a. land is fixed, or immobile.
   b. most people are not generally mobile enough to take advantage of available real estate in distant areas.
   c. local controls can have a significant impact on the market.
   d. all of the above

7. In general, when the supply of a certain commodity increases:

   a. prices tend to rise.
   b. prices tend to remain level.
   c. prices tend to drop.
   d. prices can no longer be established.

8. Special-purpose properties include those used for:

   I. office buildings.
   II. private residences.

      a. I only   c. both I and II
      b. II only   d. neither I nor II

9. Peter Dickinson is a real estate broker in a large Midwestern city. Chances are his real estate firm:

   a. performs most or all of the various real estate specializations.
   b. deals only in farm property.
   c. deals only in insurance.
   d. performs two or more of the various real estate specializations for at least two types of property.

10. In an average market, certain characteristics of the goods sold will determine how quickly the forces of supply and demand will establish the goods' prices. Which of the following is not one of these characteristics?

    a. the product's mobility
    b. the product's cost
    c. the mobility of buyer and seller
    d. whether or not the product is standardized

11. Compared with other markets, the real estate market:

    I. is relatively quick to adapt to the forces of supply and demand.
    II. is national in scope.

       a. I only   c. both I and II
       b. II only   d. neither I nor II

12. In general terms, a *market* refers to which of the following?
   a. a place where buyers and sellers come together
   b. the amount of goods available at a given price
   c. a forum where price levels are established
   d. both a and c

16

Concepts of Home Ownership

Key Terms

Actual cash value
Adjusted sales price
Apportionment clause
Capital gain
Coinsurance clause
Equity
Homeowners' insurance policy
Investment
Liability coverage
Replacement cost
Subrogation clause

Overview

Although the term *home ownership* once referred mainly to detached single-family dwellings, today's home buyer must choose among many different types of housing designed to satisfy individual needs, tastes and financial capabilities. This chapter will discuss the various types of housing available as well as the factors a potential homeowner must consider in deciding the what, where and how much of buying real estate. The chapter will also cover the many tax benefits available to all homeowners and the forms of property insurance designed to protect one of the biggest investments of a person's life. Note that this chapter is devoted to the ownership of a *residence;* the ownership of income-producing property will be discussed in Chapter 23, "Real Estate Investment."

Home Ownership   The desire to own one's home is a deep-rooted characteristic of American culture. To many people, home ownership represents financial stability, a psychological and emotional pride in ownership and a sense of belonging to the community. To others, it can represent a form of investment. Some of the expenses of home ownership, including mortgage interest and property tax payments, are partially compensated by a reduction in federal income tax.

Traditionally, the residential real estate market was composed predominantly of single-family dwellings. The typical buyer was a married couple, usually with small children. Today, however, a variety of social changes, population shifts, and economic considerations have considerably changed the real estate market. For example, many real estate buyers today are *singles,* especially unmarried women; many are *empty nesters,* married couples whose housing needs change after their children move away from home; and many are *never nesters,* married couples who choose not to have children or unmarried couples living together.

Types of Housing   As the residential market evolves, the needs of its buyers become more specialized. Thus, aside from single-family dwellings, the real estate market in any given area may include apartment complexes, condominiums and town houses, cooperatives, planned unit developments, converted-use properties, retirement communities, highrise developments, mobile homes, modular homes, time-shared occupancy and urban homesteading.

Apartment complexes continue to be popular. A complex consists of a group of apartment buildings with any number of units in each building. The buildings may be lowrise or highrise, and the amenities may include parking as well as clubhouses, swimming pools and, in some instances, golf courses.

Condominiums and *town houses* are popular forms of residential ownership, particularly for people who want the security of owning property but do not want the responsibilities of caring for and maintaining a house. Ownership of a condominium apartment or a town house—which may share party walls with other units or be separated from them by airspace—involves shared ownership of common facilities such as halls, elevators and surrounding grounds. Management and maintenance of building exteriors and grounds are provided by agreement, with expenses paid out of monthly assessments charged to owners. Office buildings and shopping centers may also be established as condominiums, allowing businesses to build equity in the space they occupy while avoiding unpredictable rent increases. The condominium form of ownership was discussed in detail in Chapter 7, "How Ownership Is Held."

A *cooperative* is very similar to a condominium in that it involves units within a larger building with common walls and facilities. An owner of a cooperative unit, however, owns not the unit itself but rather shares of stock in the corporation that holds title to the building. In return for stock in the corporation, the owner receives what is called a proprietary lease, which entitles him or her to occupancy of a particular unit in the building. Each unit owner must pay a share of the building's expenses in the same way that a condominium unit owner does. Cooperatives were discussed in Chapter 7.

Planned unit developments (PUDs) merge such diverse land uses as housing, recreation and commercial units in one self-contained development. PUDs are zoned under special cluster zoning requirements that compute roads and park areas as a percentage of the square feet of land required for homes or living units. A PUD can thus make maximum use of open space by reducing lot sizes and street areas. A community association formed as a corporation maintains common areas through fees paid by homeowners. Unlike condominium owners, PUD owners have no direct ownership interest in common areas.

Converted-use properties are existing structures, such as factories, office buildings, hotels, schools and churches, that have been converted to residential use as either rental or condominium units. For economic, structural and/or locational reasons, such buildings have been abandoned by their original owners or tenants. Rather than demolish them to make way for new structures, developers often find it both aesthetically and economically appealing to renovate the existing buildings into affordable housing. In this manner, an abandoned factory is transformed into luxury loft condominium units, a closed hotel becomes an apartment building and an old church becomes a row of town houses.

Retirement communities lend themselves particularly well to those areas of the country with temperate weather conditions. Retirement communities, often structured as PUDs, provide facilities and services to meet the physical and social needs of older persons. Under recent amendments to the federal fair housing law (see Chapter 24, "Fair Housing and Ethics") housing for older persons is defined to be occupied solely by persons 62 years of age or older or, under certain conditions, by persons at least 55 years of age.

Highrise developments that combine office space, stores, theaters and apartment units are popular across the country, particularly in metropolitan areas close to the central city. The most successful highrise developments effectively use such natural assets as rivers, lakes and forest preserves. These buildings usually are self-contained and include laundry facilities, restaurants, food stores, valet shops, beauty parlors, barbershops, swimming pools and other attractive and convenient features.

Mobile homes are one of the housing industry's fastest-growing areas of development in times of high-priced housing. Mobile homes were once considered to be useful only as temporary residences or for traveling. Now many people live in them as principal residences or use them as stationary vacation homes. The lower cost of mobile homes as compared to other types of residences, coupled with the increased living space available in the newer, double-wide models and with their appreciation in value, has made mobile homes an attractive alternative to the conventionally constructed residence. The increase in mobile-home sales has resulted in growing numbers of mobile-home parks where the owner can either lease or own space for the mobile home. These parks offer complete residential environments with permanent community facilities as well as semipermanent foundations and hookups for gas, water and electricity.

Modular homes are also gaining popularity as the base price of newly constructed homes rises. Modular homes are prefabricated structures that arrive on-site in units preassembled from the factory. As the name implies, they are modular in construction. Each preassembled room is lowered into place on the building site by a crane; workers later finish the structure and install plumbing, wiring and amenities. In this manner, entire developments can be built at a fraction of the time and cost of conventional types of construction.

Time-shared occupancy enables many people who otherwise would be unable to meet the high cost of owning a second home to enter the vacation-home market. Under this concept, many buyers purchase ownership shares or rights to use a vacation home. These interests entitle each owner to occupy the property for a period of time each year.

Factors Influencing Home Ownership	After 35 years of steady advances, the percentage of housing units occupied by their owners declined from an all-time high of 65.6 percent in 1980 to 63.8 percent in the third quarter of 1986. The high inflation of the 1970s caused housing prices to rise rapidly, but individual incomes failed to keep pace. The result is that the average home is now beyond the means of most single wage earners and even some two-income households. In 1987 the officers of the National Association of REALTORS®, the National Association of Home Builders and the Mortgage Bankers Association of America jointly drafted a document entitled "Toward a National Housing Policy." This was presented to the Congress of the United States as a set of goals and priorities to help the policymakers address the nation's most important housing issues.

The decline in home ownership is most severe among the young. First-time buyers may have difficulty saving the 10 to 20 percent down payment required for a conventional mortgage. The government-sponsored programs that provided a boost up the housing ladder for many now have more stringent requirements, and proposals for higher down payments and fees may take effect in the future.

Certainly not all individuals or families should own homes. Home ownership involves substantial commitment and responsibility, and the flexibility of renting suits some individuals' needs better than ownership. People whose work requires frequent moves from one location to another or whose financial position or future is uncertain will particularly benefit from rental situations. Renting also gives renters more leisure time by freeing them from management and maintenance responsibilities. However, rent payments provide no equity buildup. Table 16.1 illustrates the relative costs of owning and renting similar properties.

Those who choose to take on the responsibilities of home ownership must evaluate and make important decisions based on a variety of factors, including mortgage terms, ownership expenses, ability to pay, location, type of home and investment considerations.

Mortgage Terms	Liberalization of mortgage terms and payment plans over the past six decades has made the dream of home ownership a reality for many. For example, the amount of a mortgage loan in relation to the value of a home (called *loan-to-value ratio*) has increased from 40 percent in 1920 to as much as 95 percent today. Payment periods of conventional mortgages have also been extended, from five years in the

Table 16.1
First-Year Costs of Owning versus Renting

Rent an $80,000 home		Buy an $80,000 home	
Rent @ $600/month	$7,200	Mortgage payment	$7,375.20
Maintenance	120	@ $802/month ($70,000	
Insurance (renter's)	150	@ 10 percent for	
Utilities	2,400	30 years)	
Less earnings on savings:		Real estate taxes	1,500
down payment not made $10,000		Maintenance	1,200
closing costs not 5,600		Insurance (homeowner's)	300
incurred		Utilities	3,600
$202/month difference 175.20		Less income-tax savings	
between rent and		(based on marginal rate	
mortgage payment		of 28 percent) realized	
	$15,775.20	by deducting mortgage	
		interest of $7,000 and	
Assume 6 percent		real estate taxes of	
interest ($15,775.20 ×		$1,500 ($10,519 × .28)	–2,380
.06)	– 946.51	Appreciation on	
Final cost to rent	$14,828.68	property @ 5 percent	–4,000
		Final cost to buy	$7,595.20

Note: This is a simplified analysis; many other factors affect a thorough comparison. For example, remember that the market value of a home usually appreciates. Also, after the first year, a number of those variables will change, thereby altering the final costs in subsequent years.

1920s to 15 and 30 years in the 1980s. Adjustable-rate renegotiable mortgages have gained popularity among lenders in today's unsettled financial market as these loans can keep pace relative to prevailing rates.

For years, potential homeowners have been able to receive assistance in obtaining low down payment mortgage loans through the federal programs of the Federal Housing Administration (FHA) and the Veterans Administration (VA). In addition, private mortgage insurance companies offer programs to assist loan applicants in receiving higher loan-to-value ratios from private lenders than they otherwise could obtain.

Ownership Expenses

A portion of each of a homeowner's monthly mortgage payments is used to build up a reserve fund for taxes and property insurance. That portion of the loan payment that is applied to interest represents an expense to the homeowner. There are many other expenses connected with home ownership, including real estate taxes, depreciation (wearing out of the building through use), insurance, maintenance and repairs, utilities and such necessary services as garbage pickup and water supply. The owner also loses the investment return that could be realized if the money invested in a home were available for another use. The median total home ownership expenses in 1985 was 30.2 percent of income, about three times the average of the 1970s.

Ability to Pay

It is unwise for a person to buy a home without first examining the available cash reserves for making a down payment and determining whether his or her annual income is sufficient to meet all the costs of home ownership. Guides have been established to help determine the amount of debt a prospective homeowner should incur. Traditionally, lenders used as a rule of thumb the formula that the monthly cost of buying and maintaining a home (mortgage payments plus taxes and insurance) should not exceed 28 percent of a borrower's pre-tax monthly income. Some lenders have modified this percentage upward depending on such factors as the outstanding debts, potential future earnings, number of dependents and so forth. Lenders generally allow payments on all debts, including mortgage, tax and insurance, to be no more than 36 percent of monthly income.

Location

Location is the single most important influence on a home buyer's decision. The elements that contribute to the desirability of a community encompass far more than the geographic area and include such major factors as:

1. *employment opportunities:* Industrial and commercial development offering vocational opportunities;

2. *cultural advantages:* Schools, colleges, churches, libraries, theaters, museums, zoos, sports attractions and parks;

3. *governmental structure:* Police and fire protection, sanitation, water and the many public utilities (gas, power and telephone service, for instance) add to the desirability of an area, as do various quasi-municipal authorities, such as ports, public transportation, antipollution practices, forest preserves and the like;

4. *social services:* The availability and quality of hospitals, clinics, community centers and similar facilities;

5. *transportation:* A community's accessibility to people and goods depends on available air, rail, highway systems and navigable waterways. Higher energy costs and increased pollution, however, have made the development of better mass-transit facilities a greater priority, especially in urban areas. When gasoline prices were rising rapidly, the railroad systems began to attract renewed interest as an economical means of moving people and freight. Rivers, lakes and canals were the focal points of the first towns and cities in this country; and these same water routes have regained importance, particularly along the Great Lakes and adjoining tributaries.

Investment Considerations

The purchase of a home offers financial advantages to a buyer. The monthly mortgage payments a homeowner makes represent an **investment**; that is, the purchase of an asset that has the potential for profit. The profit may be in the form of present income received, or it may be a long-term gain due to increased value *(appreciation)* when the asset is sold. In the case of a residence, as the owner reduces the mortgage debt, the equity in the property increases. **Equity** represents the financial interest an owner has in the real estate in excess of the amount outstanding on any mortgage loan. Thus, the owner establishes financial security for the future by investing and building up equity in a residence that should also increase in value. In addition, as you will see in the following section, homeowners enjoy substantial tax advantages not available to renters.

Tax Benefits for Homeowners

To encourage home ownership, the federal government allows homeowners certain income-tax advantages. Even though the Tax Reform Act of 1986 (TRA) greatly restricted or eliminated tax deductions in other areas, benefits for homeowners were kept largely intact. For example, a homeowner may deduct from income—for tax purposes—the cost of mortgage interest (with a limitation we

Table 16.2 Homeowners' Tax Benefits	Income-Tax Deductions	Age 55 or Older
	Mortgage interest on first and second homes, subject to limitation Mortgage origination fees Mortgage prepayment penalties Real estate taxes	Once in lifetime, homeowner may exclude up to $125,000 of gain on sale of home owned and used as principal residence for at least three years during last five years before sale
	Deferment of Tax on Profit Tax on some or all of profit on sale postponed if another residence is purchased within 24 months before or after sale	

will discuss), real estate taxes and certain other expenses. A homeowner may even defer or eliminate tax liability on the profit received from the sale of a home. (See the illustration of these benefits in Table 16.2.)

Tax-Deductible Interest Payments

Homeowners may deduct from their taxable income:

1. mortgage interest payments on first and second homes, subject to the limitation described below;
2. real property taxes (but *not* interest paid on overdue taxes);
3. certain loan origination fees; and
4. mortgage prepayment penalties.

Interest is deductible on mortgages used to buy, build or improve a principal residence or second home provided the mortgage amount does not exceed $1 million. This mortgage amount is known as *acquisition indebtedness*. Interest on home equity loans is generally deductible only on loans of $100,000 or less. If the borrower refinances, only the outstanding balance of the old mortgage will qualify as acquisition indebtedness. Any refinancing in excess of this amount will be considered home equity indebtedness. These rules apply to home mortgages secured for a qualified residence after October 13, 1987. These rules are complicated and should be interpreted by a professional tax adviser.

Capital Gains

Capital gains are the profits realized from the sale or exchange of property. Before TRA, when property was held for a minimum of six months before a sale or exchange, profits were treated as long-term capital gains and only 40 percent of the gain was taxed. Short-term capital gains on property held less than six months were taxed at the regular rates.

The Tax Reform Act eliminated the favorable treatment for long-term capital gains. Such profits are now taxed as ordinary income; that is, the entire profit is included in the taxpayer's ordinary income to be taxed at the regular rate. Since the tax rates were decreased by TRA, however, the taxpayer reporting short-term capital gains has benefited.

Deferment of tax on capital gain. All or part of the gain on the sale of a personal residence is exempt from immediate taxation if a new residence is bought and occupied within 24 months before or 24 months after the sale of the old residence. In this situation, the capital gains tax is not avoided but is *deferred* until the property is later sold in a taxable transaction (such as when another home is not purchased).

If the new home is of value equal to or greater than that of the house sold, the entire gain may be deferred. For example, if Roger Johnson purchased a new home for $135,000, he would pay no capital gains tax.

The tax basis of the *new property* would be as follows:

Cost of new home:	$135,000
Less deferred gain from old home:	− 35,700
Tax basis of new home:	$ 99,300

If the price of the new home is lower than that of the old home, the difference between the adjusted sales price of the old residence and the sales price of the new residence is considered taxable gain. The **adjusted sales price** is the sales price less selling expenses *and* fix-up expenses. Thus, if Johnson incurred $3,000 in fix-up expenses, in addition to the selling expenses previously described, the adjusted sales price for his old residence would be $107,700.

If Johnson were to buy a new home within the allotted time for $100,000, his taxable gain, deferred gain and new tax basis would be as follows:

Old residence's adjusted sales price:		$107,700
Less cost of new home:		− 100,000
Taxable gain:		$ 7,700

Cost of new home:			$100,000
Less:			
gain from old home:	$35,700		
minus taxable gain:	− 7,700		
Deferred gain:	$28,000	−	28,000
Tax basis of new home:			$ 72,000

Over 55 exclusion. A homeowner who sells or exchanges his or her principal residence and (1) was 55 or older before the date of sale or exchange and (2) owned and used the property sold or exchanged as a principal residence for a period totaling at least three years within the five-year period ending on the date of the sale, may exclude from his or her gross income part or all of the capital gain on that sale or exchange. Taxpayers who meet these requirements can exclude the first *$125,000* of gain. Thus, if the homeowner in our example were over 55 and chose to take advantage of his once-in-a-lifetime exemption, his taxable gain would be zero.

Each homeowner may elect to exclude gains under the "over 55" provision *only once in a lifetime,* even if the total gain excluded is less than the $125,000 limit. When this exclusion is taken by a married couple selling a home, the tax laws hold that *both parties* have given up their once-in-a-lifetime exemption. Thus, if the over-55 exclusion is taken by a married couple and they subsequently divorce, neither one would be able to claim the exclusion in the future. Similarly, if the exclusion is taken by a married couple and one spouse dies, the survivor would not be able to claim the exclusion, even if he or she were to marry a person who has not claimed the exclusion.

In Practice...   *You should consult the Internal Revenue Service, a certified public accountant or a tax lawyer for further information on and precise applications of these and other income-tax issues. IRS regulations are subject to frequent revision and official interpretation. Never attempt to counsel clients and customers on tax issues, except in general terms. Always refer such parties to the aforementioned authorities for specific, accurate information and advice.*

Homeowners' Insurance

Because home ownership represents a large financial investment for most purchasers, homeowners usually protect their investment by taking out insurance on their property. Although it is possible for a homeowner to obtain individual policies for each type of risk, most residential property owners take out insurance in the form of a packaged **homeowners' insurance policy.** These standardized policies insure holders against the destruction of their property by fire or windstorm, injury to others that occurs on the property and theft of any personal property on the premises that is owned by the insured or members of the insured's family.

The package homeowner's policy also includes **liability coverage** for: (1) personal injuries to others resulting from the insured's acts or negligence, (2) voluntary medical payments and funeral expenses for accidents sustained by guests or resident employees on the property of the owner and (3) physical damage to the property of others caused by the insured. Voluntary medical payments will cover injuries to a resident employee but will not cover benefits due under any workers' compensation or occupational disease law.

Characteristics of Homeowners' Packages

Although coverage provided may vary among policies, all homeowners' policies have three common characteristics: fixed ratios of coverage, indivisible premium and first-party and third-party insurance. *Fixed ratios of coverage* require that each type of coverage in a homeowner's policy be maintained at a certain level. The amount of coverage on household contents and other items must be a fixed percentage of the amount of insurance on the building itself. Although the amount of contents coverage may be increased, it cannot be reduced below the standard percentage. In addition, theft coverage may be contingent on the full amount of the contents coverage.

An *indivisible premium* combines the rates for covering each peril into a single amount. For the single rate, the insured receives coverage for all the perils included in the policy (see the lists that follow). The insured may not pick and choose the perils to be included.

As previously discussed, *first-party and third-party insurance* not only provides coverage for damage or loss to the insured's property or its contents, but also covers the insured's legal liability for losses or damage to another's property or injuries suffered by another party while on the owner's property.

There are four major forms of homeowners' policies. The basic form, known as *HO-1,* provides property coverage against the following perils:

1. fire or lightning;

2. glass breakage;

3. windstorm or hail;

4. explosion;

5. riot or civil commotion;

6. damage by aircraft;

7. damage from vehicles;

8. damage from smoke;

9. vandalism and malicious mischief;

10. theft; and/or

11. loss of property removed from the premises when endangered by fire or other perils.

Increased coverage is provided under a broad form, known as *HO-2,* which covers the following additional perils:

12. falling objects;

13. weight of ice, snow, or sleet;

14. collapse of the building or any part of it;

15. bursting, cracking, burning or bulging of a steam or hot water heating system, or of appliances used to heat water;

16. accidental discharge, leakage or overflow of water or steam from within a plumbing, heating or air-conditioning system;

17. freezing of plumbing, heating and air-conditioning systems and domestic appliances; and

18. injury to electrical appliances, devices, fixtures and wiring from short circuits or other accidentally generated currents.

Further coverage is provided by comprehensive forms *HO-3* and *HO-5;* these policies cover all possible perils except flood, earthquake, war and nuclear attack. Other policies include *HO-4,* a form designed specifically for apartment renters, and *HO-6,* a broad-form policy for condominium owners. Apartment and condominium policies generally provide fire and windstorm, theft and public liability coverage for injuries for losses sustained within the unit, but do not usually extend to cover losses or damages to the structure. The structure is insured by either the landlord or the condominium owners' association (except, in condominium ownership, for additions or alterations made by the unit owner, which are not covered by the association's master policy). (Note: Mine subsidence insurance was discussed in Chapter 2, "Real Property.")

Claims

Most homeowners' insurance policies contain a **coinsurance clause.** This provision requires the insured to maintain fire insurance on his or her property in an amount equal to at least 80 percent of the **replacement cost** of the dwelling (not including the price of the land). If the owner carries such a policy, a claim may be made for the cost of the repair or replacement of the damaged property without deduction for depreciation.

For example, a homeowner's dwelling has a replacement cost of $100,000 and is damaged by fire. The estimated cost to repair the damaged portion of the dwelling is $71,000.

Replacement cost of dwelling	$100,000
	× 80%
Minimum coverage required on the dwelling	$ 80,000

Thus, if the homeowner carries at least $80,000 insurance on her dwelling, then her claim against the insurance company can be for the full $71,000.

If the homeowner carries coverage of less than 80 percent of the full replacement cost of the dwelling, the loss will either be settled for the **actual cash value** (cost of repairs less depreciation) or prorated by dividing the percentage of replacement cost actually covered by the policy by the minimum coverage requirement (usually 80 percent). For example, if the building is insured for only 60 percent of its value and there is a $71,000 loss, the insurance company will pay only $53,250 (60% ÷ 80%, or 75%, of $71,000 = $53,250).

In any event, *the total settlement cannot exceed the face value of the policy.* Because of coinsurance clauses, it is important for homeowners to periodically review all policies to be certain that the coverage is equal to at least 80 percent of the current replacement cost of their homes.

Most insurance policies will have an **apportionment clause**. Such a clause provides that, if the insured is covered by more than one policy, the total amount paid will be apportioned according to the amounts of coverage provided. The insured thus will not collect more than the value of the loss. For example, suppose that a building insured by Company A for $320,000 and Company B for $400,000 is damaged by fire and a $160,000 loss is incurred. Company A will be liable for $70,400 (44 percent of the loss) and Company B will be liable for $89,600 (56 percent of the loss).

Most policies will also have a **subrogation clause** providing that if the insured collects for damage from the insurance company, any rights the insured may have to sue the person who caused the damage will be assigned to the insurance company. A subrogation clause allows the insurer to pursue legal action to collect the amount paid out from the party at fault and prevents the insured from collecting twice for the same damage.

Federal Flood Insurance Program

The National Flood Insurance Act of 1968 was authorized by Congress to help owners of property located in flood-prone areas by subsidizing flood insurance. As of 1975, such property owners must obtain flood damage insurance on properties financed by mortgages or other loans, grants or guarantees obtained from federal agencies and federally insured or regulated lending institutions. The program also seeks to improve future management for flood-plain areas through land-use and control measures.

The Department of Housing and Urban Development (HUD), which administers the flood program, has prepared maps and identified specific flood-prone areas throughout the country. Property owners in the designated areas who do not obtain flood insurance (either because they do not want it or because they do not qualify as a result of their communities' not having properly entered the program) are unable to obtain federal and federally related financial assistance.

In designated areas, flood insurance coverage is required on all types of buildings—residential, commercial, industrial and agricultural—for either the value of the property or the amount of the mortgage loan, subject to the maximum limits available. Policies are written annually and can be purchased from any licensed property insurance broker, the National Flood Insurance Program or the designated servicing companies in each state.

Summary

One of the main goals of most Americans is the ownership of their own homes.

In addition to single-family homes, current trends in *home ownership* include apartment complexes, condominiums and town houses, cooperatives, planned unit developments, retirement communities, highrise developments, converted-use properties, modular homes, mobile homes and time-shared occupancy of vacation homes.

In considering the purchase of a home, a prospective buyer should be aware of both the advantages and disadvantages of home ownership. While a homeowner gains financial security and pride of ownership, the costs of ownership—both the initial price and the continuing expenses—must be considered. When purchasing a home, a prospective buyer should note its specific characteristics and evaluate the desirability of the community based on the standards of its cultural activities, employment opportunities, recreational and social facilities and transportation.

One of the *income-tax benefits* available to homeowners allows them to deduct mortgage-interest payments and property taxes from their federal income tax returns. Income tax on this gain may be deferred if the homeowner purchases and occupies another residence within 24 months before or after the sale. Homeowners over the age of 55 are given additional benefits.

To protect their investment in real estate, most homeowners purchase insurance. A standard *homeowner's insurance policy* covers fire, theft and liability and can be extended to cover many types of less common risks. Another type of insurance, which covers personal property only, is available to people who live in apartments and condominiums. In addition to homeowners' insurance, the federal government makes flood insurance mandatory for people living in flood-prone areas who wish to obtain federally regulated or federally insured mortgage loans. Many homeowners' policies contain a *coinsurance clause* that requires the policyholder to maintain fire insurance in an amount equal to 80 percent of the replacement cost of the home. If this percentage is not met, the policyholder may not be reimbursed for the full repair costs if a loss occurs.

If a homeowner carries insurance issued by more than one company, any benefits paid out will be prorated according to the insured amount under each policy. A subrogation clause enables an insurer to sue the party responsible for damage to the insured's property.

Questions

1. The real cost of owning a home includes certain costs or expenses that many people tend to overlook. Which of the following is *not* a cost or expense of owning a home?

   a. interest paid on borrowed capital
   b. homeowners' insurance
   c. maintenance and repairs
   d. taxes on personal property

2. Federal income tax laws allow for:

   I. a tax on one-half of the capital gains realized from the sale of residence.
   II. the deduction from a homeowner's taxable income of all home mortgage interest paid.

   a. I only   c. both I and II
   b. II only   d. neither I nor II

3. When a person buys a house using a mortgage loan, the difference between the amount owed on the property and what it is worth represents the homeowner's:

   a. tax basis.   c. replacement cost.
   b. equity.   d. capital gain.

4. When a homebuyer chooses a location in which to live, he or she is likely to be influenced by the area's:

   a. transportation facilities.
   b. employment opportunities.
   c. social services.
   d. all of the above

5. A typical homeowner's insurance policy covers:

   a. the cost of medical expenses for a person injured in the policyholder's home.
   b. theft.
   c. vandalism.
   d. all of the above

6. A building that is remodeled into residential units and is no longer used for the purpose for which it was originally built would be a(n):

   a. converted-use property.
   b. example of urban homesteading.
   c. planned unit development.
   d. modular home.

7. Which of the following would be likely to affect a person's decision to purchase a home?

   I. current interest rates
   II. investment considerations

   a. I only   c. both I and II
   b. II only   d. neither I nor II

8. Which of the following factors should a person consider when purchasing a home as a long-term investment?

   I. affordability
   II. the future marketability of the real estate

   a. I only   c. both I and II
   b. II only   d. neither I nor II

9. In a homeowner's insurance policy, *coinsurance* refers to:

   a. the specific form of policy purchased by the owner.
   b. the stipulation that the homeowner must purchase fire insurance coverage equal to at least 80 percent of the replacement cost of the structure in order to be able to collect the full insured amount in the event of a loss.
   c. the stipulation that the homeowner must purchase fire insurance coverage equal to at least 70 percent of the replacement cost of the structure in order to be able to collect the full insured amount in the event of a loss.
   d. a and b

10. Federal flood insurance:
    I. is required in certain areas to insure properties financed by mortgage loans against flood damage.
    II. is a common part of a homeowner's insurance policy.
       a. I only   c. both I and II
       b. II only   d. neither I nor II

11. Federal income tax laws do *not* allow a homeowner to deduct which of the following expenses from his or her taxable income?
    a. mortgage interest
    b. real estate taxes
    c. all home improvements
    d. mortgage prepayment penalties

12. Under the provisions for liability coverage in a homeowner's insurance policy, the insurance company may settle a claim for:
    a. physical damage to the insured's property.
    b. funeral expenses for the insured's child.
    c. personal injury to a delivery person who is injured on the insured's property.
    d. a and c

13. A *town house* is most closely associated with which of the following types of housing?
    a. highrise development
    b. condominium
    c. mobile home
    d. urban homestead

14. As a general rule of thumb, mortgage lenders today will not make a loan in which each monthly payment exceeds what percentage of a borrower's monthly income?
    a. 25 percent   c. 15 percent
    b. 20 percent   d. none of the above

15. A homeowner's equity in the home is:
    a. market price less purchase price.
    b. market value less debt balance.
    c. both a and b
    d. neither a nor b

16. The profit a homeowner receives from the sale of his or her residence:
    I. is the homeowner's tax basis.
    II. is not subject to federal income taxes.
       a. I only   c. both I and II
       b. II only   d. neither I nor II

17. A homeowner sold his house for $127,500. Selling expenses were $750; the house had been purchased new three years earlier for $75,000. What is the homeowner's capital gain on this transaction?
    a. $53,250   c. $51,750
    b. $52,500   d. $75,000

18. In question 17, how much of the capital gain will be subject to the homeowner's income tax?
    a. all of it   c. $21,300
    b. $20,700   d. $21,000

19. Brendon Wilson, 38, sells his home and realizes a $25,000 gain from the sale. If certain conditions are met, the capital gains taxes levied on the profits from the sale of his home might be:
    a. eliminated by claiming a once-in-a-lifetime exclusion.
    b. deferred by purchasing another home of equal or greater value.
    c. reduced by the amount of mortgage interest paid over the life of the property's ownership.
    d. a and b

20. Frieda Wilson, 62, sells her home and realizes a $52,000 gain from the sale. If certain conditions are met, the capital gains taxes on the profits from the sale of her home may be:
    a. eliminated by claiming a once-in-a-lifetime exclusion.
    b. deferred by purchasing another home of equal or greater value.
    c. reduced by the amount of mortgage interest paid over the life of the property's ownership.
    d. a and b

17

Real Estate Brokerage

Key Terms

Agency
Agency coupled with an interest
Agent
Antitrust laws
Broker
COALD
Commission
Dual agency
Employee
Express agreement
Fiduciary relationship
Finder's agreement
Fraud

General agent
Implied agreement
Independent contractor
Law of agency
Listing agreement
Principal
Procuring cause of sale
Puffing
Ready, willing and able buyer
Salesperson
Special agent
Subagent

Overview

The term *broker* can be traced back several centuries to the Norman French word *brocour*, literally meaning "wine dealer." At that time the local pub was a village's central meeting place, and it was common practice for a customer to tell the wine dealer if there was something that person wanted to buy or sell. The wine dealer would then pass the word on to other customers; if a sale was made, the *brocour* would receive a fee for the services. Although this is the essence of brokerage, *real estate brokerage* today is a much more complex operation involving strictly defined legal relationships with buyers and sellers. This chapter will discuss these legal relationships and will also examine the nature of the real estate brokerage business itself.

Agency Defined

Agency is a "consensual" relationship: the principal *delegates* authority to act; the agent *consents* to act.

An **agent** is a person who represents the interests of someone called a **principal** in dealings with third persons. The relationship of agent and principal is called an **agency.** An agent may be authorized by the principal to use the assistance of others in carrying out the purpose of the agency. Those persons would act as **subagents** of the principal.

Brokerage Defined

The business of bringing buyers and sellers together in the marketplace is *brokerage*. Buyers and sellers in many fields employ the services of brokers to facilitate complex business transactions. In the real estate business, a **broker** is defined as a person who is licensed to buy, sell, exchange or lease real property for others and to charge a fee for the services. Working on behalf of and licensed to represent the broker is the real estate **salesperson.**

The *principal* who employs the broker may be a seller, a prospective buyer, an owner who wishes to lease property or a person seeking property to rent. The real estate broker acts as the *agent* of the principal, who usually compensates the broker with a commission. Cooperating brokers assist the broker (agent) as *subagents*. This commission is contingent upon the broker's successfully performing the service for which he or she was employed, which is generally negotiating a transaction with a prospective purchaser, seller, lessor or lessee who is ready, willing and able to complete the contract.

Law of Agency

In the typical real estate transaction, the broker contracts with a seller to market his or her real estate. In this situation, the broker is an *agent* of the seller; the seller is the broker's *client*. A buyer who contacts the broker in order to review properties listed with his or her firm is merely the broker's *customer*. The client is always the principal, not as the term sometimes is erroneously used to refer to customers. Though obligated to deal fairly with all parties to a transaction and comply with all aspects of the license law, the broker is strictly accountable *only to the principal*.

The role of a broker as the agent of the principal is a **fiduciary relationship,** which falls within the requirements of the body of law that governs the rights and duties of the principal, agent and third parties, known as the **law of agency.** The fiduciary relationship is one of trust and confidence in which an agent (such as a broker or an attorney) generally is responsible for the money and/or property of others.

Types of Agent

An agent is someone who is authorized by another to perform some activity for that person. The authorized activity will be as simple or complex as the principal allows. An agent may be classified as a general agent or special agent, based upon his or her authority.

A **general agent** is someone empowered by the principal to represent the principal in a *specific range of matters.* The general agent may bind the principal to any contracts within the scope of his or her authority. This type of agency is also created by a power of attorney, which stipulates the specific areas of authority in which the agent may act.

A **special agent** is authorized to represent the principal in *one specific transaction or business activity only.* A real estate broker is generally a special agent, hired by a seller to find a ready, willing and able buyer for the seller's property. As a special agent, the broker is *not authorized* to sell the property or to bind the principal to any contract. The principals must bind themselves to the terms of contracts.

Creation of Agency

An agency relationship is created by an agreement of the parties. The real estate broker-seller relationship is generally created by an employment contract, commonly referred to as a **listing agreement.**

Because of the special nature of a real estate broker's responsibility, the Pennsylvania Real Estate Commission's Rules and Regulations stipulate that a licensee may not advertise the sale or lease of real estate or otherwise solicit prospective buyers without the authority of the seller or lessor (or this person's agent). Furthermore, the rules and regulations require that all listing agreements and other contracts of employment be *in writing.* This is creation of agency by an **express agreement.** (See discussion in Chapter 9, "Real Estate Contracts.")

An agency may also be created by **implied agreement.** This occurs by *conduct* of the parties: a person acts in behalf of others as agent; a principal delegates the authority to act. The parties may not have consciously planned to create an agency relationship. Nonetheless, it results *unintentionally, inadvertently* or *accidentally* by their actions. This can be particularly troublesome if it results in dual agency (discussed later in this chapter).

Termination of Agency

An agency between a principal and an agent may be terminated at any time, except in the case of an agency coupled with an interest. An agency may be terminated for any of the following reasons:

1. the death or incapacity of either party (notice of death is not necessary);

2. destruction or condemnation of the property;

3. expiration of the terms of the agency;

4. mutual agreement to terminate the agency;

5. breach by one of the parties, such as abandonment by the agent or revocation by the principal (the breaching party might be liable for damages);

6. by operation of law, as in a bankruptcy of the principal (since title to the property would be transferred to a court-appointed receiver); and/or

7. completion or fulfillment of the purpose for which the agency was created.

An **agency coupled with an interest** is an agency relationship in which the agent is given an interest in the subject of the agency (such as the property being sold). Such an agency *cannot be revoked by the principal, nor can it be terminated upon the principal's death.* For example, a broker might supply the financing for a condominium development, provided the developer agrees to give the broker the exclusive right to sell the completed condo units. Since this is an agency coupled with an interest, the developer would not be able to revoke the listing agreement after the broker provided the financing.

Buyer as Principal

Generally, a real estate broker is hired by a seller to locate a buyer for the seller's real property. In some cases, however, a broker may be hired by a potential buyer to find that person a parcel of real estate that possesses certain characteristics or is usable for specific purposes. A prospective purchaser seeking commercial or industrial property is particularly likely to hire a broker for this reason. In this situation, the broker and the buyer usually will draw up an agreement commonly referred to as a **finder's agreement** or *buyer agency agreement.* This document details the nature of the property desired and the amount of the broker's compensation. Note that regardless of whether an employment agreement between the broker and his or her principal is a contract to sell or to acquire property, it usually authorizes the broker to act for the principal but does not carry with it a guarantee that the broker will be able to perform. But as an agent of the principal, the broker is obligated to make a maximum effort to carry out the duties successfully.

Agent's Responsibilities to Principal

The broker, as an agent, owes the principal certain duties. These duties are clear and specific. They are not simply moral or ethical; they are *determined by* the law—the *law of agency.* An agent has a *fiduciary relationship* with the principal; that is, a relationship of trust and confidence between employer and employee. This confidential relationship carries with it certain duties that the broker must perform—the duties of **care, obedience, accounting, loyalty** and **disclosure**, easily remembered as the word **COALD** (see Figure 17.1).

Care. The broker, as an agent, must exercise a reasonable degree of care while transacting business entrusted by the principal. The principal expects the agent to have skill and expertise in real estate matters that are superior to the average person. This requires the agent to discover all facts that are pertinent to the principal's affairs. Remember, the broker is liable to the principal for any loss resulting from negligence or carelessness.

Obedience. The broker is obligated at all times to act in good faith and in conformity with the principal's instructions and authority. Again, a broker is liable for any losses incurred by the principal due to any acts the broker performs that are not within the scope of authority. The agent's duty is to obey *lawful and ethical* instructions, promptly and efficiently. Obedience to *unlawful* instructions violates the agent's duty of loyalty. Refusing to make a property available to minorities or concealing the condition of a property, per a principal's request, are examples of unlawful instructions. The broker may disobey a principal or perform acts beyond his or her authority in an emergency situation so long as the broker's actions are in the principal's best interests.

Accounting. The broker must be able to report the status of all funds received from, or on behalf of, the principal. Most state real estate license laws require

Figure 17.1
Agent's
Responsibilities

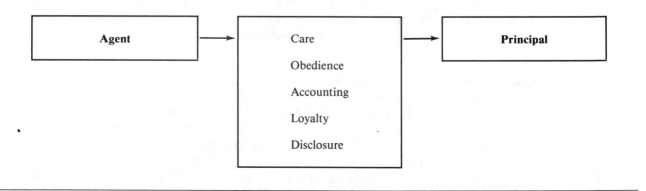

brokers to give copies of all documents to all parties affected by them and to keep copies of such documents on file for a specified period of time. In addition, the license laws generally require the broker to immediately deposit all funds entrusted to the broker in a special trust, or escrow, account; the laws make it illegal for the broker to commingle such monies with personal funds.

Loyalty. Loyalty is a must—the broker owes the principal 100 percent, the utmost in loyalty. An agent must always place a principal's interests exclusively above all other persons, including the broker. Thus, an agency cannot disclose such information as the principal's financial condition, the fact that the principal (if the seller) will accept a price lower than the listing price for the real estate or any similar confidential facts that might harm the principal's bargaining position.

The state law forbids brokers and salespeople to buy property listed with them for their own accounts or for accounts in which they have a personal interest without first notifying the principal of such interest and receiving his or her consent. Likewise, by law neither brokers nor salespeople may sell property in which they have a personal interest without informing the purchaser of that interest.

Disclosure. Along with these four responsibilities goes the duty of disclosure. It is the broker's duty to keep the principal fully informed at all times of all facts or information that could affect the principal's transaction. Duty of disclosure includes relevant and material information the agent knows or *should have known*. This duty of discovery includes facts that are favorable or unfavorable to the principal's position because of their impact on the principal. The broker may be held liable for damages for failure to disclose such information.

For example—an agent for the seller would disclose the following: all offers; the identity of the purchasers, including the agent's relationship to them (such as a relative or the broker as a participating purchaser); the ability of the purchaser to complete the sale or offer a higher price; any interest the broker has in the buyer (such as the buyer asking the broker to manage the property after it is purchased); or a buyer's intention to resell the property for a profit.

Agent's Responsibilities to Third Parties

Even though an agent's primary responsibility is to the principal, the agent also has duties to the third parties with whom he or she deals. The duties of agent to buyer include:

1. reasonable care and skill in performance of the agent's duties;

2. honest and fair dealing;

3. disclosure of all facts known to the agent that materially affect the value or desirability of the property and that are not known to the buyer.

The old doctrine of *caveat emptor* ("let the buyer beware") has no place in the modern real estate transaction. The duty of disclosure has been expanded by the courts and legislatures to include not only facts of which the broker is aware, but facts of which the broker, by a reasonably diligent property inspection, *should* have been aware. In other words, the broker could be liable for damages to a buyer if there is a property defect that the broker could have discovered and revealed to the buyer, but did not.

In dealing with a buyer, a broker, as an agent of the seller, must exercise extreme caution and be aware of the laws and ethical considerations that affect this relationship. For example, brokers must be careful about the statements they or their staff members make about a parcel of real estate. Statements of opinion are permissible as long as they are offered as opinions and without any intention to deceive.

Statements of fact, however, must be accurate. Statements that exaggerate a property's benefits are called **puffing.** Brokers and salespeople must be alert to ensure that none of their statements can in any way be interpreted as involving *fraud.* **Fraud** is the *intentional* misrepresentation of a material fact in such a way as to harm or take advantage of another person. In addition to false statements about a property, the concept of fraud covers intentional concealment or nondisclosure of important facts. The Pennsylvania Real Estate Commission's Rules and Regulations specifically state that a licensee may not make representations to give assurances or advice concerning any aspect of a real estate transaction that is known (or should be known) to be incorrect, inaccurate or improbable.

If a contract to purchase real estate is obtained as a result of fraudulent misstatements made by a broker or by that broker's salespeople, the contract may be disaffirmed or renounced by the purchaser. In such a case, the broker will lose a commission. If either party suffers loss because of a broker's misrepresentations, the broker can be held liable for damages. If the broker's misstatements are based upon the owner's own inaccurate statements to the broker, however, and the broker had no independent duty to investigate their accuracy, the broker may be entitled to a commission even if the buyer rescinds the sales contract.

A seller is also responsible for revealing to a buyer any hidden, or latent, defects in a building. *A latent defect is one that is known to the seller but not to the buyer and that is not discoverable by ordinary inspection.* Buyers have been able to either rescind the sales contract or to receive damages when such defects had not been revealed. Examples of such circumstances are cases in which a house was built over a ditch that was covered with decaying timber, a buried drain tile caused water to accumulate or a driveway was built partly on adjoining property. Cases in which the seller neglected to reveal violations of zoning or building codes have also been decided in favor of the buyer.

In Practice...

Because of the enormous exposure to liability that real estate licensees have under the law, some brokers purchase what is known as errors and omissions insurance policies *for their firms. Operating similarly to malpractice insurance in the medical field, such policies generally cover liabilities for errors, mistakes, and negligence in the usual listing and selling activities of a real estate office. Individual salespeople, likewise, obtain insurance for themselves.*

Dual Agency

In dealing with buyers, the broker must be careful of any situation that might be considered a **dual agency.** Sometimes a broker may have the opportunity to receive compensation from both the buyer and seller in a transaction. Theoretically, however, an agent cannot be loyal to two or more distinct principals in the same transaction. Thus, state real estate license laws generally prohibit a broker from representing and collecting compensation from both parties to a transaction without their prior mutual knowledge and consent. Note, however, that although the courts tend to accept this *informed consent exception,* many indicate a reluctance to permit brokers to act as dual agents. In fact, some courts reject the consent exception altogether because of public policy considerations. Many brokers today believe in what is known as the *single agency* concept, which strictly holds that a broker can effectively be a principal to only one party at a time in a given transaction.

Dual agency is a concern for licensees, not only because of Pennsylvania license law requirements but also because an *undisclosed* dual agency can result in a sales contract being rescinded (see Chapter 9, "Real Estate Contracts"), a commission being forfeited or a suit for damages. Whether by careless "salesmanship," a lack of understanding of fiduciary loyalty or an interest in bringing buyers and sellers to a mutually satisfactory agreement, the licensee may make statements that unintentionally or inadvertently create an agency to the buyer while an expressed agency exists with the seller. The agent who tells a buyer, for example, that the sellers will come down from their list price, or suggests offering the seller less while the agent convinces the seller to take the offer, leads the buyer to believe that the agent is now working for the buyer. Confiding the seller's intentions or giving the appearance of persuading the seller to accept an offer in the buyer's interest has, by the agent's actions, created an implied agency to the buyer and should be avoided.

In Practice...

Before entering into a listing agreement, a licensee should fully explain to a seller/ principal the nature of the agency relationship and the provisions of the document that creates it. Also, to avoid potential problems arising from misunderstanding under current Pennsylvania license law, a licensee must inform each buyer/ customer (at first meeting) that he or she represents the seller and owes the seller 100-percent loyalty. However, giving this information does not relieve the licensee from dealing fairly and honestly with the buyer/customer.

Nature of the Brokerage Business

Whether affiliated with any national franchise or marketing organization, a real estate broker is an independent businessperson who sets the policies of his or her own office. A broker engages employees and salespeople, determines their compensation and directs their activities. A broker is free to accept or reject agency relationships with principals. This is an important characteristic of the brokerage business: *A broker has the right to reject agency contracts that in his or her judgment violate the ethics or high standards of the office.* However, once a brokerage relationship has been established, the broker represents the principal. The broker owes that person the duty to exercise care, skill and integrity in carrying out instructions.

Real Estate License Laws

Every state and Canadian province requires real estate brokers and salespeople to be licensed. Knowledge of the Pennsylvania Real Estate Licensing and Registration Act and the Rules and Regulations of the Pennsylvania Real Estate Commission is essential to the understanding of brokers' and salespeople's authority and responsibilities. The specific details of the license law and rules and regulations were covered in Chapter 14, "Pennsylvania Real Estate Licensing and Registration Act."

The state real estate license laws generally regulate many of the day-to-day business operations of a real estate brokerage. Such matters include location of a definite, regular place of business for the firm, placement of business signs, requirements for establishing and maintaining branch brokerage offices, proper accounting procedures, correct handling of client trust fund accounts and specific manner of execution and retention of documents involved in the real estate transaction.

Broker-Salesperson Relationship

A person licensed to perform real estate activities on behalf of a licensed real estate broker is known as a real estate salesperson. *The salesperson is responsible only to the broker under whom he or she is licensed.* A salesperson can carry out only those responsibilities assigned by that broker. The salesperson is the agent of the broker.

A broker is licensed to act as the principal's agent and can thus collect a commission for performing the assigned duties. A salesperson, on the other hand, has no authority to make contracts or receive compensation directly from a principal. The broker is fully responsible for the actions of all salespeople licensed under him or her. *All of a salesperson's activities must be performed in the name of the supervising broker.*

Independent contractor versus employee. The agreement between a broker and a salesperson should be set down in a written contract that defines the obligations and responsibilities of the relationship. State license laws generally treat the salesperson as the employee of the broker in defining legal responsibilities. The broker is thus liable for all acts performed by the salesperson within the "scope" of the salesperson's employment; that is, the real estate business. This is without regard to the fact that a salesperson may enter into a contractual agreement and be considered by a broker for tax purposes as either an employee or an independent contractor. Whether a salesperson is treated as an employee or an independent contractor will affect the structure of the salesperson's work responsibilities and the broker's liability to pay and withhold taxes from the salesperson's earnings (see Figure 17.2).

The nature of the employer-employee relationship allows a broker to exercise certain *controls* over salespeople who are employees. The broker may require an **employee** to adhere to regulations concerning such matters as working hours, office routine, and dress or language standards. As an employer, a broker is required by the federal government to withhold social security tax and income tax from wages

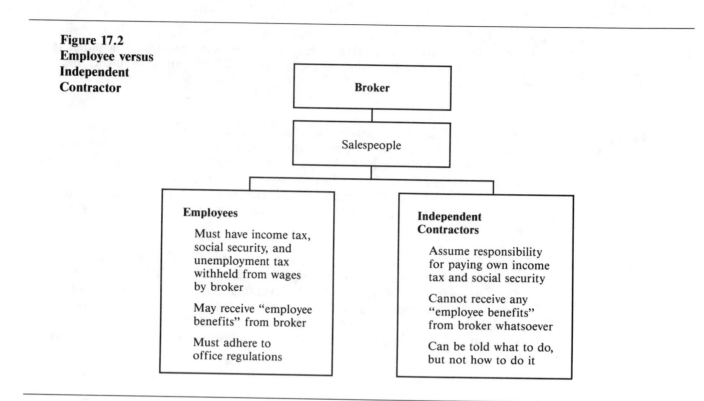

**Figure 17.2
Employee versus
Independent
Contractor**

paid to employees. The broker is also required to pay unemployment compensation tax on wages paid to one or more employees, as defined by state and federal laws. In addition, a broker may provide employees with such benefits as health insurance and profit-sharing plans.

A broker's relationship with an independent contractor is very different. The **independent contractor**-salesperson operates more independently than an employee, and the broker may not control the activities in the same way. Basically, the broker may control *what* the independent contractor will do but not *how* it will be done. An independent contractor assumes responsibility for paying his or her own income and social security taxes and provides his or her own health insurance if such coverage is desired. An independent contractor receives nothing from the broker that could be construed as an employee benefit.

In Practice...

The Internal Revenue Service often investigates the independent contractor/ employee situation in many brokers' offices. The best way to ensure either status officially is for a broker to have a clearly drawn employee or independent-contractor agreement with each salesperson on the staff. The broker should have an attorney verify that such agreements are in effect and are being followed explicitly. Brokers' difficulties in this area seem to stem primarily from an overreliance on signed agreements; a signed agreement would mean little to an IRS auditor if the actions of the parties were contrary to the document's provisions.

**Broker's
Compensation**

The broker's compensation is specified in the listing agreement, management agreement or other contract with the principal. Compensation can be in the form of a **commission** or brokerage fee computed as a *percentage of the total amount of* *money involved* or as a flat fee. Such commission is usually considered to be earned when the broker has accomplished the work for which the broker was hired, and it is due at the closing of the sale or other transaction. Most sales commissions are earned and payable when the sale is consummated by *delivery of the seller's deed,* and this provision is generally included in the listing agreement or in the real estate sales contract. When no time is specified in the sales or listing agreement for the payment of the broker's commission, it is generally earned when a completed sales contract has been executed by a ready, willing and able buyer; accepted and executed by the seller; and copies of the contract are in the possession of all parties.

In order to be entitled to a sales commission, a selling agent must be able to show that he or she: (1) is a licensed broker, (2) was the procuring cause of the sale and (3) was employed by the seller to make the sale. In order to be considered the **procuring cause of sale,** the broker must have taken action to start or cause a chain of events that resulted in the sale. A broker who causes or completes such action without a contract or promise to be paid is termed a *volunteer* and has no legal claim for compensation. In order for a broker to collect a sales commission from a seller, the broker must be able to prove that the seller agreed to pay a commission for the sale. In other words, the broker must have been employed by the seller.

"Procuring cause" must be decided by the specific actions in a transaction—the contributions of the salesperson to a buyer's decision to purchase. For example, commission disputes arise after "salesperson B" shows a property to a buyer who had already previewed the same property with "salesperson A"; the buyer purchased the property through "salesperson B." "Procuring cause" cannot be decided merely on the evidence of which salesperson introduced the buyer to the property versus the salesperson who obtained the signed agreement of sale. This dispute would be decided by determining which salesperson's efforts, such as dissemination of information and follow-up with the customer, effected the sale.

Once a seller accepts an offer from a ready, willing and able buyer, the seller is technically liable for the broker's commission regardless of whether or not the buyer completes the purchase. A **ready, willing and able buyer** is one who is *prepared to buy on the seller's terms and ready to take positive steps toward consummation of the transaction.* Courts may prevent the broker from receiving a commission if the broker knew the buyer is financially unable to perform.

A broker who has produced a buyer who is ready, willing and able to meet the listing terms is usually still entitled to a commission if the transaction is *not* consummated for any of the following reasons:

1. the owner changes his or her mind and refuses to sell;

2. the owner's spouse refuses to sign the deed;

3. there are defects in the owner's title that are not corrected;

4. the owner commits fraud with respect to the transaction;

5. the owner is unable to deliver possession within a reasonable time;

6. the owner insists on terms not in the listing (for example, the right to restrict the use of the property); and/or

7. the owner and the buyer agree to cancel the transaction.

In other words, *a broker is generally due a commission if a sale is not consummated because of the principal's default.*

The rate of a broker's commission is *negotiable in every case.* For members of the profession to attempt, however subtly, to impose uniform commission rates would be a clear violation of state and federal antitrust laws (which will be discussed later in this chapter). Yet, a broker is free to set the minimum rate that is acceptable. The important point is for broker and client to agree on a rate before the agency relationship is established. If no amount or percentage rate of commission is stated in the listing contract, and a legal action results, the court may determine a reasonable amount of commission by evidence of the custom in a particular community.

Most license laws (including the Pennsylvania license law) make it illegal for a broker to share a commission with someone who is not licensed as a salesperson or broker and performs, or attempts to perform, services for which a license is required. This has been construed to include the giving of certain items of personal property (a new television or other premiums—vacations and the like). This is not to be confused with a referral fee paid between brokers for a "lead." These are legal as the individuals are licensed.

Salesperson's Compensation

The compensation of a salesperson is set by a mutual agreement between the broker and salesperson. A broker may agree to pay a salary or a share of the commissions from transactions originated by a salesperson. A salesperson may have a drawing account against an earned share of commissions. Some brokers require salespeople to pay all or part of the expenses of advertising listed properties.

A recent innovation in salespeople's compensation is the *100-percent commission plan.* In a brokerage firm where this system has been adopted, all salespeople pay a monthly service charge to their broker (to cover the costs of office space, telephones, and supervision) and receive 100 percent of the commissions from the sales they negotiate.

However the salesperson's compensation is structured, it may come only from the employing broker. The salesperson cannot receive any fee or other compensation initiating from a seller, a buyer or outside broker unless the employing broker first agrees in writing to the payment.

Legal Rights and Obligations

Every real estate transaction involves legal rights. As each contract is prepared for signature, the broker should advise the parties of the desirability of securing legal counsel to protect their interests.

During the past several years, discussions (and, in some cases, court suits) have arisen between bar associations and real estate boards. These discussions are concerned with the protection of the legal rights and obligations of the parties to a real estate transaction.

While real estate brokers and salespeople do bring buyers and sellers together, they cannot offer legal advice—only a licensed attorney may do this. This matter has been brought before the supreme courts of some states. These courts uniformly recognize that a real estate broker must have the authority to secure some form of agreement between a buyer and seller, evidencing the transaction and providing for payment of the broker's commission.

In many states a special form of sales contract that must be used by real estate brokers has been approved by the bar associations and real estate boards. A broker has no authority in these states to use any other form of contract, and in some instances, if a broker were to use another form his or her license could be revoked. Other states have not adopted a specific form of contract. The Pennsylvania License Law does not have a specific form of contract. However, it does require certain language to be included in contracts, as noted in Chapter 14. The Pennsylvania Association of REALTORS®, local bar associations and Boards of REALTORS® have available standard forms that can be used in real estate transactions.

In Practice...   *If there is any ambiguity in a contract, the courts generally will interpret the agreement against the party who prepared it. For example, a broker is responsible for preparing all listing agreements for the firm. If there were any doubt whether a listing agreement was an exclusive agency or an exclusive right to sell, the courts would probably construe it to be an exclusive agency, thus ruling against the broker who was responsible for preparing the document.*

Antitrust Laws   The real estate industry is subject to federal and state **antitrust laws.** Generally, these laws prohibit monopolies and contracts, combinations and conspiracies that unreasonably restrain trade. The most common antitrust violations that can occur in the real estate business are price fixing and allocation of customers or markets.

Illegal *price fixing* occurs when brokers conspire to set prices for the services they perform (sales commissions, management rates) rather than let those prices be established through competition in the open market.

Leading the public to believe that there is a "going rate" of commission or fee perpetuates an impression that both are standardized or fixed by the industry. Multi-list organizations, Boards of REALTORS® and other professional organizations are prohibited from setting fees and commission splits between brokers and also from denying membership in these organizations on the basis of fees charged. Discussions of rates of commission between licensees from different firms could be construed as a price fixing activity. Not only is an ethical question raised by leading the public to believe that brokers discriminate against other brokers by failing to cooperate with them because of the rates charged, but also such action could be viewed as an attempt to standardize practices by restricting open market competition.

Allocation of customers or markets involves an agreement between brokers to divide their markets and refrain from competing for each other's business. Allocations may take place on a geographic basis, with brokers agreeing to specific territories within which they will operate exclusively. The division may also take place along other lines; for example, two brokers may agree that one will handle only residential properties under $100,000 in value, while another will handle residential properties over $100,000 in value.

The penalties for such acts are severe. For example, under the Sherman Antitrust Act people who fix prices or who allocate markets may be found guilty of a misdemeanor, punishable by a maximum $100,000 fine and three years in prison. For corporations, the penalty may be as high as $1 million. In a civil suit, a person who has suffered a loss because of the antitrust activities of a guilty party may recover triple the value of the actual damages plus attorney's fees and costs.

Summary

Real estate brokerage is the bringing together, for a fee or commission, of people who wish to buy, sell, exchange or lease real estate. All states and Canadian provinces require that real estate brokers and salespeople be licensed.

An important part of real estate brokerage is the *law of agency.* The person who hires the broker is the *principal.* The principal and the agent have a *fiduciary relationship,* under which the agent owes the principal the duties of care, obedience, accounting, loyalty and disclosure.

The broker's compensation in a real estate sale may take the form of a *commission,* or a flat fee. The broker is considered to have earned a commission when he or she procures a *ready, willing and able buyer* for a seller.

A broker may hire salespeople to assist him or her in this work. The salesperson works on the broker's behalf as either an *employee* or an *independent contractor.*

Many of the general operations of a real estate brokerage are regulated by the real estate license laws. In addition, state and federal *antitrust laws* prohibit brokers from conspiring to fix prices or allocate customers or markets.

Questions

1. Under the law of agency, a real estate broker owes his or her principal the duty of:

   a. care.
   b. obedience.
   c. disclosure.
   d. all of the above

2. A real estate broker acting as the agent of the seller:

   a. is obligated to render faithful service to the seller.
   b. can make a profit if possible in addition to his or her commission.
   c. can agree to a change in price without the seller's approval.
   d. can accept a commission from the buyer without the seller's approval.

3. To establish a firm legal contract between a broker and seller, the broker should:

   I. get an oral listing agreement from the seller.
   II. file a suit in court.

   a. I only   c. both I and II
   b. II only   d. neither I nor II

4. A real estate broker may lose the right to a commission in a real estate transaction if he or she:

   a. did not advertise the property.
   b. was not licensed when hired as an agent.
   c. did not have a written agreement.
   d. b and c

5. The statement "a broker must be employed to recover a commission for his or her services" means:

   a. the broker must work in a real estate office.
   b. the seller must have made an agreement to pay a commission to the broker for selling the property.
   c. the broker must have asked the seller the price of the property and then found a ready, willing and able buyer.
   d. the broker must have a salesperson employed in the office.

6. A real estate broker hired by an owner to sell a parcel of real estate must comply with the:

   I. instructions of the owner.
   II. law of agency.

   a. I only   c. both I and II
   b. II only   d. neither I nor II

7. As an employee of a real estate broker, a real estate salesperson has the authority to:

   a. act as an agent for a seller.
   b. assume responsibilities assigned by the broker.
   c. accept a commission from another broker.
   d. a and b

8. Mickie Michaels, a licensed broker, learns that his neighbor, Paul Cella, wishes to sell his house. Michaels knows the property well, and while Cella is out of town for a week, Michaels is able to convince Barney Schultz to buy the property. Michaels obtains Schultz's signature on a purchase offer together with a check for an earnest money deposit. When Cella returns, Michaels obtains Cella's acceptance of Schultz's offer. In this situation:

   a. Cella is not obligated to pay Michaels a commission.
   b. Schultz is obligated to pay Michaels a commission for locating the property.
   c. Cella must pay Michaels a commission.
   d. b and c

9. A person who has the authority to enter into contracts concerning all business affairs of another is called a(n):

   a. general agent.
   b. secret agent.
   c. special agent.
   d. attorney.

10. The document that creates the situation detailed in question 9 is a:
    I. listing agreement.
    II. power of attorney.
    - a. I only
    - b. II only
    - c. both I and II
    - d. neither I nor II

11. The term *fiduciary* refers to:
    - a. the sale of another's property by an authorized agent.
    - b. principles by which a real estate broker must conduct his or her business.
    - c. one who provides the financing for a condominium development.
    - d. the principal in a principal-agent relationship.

12. The legal relationship between broker and seller is generally a(n):
    - a. special agency.
    - b. general agency.
    - c. ostensible agency.
    - d. universal agency.

13. Broker Duncan Rivera lists Sam and Adele Kaufmann's house for $87,000. Adele has been transferred to another state and the couple must sell their house within three months. To expedite the sale, Rivera tells a prospective buyer that the couple will accept at least $5,000 less for the house. In this situation:
    I. Rivera has violated his agency responsibilities to the Kaufmanns.
    II. Rivera should not have disclosed this information to the prospective buyer, as it is not in the sellers' best financial interests.
    - a. I only
    - b. II only
    - c. both I and II
    - d. neither I nor II

14. An agency relationship may be terminated by all except which of the following means?
    - a. The owner decides not to sell the house.
    - b. The broker discovers that the market value of the property is such that he or she will not make an adequate commission.
    - c. The owner dies.
    - d. The broker secures a ready, willing and able buyer for the seller's property.

15. A real estate broker who engages salespeople as independent contractors must:
    I. withhold income tax and social security from all commissions earned by them.
    II. require them to attend sales meetings and to participate in office insurance plans if he requires other salespeople hired as employees to do so.
    - a. I only
    - b. II only
    - c. both I and II
    - d. neither I nor II

16. A broker may be hired by which of the following?
    - a. an owner of a large apartment building, to find suitable tenants and collect rents
    - b. a seller of real estate, to find a buyer who is ready, willing and able to purchase the property
    - c. a person looking for a three-flat apartment building at a certain price in a specific area of town
    - d. all of the above

17. Which of the following would be considered a violation of antitrust laws?
    - a. Brokers representing the Temple, ABC and All-American Property Management Companies decide to de-escalate their current price war by charging more uniform rates.
    - b. Salespeople Joe Black and Emma Marie Mitsubushi, working on behalf of two local firms, agree that Black should seek listings only from the east side of town and Mitsubushi should seek listings only from the west side of town.
    - c. both
    - d. neither

18. A real estate broker:
    - a. who makes deliberate misstatements about real property he or she is selling is committing fraud.
    - b. generally enters into a finder's agreement with a seller to find a buyer for the property.
    - c. is usually the seller's universal agent.
    - d. a and c

19. A broker is entitled to collect a commission from both the seller and the buyer:

   a. when the broker holds a state license.
   b. when the buyer and the seller are related.
   c. when both parties agree to such a transaction.
   d. when both parties have attorneys.

18

Listing Agreements

Key Terms
Automatic extension
Competitive market analysis
Exclusive-agency listing
Exclusive-right-to-sell listing
Listing agreement
Multiple listing
Net listing
Open listing
Special agency

Overview
A retailer may employ the best salespeople in the business, maintain the most attractive shop in town and spend thousands of dollars on public relations and advertising to further the company's image only to go out of business because he or she does not have an adequate supply of goods on hand to sell. Such is the case in the real estate business. Without a well-stocked inventory of listed property to sell, a broker or salesperson is no more than an office clerk without an income. The listing agreement that secures the broker's inventory can take many forms, each with its own rights and responsibilities for principal and agent. This chapter will examine these forms of listing agreements as well as some of the factors a broker or salesperson must consider when "taking a listing."

Listing Property

Every real estate sale involves two parties. The first is the seller. The second, of course, is the buyer. It is the seller who furnishes the real estate broker and salesperson with the necessary inventory: that is, the *listing*. How complete and accurately priced this inventory is will determine the broker's ultimate success.

To acquire their inventories, brokers and salespeople must obtain listings. As discussed in Chapter 17, "Real Estate Brokerage," a listing agreement creates a **special agency** relationship between a broker (agent) and a seller (principal), whereby the agent is authorized to represent the principal's property for sale, solicit offers and submit the offers to the principal. Listing agreements are written contracts of employment. A broker cannot institute a court action to collect a commission unless the broker can prove employment with the seller.

Under the provisions of the state real estate license laws, only a broker can act as agent to list, sell or rent another person's real estate. Throughout this chapter, unless otherwise stated, the terms *broker, agent* and *firm* are intended to include both broker and salesperson. However, the parties to a listing contract are the seller and the broker. While salespersons have the authority to list, lease and sell property and provide other services to a principal, state real estate license laws stipulate that these acts must be done in the name and under the supervision of the broker, never in the name of the salesperson.

Listing Agreements

The forms of **listing agreements,** or employment contracts, generally used are: (1) open listing, (2) exclusive-agency listing and (3) exclusive-right-to-sell listing.

Open listing. In an **open listing** (also known in some areas as a *general* or *simple listing*), the seller retains the right to employ any number of brokers as agents. These brokers can act simultaneously, and the seller is obligated to pay a commission only to that broker who successfully produces a ready, willing and able buyer. If the seller personally sells the property *without the aid of any of the brokers,* the seller is not obligated to pay any of them a commission. If a broker was in any way a procuring cause in the transaction, however, he or she may be entitled to a commission. A listing contract usually creates an open listing unless wording that specifically provides otherwise is included. The Pennsylvania Real Estate Commission's (PREC's) rules and regulations stipulate that any broker taking an open listing must give the parties involved a written memorandum stating all the terms of the listing agreement.

Exclusive-agency listing. In an **exclusive-agency listing,** *only one broker* is specifically authorized to act as the exclusive agent of the principal. The *seller* under this form of agreement *retains the right to sell the property himself or herself* without obligation to the broker. The seller is obligated to pay a commission to the broker if the broker has been the procuring cause of the sale or if any other broker sells the property.

Exclusive-right-to-sell listing.   In an **exclusive-right-to-sell listing,** one broker is appointed sole agent of the seller and is given the exclusive right, or *authorization,* to represent the property in question. Under this form of contract, the seller must pay the broker a commission *regardless of who sells the property* if it is sold while the listing is in effect. In other words, if the seller gives a broker an exclusive-right-to-sell listing but finds a buyer without the broker's assistance, the seller still must pay the broker a commission. Note that, according to the PREC's rules and regulations, all exclusive-right-to-sell listings must contain statements in bold type that the broker will earn a commission upon the property's sale, regardless of who, including the owner, makes the sale during the listing period. This is usually the most popular form of listing agreement among brokers. (An example of this form of agreement is reproduced in Figure 18.1 near the end of this chapter.)

The PREC's rules and regulations also require that certain terms be included in every exclusive-agency and exclusive-right-to-sell listing: the seller's asking price; the broker's expected commission on that price; the terms of payment; that the commission and time period of contract are negotiable; the duration of the contract (when it will expire) not to exceed 12 months; notice of the Real Estate Recovery Fund; and that monies received are held by the broker in an escrow account.

Special Listing Provisions

Multiple listing. **Multiple listing** contracts are used by brokers who are members of a *multiple listing service*. Such an organization consists of a group of brokers within an area who agree to pool their listings.

The multiple listing agreement is an *exclusive listing* with an additional authority and obligation to the listing broker to *distribute the listing to other brokers who belong to the multiple listing service*. The contractual obligations among the member brokers of a multiple listing organization vary widely. Most provide that upon sale of the property *the commission is divided between the listing broker and the selling broker.* Terms for division of the commission are agreed upon individually by the brokers, however, rather than by multilist agreement.

Under most multiple listing contracts, the broker who secures the listing is not only authorized but *obligated* to turn over the listing to the multiple listing service within a definite period of time so that it can be distributed to the other member brokers. The length of time during which the listing broker can offer the property exclusively without notifying the other member brokers varies.

A multiple listing offers advantages to both broker and seller. Brokers develop a sizable inventory of properties to be sold and are assured a portion of the commission if they list the property or participate in its sale. Sellers also gain under this form of listing agreement because all members of the multiple listing organization are eligible to sell their property.

Net listing.   A **net listing** refers to the amount of money the seller will receive if the property is sold. The seller's property is listed for this net amount and the broker is free to offer the property for sale at any price higher than the listing price. If the property is sold, the broker pays the seller only the net amount for which the property was listed. Although net listings are not prohibited in Pennsylvania, they are outlawed in many states. The question of fraud is frequently raised because of uncertainty over the sale price set or received by the broker.

Termination of Listings

As discussed in Chapter 17, a listing agreement may be terminated for any of the following reasons: (1) fulfillment of the purpose of the listing; (2) expiration of the time period stated in the agreement; (3) breach or cancellation by one of the parties, although that party may be liable to the other for damages; (4) transfer of title to the property by operation of law, as in a bankruptcy; (5) mutual consent; (6) death or incapacity of either party; (7) destruction of the property or a change in property use by outside forces (such as a change in zoning or condemnation by eminent domain).

Remember that a listing agreement is a *personal service contract*. As such, its success depends on the personal efforts of the broker who is a party to the agreement. The broker cannot turn the listing over to another broker. If the broker abandons the listing by failing to perform any work toward its fulfillment, or revokes the agreement, the property owner cannot force the broker to comply with it. The property owner can, however, sue the broker for damages.

The property owner could fail to fulfill the terms of the agreement by refusing to cooperate with reasonable requests of the broker (such as allowing tours of the property by prospective buyers) or refusing to proceed with a sales contract. The property owner could also simply cancel the listing agreement. In either case, the property owner could be liable for damages to the broker.

Expiration of listing period. All listings should specify a definite period of time during which the broker is to be employed. The use of automatic extensions of time in exclusive listings is *prohibited*, as is a cancellation notice to terminate, in Pennsylvania. An example of an **automatic extension** is a listing that provides for a base period of 90 days and "continues thereafter until terminated by either party hereto by 30 days' notice in writing." Some court decisions have held that such an extended period is to be considered an open listing rather than part of the original exclusive-agency listing.

Obtaining Listings

All legal owners of the listing property or their authorized agents, as well as the listing salesperson and/or broker, should sign the listing agreement. The listing salesperson can sign the contract in the broker's name if authorized by the broker.

Information needed for listing agreements. It is important to obtain as much information as possible concerning a parcel of real estate when taking a listing. This ensures that all possible contingencies can be anticipated and provided for, particularly when the listing will be shared with other brokers and salespeople in a multiple listing arrangement. This information generally includes (where appropriate):

1. names and addresses of owners;
2. asking price;
3. legal (or other sufficient) description of the property;
4. number and sizes of rooms;
5. construction and age of the building;
6. information about the neighborhood (schools, churches, transportation);
7. current taxes;

8. financing (interest, payments, other costs and whether or not the loan is assumable);

9. utilities and average payments;

10. appliances to be included in the transaction;

11. date of occupancy or possession;

12. possibility of seller financing;

13. zoning classification (especially important for vacant land); and

14. a detailed list of what will and will not be included in the sales price.

Remember that a real estate broker, as an agent of the seller, is responsible for the disclosure of any material information regarding the property. Obtaining as much initial information from the seller as possible—even if it becomes necessary to ask penetrating and possibly embarrassing questions—will pay off in the long run by saving both principal and agent from potential legal difficulties. The agent also should assume the responsibility of searching the public records for such pertinent information as legal description, lot size and yearly taxes.

In Practice...

Some brokers use a separate information sheet (also known as a profile or data sheet) for recording many of the foregoing property features, including room sizes, lot sizes, and taxes. In these firms, listing agreements contain mainly the specific contract terms—listing price, duration of the agreement, signatures of the parties and so forth.

Pricing the Property

The pricing of the real estate is of primary importance. Although it is the responsibility of the broker or salesperson to advise, counsel and assist, it is ultimately the *seller* who must determine a listing price for his or her own property. However, as the average seller does not usually have the background to make an informed decision about a fair market price, the real estate agent must be prepared to offer his or her knowledge, information and expertise in this area. A broker should reject any listing in which the price has been substantially exaggerated.

A salesperson can help the seller determine a listing price for the property through a **competitive** (or *comparative*) **market analysis** (CMA). This is a comparison of the prices of recently sold homes that are similar in location, style and amenities to that of the listing seller. If no such comparisons can be made or if the seller thinks the property is unique in some way, a formal real estate appraisal, prepared by a broker—a professional, detailed estimate of a property's value—may be warranted. (See Chapter 19, "Real Estate Appraisal.")

Seller's return. One of the main concerns of every seller is how much money will be made from the sale. To find the price at which a property must be sold in order for the seller to receive a given amount from the sale when, for example, the seller is considering a counteroffer, the following computations can be made:

Assume that a seller wants to receive $100,000 after paying the broker's commission, closing costs and necessary repair costs (such as those indicated by a termite inspection). The selling price, therefore, should be $100,000 *plus* estimated closing costs, repair costs and the broker's commission (7 percent in this hypothetical situation).

1. The unknown selling price is: 100%
   Subtract the broker's commission that will be
   included in the selling price: −7%
   The seller's portion of the selling price
   will therefore be: **93%**

2. The seller wants to net $100,000, to which are added estimated
   closing costs of $2,000 and repairs of $1,500 for a total of $103,500. This is
   93 percent of the full sales price, so:

$$93\% = .93 \qquad .93\overline{)\$103,500}^{\displaystyle \$111,290.32 \text{ selling price}}$$

3. The broker's commission will be: $111,290.32
                                          ×   .07
                                          $ 7,790.32

4. The seller receives: $111,290.32
                                           −7,790.32
                                           $103,500.00
                                           −3,500.00
                                           $100,000.00

The example assumes that the seller owns the property free and clear. In most cases, the seller must also account for any outstanding loan balance(s). With a remaining mortgage loan balance of, for example, $57,000 as of the date of closing, the seller in the example would receive $43,000 ($100,000–$57,000), less various closing costs incurred by the seller.

The selling price reached in this way—by considering the seller's expected return—should still fall within the acceptable range determined for the property's market value by the competitive market analysis.

Sample Listing Agreement

Figure 18.1 is a typical listing agreement; note that the individual specifics of a listing may vary from area to area. Following is a section-by-section analysis of the sample agreement; numerical references are to the specific provisions of the contract.

1. *Exclusive Right to Sell.* The title specifies that this document is an "exclusive right to sell" real property.

2. *Date.* The date of the listing contract is the date it is executed; however, this may not necessarily be the date that the contract becomes effective.

3. *Names and Signatures.* The names of all persons having an interest in the property should be specified and should enter into the agreement. If the property is owned under one of the forms of co-ownership discussed in Chapter 7, "How Ownership Is Held," that fact should be clearly established. All owners of the property must sign the contract. If one or more of the owners is married, it is wise to obtain the spouse's signature to release marital rights.

4. *Broker or Firm.* The name of the broker or firm entering into the listing must be clearly stated in the agreement.

5. *Owner's Granting of the Listing.* This section establishes the document as a *legal contract* and states the promises by both parties that create and bind the agreement.

6, 7. *Commission Rate.* This paragraph establishes the broker's rate of commission, or a minimum amount of commission, and must be so stated in the contract.

8. *Protection Clause.* This section will protect the broker if the owner or another person sells the property after the listing expires to a person with whom the original broker negotiated. In other words, the broker is guaranteed a commission for a set period of time after the agreement expires (generally three to six months) if he or she was the procuring cause of the sale, even if the broker did not actually consummate the transaction. This protection clause does not apply, however, if the owner signs a new listing agreement with another broker after the original agreement expires.

9. *Broker's Responsibilities.* This paragraph defines the rights and duties of the broker.

10. *Broker's Authority.* Here the broker is given the authority to place a sign on the property and show it to buyers, as well as the permission to supply the buyers with any and all information that may appear on the listing form. Without such permission, this information would be confidential and could not be revealed to anyone without breaching the agency doctrine of confidence.

11. *Listing Price.* The listing price is a gross sales price and the owner should understand that any obligations such as taxes, mortgages and assessments remain the owner's responsibility and must be paid out of the proceeds of the sale.

12. *Encumbrances.* This paragraph points out responsibilities of encumbrances, especially important to the broker because they determine whether or not the property is in fact salable.

13. *Evidence of Ownership and Deed.* The type of deed to be executed and proof of ownership in the form of a title are stated here.

14. *Liabilities.* The owner protects both buyer and broker with this statement.

15. *Civil Rights Legislation.* This clause serves to alert the owner that both federal and state legislation exist to protect against discrimination. The "Official Notice" required by the Pennsylvania Human Relations Act is discussed in Chapter 24.

16. *Termination of Agreement.* Both the exact time and the date serve to remove any ambiguity in regard to termination of the contract. A particular termination date does not necessarily include that day itself unless the phrase "up to and including" is used.

17. *Disclosures Required by the Pennsylvania Real Estate Licensing and Registration Act, Sec. 606.*
    a. Statement that the broker's commission and time period of the listing are negotiable.
    b. Statement describing the purpose of the Real Estate Recovery Fund established by the Act and the telephone number of the commission at which the seller can receive further information about the fund.

**Figure 18.1
Exclusive
Right-to-Sell
Agreement**

(4)

**LISTING
FOR SALE**

This form recommended and approved for, but not restricted to, use by
members of the Pennsylvania Association of REALTORS®

XLS-1970
(Rev. 5-88)

─AGENT:─

─PA. LICENSED BROKER─

There are 3 copies
of this listing
agreement.
1. Yellow. . .Agent
2. White . . .Owner
3. Blue . . . .

(3)

**OWNERS,
OCCUPANTS &
POSSESSION**
(9-83)

PROPERTY DESCRIPTION, TERMS & STATISTICAL INFORMATION   **LISTED PRICE $** _____
PROPERTY LISTED _____
MUNICIPALITY _____
DEED BOOK# _____ PAGE# _____ RECORDING DATE _____
OWNERS _____ RES. TEL.# _____
OWNERS _____ BUS. TEL.# _____
ADDRESS _____ S.S.# _____
OCCUPANT (#1) _____ TEL.# _____
LEASE TERM _____ EXPIRES _____ SEC. DEP. $ _____
RENT $ _____ RENT INCLUDES _____
OCCUPANT (#2) _____ TEL.# _____
LEASE TERM _____ EXPIRES _____ SEC. DEP. $ _____
RENT $ _____ RENT INCLUDES _____
AGREED SETTLEMENT DATE □ _____ DAYS AFTER AGREEMENT □ AFTER _____ 19 ____
POSSESSION BY DEED □ AND PHYSICAL POSSESSION □ AT SETTLEMENT □ _____
□ AND ASSIGNMENT OF LEASE(S) _____

**BUILDINGS &
IMPROVEMENTS**
(1-82)

TYPE BUILDING AND ARCHITECTURE _____ YEAR BUILT _____
CONSTRUCTION _____ SQUARE FOOTAGE _____
BASEMENT OR GROUND LEVEL _____
FIRST LEVEL _____

SECOND LEVEL _____

THIRD LEVEL _____

GARAGE _____ OUTBUILDINGS _____
DOM. H.W. HEATER _____ TYPE ROOF _____ AGE OF ROOF _____
HEAT TYPE _____ FUEL _____ CONSUMPTION _____
□ _____
□ OWNER AUTHORIZES WOOD INFESTATION INSPECTION BY: _____
□ _____

EXCLUSIONS
(1-82)
**FEATURES
INCLUDED**
(4-83)

□ COMB. ST. DOORS	□ AIR COND. UNIT_____	□ SUN DECK	□ DRAPERIES	□ _____A SERVICE
□ COMB. ST. WINDS.	□ CENT. AIR CON.	□ T.V. ANTENNA	□ DRAP. RODS & HDW.	□ 220V SERVICE
□ FENCING	□ CHANDELIER	□ ROTOR SYSTEMS	□ GARB. DISPOSAL	□ SUMP PUMP
□ VEN. BLINDS	□ PORCH _____	□ CORNICES	□ DISHWASHER	□ RANGE/OVEN
□ RADIATOR COVERS	□ PATIO _____	□ CUR. RODS & HDW.	□ LAUND. FACIL.	□ REFRIG.
□ CARPETING _____				□ SMOKE DETECTOR___

INSULATION: □ WALLS R- _____ □ CEILINGS R- _____ □ FLOORS R- _____ □ _____
□ _____
□ _____

**DEFECTS
DISCLOSURE**
(5-88)

OWNER HAS BEEN ADVISED OF OWNER'S DUTY TO DISCLOSE MATERIAL DEFECTS OR CONDITIONS
AND KNOWS OF NO PROPERTY DEFECTS EXCEPT AS FOLLOWS: _____

**LAND
IMPROVEMENTS
AND SERVICES**
(1-82)

LOT SIZE _____ ZONING _____

□ PUBLIC WATER	□ PUBLIC SEWER	□ SAND MOUND	□ SIDEWALKS	□ PRIVATE DRIVE
□ WELL (_____depth)	□ CESSPOOL	□ STREET LIGHTS	□ REAR ALLEY	□ COMMON DRIVE
□ GAS	□ SEP. TANK (___gal.)	□ PAVED STREETS	□ OFF STREET PARK.	□ TRASH/GAR. COLL.

CONVENIENCES
(1-82)

SCHOOLS _____
TRANSPORTATION _____ SHOPPING _____

**FINANCIAL
INFORMATION**
(1-82)

FINANCING TERMS ACCEPTABLE TO OWNER _____

MORTGAGEE & ACCT.# _____ TYPE _____
ORIG. AMT. $ _____ PRESENT BAL. $ _____ ORIG. TERM (MOS.) _____
REMAINING TERM (MOS.) _____ INTEREST RATE _____% TOTAL PMT. $ _____
DEBTS OR JUDGMENTS _____ BAL. DUE $ _____
ASSESSMENT $ _____ YEARLY TAXES $ _____ MONTHLY TAXES $ _____

**TAX
INFORMATION**
(1-82)

TRASH $ _____ SEWER $ _____ PER CAPITA $ _____ OTHER $ _____
UNPAID ASSESS./NOTICES $ _____
PAYMENT OF TRANSFER TAXES _____

(7)

**OWNER
AUTHORIZES**
(1-82)

□ SALE SIGN   □ SOLD SIGN   □ KEY IN OFFICE   □ KEY LOCK BOX

(6)

**AGENT'S
FEE &
EXPIRATION**
(5-88)

(8)

THE AGENT'S FEE AND EXPIRATION DATE OF THIS AGREEMENT HAVE NOT BEEN ESTABLISHED OR RECOMMENDED BY
ANY ASSOCIATION OF REALTORS, OR BY ANY OTHER ORGANIZATION OR INDIVIDUAL.
BEFORE SIGNING THIS AGREEMENT THE OWNER WAS INFORMED THAT THE AGENT'S FEE AND THE EXPIRATION DATE
OF THIS AGREEMENT ARE NEGOTIABLE. OWNER AGREES THAT AGENT'S RESPONSIBILITY TO PRESENT OFFERS
TERMINATES WITH AN ACCEPTANCE OF AN OFFER.
AGENT'S FEE _____ OF/FROM THE AGREED SALE PRICE.
AGENT'S FEE IN THE EVENT OF BUYER DEFAULT _____ of/from any monies paid on account.
EXPIRATION DATE OF AGENCY _____ Maximum permissible term is one year.
AGENT'S FEE PROTECTION PERIOD for prospective buyers after expiration of agency _____

(OVER)

Figure 18.1 (cont.)

(1)

(5)

AGENCY & TERM
(9-83)

(1)

(8)

POSSESSION
(1-82)

PROPERTY DEFECTS
(5-88)

DEPOSIT
(4-83)

RECOVERY FUND
(5-85)

TITLE ASSIGNS, ETC.
(3-85)

OFFICIAL NOTICE TO PERSONS OFFERING TO SELL OR RENT HOUSING IN PENNSYLVANIA
(5-88)

NO OTHER CONTRACTS
(2-88)

APPROVAL
(3-85)

(2)

(3)

EXCLUSIVE RIGHT TO SELL AGREEMENT FOR SALE OF REAL ESTATE
COPYRIGHT PENNSYLVANIA ASSOCIATION OF REALTORS® 1973

1. In consideration of your agreement to endeavor to procure a buyer therefore, I hereby employ you as the sole and exclusive agent for the sale of the property described on the reverse side of this form and grant you the sole and exclusive right to sell the said property (herein referred to as agency), for the price and terms therein mentioned, or for or upon any other price or terms to which I may agree.

This agency shall continue in effect until the "EXPIRATION DATE OF AGENCY" as specified on the reverse side of this form unless extended in writing by the parties hereto. After the "EXPIRATION DATE OF AGENCY" or any extension thereof, the Agent's authority shall continue as to negotiations pending at time of such expiration.

I agree that if said property is sold or exchanged during the term of said agency, WHETHER EFFECTED BY WHOMSOEVER INCLUDING MYSELF, THE OWNER, I will pay you the "AGENTS FEE" and I will pay you the same fee:

    (a.) if you alone or in cooperation with another agent produce a Buyer who is ready, willing and able to purchase the property.

    (b.) if during the "AGENTS FEE PROTECTION PERIOD" the said property is sold or exchanged in whole or in part to anyone with whom you, any other agent or I have negotiated with during the term of said agency and providing the property is not listed exclusively with another Broker at the time.

    (c.) or the "AGENTS FEE IN THE EVENT OF BUYERS DEFAULT" as specified on the reverse side of this form, but in no case will the sum paid be in excess of the "AGENTS FEE".

In the event Eminent Domain proceedings are instituted against all or part of the subject property during the term of this listing or during the term of any agreement of sale secured through this agency which would render the property unmarketable in its total state as offered, I agree to pay to you your same fee from the gross compensation received through said proceedings at such time when the said compensation has been received by me.

2. It is agreed that possession will be given to any buyer as specified on the reverse side under "POSSESSION AVAILABLE" and upon the terms set forth in this Agency. It is further agreed that I will not enter into or renew any lease for any term whatsoever during the term of this agency except as noted herein.

3. I hereby authorize you to disclose material property defects specified on the front side of this form and agree to indemnify you and any subagents against liability, including court costs and attorney fees, caused by my failure to disclose accurately and completely any material condition of the property that may affect its desirability.

4. I agree that deposit or hand monies will be retained by you in an escrow account in accordance with the Real Estate Licensing Act as amended, until consumation or termination of any sale or exchange that may occur as a result of this Agency.

It shall be the sole option of the Agent to hold any uncashed check tendered as deposit or hand monies, pending the acceptance of any offers obtained on the property.

5. A real estate recovery fund exists to reimburse persons who have suffered monetary loss and have obtained an uncollectable judgment due to fraud, misrepresentation or deceit in a real estate transaction by a Pennsylvania licensee. For complete details, call 717-783-3658.

6. I further certify that I own the subject property free and clear except as noted on this form, with a fee simple title and that I am legally able to sell or exchange the property as offered.

7. This Agency shall inure to the benefit of and be binding upon, the parties hereto, and their respective personal representatives, guardians, assigns and successors.

8. Responsibilities of Owners of Real Property under the PENNSYLVANIA HUMAN RELATIONS ACT of October 27, 1955, P.L. 744, as amended. The Pennsylvania Legislature has made it illegal: To refuse to sell, lease, finance, or otherwise deny or withhold residential or commercial property located in the Commonwealth of Pennsylvania because of any person's RACE, COLOR, SEX, RELIGIOUS CREED, ANCESTRY, NATIONAL ORIGIN, HANDICAP or DISABILITY, or To refuse to lease, or discriminate in the terms of selling or leasing, or in furnishing facilities, services or privileges in connection with the ownership, occupancy or use of any residential or commercial property because of any person's RACE, COLOR, SEX, RELIGIOUS CREED, ANCESTRY, NATIONAL ORIGIN, HANDICAP or DISABILITY, USE of a GUIDE or SUPPORT ANIMAL BECAUSE of the BLINDNESS, DEAFNESS or PHYSICAL HANDICAP of the USER or BECAUSE the USER is a HANDLER or TRAINER of SUPPORT or GUIDE ANIMALS or To evict or attempt to evict any occupant of residential housing before the end of the term of a lease because of pregnancy or birth of a child.

OTHER APPLICABLE LAWS EXPLAINED: The CIVIL RIGHTS ACT OF 1866 provides that all citizens of the United States shall have the same right in every state and territory thereof to inherit, purchase, lease, sell, hold and convey real and personal property, and prohibits all racial and ethnic discrimination without exception in the sale or rental of property.

TITLE VIII of the FEDERAL CIVIL RIGHTS ACT OF 1968 prohibits discrimination in housing based on race, color, sex, religion or national origin. COURT AWARDS: Under either of the above laws, federal courts may award successful plaintiffs actual and punitive damages, attorney's fees, and injunctive relief.

TITLE IX of the CIVIL RIGHTS ACT OF 1968 provides criminal penalties for the willful or attempted injury, intimidation or interference with any person because of his/her race, color, sex, religion or national origin who is selling, purchasing, renting, financing or occupying any dwelling or contracting or negotiating for the sale, purchase, rental, financing or occupation of any dwelling or applying for or participating in any service, organization or facility relating to the business of selling or renting dwellings.

REAL ESTATE BROKERS LICENSE ACT OF MAY 1, 1929, P.L. 1216, as amended, makes it unlawful for a real estate broker or salesperson to accept a listing with an understanding that illegal discrimination in the sale or rental of property is to be practiced.

LOCAL ORDINANCES prohibiting discrimination in housing may exist in your locality, and should be consulted for any additional protection these ordinances may provide.

TO OWNERS OF REAL PROPERTY WITHIN THE COMMONWEALTH: YOU ARE LEGALLY RESPONSIBLE for your own actions and the actions of any agent acting on your behalf. Under the Pennsylvania Human Relations Act and other state and federal legislation which prohibit discrimination in housing, you bear the responsibility for seeing that discriminatory acts do not occur.

PROTECT YOURSELF by providing your agent with verbal and written instructions that in all transactions relating to your property — including all services provided in connection with the transactions — you wish to comply with all civil rights ordinances including, but not limited to: The Pennsylvania Human Relations Act, The Civil Rights Act of 1866 and Title VIII of the Civil Rights Act of 1968.

Under the Pennsylvania Human Relations Act, neither you nor your broker/salesperson or agent may

1. Steer or otherwise direct a property seeker's attention to a particular neighborhood based on the race, color, religion, national origin, ancestry, sex, handicap or disability, or use of a guide or support animal because of the blindness, deafness or physical handicap of the user, or because the user is a handler or trainer of support or guide animals, of either the property seekers or persons already residing in that neighborhood.

2. Volunteer information to or invite questions from property seekers concerning the race, color, religion, national origin, ancestry, sex, handicap or disability, use of a guide or support animal because of the blindness, deafness or physical handicap of the user or because the user is a handler or trainer of support or guide animals of persons already residing in a neighborhood.

3. Answer questions from or initiate a discussion with persons who are selling, renting, or otherwise making housing or commercial property available concerning the race, color, religion, national origin, ancestry, sex, handicap or disability, or use of a guide or support animal of the blindness, deafness or physical handicap of the user or because the user is a handler or trainer of support or guide animals of prospective buyers, applicants or others seeking housing.

4. Engage in certain practices which attempt to induce the sale, or discourage the purchase or lease, of housing accommodations or commercial property by making direct or indirect reference to the present or future composition of the neighborhood in which the facility is located with respect to race, color, religion, sex, ancestry, national origin, hanidcap or disability, or guide or support animal dependency.

5. Engage in any course of action which could be construed as reluctant or delayed service having the effect of withholding or making unavailable housing accommodations or commercial property to persons because of their race, color, religion, national origin, ancestry, sex, handicap or disability, or use of a guide or support animal.

RULES AND REGULATIONS OF THE PENNSYLVANIA HUMAN RELATIONS COMMISSION (16 Pennsylvania Code 43.14) require that all licensed brokers or salespersons who list your property for sale or rent shall provide you with a copy of this notice in order that you may be made aware of the laws you are required to obey.

9. No listing agreement for a term beginning before the expiration date of this listing may be entered into by owner with another agent during the term of this agreement.

AGENT _____ (S)   OWNER _____ (S)

BY _____ (S)   OWNER _____ (S)

DATE _____ 19 ____   OWNER _____ (S)

PROPERTY DESCRIPTION, TERMS & STATISTICAL INFORMATION ON REVERSE SIDE.

**Figure 18.2
Radon
Addendum**

RADON DISCLOSURE ADDENDUM TO EXCLUSIVE RIGHT TO SELL AGREEMENT
_____ 19_____

RE: PROPERTY _____
AGENT: _____
OWNERS: _____

PENNSYLVANIA REALTORS ASSOCIATION

Form 113-3

NOTICE TO SELLERS REGARDING RADON GAS

1. Radon is a radioactive gas produced naturally in the ground by the normal decay of uranium and radium. Uranium and radium are widely distributed in trace amounts in the earth's crust. Descendants of Radon gas are called Radon daughters, or Radon progeny. Several Radon daughters emit alpha radiation, which has high energy but short range.

2. Studies indicate the result of extended exposure to high levels of Radon gas/Radon daughters is an increased risk of lung cancer.

3. Radon gas originates in soil and rocks. It diffuses, as does any gas, and flows along the path of least resistance to the surface of the ground, and then to the atmosphere. Being a gas, Radon can also move into any air space, such as basements, crawl spaces and living areas.

4. If a house has a Radon problem, it can usually be cured by (a) increased ventilation and/or (b) preventing Radon entry.

5. The EPA advises corrective action if the annual average exposure to Radon daughters exceeds 0.02 working levels.

6. Further information can be secured from the DER Radon Project Office, 1100 Grosser Road, Gilbertsville, PA 19525; Call 1-800-23RADON or (215) 369-3590.

RADON CERTIFICATION

I hereby acknowledge that I have been provided with a copy of "Notice to Sellers Regarding Radon" and certify that:

( ) The property was tested and Radon was found to be at or below 0.02 working levels (4 picocuries/liter).

( ) The property was tested and Radon was found to be above 0.02 working levels (4 picocuries/liter).

( ) The property was modified after which it was retested and Radon was found to be at or below 0.02 working levels (4 picocuries/liter).

Seller does not warrant either the method or result of the test.

( ) I have no knowledge concerning the presence or absence of Radon.

I hereby authorize you, as my agent, and any subagents, to disclose the foregoing information to prospective purchasers.

AGENT _____ OWNER _____ (s)
BY _____ (s) OWNER _____ (s)
DATE _____, 19_____ OWNER _____ (s)

COPIES: WHITE: OWNER.   YELLOW: AGENT.   BLUE: _____   8/87

**Figure 18.3
U.F.F.I.
Addendum**

U.F.F.I. ADDENDUM TO EXCLUSIVE RIGHT TO SELL AGREEMENT
_____ 19_____

RE PROPERTY: _____
AGENT _____
OWNERS _____

NOTICE TO SELLERS REGARDING UREA-FORMALDEHYDE FOAM INSULATION

Urea-formaldehyde foam insulation (UFFI) is a thermal insulation material that is manufactured at the site of installation and pumped into the space between the walls of the building being insulated where it hardens to form a layer of insulation.

Effective August 9, 1982, the United States Consumer Product Safety Commission (CPSC) banned the future sale of UFFI, having determined that such insulation presented an unreasonable health risk to those exposed to it because of the formaldehyde gas which may be released from the product into the interiors of buildings in which it had been installed. The health risks identified by the CPSC included cancer, acute illness such as eye, nose, and throat irritation and sensitization.

On April 7, 1983, the United States Court of Appeals for the Fifth Circuit overturned the CPSC's UFFI Ban. The court found that the record developed by the CPSC did not contain the substantial evidence necessary to support the ban. The court's decision found that both of the CPSC's findings that UFFI was carcinogenic and that it caused acute irritant effects were not supported by substantial evidence. Additionally, the court held that the CPSC should have addressed the alleged health hazards of UFFI by a proceeding under the Federal Hazardous Substances Act rather than the Consumer Product Safety Act.

Notwithstanding the overturn of the ban, it is recommended that all prospective purchasers continue to be advised if UFFI is or has been present in a residence. Such disclosure is recommended for several reasons. First, the court's opinion, while noting multiple flaws in the CPSC's findings, did not state that UFFI posed no health risk. In fact, the court stated that "the Commission's defense of its investigations persuades us that UFFI is not completely innocent. We agree that 'taken as a whole, the complaints do identify a real problem.'" What the CPSC failed to establish, however, is that the health risk is "unreasonable."

Second, articles have appeared in major newspapers reporting litigation brought by UFFI homeowners in their homes. These lawsuits, estimated by one law firm to run upwards of 700, indicate that UFFI has not ceased to be an issue of importance to homeowners. The presence of UFFI in a home therefore still remains a fact about which prospective purchasers should be advised to avoid later claims against sellers and their agents based on misrepresentation or even fraud.

In the event liability is imposed for failure to disclose the presence of UFFI, such finding could result in the rescission of the purchase agreement by the buyer and/or an award of damages against the seller or any person responsible for disclosing information regarding the property.

Insulation Certification

I hereby acknowledge that I have been provided with a copy of "Notice to Sellers Regarding Urea-Formaldehyde Foam Insulation" and certify that

( ) urea-formaldehyde foam insulation was installed in _____ (date)

( ) urea-formaldehyde foam insulation was installed in _____ (date) but was removed in _____ (date)

( ) urea-formaldehyde foam insulation has not been installed

( ) I have no knowledge concerning the presence or absence of urea-formaldehyde foam insulation, but it has not been installed since _____ (date)

I hereby authorize you, as my agent, and any subagents appointed by you, to disclose the foregoing information to prospective purchasers.

AGENT _____ (S) OWNER _____
BY _____ (S) OWNER _____
DATE _____, 19_____ OWNER _____

110-3

COPIES: White; Owner,   Yellow; Agent,   Blue; _____   6/84

The sample Exclusive-Right-to-Sell Agreement and other suggested addenda (Figures 18.2, 18.3) are published by the Pennsylvania Association of REALTORS® for use by any licensee throughout the state. A local MLS may publish a similar form for use by its members.

Summary

To acquire an inventory of property to sell, brokers and salespeople must obtain listings. The various kinds of listing agreements include open listings, exclusive-agency listings and exclusive-right-to-sell listings.

An *open listing* is one in which, to obtain a commission, the broker must find a buyer before the property is sold by the seller or another broker. Under an *exclusive-agency listing,* the broker is given the exclusive right to represent the seller, but the seller can avoid paying the broker a commission if the owner sells the property without the broker's help. With an *exclusive-right-to-sell listing,* the seller employs only one broker and must pay that broker a commission regardless of whether it is the broker or the seller who finds a buyer—so long as the buyer is found within the listing period.

A *multiple listing* provision may appear in an exclusive listing and gives the broker additional authority and obligation to distribute the listing to other brokers in the multiple listing organization. A *net listing,* outlawed in some states and considered unethical in most other areas, is based on the net price the seller will receive if the property is sold. The broker under a net listing is free to offer the property for sale at the highest available price and retain as his or her commission any amount over and above the seller's net.

A listing agreement may be terminated for the same reasons as any other agency relationship.

Questions

1. A listing agreement is:
   a. the broker's employment contract with his or her salespeople.
   b. the broker's employment contract with a principal.
   c. generally an oral agreement.
   d. none of the above

2. Which of the following is a similarity between an exclusive-agency and an exclusive-right-to-sell listing?
   a. Under both types of listing the seller retains the right to sell his or her real estate without the broker's help and not be liable to the broker for a commission.
   b. Both are open listings.
   c. Both give the responsibility of representing the seller to one broker only.
   d. Under both the seller authorizes only one particular salesperson to show his or her property.

3. If a seller wanted a minimum return of $90,000 and the broker were to receive a six percent commission, what would the minimum gross selling price have to be?
   I. $90,000 plus six percent of $90,000
   II. $94,680.85
      a. I only   c. both I and II
      b. II only   d. neither I nor II

4. Which of the following is a similarity between an open listing and an exclusive-agency listing?
   a. Under both the seller avoids paying the broker a commission if the seller sells the property himself or herself.
   b. Both listings grant a commission to any licensed broker who finds a buyer for the seller's property.
   c. Both are net listings.
   d. Under both, the broker earns a commission regardless of who sells the property so long as it is sold within the listing period.

5. A multiple listing clause:
   a. involves more than one parcel of real estate.
   b. is the same as an open listing agreement.
   c. benefits only the seller.
   d. benefits both broker and seller.

6. A listing may be terminated by:
   I. the broker's failure to spend time on it.
   II. expiration of the time period stated in the listing.
      a. I only   c. both I and II
      b. II only   d. neither I nor II

7. A broker sold a residence for $88,000 and received $6,160 as her commission in accordance with the terms of the listing agreement. What percentage of the sales price was the broker's commission?
      a. 6 percent   c. 7 percent
      b. 6½ percent   d. 7½ percent

8. A listing agreement that runs for a set period of time and renews itself for another listing period after the initial period ends:
   I. contains an automatic extension provision.
   II. is prohibited in Pennsylvania.
      a. I only   c. both I and II
      b. II only   d. neither I nor II

9. When a broker or salesperson takes a listing, who should sign the agreement?
   a. the seller
   b. the listing broker or salesperson
   c. all brokers in a multiple listing situation
   d. a and b

10. The selling price of a parcel of real estate is determined by:
    I. the seller.
    II. the salesperson.
       a. I only   c. both I and II
       b. II only   d. neither I nor II

11. Which of the following provisions must, by state regulation, be included in exclusive listing agreements?
   a. the rate of commission
   b. the seller's asking price
   c. the date the agreement terminates
   d. all of the above

12. Salesperson Joseph Franks has just secured a listing to sell Joyce Randolph's home. When completing the listing agreement, Franks should:
   a. submit the completed form to his broker.
   b. obtain as much information about the property from Randolph as possible.
   c. refuse the listing if he thinks Randolph wants to price it far higher than the fair market value.
   d. all of the above

13. A competitive market analysis:
   I. can help the seller set a fair price.
   II. is a comparison of recently sold properties similar to a seller's parcel of real estate.
      a. I only   c. both I and II
      b. II only   d. neither I nor II

14. A seller's residence is listed with a broker, stipulating that he wants to receive $85,000 from the sale but that the broker can sell the residence for as much as possible and keep the difference as his commission. The broker agrees. This type of listing is:
   I. called an open listing.
   II. illegal in Pennsylvania.
      a. I only   c. both I and II
      b. II only   d. neither I nor II

15. A property was listed with a broker who belonged to a multiple listing service and was sold for $53,500 by another broker member. The total commission was six percent of the sales price; of this commission the selling broker received 60 percent, and the listing broker received the balance. How much was the listing broker's commission?
   a. $2,142   c. $1,464
   b. $1,926   d. $1,284

19

Real Estate Appraisal

Key Terms

Appraisal
Capitalization rate
Cost approach
Depreciation
Direct sales comparison approach
External depreciation
Functional obsolescence
Gross rent multiplier
Highest and best use
Income approach
Market value
Physical deterioration
Plottage
Quantity-survey method
Reconciliation
Regression/progression
Replacement cost
Reproduction cost
Square-foot method
Substitution
Unit-in-place method
Value

Overview

Real estate is the business of value. Members of the general public informally estimate this value when they buy, sell or invest in real estate. A formal estimate of value is generally conducted by a professional real estate appraiser and serves as a basis for the pricing, financing, insuring or leasing of real property. This chapter will examine value—what determines it, adds to it and detracts from it. It will also discuss in detail the various methods professional appraisers use to estimate the value of residential as well as commercial and industrial real estate.

Appraising

An **appraisal** is a supportable estimate or opinion of value. In the real estate business, the highest level of appraisal activity is conducted by professional real estate appraisers, who are recognized for their knowledge, training, skill and integrity in this field. In Pennsylvania, appraisers must be licensed real estate brokers. Salesperson licensees in Pennsylvania may work as an *assistant* to the appraiser who is a broker. These activities involve gathering information about the property and compiling data. The broker, who signs the report is, therefore, responsible for the appraisal, including its preparation, conclusions and a personal inspection of the property. Formal appraisal reports are relied upon in decisions made by mortgage lenders, investors, public utilities, governmental agencies, businesses and individuals.

This is not to be confused with the sales agent's service of assisting a seller to arrive at a market value for the property. A formal appraisal is seldom used; rather, the seller relies on a *competitive market analysis* prepared by a salesperson. This is a report compiled from research of the marketplace, primarily other similar properties that have sold recently. The salesperson must be knowledgeable of the fundamentals of valuation in compiling the market data. The competitive market analysis is not as comprehensive or technical as a formal appraisal and may be biased by a salesperson anticipating an agency relationship.

Appraising is a professional service performed on a "fee for time and effort" basis. This is not a contractual relationship resulting in a fiduciary as described in Chapter 17, "Real Estate Brokerage." Therefore, the appraiser is an independent third party required to provide an unbiased estimate of value.

Value

Value is an abstract word with many acceptable definitions. In a broad sense, **value** may be defined as the relationship between an object desired and a potential purchaser. It is the power of a good or service to command other goods or services in exchange. In terms of real estate appraisal, value may be described as the *present worth of future benefits arising from the ownership of real property.*

To have value in the real estate market, a property must have four characteristics:

1. *utility,* the capacity to satisfy human needs and desires;

2. *scarcity,* a finite supply;

3. *demand,* the need or desire for possession or ownership backed by the financial means to satisfy that need (Note: When the word *demand* is used in economics, *effective demand* is usually assumed.);

4. *transferability,* the transfer of ownership rights with relative ease.

Market Value

While a given parcel of real estate may have many different kinds of value at the same time (as illustrated in Figure 19.1), generally the goal of an appraiser is an estimate of *market value.* The **market value** of real estate is the most probable price that a property should bring in a competitive and open market under all

**Figure 19.1
Kinds of Value**

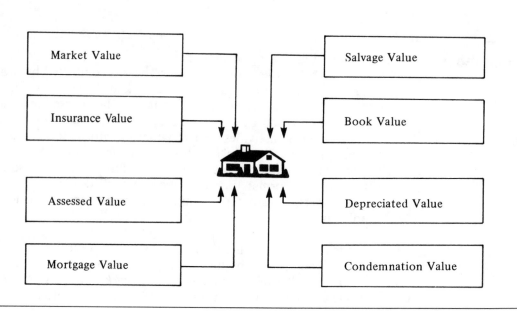

conditions requisite to a fair sale, given that the buyer and seller are each acting prudently and knowledgeably and assuming the price is not affected by undue stimulus. Included in this definition are that:

1. most probable price is not the average or highest price;

2. buyer and seller are typically motivated;

3. both parties are well informed or advised and each is acting in what is considered his or her own best interests without undue pressure;

4. a reasonable time is allowed for exposure in the open market;

5. payment is made in cash or its equivalent;

6. financing, if any, is on terms generally available in the community at the specific date and typical for the property type in its locale; and

7. the price represents a normal consideration for the property sold, unaffected by special financing amounts and/or terms, services, fees, costs or credits incurred in the market transaction.

Market value versus market price. Market value is an opinion of value based on an analysis of data, which may include not only an analysis of comparable sales but also an analysis of potential income and expenses and replacement costs (less depreciation). *Market price,* on the other hand, is what a property *actually* sells for—its selling price. Theoretically, the ideal market price would be the same as the market value; however, there are circumstances under which a property may be sold at below market value, such as when the seller is forced to sell quickly or when a sale is arranged between relatives. Thus, the market price can be taken as accurate evidence of current market value only after considering the relationship of the buyer and seller, the terms and conditions of the market and the effect of the passage of time since the sale was made.

Market value versus cost. It is also important to distinguish between market value and *cost*. One of the most common misconceptions about valuing property is that cost represents market value. Cost and market value *may* be equal and often are when the improvements on a property are new and represent the highest and best use of the land. But more often, cost does not equal market value. For example, two homes are identical in every respect except that one is located on a street with heavy traffic and the other is on a quiet, residential street. The value of the former may be less than that of the latter, although the cost of each may be exactly the same. Another example would be a situation in which the demand for homes greatly exceeds the available supply to such an extent that buyers actually pay more than it would cost to construct such homes in order to secure housing without long delay. In this instance, market value could easily exceed cost.

Basic Principles of Value

There are a number of economic principles at work that affect the value of real estate. The most important of these principles are defined in the following paragraphs.

Highest and best use. Land has no value if it has no use; use is derived from the satisfaction of a need or want. **Highest and best use** of a site is that reasonable and probable use that supports the highest present value on the effective date of the appraisal. Improvements must be legally permitted, financially feasible, physically possible and provide more profit than any other use of the site. Highest and best use of a site can change with social, political and economic forces. A highest-and-best-use study may show that a parking lot in a busy downtown area should, in fact, be replaced by an office building. To place a value on the property based on its present use would be erroneous, for a parking lot is not the highest and best use of the land. In appraising a residential location, the determination of highest and best use will not involve just the income available in money. Amenities or owner satisfaction—an unusual view of the mountains, for instance—may be a key factor.

Substitution. The principle of **substitution** states that the maximum value of a property tends to be set by the cost of purchasing an equally desirable and valuable substitute property, assuming that no costly delay is encountered in making the substitution. For example, if there are two similar houses for sale in an area, the one with the lower asking price would normally be purchased first.

Supply and demand. This principle states that the value of a property will increase if the supply decreases and the demand either increases or remains constant—and vice versa. For example, the last lot to be sold in a residential area where the demand for homes is high would probably be worth more than the first lot sold in that area.

Conformity. This means that maximum value is realized if the use of land conforms to existing neighborhood standards. In residential areas of single-family houses, for example, buildings should be similar in design, construction, size and age to other buildings in the neighborhood. Subdivision restrictions rely on the principle of conformity to ensure maximum future value.

Anticipation. This principle holds that value can increase or decrease in anticipation of some future benefit or detriment affecting the property. For example, the value of a house may be affected if there are rumors that an adjacent property may be converted to commercial use in the near future.

Increasing and diminishing returns. Improvements to land and structures will eventually reach a point at which they will no longer have an effect on property values. As long as money spent on improvements produces an increase in income or value, the *law of increasing returns* is applicable. But at the point where additional improvements will not produce a proportionate increase in income or value, the *law of diminishing returns* applies.

Regression and progression. The principle that, between dissimilar properties, the worth of the better property is adversely affected by the presence of the lesser-quality property is known as **regression**. Thus, in a neighborhood of modest homes, a structure that is larger, better maintained, and/or more luxurious, would tend to be valued in the same range as the others. Conversely, the principle of **progression** states that the worth of a lesser property tends to increase if it is located among better properties.

Plottage. The principle of **plottage** holds that the merging or consolidation of adjacent lots held by separate land owners into one larger lot may produce a higher total land value than the sum of the two sites valued separately. For example, if two adjacent lots are valued at $35,000 each, their total value if consolidated into one larger lot under a single use might be $90,000. The process of merging the two lots under one owner is known as *assemblage.*

Contribution. The value of any component of a property consists of what its addition contributes to the value of the whole or what its absence detracts from that value. For example, the cost of installing an air-conditioning system and remodeling an older office building may be greater than is justified by any increase in market value (a function of expected net increase) that may result from the improvement to the property.

Competition. This principle states that excess profits tend to attract competition. For example, the success of a retail store may attract investors to open similar stores in the area. This tends to mean less profit for all stores concerned unless the purchasing power in the area increases substantially.

Change. No physical or economic condition remains constant. Real estate is subject to natural phenomena, such as tornadoes, fires and routine wear and tear of the elements. The real estate business is also subject to the demands of its market, just as is any business. It is an appraiser's job to be knowledgeable about the past and, perhaps, predictable effects of natural phenomena and the behavior of the marketplace.

The Three Approaches to Value	In order to arrive at an accurate estimate of value, three basic approaches, or techniques, are traditionally used by appraisers: the direct sales comparison approach, the cost approach and the income approach. Each method serves as a check against the others and narrows the range within which the final estimate of value will fall. Each method is generally considered most reliable for specific types of property.
The Direct Sales Comparison Approach	In the **direct sales comparison approach** (formerly known as the sales comparison approach), an estimate of value is obtained by comparing the subject property (the property under appraisal) with recently sold comparable properties (proper-

ties similar to the subject). Because no two parcels of real estate are exactly alike, each comparable property must be analyzed for differences and similarities between it and the subject property. The sales prices must be adjusted for any dissimilarities. The principal factors for which adjustments must be made fall into four basic categories:

1. *Date of sale:* An adjustment must be made if economic changes occur between the date of sale of the comparable property and the date of the appraisal.

2. *Location:* An adjustment may be necessary to compensate for locational differences. For example, similar properties might differ in price from neighborhood to neighborhood, or in more desirable locations within the same neighborhood.

3. *Physical features:* Physical features that may cause adjustments include age of building, size of lot, landscaping, construction, number of rooms, square feet of living space, interior and exterior condition, presence or absence of a garage, fireplace, or air-conditioner and so forth.

4. *Terms and conditions of sale:* This consideration becomes important if a sale is not financed by a standard mortgage procedure.

After a careful analysis of the differences between comparable properties and the subject property, the appraiser must adjust the comparables to reflect the market's reaction to the differences. Following the principle of contribution, the value of an amenity or the impact of date of sale, location or terms of a sale are assigned by the market. The appraiser estimates either dollar or percentage adjustments reflective of the value of these differences. (See Table 19.1 for application of adjustments.) The value of a feature present in the subject but not in the comparable property is *added* to the sales price. This presumes that, all other comparables being equal, a property having a feature not present in the comparable property (such as a fireplace or wet bar) would tend to have a higher market value solely because of this feature. (The feature need not be a physical amenity; it may be a locational or aesthetic feature.) Likewise, the value of a feature present in the comparable but not the subject property is *subtracted*. The adjusted sales prices of the comparables represent the probable value range of the subject property. From this range, a single market value estimate can be selected.

The direct sales comparison approach is essential in almost every appraisal of real estate. It is considered the most reliable of the three approaches in appraising residential property, where the amenities (intangible benefits) are so difficult to measure. Most appraisals will include a minimum of three comparable sales reflective of the subject property. An example of the direct sales comparison approach is shown in Table 19.1.

The Cost Approach

The **cost approach** to value is based on the principle of substitution, which states that the maximum value of a property tends to be set by the cost of acquiring an equally desirable and valuable substitute property, assuming that no costly delay is encountered in making the substitution.

**Table 19.1
Direct Sales
Comparison
Approach
to Value**

	Subject Property	Comparables				
		A	B	C	D	E
Sales Price		$68,000	$67,500	$69,500	$68,000	$65,000
Location	good	same	poorer +1500	same	same	same
Age	6 years	same	same	same	same	same
Size of Lot	60' × 135'	same	same	larger −1500	same	larger −1500
Landscaping	good	same	same	same	same	same
Construction	brick	same	same	same	same	same
Style	ranch	same	same	same	same	same
No. of Rooms	6	same	same	same	same	same
No. of Bedrooms	3	same	same	same	same	same
No. of Baths	1½	same	same	same	same	same
Sq. Ft. of Living Space	1500	same	same	same	same	same
Other Space (Basement)	full basement	same	same	same	same	same
Condition— Exterior	average	better −500	poorer +1000	better −500	same	poorer +500
Condition— Interior	good	same	same	better −500	same	same
Garage	2-car attached	same	same	same	same	none +2500
Other Improvements						
Financing Date of Sale	current	1 yr. ago +2500	current	current	current	
Net Adjustments		−500	+5000	−2500	-0-	+1500
Adjusted Value		$67,500	$72,500	$67,000	$68,000	$66,500

Note: Because the value range of the properties in the comparison chart (excluding comparable B) is close and comparable D required no adjustment, an appraiser would conclude that the indicated market value of the subject is $68,000.

The cost approach consists of five steps:

1. estimate the value of the land as if it were vacant and available to be put to its highest and best use;

2. estimate the current cost of constructing buildings and site improvements;

3. estimate the amount of accrued depreciation of the building resulting from physical deterioration, functional obsolescence and/or external depreciation;

4. deduct accrued depreciation from the estimated construction cost of new building(s) and site improvements; and

5. add the estimated land value to the depreciated cost of the building(s) and site improvements to arrive at the total property value.

Land value (step 1) is usually estimated by using the direct sales comparison approach; that is, the location and improvements of the subject site are compared to those of similar nearby sites, and adjustments are made for significant differences.

Table 19.2 Cost Approach to Value			
Land Valuation: Size 60 × 135 @ $450 per front foot			= $27,000
Plus site improvements: driveway, walks, landscaping, etc.			= 4,000
Total Land Valuation			$31,000
Building Valuation: Replacement Cost			
1,500 sq. ft. @ $65 per sq. ft. =		$97,500	
Less Depreciation:			
Physical depreciation,			
curable			
(items of deferred maintenance)			
exterior painting	$4,000		
incurable (structural deterioration)	5,200		
Functional obsolescence	2,000		
External depreciation	-0-		
Total Depreciation		–11,200	
Depreciated Value of Building			$ 86,300
Indicated Value by Cost Approach			$117,300

There are two ways to look at the construction cost of a building for appraisal purposes (step 2): reproduction cost and replacement cost. **Reproduction cost** is the dollar amount required to construct an *exact duplicate* of the subject building at current prices. **Replacement cost** of the subject property would be the construction cost at current prices of a property that is not necessarily an exact duplicate but serves the same purpose or functional utility as the original. Replacement cost is most often used in appraising as it eliminates obsolete features and takes advantage of current construction materials and techniques.

An example of the cost approach to value is shown in Table 19.2.

Determining reproduction or replacement cost. An appraiser using the cost approach computes the reproduction or replacement cost of a building using one of the following methods:

1. **Square-foot method:** The cost per square foot of a recently built comparable structure is multiplied by the number of square feet (using exterior dimensions) in the subject building. This is the most common and easiest method of cost estimation. (See Table 19.2.) The *cubic-foot method* (use of cubic feet) may be used for certain buildings.

2. **Unit-in-place method:** Major construction components, such as exterior walls, interior walls, foundation, roof, heating and coooling, are segregated. The cost of each, including material and labor, is calculated. The sum of the components is the cost of the new structure. Lineal foot or square foot measures are used, depending on the component. Computations also include indirect costs such as overhead, building permits and builder's profits.

3. **Quantity-survey method:** An estimate is made of the quantities of raw materials needed (lumber, brick, plaster and so on) as well as of the current price of such materials and their installation costs. Indirect costs as mentioned before are also included in the computations. This is a highly technical and time-consuming method. Reproduction might be stated as: 10,000 concrete slabs at $3.50 per slab, 1500 doorknobs at $7.00 each and so forth.

Depreciation. In a real estate appraisal, **depreciation** refers to any condition that adversely affects the value of an improvement to real property. Land does not depreciate—it retains its value indefinitely, except in such rare cases as down-zoned urban parcels, improperly developed land or misused farmland. For appraisal purposes (as opposed to depreciation for tax purposes, which will be discussed in Chapter 23, "Real Estate Investment"), depreciation is divided into three classes according to its cause. Depreciation is considered to be curable or incurable depending on the contribution of the expenditure to the value of the property.

1. **Physical deterioration—curable:** Repairs that are economically feasible, considering the remaining years of life of the building, and would result in an increase in appraised value equal to or exceeding their cost. Routine maintenance, such as painting, or a new roof on a 40-year-old building that is otherwise in good condition are examples.

   Physical deterioration—incurable: Repairs that would not contribute a comparable value to the building. Near the end of a building's useful life, major repair work, such as replacement of weatherworn siding, may not warrant the financial investment.

2. **Functional obsolescence—curable:** Outmoded or unacceptable physical or design features that could be replaced or redesigned at a cost that would be offset by the anticipated increase in ultimate value. Outmoded plumbing fixtures are usually easily replaced. Room function may be redefined at no cost if the basic room layout allows for it. A bedroom adjacent to a kitchen may be converted to a family room.

   Functional obsolescence—incurable: Currently undesirable physical or design features that could not be easily remedied because the cost of effecting a cure would be greater than its contribution to the value. Many older multistory industrial buildings are considered less suitable than one-story buildings. An office building that cannot be air-conditioned suffers from functional obsolescence.

3. **External depreciation—incurable only:** Caused by factors not on the subject property, such as environmental, social or economic forces. This type of depreciation cannot usually be considered curable because the loss in value cannot be affected by expenditures to the property. Proximity to a nuisance, such as a polluting factory or a deteriorating neighborhood, would be unchangeable factors that could not be cured by the owner of the subject property.

In determining a property's depreciation, most appraisers use the *breakdown method,* in which depreciation is broken down into all three classes, with separate estimates for curable and incurable factors in each class. Depreciation, however, is difficult to measure, and the older the building, the more difficult it is to estimate. Much of the functional obsolescence and all of the external depreciation can be evaluated only by considering the actions of buyers in the marketplace.

In Practice...   *The cost approach is most helpful in the appraisal of special-purpose buildings such as schools, churches and post offices. Such properties are difficult to appraise using other methods because there seldom are many local sales to use as comparables and the properties do not usually generate income.*

**Table 19.3
Income Approach
to Value**

Gross Annual Income Estimate (potential rent income)	=	$60,000
Less vacancy and loss of rent (estimated) @ 5%	=	–3,000
Effective Gross Income		$57,000

Expenses:

Real estate taxes	$9,000	
Insurance	1,000	
Heat	2,800	
Janitor	5,200	
Utilities, electricity, water, gas	800	
Repairs	1,200	
Decorating	1,400	
Reserve for replacements	800	
Maintenance	1,200	
Legal and accounting	600	
Management	3,000	
Total Expenses		$27,000
Annual Net Income		$30,000

Capitalization Rate = 10%

Capitalization of annual net income: $\dfrac{\$30,000}{.10}$

Indicated Value by Income Approach = $300,000

The Income Approach

The **income approach** to value is based on the present worth of the future rights to income. It assumes that the income derived from a property will, to a large extent, control the value of that property. The income approach is used for valuation of income-producing properties—apartment buildings, central business districts, shopping centers and the like. In estimating value using the income approach, an appraiser must go through the following steps:

1. Estimate annual potential *gross rental income.* An estimate of economic rental income must be made based on market studies. Current rental income may not reflect the current market rental rates, especially in the cases of short-term leases or leases about to terminate.

2. Deduct an appropriate allowance for vacancy and rent loss, based on the appraiser's experience, and add income from concessions and vending machines to arrive at *effective gross income.*

3. Deduct the annual *operating expenses* from the effective gross income to arrive at the annual *net operating income.* See Table 19.3, "Income Approach to Value" for expenses. Management costs are always included, even if the current owner manages the property. Mortgage payments (principal and interest) are *debt service* and are not considered operating expenses.

4. Estimate the price a typical investor would pay for the income produced by this particular type and class of property. This is done by estimating the rate of return (or yield) that an investor will demand for the investment of capital in this type of building. This rate of return is called the **capitalization** (or "cap") **rate** and is determined by comparing the relationship of net operating income to the sales prices of similar properties that have sold in the current market. For example, a comparable property that is producing an annual net income of $15,000 is sold for $187,500. The capitalization rate is $15,000 ÷ $187,500, or eight percent. If other comparable properties sold at

prices that yield substantially the same rate, it may be concluded that eight percent is the rate that the appraiser should apply to the subject property.

5. Finally, the capitalization rate is applied to the property's annual net operating income, resulting in the appraiser's estimate of the property's value.

With the appropriate capitalization rate and the projected annual net operating income, the appraiser can obtain an indication of value by the income approach in the following manner:

$$\text{Net Operating Income} \div \text{Capitalization Rate} = \text{Value}$$

$$\text{Example: } \$15,000 \text{ income} \div 8\% \text{ cap rate} = \$187,500 \text{ value}$$

This formula and its variations are important in dealing with income property.

$$\frac{\text{Income}}{\text{Rate}} = \text{Value} \qquad \frac{\text{Income}}{\text{Value}} = \text{Rate} \qquad \text{Value} \times \text{Rate} = \text{Income}$$

A very simplified version of the computations used in applying the income approach is illustrated in Table 19.3.

In Practice...   *The most difficult step in the income approach to value is determining the appropriate capitalization rate for the property. This rate must be selected to accurately reflect the recapture of the original investment over the building's economic life, give the owner an acceptable rate of return on investment and provide for the repayment of borrowed capital. Note that an income property that carries with it a great deal of risk as an investment generally requires a higher rate of return than a property considered a safe investment.*

Gross rent or income multipliers. Certain properties, such as single-family homes or two-flat buildings, are not purchased primarily for income. As a substitute for the income approach, the **gross rent multiplier** (GRM) method is often used in appraising such properties. The GRM relates the sales price of a property to its rental income. (Gross *monthly* income is used for residential property; gross *annual* income is used for commercial and industrial property.) The formula is as follows:

$$\frac{\text{Sales Price}}{\text{Rental Income}} = \text{Gross Rent Multiplier}$$

For example, if a home recently sold for $82,000 and its monthly rental income was $650, the GRM for the property would be computed thus:

$$\frac{\$82,000}{\$650} = 126.2 \text{ GRM}$$

To establish an accurate GRM, an appraiser must have recent sales and rental data from at least four properties that are similar to the subject property. The resulting GRM can then be applied to the estimated fair market rental of the subject property in order to arrive at its market value. The formula would then be:

$$\text{Rental Income} \times \text{GRM} = \text{Estimated Market Value}$$

Table 19.4 shows some examples of GRM comparisons.

Comparable No.	Sales Price	Monthly Rent	GRM
1	$93,600	$650	144
2	78,500	450	174
3	95,500	675	141
4	82,000	565	145
Subject	?	625	?

Table 19.4 Gross Rent Multiplier

Note: Based on an analysis of these comparisons, a GRM of 145 seems reasonable for homes in this area. In the opinion of an appraiser, then, the estimated value of the subject property would be 625×145, or $90,625.

In Practice...

Much skill is required to use multipliers accurately, because there is no fixed multiplier for all areas or all types of properties. Therefore, many appraisers view the technique simply as a quick, informal way to check the validity of a property value obtained by one of the other appraisal methods.

Reconciliation

When the three approaches to value are applied to the same property, they will normally produce three separate indications of value. **Reconciliation** is the art of analyzing and effectively weighing the findings from the three approaches.

Although each approach may serve as an independent guide to value, whenever possible all three approaches should be used as a check on the final estimate of value. The process of reconciliation is more complicated than simply taking the average of the three derived value estimates. An average implies that the data and logic applied in each of the approaches are equally valid and reliable and should therefore be given equal weight. In fact, however, certain approaches are more valid and reliable with some kinds of properties than with others.

For example, in appraising a home the income approach is rarely valid and the cost approach is of limited value unless the home is relatively new; therefore, the direct sales comparison approach is usually given greatest weight in valuing single-family residences. In the appraisal of income or investment property, the income approach would normally be given the greatest weight. In the appraisal of churches, libraries, museums, schools and other special-use properties where there is little or no income or sales revenue, the cost approach would usually be assigned the greatest weight. From this analysis, or reconciliation, a single estimate of market value is produced.

The Appraisal Process

The key to an accurate appraisal lies in the methodical collection of data. The appraisal process is an orderly set of procedures used to collect and analyze data in order to arrive at an ultimate value conclusion. The data are divided into two basic classes:

1. *general data,* covering the nation, region, city and neighborhood. Of particular importance is the neighborhood, where an appraiser finds the physical, economic, social and political influences that directly affect the value and potential of the subject property;

**Figure 19.2
The Appraisal
Process**

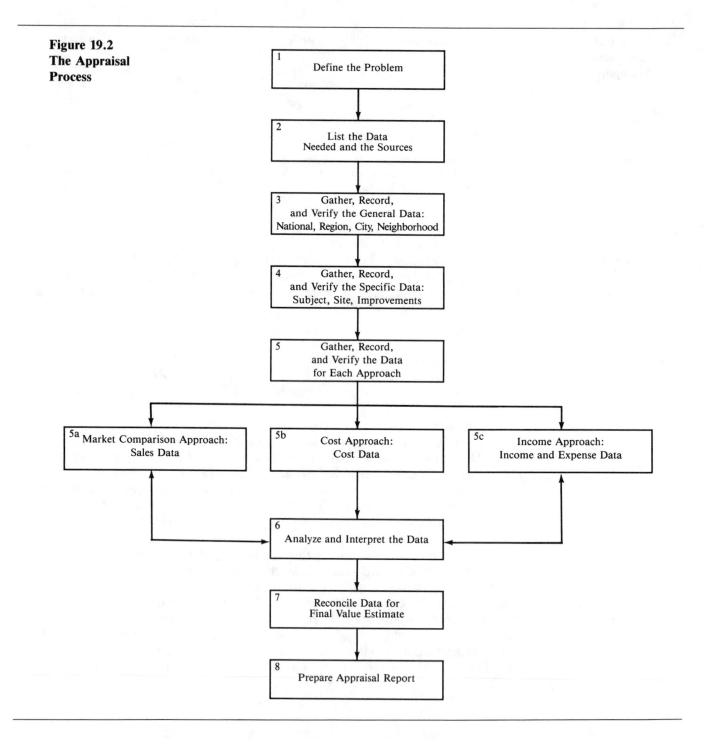

2. *specific data,* covering details of the subject property as well as comparative data relating to costs, sales and income and expenses of properties similar to and competitive with the subject property.

Figure 19.2 outlines the steps an appraiser takes in carrying out an appraisal assignment. The numbers in the following list correspond to the numbers on the flowchart.

1. *Define the problem:* The kind of value to be estimated must be specified and the valuation approach(es) most valid and reliable for the kind of property under appraisal must be selected.

2. *List the data needed and their sources:* Based on the approach(es) the appraiser will be using, the types of data needed and the sources to be consulted are listed.

3. *Gather, record and verify the general data:* Detailed information concerning the economic, political and social conditions of the region and/or city and comments on the effects of these data on the subject property must be obtained.

4. *Gather, record and verify the specific data on the subject property:* Specific data include information about the subject site and improvements.

5. *Gather, record and verify the data for the valuation approach used:* Depending upon the approach(es) used, comparative information relating to sales, income and expenses and construction costs of comparable properties must be collected. As with steps 3 and 4, all data should be verified, usually by checking the same information against two different sources. In the case of sales data, one source should be a person directly involved in the transaction.

6. *Analyze and interpret the data:* All information collected must be reviewed to ensure that all relevant facts have been considered and handled properly and that no errors have been made in calculations.

7. *Reconcile data for final value estimate:* The appraiser finally makes a definite statement of conclusions reached. This is usually in the form of a value estimate of the property.

8. *Prepare appraisal report:* After the three approaches have been reconciled and an opinion of value reached, the appraiser prepares a formal written report for the client. The statement may be a completed *form*, a *letter* or a lengthy written *narrative*. It should contain:

   a. the estimate of value and the date to which it applies;

   b. the purpose and function for which the appraisal was made;

   c. a description of the neighborhood and the subject property;

   d. factual data covering costs, sales and income and expenses of similar, recently sold properties;

   e. an analysis and interpretation of the data collected;

   f. a presentation of one or more of the three approaches to value in enough detail to support the appraiser's final value conclusion;

   g. any qualifying conditions;

   h. supportive material, such as charts, maps, photographs, floor plans, leases and contracts;

   i. the certification, qualifications and signature of the appraiser.

Figure 19.3 is a typical report form used in appraising for residential mortgage purposes. Note that, even in such a brief report detailed descriptions of the neighborhood and property being appraised are required.

Figure 19.3
Residential Appraisal
Report

Property Description & Analysis UNIFORM RESIDENTIAL APPRAISAL REPORT File No.

SUBJECT

Property Address	Census Tract	LENDER DISCRETIONARY USE
City County State	Zip Code	Sale Price $
Legal Description		Date
Owner/Occupant	Map Reference	Mortgage Amount $
Sale Price $ Date of Sale	PROPERTY RIGHTS APPRAISED	Mortgage Type
Loan charges/concessions to be paid by seller $	☐ Fee Simple	Discount Points and Other Concessions
R.E. Taxes $ Tax Year HOA $/Mo.	☐ Leasehold	Paid by Seller $
Lender/Client	☐ Condominium (HUD/VA)	
	☐ De Minimis PUD	Source

NEIGHBORHOOD

	Urban	Suburban	Rural	NEIGHBORHOOD ANALYSIS	Good	Avg	Fair	Poor
LOCATION	☐	☐	☐	Employment Stability				
BUILT UP	Over 75%	25-75%	Under 25%	Convenience to Employment				
GROWTH RATE	Rapid	Stable	Slow	Convenience to Shopping				
PROPERTY VALUES	Increasing	Stable	Declining	Convenience to Schools				
DEMAND/SUPPLY	Shortage	In Balance	Over Supply	Adequacy of Public Transportation				
MARKETING TIME	Under 3 Mos.	3-6 Mos.	Over 6 Mos.	Recreation Facilities				

PRESENT LAND USE %	LAND USE CHANGE	PREDOMINANT OCCUPANCY	SINGLE FAMILY HOUSING PRICE $(000) AGE (yrs)	
Single Family	Not Likely	Owner		Adequacy of Utilities
2-4 Family	Likely	Tenant	Low	Property Compatibility
Multi-family	In process	Vacant (0-5%)	High	Protection from Detrimental Cond.
Commercial	To:	Vacant (over 5%)	Predominant	Police & Fire Protection
Industrial			—	General Appearance of Properties
Vacant				Appeal to Market

Note: Race or the racial composition of the neighborhood are not considered reliable appraisal factors.
COMMENTS:

SITE

		Topography
Dimensions		
Site Area	Corner Lot	Size
Zoning Classification	Zoning Compliance	Shape
HIGHEST & BEST USE: Present Use	Other Use	Drainage

UTILITIES	Public	Other	SITE IMPROVEMENTS	Type	Public	Private	
Electricity			Street				View
Gas			Curb/Gutter				Landscaping
Water			Sidewalk				Driveway
Sanitary Sewer			Street Lights				Apparent Easements
Storm Sewer			Alley				FEMA Flood Hazard Yes* No
							FEMA* Map/Zone

COMMENTS (Apparent adverse easements, encroachments, special assessments, slide areas, etc.):

IMPROVEMENTS

GENERAL DESCRIPTION	EXTERIOR DESCRIPTION	FOUNDATION	BASEMENT	INSULATION
Units	Foundation	Slab	Area Sq. Ft.	Roof
Stories	Exterior Walls	Crawl Space	% Finished	Ceiling
Type (Det./Att.)	Roof Surface	Basement	Ceiling	Walls
Design (Style)	Gutters & Dwnspts.	Sump Pump	Walls	Floor
Existing	Window Type	Dampness	Floor	None
Proposed	Storm Sash	Settlement	Outside Entry	Adequacy
Under Construction	Screens	Infestation		Energy Efficient Items:
Age (Yrs.)	Manufactured House			
Effective Age (Yrs.)				

ROOM LIST

ROOMS	Foyer	Living	Dining	Kitchen	Den	Family Rm.	Rec. Rm.	Bedrooms	# Baths	Laundry	Other	Area Sq. Ft.
Basement												
Level 1												
Level 2												

Finished area **above** grade contains: Rooms,   Bedroom(s);   Bath(s);   Square Feet of Gross Living Area

INTERIOR

SURFACES	Materials/Condition	HEATING	KITCHEN EQUIP.	ATTIC	IMPROVEMENT ANALYSIS	Good	Avg	Fair	Poor
Floors		Type	Refrigerator	None	Quality of Construction				
Walls		Fuel	Range/Oven	Stairs	Condition of Improvements				
Trim/Finish		Condition	Disposal	Drop Stair	Room Sizes/Layout				
Bath Floor		Adequacy	Dishwasher	Scuttle	Closets and Storage				
Bath Wainscot		COOLING	Fan/Hood	Floor	Energy Efficiency				
Doors		Central	Compactor	Heated	Plumbing-Adequacy & Condition				
		Other	Washer/Dryer	Finished	Electrical-Adequacy & Condition				
		Condition	Microwave		Kitchen Cabinets-Adequacy & Cond.				
Fireplace(s) #		Adequacy	Intercom		Compatibility to Neighborhood				

AUTOS

CAR STORAGE:	Garage	Attached	Adequate	House Entry	Appeal & Marketability				
No. Cars	Carport	Detached	Inadequate	Outside Entry	Estimated Remaining Economic Life				Yrs.
Condition	None	Built-In	Electric Door	Basement Entry	Estimated Remaining Physical Life				Yrs.

Additional features:

COMMENTS

Depreciation (Physical, functional and external inadequacies, repairs needed, modernization, etc.):

General market conditions and prevalence and impact in subject/market area regarding loan discounts, interest buydowns and concessions:

Freddie Mac Form 70 10/86   Fannie Mae Form 1004 10/86

Figure 19.3 (cont.)

UNIFORM RESIDENTIAL APPRAISAL REPORT   File No.

Valuation Section

Purpose of Appraisal is to estimate Market Value as defined in the Certification & Statement of Limiting Conditions.

COST APPROACH

BUILDING SKETCH (SHOW GROSS LIVING AREA ABOVE GRADE)
If for Freddie Mac or Fannie Mae, show only square foot calculations and cost approach comments in this space.

ESTIMATED REPRODUCTION COST-NEW-OF IMPROVEMENTS:

Dwelling _____ Sq. Ft. @ $ _____	= $ _____
_____ Sq. Ft. @ $ _____	= _____
Extras _____	= _____
	= _____
Special Energy Efficient Items _____	= _____
Porches, Patios, etc. _____	= _____
Garage/Carport _____ Sq. Ft. @ $ _____	= _____
Total Estimated Cost New	= $ _____

	Physical	Functional	External
Less Depreciation			= $ _____

Depreciated Value of Improvements .... = $ _____
Site Imp. "as is" (driveway, landscaping, etc.) = $ _____
ESTIMATED SITE VALUE .... = $ _____
(If leasehold, show only leasehold value.)
INDICATED VALUE BY COST APPROACH .... = $ _____

(Not Required by Freddie Mac and Fannie Mae)
Does property conform to applicable HUD/VA property standards? ☐ Yes ☐ No
If No, explain: _____

Construction Warranty ☐ Yes ☐ No
Name of Warranty Program _____
Warranty Coverage Expires _____

SALES COMPARISON ANALYSIS

The undersigned has recited three recent sales of properties most similar and proximate to subject and has considered these in the market analysis. The description includes a dollar adjustment, reflecting market reaction to those items of significant variation between the subject and comparable properties. If a significant item in the comparable property is superior to, or more favorable than, the subject property, a minus (–) adjustment is made, thus reducing the indicated value of subject; if a significant item in the comparable is inferior to, or less favorable than, the subject property, a plus (+) adjustment is made, thus increasing the indicated value of the subject.

ITEM	SUBJECT	COMPARABLE NO. 1		COMPARABLE NO. 2		COMPARABLE NO. 3	
Address							
Proximity to Subject							
Sales Price	$	$		$		$	
Price/Gross Liv. Area	$	$		$		$	
Data Source							
VALUE ADJUSTMENTS	DESCRIPTION	DESCRIPTION	+ (–) $ Adjustment	DESCRIPTION	+ (–) $ Adjustment	DESCRIPTION	+ (–) $ Adjustment
Sales or Financing Concessions							
Date of Sale/Time							
Location							
Site/View							
Design and Appeal							
Quality of Construction							
Age							
Condition							
Above Grade Room Count	Total ┆ Bdrms ┆ Baths	Total ┆ Bdrms ┆ Baths		Total ┆ Bdrms ┆ Baths		Total ┆ Bdrms ┆ Baths	
Gross Living Area	Sq. Ft.	Sq. Ft.		Sq. Ft.		Sq. Ft.	
Basement & Finished Rooms Below Grade							
Functional Utility							
Heating/Cooling							
Garage/Carport							
Porches, Patio, Pools, etc.							
Special Energy Efficient Items							
Fireplace(s)							
Other (e.g. kitchen equip., remodeling)							
Net Adj. (total)		☐ + ☐ – $		☐ + ☐ – $		☐ + ☐ – $	
Indicated Value of Subject		$		$		$	

Comments on Sales Comparison: _____

RECONCILIATION

INDICATED VALUE BY SALES COMPARISON APPROACH .... $ _____
INDICATED VALUE BY INCOME APPROACH (If Applicable) Estimated Market Rent $ _____ /Mo. x Gross Rent Multiplier _____ = $ _____

This appraisal is made ☐ "as is" ☐ subject to the repairs, alterations, inspections or conditions listed below ☐ completion per plans and specifications.
Comments and Conditions of Appraisal: _____

Final Reconciliation: _____

This appraisal is based upon the above requirements, the certification, contingent and limiting conditions, and Market Value definition that are stated in
☐ FmHA, HUD &/or VA instructions.
☐ Freddie Mac Form 439 (Rev. 7/86)/Fannie Mae Form 1004B (Rev. 7/86) filed with client _____ 19 _____ ☐ attached.
I (WE) ESTIMATE THE MARKET VALUE, AS DEFINED, OF THE SUBJECT PROPERTY AS OF _____ 19 _____ to be $ _____

I (We) certify: that to the best of my (our) knowledge and belief the facts and data used herein are true and correct; that I (we) personally inspected the subject property, both inside and out, and have made an exterior inspection of all comparable sales cited in this report; and that I (we) have no undisclosed interest, present or prospective therein.

Appraiser(s) SIGNATURE _____
NAME _____

Review Appraiser SIGNATURE _____ (if applicable) NAME _____

☐ Did ☐ Did Not Inspect Property

Freddie Mac Form 70 10/86   Fannie Mae Form 1004 10/86

In Practice...   *The role of an appraiser is not to determine value, but to develop a supportable and objective report about the value of the subject property. The appraiser relies on experience and expertise in valuation theories to evaluate market data. The appraiser does not create numbers or "pick them from the air." In other words, it is not what the appraiser thinks the property is worth, but what the market indicates is the value that the appraiser can verify. This is an important point to remember, particularly when dealing with a property owner who may, understandably, lack the necessary objectivity to see the property realistically. This possible lack of objectivity can complicate the salesperson's ability to list a property within the most probable range of market value, as well.*

The Profession of Appraising

In 1932 the American Institute of Real Estate Appraisers was founded. A few years later another organization, now known as the Society of Real Estate Appraisers, was formed. Through the years a number of other professional appraisal organizations have come into existence, including the American Society of Appraisers, the National Association of Review Appraisers, the National Association of Independent Fee Appraisers, and the American Society of Farm Managers and Rural Appraisers.

The American Institute offers the professional designations of RM (Resident Member) and MAI (Member of the Appraisal Institute). The Society offers the designations of SRA (Senior Residential Appraiser), SRPA (Senior Real Property Appraiser), and SREA (Senior Real Estate Analyst). The National Association of Independent Fee Appraisers offers the designations of IFA (member) and IFAS (senior member).

Appraising has now become the most specialized branch of real estate. Through these groups, courses have been established in universities and colleges and books, journals and other publications devoted to various aspects of appraising have come into existence.

Summary

To *appraise* real estate means to *estimate its value.* Although there are many types of value, the most common objective of an appraisal is to estimate *market value*—the most probable sale price of a property.

Appraisals are concerned with values, prices and costs; it is vital to understand the distinctions among the terms. *Value* is an estimate of future benefits, *cost* represents a measure of past expenditures, and *price* reflects the actual amount of money paid for a property.

Basic to appraising are certain underlying economic principles, such as highest and best use, substitution, supply and demand, conformity, anticipation, increasing and diminishing returns, regression and progression, plottage, contribution, competition and change.

A professional appraiser analyzes a property through three approaches to value. In the *direct sales comparison approach,* the value of the subject property is compared with the values of others like it that have sold recently. Because no two properties are exactly alike, adjustments must be made to account for any differences. With the *cost approach,* an appraiser calculates the cost of building a similar structure on a similar site. The appraiser then subtracts depreciation (losses in value), which reflects the differences between new properties of this type and the present condition of the subject property. The *income approach* is an analysis based on the relationship between the rate of return that an investor requires and the net income that a property produces.

An informal version of the income approach, called the *gross rent multiplier* (GRM), may be used to estimate the value of single-family residential properties that are not usually rented but could be. The GRM is computed by dividing the sales price of a property by its gross monthly rent.

Normally, the application of the three approaches will result in three different estimates of value. In the process of *reconciliation*, the validity and reliability of each approach are weighed objectively to arrive at the single best and most supportable estimate of value.

Questions

1. Which of the following approaches to value makes use primarily of comparables?
   a. direct sales comparison
   b. cost
   c. income
   d. all of the above

2. The elements of value include which of the following?
   a. utility
   b. scarcity
   c. demand
   d. all of the above

3. The principle of value that states that two adjacent parcels of land combined into one larger parcel would have a greater value than the two parcels valued separately is called:
   a. substitution.
   b. plottage.
   c. highest and best use.
   d. contribution.

4. The amount of money a property commands in the marketplace is its:
   a. market price.
   b. market value.
   c. capitalization rate.
   d. index.

5. Joe Hamel has his "dream house" constructed for $100,000 in an area where most newly constructed homes are not as well equipped as his and typically sell for only $80,000. The value of Hamel's house is likely to be affected by the principle of:
   a. progression.   c. change.
   b. assemblage.   d. regression.

6. In question 5, the owners of the lesser-valued homes in Hamel's immediate area are likely to be affected by the principle of:
   a. progression.
   b. increasing returns.
   c. competition.
   d. regression.

7. Depreciation, as used in real estate appraisals, can be caused by which of the following?
   a. functional obsolescence
   b. physical deterioration
   c. external depreciation
   d. all of the above

8. *Reconciliation* refers to which of the following?
   a. loss of value due to any cause
   b. separating the value of the land from the total value of the property in order to compute depreciation
   c. analyzing the results obtained by the three approaches to value to determine a final estimate of value
   d. the process by which an appraiser determines the highest and best use for a parcel of land

9. One method an appraiser uses to determine a building's replacement cost involves an estimate of the raw materials needed to build the structure, plus the cost of such materials, labor and other expenses. This is called the:
   a. square-foot method.
   b. quantity-survey method.
   c. cubic-foot method.
   d. unit-in-place method.

10. If a property's annual net income is $24,000 and it is valued at $300,000, what is its capitalization rate?
    a. 12.5 percent   c. 15 percent
    b. 10.5 percent   d. 8 percent

11. Certain data must be determined by an appraiser before value can be computed by the income approach. Which one of the following is *not* required for this process?
    a. annual net income
    b. proper capitalization rate
    c. accrued depreciation
    d. annual gross income

12. The income approach would be given the most weight in the valuation of a(n):
    a. single-family residence.
    b. industrial property.
    c. strip shopping center.
    d. school.

13. The value of a parcel of real estate is:
    I. an estimate of its future benefits.
    II. the amount of money paid for the property.
       a. I only
       b. II only
       c. both I and II
       d. neither I nor II

14. Capitalization is the process by which annual net income is used as the basis to:
    a. determine cost.
    b. estimate value.
    c. establish depreciation.
    d. determine potential tax value.

15. From the reproduction or replacement cost of the building, an appraiser deducts depreciation, which represents:
    a. the remaining economic life of the building.
    b. remodeling costs to increase rentals.
    c. loss of value due to any cause.
    d. costs to modernize the building.

16. In the direct sales comparison approach to value, the probable sales price of a building may be estimated by:
    I. capitalizing net income.
    II. considering sales of similar properties.
       a. I only
       b. II only
       c. both I and II
       d. neither I nor II

17. Which of the following factors would *not* be important in comparing properties under the direct sales comparison approach to value?
    a. difference in dates of sale
    b. difference in real estate taxes
    c. difference in appearance and condition
    d. difference in original cost

18. In the income approach to value:
    I. the reproduction or replacement cost of the building must be computed.
    II. the capitalization rate must be estimated.
       a. I only
       b. II only
       c. both I and II
       d. neither I nor II

19. In the cost approach to value, it is necessary to:
    a. determine a dollar value for depreciation.
    b. estimate future expenses and operating costs.
    c. check sales prices of recently sold homes in the area.
    d. a and b

20. Which of the following formulas would be used to determine the capitalization rate of an office building?
    a. $Income = Rate \times Value$
    b. $\dfrac{Income}{Rate} = Value$
    c. $\dfrac{Income}{Value} = Rate$
    d. a and b

21. The appraised value of a residence with five bedrooms and one bathroom would probably be adversely affected because of:
    a. external depreciation.
    b. functional obsolescence.
    c. physical deterioration—curable.
    d. physical deterioration—incurable.

20

Financing the Real Estate Transaction

Key Terms

Adjustable rate mortgage (ARM)
Balloon payment
Blanket mortgage
Construction loan
Conventional loan
Discount points
ECOA
FHA loan
Graduated payment mortgage (GPM)
Growing equity mortgage (GEM)
Installment contract
Loan-to-value ratio

Open-end mortgage
Package mortgage
Private mortgage insurance (PMI)
Purchase-money mortgage
Renegotiable rate mortgage (RRM)
Reverse annuity mortgage (RAM)
Regulation Z
Shared-appreciation mortgage (SAM)
Sale and leaseback
VA loan
Wraparound mortgage

Overview

Rarely is real estate purchased on a cash basis; the buyer relies on a mortgage loan. The choice of a loan program is influenced by the cash available for a down payment, the affordability of the monthly payment and the type of property pledged as collateral. The real estate licensee must be familiar with alternative types of financing and payment plans. These will be discussed in this chapter, as well as federal legislation affecting disclosure of finance charges and closing costs and the availability of credit.

Cost of Credit

As discussed in Chapter 13, "Real Estate Financing," the borrower incurs costs for the mortgage loan. From the borrower's point of view, the loan is a means of financing an expenditure; from a lender's point of view, it is an investment. The investment must generate sufficient income to be attractive to the lender. Income on the loan is realized from (1) finance charges collected at closing and (2) recurring income—interest—collected during the term of the loan.

At closing, in addition to the cash requirements for down payment and other settlement costs (see Chapter 21, "Closing the Real Estate Transaction"), the borrower pays a *loan origination fee*, or service fee. Generally this is one percent of the mortgage loan. The lender may charge more than one percent, depending on the lender's income requirements. In addition to the origination fee, there may be other charges, represented as *points*, which will be discussed later. Discount points may be charged to the buyer or negotiated between the buyer and seller. However, VA regulations prohibit charging discount points to the buyer; in VA loans the points *must* be paid by the seller. If a borrower's down payment is small relative to the amount of the mortgage loan and the value of the property, the lender also may require insurance on the loan. The *insurance premium* would be paid at closing (it may also recur during the term of the loan).

Discount Points

The institution that originates a loan may sell it instead of collecting the principal and interest over the long term. By selling loans, lending institutions replenish their supply of funds for additional loans.

For an investor to be interested in purchasing a mortgage loan the yield must be competitive, and similarly for the borrower to be interested, the rate must be competitive. **Discount points** may be charged by a lending institution when the interest rate is less than the money market. This may be particularly true in the case of VA loans, where the government sets the maximum interest that may be charged by the lender. One discount point equals one percent of the mortgage amount.

If a mortgage loan made at a fixed interest rate of 10 percent is compared to a similar mortgage loan at 10½ percent, the loan at 10 percent yields ½ percent less interest. If both loans were offered to the investor, the investor would choose the 10½ percent loan. The only way to sell the 10 percent loan is to reduce the price or discount it to increase its yield.

Generally, one point of the mortgage principal is deducted for each ⅛ percent difference in the interest yield. In the case of the 10 percent and 10½ percent loans, there is ½ percent difference in yield, which equals ⁴⁄₈. Therefore, a difference of four percentage points would be discounted. For example, if the mortgage amount is $50,000, then a four point discount would represent four percent of $50,000, or $2,000. The discounted value of the loan would be $50,000 minus $2,000, or $48,000. The investor who pays $48,000 for a $50,000 10 percent mortgage note will receive $5,000 per year interest, which would be nearly a 10½ percent yield on the $48,000 investment. Discount points, then, represent the percentage by which the face amount of a mortgage loan is discounted, or reduced, when it is sold to an investor.

Application for Credit

All mortgage lenders require prospective borrowers to file an application for credit that provides the lender with the basic information needed to evaluate the acceptability of the proposed loan. The application includes information regarding the purpose of the loan, the amount, rate of interest and the proposed terms of repayment. This is considered a preliminary offer of a loan agreement; final terms may require lengthy negotiations.

A prospective borrower must submit personal information to the lender, including employment, earnings, assets and financial obligations. Details of the real estate that will be the security for the loan must be provided, including legal description, improvements, title, survey and taxes. For loans on income property or those made to corporations, additional information is required, such as financial and operating statements, schedules of leases and tenants and balance sheets.

The lender carefully investigates the application information, studying credit reports and an appraisal of the property before deciding whether or not to grant the loan. The lender's acceptance of the application is written in the form of a *loan commitment,* which creates a contract to make a loan and sets forth the details. With borderline cases, a commitment may be made based on the lender's current financial position.

In Practice...

Because interest rates and loan terms change frequently, you should check with local sources of real estate financing on a regular basis to learn of specific loan rates and terms. As a licensee, you can better serve your customers—and thus more effectively sell your clients' properties—if you can knowledgeably refer buyers to local lenders offering the most favorable terms.

Loan Repayment

There are a variety of mortgage repayment plans. As discussed in Chapter 13, the majority are *amortized* loans involving principal and interest payments during the term, as opposed to payment of interest only in a *straight* loan. Interest on amortized loans may be paid at a *fixed* rate or *variable* rate, wherein a new note is written periodically for the remaining balance at a new interest rate or the terms of the original note provide for fluctuating interest. In addition to a fully amortized, fixed interest/fixed payment loan, the following payment programs have been developed.

Adjustable rate mortgage (ARM). An **adjustable rate mortgage** is generally originated at one rate of interest, with the rate fluctuating up or down during the loan term based on a certain economic indicator, such as the cost-of-funds index for federally chartered savings and loan associations. Details of how and when the rate of interest on the loan will change are included in the provisions of the note. Generally, interest rate adjustments are limited to one each year, and there is a set maximum number of increases that may be made over the life of the loan. The borrower is usually given the right to prepay the loan in full without penalty whenever the interest rate is changed.

Graduated payment mortgage (GPM). The mortgagor may elect to take advantage of a *flexible payment plan,* such as a **graduated payment mortgage,** generally used to enable younger buyers and buyers in times of high interest rates to purchase real estate. Under this plan, a mortgagor makes lower monthly payments for the first few years of the loan (typically the first five years), and larger payments for the remainder of the term, when the mortgagor's income is expected to have increased. This is a fixed rate loan.

Balloon payment loan. When a mortgage loan requires periodic payments that will not fully amortize the amount of the loan by the time the final payment is due, the final payment is a larger amount than the others. This is called a **balloon payment,** and this type of loan is a *partially amortized loan.* For example, a loan made for $80,000 at 11½ percent interest may be computed on a 30-year amortization schedule but paid over a 20-year term with a final balloon payment due at the end of the twentieth year. In this case, each monthly payment would be $792.24 (the amount taken from a 30-year amortization schedule), with a final balloon payment of $56,340 (the amount of principal still owing after 20 years). It is frequently assumed that if the payments are promptly made, the lender will extend the balloon payment for another limited term. The lender, however, is in no way legally obligated to grant this extension and can require payment in full when the note is due.

Growing equity mortgage (GEM). The **growing equity mortgage,** or *rapid-payoff mortgage,* makes use of a fixed interest rate, but payments of principal are increased according to an index or schedule. The total payment thus increases, but the borrower's income is expected to keep pace, and the loan is paid off more quickly.

Renegotiable rate mortgage (RRM). A **renegotiable rate mortgage** is a long-term loan that is renewable every three, four or five years, at which time the interest rate is increased or decreased. These adjustments are based on a national index—for instance, the interest rates on previously occupied homes as compiled by the Federal Home Loan Bank Board. Interest rates may change at a maximum rate of one-half percent per year, with a five percent maximum over the life of the loan; specifics are included in the provisions of the note. Often such limitations are self-imposed by lenders. Borrowers must be notified of any rate change at least 30 days in advance of the change. Downward interest adjustments are mandatory, while upward adjustments are optional. Borrowers are usually allowed to prepay without penalty within a reasonable time after receiving notice of a rate change.

Shared-appreciation mortgage (SAM). A **shared-appreciation mortgage** is one in which the lender originates a mortgage loan at a favorable interest rate (several points below the going rate) in return for a guaranteed share of the gain (if any) the borrower will realize when the property is eventually sold. This type of loan was originally made to developers of large real estate projects, but in times of expensive mortgage money it has appeared in the residential financing market. The specific details of the shared-appreciation agreement are set forth in the mortgage and note documents.

Reverse annuity mortgage (RAM). A **reverse annuity mortgage** is one in which regular monthly payments are made *to the borrower,* based on the equity the homeowner has invested in the property given as security for the loan. A reverse loan allows senior citizens on fixed incomes to realize the equity buildup in their homes without having to sell. The borrower is charged a fixed rate of interest and the loan is eventually paid from the sale of the property or from the borrower's estate upon his or her death.

It is common in loans with fluctuating interest rates for the lender to include a "cap rate." This is the maximum interest that can be charged anytime during the loan.

In Practice...   *Interest payments made under a mortgage loan secured by a first or second home are deductible for federal income-tax purposes. This deduction, in effect, reduces the borrower's total cost of housing for the year. Interest deductions are limited, however, to the interest paid on mortgages used to buy, build or improve a principal or second home, provided the loan amount does not exceed $1 million. Tax deductions for the homeowner were discussed in greater detail in Chapter 16.*

Points (prepaid interest) paid at the time of financing a home purchase are fully deductible for the year paid. Points on a loan to finance property improvements are also fully deductible for the year paid. Points paid on a loan refinancing are deductible, but only in portions each year over the stated term of the loan. If advance payments of loan principal are made, there is no increase in the deduction. If the entire loan is repaid, however, any undeducted points may be deducted for that year.

Loans   Mortgage loans are generally classified as to whether or not they are conventional based on their **loan-to-value ratio,** that is, the ratio of debt to value of the property. The lower the ratio of debt to value (the higher the borrower's down payment), the more secure the loan is considered, minimizing the lender's risk.

Conventional Loans   Loans are classified as **conventional loans** when the payment of the debt rests upon the ability of the borrower to pay, with security provided solely by the mortgage. In making these loans the lender relies primarily on its appraisal of the security and information from credit reports indicating the reliability of the prospective borrower. These loans require no additional insurance or guarantee to protect the lender's interest. Qualifications for these loans have been influenced considerably in recent years by increased participation in the secondary mortgage market. The Federal National Mortgage Association and Federal Home Loan Mortgage Association have set standards that must be met for any loan to be salable to them.

Private Mortgage Insurance (PMI)   Under the provisions of **private mortgage insurance** programs, home purchasers can obtain conventional mortgage loans of up to 95 percent of the appraised property value at prevailing interest rates and reasonable insurance premium costs. Since the loan-to-value ratio is higher than other conventional loans, the lender's interest is secured by insurance in addition to the mortgage. The leader in the insurance field is the *Mortgage Guaranty Insurance Corporation (MGIC)* of Milwaukee, Wisconsin, which instituted the program in 1957. MGIC is one of a number of mortgage insurance companies. Generally, the first-year insurance premium is paid at closing. Monthly premiums are paid into an escrow account in addition to the mortgage payment.

FHA-Insured Loans   The Federal Housing Administration (FHA) was created in 1934 under the National Housing Act to encourage improvement in housing standards and conditions, provide an adequate home-financing system through insurance of housing credit and exert a stabilizing influence on the mortgage market. The FHA was the government's response to the lack of housing, excessive foreclosures and collapsed building industry that occurred during the Depression.

The FHA, which operates under the Department of Housing and Urban Development (HUD), neither builds homes nor lends money itself. Rather, *it insures loans on real property made by approved lending institutions.* These are high loan-to-value ratio loans—up to 97%. It does not insure the property, but it does insure the lender against loss. The common term **FHA loan,** then, refers to a loan that is not made by the agency but insured by it.

The most popular FHA program is Title II, Section 203(b), which applies to loans on one-family to four-family residences. Although interest rates on these loans are no longer fixed by the FHA, such rates are generally one-half percent lower than those charged under conventional loans. These rates are generally lower because the protection of the FHA mortgage insurance makes them a lesser risk to the lender. Technical requirements of the loan established under congressional authority must be met before the FHA will issue the insurance. Three of these requirements are:

1. In addition to paying interest, the *borrower is charged between 2.9 and 3.8 percent* of the outstanding loan amount as a *premium for the FHA insurance.* This amount is payable in cash at the closing or it may be financed for the term of the loan.

2. The FHA regulations set *standards* for type and construction of buildings, quality of neighborhood, and credit requirements for borrowers.

3. The mortgaged real estate must be appraised by an *approved FHA appraiser.* The loan amount insured generally cannot exceed 97 percent on the first $25,000 of appraised value or purchase price, whichever is less, and 95 percent of the remainder. For a single-family owner-occupied house or condominium with a maximum appraised value or purchase price (whichever is less) of $50,000 (including closing costs), the maximum loan is 97 percent of the entire appraised value. For houses less than one year old, and not insured prior to the beginning of construction, the loan ratio is 90 percent of the appraised value or selling price, whichever is less. Note that if the purchase price exceeds the FHA-appraised value, the buyer may pay the difference in cash as part of the down payment. In addition, the FHA has set maximum loan amounts for various regions of the country. Contact your local FHA office for such amounts in your area. FHA regulations require that both buyer and seller sign a statement indicating that they have examined the FHA appraisal.

To determine the maximum allowable mortgage, the *acquisition cost* (appraised value + closing costs) may be used instead of the appraised value alone. Thus, if the appraised value of a home is $60,000 and allowable closing costs are $1,800, the total acquisition cost is $61,800. The maximum allowable mortgage is $59,200. (97% of the first $25,000 = $24,250; 95% of the remaining $36,800 = $34,960. $24,250 + $34,960 = $59,210. Round down to the nearest 50 or 100.)

Prepayment privileges. When a mortgage loan is insured by the FHA and the real estate given as security is a single-family dwelling or an apartment building with no more than four units, the borrower retains the privilege of prepaying the debt without penalty. On the first day of any month before the loan matures, the borrower may pay the entire debt or an amount equal to one or more monthly payments on the principal. The borrower must give the lender written notice of intention to exercise this privilege at least 30 days beforehand, or the lender may charge up to 30 days' interest in lieu of such notification.

Other FHA loan programs. In addition to loans made under Title II, Section 203(b), FHA loans are also granted under the following programs:

1. Title I: Home improvement loans are covered under this title; such loans are for relatively low amounts with a repayment term of no longer than seven years and 32 days.

2. Title II, Section 246: Loans made to purchase condominiums are covered under this program, which in most respects is similar to the basic 203(b) program.

3. Title II, Section 245: Graduated payment mortgages, as discussed in this chapter, are allowed under this program; depending on interest rates, the loan-to-value ratio of such loans might range from 87 to 93 percent.

Points. Since December 1, 1983, a lender of an FHA-insured loan can charge points in addition to a one percent loan fee. The FHA limits seller contributions (including discount points, temporary buydown costs and closing costs) to five percent of the property's acquisition cost. With that limitation, payment of points is a matter of negotiation between buyer and seller.

VA-Guaranteed (GI) Loans

Under the Servicemen's Readjustment Act of 1944 and subsequent federal legislation, the Veterans Administration is authorized to guarantee loans to purchase or construct homes for eligible veterans—those who have served a minimum of 181 days' active service since September 16, 1940; 90 days for veterans of World War II, the Korean War and/or the Vietnam conflict; two full years for those enlisting for the first time after September 7, 1980. The VA also guarantees loans to purchase mobile homes and plots on which to place them. VA loans assist veterans in financing the purchase of homes with little or no down payments, at comparatively low interest rates. Rules and regulations are issued from time to time by the VA, setting forth the qualifications, limitations and conditions under which a loan may be guaranteed. (Table 20.1 is a comparison of VA and FHA loan programs.)

As with the term *FHA loan,* **VA loan** is something of a misnomer. The VA does not normally lend money itself; it guarantees loans made by lending institutions approved by the agency. The term *VA loan,* then, refers to a loan that is not made by the agency but is guaranteed by it.

There is no VA limit on the amount of the loan a veteran can obtain; this is determined by the lender. The VA does, however, set a limit on the amount of the loan that it will guarantee, currently $36,000 of the loan amount, toward the purchase, construction, repair or alteration of a house, condominium or farm residence.

Note that the $36,000 figure is the amount of the guarantee and refers to the maximum amount the lender would receive from the VA in the case of a default and foreclosure if the sale did not bring enough to cover the outstanding balance. For example, if a $60,000 loan were in default, the property could sell at foreclosure for as little as $24,000 ($60,000–$36,000) and the lender would recoup the full value of the loan.

To determine what portion of a mortgage loan the VA will guarantee, the veteran must apply for a *certificate of eligibility.* This certificate does not mean that the

Table 20.1	Federal Housing Administration	Veterans Administration
Comparison of FHA and VA Loan Programs	1. Financing is available to veterans and nonveterans alike 2. Financing programs for owner-occupied, rental and other types of construction; owner-occupied has greater loan-to-value ratio 3. Requires a larger down payment than VA 4. Different evaluation methods; like VA, there are prescribed valuation procedures for the approved appraisers to follow 5. FHA valuation sets the maximum loan FHA will insure but does not limit the sales price 6. No prepayment penalty 7. On default, foreclosure and claim, the FHA lender usually gets U.S. debentures 8. Insures the loan by way of mutual mortgage insurance; premiums paid by borrower 9. Discount points can be charged, payable by either seller (no more than 5 points) or buyer 10. Borrower is subject to one percent loan origination fee; 2½ percent for buildings to be constructed 11. FHA loan can be assumed without FHA approval after two years	1. Financing available only to veterans and certain unremarried widows and widowers 2. VA financing limited to owner-occupied residential (one- to four-family) dwellings—must sign occupancy certificate on two separate occasions 3. Does not normally require down payment, though lender may require small down payment 4. Methods of valuation differ—VA issues a certificate of reasonable value 5. With regard to home loans, the VA loan may not exceed the appraised value of the home 6. No prepayment penalty 7. Following default, foreclosure and claim, the lender usually receives cash 8. Guarantees up to $36,000 of the loan 9. Borrower prohibited from paying discount points (except in refinancing and certain defined circumstances) 10. VA loan can be assumed by nonveteran without VA approval 11. Borrower must pay VA a one percent funding fee at closing

Note: Provisions for assumption of FHA and VA loans were discussed in Chapter 13, "Real Estate Financing."

veteran will automatically receive a mortgage. It merely sets forth the maximum guarantee the veteran is entitled to.

The VA will also issue a *certificate of reasonable value* (CRV) for the property being purchased, stating its current market value based on a VA-approved appraisal. The CRV places a ceiling on the amount of a VA loan allowed for the property; if the purchase price is greater than the amount cited in the CRV, the veteran must pay the difference in cash.

Only in certain situations (such as in isolated rural areas) where financing is not reasonably available does the VA lend money itself; otherwise, a veteran obtains a loan from a VA-approved lending institution. The VA does not require a down payment. Although the VA guarantee is never more than $36,000, in practice the veteran may be able to obtain a 100-percent loan if the appraised valuation of the property is $110,000 or less and the veteran is entitled to a full $36,000 guarantee. Maximum loan terms are 30 years for one-family to four-family dwellings and 40 years for farm loans. The interest rate cannot exceed the rate set periodically by the VA Administrator. Residential property purchased with a VA loan must be owner-occupied.

VA loans can be assumed by purchasers who do not qualify as veterans. The original veteran borrower remains liable for the loan but could obtain a release of the certificate of eligibility if another veteran used his or her own entitlement in assuming the loan.

Prepayment. As with an FHA loan, the borrower under a VA loan can prepay the debt at any time without penalty. Also, the veteran may not be required to pay more than a one percent origination fee.

At the closing of a purchase financed by a VA loan, the *seller* is charged discount points, as previously discussed. The VA allows lenders to charge reasonable closing costs plus a loan origination fee that may not exceed one percent of the loan amount. There is also a one percent funding fee, which the veteran pays the VA at closing.

In Practice...	*Regulations and requirements regarding FHA and VA loans change frequently. Check with local lenders, as well as with your local FHA and VA offices, from time to time for current information regarding these government-backed loan programs.*

Other Financing Techniques

By altering the terms of the basic mortgage and note, a borrower and a lender can tailor financing instruments to best suit the type of transaction and the financial needs of both parties. Especially in times of tight, expensive mortgage money, such "creative financing" gains prominence. In addition, real estate may be financed using instruments other than mortgages, as will be discussed in the following section.

Purchase-Money Mortgages

A **purchase-money mortgage** is a note and mortgage created at the time of purchase to facilitate the sale. The term is used in two ways—to refer to *any* security instrument originating at the time of sale and (most often) to refer to the instrument *given by the purchaser to a seller who "takes back" a note for part or all of the purchase price.* This may be a first or second mortgage and it becomes a lien on the property when the title passes. In the event of the foreclosure of a purchase-money mortgage, the lien takes priority over judgment liens against the borrower. In Pennsylvania, a purchase-money mortgage lien takes priority from the date of the mortgage if recorded within 30 days of that date.

Package Mortgages

A **package mortgage** not only includes the real estate but also *expressly includes all personal property and appliances installed on the premises.* In recent years, this kind of loan has been used extensively in financing furnished condominium units in some parts of the country. Such loans usually include furniture, drapes, carpets, the kitchen range, refrigerator, dishwasher, garbage disposal unit, washer and dryer, food freezer and other appliances as part of the real estate in the sales price of the home.

Package mortgages are not permitted in Pennsylvania, however. State law stipulates that only real estate and fixtures may be made subject to the lien of a mortgage on real estate.

Blanket Mortgages

A **blanket mortgage** covers *more than one parcel or lot* and is usually used to finance subdivision developments (though it can be used to finance the purchase of improved properties or to consolidate loans as well). These loans usually include a provision, known as a *partial release clause,* that the borrower may obtain the release of any one lot or parcel from the lien by repaying a definite amount of the loan. The lender issues a partial release for each parcel released from the mortgage lien; this release form includes a provision that the lien will continue to cover all other unreleased lots.

Wraparound Encumbrances

A **wraparound mortgage** enables a borrower who is paying off an existing mortgage loan to obtain additional financing from a second lender. *The new lender assumes payment of the existing loan and gives the borrower a new, increased loan at a higher interest rate.* The total amount of the new loan includes the existing loan as well as the additional funds needed by the borrower. The borrower makes payments to the new lender on the larger loan, and the new lender makes the payments on the original loan.

A wraparound mortgage is frequently used as a method of refinancing real property or financing the purchase of real property when an existing mortgage cannot be prepaid. It is also used to finance the sale of real estate when the buyer wishes to put up a minimum of initial cash for the sale. The buyer executes a wraparound document to the seller, who will collect payments on the new loan and continue to make payments on the old loan. The buyer should require a protective clause in the document granting the right to make payments directly to the original lender in the event of a potential default on the old loan by the seller.

In Practice...

A wraparound loan is possible only if the original loan permits such a refinancing. An acceleration and alienation or due-on-sale clause in the original loan documents may prevent a sale under such terms. A real estate licensee should neither encourage nor assist in any financing that violates loan provisions. To do so could result in suspension or revocation of the agent's license.

Open-End Mortgages

An **open-end mortgage** secures a *note* executed by the borrower to the lender as well as any future *advances* of funds made by the lender to the borrower or successors in title.

The mortgage usually includes a statement of the maximum amount to be secured. Any sums the lender may have to pay to protect the security due to the borrower's neglect of such items as taxes, assessments or insurance premiums are added to this maximum amount.

An open-end mortgage is frequently used by borrowers to obtain additional funds in order to improve their property. The borrower "opens" the mortgage to increase the debt to its original amount, or the amount stated in the note, after the debt has been reduced by payments over a period of time. The lender is not obligated to advance the additional funds.

Construction Loans

A **construction loan** is made to *finance the construction of improvements* on real estate (homes, apartments, office buildings and so forth). Under a construction loan, the lender disburses the loan proceeds while the building is being constructed.

Payments are made from time to time to the *general contractor* for that part of the construction work that has been completed since the previous payment. Prior to each payment, the lender inspects the work. The general contractor must provide the lender with adequate waivers of lien releasing all mechanics' lien rights (see Chapter 11, "Real Estate Taxes and Other Liens") for the work covered by the payment. This kind of loan generally bears a higher interest rate because of the risks assumed by the lender. These risks include the inadequate releasing of mechanics' liens, possible delays in completing the building or the financial failure of the contractor or subcontractors. This type of financing is generally short-term, or *interim, financing*. The borrower pays interest only, periodically, on the monies that have been disbursed to that payment date. The borrower is expected to arrange for a permanent loan (also known as an *end loan* or *take-out loan*) that will repay or "take out" the construction financing lender when the work is completed.

Sale and Leaseback

Sale-and-leaseback arrangements are used rather extensively as a means of financing large commercial or industrial plants. The land and building, usually used by the seller for business purposes, are sold to an investor, such as an insurance company. The real estate is then leased back by the buyer (the investor) to the seller, who continues to conduct business on the property as a tenant. The buyer becomes the lessor and the original owner becomes the lessee. This enables a business firm that has money invested in the real estate to free that money so it can be used as working capital.

Sale-and-leaseback arrangements are very complex. They involve complicated legal procedures and their success is usually related to the effects the transaction has on the firm's tax situation. A real estate broker should consult with legal and tax experts when involved in this type of transaction.

Installment Contracts/ Contracts for Deed

As discussed in Chapter 9, "Real Estate Contracts," real estate can be purchased under an **installment contract,** also known as a contract for deed, land contract of sale, agreement of sale or articles of agreement for warranty deed. Real estate is often sold on contract in one of two situations: (1) when mortgage financing is unavailable or too expensive and (2) when the purchaser does not have a sufficient down payment to cover the difference between a mortgage loan and the selling price of the real estate.

Investment Group Financing

Large real estate projects, such as highrise apartment buildings, office complexes and shopping centers, are often financed as a joint venture through group financing arrangements, such as syndicates, limited partnerships and real estate investment trusts. These complex investment agreements are discussed in Chapter 23, "Real Estate Investment."

Financing Legislation

The federal government regulates the lending practices of mortgage lenders through the Truth-in-Lending Act, Equal Credit Opportunity Act and the Real Estate Settlement Procedures Act.

Regulation Z

Regulation Z, which was promulgated pursuant to the *Truth-in-Lending Act,* requires credit institutions to inform borrowers of the true cost of obtaining credit so that the borrower can compare the costs of various lenders and avoid the uninformed use of credit. When credit is extended to individuals for personal, family or household uses and the amount of credit is $25,000 or less, Regulation Z applies. If a credit transaction is secured by a residence, such as a mortgage loan, Regulation Z always applies, regardless of the amount. The regulation does not apply to business, commercial or agricultural loans over $25,000.

The regulation requires that the customer be fully informed of all finance charges, as well as the true annual interest rate, before a transaction is consummated. The finance charges must include any loan fees, finders' fees, service charges, points and interest. In the case of a mortgage loan made to finance the purchase of a dwelling, the lender must compute and disclose the *annual percentage rate* (APR) but does not have to indicate the total interest payable during the term of the loan. Also, the lender does not have to include as part of the finance charge such actual costs as title fees, legal fees, appraisal fees, credit reports, survey fees and closing expenses.

Advertising. Regulation Z provides strict regulation of real estate advertisements that include mortgage financing terms. General phrases like "liberal terms available" may be used, but if details are given they must comply with this act. By the provisions of the act, the annual percentage rate—which includes all charges— rather than the interest rate alone *must be stated.* The total finance charge must be specified as well.

Specific credit terms, such as the down payment, monthly payment, dollar amount of the finance charge or term of the loan, may not be advertised unless the following information is set forth as well: cash price; required down payment; number, amount and due dates of all payments; and annual percentage rate. The total of all payments to be made over the term of the mortgage must also be specified unless the advertised credit refers to a first mortgage to finance acquisition of a dwelling.

Three-day right of rescission. In the case of most consumer credit transactions covered by Regulation Z, the borrower has three days in which to rescind the transaction by merely notifying the lender. However, this right of rescission does not apply to residential first mortgage loans.

Penalties. Regulation Z provides penalties for noncompliance. The penalty for violation of an administrative order enforcing Regulation Z is $10,000 for each day the violation continues. A fine of up to $10,000 may be imposed for engaging in an unfair or deceptive practice. In addition, a creditor may be liable to a consumer for violation of Regulation Z for twice the amount of the finance charge, for a minimum of $100 and a maximum of $1,000, plus court costs, attorney's fees and any actual damages. Willful violation is a misdemeanor punishable by a fine of up to $5,000, one year's imprisonment or both.

Federal Equal Credit Opportunity Act

The **Federal Equal Credit Opportunity Act (ECOA),** in effect since 1975, prohibits lenders and others who grant or arrange credit to consumers from discriminating against credit applicants on the basis of race, color, religion, national origin, sex, marital status, age (provided the applicant is of legal age) or dependency upon public assistance. In addition, lenders and other creditors must inform all rejected credit applicants, in writing, of the principal reasons why credit was denied or terminated.

Real Estate Settlement Procedures Act

The federal Real Estate Settlement Procedures Act (RESPA) was created to ensure that the buyer and seller in a residential real estate transaction involving a new first mortgage loan have knowledge of all settlement costs. This important federal law will be discussed in detail in Chapter 21, "Closing the Real Estate Transaction."

Summary

The borrower incurs costs in financing the real estate purchase: (1) finance charges paid at closing, such as loan origination fees, points and, in some cases, mortgage insurance premiums; (2) the recurring cost of interest and any mortgage insurance premiums.

In order for the lender to sell a mortgage loan its income must be competitive in the money market. *Discount points* may be charged to increase the yield of the loan. Points may be paid by the buyer, shared by buyer and seller or, in the case of a VA loan, *must* be paid by the seller.

There are many types of loan repayment plans, in addition to a fully amortized, fixed interest and straight loans. Adjustable rate mortgages, graduated payment mortgages, growing equity mortgages, renegotiable rate mortgages, shared-appreciation mortgages and reverse annuity mortgages have been developed.

The types of mortgage programs available include conventional loans and those insured by FHA or private mortgage insurance companies or guaranteed by the VA. FHA and VA loans must meet certain requirements in order for the borrower to obtain the benefits of the government backing, which induces the lender to lend its funds. The interest rates for these loans may be lower than those charged for conventional loans.

Other types of real estate financing include purchase-money mortgages, blanket mortgages, package mortgages, open-end mortgages, wraparound mortgages, construction loans, sale-and-leaseback agreements, installment contracts and investment group financing.

Regulation Z requires lenders to inform prospective buyers, who use their homes as security for credit, of all finance charges involved in such a loan. Severe penalties are provided for noncompliance. The *Federal Equal Credit Opportunity Act* prohibits creditors from discriminating against credit applicants on the basis of race, color, religion, national origin, sex, marital status, age or dependency on public assistance. The *Real Estate Settlement Procedures Act* requires lenders to inform both buyers and sellers, in advance, of all fees and charges required for the settlement or closing of a residential real estate transaction.

Questions

1. The McBains are purchasing a lakefront summer home in a new resort development. The house is completely equipped and the McBains are seeking a loan that covers the purchase price of the residence, including furnishings and appliances. This kind of financing is:

   a. a wraparound loan.
   b. a blanket loan.
   c. an unconventional loan.
   d. not permitted in Pennsylvania.

2. Discount points on a VA loan:

   I. represent the percentage by which the face amount of a VA loan is reduced when it is sold to an investor in order to make its rate of return competitive with that of other loan investments.
   II. are charged to the seller.

   a. I only   c. both I and II
   b. II only   d. neither I nor II

3. A developer has obtained a large loan in order to finance the construction of a planned unit development.

   I. This is a short-term loan and the developer arranged for long-term financing in order to repay it when the construction is completed.
   II. The borrowed money is disbursed in installments and the lender inspects the construction to ensure that all subcontractors and laborers have properly completed work under their contracts before disbursing each installment of the loan.

   a. I only   c. both I and II
   b. II only   d. neither I nor II

4. The Carters purchased a residence for $75,000. They made a down payment of $15,000 and agreed to assume the seller's existing mortgage, which had a current balance of $23,000. The Carters financed the remaining $37,000 of the purchase price by executing a mortgage and note to the seller. This type of loan, by which the seller becomes the mortgagee, is called a:

   a. blanket mortgage.
   b. package mortgage.
   c. balloon note.
   d. purchase-money mortgage.

5. In a sale and leaseback:

   I. the seller/vendor retains title to the real estate.
   II. the buyer/vendee gets possession of the property.

   a. I only   c. both I and II
   b. II only   d. neither I nor II

6. A borrower obtains a mortgage loan that is not insured or guaranteed by a government agency. This borrower has obtained:

   a. wraparound mortgage.
   b. conventional loan.
   c. land contract.
   d. growing equity mortgage.

7. A graduated payment mortgage:

   a. allows for smaller payments to be made in the early years of the loan.
   b. allows for the debt's interest rate to increase or decrease from time to time, depending on certain economic factors.
   c. is also called a growing equity mortgage.
   d. all of the above

8. A loan at $9\frac{1}{2}\%$ interest, originated with a charge of two points, has an effective yield of approximately:

   a. $11\frac{1}{2}$ percent.   c. $9\frac{3}{4}$ percent.
   b. $9\frac{1}{4}$ percent.   d. 9.625 percent.

9. FHA-insured loans are made from funds furnished by:

   a. the FHA.
   b. private lenders approved by the FHA.
   c. approved lending institutions.
   d. a and b

10. Regulation Z requires lenders to:

    I. properly inform buyers and sellers of commercial property of all settlement costs in a real estate transaction.
    II. inform prospective home mortgage borrowers of all charges, fees and interest involved in making a home mortgage loan.

       a. I only   c. both I and II
       b. II only   d. neither I nor II

11. The Federal Equal Credit Opportunity Act prohibits lenders from discriminating against potential borrowers on the basis of which of the following?

    a. race   c. national origin
    b. sex   d. all of the above

12. Which of the following is an example of a conventional loan?

    a. a mortgage loan insured by the Federal Housing Administration
    b. a second loan for home improvements secured through a credit union
    c. a loan obtained through a private lender with a VA guarantee
    d. all of the above

13. A renegotiable rate mortgage is one in which:

    I. the lender profits from the property's appreciation when it is sold.
    II. the interest rate is lower in the early years of the loan and higher in later years, when the mortgagor's salary is expected to rise.

       a. I only   c. both I and II
       b. II only   d. neither I nor II

21

Closing the Real Estate Transaction

Key Terms

Accrued item
Closing agent
Closing statement
Credit
Debit
Escrow
Prepaid item
Proration
Real Estate Settlement Procedures Act (RESPA)
Uniform Settlement Statement

Overview

After securing and servicing a listing, advertising the property, finding and qualifying potential buyers and negotiating for and obtaining a signed sales contract on the seller's property, a real estate licensee is one step away from receiving his or her commission. That last step is the real estate closing, a procedure that includes both title and financial considerations. This chapter will discuss both aspects of real estate closing. Special emphasis will be placed on the computations necessary to settle all necessary expenses between buyer and seller and between seller and broker. The chapter also includes a detailed example of a real estate closing.

Closing the Transaction

The preceding chapters discuss the various elements involved in and leading up to the closing of a sale. A real estate professional should be able to assist in preclosing arrangements and advise the parties in estimating their expenses and the approximate amounts the buyer will need and the seller will actually receive at the closing. The closing represents the culmination of the service the broker's firm provides. The sale, which the broker has negotiated, is completed, and the broker's commission (and thus the salesperson's commission) is generally paid out of the proceeds at the closing.

At the Closing

Generally speaking, the closing of a real estate transaction involves a gathering of interested parties at which the promises made in the *real estate sales contract* are kept, or *executed;* that is, the seller's deed is delivered in exchange for the purchase price. In many sales transactions, two closings actually take place at this time: (1) the closing of the buyer's loan—the disbursal of mortgage funds by the lender and (2) the closing of the sale. A closing involving all interested parties is often called a "round table close."

As discussed in Chapter 9, "Real Estate Contracts," a sales contract is the blueprint for the completion of a real estate transaction. A contract should be complete and should provide for all possibilities in order to avoid misunderstandings that could delay or even prevent the closing of the sale. Before going ahead with this exchange, the parties should be assured that the various conditions and stipulations of their sales contract have been met.

The buyer will want to be sure that the seller is delivering good title and that the property is in the promised condition. This involves inspecting the title evidence, the deed the seller will give, any documents representing the removal of undesired liens and encumbrances, the survey, the termite report and any leases, including security deposits (if there are tenants on the premises). The seller will want to be sure that the buyer has obtained the stipulated financing and has sufficient funds to complete the sale. Both parties will wish to inspect the closing statement to make sure that all monies involved in the transaction have been properly accounted for. In doing this, the parties will most likely be represented by attorneys.

When the parties are satisfied that everything is in order, the exchange is made and all pertinent documents are then recorded. The documents must be recorded in the correct order to avoid creating a defect in the title. For example, if the seller is paying off an existing loan and the buyer is obtaining a new loan, the seller's satisfaction of mortgage must be recorded before the seller's deed to the buyer. The buyer's new mortgage must then be recorded after the deed, for the lender cannot have a security interest in the buyer's property until the buyer's ownership has been recorded.

Where Closings Are Held and Who Attends

Closings may be held at a number of locations, including the offices of the title company, the lending institution, the office of one of the parties' attorneys, the broker, the county recorder (or other local recording official) or the escrow company. Those attending a closing may include:

1. the buyer;

2. the seller;

3. the real estate agent (broker and/or salesperson);

4. the attorney(s) for the seller and/or buyer;

5. the representatives and/or attorneys for lending institutions involved with the buyer's new mortgage loan, the buyer's assumption of the seller's existing loan or the seller's payoff of an existing loan; and/or

6. the representative of the title insurance company.

Closing agent or closing officer. One person usually conducts the proceedings at a closing and calculates the official settlement, or division of charges and expenses between the parties. In some areas of Pennsylvania, real estate brokers preside; in others, the **closing agent** is the buyer's or seller's attorney, a representative of the lender or a representative of a title company. Some title companies and law firms employ paralegal assistants, called *closers,* who conduct closings for their firms. The closer is the person in such an office who arranges the time for closing with the parties involved, prepares the closing statements, compares figures with lenders and orders title evidence, surveys and other miscellaneous items needed.

IRS reporting requirements. The Tax Reform Act of 1986 requires the reporting of real estate transactions to the Internal Revenue Service. The gross proceeds involved in the transaction, along with other information, must be reported by the person (including any attorney or title company) responsible for closing the transaction. If that person does not report, the responsibility then falls on (in the following order): the mortgage lender, the seller's broker, the buyer's broker or such other person as the regulations designate.

Broker's Role at Closing

Depending on the local practice, the broker's role at a closing can vary from simply collecting the commission to conducting the proceedings. A real estate broker is not authorized to give legal advice or otherwise engage in the practice of law. In some areas, this means that a broker's job is essentially over when the sales contract is signed; at that point, the attorneys take over. Even so, a broker's service generally continues after the contract is signed in that the broker advises the parties in practical matters and makes sure all the details are taken care of so that the closing can proceed smoothly. In this capacity the broker might make arrangements for such items as title evidence, surveys, appraisals, inspections or repairs for wood-boring insects, structural conditions, water supplies, sewage facilities or toxic substances such as radon. Caution should be exercised in recommending sources for any inspections or testing services since this creates liability in the event the buyer is injured by a provider's service. The broker is usually responsible for ordering or coordinating various exhibits, as described in this chapter.

Lender's Interest in Closing

Whether a buyer is obtaining new financing or assuming the seller's existing loan, the lender wants to protect its security interest in the property—to make sure that the buyer is getting good, marketable title and that tax and insurance payments are maintained—so that there will be no liens with greater priority than the mortgage lien and the insurance will be paid up if the property is damaged or destroyed. For this reason, the lender will frequently require the following items: (1) a title insurance policy; (2) a fire and hazard insurance policy, with receipt for the premium; (3) additional information, such as a survey, a termite or other inspection report or a certificate of occupancy; (4) establishment of a reserve, or escrow, account for tax and insurance payments; and (5) representation by its own attorney at the closing.

RESPA Requirements

The federal **Real Estate Settlement Procedures Act (RESPA),** enacted in 1974 and revised in 1975, was created to ensure that the buyer and seller in a residential real estate sale or transfer have knowledge of all settlement costs. In this context, residential real estate includes one-family to four-family homes, cooperatives and condominiums. *RESPA requirements apply when the purchase is financed by a federally related mortgage loan.* Federally related loans include those (1) made by banks, savings and loan associations or other lenders whose deposits are insured by federal agencies (FDIC or FSLIC); (2) insured by the FHA or guaranteed by the VA; (3) administered by the U.S. Department of Housing and Urban Development; or (4) intended to be sold by the lender to Fannie Mae, Ginnie Mae or Freddie Mac.

RESPA regulations apply only to transactions involving new first mortgage loans. A transaction financed solely by a purchase-money mortgage taken back by the seller, an installment contract (land contract of sale, contract for deed) or the buyer's assumption of the seller's existing loan would not be covered by RESPA, unless the terms of the assumed loan are modified or the lender imposes charges of more than $50 for the assumption. As of June 20, 1976, when a transaction is covered by RESPA, the following requirements must be complied with:

1. *Special information booklet:* Lenders must give a copy of the HUD booklet *Settlement Costs and You* to every person from whom they receive or for whom they prepare a loan application. This booklet provides the borrower with general information about settlement (closing) costs and explains the various RESPA provisions, including a line-by-line discussion of the Uniform Settlement Statement (see item 3).

2. *Good faith estimate of settlement costs:* At the time of the loan application, or within three business days, the lender must provide the borrower with a good faith estimate of the settlement costs the borrower is likely to incur. This estimate may be a specific figure or a range of costs based upon comparable past transactions in the area. In addition, if the lender requires use of a particular attorney or title company to conduct the closing, the lender must state whether it has any business relationship with that firm and must estimate the charges for this service. Under Pennsylvania license laws, buyer's and seller's estimated settlement fees must be disclosed by the licensee to each party on an appropriate form prior to their signing the sales agreement. Figures 21.1 and 21.2 are examples of these forms.

3. *Uniform Settlement Statement (HUD Form 1):* RESPA provides that loan closing information must be prepared on a special HUD form, the **Uniform Settlement Statement,** designed to detail all financial particulars of a transaction. A copy of this form is illustrated in Figure 21.4. The completed statement must itemize all charges imposed by the lender. Charges incurred by the buyer and seller, contracted for separately and outside the closing, do not have to be

**Figure 21.1
Buyer's Estimated
Closing Costs**

PENNSYLVANIA ASSOCIATION OF REALTORS'
This form recommended and approved for, but not restricted to, use by members of the Pennsylvania Association of REALTORS'

BUYER'S CLOSING COSTS
ESTIMATED

RE PROPERTY: _____

SETTLEMENT DATE: _____   PURCHASE PRICE $ _____

1. Title		Charges
(a) Title Search	$	
(b) Settlement/Notary Fees	$	
(c) Title Insurance	$	
(d) End's #100, #300, #710 others	$	
(e) Mechanics Lien Insurance	$	
(f) Recording Fees: Mortgage and/or Deed	$	
(g) Transfer Tax	$	
(h) Survey	$	
2. Agent's Services	$	
3. Hazard Insurance	$	
4. Tax Adjustments: (+/−)		
(a) School	$	
(b) County	$	
(c) Municipality	$	
(d)	$	
(e)	$	
5. Lienable (+/−) e.g. water, sewer, condo/associations		
(a)	$	
(b)	$	
6.	$	
7.	$	
8. Lender		
(a) Fees (Part payment may be required before settlement)	$	
(b) Appraisal & Credit Report (s) (Paid with application)	$	
(c) Mortgage Insurance Premium	$	
(d) Preparation Mortgage Documents	$	
(e) VA Funding Fee	$	
(f) Interest from to	$	
(g)	$	
(h)	$	
9. Reserves Deposited With Lender (Escrow Account)		
(a) Hazard Insurance	$	
(b) Mortgage Insurance Premium	$	
(c) Taxes:		
(1) School	$	
(2) County	$	
(3) Municipality	$	
(d)	$ _____	

                                    Estimated Costs $

I/We understand the estimated costs are based on the best information available at this date and may be higher or lower at settlement.
MORTGAGE TYPE: ☐ **FIXED RATE** ☐ **ADJUSTABLE RATE** ☐ _____

Estimated Monthly Payments	Estimated Maximum Monthly Payments
INITIALLY	**INITIALLY**
Based on $, for years, at %	Based on $, for years, at %
Prinicpal and Interest .... $	Prinicpal and Interest .... $
Taxes........................ $	Taxes........................ $
Hazard Insurance .... $	Hazard Insurance .... $
Mortgage Insurance Premium ... $	Mortgage Insurance Premium ... $
$ _____	$ _____
Estimated Total $	**Estimated Total** $

If the interest rate charged by the mortgage lender is higher or lower than the above rates, the total monthly payments will be higher or lower.   Because mortgage types and terms vary greatly, Buyer should consult the mortgage lender in regards to mortgage costs and terms.
An agreement for the sale of real estate must contain the zoning classification of the property except for a single family dwelling.
A real estate recovery fund exists to reimburse persons who have suffered monetary loss and have obtained an uncollectable judgment due to fraud, misrepresentation or deceit in a real estate transaction by a Pennsylvania licensee.   For complete details, call 717-783-3658.
THE AGENT REPRESENTS THE SELLER, however, the Agent may perform services for the Buyer in connection with financing, insurance and document preparation.
We also understand and have received a copy of these estimated closing costs and estimated monthly payments before signing the agreement of sale.

AGENT: _____   BUYER: _____(seal)
Prepared by: _____   BUYER: _____(seal)
DATE: _____   BUYER: _____(seal)
404   5/85

Figure 21.2
Seller's Estimated
Closing Costs

PENNSYLVANIA ASSOCIATION OF REALTORS®
This form recommended and approved for, but not restricted to, use by members of the Pennsylvania Association of REALTORS

SELLER'S CLOSING COSTS
ESTIMATED

RE PROPERTY:_____
SETTLEMENT DATE: _____   SALE PRICE $ _____

Charges

1. Agents Fee .... $ _____

2. Preparation of Deed .... $ _____

3. Transfer Tax .... $ _____

4. Tax Adjustments (+/−)
    (a) School .... $ _____
    (b) County .... $ _____
    (c) Municipality .... $ _____
    (d) _____ $ _____
    (e) _____ $ _____

5. Lienable Items (+/−) e.g. water, sewer, condo/associations
    (a) _____ $ _____
    (b) _____ $ _____

6. Mortgage Placement Fee .... $ _____

7. Wood-Infestation Report .... $ _____

8. Municipal Certification .... $ _____

9. Settlement Fee .... $ _____

10. Notary Fees .... $ _____

11. Survey .... $ _____

12. _____ $ _____

13. _____ $ _____

                 Estimated Costs $ _____

Sale Price _____ $ _____
Less Estimated Costs _____ $ _____
            Estimated Proceeds $ _____

The estimated proceeds do not take into account any mortgages, liens, assessments or other obligations which may be against the property.

The above figures are approximated closing costs and will be adjusted as of date of final settlement, if necessary.

I/We understand and have received a copy of these estimated closing costs.

AGENT: _____   SELLER: _____(seal)
BY: _____   SELLER: _____(seal)
                                    SELLER: _____(seal)
DATE: _____   SELLER: _____(seal)

10/83

disclosed. Items paid for prior to the closing must be clearly marked as such on the statement and are omitted from the totals. This statement must be made available for inspection by the borrower *at or before* the closing. Upon the borrower's request, *the closing agent must permit the borrower to inspect the settlement statement, to the extent that the figures are available, one business day before the closing.* Lenders must retain these statements for two years after the date of closing unless the loan (and its servicing) is sold or otherwise disposed of. The Uniform Settlement Statement may be altered to allow for local custom and certain lines may be deleted if they do not apply in the area. RESPA requires the lender to account to HUD for the charges assessed at closing, including *reasonable* escrow amounts, thus preventing the lender from taking advantage of the borrower.

4. *Prohibition against kickbacks:* RESPA explicitly prohibits the payment of kickbacks, or unearned fees, such as when an insurance agency pays a kickback to a lender for referring one of the lender's recent customers to the agency or the payment to the broker for a loan referral. This prohibition does *not* include fee splitting between cooperating brokers or members of multiple listing services, brokerage referral arrangements or the division of a commission between a broker and his or her salespeople.

RESPA is administered by the U.S. Department of Housing and Urban Development (HUD).

In Practice...   *Note that although RESPA requires the lender to keep statements for two years after closing, the State Real Estate Commission requires that documents of all real estate transactions be kept by the broker for three years following settlement.*

The Title Procedure

As discussed earlier, the purchaser and the purchaser's lender assure themselves that the seller's property and title comply with the contract requirements. The sales contract usually includes time limitations for the parties to obtain and present title evidence and remove any objections to the title. A contract that includes the provision "time is of the essence" expresses the agreement of the parties that all *time limitations are to be met exactly as stated.*

In Pennsylvania, the buyer is responsible for being assured that he or she is taking good title to the property by ordering and paying for a current *abstract of title* from the title insurance company. This opinion sets forth the status of the seller's title, showing liens, encumbrances, easements, conditions or restrictions that appear on the record and to which the seller's title is subject. It is important for the broker or salesperson, buyer and seller to review the title report *before* closing to allow time to resolve problems that could delay closing.

On the date when the sale is actually completed, that is, the date of delivery of the deed, the buyer has a title abstract that was issued several days or weeks before the closing. For this reason, the title or abstract company is usually required to make two searches of the public records. The first, as discussed, shows the status of the seller's title on the date of the sales contract. The second search is made after the closing and covers the date when the deed is recorded to the purchaser.

In some areas where real estate sales transactions are customarily closed through an escrow, the escrow agreement generally includes provision for an extended-coverage policy to be issued to the buyer as of the date of closing. In such cases, there is no gap between the date of commitment and the closing.

Checking the Premises

In general, it is important for the buyer to inspect the property to determine the interests of any parties in possession or other interests that cannot be determined from inspecting the public record. A *survey* is frequently required so that the purchaser will know the location and size of the property. The contract will specify who is to pay for this. It is usual for the survey to "spot" the location of all buildings, driveways, fences and other improvements located primarily on the premises being purchased as well as any such improvements located on adjoining property that may encroach upon the premises being bought. The survey also sets out, in full, any existing easements and encroachments. So that the survey will clearly identify the location of the property, the house number, if any, should be stated.

Shortly before the closing takes place, the buyer will usually make a *final inspection* of the property with the broker. The purposes of the final inspection are to make sure that necessary repairs have been made, that the property has been well maintained (both inside and outside), that all fixtures are in place and that there has been no unauthorized removal or alteration of any part of the improvements.

There is little uniformity in the rules covering *chattels and fixtures*. Each area has established customs that are usually followed. However, the following items are normally considered to be fixtures and are included in the conveyance free and clear of liens, unless there is an agreement otherwise: draperies, shades, blinds, screens, storm doors and windows, plumbing and heating equipment, built-in appliances, and tools. In apartment buildings, the following may also be included: hall carpets, refrigerators, gas and electric stoves, and such garden tools as lawn mowers and hoses.

Releasing Existing Liens

When the purchaser is paying cash or is obtaining a new mortgage in order to purchase the property, the seller's existing mortgage usually is paid in full and the record marked satisfied. In order to know the exact amount required to pay the existing mortgage, the seller secures a *payoff statement* from the mortgagee effective the date of closing. This payoff statement sets forth the unpaid amount of principal, interest due through the date of payment, the fee for issuing the satisfaction piece; and credits, if any, for tax and insurance reserves. The same procedure would be followed for any other liens that must be released before the buyer takes title.

For transactions in which the buyer is assuming the seller's existing mortgage loan, the buyer will want to know the exact balance of the loan as of the closing date. In some areas it is customary for the buyer to obtain an *estoppel certificate* from the seller, which certifies the amount owed on the mortgage loan, the interest rate and the last interest payment made.

Closing in Escrow

As discussed in Chapter 9, a real estate transaction may be closed through an escrow. Although there are a few states, such as Pennsylvania, where transactions are never closed in escrow, escrow closings are used to some extent in most states; in the western section of the country, most transactions are closed in escrow.

An **escrow** is a method of closing a real estate transaction in which a disinterested third party is authorized to act as escrow agent and is given the responsibility to coordinate the closing activities. The escrow agent may also be called the *escrowee* or *escrow holder.* The escrow agent may be an attorney, a title company, a trust company, an escrow company or the escrow department of a lending institution. Though many brokerages do offer escrow services, a broker cannot be a disinterested party in a transaction from which a commission is collected. Because the escrow agent is placed in a position of great trust, many states have laws regulating escrow agents and limiting who may serve in this capacity.

Preparation of Closing Statements	A typical real estate sales transaction involves numerous expenses for both parties in addition to the purchase price. Furthermore, there are a number of property expenses that the seller will have already paid in advance for a set period of time or that the buyer will pay in the future. The financial responsibility for these items must be *prorated,* or divided, between the buyer and the seller. In closing a transaction, it is customary to account for all these items by preparing a written statement, such as the HUD Form 1, to determine how much money the buyer needs and how much the seller will net after the broker's commission and expenses.
How the Closing Statement Works	The completion of a **closing statement** involves an accounting of the parties' debits and credits. A **debit** is a charge, an amount that the party being debited owes and must pay at the closing. A **credit** is an amount entered in a person's favor—either an amount that has already been paid, an amount being reimbursed or an amount the buyer promises to pay in the form of a loan.

To determine the amount the buyer needs at the closing, the buyer's debits are totaled—any expenses and prorated amounts for items prepaid by the seller are added to the purchase price. Then the buyer's credits are totaled. These would include the earnest money (already paid), the balance of the loan the buyer is obtaining or assuming and the seller's share of any prorated items that the buyer will pay in the future. Finally, the total of the buyer's credits is subtracted from the total amount the buyer owes (debits) to arrive at the actual amount of cash the buyer must bring to the closing. Usually the buyer brings a bank cashier's check or a certified personal check.

A similar procedure is followed to determine how much money the seller will actually receive. The seller's debits and credits are each totaled. The credits would include the purchase price plus the buyer's share of any prorated items that the seller has prepaid.

The seller's debits would include expenses, the seller's share of prorated items to be paid later by the buyer, and the balance of any mortgage loan or other lien that the seller is paying off. Finally, the total of the seller's charges is subtracted from the total credits to arrive at the amount the seller will receive.

Expenses

In addition to the payment of the sales price and the proration of taxes, interest and the like, a number of other expenses and charges may be involved in a real estate transaction. These may include the following items.

Broker's commission. The broker's commission is usually paid by the seller, for the broker is usually the seller's agent. When the buyer has employed the broker, the buyer pays the commission. As discussed in Chapter 17, "Real Estate Brokerage," it is important that the broker's rate of commission be negotiated between the broker and the principal for each transaction and be specifically stated in the listing agreement.

Attorney's fees. If either of the parties' attorneys will be paid from the closing proceeds, that party will be charged with the expense in the closing statement.

Recording expenses. In Pennsylvania, the charge for recording a document varies according to the size of the document and the number of additional registrations involved.

The *seller* usually pays for recording charges (filing fees), which are necessary in order to clear all defects and furnish the purchaser with a clear title in accordance with the terms of the contract. Items usually charged to the *seller* would include the recording of satisfaction of mortgages, quitclaim deeds, affidavits and satisfaction of mechanic's lien claims. The *purchaser* pays for recording charges incident to the actual transfer of the title. Items usually charged to the *purchaser* include the recording of the deed, which conveys title to the purchaser, and of a mortgage executed by the purchaser.

Transfer tax. The State of Pennsylvania, like many states (as discussed in Chapter 10, "Transfer of Title"), requires that transfer tax be paid on real estate transactions. Transfer tax stamps are charged at one percent of consideration or one percent of value if there is no consideration. Many cities and local municipalities in Pennsylvania charge transfer tax in addition to the state transfer tax. In Pennsylvania, it is customary for the buyer and the seller to share this expense equally.

Title expenses. The responsibility for title expenses varies according to local custom. As discussed earlier, in Pennsylvania the buyer is required to furnish evidence of good title and pay for the title search.

The Pennsylvania Title Insurance Rating Bureau regulates the issuance of title insurance and has a set of combined, all-inclusive title insurance rates for buyers of real estate. The set rate covers the initial title search, the later date search to "bring the title down" to the closing date and the title insurance policy. (See Figure 21.3—Schedule of All-Inclusive Title Insurance Rates.)

Municipal lien and sewage lien letters are required in some areas as further evidence that there are no pending liens. Any fees for these letters are, by custom, generally paid by the seller.

Tax certification letters, sometimes requiring a fee, may be necessary in cases when the seller does not have any of the immediate past three years tax receipts to deliver to the buyer. As discussed in Chapter 12, "Title Records," real estate tax liens are not immediately filed in the recorder's office. Therefore, it is necessary to provide the buyer evidence that the taxes have been paid.

**Figure 21.3
Schedule of
All-Inclusive
Title Insurance
Rates**

ALL-INCLUSIVE SCHEDULE OF RATES
Effective February 17, 1983

UNIT OF INSURANCE OR FRACTION THEREOF	AREA II BASIC	RE ISSUE
$ 0 - $10,000	$146	$121
$10,001 - $11,000	164	136
$11,001 - $12,000	172	142
$12,001 - $13,000	180	150
$13,001 - $14,000	186	155
$14,001 - $15,000	195	162
$15,001 - $16,000	201	169
$16,001 - $17,000	207	174
$17,001 - $18,000	214	181
$18,001 - $19,000	221	186
$19,001 - $20,000	228	192
$20,001 - $21,000	234	198
$21,001 - $22,000	242	205
$22,001 - $23,000	249	211
$23,001 - $24,000	256	217
$24,001 - $25,000	262	222
$25,001 - $26,000	268	229
$26,001 - $27,000	275	234
$27,001 - $28,000	282	241
$28,001 - $29,000	289	247
$29,001 - $30,000	295	252
$30,001 - $31,000	299	259
$31,001 - $32,000	305	263
$32,001 - $33,000	310	268
$33,001 - $34,000	317	274
$34,001 - $35,000	322	279
$35,001 - $36,000	328	285
$36,001 - $37,000	335	290
$37,001 - $38,000	340	295
$38,001 - $39,000	346	300
$39,001 - $40,000	352	306
$40,001 - $41,000	358	312
$41,001 - $42,000	364	317
$42,001 - $43,000	370	322
$43,001 - $44,000	376	327
$44,001 - $45,000	382	333
$45,001 - $46,000	388	339
$46,001 - $47,000	394	343
$47,001 - $48,000	399	349
$48,001 - $49,000	405	354
$49,001 - $50,000	412	359
$50,001 - $51,000	413	364
$51,001 - $52,000	417	369
$52,001 - $53,000	422	373
$53,001 - $54,000	428	379
$54,001 - $55,000	433	383

UNIT OF INSURANCE OR FRACTION THEREOF	AREA II BASIC	RE ISSUE
$55,001 - $ 56,000	$438	$387
$56,001 - $ 57,000	444	392
$57,001 - $ 58,000	449	397
$58,001 - $ 59,000	453	402
$59,001 - $ 60,000	459	406
$60,001 - $ 61,000	464	411
$61,001 - $ 62,000	470	416
$62,001 - $ 63,000	475	420
$63,001 - $ 64,000	480	426
$64,001 - $ 65,000	485	430
$65,001 - $ 66,000	490	434
$66,001 - $ 67,000	495	440
$67,001 - $ 68,000	501	444
$68,001 - $ 69,000	506	449
$69,001 - $ 70,000	511	453
$70,001 - $ 71,000	517	458
$71,001 - $ 72,000	521	463
$72,001 - $ 73,000	526	467
$73,001 - $ 74,000	532	472
$74,001 - $ 75,000	537	477
$75,001 - $ 76,000	542	481
$76,001 - $ 77,000	548	487
$77,001 - $ 78,000	553	491
$78,001 - $ 79,000	557	495
$79,001 - $ 80,000	563	501
$80,001 - $ 81,000	568	505
$81,001 - $ 82,000	573	510
$82,001 - $ 83,000	579	514
$83,001 - $ 84,000	583	519
$84,001 - $ 85,000	588	524
$85,001 - $ 86,000	594	528
$86,001 - $ 87,000	599	534
$87,001 - $ 88,000	604	538
$88,001 - $ 89,000	610	542
$89,001 - $ 90,000	615	548
$90,001 - $ 91,000	619	552
$91,001 - $ 92,000	625	557
$92,001 - $ 93,000	630	562
$93,001 - $ 94,000	635	566
$94,001 - $ 95,000	641	571
$95,001 - $ 96,000	646	575
$96,001 - $ 97,000	650	581
$97,001 - $ 98,000	656	585
$98,001 - $ 99,000	661	589
$99,001 - $100,000	666	595

On the excess over $100,000	Basic Rate	Re-issue Rate
$ 100,001 - $ 500,000 - Add per $1,000	$4 50	$4 00
$ 500,001 - $1,000,000 - Add per $1,000	$3 50	$3 25
Over $1,000,000 - Direct Inquiries Requested		

*ALL INCLUSIVE INCLUDES
Examination, Title Insurance Premium and Settlement

Deed preparation fee. This is the fee charged by the preparer of the deed. It is customarily paid by the seller.

Loan fees. When the purchaser is securing a mortgage to finance the purchase, the lender (mortgage company) will usually charge a service charge or loan origination fee of from one to three percent (or more) of the loan. The fee is a flat charge and is usually paid by the purchaser at the time the transaction is closed. If calculated as a percentage of the loan principal, such fees are spoken of as *points;* for example, a two percent fee is called *two points*. In addition, the buyer may be charged an assumption fee if he or she assumes the seller's existing financing.

The seller may also be charged fees by a lender. If the buyer finances the purchase with a VA loan, the seller may be required to pay discount points as discussed in Chapter 20, "Financing the Real Estate Transaction." Also, under the terms of some mortgage loans, the seller may be required to pay a prepayment charge or penalty for paying off the mortgage loan in advance of its due date.

Tax reserves and insurance reserves (escrows). Many mortgage lenders require borrowers to provide a reserve fund or escrow account to meet future real estate taxes and insurance premiums. As discussed in Chapter 13, "Real Estate Financing," the borrower starts the account at closing by depositing funds to cover at least the amount of unpaid real estate taxes from the date of lien to the end of the current month. (The buyer receives a credit from the seller at closing for any unpaid taxes.) Thereafter, the borrower is required to pay an amount equal to one month's portion of the estimated taxes.

The borrower is responsible for a fire insurance policy (many choose a homeowner's policy, as discussed in Chapter 16, "Concepts of Home Ownership"), as a condition of the mortgage loan. Generally, the first year's premium is paid in full at closing. An amount equal to one month's premium is paid, thereafter. The borrower's monthly loan payment includes the principal and interest on the loan plus one-twelfth of the taxes and insurance (PITI).

Appraisal fees. Either the seller or the purchaser pays the appraisal fees, depending on who orders the appraisal. When the buyer obtains a mortgage, it is customary for the lender to require an appraisal, which the buyer pays for. A residential mortgage appraisal may cost from $150 to $300.

Survey fees. The purchaser who obtains new mortgage financing customarily pays the survey fees. In some cases the sales contract may require the seller to furnish a survey.

Prorations

Most closings involve the division of financial responsibility between the buyer and seller for such items as loan interest, taxes, rents, fuel and utility bills. These allowances are called **prorations.** Prorations are necessary to ensure that expenses are fairly divided between the seller and the buyer. For example, in states where taxes must be paid in advance, such as Pennsylvania, the seller would be entitled to a rebate at the closing. If the buyer assumes the seller's existing mortgage, the seller usually owes the buyer an allowance for accrued interest through the date of closing.

Accrued items are items to be prorated that have been earned during the occupancy or ownership of the seller but have not been paid by the seller and are credited to the purchaser. (*Earned,* as used here, means owed by the seller.) Each accrued item will be paid by the purchaser at some later time, so the seller must pay a share (the earned portion) at the closing by giving a credit to the purchaser.

Prepaid items are items to be prorated that have been prepaid by the seller but not fully earned (not fully used up). They are therefore credits to the seller.

General rules for prorating. The rules or customs governing the computation of prorations for the closing of a real estate sale vary widely from state to state. In many states the real estate boards and the bar association have established closing rules and procedures. In some cases these rules and procedures control closings for the entire state; in others they merely affect closings within a given city, town or county.

Here are some general rules to guide you in studying the closing procedure and preparing the closing statement:

1. In most states, the seller owns the property on the day of closing, and prorations or apportionments are usually made *to and including the day of closing.* In a few states, however, it is specifically provided that the buyer owns the property on the closing date and that adjustments shall be made as of the day preceding the day on which title is closed.

2. Mortgage interest, general real estate taxes, water taxes, insurance premiums and similar expenses are usually computed by using *360 days in a year and 30 days in a month.* However, the rules in some areas provide for computing prorations on the basis of the actual number of days in the calendar month of closing. The sales contract may specify which method is to be used.

3. Accrued or prepaid *general real estate taxes* are usually prorated at the closing. In Pennsylvania, taxes are generally prepaid and may be due in the early part of the year. The tax proration, then, could be for accrued or prorated taxes depending on the time of year and the tax payment schedule. *Special assessments* for such municipal improvements as sewers, water mains or streets are usually paid in annual installments over several years. The municipality usually charges the property owner annual interest on the outstanding balance of future installments. In a sales transaction, the seller pays the current installment and the buyer assumes all future installments. *The special assessment installment is not generally prorated at the closing;* some buyers, however, insist that the seller allow them a credit for the seller's share of the interest to the closing date.

4. *Rents* are usually adjusted on the basis of the *actual* number of days in the month of closing. It is customary for the seller to receive the rents for the day of closing and to pay all expenses for that day. If any rents for the current month are uncollected when the sale is closed, the buyer will often agree by a separate letter to collect the rents if possible and remit the pro rata share to the seller.

5. *Security deposits* made by tenants to cover the last month's rent of the lease or to cover the cost of repairing damage caused by the tenant are generally transferred by the seller to the buyer. Because of Pennsylvania's regulations regarding security deposits, as discussed in Chapter 8, it is wise to get the tenant's consent to such a transfer of the deposit.

6. Depending on customary settlement procedures evidence of *water and sewage charges*, whether billed monthly or quarterly, are presented at closing. The earned portion is debited to the seller through the date of closing; the prepaid portion is credited to the seller. *Other utilities* are not normally handled at closing; the utility company handles final billing.

You should verify these proration rules with the customs in your area.

Accounting for Credits and Charges

The items that must be accounted for in the closing statement fall into two general categories: (1) prorations or other amounts due to either the buyer or seller (credit to) and paid for by the other party (debit to) and (2) expenses or items paid by the seller or buyer (debit only).

The following list shows which items are commonly credited to the buyer and which to the seller. Other items may be included in such a list, depending upon the customs of your area.

Items Credited to Buyer (debited to seller)	**Items Credited to Seller** (debited to buyer)
1. buyer's earnest money*	1. sales price*
2. unpaid principal balance of outstanding mortgage being assumed by buyer*	2. prorated premium for unearned (prepaid) portion of fire insurance
3. earned interest on existing assumed mortgage not yet payable (accrued)	3. coal or fuel oil on hand, usually figured at current market price (prepaid)
4. earned portion of general real estate tax not yet due (accrued)	4. insurance and tax reserve (if any) when outstanding mortgage is being assumed by buyer (prepaid)
5. unearned portion of current rent collected in advance	5. refund to seller of prepaid water charge and similar expenses
6. tenants' security deposits*	6. unearned portion of general real estate tax, if paid in advance
7. purchase-money mortgage	

*These items are not prorated; they are entered in full as listed.

Note that the *buyer's earnest money,* although credited to the buyer, *is not debited to the seller.* The buyer receives a credit because that amount has already been paid toward the purchase price; however, as prescribed by state law, the money is held by the broker or escrow agent until the settlement, when it will be included as part of the total amount due the seller. Note also that if the seller is paying off an existing loan and the buyer is obtaining a new one, these two items are accounted for with a debit only to the seller for the amount of the payoff and a credit only to the buyer for the amount of the new loan.

Accounting for expenses. Expenses paid out of the closing proceeds are debited only to the party making the payment. Occasionally, an expense item—such as the state transfer tax—is shared by the buyer and the seller, and each party will be debited for one-half the expense.

The Arithmetic of Prorating

Accurate prorating involves four considerations: (1) what the item being prorated is, (2) whether it is an accrued item that requires the determination of an earned amount, (3) whether it is a prepaid item that requires the unearned amount—a refund to the seller—to be determined and (4) what arithmetic processes must be used. The information contained in the previous sections will assist in answering the first three questions.

The computation of a proration involves identifying a yearly charge for the item to be prorated, then dividing by 12 to determine a monthly charge for the item. It is usually also necessary to identify a daily charge for the item by dividing the monthly charge by the number of days in the month. These smaller portions are then multiplied by the number of months and/or days in the prorated time period to determine the accrued or unearned amount that will be figured in the settlement.

Using this general principle, there are three methods of calculating prorations:

1. The yearly charge is divided by a *360-day year,* or 12 months of 30 days each.

2. The monthly charge is divided by the *actual number of days in the month of closing* to determine the amount.

3. The *yearly charge is divided by 365* to determine the daily charge. Then the actual number of days in the proration period is determined, and this number is multiplied by the daily charge.

In some cases, when a sale is closed on the 15th of the month the one-half month's charge is computed by simply dividing the monthly charge by two.

The final proration figure will vary slightly, depending on which computation method is used. The final figure will also vary according to the number of decimal places to which the division is carried. *All of the computations in this text are computed by carrying the division to three decimal places.* The third decimal place is rounded off to cents only after the final proration figure is determined.

Accrued Items

Consider unpaid real estate taxes, which may be an accrued item. When the taxes are levied for the calendar year but have not yet been paid, the accrued portion is for the period from January 1 to the date of closing. If the current tax bill has not yet been issued, the parties must agree on an estimated amount based on the previous year's bill and any known changes in assessment or tax levy for the current year.

For example, assume a sale is to be closed on April 17, and current real estate taxes of $1,200 are to be prorated accordingly. The accrued period, then, is three months and 17 days. First determine the prorated cost of the real estate tax per month and day:

$$\frac{\$100 \text{ per month}}{12)\$1,200} \qquad \frac{3.333 \text{ per day}}{30)\$100.000}$$
$$\text{months} \qquad\qquad\qquad \text{days}$$

Next, multiply these figures by the accrued period and add the totals to determine the prorated real estate tax:

$100	$ 3.333	$300.000
× 3 months	× 17 days	+ 56.661
$300	$56.661	$356.661

Thus, the accrued real estate tax for 3 months and 17 days is $356.66 (rounded off to two decimal places after the final computation). This amount represents the seller's accrued earned tax; it will be *a credit to the buyer and a debit to the seller.*

To compute this proration according to the actual number of days in the accrued period, the following method is used. The accrued period from January 1 to April 17 runs 107 days (January's 31 days, February's 28 days and so on). A tax bill of $1,200 ÷ 365 days = $3.288 per day. $3.288 × 107 days = $351.816, or $351.82.

In Practice...

On state licensing examinations, tax prorations are usually based on a 30-day month (360-day year) unless specified otherwise in the problem. Note that this may differ with your local customs regarding tax prorations. Many title insurance companies provide proration charts that detail tax factors for each day in the year. To determine a tax proration using one of these charts, you would multiply the factor given for the closing date by the annual real estate tax.

Prepaid Items

In Pennsylvania, a tax proration can also be a prepaid item. As real estate tax may be paid in the early part of the year, tax prorations calculated for closings taking place later in the year must reflect the fact that the seller has already paid the tax. For example, in the above problem, suppose that the closing did not take place until September 17 and that the taxes had been paid. The buyer, then, must reimburse the seller; the proration is *credited to the seller and debited to the buyer.*

In figuring the tax proration, it is necessary to ascertain the number of future days, months and years for which the taxes have been paid. The formula commonly used for this purpose is as follows:

	Years	Months	Days
Taxes paid to (Dec. 31, end of tax year)	1989	12	31
Date of closing (Sept. 17, 1989)	1989	9	17
Period for which tax must be paid		3	14

With this formula we can find the amount the buyer will reimburse the seller for the *unearned* portion of the real estate tax. The prepaid period, as determined using the formula for prepaid items, is three months and 14 days. Three months at $100 per month equals $300, plus 14 days × 3.333 per day = $46.662. Add this up to determine that the proration is $346.662, or $346.66 *credited to the seller and debited to the buyer.*

Another example of a prepaid item is a water bill. Assume that the water is billed in advance by the city without using a meter. The six months' billing is $8 for the period ending October 31. The sale is to be closed on August 3. Because the water is paid to October 31, the prepaid time must be computed. Using a 30-day basis, the time period is the 27 days left in August plus two full months: $8 ÷ 6 = $1.333 per month. For one day, divide $1.333 by 30, which equals $.044 per day. The prepaid period is two months and 27 days, so:

$$\begin{aligned} 27 \text{ days} \times \$.044 &= \$1.188 \\ 2 \text{ months} \times \$1.333 &= \underline{\$2.666} \\ &\quad \$3.854, \text{ or } \$3.85 \end{aligned}$$

This is a prepaid item and is *credited to the seller* and *debited to the buyer* on the closing statement.

To figure this on the basis of the actual days in the month of closing, the following process would be used:

$1.333 per month ÷ 31 days in August = $.043 per day
August 4 through August 31   = 28 days
28 days × $.043   = $1.204
2 months × $1.333   = $2.666
$1.204 + $2.666   ≈ $3.870, or *$3.87*

In Practice...   *Homeowner's insurance policies are not generally assumed. The typical policy is for one year. The seller will cancel the policy effective the date of closing and receive a refund of unused premium from the insurance company. The buyer purchases a new policy, effective the date of closing. Evidence of insurance coverage is required by the mortgage lender at closing.*

The Closing Statement

The remaining portion of this chapter illustrates a sample transaction using the HUD Uniform Settlement Statement that appears in Figure 21.4. The requirements of the Real Estate Settlement Procedures Act (RESPA) were discussed earlier.

Basic Information of Offer and Sale

John and Joanne Iuro listed their home at 3045 North Racine Avenue in Riverdale, Pennsylvania, with the Open Door Real Estate Company. The listing price was $118,500, and possession could be given within four weeks after all parties had signed the contract. Under the terms of the listing agreement, the sellers agreed to pay the broker a commission of six percent of the sales price.

The Open Door Real Estate Company submitted a contract offer to the Iuros from Brook Redemann, a bachelor, presently residing at 22 King Court, Riverdale. Redemann offered $115,000, with earnest money/down payment of $23,000, and the remaining $92,000 of the purchase price to be obtained through a new conventional loan. No private mortgage insurance will be necessary as the loan-to-value ratio will not exceed 80 percent. The Iuros signed the contract on May 15, 1989. Closing was set for June 15, 1989 at the office of the Open Door Real Estate Company, 720 Main Street, Riverdale.

The unpaid balance of the sellers' mortgage as of June 1, 1989 will be $57,700. Payments are $680 per month at 11 percent per annum on the unpaid balance.

The sellers will pay $20 for recording two instruments to clear defects in the sellers' title; $200 for preparation of deed and legal representation; $10 to record the mortgage satisfaction; and $85 for a pest inspection.

The buyer will pay $861 for evidence of title in the form of title insurance; $10 to record the deed; $10 to record the mortgage; and $175 for a survey.

Transfer tax of one percent of the consideration will be collected by the municipality; one percent by the state. The total cost of $2,300 will be divided equally between the buyer and the sellers.

County real estate taxes for the calendar year 1988, amounting to $1,725, have been paid, but taxes for the calendar year 1989, estimated to be in the same amount, have not been paid. According to the contract, real estate taxes and mortgage interest are to be prorated on the basis of 30 days per month.

**Figure 21.4
RESPA Uniform
Settlement Statement**

A. **Settlement Statement**	U.S. Department of Housing and Urban Development

OMB No. 2502-0265

B. Type of Loan

1. ☐ FHA   2. ☐ FmHA   3. ☒ Conv. Unins.
4. ☐ VA   5. ☐ Conv. Ins.

6 File Number	7. Loan Number	8 Mortgage Insurance Case Number

C. Note: This form is furnished to give you a statement of actual settlement costs. Amounts paid to and by the settlement agent are shown. Items marked "(p.o.c.)" were paid outside the closing; they are shown here for informational purposes and are not included in the totals.

D. Name and Address of Borrower	E. Name and Address of Seller	F. Name and Address of Lender
Brook Redemann 22 King Court Riverdale, Pennsylvania	John and Joanne Iuro 3045 North Racine Ave. Riverdale, Pennsylvania TIN:	Thrift Federal Savings 1100 Fountain Plaza Riverdale, Pennsylvania

G. Property Location	H. Settlement Agent
3045 North Racine Avenue Riverdale, Pennsylvania	Address Open Door Real Estate Company 720 Main Street TIN: Riverdale, Pennsylvania

Place of Settlement Open Door Real Estate	I. Settlement Date June 15, 1988

J. Summary of Borrower's Transaction		K. Summary of Seller's Transaction	
100. Gross Amount Due From Borrower		**400. Gross Amount Due To Seller**	
101. Contract sales price	$115,000.00	401. Contract sales price	$115,000.00
102. Personal property		402. Personal property	
103. Settlement charges to borrower (line 1400)	6700.59	403.	
104.		404.	
105.		405.	
Adjustments for items paid by seller in advance		**Adjustments for items paid by seller in advance**	
106. City/town taxes to		406. City/town taxes to	
107. County taxes to		407. County taxes to	
108. Assessments to		408. Assessments to	
109.		409.	
110.		410.	
111.		411.	
112.		412.	
120. Gross Amount Due From Borrower	$121,700.59	**420. Gross Amount Due To Seller**	$115,000.00
200. Amounts Paid By Or In Behalf Of Borrower		**500. Reductions In Amount Due To Seller**	
201. Deposit or earnest money	23,000.00	501. Excess deposit (see instructions)	
202. Principal amount of new loan(s)	92,000.00	502. Settlement charges to seller (line 1400)	8,365.00
203. Existing loan(s) taken subject to		503. Existing loan(s) taken subject to	
204.		504. Payoff of first mortgage loan	57,964.47
205.		505. Payoff of second mortgage loan	
206.		506.	
207.		507.	
208.		508.	
209.		509.	
Adjustments for items unpaid by seller		**Adjustments for items unpaid by seller**	
210. City/town taxes to		510. City/town taxes to	
211. County taxes 1/1/88 to 6/15/88	790.63	511. County taxes 1/1/88 to 6/15/88	790.63
212. Assessments to		512. Assessments to	
213.		513.	
214.		514.	
215.		515.	
216.		516.	
217.		517.	
218.		518.	
219.		519.	
220. Total Paid By/For Borrower	$115,790.63	**520. Total Reduction Amount Due Seller**	$ 67,120.10
300. Cash At Settlement From/To Borrower		**600. Cash At Settlement To/From Seller**	
301. Gross Amount due from borrower (line 120)	121,700.59	601. Gross amount due to seller (line 420)	115,000.00
302. Less amounts paid by/for borrower (line 220)	(115,790.63)	602. Less reductions in amt. due seller (line 520)	(67,120.10)
303. Cash ☒ From ☐ To Borrower	$ 5909.96	**603. Cash** ☒ To ☐ From Seller	$ 47,879.90

SUBSTITUTE FORM 1099 SELLER STATEMENT

The information contained in Blocks E, G, H and I and on line 401 (or, if line 401 is asterisked, lines 403 and 404) is important tax information and is being furnished to the Internal Revenue Service. If you are required to file a return, a negligence penalty or other sanction will be imposed on you if this item is required to be reported and the IRS determines that it has not been reported.

You are required by law to provide _____ with your correct taxpayer identification number. If you do not provide _____ with your correct taxpayer identification number, you may be subject to civil or criminal penalties imposed by law. Under penalties of perjury, I certify that the number shown on this statement is my correct taxpayer identification number.

Seller's Signature _____

SELLER INSTRUCTIONS

If this real estate was your principal residence, file Form 2119, Sale or Exchange of Principal Residence, for any gain, with your income tax return, for other transactions, complete the applicable parts of Form 4797, Form 6252 and/or Schedule D (Form 1040).

Previous Edition Is Obsolete   7/87   HUD-1 (3-86)
RESPA HB 4305.2

Figure 21.4 (cont.)

L. Settlement Charges

700. Total Sales/Broker's Commission based on price $ 115,000 @ 6 % = 6,900.00	Paid From Borrowers Funds at Settlement	Paid From Seller's Funds at Settlement
Division of Commission (line 700) as follows:		
701. $ to		
702. $ to		
703. Commission paid at Settlement		$6,900.00
704.		

800. Items Payable In Connection With Loan		
801. Loan Origination Fee 1 %	$ 920.00	
802. Loan Discount 2 %	1,840.00	
803. Appraisal Fee $150.00 to Swift Appraisal	POC	
804. Credit Report $ 60.00 to ACME Credit Bureau	POC	
805. Lender's Inspection Fee		
806. Mortgage Insurance Application Fee to		
807. Assumption Fee		
808.		
809.		
810.		
811.		

900. Items Required By Lender To Be Paid In Advance		
901. Interest from 6/16/88 to 6/30/88 @ $ 25.556 /day	383.34	
902. Mortgage Insurance Premium for months to		
903. Hazard Insurance Premium for 1 years to Hite Insurance	345.00	
904. years to		
905.		

1000. Reserves Deposited With Lender		
1001. Hazard insurance months @ $ per month		
1002. Mortgage insurance months @ $ per month		
1003. City property taxes months @ $ per month		
1004. County property taxes 7 months @ $ 143.75 per month	1,006.25	
1005. Annual assessments months @ $ per month		
1006. months @ $ per month		
1007. months @ $ per month		
1008. months @ $ per month		

1100. Title Charges		
1101. Settlement or closing fee to		
1102. Abstract or title search to		
1103. Title examination to		
1104. Title insurance binder to		
1105. Document preparation to		
1106. Notary fees to		
1107. Attorney's fees to		200.00
(includes above items numbers:)		
1108. Title insurance to	861.00	
(includes above items numbers:)		
1109. Lender's coverage $		
1110. Owner's coverage $		
1111.		
1112.		
1113.		

1200. Government Recording and Transfer Charges		
1201. Recording fees: Deed $ 10.00 ; Mortgage $ 10.00 ; Releases $ 10.00	20.00	10.00
1202. City/county/stamps: Deed $; Mortgage $		
1203. State tax/stamps: Deed $ 2300 ; Mortgage $	1,150.00	1,150.00
1204. Record two documents to clear title		20.00
1205.		

1300. Additional Settlement Charges		
1301. Survey to	175.00	
1302. Pest inspection to		85.00
1303.		
1304.		
1305.		

1400. Total Settlement Charges (enter on lines 103, Section J and 502, Section K)	$ 6,700.59	$8,365.00

I have carefully reviewed the HUD-1 Settlement Statement and to the best of my knowledge and belief, it is a true and accurate statement of all receipts and disbursements made on my account or by me in this transaction. I further certify that I have received a copy of the HUD-1 Settlement Statement.

_____   _____

Borrowers   Sellers

     The HUD-1 Settlement Statement which I have prepared is a true and accurate account of this transaction. I have caused the funds to be disbursed in accordance with this statement.

_____   _____

Settlement Agent   Date

WARNING: It is a crime to knowingly make false statements to the United States on this or any other similar form. Penalties upon conviction can include a fine and imprisonment. For details see: Title 18 U. S. Code Section 1001 and Section 1010.

The buyer's new loan is from Thrift Federal Savings, 1100 Fountain Plaza, Riverdale, in the amount of $92,000 at ten percent interest. In connection with this loan he will be charged $150 to have the property appraised by Swift Appraisal and $60 for a credit report from the Acme Credit Bureau. Redemann willl pay a one percent loan origination fee of $920, and two discount points. In addition, the buyer will pay for interest on his loan for the remainder of the month of closing—15 days at $25.556 per day, or $383.34. His first full payment (including July's interest) will be due August 1. He must deposit $1,006.25 or $7/12$ of the anticipated 1989 real estate tax into an escrow account. A one-year hazard insurance premium at $3 per $1,000 of appraised value ($115,000 ÷ 1,000 × 3 = $345) is paid to Hite Insurance Company. Since the appraisal and credit report are performed prior to loan approval, they are paid at the time of loan application, regardless of whether or not the transaction eventually closes. These items will be noted as POC—paid outside closing—on the settlement statement.

Computing the Prorations and Charges

Following are illustrations of the various steps in computing the prorations and other amounts to be included in the settlement thus far.

1. *Closing date:* June 15, 1989

2. *Commission:* 6% × $115,000 (sales price) = *$6,900*

3. *Seller's mortgage interest:*
   11% × $57,700 (principal due after June 1 payment) = $6,347 interest per year
   $6,347 ÷ 360 days = $17.631 interest per day
   15 days of accrued interest to be paid by the seller
   15 × $17.631 = $264.465, or $264.47 interest owed by the seller
   $57,700 + $264.465 = $57,964.47 payoff of seller's mortgage

4. *Real estate taxes* (estimate based on 1988 tax bill of $1,725):
   $1,725.00 ÷ 12 months = $143.75 per month
   $ 143.75 ÷ 30 days = $ 4.792 per day
   The earned period is from January 1, 1989, to and including June 15, 1989, and equals 5 months, 15 days:
   $143.75 × 5 months = $718.750
   $4.792 × 15 days   = $ 71.880
   $790.630, or *$790.63 seller owes buyer*

The Uniform Settlement Statement is divided into 12 sections. The most important information is included in Sections J, K and L. The borrower's and seller's summaries (J and K) are very similar to one another. For example, in Section J, the summary of the borrower's transaction, the buyer-borrower's debits are listed in lines 100 through 112 and totaled on line 120 (gross amount due from borrower). The total of the settlement costs itemized in Section L of the statement is entered on line 103 as one of the buyer's charges. The buyer's credits are listed on lines 201 through 219 and totaled on line 220 (total paid by/for borrower). Then, as with the other statements, the buyer's credits are subtracted from the charges to arrive at the cash due from the borrower to close (line 303).

In Section K, the summary of the seller's transaction, the sellers' credits are entered on lines 400 through 412 and totaled on line 420 (gross amount due to seller). The sellers' debits are entered on lines 501 through 519 and totaled on line 520 (total reduction amount due seller). The total of the sellers' settlement charges is on line 502. Then the debits are subtracted from the credits to arrive at the cash due to the sellers in order to close (line 603).

Section L is a summary of all the settlement charges for the transaction; the buyer's expenses are listed in one column and the seller's expenses are listed in the other. Note that if an attorney's fee is listed as a lump sum in line 1107, the settlement should list by line number the services that were included in that total fee.

Summary

Closing a sale involves both title procedures and financial matters. The broker, as agent of the seller, should be present at the closing to see that the sale is actually concluded and to account for the earnest money deposit.

The federal *Real Estate Settlement Procedures Act (RESPA)* requires disclosure of all settlement costs when a real estate purchase is financed by a federally related mortgage loan. RESPA requires lenders to use a *Uniform Settlement Statement* to detail the financial particulars of a transaction.

Usually the buyer orders and pays for the title evidence, such as title insurance, to ensure that the seller's title is acceptable.

The actual amount to be paid by the buyer at the closing is computed by preparation of a *closing,* or *settlement, statement.* This lists the sales price, earnest money deposit and all adjustments and prorations due between buyer and seller. The purpose of this statement is to determine the net amount due the seller at closing and the cash requirements of the buyer. The form is signed by both parties to evidence their approval.

Questions

1. Which of the following is true of real estate closings in Pennsylvania?
   a. Closings are generally conducted by real estate salespeople.
   b. The buyer usually receives the rents for the day of closing.
   c. The buyer pays for title evidence.
   d. The buyer usually pays the expenses for the day of closing.

2. When an item to be prorated has been earned (is owing) but has not been paid by the seller:
   a. the amount owed is a credit to the buyer.
   b. the amount owed is a debit to the seller.
   c. the amount owed is a debit to the buyer.
   d. a and b

3. When the item to be prorated has been paid by the seller but not fully earned (or used up):
   a. the unused portion is a credit to the seller.
   b. the unused portion is a credit to the buyer.
   c. the unused portion is prorated.
   d. the unused portion is a debit to the seller.

4. Certain amounts included in a closing statement are not prorated but are listed at the full amount. Which of the following is always prorated?
   a. state transfer tax
   b. earnest money
   c. the unpaid principal balance of the seller's mortgage assumed by the buyer
   d. interest on the seller's mortgage assumed by the buyer that has accrued since the last interest was paid

5. All encumbrances and liens shown on the report of title, other than those waived or agreed to by the purchaser and listed in the contract, must be removed so that the title can be delivered free and clear. The removal of such encumbrances is the duty of the:
   a. buyer.   c. broker.
   b. seller.   d. title company.

6. Legal title always passes from the seller to the buyer:
   a. on the date of execution of the deed.
   b. when the closing statement has been signed.
   c. when the deed is placed in escrow.
   d. when the deed is delivered.

7. In Pennsylvania, transfer taxes may be:
   I. debited to buyer.
   II. debited to seller.
      a. I only   c. both I and II
      b. II only   d. neither I nor II

8. The closing statement will disclose to the seller:
   I. the amount of money he or she will receive at the closing.
   II. the amount the buyer must bring to the closing.
      a. I only   c. both I and II
      b. II only   d. neither I nor II

9. Which one of the following items is *not* usually prorated between buyer and seller at the closing?
   a. recording charges
   b. general taxes
   c. rents
   d. mortgage interest

Questions 10 through 16 pertain to certain items as they would normally appear on a closing statement.

10. The sales price of the property is a:
    I. credit to the seller.
    II. debit to the buyer.
        a. I only   c. both I and II
        b. II only   d. neither I nor II

11. The earnest money left on deposit with the broker is a:
    a. credit to the seller.
    b. credit to the buyer.
    c. debit to the seller.
    d. debit to the buyer.

12. The principal amount of the purchaser's new mortgage loan is a:
    a. credit to the seller.
    b. credit to the buyer.
    c. debit to the seller.
    d. none of the above

13. Unpaid real estate taxes, water service and so forth are a:
    I. credit to the buyer.
    II. debit to the seller.
        a. I only   c. both I and II
        b. II only   d. neither I nor II

14. The broker's commission is a:
    a. credit to the buyer.
    b. debit to the seller.
    c. debit to the buyer.
    d. a and b

15. Unpaid interest proration on an existing assumed mortgage is a:
    a. credit to the seller.
    b. debit to the buyer.
    c. debit to the seller.
    d. a and b

16. Fuel oil left in a holding tank on the property is a:
    I. credit to the buyer.
    II. debit to the seller.
        a. I only   c. both I and II
        b. II only   d. neither I nor II

17. In Pennsylvania, prorated real estate taxes are:
    I. an accrued item.
    II. a prepaid item.
        a. I only   c. either I or II
        b. II only   d. neither I nor II

18. The RESPA Uniform Settlement Statement must be used to illustrate all settlement charges:
    a. for every real estate transaction.
    b. for transactions financed by VA and FHA loans only.
    c. for transactions financed by federally related mortgage loans.
    d. for all transactions in which mortgage financing is involved.

19. Which of the following would a lender generally require to be produced at the closing?
    a. title insurance policy
    b. market value appraisal
    c. fire and hazard insurance policy
    d. a and c

20. In Pennsylvania, which of the following forms of title insurance is (are) customarily paid for by the buyer?
    I. owner's title insurance policy
    II. lender's title insurance policy
        a. I only   c. both I and II
        b. II only   d. neither I nor II

22

Property Management Insurance

Overview

A real estate owner who rents the upstairs apartment in the building where he or she resides generally has no problem with property management—setting and collecting rents, maintenance and repairs are easy enough with only one tenant. But the owners of large multiunit developments often lack the time and/or expertise to successfully manage their properties. Enter the *property manager,* hired to maintain the property and ensure the profitability of the owner's investment. This chapter will examine the growing property management profession and will include discussions of the types of property insurance available to further protect an owner's real estate investment.

Property Management	In recent years the increased size of buildings; the technical complexities of construction, maintenance and repair; and the trend toward absentee ownership by individual investors and investment groups have led to the expanded use of professional property managers for both residential and commercial properties.

Property management has become so important that many brokerage firms maintain separate management departments staffed by carefully selected, well-trained people. In Pennsylvania, property managers must be licensed real estate brokers. Many corporate and institutional owners of real estate have also established property management departments. However, many real estate investors still manage their own property and thus must acquire the knowledge and skills of a property manager. |
| **Functions of the Property Manager** | In the simplest terms, a **property manager** is someone who *preserves the value of an investment property while generating income as an agent for the owners.* More specifically, a property manager is expected to merchandise the property and control operating expenses so as to maximize income. In addition, a manager should maintain and modernize the property to preserve and enhance the owner's capital investment. The manager carries out these objectives by: (1) securing suitable tenants, (2) collecting the rents, (3) caring for the premises, (4) budgeting and controlling expenses, (5) hiring and supervising employees and (6) keeping proper accounts and making periodic reports to the owner. |
| **Securing Management Business** | In today's market, property managers may look to corporate owners, apartments and condominiums, investment syndicates, trusts and absentee owners as possible sources of management business. In securing business from any of these sources, word of mouth is often the best advertising. A manager who consistently demonstrates the ability to increase property income over previous levels should have no difficulty finding new business.

However, before contracting to manage any property, the professional property manager should be certain that the building owner has realistic income expectations and is willing to spend money on necessary maintenance. Attempting to meet impossible owner demands by dubious methods can endanger the manager's reputation and prove detrimental to obtaining future business. |
| **The Management Agreement** | The first step in taking over the management of any property is to enter into a **management agreement** with the owner (see Figure 22.1). This agreement creates an agency relationship between the owner and the property manager, just as a listing agreement creates an agency relationship between selling owner and listing broker. The property manager is usually considered to be a *general agent,* whereas a real estate broker is usually considered to be a *special agent.* As agent, the property manager is charged with the same agency responsibilities, fiduciary to the owner, as the listing broker—care, obedience, accounting, loyalty and disclosure (COALD). (Agency responsibilities were discussed at length in Chapter 17, "Real Estate Brokerage.") |

**Figure 22.1
Property Management
Agreement**

NCR (No Carbon Required)

MANAGEMENT AGREEMENT

IN CONSIDERATION of the covenants herein contained, _____

_____, hereinafter designated as Owner,

agrees to employ _____, hereinafter designated as Agent,

to rent, lease, operate and manage the real property situated in the City of _____

County of _____, State of _____, Known as _____

for a period commencing this date and terminating at midnight of _____, and continuing on a month to month basis
thereafter subject to _____ days written notice of intent to terminate by either party, upon the following TERMS AND CONDITIONS:

AGENT'S AUTHORITIES AND OBLIGATIONS

Owner hereby confers upon Agent the following authorities and obligations, where initialed by Owner:

_____ To advertise the availability "for rent" or "for lease" of the premises and to display "For Rent" or "For Lease" signs. To screen and use diligence in the selection of prospective tenants and to abide by all fair housing laws.

_____ To negotiate leases as may be approved by Owner. Lease terms not to exceed _____

_____ To execute leases and rental agreements on behalf of Owner.

_____ To collect rents, security deposits, and all other receipts, and to deposit such monies in a trust account with a qualified banking institution.

_____ To serve notice of termination of tenancies, notices to quit or pay rent, and such other notices as Agent may deem appropriate.

_____ To employ attorneys approved by Owner for the purpose of enforcing Owner's rights under leases and rental agreements and instituting legal action on behalf of Owner.

_____ To provide all services reasonably necessary for the proper management of the property including periodic inspections, supervision of maintenance, and arranging for such improvements, alterations and repairs as may be required of Owner.

_____ To hire, supervise and discharge all employees and independent contractors required in the operation and maintenance of the property. Compensation shall be in such amounts as approved by Owner and the employment of any employee shall be terminable at will. It is agreed that all such employees are employees of the Owner and not of the Agent. To prepare payroll tax returns for Owner, where applicable, and to make payments of such taxes to the appropriate agencies from gross revenue.

_____ To contract for repairs or alterations at a cost to Owner not to exceed $_____

_____ To contract for emergency repairs at a cost to Owner not to exceed $_____ per repair.

_____ In the event Owner is not available for consultation, to contract for such repairs and expenditures as are necessary for the protection of the property from damage, or to perform services to the tenants provided for in their leases.

_____ To execute service contracts for utilities and services for the operation, maintenance, and safety of the property as Agent deems necessary or advisable. Provided that the terms of any such contract shall not exceed _____ months and the amount payable each month shall not exceed $_____ without written approval of Owner.

To pay from gross receipts all operating expenses and such other expenses as may be authorized by Owner, including:

_____ Mortgage Payments

_____ Property Taxes

_____ Payroll Taxes

_____ Insurance Premiums

_____ Other: _____

_____

_____ To maintain accurate records of all monies received and disbursed in connection with the management of the property. Said records shall be open for inspection by Owner during regular business hours and upon reasonable notice.

_____ To submit monthly statements of all receipts and disbursements no later than the _____ day of the following month.

OWNER'S OBLIGATIONS

Owner agrees to pay to Agent fees for services rendered at the rates hereinafter set forth. Such compensation is due and payable on demand and may be deducted by the Agent from receipts.

COMPENSATION FOR MANAGEMENT SERVICES (initial where applicable):

_____ $_____ per month for each single family residence.

_____ _____% of gross monthly collections, provided that the minimum compensation is at least $_____ per month.

_____ $_____ flat fee per unit per month.

COMPENSATION FOR LEASING:

_____ New leases: _____

_____ Renegotiated leases: _____

COMPENSATION FOR MODERNIZATION OR CAPITAL IMPROVEMENTS: _____

COMPENSATION FOR REFINANCING: _____

COMPENSATION FOR OTHER SERVICES: _____

Owner shall indemnify and save the Agent harmless from any and all costs, expenses, attorney's fees, suits, liabilities, damages from or connected with the management of the property by Agent, or the performance or exercise of any of the duties, obligations, powers, or authorities herein or hereafter granted to Agent.

Owner shall not hold Agent liable for any error of judgement, or for any mistake of fact or law, or for anything which Agent may do or refrain from doing hereinafter, except in cases of willful misconduct or gross negligence.

Owner agrees to carry, at Owner's expense, Workers Compensation Insurance for Owner's employees. Owner also agrees to carry, at Owner's expense, bodily injury, property damage and personal injury public liability insurance in the amount of not less than $500,000 combined single limit for bodily injury and property damage. The policy shall be written on a comprehensive general liability form and shall name the Agent as additional insured.

Owner shall immediately furnish Agent with a certificate of insurance evidencing that the above coverage is in force with a carrier acceptable to Agent. In the event Agent receives notice that said insurance coverage is to be cancelled, Agent shall have the option to immediately cancel this agreement.

Owner assumes full responsibility for the payment of any expenses and obligations incurred in connection with the exercise of Agent's duties set forth in this agreement.

Owner shall deposit with Agent $_____ as an initial operating reserve and will cover any excess of expenses over income within ten days of any request by Agent. The Agent may terminate this agreement immediately if the request for additional funds is not paid. Owner understands that it is not Agent's obligation to advance its own funds for payment of Owner's operating expenses.

OTHER TERMS

All notices required to be given hereunder shall be in writing and mailed to the parties hereto at the addresses set forth below.

In the event of any legal action by the parties arising out of this agreement, the prevailing party shall be entitled to reasonable attorney's fees and costs, to be determined by the court in which such action is brought.

ADDITIONAL TERMS: _____

_____

_____

_____

_____

Agent accepts the employment under the terms hereof and agrees to use diligence in the exercise of the obligations, duties, authorities and powers conferred herein upon Agent.

Dated: _____

_____ Agent   _____ Owner

By _____   _____ Owner

Title _____   Soc. Sec. # _____

Address _____   Address _____

Phone _____   Phone _____

FORM 115 (3-85)   COPYRIGHT © 1985, BY PROFESSIONAL PUBLISHING CORP, 122 PAUL DR, SAN RAFAEL, CA 94903   **PROFESSIONAL PUBLISHING**

The management agreement should be in writing and should cover the following points:

1. *Description* of the property.

2. *Time period* the agreement will cover.

3. *Definition of management's responsibilities:* All of the manager's duties should be stated in the contract; exceptions should be noted.

4. *Statement of owner's purpose:* This statement should indicate what the owner desires the manager to accomplish with the property. One owner may wish to maximize net income and therefore instruct the manager to cut expenses and minimize reinvestment. Another owner may want to increase the capital value of the investment, in which case the manager should initiate a program for improving the property's physical condition.

5. *Extent of manager's authority:* This provision should state what authority the manager is to have in such matters as hiring, firing and supervising employees, fixing rental rates for space, making expenditures and authorizing repairs within the limits established previously with the owner. (Repairs that exceed a certain expense limit may require the owner's written approval.)

6. *Reporting:* Agreement should be reached on the frequency and detail of the manager's periodic reports on operations and financial position. These reports serve as a means for the owner to monitor the manager's work and as a basis for both the owner and the manager to assess trends that can be used in shaping future management policy.

7. *Management fee:* The fee can be based on a percentage of gross or net income, a commission on new rentals, a fixed fee or a combination of these.
   (Note: Management fees are subjected to the same antitrust considerations as sales commissions. They cannot be standardized in the marketplace since that would be viewed as "price fixing." The fee is the result of negotiation between the agent and principal.)

8. *Allocation of costs:* The agreement should state which of the property manager's expenses, such as office rent, office help, telephone, advertising, association fees, and social security, will be paid by the manager and which will be charged to the property's expenses and paid by the owner.

After entering into an agreement with a property owner, a manager must handle the property as if it were his or her own. In all activities, the manager must be aware that the first responsibility is to *realize the highest return on the property that is consistent with the owner's instructions.*

| **Management Considerations** | A property manager must protect the interest of the property owner by: (1) constantly *improving the reputation* as well as the *physical condition* of the property, (2) protecting the owner from *insurable losses,* (3) protecting the owner by helping the neighborhood and the community to offer the best possible *residential and business environments,* (4) keeping constant *check on all expenditures* to be sure that costs are kept as low as possible for the results that must be accomplished and (5) *adjusting the rental rate* as necessary to produce the highest total income. |

A property manager must live up to his or her side of the management agreement in both the letter and the spirit of the contract. The owner must be kept well informed on all matters of policy as well as on the financial condition of the property and its operation. Finally, a manager must keep in contact with others in the field, improving his or her knowledge of the subject and keeping informed on current policies pertaining to the profession.

Budgeting Expenses

Before attempting to rent any property, a property manager should develop an operating budget based on anticipated revenues and expenses and reflecting the long-term goals of the owner. In preparing a budget, a manager should begin by allocating money for such continuous, *fixed expenses* as employees' salaries, real estate taxes, property taxes and insurance premiums.

Next, the manager should budget for such *variable expenses* as repairs, decorating and supplies. The amount allocated can be computed from the previous yearly costs of the variable expenses.

Capital expenditures. If an owner and a property manager decide that modernization or renovation of the property would enhance its value, the manager should budget money to cover the costs of remodeling. Budgeting for *reserves for replacements* is commonly the way capital expenditures are allocated. In the case of large-scale construction, the expenses charged against the property's income should be spread over several years.

Although budgets should be as accurate an estimate of cost as possible, adjustments may sometimes be necessary, especially in the case of new properties.

Renting the Property

Effective rental of the property is essential to the success of a property manager. However, the role of the manager in managing a property should not be confused with that of a broker acting as leasing agent solely concerned with renting space. The property manager may use the services of a leasing agent to solicit prospective tenants or collect rents, but that agent does not undertake the full responsibility of maintenance and management of the property.

Setting rental rates. In establishing rental rates for a property, a basic concern must be that, in the long term, the income from the rentable space cover the fixed charges and operating expenses and also provide a fair return on the investment. Consideration must also be given to the prevailing rates in comparable buildings and the current level of vacancy in the property to be rented. In the short term, rental rates are primarily a result of supply and demand. Decisions about rental rates should start with a detailed survey of the competitive space available in the neighborhood. Prices should be noted and adjusted for differences between neighboring properties and the property being managed.

Note that while apartment rental rates are stated in monthly amounts, office and commercial space rentals are usually stated according to either the annual or the monthly rate per square foot of space.

If a high level of vacancy exists, an immediate effort should be made to determine the reason. *A high level of vacancy does not necessarily indicate that rents are too high.* The trouble may be inept management or defects in the property. The manager should attempt to identify and correct the problems first rather than lower the rent. Conversely, *while a high percentage of occupancy may appear to indicate an effective rental program, it could also mean that rental rates are too low.* With an apartment house or office building, any time the occupancy level exceeds 95 percent serious consideration should be given to raising the rents.

Tenant selection. Generally, the highest rents can be secured from satisfied tenants. While a broker may sell a property and then have no further dealings with the purchaser, a building manager's success is greatly dependent on retaining sound, long-term relationships. In selecting prospective commercial or industrial tenants, a manager should be sure that each person will "fit the space." The manager should be certain that: (1) the *size of the space* meets the tenant's requirements, (2) the tenant will have the *ability to pay* for the space for which he or she contracts, (3) the *tenant's business will be compatible* with the building and the other tenants and (4) if the tenant is likely to expand in the future, there will be *expansion space available.* After a prospect becomes a tenant, *the manager must be sure that the tenant remains satisfied in all respects commensurate with fair business dealing.*

Note that in selecting residential and commercial tenants, the property manager must comply with all federal and local fair housing laws (see Chapter 24, "Fair Housing Laws and Ethical Practices").

Collecting rents. A building will not be a profitable operation unless the property manager can collect all rents when they are due. Any substantial loss resulting from nonpayment of rent will quickly eliminate the margin of profitability in an operation.

The best way to minimize problems with rent collection is to make a *careful selection* of tenants in the first place. A property manager's desire to have a high level of occupancy should not override good judgment in accepting only those tenants who can be expected to meet their financial obligations to the property owner. A property manager should investigate financial references given by the prospect, local credit bureaus and, when possible, the prospective tenant's former landlord.

The terms of rental payment should be spelled out in detail in the lease agreement. These details include the time and place of payment, provisions and penalties for late payment and provisions for cancellation and damages in case of nonpayment. A *firm and consistent collection plan* with a sufficient system of notices and records should be established by the property manager. In cases of delinquency, every attempt must be made to make collections without resorting to legal action. For those cases in which it is required, a property manager must be prepared to initiate and follow through with the necessary steps in conjunction with the property owner's or management firm's legal counsel.

Maintaining the Property

One of the most important functions of a property manager is the supervision of property maintenance. A manager must learn to balance services provided with the costs they entail so as to satisfy the tenants' needs while minimizing operating expenses.

The term *maintenance* actually covers several types of activities. First, the manager must *protect the physical integrity of the property* to ensure that the condition of the building and its grounds is kept at its present level. Over the long term, preserving the property by repainting the exterior or replacing the heating plant will help to keep the building functional and decrease routine maintenance costs.

A property manager must also *supervise the routine cleaning and repairs* of the building. Such day-to-day duties as cleaning common areas, minor carpentry and plumbing and regularly scheduled upkeep of heating, air-conditioning and landscaping are generally handled by regular building employees or by outside firms that have contracted with the manager to provide certain services.

In addition, especially when dealing with commercial or industrial space, a property manager will be called on to *alter the interior of the building to meet the functional demands of the tenant.* These alterations range from repainting to completely gutting the interior and redesigning the space.

Designing interior space is especially important when renting new buildings, for the interior is usually left incomplete so that it can be adapted to the needs of the individual tenants. Another portion of a manager's responsibility is the supervision of modernization or renovation of buildings that have become functionally obsolete and thus unsuited to today's building needs. (See Chapter 19, "Real Estate Appraisal," for a definition of *functional obsolescence.*) The renovation of a building often increases the building's marketability and thus its possible income.

Employees versus contracted services. One of the major decisions a property manager faces is whether to contract for maintenance services from an outside firm or hire on-site employees to perform such tasks. This decision should be based on a number of factors, including size of the building, complexity of tenants' requirements and availability of suitable labor.

The Management Profession

For those interested in pursuing a career in property management, most metropolitan areas have local associations of building and property owners and managers that are affiliates of regional and national associations. The Institute of Real Estate Management was founded in 1933 and is part of the NATIONAL ASSOCIATION OF REALTORS®. The Institute awards the designation of *Certified Property Manager* (CPM) to persons who have met certain requirements. The Building Owners and Managers Association International (BOMA International) is a federation of local associations of owners and managers, primarily of office buildings. Training courses leading to the designation *Real Property Administrator* are offered by the Building Owners and Managers Institute International (BOMI International), an independent institute affiliated with BOMA. In addition, there are many specialized professional organizations for apartment managers, community association managers, shopping center managers and others. Participation in groups such as these allows property managers to gain valuable professional knowledge and to discuss their problems with other managers facing similar issues.

Insurance

One of the most important responsibilities of a property manager is to protect the property owner against all major insurable risks. A competent, reliable insurance agent who is well-versed in all areas of insurance pertaining to property should be selected to survey the property and make recommendations. Final decisions, however, must be made by the property owner.

Awareness of the purposes of insurance coverage, and how to make best use of the many types of insurance available are part of what is called *risk management*.

Risk management involves answering the question, "What will happen if something goes wrong?" The perils of any risk must be evaluated in terms of options. In considering the possibility of a loss, the property manager must decide whether it is better to:

- *avoid it,* by removing the source of risk, such as a swimming pool;

- *retain it,* to a certain extent, by insuring with a large *deductible* (loss not covered by the insurer);

- *control it,* by installing sprinklers, fire doors and other preventive measures; or

- *transfer it,* by taking out an insurance policy.

Types of Coverage   There are many kinds of insurance coverage available to income-property owners and managers. Some of the more common types are:

1. **Fire and hazard insurance:** Fire insurance policies provide coverage against direct loss or damage to property from a fire on the premises. Standard fire coverage can be extended to cover hazards such as windstorm, hail, smoke damage or civil insurrection.

2. **Business interruption insurance:** Most hazard policies insure against the actual loss of property but do not cover loss of revenues from income property. Interruption insurance covers the loss of income that occurs if the property cannot be used to produce income.

3. **Contents and personal property insurance:** This covers building contents and personal property during periods when they are not actually located on the business premises.

4. **Liability insurance:** Public liability insurance covers the risks an owner assumes when the public enters the building. Claims are used to pay medical expenses for a person injured in the building as a result of the landlord's negligence. Another liability risk is that of medical or hospital payments for injuries sustained by building employees hurt in the course of their employment. These claims are covered by state laws known as **workers' compensation acts.** These laws require a building owner who is an employer to obtain a workers' compensation policy from a private insurance company.

5. **Casualty insurance:** Casualty insurance policies include coverage against theft, burglary, vandalism, machinery damage and health and accident insurance. Casualty policies are usually written on specific risks, such as theft, rather than being all-inclusive.

6. **Surety bonds:** Surety bonds cover an owner against financial losses resulting from an employee's criminal acts or negligence while carrying out his or her duties.

Today, many insurance companies offer **multiperil policies** for apartment and business buildings. These policies offer the property manager an insurance package that includes such standard types of commercial coverage as fire, hazard, public liability and casualty.

Claims
When a claim is made under a policy insuring a building or other physical object, there are two possible methods of determining the amount of the claim. One is the *depreciated,* or actual, cash value of the damaged property, and the other is replacement cost. If a 30-year-old building is damaged, the timbers and materials are 30 years old and therefore do not have the same value as new material. Thus, in determining the amount of the loss under what is called *actual cash value,* the cost of new material would be reduced by the estimated depreciation the item had suffered during the time it had been in the building.

The alternate method is to cover *replacement cost.* This would represent the actual amount a builder would charge to replace the damaged property at the time of the loss, including materials.

When purchasing insurance, a manager must assess whether the property should be insured at full replacement cost or at a depreciated cost. As with the homeowners' policies discussed in Chapter 16, "Concepts of Home Ownership," commercial policies include *coinsurance clauses* that require the insured to carry fire coverage, usually in an amount equal to 80 percent of the building's replacement value.

Summary
Property management is a specialized service to owners of income-producing properties in which the managerial function may be delegated to an individual or a firm with particular expertise in the field. The manager, as agent of the owner, becomes the administrator of the project and assumes the executive functions required for the care and operation of the property.

A management agreement must be carefully prepared to define and authorize the manager's duties and responsibilities. This agreement establishes the agency relationship between owner and manager.

The first step a property manager should take when managing a building is to draw up a budget of estimated variable and fixed expenses. The budget should also allow for any proposed expenditures for major renovations or modernizations agreed on by the manager and the owner. These projected expenses, combined with the manager's analysis of the condition of the building and the rent patterns in the neighborhood, will form the basis on which rental rates for the property are determined.

Once a rent schedule is established, the property manager is responsible for soliciting tenants whose needs are suited to the available space and who are financially capable of meeting the proposed rents. The manager is generally obligated to collect rents, maintain the building, hire necessary employees, pay taxes for the building and deal with tenant problems.

Once the property is rented, one of the manager's primary responsibilities is supervising its maintenance. Maintenance includes safeguarding the physical integrity of the property and performing routine cleaning and repairs as well as adapting the interior space and overall design of the property to suit the tenants' needs and meet the demands of the market.

In addition, the manager is expected to secure adequate insurance coverage for the premises. The basic types of coverage applicable to commercial structures include *fire and hazard insurance* on the property and fixtures, *business interruption insurance* to protect the owner against income losses and *casualty insurance* to provide coverage against such losses as theft, vandalism and destruction of machinery. The manager should also secure *public liability insurance* to insure the owner against claims made by people injured on the premises and *workers' compensation policies* to cover the claims of employees injured on the job.

Questions

1. Which of the following types of insurance coverage insures the property owner against the claims of employees injured while on the job?

    a. business interruption
    b. workers' compensation
    c. casualty
    d. surety bond

2. In renting units in an apartment building, a property manager must comply with which of the following?

    a. the terms of the management agreement
    b. the owner
    c. fair housing laws
    d. all of the above

3. From a management point of view, apartment building occupancy that reaches as high as 98 percent would tend to indicate that:

    a. the building is poorly managed.
    b. the building is well-managed.
    c. the building is a desirable place to live.
    d. rents should be raised.

4. A deliveryman slips on a defective stair in an apartment building and is hospitalized. A claim against the building owner for medical expenses will be made under which of the following policies held by the owner?

    a. workers' compensation
    b. casualty
    c. liability
    d. fire and hazard

5. The relationship between a building owner and a property manager is:

    I. an agency relationship.
    II. established in the management agreement.

    a. I only   c. both I and II
    b. II only   d. neither I nor II

6. Which of the following should *not* be a consideration in selecting a tenant?

    a. the size of the space versus the tenant's requirements
    b. the tenant's ability to pay
    c. the racial and ethnic background of the tenant
    d. the compatibility of the tenant's business to other tenants' business

7. Risk management alternatives include:

    a. avoiding losses.
    b. controlling losses.
    c. transferring losses.
    d. all of the above

8. In drawing up an operating budget, the property manager should consider:

    a. the variable expenses.
    b. the long-range desires of the owner.
    c. anticipated revenues.
    d. all of the above

9. Generally, the provisions of the manager-owner agreement should include:

    I. a definition of the manager's responsibilities.
    II. a listing of previous owners of the property.

    a. I only   c. both I and II
    b. II only   d. neither I nor II

10. Rents should be determined on the basis of:

    a. prevailing rental rates in the area.
    b. operating expenses, fixed charges and a proper net profit to the owner.
    c. current level of vacancy.
    d. all of the above

11. Property manager Frieda Jacobs hires Albert Weston as the full-time janitor for one of the buildings she manages. While repairing a faucet in one of the apartments, Weston steals a television set. Jacobs could protect the owner against liability for this type of loss by purchasing:

   a. liability insurance.
   b. workers' compensation insurance.
   c. a surety bond.
   d. casualty insurance.

12. Before accepting a tenant, the property manager should:

   a. determine if the available space fits the tenant's needs.
   b. check the tenant's ability to pay.
   c. check whether the tenant is compatible with other tenants.
   d. all of the above

13. The possible methods of determining the amount of a claim under an insurance policy covering damage to a building include the:

   I. replacement cost method.
   II. actual cash value method.

     a. I only   c. both I and II
     b. II only   d. neither I nor II

14. In assuming responsibility for the maintenance of a property, the manager is expected to:

   I. directly or indirectly supervise the routine cleaning and repair work of the building.
   II. adapt the interior space of the building to meet the requirements of individual tenants.

     a. I only   c. both I and II
     b. II only   d. neither I nor II

23

Real Estate Investment

Key Terms

Adjusted basis
Appreciation
Basis
Boot
Capital gain
Cash flow
Cost recovery
Depreciation
Equity buildup
Exchange
General partnership

Inflation
Installment sale
Intrinsic value
Leverage
Limited partnership
Pyramiding
Real estate investment syndicate
Real estate investment trust
Real estate mortgage investment conduit
Tax credits

Overview

The market for real estate investment is one of the most active in the country. Real estate can be used to generate income, build up equity and, to a limited extent, provide tax deductions that can be used to offset income from other sources. This chapter will present a basic introduction to real estate investment. Major emphasis is placed on investment opportunities open to small or beginning investors. Note that the examples and computations given in this chapter are symbolic and used for *illustrative purposes only*. Such examples are included in the discussion in order to explain a particular feature or concept of investment, *not to teach the reader how, when or what amount of money to invest*.

Investing in Real Estate

Often, customers ask a real estate broker or salesperson to act as an investment counselor. Too often, the licensee is placed in that role by eager, inexperienced investors with high hopes for quick profits. Although it may be the real estate licensee's responsibility to analyze and discuss with the potential investor his or her financial status, future goals and investment motivations, the broker or salesperson should always *refer a potential real estate investor to a competent tax accountant, attorney or investment specialist* who can give expert advice regarding the investor's specific interest.

Real estate practitioners should possess an essential knowledge of real estate investment so they can counsel customers on a basic level. Such knowledge should begin with an examination of the traditional advantages and disadvantages of investing in real estate as opposed to other commodities.

Advantages of Real Estate Investment

Traditionally, real estate investments have shown a *high rate of return,* generally higher than the prevailing interest rate charged by mortgage lenders. Theoretically, this means that an investor can use the leverage of borrowed money to finance a real estate purchase and feel relatively sure that the asset will yield more money than it costs to finance the purchase.

Real estate values usually keep pace with the rate of inflation. Such an *inflation hedge* provides the real estate investor with relative assurance that if purchasing power of the dollar decreases, the value of the assets will increase to offset the inflationary effects. Inflation will also be discussed in detail later in this chapter.

Finally, a distinct advantage of real estate investment is that an investor can use borrowed money to finance the assets, which significantly increases the investor's buying power. In addition to the advantage of using borrowed money, the portion of an investor's mortgage payments applied to the principal represents *equity buildup* and increases the value of the investor's ownership interest in the asset with each remittance. This means the investor can refinance the property, receiving a certain amount of cash, should the need arise.

Disadvantages of Real Estate Investment

Unlike stocks and bonds, *real estate is not highly liquid* over a short period of time. This means that an investor cannot usually sell his or her real estate quickly without taking some sort of loss. An investor in listed stocks need only call a stockbroker in order to liquidate a certain portion of such assets quickly when funds are needed. In contrast, even though a real estate investor may be able to raise a limited amount of cash by refinancing the property, that property is usually listed with a real estate broker and the investor may have to sell the property at a substantially lower price than its market value in order to facilitate a quick sale.

Finally, and most important, *a high degree of risk* is often involved in real estate investment. There is always the possibility that an investor's property will decrease in value during the period it is held or that it will not generate an income sufficient to make it profitable.

The Investment	The most important form of real estate investment is *direct ownership*. Both individuals and corporations may own real estate directly and manage it for appreciation or cash flow (income). Property held for **appreciation** is generally expected to increase in value and show a profit when sold at some future date. Income property is just that—property held for current income as well as a profit upon its sale.
Appreciation	Real estate is an avenue of investment open to those interested in holding property primarily for appreciation.

Two main factors affect appreciation: inflation and intrinsic value. **Inflation** is defined as the *increase in the amount of money in circulation, which results in a decline in its value coupled with a rise in wholesale and retail prices.* The **intrinsic value** of real estate is the result of a person's individual choices and preferences for a given geographical area, based on the features and amenities that the area has to offer. For example, property located in a well-kept suburb near business and shopping areas would have a greater intrinsic value to most people than similar property in a more isolated location. As a rule, the greater the intrinsic value, the more money a property can command upon its sale.

Quite often an investor speculates in purchases of either agricultural (farm) land or undeveloped (raw) land, located in what is expected to be a major path of growth. This type of investment carries with it many inherent risks. The investor must consider such questions as: How fast will the area develop? Will it grow sufficiently for the investor to make a good profit? Will the expected growth even occur? More important, will the profits eventually realized from the property be great enough to offset the costs (such as property taxes) of holding the land?

Despite these risks, land has historically been a good inflation hedge if held for a long term. It can also be a source of income to offset some of the holding costs. For example, agricultural land can be leased out for crops or timber production, or grazing. On the downside, the Internal Revenue Service does not allow the depreciation (cost recovery) of land. Also, such land may not be liquid (salable) at certain times under certain circumstances, because few people are willing to purchase raw or agricultural land on short notice.

Income	The wisest initial investment a person who wishes to buy and personally manage real estate can make is the purchase of rental income property.

Cash flow. The object of an investor's directing funds into income property is to generate spendable income, usually called cash flow. The **cash flow** is the total amount of money remaining after all expenditures have been paid, including taxes, operating costs and mortgage payments. The cash flow produced by any given parcel of real estate is determined by at least three factors: amount of rent received, operating expenses and method of debt repayment.

Generally, the amount of *rent* (income) that a property may command depends on a number of factors, including location, physical appearance and amenities. If the cash flow from rents is not enough to cover all expenses, a *negative cash flow* will result.

To keep cash flow high, an investor should *keep operating expenses low.* Such operating expenses include general maintenance of the building, repairs, utilities, taxes and tenant services (switchboard facilities, security systems and so forth). As with inadequate rental income, poor or overly expensive management can result in negative cash flow.

An investor often stands to make more money by investing borrowed money, usually obtained through a mortgage loan or deed of trust loan. *Low mortgage payments* spread over a long period of time result in a higher cash flow because they allow the investor to retain more income each month; conversely, higher mortgage payments would contribute to a lower cash flow.

Investment opportunities. Traditional income-producing property investments include apartment buildings, hotels, motels, commercial properties, shopping centers, office buildings and industrial properties. Investors in recent years have found single-family dwellings, town houses and condominium units to be favorable investments in certain situations.

Leverage

Essentially, **leverage** is the use of *borrowed money to finance the bulk of an investment.* As a rule, an investor can receive a maximum return from an initial investment (the down payment) by:

1. making a small down payment;

2. paying low interest rates; and

3. spreading mortgage payments over as long a period as possible.

As an example, the use of leveraging allows a person of modest income to buy a home valued at several times that amount, as the figure below illustrates.

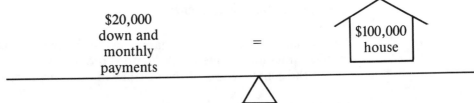

The amount of the monthly payments will depend upon the interest rate charged and the loan term over which the principal (amount borrowed) must be repaid. When interest rates are comparatively low, borrowers frequently increase the amount of principal, by buying a more expensive home, taking a loan with a shorter term or making advance payments of principal. The 15-year mortgage loan, once a rarity, has now become commonplace thanks to the lowering of interest rates in the mid-1980s.

The effect of leveraging on an investor is to provide, on a sale of the asset, a return that is a reflection of the effect of market forces on the entire amount of the original purchase price, but is measured against only the actual cash invested. For example, if an investor spends $100,000 for rental property and makes a $20,000 down payment, then sells that property five years later for $125,000, the return over five years is $25,000. Disregarding ownership expenses, the return is not 25 percent ($25,000 compared to $100,000), but 125 percent of the original amount invested ($25,000 compared to $20,000).

Risks are generally proportionate to leverage. A high degree of leverage gives the investor and lender a high degree of risk; lower leverage results in a lower risk.

Equity buildup. **Equity buildup** is that portion of the payment directed toward the principal rather than the interest, *plus* any gain in property value due to appreciation. In a sense, equity buildup is like money in the bank to the investor. Although this accumulated equity is not realized as cash unless the property is sold or refinanced, the equity interest may be sold, exchanged or mortgaged (refinanced) to be used as leverage for other investments.

Pyramiding through refinancing. By holding and refinancing using equity and appreciation buildup, rather than selling or exchanging already-owned properties, an investor can increase holdings substantially without investing any additional capital. This practice is known as **pyramiding.** By reinvesting and doubling holdings periodically, it is conceivable that an investor who started out with a small initial cash down payment could own (heavily mortgaged) properties worth hundreds of thousands or millions of dollars. With sufficient cash flow to cover all costs, if market values hold steady, the income derived from such assets could pay off the various mortgage debts and show a handsome profit.

Tax Benefits

One of the main reasons real estate investments were popular—and profitable—in the past was that federal law allowed investors to use losses generated by the investments to shelter income from other sources.

The Tax Reform Act of 1986 (TRA) has eliminated some tax advantages of owning investment real estate, but, with professional tax advice, the investor can still make a wise real estate purchase.

We have already discussed in Chapter 16 the change in the status of capital gains and the limitation on interest deductions brought about by TRA. We will now look at the consequences of the new law in other areas of importance to investors.

The discussions and examples used in this section are designed to introduce the reader to general tax concepts—a tax attorney or CPA should be consulted for further details on specific regulations. Internal Revenue Service regulations are subject to frequent change; again, consult a tax expert for up-to-date information.

Capital Gains

The tax law no longer favors long-term investments by reducing the taxable gain (profit) on their sale or exchange. What we term **capital gain** is still defined as the difference between the adjusted basis of property and its net selling price. The distinction between long-term and short-term capital gain has been eliminated. All such profit is now taxed as ordinary income. As pointed out earlier, the taxpayer who profits from a transaction involving property held for less than six months will actually benefit by the new, overall lower tax rates.

Basis. A property's cost basis will determine the amount of gain to be taxed. The **basis** of property is the investor's initial cost for the parcel of real estate. The investor adds to the basis the cost of any physical improvements subsequently made to the property, and subtracts from the basis the amount of any depreciation claimed as a tax deduction (explained later), to derive the property's **adjusted basis.** When the property is sold by the investor, the amount by which the sale price exceeds the property's adjusted basis is the capital gain taxable as income.

For example, assume an investor purchased a one-family dwelling for rental purposes ten years ago for $45,000. The value of the land was set at $10,000; the value of the improvements totaled $35,000. The investor is now selling the home for $100,000; of this sum, $20,000 represents the new value of the land. Shortly before selling the property, the investor made $3,000 worth of capital improvements to the structure. Depreciation has been taken on a straight-line 35-year basis. (Depreciation, now called "cost recovery," will be discussed later in this section.) The investor paid the selling broker a seven percent commission and also paid $600 in closing costs. So the investor's capital gain would be computed as follows:

Selling price:		$ 100,000
Less:		
7% commission	$ 7,000	
closing costs	+ 600	
	$ 7,600	− 7,600
Net sales price:		$ 92,400
Less value of land:		− 20,000
		$ 72,400
Basis:		
building	$ 35,000	
improvements	+ 3,000	
	$ 38,000	
Less depreciation:		
($35,000 ÷ 35 years =		
$1,000; $1,000 × 10		
years' ownership)	− 10,000	
Adjusted basis:	$ 28,000	− 28,000
Capital gain on improvements:		$ 44,400
Plus capital gain on land:		
value at sale	$ 20,000	
less original value	− 10,000	
	$ 10,000	+ 10,000
Total capital gain:		$ 54,400
Amount taxable as ordinary income:		$ 54,400

Exchanges

Through **exchange,** trading one property for another, a real estate investor can defer capital-gains tax. Tax laws generally provide that an investor's capital gains are not taxed when the property is exchanged for income-producing properties of like kind. Note, however, that *the tax is deferred, not eliminated.* If the property is sold, the investor will be required to pay tax on the total capital gain. Or an investor can keep exchanging upward in value, adding to any assets as long as the investor lives without ever personally having to pay any capital-gains tax.

To qualify as a tax-deferred exchange, the properties involved must be of *like kind*—for example, real estate for real estate. Any additional capital or personal property included with the transaction to even out the exchange is considered **boot,** and the party receiving it is taxed at the time of the exchange. The value of the boot is added to the basis of the property with which it is given.

For example, investor Brown owns an apartment building with an adjusted basis of $225,000 and a market value of $375,000. Brown exchanges the building plus $75,000 cash for another apartment building having a market value of $450,000. That building, owned by investor Grey, has an adjusted basis of $175,000. Brown's basis in the new building will be $300,000 (the $225,000 basis of the building exchanged plus the $75,000 cash boot paid) and Brown has no tax liability on the exchange. Grey must pay tax on the $75,000 boot received and has a basis of $175,000 (the same as the previous building) in the building now owned.

Depreciation (Cost Recovery)

Depreciation is an accounting concept (as opposed to depreciation for appraisal purposes). The Internal Revenue Service Code now calls depreciation **cost recovery.** Depreciation allows an investor to recover the cost of an income-producing asset by way of tax deductions over the period of the asset's useful life.

While investors rarely purchase property without the expectation that it will appreciate over time, the view of the Internal Revenue Service is that all physical structures will deteriorate and hence lose value over time. Cost recovery deductions may be taken only on personal property and improvements to land, and only if they are used in a trade or business or for the production of income. Thus, a cost recovery deduction cannot be claimed on an individual's personal residence. *Land cannot be depreciated*—technically it never wears out or becomes obsolete.

If depreciation is taken in equal amounts over an asset's useful life, the method used is called *straight-line depreciation.* For certain property, it is also possible to use an *accelerated cost recovery system (ACRS)* to claim greater deductions in the early years of ownership, gradually reducing the amount deducted in each year of the useful life.

ACRS allows "recovery" (tax deduction) of a greater share of property value in the first years that the property is depreciated. In contrast, the *straight-line* method of depreciation allows for depreciation to be spread out evenly over the recovery period. The ability to take a larger deduction than that allowed under the straight-line method provides investors with a useful tool in developing an investment strategy.

Unfortunately, the treatment of real estate for depreciation purposes has undergone many changes over the last decade, and the new tax law has removed some of the advantageous provisions of the past.

For real property placed in service (acquired and producing income) before 1981, depreciation could be taken over the property's useful life (for example, 35 to 40 years in the case of a new building). The recovery period was reduced to 15 years for property placed in service as of January 1, 1981. The term was increased to 18 years for property placed in service after March 15, 1984, and 19 years for property placed in service after May 8, 1985. Either a straight-line or accelerated recovery system could be used. Those properties retain their former depreciation schedules.

For property placed in service as of January 1, 1987, however, the Tax Reform Act has increased the recovery period on residential rental property to 27.5 years and nonresidential property to 31.5 years. Just as important, only straight-line depreciation is allowed.

The impact on investors of the change in depreciation schedules will be to greatly decrease the allowable tax deductions in the early years of property ownership. The entire property value is still eventually recovered, but the investor must be prepared to have far less benefit from deductions in the early years of ownership.

Deductions and TRA '86

The Tax Reform Act of 1986 limits the deductibility of losses from rental property. The first $25,000 of loss can be used to offset income from any source provided that the investor *actively participates* in the management and operation of the property and has taxable income of no more than $100,000 before the deduction is made. The deduction is reduced by $.50 for every dollar of income over $100,000, and is thus eliminated completely when income reaches $150,000. Two examples will help to illustrate the impact of this law.

1. Harvey has an adjusted gross income of $130,000 and losses of $20,000 from three apartment buildings that he owns and personally manages. Harvey is entitled to a deduction of only $10,000 (as the $25,000 maximum is reduced by $.50 for every dollar of the $30,000 Harvey earned over $100,000), reducing his taxable income to $120,000.

2. Helen has an adjusted gross income of $100,000 and losses of $20,000 from rental property that she actively manages. Helen is entitled to a deduction of the full $20,000 (as her income doesn't exceed $100,000), reducing her taxable income to $80,000.

The deduction applies only when the taxpayer actively participates in managing the rental property. The involvement may be as great as personally managing the day-to-day operation of the rental property with no outside assistance or as minimal as simply making management decisions, such as the approval of new tenants and lease terms, while hiring others to provide services.

The Tax Reform Act prevents an investor from using a loss from a passive activity (one in which the taxpayer is not an active participant) to shelter "active income" (such as wages) or "portfolio income" (such as stock dividends, bank interest and capital gains). An example of a passive investor is a limited partner, someone who contributes investment monies but has no voice in the operation of the investment.

While the deduction restrictions do not apply to people who invest in and *actively* run a trade or business, deduction of losses is restricted for those who invest in a business and then play only a passive role in its operation. Active involvement in the running of a trade or business must be "regular, continuous and substantial" —a greater degree of involvement than that required for rental real estate. The co-owner of a restaurant, for instance, would be required to take a participatory role in the day-to-day running of the business.

Generally, a passive investor can offset investment losses only against investment income. If the passive investor has no other current investment income, the loss may be carried over to offset investment income in future years. If the investment is sold before the loss is used, it may offset what would otherwise be taxable gain on the sale.

To ease the effect of the new law, investors can write off 65 percent of passive losses against noninvestment income in 1987, 40 percent in 1988, 20 percent in 1989 and 10 percent in 1990.

Tax credits. A **tax credit** is a direct reduction in tax due, rather than a deduction from income before tax is computed. A tax credit is therefore of far greater value.

Investors in older building renovations and low-income housing projects may use the designated tax credits (described below) to offset tax on up to $25,000 of other income. This is a major exception to the rule requiring active participation in the project. Even passive investors can take advantage of the tax credits. The maximum income level at which the credits can be taken is also higher. Investors with adjusted gross income of up to $200,000 are entitled to the full $25,000 offset, which is reduced by $.50 for every additional dollar of income, and eliminated entirely for incomes above $250,000.

Since 1976, tax credits have been provided for taxpayers who renovate historic property. Historic property is property so designated by the Department of the Interior and listed in the *National Register of Historic Landmarks* or is property of historic significance that is located in an area certified by a state as a historic district.

The Tax Reform Act has reduced the allowable credit from 25 percent of the money spent on renovation of historic property to 20 percent of money so spent. The property can be depreciated, but the full amount of the tax credit must be subtracted from the basis derived by adding purchase cost and renovation expenses. (Formerly, only one-half of the amount of the tax credit had to be subtracted.)

The work must be accomplished in accordance with federal historic property guidelines and certified by the Department of the Interior. After renovation, the property must be used as a place of business or rented—it cannot be used as the personal residence of the person taking the tax credit.

Prior to the Tax Reform Act, a credit of 15 percent of renovation expenses was allowed for buildings at least 30 years old, even though not designated "historic." The credit was 20 percent for buildings at least 40 years old.

Under the new law, there is a credit of 10 percent of rehabilitation costs for nonhistoric buildings placed in service before 1936. Nonhistoric buildings must be nonresidential property.

Note: Special transition rules may make a rehabilitated property eligible for a 19-year recovery period.

The new law also provides tax credits ranging from four percent to nine percent each year over a ten-year period for expenditures on new construction or renovation of low-income housing placed in service or acquired after 1986 and before 1990.

The new law is designed to eliminate the depreciation "losses" that shielded non-investment income from taxation and formed the basis for tax shelters in the past. Coupled with the significant changes in the deductibility of passive investment losses, the depreciation changes place new emphasis on sound economic analysis of potential investments.

Installment Sales

A taxpayer who sells real property valued at $150,000 or less and held for rental or for sale in the ordinary course of business and who receives payment on an installment basis, may report any profit on the transaction in the year actually received. Taxable income is based on the proportion of the profit to the total contract price received in the year reported. If the property value exceeds $150,000, all gain must be reported in the year of sale, no matter how little cash the seller actually receives at that time.

There are many complex provisions regarding installment sales. The details of any proposed transaction require consultation with an accountant and attorney.

Real Estate Investment Syndicates

A **real estate investment syndicate** is a form of business venture in which a group of people pool their resources to own and/or develop a particular piece of property. In this manner, people with only modest capital can invest in large-scale, high-profit operations, such as high-rise apartment buildings and shopping centers. A certain amount of profit is realized from rents collected on the investment, but the main return usually comes when the syndicate sells the property after sufficient appreciation.

Syndicate participation can take many different legal forms, from tenancy in common and joint tenancy to various kinds of partnerships, corporations and trusts. *Private syndication,* which generally involves a small group of closely associated and/or widely experienced investors, is distinguished from *public syndication,* which generally involves a much larger group of investors who may or may not be knowledgeable about real estate as an investment. The distinction between the two is usually based on the nature of the arrangement between syndicator and investors, not on the type of syndicate.

Any pooling of individuals' funds raises questions about the form of the investors' ownership and the requirement of the syndicator to register the security under federal or state laws. A distinction must be made between direct ownership in real estate versus a security. Blue sky laws are state security laws that require extensive disclosure by the syndicator about the venture to prospective investors. The Pennsylvania Security Laws were passed in 1972.

Securities laws include provisions to control and regulate the offering and sale of securities. This is to protect members of the public who are not sophisticated investors but may be solicited to participate. Real estate securities must be registered with state officials and/or with the federal Securities and Exchange Commission (SEC) when they meet the defined conditions of a public offering. The number of prospects solicited, the total number of investors or participants, the financial background and sophistication of the investors and the value or price per unit of investment are pertinent facts. *Salespeople of such real estate securities may be required to obtain special licenses.*

Forms of Syndicates

Real estate investment syndicates are usually organized as either general or limited partnerships.

A **general partnership** is organized so that *all members of the group share equally in the managerial decisions, profits and losses involved with the investment.* A certain member (or members) of the syndicate is designated to act as trustee for the group and holds title to the property and maintains it in the syndicate's name.

Under a **limited partnership** agreement, *one party* (or parties), usually a property developer or real estate broker, *organizes, operates and is responsible for the entire syndicate.* The person is called the *general partner.* The other members of the partnership are merely investors; they have no voice in the organization and direction of the operation. These passive investors are called *limited partners.* The limited partners share in the profits and compensate the general partner out of such profits. The general partner is not only responsible for the assembled investors but has direct control over the invested commodity—be it real estate, horses or energy resources. The general partner acts as property manager for the real estate and is compensated by the limited partnership for that activity as well as for administrative tasks involving the limited partners. It is said that a limited partnership is only as good as the general partner. For protection of their investment, the investors are totally dependent on the general partner's real estate expertise and prudent decision-making, even though the risk is limited. Unlike a general partnership, in which each member is responsible for the total losses (if any) of the syndicate, the limited partners stand to lose only as much as they invest—nothing more. The general partner(s) will be totally responsible for any excess losses incurred by the investment. The sale of a limited partnership interest involves the sale of an *investment security,* as defined by the SEC. Therefore, such sales are subject to state and federal laws concerning the sale of securities. Unless exempt, the securities must be registered with the federal Securities and Exchange Commission and the appropriate state authorities.

Investors in investment syndicates must be particularly cautious in light of the new tax rules. Passive investors (such as limited partners) are now subject to the passive loss rules and must make investment decisions based on sound income and appreciation projections.

Real Estate Investment Trusts

By directing their funds into **real estate investment trusts** (REITs), real estate investors can take advantage of the same tax benefits as mutual fund investors. A real estate investment trust does not have to pay corporate income tax as long as 95 percent of its income is distributed to its shareholders and certain other conditions are met. There are three types of investment trusts: equity trusts, mortgage trusts and combination trusts. In order to form a REIT legally, a group of 100 or more members must hold shares in the trust. To qualify as a REIT, at least 75 percent of the trust's income must come from real estate.

Equity trusts. Much like mutual fund operations, equity REITs pool an assortment of large-scale income properties and sell shares to investors. This is in contrast to a real estate syndicate, through which several investors pool their funds in order to purchase *one* particular property. An equity trust also differs from a syndicate in that the trust realizes and directs its main profits through the *income* derived from the various properties it owns rather than from the sale of those properties.

Mortgage trusts. Mortgage trusts operate similarly to equity trusts, except that the mortgage trusts buy and sell real estate mortgages (usually short-term, junior instruments) rather than real property. A mortgage trust's major sources of income are mortgage interest and origination fees. Mortgage trusts may also make construction loans and finance land acquisitions.

Combination trusts. Combination trusts invest shareholders' funds in both real estate assets and mortgage loans. It has been predicted that these types of trusts are best able to withstand economic slumps because they can balance their investments and liabilities more efficiently than the other types of trusts.

Real Estate Mortgage Investment Conduits

The Tax Reform Act has created a new tax entity that may issue multiple classes of investor interests (securities) backed by a pool of mortgages.

The **real estate mortgage investment conduit** (REMIC) has complex qualification, transfer and liquidation rules. Qualifications include the "asset test" (substantially, all assets after a startup period must consist of qualified mortgages and permitted investments) and the requirement that investors' interests consist of one or more classes of regular interests and a single class of residual interests. Holders of regular interests receive interest or similar payments based on either a fixed rate or variable rate, as allowed. Holders of residual interests receive distributions (if any) on a pro rata basis.

Summary

Traditionally, real estate investment has offered a *high rate of return,* while at the same time acting as an effective *inflation hedge,* and allowing an investor to make investments through *leverage.* On the other hand, real estate is *not a highly liquid investment* and often carries a *high degree of risk.* Also, it is difficult to invest in real estate without *expert advice;* a certain amount of involvement is required to establish and maintain the investment.

Investment property held for *appreciation* purposes is generally expected to increase in value to a point where its selling price is enough to cover holding costs and show a profit as well. The two main factors affecting appreciation are *inflation* and the property's present and future *intrinsic value.* Real estate held for *income* purposes is generally expected to generate a steady flow of income, usually called *cash flow,* and to show a profit upon its sale.

An investor hoping to take advantage of maximum *leverage* in financing an investment should attempt to make a small down payment, pay low interest rates and spread mortgage payments over as long a period as possible. By holding and refinancing properties, or *pyramiding,* an investor can substantially increase any holdings without investing additional capital.

By *exchanging* one property for another with an equal or greater selling value, an investor can *defer* paying tax on the gain realized until a sale is made. A total tax deferment is possible only if the investor receives no cash or other incentive to even out the exchange. If received, such cash or property is called *boot* and is taxed at the taxpayer's regular income-tax rate.

Depreciation (cost recovery) is a concept that allows an investor to recover in tax deductions the basis of an asset over the period of its useful life. Only costs of improvements to land may be recovered, not costs for the land itself.

The Tax Reform Act of 1986 has greatly limited the potential for investment losses to shelter other income, but *tax credits* are still allowed for projects involving low-income housing and older buildings.

An investor may defer federal income taxes on gain realized from the sale of an investment property through an *installment sale* of property valued at less than $150,000.

Individuals may also invest in real estate through an *investment syndicate;* this usually includes *general and limited partnerships.* Other forms of real estate investments are the *real estate investment trust* (REIT) and the *real estate mortgage investment conduit* (REMIC).

Questions

1. In 1988, the Smiths received capital gains of $22,000, which are:

   a. deductible only from passive income.
   b. taxed at their regular rate on 40 percent of value.
   c. included in their ordinary income.
   d. subject to the purchase price rule.

2. Harvey, a limited partner in a partnership that is renovating a historic waterfront property, is entitled to:

   a. offset no more than the amount he has at risk.
   b. offset his share of tax credits on income up to $100,000.
   c. offset his share of tax credits on income up to $200,000.
   d. offset his share of tax credits on income up to $250,000.

3. Helen has purchased a dilapidated townhouse that is 40 years old and of no particular historic value. Helen intends to renovate the townhouse and live in it. On her renovation expenditures, Helen will be entitled to tax credits of:

   a. $25,000.   c. $12,500.
   b. $0.   d. 25%.

4. Jim traded his office building purchased for $475,000 and valued at $650,000 for an office building valued at $750,000. Jim also paid $100,000 cash to the owner of the other building. Jim:

   a. received $100,000 "boot."
   b. must report $100,000 as income.
   c. must reduce his adjusted basis by $100,000.
   d. now has a property basis of $575,000.

5. When an investor attempts to purchase a parcel of real estate through the use of borrowed funds, he or she is taking advantage of:

   a. leverage.   c. capital gains.
   b. depreciation.   d. exchange.

6. An investment syndicate in which all members share equally in the managerial decisions, profits and losses involved in the venture would be an example of which of the following?

   a. real estate investment trust
   b. limited partnership
   c. real estate mortgage trust
   d. general partnership

7. The increase of money in circulation coupled with a rise in prices, resulting in a decline in the value of money, is called:

   a. appreciation.   c. negative cash flow.
   b. inflation.   d. recapture.

8. If an investor holding an income property wishes to maintain a high degree of cash flow, he or she should:

   I. keep operating expenses low.
   II. charge low rents so there will be few vacancies.

   a. I only   c. both I and II
   b. II only   d. neither I nor II

9. Investor Mary Clark is contemplating purchasing an apartment building for both income and appreciation purposes for $150,000. All else being equal, which of the following choices should yield Clark the largest percentage of return on her initial investment after the first year?

   a. Clark pays $150,000 cash for the property.
   b. Clark gives the seller a $75,000 down payment and a 15-year purchase-money mortgage for the balance at 10.5 percent interest.
   c. Clark gives the seller $15,000 down and obtains a 30-year mortgage for the balance at 11 percent interest.
   d. Clark gives the seller $20,000 down and agrees to pay the seller ten percent of the unpaid balance each year for ten years, plus 10.5 percent interest.

10. For tax purposes, the initial cost of an investment property, plus the cost of any subsequent improvements to the property, less recovery deductions, represents the investment's:

    a. adjusted basis.   c. basis.
    b. capital gains.   d. salvage value.

11. Julia Kinder is exchanging her apartment building for an apartment building of greater market value and must include a $10,000 boot to even out the exchange. Which of the following may she use as a boot?

    a. $10,000 cash
    b. common stock with a current market value of $10,000
    c. an auto with a current market value of $10,000
    d. any of the above if acceptable to the exchangers

12. Capital gains:

    I. may be realized only from the sale of improvements to real estate, not from the sale of land itself.
    II. are limited to 25 percent of an income property's gross income for the year of sale.

        a. I only   c. both I and II
        b. II only   d. neither I nor II

13. Toward which of the following might an investor direct his or her funds in order to hold real estate primarily for appreciation purposes?

    I. farmland
    II. shopping center

        a. I only   c. both I and II
        b. II only   d. neither I nor II

14. A property's equity represents its current value less which of the following?

    a. recovery deductions
    b. mortgage indebtedness
    c. physical improvements
    d. selling costs and recovery deductions

15. When an investor holds and refinances investment properties, using their equities as leverage, he or she is taking advantage of which of the following concepts?

    a. pyramiding   c. recapture
    b. negative cash flow   d. useful life

16. A new tax entity that issues securities backed by a pool of mortgages is a:

    a. REIT.   c. TRA.
    b. REMIC.   d. general partnership.

24

Fair Housing Laws and Ethical Practices

Key Terms

Blockbusting
Civil Rights Act of 1866
Code for Equal Opportunity
Code of Ethics
Department of Housing and Urban Development
Fair Housing Amendments Act of 1988
Federal Fair Housing Act of 1968
Housing and Community Development Act
Office of Fair Housing and Equal Opportunity
Pennsylvania Human Relations Commission Act
Redlining
Steering

Overview

In order to achieve and maintain a favorable reputation in the community, a real estate licensee must be able to demonstrate more than good business ability. It is crucial that the licensee's *ethics,* or business principles, be above reproach. The various state license laws require licensees to adhere to certain ethical practices, as do the codes of ethics subscribed to by members of professional real estate organizations. Further, the federal and state governments have enacted laws that require licensees to follow ethical practices when dealing with the public in order to insure equal opportunity in housing for everyone. This chapter will deal with such fair housing laws and will examine the codes of ethical practices to which most brokers and salespeople adhere.

| **Equal Opportunity in Housing** | Brokers and salespeople who offer residential property for sale anywhere in the United States must be aware of the federal, state and local laws pertaining to human rights and nondiscrimination. These laws, under such titles as open housing, fair housing or equal opportunity housing, generally prohibit undesirable and discriminatory activities. Their provisions affect every phase of the real estate sales process from listing to closing, and *all brokers and salespeople must comply with them.* |

The goal of legislators who have enacted fair housing laws and regulations is to create a single, unbiased housing market—one in which every home seeker has the opportunity to buy any home in the area he or she chooses, providing that the home is within the home seeker's financial means. Because most of the housing in the United States is produced and marketed through the private real estate market, owners, real estate brokers, apartment management companies, real estate boards, lending agencies, builders and developers must all take a part in creating this single housing market.

As a potential licensee, the student of real estate must be aware of undesirable and illegal housing practices in order to avoid them. The licensee must realize that failure to comply with fair housing practices is not only a criminal act but also grounds for license revocation.

| **Federal Fair Housing Laws** | The efforts of the federal government to guarantee equal housing opportunities to all U.S. citizens began over 100 years ago with the passage of the **Civil Rights Act of 1866.** This law, an outgrowth of the Fourteenth Amendment, prohibits any type of discrimination based on race. "All citizens of the United States shall have the same right in every state and territory as is enjoyed by white citizens thereof to inherit, purchase, lease, sell, hold, and convey real and personal property." A summary of federal fair housing laws appears in Table 24.1. |

Aside from a few isolated court decisions, little effort was made to enforce the principles of fair housing until 1962, when President John Kennedy issued *Executive Order No. 11063.* This order guaranteed nondiscrimination in all housing financed by FHA and VA loans. Because of the relatively small percentage of housing affected by Executive Order No. 11063, however, it had limited impact.

The scope of the federal government's fair housing regulation was expanded by the *Civil Rights Act of 1964,* which prohibited discrimination in any housing program that receives whole or partial federal funding. However, as only a very small percentage of housing in the United States is government-funded, this law also had little impact on the housing industry.

Fair Housing Act of 1968. In 1968, two major events occurred that greatly encouraged the progress of fair housing. The first of these was the passage of the **Federal Fair Housing Act,** which is contained in *Title VIII of the Civil Rights Act of 1968.* This law provides that it is unlawful to discriminate on the basis of race, color, religion or national origin when selling or leasing residential property. It

Table 24.1 Summary of Federal Fair Housing Laws	Law	Purpose
	Civil Rights Act of 1866	Prohibits discrimination in housing based on race without exception
	Executive Order No. 11063	Prohibits discrimination in housing funded by FHA or VA loans
	Civil Rights Act of 1964	Prohibits discrimination in federally funded housing programs
	Title VIII of the Civil Rights Act of 1968 (Federal Fair Housing Act)	Prohibits discrimination in housing based on race, color, religion, or national origin with certain exceptions
	Housing and Community Development Act of 1974	Extends prohibitions to discrimination in housing based on sex
	Fair Housing Amendments Act of 1988	Prohibits discriminatory housing practices based on handicap and familial status with certain exceptions for housing for older persons

covers dwellings, apartments and vacant land acquired for the construction of residential buildings and prohibits discriminatory acts such as:

1. refusing to sell, rent or negotiate with any person, or otherwise making a dwelling unavailable to any person;

2. changing terms, conditions or services for different individuals as a means of discrimination;

3. practicing discrimination through any statement or advertisement that indicates a preference or limitation or restricts the sale or rental of residential property;

4. representing to any person, as a means of discrimination, that a dwelling is not available for sale or rental;

5. making a profit by inducing owners of housing to sell or rent because of the prospective entry into the neighborhood of persons of a particular race, color, religion or national origin;

6. altering the terms or conditions for a home loan to any person who wishes to purchase or repair a dwelling, or otherwise denying such a loan as a means of discrimination; and

7. denying people membership or limiting their participation in any multiple listing service, real estate brokers' organization or other facility related to the sale or rental of dwellings as a means of discrimination.

The following exemptions to the Federal Fair Housing Act are also provided:

1. The sale or rental of a single-family home is exempted when the home is owned by an individual who does not own more than three such homes at one time and when the following conditions exist: (a) a broker, salesperson or agent is not used, and (b) discriminatory advertising is not used. If the owner is not living in the dwelling at the time of the transaction or was not the most

recent occupant, only one such sale by an individual is exempt from the law within any 24-month period.

2. The rental of rooms or units is exempted in an owner-occupied one-family to four-family dwelling.

3. Dwelling units owned for other than commercial purposes by religious organizations may be restricted to people of the same religion if membership in the organization is not restricted on the basis of race, color or national origin.

4. A private club that is not in fact open to the public may restrict the rental or occupancy of lodgings that it owns to its members, as long as the lodgings are not operated commercially.

In addition to the general provisions of the Federal Fair Housing Law, the Department of Housing and Urban Development has issued numerous rules and regulations that establish guidelines for the real estate industry in such specific areas as advertising and marketing procedures.

Jones v. Mayer. The second significant fair housing development of 1968 was the Supreme Court decision in the case of *Jones* v. *Alfred H. Mayer Company,* 392 U.S. 409 (1968). In its ruling, the Court upheld the previously discussed Civil Rights Act of 1866, which "prohibits all racial discrimination, private or public, in the sale and rental of property."

The importance of this decision rests in the fact that although the 1968 federal law exempts individual homeowners and certain groups, the 1866 law *prohibits all racial discrimination without exception.* So despite any exemptions in the 1968 law, an aggrieved person may seek a remedy for racial discrimination under the 1866 law against *any* homeowner, regardless of whether or not the owner employed a real estate broker and/or advertised the property.

Amendment to Fair Housing Law. A 1972 amendment to the Federal Fair Housing Act of 1968 instituted the use of an equal housing opportunity poster. This poster, which can be obtained from HUD (illustrated in Figure 24.1), features the equal housing opportunity slogan, an equal housing statement pledging adherence to the fair housing act and support of affirmative marketing and advertising programs, and the equal housing opportunity logo shown in Figure 24.2. When HUD investigates a broker for discriminatory practices, it considers failure to display the poster evidence of discrimination.

In 1974 the **Housing and Community Development Act** was passed, extending prohibitions of discrimination in housing based on *sex.*

Supreme Court interpretation. In 1987 the federal Supreme Court further interpreted the concept of *race* as the court viewed it to be understood in the 19th century when the Civil Rights Act of 1866 was passed. Ancestry or ethnic characteristics, meaning that one possesses certain physical, cultural or linguistic characteristics commonly shared by a "national origin group" were criteria used in the court's decision of two cases. These rulings are significant as the common use of "race," referring to nonwhite persons, is further clarified and expanded. Discrimination on the basis of race, as it is now defined, affords due process of complaints under the provisions of the Civil Rights Act of 1866. These cases are taken to federal court.

Fair Housing Amendments Act. In the 20th anniversary year of the passage of the Federal Fair Housing Act additional progress was made in efforts to create an open housing market. Discrimination in the sale, rental and financing (including appraising) of dwellings based on race, color, religion, sex and national origin as it is prohibited by the previous laws has been further expanded by the passage of the **Fair Housing Amendments Act** on September 13, 1988, to become effective March 12, 1989. It prohibits discriminatory housing practices based on *handicap* and *familial status*, establishes administrative enforcement mechanisms for cases that cannot be resolved informally and provides for monetary penalties in housing discrimination. In addition to prohibiting discrimination against persons with handicaps, the Act makes it unlawful to refuse to permit, at the expense of the handicapped person, reasonable modifications of the existing premises to afford such person full enjoyment of the property. The Act defines provisions for handicap accessibility and interior and exterior design and construction requirements of certain multifamily dwellings for occupancy on or after March 12, 1991. The law does not prohibit the restricting of occupancy exclusively to handicapped persons in dwellings that are designed specifically for their accommodation.

The purpose of protecting familial status is to assure that families, particularly those with children, would have access to housing accommodations. However, the Act provides for certain exceptions for housing for older persons so as to not unfairly limit their housing choices. If all persons occupying a housing facility are 62 or older, then the housing facility is exempt from the prohibitions against discrimination because of familial status. A housing facility that meets the requirements for physical and social needs of older persons may qualify for the "55 or over housing" exemption as well, provided that 80 percent of the units are occupied by persons over this age.

In addition to exemptions to protect housing for older persons and certain types of housing as defined by the Federal Fair Housing Act, nothing in this Act prohibits the refusal to sell or rent a dwelling to or otherwise make it unavailable to any person who has been *convicted* of illegal manufacture or a distribution of a controlled substance, as defined by the Controlled Substance Act. This exemption is intended to allow landlords to protect tenants by refusing housing to such a person.

The law explains the definitions of the terms used above. The Department of Housing and Urban Development (HUD) has also adopted regulations to further define and implement this Act.

Blockbusting and Steering

Blockbusting and steering are practices frequently discussed in connection with fair housing. Though they are not mentioned by name in the Federal Fair Housing Act of 1968, both are prohibited by HUD regulations.

Blockbusting means inducing homeowners to sell by making representations regarding the entry, or prospective entry, of a person of a particular race, color, religion, sex, familial status, national origin or handicap into a neighborhood. This is not to be confused with the rights protected under the law for all persons to choose a neighborhood regardless of the profile of its population, be it homogeneous or otherwise. Rather, it is an act to induce *panic selling,* wherein the blockbuster asserts that the entry of such persons will result in undesirable consequences (such as the lowering of property values) and capitalizes on fears of property owners who then flee the neighborhood. This results in *financial gain*

Figure 24.1
Equal Housing
Opportunity Poster*

*Pursuant to the Federal Fair Housing Amendments Act of 1988, the equal housing opportunity poster will be amended to include discrimination on the basis of handicap and familial status, discrimination in the appraisal of housing, and a toll-free number for determining where complaints can be filed.

Figure 24.2
Equal Housing
Opportunity Symbol

for the blockbuster. The blockbuster purchases the properties cheaply from the homeowners and resells them at a higher price to minority persons. Real estate licensees may be accused of blockbusting if they solicit homeowners using the same representations, thereby realizing financial gain resulting from additional sales activity generated in a neighborhood. To avoid accusations of blockbusting, licensees should use good judgment when choosing methods used for soliciting listings.

Steering is the channeling of home seekers to particular neighborhoods, having the *effect* of limiting their choices. This practice makes certain homes unavailable, which is contrary to the freedoms protected under the fair housing laws. It may be done to either preserve the homogeneity of a neighborhood or to purposely change its character to create a speculative situation leading to blockbusting. Many cases of steering are subtle, motivated by *assumptions or perceptions* on the part of the licensee about a home seeker's desires or preferences for a neighborhood, or an assumption about financial ability. Assumptions are dangerous—they could be *wrong*. The role of the salesperson, consistent with the expertise sought from a licensee, is to *objectively* qualify the prospective home seeker's housing requirements and financial ability and make recommendations based on the individual's personal needs and abilities. The prospective home seeker, then, narrows the field of choices, particularly the neighborhoods to be explored. The licensee is cautioned not to assume that a prospective home seeker expects to be directed to certain neighborhoods. Steering nonminorities is as illegal as steering minorities.

Redlining

The practice of refusing to make mortgage loans or issue insurance policies in specific areas without regard to the economic qualifications of the applicant is known as **redlining.** This practice, which often contributes to the deterioration of older, transitional neighborhoods, is frequently based on racial grounds rather than on any real objections to the applicant.

In an effort to counteract redlining, the federal government passed the *Home Mortgage Disclosure Act* in 1975. This act requires all institutional mortgage lenders with assets in excess of $10 million and one or more offices in a given geographic area to make annual reports by census tracts of all mortgage loans the institution makes or purchases. This law enables the government to detect lending or insuring patterns that might constitute redlining.

It is important to note that a lending institution that refuses a loan solely on sound economic grounds cannot be accused of redlining.

Pennsylvania Human Relations Commission Act

The **Pennsylvania Human Relations Commission Act**, as amended December 16, 1986, prohibits the following activities when they result in discrimination on the basis of sex, race, color, religious creed, ancestry, national origin, handicap or disability, use of guide or support animal due to blindness, deafness or physical handicap or the users of animals as trainers:

1. refusing to sell, lease or finance, or denying or withholding housing accommodations or commercial property;

2. refusing to lend money for the purchase, construction, rehabilitation, maintenance or repair of housing accommodations or commercial property;

3. changing the terms or conditions of selling, leasing, furnishing or servicing housing accommodations or commercial property;

4. lending money under special terms or conditions;

5. printing, publishing or circulating any statement or advertisement that indicates preferences, limitations or specifications; and

6. making inquiries, gathering information and making or keeping records that can lead to illegal action of this kind.

7. evicting or attempting to evict an occupant of any housing accommodation before the end of the term of a lease because of pregnancy or childbirth.

Note that the Pennsylvania Human Relations Act includes commercial property, whereas the federal laws only affect housing accommodations.

Prior to the passage of the federal Fair Housing Amendments Act of 1988 the Pennsylvania Human Relations Act was more protective by prohibiting discrimination on the basis of handicap. The recent federal amendment includes handicap, expands protection to familial status and provides for stronger enforcement mechanisms. Due to these recent developments, the best advice to the real estate licensee is to follow the Pennsylvania law and the protection of familial status under the federal law. The states have until January 13, 1992, to address their own laws and become substantially equivalent to the federal law.

Exemptions

Exemptions as defined in the Federal Fair Housing Act have limited application under Pennsylvania law. The federal *seller* and *rental* property exemptions apply only to privately owned or government housing located in Pennsylvania that is *federally assisted*. The seller and rental property exemptions in the Pennsylvania Human Relations Act would apply in all other situations. Refer to Tables 24.2 and 24.3 for a comparison of the exemptions under the various fair housing laws.

Table 24.2

SELLER[1] EXEMPTIONS UNDER PENNSYLVANIA & FEDERAL FAIR HOUSING

PROTECTED CLASS	PENNSYLVANIA HUMAN RELATIONS ACT	TITLE VIII, CIVIL RIGHTS ACT OF 1968 FAIR HOUSING AMENDMENTS ACT OF 1988	CIVIL RIGHTS ACT OF 1866	PROTECTED CLASS
RACE	Housing offered for sale by a religious, charitable, educational, private or fraternal organization may be sold preferentially to its own members.	1. Single family if: a. the owner is a private individual who owns less than 4 such houses, and b. the owner does not use a broker or other agent, and c. discriminatory advertising is not used. d. No more than one house in which the owner was not the most recent resident is sold during any 2 year period. 2. Any home offered for sale by a religious organization for other than commercial purposes and for its own members—provided that membership is not restricted because of race, color or national origin.	NONE	RACE
COLOR			NONE	COLOR
RELIGION			NONE	RELIGION
NATIONAL ORIGIN			Provided that the basis of the discrimination is ETHNICITY[2]	NATIONAL ORIGIN
ANCESTRY				ANCESTRY
SEX			NOT APPLICABLE	SEX
HANDICAP DISABILITY			NOT APPLICABLE	HANDICAP DISABILITY
FAMILIAL STATUS	NOT APPLICABLE		NOT APPLICABLE	FAMILIAL STATUS
USE OF GUIDE/SUPPORT ANIMAL		NOT APPLICABLE	NOT APPLICABLE	USE OF GUIDE/SUPPORT ANIMAL

1. Excluding privately owned or governmental housing which is federally assisted and subject to prohibitions against discrimination based on handicap or age.

2. This statute does not prohibit discrimination based solely on religion (holding certain religious beliefs) or national origin (being born in a certain nation). It does prohibit discrimination against individuals (1) whose religion is part of the ethnic characteristics commonly shared by a national origin group, or (2) whose national origin or ancestry is revealed by certain physical, cultural or linguistic characteristics commonly shared by or associated with persons of a particular national origin group.

NOTE: Always consult local laws to determine if they provide protection to other classes or allow fewer exemptions.

PREPARED BY THE PENNSYLVANIA HUMAN RELATIONS COMMISSION (Amended)

Table 24.3

RENTAL PROPERTY[1] EXEMPTIONS UNDER PENNSYLVANIA & FEDERAL FAIR HOUSING LAWS

PROTECTED CLASS	PENNSYLVANIA HUMAN RELATIONS ACT	TITLE VIII, CIVIL RIGHTS ACT OF 1968 FAIR HOUSING AMENDMENTS ACT OF 1988	CIVIL RIGHTS ACT OF 1866	PROTECTED CLASS
RACE	1. Owner-occupied building of 2 units. 2. Owner-occupied rooming house with a common entrance. 3. Housing provided by a religious, charitable, educational, private or fraternal organization may be given preferentially to its members.	1. Owner-occupied building with less than 5 units. 2. Single family houses if: a. the owner is a private individual who owns less than 4 such houses, and b. the owner does not use a broker or other agent, and c. discriminatory advertising is not used. 3. Housing provided by a religious organization or a private club for other than commercial purposes and for its own members—provided that membership is not restricted because of race, color or national origin.	NONE	RACE
COLOR			NONE	COLOR
RELIGION			NONE	RELIGION
NATIONAL ORIGIN			Provided that the basis of the discrimination is ETHNICITY[2]	NATIONAL ORIGIN
ANCESTRY				ANCESTRY
SEX			NOT APPLICABLE	SEX
HANDICAP DISABILITY	NOT APPLICABLE		NOT APPLICABLE	HANDICAP DISABILITY
FAMILIAL STATUS			NOT APPLICABLE	FAMILIAL STATUS
USE OF GUIDE/ SUPPORT ANIMAL		NOT APPLICABLE	NOT APPLICABLE	USE OF GUIDE/ SUPPORT ANIMAL

1. Excluding privately owned or governmental housing which is federally assisted and subject to prohibitions against discrimination based on handicap or age.

2. This statute does not prohibit discrimination based solely on religion (holding certain religious beliefs) or national origin (being born in a certain nation). It does prohibit discrimination against individuals (1) whose religion is part of the ethnic characteristics commonly shared by a national origin group, or (2) whose national origin or ancestry is revealed by certain physical, cultural or linguistic characteristics commonly shared by or associated with persons of a particular national origin group.

NOTE: Always consult local laws to determine if they provide protection to other classes or allow fewer exemptions.

PREPARED BY THE PENNSYLVANIA HUMAN RELATIONS COMMISSION (Amended)

However, *none* of these exemptions is applicable involving race, as previously mentioned, nor in transactions involving a Pennsylvania real estate licensee. Section 604 of the Pennsylvania Real Estate Licensing and Registration Act prohibits brokers and salespeople from accepting listings that discriminate in the sale or rental of a property to a person or group, from giving false information for the purpose of discrimination and from making distinctions, for discriminatory purposes, in the location of housing or dates of availability.

Enforcement of Fair Housing Laws

Federal law. *Complaints brought under the Civil Rights Act of 1866 must be taken directly to a federal court.* The real estate licensee should be aware that discrimination cases that are processed directly to a federal court can be the most costly to defend and can result in judgments amounting to thousands of dollars—the most costly price to pay if a defendant is found guilty of discrimination.

The Federal Fair Housing Act is administered by the **Office of Fair Housing and Equal Opportunity** (OFHEO) under the direction of the Secretary of the Department of Housing and Urban Development (HUD). Any aggrieved person may file a complaint with the secretary or his or her delegate within one year after an alleged discriminatory action occurs. HUD may also initiate its own complaint. Complaints may be reported to: Office of Fair Housing and Equal Opportunity, Dept. of Housing and Urban Development, Washington, DC 20410, or to Office of Fair Housing and Equal Opportunity c/o the nearest HUD regional office.

Upon receipt of a complaint the secretary shall initiate an investigation and, within 100 days of the filing of the complaint, determine that reasonable cause exists to bring a charge that discrimination has occurred or to dismiss the complaint. During this investigation period the secretary can attempt to resolve the dispute informally through conciliation. *Conciliation* is a process initiated to resolve the complaint by obtaining assurance that the respondent (the person against whom the complaint was filed) will remedy any violation of the rights of the aggrieved party and take such action as will assure the elimination or prevention of discriminatory practices in the future. These agreements can be enforced through civil action, if necessary.

The aggrieved person has the right to seek relief through administrative proceedings (before an administrative law judge) at any time during the investigation period or after a charge has been decided or may elect civil (judicial) action at any time within two years of the discriminatory act. These procedures are described in detail in the Fair Housing Amendments Act, including penalties. Findings of discriminatory acts may result in civil penalites of $10,000 for the first offense; $25,000 for the second offense within five years; and $50,000 for a third or more offenses within seven years.

Whenever the Attorney General has reasonable cause to believe that any person or group is engaged in a pattern or practice of resistance to the full enjoyment of any of the rights granted by the federal fair housing laws, the Attorney General may commence a civil action in any federal district court. Civil penalites may result in an amount not to exceed $50,000 for a first violation and an amount not to exceed $100,000 for second and subsequent violations.

State law. Whenever a state or municipality has a fair housing law that has been ruled *substantially equivalent* to the federal law, such as Pennsylvania and the cities of Pittsburgh and Philadelphia, all complaints in the state or locality, including those filed with HUD, are referred to and handled by the Pennsylvania Human Relations Commission. To be considered substantially equivalent, the local law and its related regulations must contain prohibitions comparable to the federal law. In addition, the state or locality must show that its local enforcement agency is taking sufficient affirmative action in processing and investigating complaints and in finding remedies for discriminatory practices.

Contact the Pennsylvania Human Relations Commission at any one of the following regional offices:

REGION I	REGION II	REGION III
Pittsburgh Regional Office	Harrisburg Regional Office	Philadelphia Regional Office
State Office Building	3405 North Sixth Street	711 State Office Building
300 Liberty Avenue	Harrisburg, PA	1400 Spring Garden Street
11th Floor	(717) 787-9784	Philadelphia, PA
Pittsburgh, PA		(215) 560-2496
(412) 565-5395		

Additionally, local municipalities have ordinances or commissions that deal with discriminatory housing practices.

Under the Pennsylvania Human Relations Act, complaints are processed in the following manner:

1. The complaint, stating discriminatory practice, can be brought by the injured individual including brokers or agents, the commission itself, the attorney general of Pennsylvania, or an employer or organization.

2. The commission makes an investigation.

3. Based on the investigation, the commission either finds no grounds for the complaint and dismisses it or finds grounds and then acts to correct the discriminatory practice.

4. If the commission upholds the complaint, it will require in a formal conciliation agreement that the violator either make available the formerly denied housing or compensate the injured party to the extent of any losses caused by the discrimination. The violator will also have to take affirmative action to eliminate the discriminatory practice. This agreement has the same effect as a final order issued after a public hearing.

5. When a complaint is not resolved in the conciliation stage, a public hearing is convened, a decision rendered and a legally enforceable order issued.

6. Violations of commission orders are *misdemeanors* with fines ranging from *$100 to $500 and/or imprisonment of 30 days or less.*

The Pennsylvania Human Relations Commission prepares and distributes fair housing practices notices and posters, which any person subject to the Pennsylvania Human Relations Act *must* prominently exhibit in his or her place of business. In addition, the commission requires all licensees to furnish an individual seeking to list a property with an "Official Notice" (Figure 24.3) of Pennsylvania law intended to help a seller or lessor comply with the fair housing provisions. It lists the types of practices considered discriminatory under the Pennsylvania Human Relations Act and it also summarizes the Civil Rights Act of 1866, applicable federal laws and the parts of the Pennsylvania Real Estate Licensing and Registration Act that relate to discriminatory practices.

Threats or Acts of Violence

The Federal Fair Housing Act of 1968 contains criminal provisions protecting the rights of those who seek the benefits of the open housing law as well as owners, brokers or salespeople who aid or encourage the enjoyment of open housing rights. Unlawful actions involving threats, coercion and intimidation are punishable by appropriate civil action. In such cases, the victim should report the incident immediately to the local police and to the nearest office of the Federal Bureau of Investigation.

In Pennsylvania, a victim of such harassment is further protected by the Pennsylvania Human Relations Act, and the Ethnic Intimidation and Vandalism Act, which prohibit coercion, intimidation or threats. The Pennsylvania Human Relations Act prohibits retaliation against those who seek protection under this Act by filing a complaint or against those who are fair housing activists. In Pennsylvania Interagency Task Force on Civil Tension has been established to investigate incidents of this kind. The Pennsylvania Real Estate Commission also investigates discrimination complaints. Complaints can be referred through any commission office.

Implications for Brokers and Salespeople

To a large extent, the laws place the burden or responsibility for effecting and maintaining fair housing on real estate licensees—brokers and salespeople. And brokers and salespeople *must* comply with the laws; it is as simple as that. The laws are explicit and widely known. Anyone who violates them, whether intentionally or unintentionally, should be aware of the legal ramifications. In such cases, the complainant does not have to prove guilty knowledge or specific intent—only the fact that discrimination occurred.

How does a broker go about complying with the laws and making that policy known? As mentioned earlier, HUD regulations require that a public statement in the form of an approved fair housing poster must be displayed by a broker in any place of business where housing is offered for sale or rent (including model homes). HUD also offers guidelines for nondiscriminatory language and illustrations for use in real estate advertising. The agency further requires every broker to take affirmative marketing action in the choice of advertising media and in individual canvassing in order to assure that all interested individuals have the same range of housing options.

In addition, the National Association of REALTORS® suggests that a broker's position can be emphasized and problems can be avoided by the prominent display of a sign stating that it is against company policy as well as state and federal laws to offer any information on the racial, ethnic or religious composition of a neighborhood or to place restrictions on listing, showing or providing information on the availability of homes for any of these reasons. If a prospect still expresses a locational preference for housing based upon race, the association's guidelines suggest the following response: "I cannot give you that kind of advice. I will

Figure 24.3
Official Notice

The Commonwealth of Pennsylvania
Human Relations Commission

Official Notice

Responsibilities of Owners of Real Property
under
the PENNSYLVANIA HUMAN RELATIONS ACT of
October 27, 1955, P.L. 744, as amended

The Pennsylvania Legislature has made it illegal: To refuse to sell, lease, finance, or otherwise deny or withhold residential or commercial property located in the Commonwealth of Pennsylvania because of any person's

---

RACE, COLOR, SEX, RELIGIOUS CREED, ANCESTRY, NATIONAL ORIGIN, HANDICAP or DISABILITY

---

or

To refuse to lease, or discriminate in the terms of selling or leasing, or in furnishing facilities, services or privileges in connection with the ownership, occupancy or use of any residential or commercial property because of any person's

---

RACE, COLOR, SEX, RELIGIOUS CREED, ANCESTRY, NATIONAL ORIGIN, HANDICAP or DISABILITY, USE of a GUIDE or SUPPORT ANIMAL BECAUSE of the BLINDNESS, DEAFNESS or PHYSICAL HANDICAP of the USER or BECAUSE the USER is a HANDLER or TRAINER of SUPPORT or GUIDE ANIMALS

---

or

To evict or attempt to evict any occupant of residential housing before the end of the term of a lease because of pregnancy or birth of a child.

Figure 24.3
(cont.)

OTHER APPLICABLE LAWS EXPLAINED:

The **CIVIL RIGHTS ACT OF 1866** provides that all citizens of the United States shall have the same right in every state and territory thereof to inherit, purchase, lease, sell, hold and convey real and personal property, and prohibits **all racial and ethnic discrimination** without exception in the sale or rental of property.

TITLE VIII of the **FEDERAL CIVIL RIGHTS ACT OF 1968** prohibits discrimination in housing based on **race, color, sex, religion** or **national origin.**

COURT AWARDS: Under either of the above laws, federal courts may award successful plaintiffs actual and punitive damages, attorney's fees, and injunctive relief.

TITLE IX of the **CIVIL RIGHTS ACT OF 1968** provides criminal penalties for the willful or attempted injury, intimidation or interference with any person because of his/her **race, color, sex, religion** or **national origin** who is selling, purchasing, renting, financing or occupying any dwelling or contracting or negotiating for the sale, purchase, rental, financing or occupation of any dwelling or applying for or participating in any service, organization or facility relating to the business of selling or renting dwellings.

REAL ESTATE BROKERS LICENSE ACT OF MAY 1, 1929, P.L. 1216, as amended, makes it unlawful for a real estate broker or salesperson to accept a listing with an understanding that illegal discrimination in the sale or rental of property is to be practiced.

LOCAL ORDINANCES prohibiting discrimination in housing may exist in your locality, and should be consulted for any additional protection these ordinances may provide.

TO OWNERS OF REAL PROPERTY WITHIN THE COMMONWEALTH:

YOU ARE LEGALLY RESPONSIBLE for your own actions and the actions of any agent acting on your behalf. Under the Pennsylvania Human Relations Act and other state and federal legislation which prohibit discrimination in housing, you bear the responsibility for seeing that discriminatory acts do not occur.

PROTECT YOURSELF by providing your agent with verbal and written instructions that in all transactions relating to your property— including all services provided in connection with the transactions— you wish to comply with all civil rights ordinances including, but not limited to: **The Pennsylvania Human Relations Act, The Civil Rights Act of 1866 and Title VIII of the Civil Rights Act of 1968.**

**Figure 24.3
(cont.)**

Under the Pennsylvania Human Relations Act, neither you nor your broker/salesperson or agent may

1. Steer or otherwise direct a property seeker's attention to a particular neighborhood based on the race, color, religion, national origin, ancestry, sex, handicap or disability, or use of a guide or support animal because of the blindness, deafness or physical handicap of the user, or because the user is a handler or trainer of support or guide animals, of either the property seekers or persons already residing in that neighborhood.

2. Volunteer information to or invite questions from property seekers concerning the race, color, religion, national origin, ancestry, sex, handicap or disability, or use of a guide or support animal because of the blindness, deafness or physical handicap of the user or because the user is a handler or trainer of support or guide animals of persons already residing in a neighborhood.

3. Answer questions from or initiate a discussion with persons who are selling, renting, or otherwise making housing or commercial property available concerning the race, color, religion, national origin, ancestry, sex, handicap or disability, or use a guide or support animal because of the blindness, deafness or physical handicap of the user or because the user is a handler or trainer of support or guide animals of prospective buyers, applicants, or others seeking housing.

4. Engage in certain practices which attempt to induce the sale, or discourage the purchase or lease, of housing accommodations or commercial property by making direct or indirect reference to the present or future composition of the neighborhood in which the facility is located with respect to race, color, religion, sex, ancestry, national origin, handicap or disability, or guide or support animal dependency.

5. Engage in any course of action which could be construed as reluctant or delayed service having the effect of withholding or making unavailable housing accommodations or commercial property to persons because of their race, color, religion, national origin, ancestry, sex, handicap or disability, or use of a guide or support animal.

RULES AND REGULATIONS OF THE PENNSYLVANIA HUMAN RELATIONS COMMISSION (16 Pennsylvania Code 43.14) require that all licensed brokers or salespersons with whom you list your property for sale or rent **shall provide you with a copy of this notice** in order that you may be made aware of the laws you are required to obey.

Figure 24.3
(cont.)

COMMONWEALTH OF PENNSYLVANIA
ROBERT P. CASEY, Governor
PENNSYLVANIA HUMAN RELATIONS COMMISSION
THOMAS L. MCGILL, JR., Chairperson

October, 1987

For further information, write, phone or visit the Pennsylvania Human
Relations Commission:
Headquarters Office, Executive House, 101 S. 2nd Street, Suite 300 •
P.O. Box 3145 • Harrisburg, PA 17105-3145
Telephone: (717) 783-8274

To file a complaint contact the regional Office nearest you:

Pittsburgh	**Harrisburg**	**Philadelphia**
300 Liberty Avenue	3405 N. Sixth Street	711 State Office Building
Pittsburgh, PA 15222	Harrisburg, PA 17110	Philadelphia, PA 19130
(412) 565-5395	(717) 787-9784	(215) 560-2496

show you several homes that meet your specifications. You will have to decide which one you want."

It is important for brokers and salespeople to develop consistent work habits that reflect full compliance with the letter and spirit of fair housing laws. This requires not only thorough knowledge of the laws, but a sensitivity to the human emotions involved and an understanding of how compliance is measured. One criterion of compliance is "equal treatment." Within an individual's property requirements, financial ability and experience in the marketplace, all parties deserve the same standard of service from the licensee. A good test is to answer the question, "Are we doing this for everyone?" If the act is not consistently done, it could be construed as discriminatory. A second criterion of compliance is the "effects test." Licensees encounter potential pitfalls in innocent actions that may be viewed later as prejudicial. For instance, a seller asks the nationality of a prospective purchaser. The licensee must consider the *effect* of possible responses on the transaction. If the seller refuses to negotiate or decides to pursue a different course of negotiations, the question of discrimination could arise. Another example is eliminating the showing of a property in a neighborhood because the licensee assumed the profile of the neighborhood would be undesirable to the purchaser. This could have the *effect* of denying a prospective purchaser access to a neighborhood (steering). One cannot control the effects of one's actions. Thus, one must be conscious of how one's actions could be construed. The licensee must remember that issues of nationality, race or other protected classes can have no bearing on a transaction in an open housing market.

For every broker and salesperson, a sincere, positive attitude toward fair housing laws is a good start in dealing with this sensitive issue. It provides effective models for all who come in contact with the licensee. Active cooperation with local real estate board programs and community committees is also an excellent idea. This evidences the licensee's willingness to serve the community and observe the laws and it helps to change public attitudes. Both factors can result in good public relations and, ultimately, more business for the licensee.

In Pennsylvania, efforts have been made to develop positive attitudes and uniform procedures. A memorandum of understanding between the Pennsylvania Association of REALTORS® and the Pennsylvania Human Relations Commission was signed on June 25, 1974, in Harrisburg, Pennsylvania. It is a model for voluntary agreements between the commission and local boards of REALTORS®. In April 1987 the Pennsylvania Association of REALTORS® and the Pennsylvania Human Relations Commission jointly adopted Fair Housing Guidelines. These set forth recommended brokerage practices in sales and listings, marketing and advertising and rentals.

Standards of Professional Practice

Professional Organizations

Years ago, real estate brokers realized the need for an organization to assist them in improving their business abilities and educating the public about the value of qualified real estate brokers. The National Association of REALTORS® (NAR) was organized in 1908 (as the National Association of Real Estate Boards) to meet this need. This association has grown with the business and today is one of the leading trade organizations in the country. It is the parent organization of local real estate boards operating throughout the United States. The professional activities of all REALTORS®—brokers and salespeople who are active members of local boards that are affiliated with the national association—are governed by the association's Code of Ethics. (Note that a licensed broker or salesperson is not required to become a REALTOR®.)

There are also many independent real estate boards and other professional associations that were organized to set high standards for their members, promote their members' best interests and educate the public about the real estate profession. The National Association of Real Estate Brokers (Realtists) was founded in 1947. Its membership includes individual members, as well as brokers, who belong to state and local real estate boards affiliated with the organization. The members also subscribe to a code of ethics that sets professional standards for all Realtists.

Code of Ethics

The importance of adhering to a set of ethical business standards cannot be overemphasized. At least one state real estate commission has adopted a code of ethics as part of its real estate license law and others may follow this example.

The NAR adopted its **Code of Ethics** in 1913. Through the years it has proved helpful to everyone in the real estate business because it contains practical applications of business ethics and statements of good practices that everyone in the business should know and carefully follow. A real estate business is only as good as its reputation and reputations are built on sound business practices and fair dealings with clients, other real estate brokers, and the general public. The NAR publishes interpretations of the Code known as Standards of Practice. The interpretations establish precedents for local boards to follow in hearings that involve violations of the Code. The association's Code of Ethics governs the professional activities of all REALTORS®—the active members of local boards affiliated with NAR. The REALTORS® Code of Ethics and Standards of Practice appear in Figure 24.4

Code for Equal Opportunity

In order to better support fair housing opportunities in its members' communities, the NAR has adopted a **Code for Equal Opportunity.** The Code basically sets forth suggested standards of conduct for REALTORS® so that they may comply with the letter as well as the spirit of the fair housing laws. The Code provides that:

1. In the sale, purchase, exchange, rental or lease of real property, REALTORS® and their REALTOR-Associates® have the responsibility to offer equal service to all clients and prospects without regard to race, color, religion, sex or national origin. This encompasses:

   a. standing ready to enter broker-client relationships or to show property equally to members of all races, creeds or ethnic groups;

   b. receiving all formal written offers and communicating them to the owner;

   c. exerting their best efforts to conclude all transactions; and

   d. maintaining equal opportunity employment practices.

Figure 24.4

Code of Ethics and Standards of Practice

of the
NATIONAL ASSOCIATION OF REALTORS®

Where the word REALTOR® is used in this Code and Preamble, it shall be deemed to include REALTOR-ASSOCIATE®. Pronouns shall be considered to include REALTORS® and REALTOR-ASSOCIATE®s of both genders.

Preamble...

Under all is the land. Upon its wise utilization and widely allocated ownership depend the survival and growth of free institutions and of our civilization. The REALTOR® should recognize that the interests of the nation and its citizens require the highest and best use of the land and the widest distribution of land ownership. They require the creation of adequate housing, the building of functioning cities, the development of productive industries and farms, and the preservation of a healthful environment.

Such interests impose obligations beyond those of ordinary commerce. They impose grave social responsibility and a patriotic duty to which the REALTOR® should dedicate himself, and for which he should be diligent in preparing himself. The REALTOR®, therefore, is zealous to maintain and improve the standards of his calling and shares with his fellow REALTORS® a common responsibility for its integrity and honor. The term REALTOR® has come to connote competency, fairness, and high integrity resulting from adherence to a lofty ideal of moral conduct in business relations. No inducement of profit and no instruction from clients ever can justify departure from this ideal.

In the interpretation of this obligation, a REALTOR® can take no safer guide than that which has been handed down through the centuries, embodied in the Golden Rule, "Whatsoever ye would that men should do to you, do ye even so to them."

Accepting this standard as his own, every REALTOR® pledges himself to observe its spirit in all of his activities and to conduct his business in accordance with the tenets set forth below.

Articles 1 through 5 are aspirational and establish ideals the REALTOR® should strive to attain.

ARTICLE 1
The REALTOR® should keep himself informed on matters affecting real estate in his community, the state, and nation so that he may be able to contribute responsibly to public thinking on such matters.

ARTICLE 2
In justice to those who place their interests in his care, the REALTOR® should endeavor always to be informed regarding laws, proposed legislation, governmental regulations, public policies, and current market conditions in order to be in a position to advise his clients properly.

ARTICLE 3
The REALTOR® should endeavor to eliminate in his community any practices which could be damaging to the public or bring discredit to the real estate profession. The REALTOR® should assist the governmental agency charged with regulating the practices of brokers and salesmen in his state. (Revised 11/87)

ARTICLE 4
To prevent dissension and misunderstanding and to assure better service to the owner, the REALTOR® should urge the exclusive listing of property unless contrary to the best interest of the owner. (Revised 11/87)

ARTICLE 5
In the best interests of society, of his associates, and his own business, the REALTOR® should willingly share with other REALTORS® the lessons of his experience and study for the benefit of the public, and should be loyal to the Board of REALTORS® of his community and active in its work.

Articles 6 through 23 establish specific obligations. Failure to observe these requirements subjects the REALTOR® to disciplinary action.

ARTICLE 6
The REALTOR® shall seek no unfair advantage over other REALTORS® and shall conduct his business so as to avoid controversies with other REALTORS®. (Revised 11/87)

- **Standard of Practice 6-1**
"The REALTOR® shall not misrepresent the availability of access to show or inspect a listed property. (Cross-reference Article 22.)" (Revised 11/87)

ARTICLE 7
In accepting employment as an agent, the REALTOR® pledges himself to protect and promote the interests of the client. This obligation of absolute fidelity to the client's interests is primary, but it does not relieve the REALTOR® of the obligation to treat fairly all parties to the transaction.

- **Standard of Practice 7-1**
"Unless precluded by law, government rule or regulation, or agreed otherwise in writing, the REALTOR® shall submit to the seller all offers until closing. Unless the REALTOR® and the seller agree otherwise, the REALTOR® shall not be obligated to continue to market the property after an offer has been accepted. Unless the subsequent offer is contingent upon the termination of an existing contract, the REALTOR® shall recommend that the seller obtain the advice of legal counsel prior to acceptance. (Cross-reference Article 17.)" (Revised 5/87)

- **Standard of Practice 7-2**
"The REALTOR®, acting as listing broker, shall submit all offers to the seller as quickly as possible."

- **Standard of Practice 7-3**
"The REALTOR®, in attempting to secure a listing, shall not deliberately mislead the owner as to market value."

- **Standard of Practice 7-4**
(Refer to Standard of Practice 22-1, which also relates to Article 7, Code of Ethics.)

- **Standard of Practice 7-5**
(Refer to Standard of Practice 22-2, which also relates to Article 7, Code of Ethics.)

- **Standard of Practice 7-6**
"The REALTOR®, when acting as a principal in a real estate transaction, cannot avoid his responsibilities under the Code of Ethics."

ARTICLE 8
The REALTOR® shall not accept compensation from more than one party, even if permitted by law, without the full knowledge of all parties to the transaction.

ARTICLE 9
The REALTOR® shall avoid exaggeration, misrepresentation, or concealment of pertinent facts relating to the property or the transaction. The REALTOR® shall not, however, be obligated to discover latent defects in the property or to advise on matters outside the scope of his real estate license.

**Figure 24.4
(cont.)**

- **Standard of Practice 9-1**

  "The REALTOR® shall not be a party to the naming of a false consideration in any document, unless it be the naming of an obviously nominal consideration."

- **Standard of Practice 9-2**

  (Refer to Standard of Practice 21-3, which also relates to Article 9, Code of Ethics.)

- **Standard of Practice 9-3**

  (Refer to Standard of Practice 7-3, which also relates to Article 9, Code of Ethics.)

- **Standard of Practice 9-4**

  "The REALTOR® shall not offer a service described as 'free of charge' when the rendering of a service is contingent on the obtaining of a benefit such as a listing or commission."

- **Standard of Practice 9-5**

  "The REALTOR® shall, with respect to the subagency of another REALTOR®, timely communicate any change of compensation for subagency services to the other REALTOR® prior to the time such REALTOR® produces a prospective buyer who has signed an offer to purchase the property for which the subagency has been offered through MLS or otherwise by the listing agency."

- **Standard of Practice 9-6**

  "REALTORS® shall disclose their REALTOR® status when seeking information from another REALTOR® concerning real property for which the other REALTOR® is an agent or subagent."

- **Standard of Practice 9-7**

  "The offering of premiums, prizes, merchandise discounts or other inducements to list or sell is not, in itself, unethical even if receipt of the benefit is contingent on listing or purchasing through the REALTOR® making the offer. However, the REALTOR® must exercise care and candor in any such advertising or other public or private representations so that any party interested in receiving or otherwise benefiting from the REALTOR®'s offer will have clear, thorough, advance understanding of all the terms and conditions of the offer. The offering of any inducements to do business is subject to the limitations and restrictions of state law and the ethical obligations established by Article 9, as interpreted by any applicable Standard of Practice."

- **Standard of Practice 9-8**

  "The REALTOR® shall be obligated to discover and disclose adverse factors reasonably apparent to someone with expertise in only those areas required by their real estate licensing authority. Article 9 does not impose upon the REALTOR® the obligation of expertise in other professional or technical disciplines. (Cross-reference Article 11.)"

ARTICLE 10

The REALTOR® shall not deny equal professional services to any person for reasons of race, creed, sex, or country of national origin. The REALTOR® shall not be party to any plan or agreement to discriminate against a person or persons on the basis of race, creed, sex, or country of national origin.

ARTICLE 11

A REALTOR® is expected to provide a level of competent service in keeping with the standards of practice in those fields in which the REALTOR® customarily engages.

The REALTOR® shall not undertake to provide specialized professional services concerning a type of property or service that is outside his field of competence unless he engages the assistance of one who is competent on such types of property or service, or unless the facts are fully disclosed to the client. Any person engaged to provide such assistance shall be so identified to the client and his contribution to the assignment should be set forth.

The REALTOR® shall refer to the Standards of Practice of the National Association as to the degree of competence that a client has a right to expect the REALTOR® to possess, taking into consideration the complexity of the problem, the availability of expert assistance, and the opportunities for experience available to the REALTOR®.

- **Standard of Practice 11-1**

  "Whenever a REALTOR® submits an oral or written opinion of the value of real property for a fee, his opinion shall be supported by a memorandum in his file or an appraisal report, either of which shall include as a minimum the following:

  1. Limiting conditions
  2. Any existing or contemplated interest
  3. Defined value
  4. Date applicable
  5. The estate appraised
  6. A description of the property
  7. The basis of the reasoning including applicable market data and/or capitalization computation

  "This report or memorandum shall be available to the Professional Standards Committee for a period of at least two years (beginning subsequent to final determination of the court if the appraisal is involved in litigation) to ensure compliance with Article 11 of the Code of Ethics of the NATIONAL ASSOCIATION OF REALTORS®."

- **Standard of Practice 11-2**

  "The REALTOR® shall not undertake to make an appraisal when his employment or fee is contingent upon the amount of appraisal."

- **Standard of Practice 11-3**

  "REALTORS® engaged in real estate securities and syndications transactions are engaged in an activity subject to regulations beyond those governing real estate transactions generally, and therefore have the affirmative obligation to be informed of applicable federal and state laws, and rules and regulations regarding these types of transactions."

ARTICLE 12

The REALTOR® shall not undertake to provide professional services concerning a property or its value where he has a present or contemplated interest unless such interest is specifically disclosed to all affected parties.

- **Standard of Practice 12-1**

  (Refer to Standards of Practice 9-4 and 16-1, which also relate to Article 12, Code of Ethics.)

ARTICLE 13

The REALTOR® shall not acquire an interest in or buy for himself, any member of his immediate family, his firm or any member thereof, or any entity in which he has a substantial ownership interest, property listed with him, without making the true position known to the listing owner. In selling property owned by himself, or in which he has any interest, the REALTOR® shall reveal the facts of his ownership or interest to the purchaser.

- **Standard of Practice 13-1**

  "For the protection of all parties, the disclosures required by Article 13 shall be in writing and provided by the REALTOR® prior to the signing of any contract."

ARTICLE 14

In the event of a controversy between REALTORS® associated with different firms, arising out of their relationship as REALTORS®, the REALTORS® shall submit the dispute to arbitration in accordance with the regulations of their Board or Boards rather than litigate the matter.

- **Standard of Practice 14-1**

  "The filing of litigation and refusal to withdraw from it by a REALTOR® in an arbitrable matter constitutes a refusal to arbitrate."

Figure 24.4
(cont.)

• Standard of Practice 14-2

"The obligation to arbitrate mandated by Article 14 includes arbitration requests initiated by the REALTOR®'s client."

• Standard of Practice 14-3

"Article 14 does not require a REALTOR® to arbitrate in those circumstances when all parties to the dispute advise the Board in writing that they choose not to arbitrate before the Board." (Approved 5/88)

ARTICLE 15

If a REALTOR® is charged with unethical practice or is asked to present evidence in any disciplinary proceeding or investigation, he shall place all pertinent facts before the proper tribunal of the Member Board or affiliated institute, society, or council of which he is a member.

• Standard of Practice 15-1

"The REALTOR® shall not be subject to disciplinary proceedings in more than one Board of REALTORS® with respect to alleged violations of the Code of Ethics relating to the same transaction."

• Standard of Practice 15-2

"The REALTOR® shall not make any unauthorized disclosure or dissemination of the allegations, findings, or decision developed in connection with an ethics hearing or appeal."

• Standard of Practice 15-3

"The REALTOR® shall not obstruct the Board's investigative or disciplinary proceedings by instituting or threatening to institute actions for libel, slander or defamation against any party to a professional standards proceeding or their witnesses." (Approved 11/87).

• Standard of Practice 15-4

"The REALTOR® shall not intentionally impede the Board's investigative or disciplinary proceedings by filing multiple ethics complaints based on the same event or transaction." (Adopted 11/88)

ARTICLE 16

When acting as agent, the REALTOR® shall not accept any commission, rebate, or profit on expenditures made for his principal-owner, without the principal's knowledge and consent.

• Standard of Practice 16-1

"The REALTOR® shall not recommend or suggest to a client or a customer the use of services of another organization or business entity in which he has a direct interest without disclosing such interest at the time of the recommendation or suggestion." (Revised 5/88)

• Standard of Practice 16-2

"When acting as an agent or subagent, the REALTOR® shall disclose to a client or customer if there is any financial benefit or fee the REALTOR® or the REALTOR®'s firm may receive as a direct result of having recommended real estate products or services (e.g., homeowner's insurance, warranty programs, mortgage financing, title insurance, etc.) other than real estate referral fees." (Approved 5/88)

ARTICLE 17

The REALTOR® shall not engage in activities that constitute the unauthorized practice of law and shall recommend that legal counsel be obtained when the interest of any party to the transaction requires it.

ARTICLE 18

The REALTOR® shall keep in a special account in an appropriate financial institution, separated from his own funds, monies coming into his possession in trust for other persons, such as escrows, trust funds, clients' monies, and other like items.

ARTICLE 19

The REALTOR® shall be careful at all times to present a true picture in his advertising and representations to the public. The REALTOR® shall also ensure that his status as a broker or a REALTOR® is clearly identifiable in any such advertising.

• Standard of Practice 19-1

"The REALTOR® shall not submit or advertise property without authority, and in any offering, the price quoted shall not be other than that agreed upon with the owners."

• Standard of Practice 19-2

(Refer to Standard of Practice 9-4, which also relates to Article 19, Code of Ethics.)

• Standard of Practice 19-3

"The REALTOR®, when advertising unlisted real property for sale in which he has an ownership interest, shall disclose his status as both an owner and as a REALTOR® or real estate licensee."

• Standard of Practice 19-4

"The REALTOR® shall not advertise nor permit any person employed by or affiliated with him to advertise listed property without disclosing the name of the firm."

• Standard of Practice 19-5

"The REALTOR®, when acting as listing broker, retains the exclusive right to represent that he has 'sold' the property, even if the sale resulted through the cooperative efforts of another broker. However, after the transaction has been consummated, the listing broker may not prohibit a successful cooperating broker from advertising his 'participation' or 'assistance' in the transaction, or from making similar representations provided that any such representation does not create the impression that the cooperating broker had listed or sold the property. (Cross-reference Article 21.)" (Approved 5/87)

ARTICLE 20

The REALTOR®, for the protection of all parties, shall see that financial obligations and commitments regarding real estate transactions are in writing, expressing the exact agreement of the parties. A copy of each agreement shall be furnished to each party upon his signing such agreement.

• Standard of Practice 20-1

"At the time of signing or initialing, the REALTOR® shall furnish to the party a copy of any document signed or initialed."

• Standard of Practice 20-2

"For the protection of all parties, the REALTOR® shall use reasonable care to ensure that documents pertaining to the purchase and sale of real estate are kept current through the use of written extensions or amendments."

ARTICLE 21

The REALTOR® shall not engage in any practice or take any action inconsistent with the agency of another REALTOR®.

• Standard of Practice 21-1

"Signs giving notice of property for sale, rent, lease, or exchange shall not be placed on property without the consent of the owner."

• Standard of Practice 21-2

"The REALTOR® obtaining information from a listing broker about a specific property shall not convey this information to, nor invite the cooperation of a third party broker without the consent of the listing broker."

• Standard of Practice 21-3

"The REALTOR® shall not solicit a listing which is currently listed exclusively with another broker. However, if the listing broker, when asked by the REALTOR®, refuses to disclose the expiration date and nature of such listing; i.e., an exclusive right to sell, an exclusive agency, open listing, or other form of contractual agreement between the listing broker and his client, the REALTOR®, unless precluded by law, may contact the owner to secure such information and may discuss the terms upon which he might take a future listing or, alternatively, may take a listing to become effective upon expiration of any existing exclusive listing."

**Figure 24.4
(cont.)**

- **Standard of Practice 21-4**

''The REALTOR® shall not use information obtained by him from the listing broker, through offers to cooperate received through Multiple Listing Services or other sources authorized by the listing broker, for the purpose of creating a referral prospect to a third broker, or for creating a buyer prospect unless such use is authorized by the listing broker.''

- **Standard of Practice 21-5**

''The fact that a property has been listed exclusively with a REALTOR® shall not preclude or inhibit any other REALTOR® from soliciting such listing after its expiration.''

- **Standard of Practice 21-6**

''The fact that a property owner has retained a REALTOR® as his exclusive agent in respect of one or more past transactions creates no interest or agency which precludes or inhibits other REALTORS® from seeking such owner's future business.''

- **Standard of Practice 21-7**

''The REALTOR® shall be free to list property which is 'open listed' at any time, but shall not knowingly obligate the seller to pay more than one commission except with the seller's knowledgeable consent. (Cross-reference Article 7.)'' (Revised 5/88)

- **Standard of Practice 21-8**

''When a REALTOR® is contacted by an owner regarding the sale of property that is exclusively listed with another broker, and the REALTOR® has not directly or indirectly initiated the discussion, unless precluded by law, the REALTOR® may discuss the terms upon which he might take a future listing or, alternatively, may take a listing to become effective upon expiration of any existing exclusive listing.''

- **Standard of Practice 21-9**

''In cooperative transactions a REALTOR® shall compensate the cooperating REALTOR® (principal broker) and shall not compensate nor offer to compensate, directly or indirectly, any of the sales licensees employed by or affiliated with another REALTOR® without the prior express knowledge and consent of the cooperating broker.''

- **Standard of Practice 21-10**

''Article 21 does not preclude REALTORS® from making general announcements to property owners describing their services and the terms of their availability even though some recipients may have exclusively listed their property for sale or lease with another REALTOR®. A general telephone canvass, general mailing or distribution addressed to all property owners in a given geographical area or in a given profession, business, club, or organization, or other classification or group is deemed 'general' for purposes of this standard.

Article 21 is intended to recognize as unethical two basic types of solicitation:

First, telephone or personal solicitations of property owners who have been identified by a real estate sign, multiple listing compilation, or other information service as having exclusively listed their property with another REALTOR®; and

Second, mail or other forms of written solicitations of property owners whose properties are exclusively listed with another REALTOR® when such solicitations are not part of a general mailing but are directed specifically to property owners identified through compilations of current listings, 'for sale' signs, or other sources of information required by Article 22 and Multiple Listing Service rules to be made available to other REALTORS® under offers of subagency or cooperation.''

- **Standard of Practice 21-11**

''The REALTOR®, prior to accepting a listing, has an affirmative obligation to make reasonable efforts to determine whether the property is subject to a current, valid exclusive listing agreement.''

Form No. 166-288-1 (11/88)

- **Standard of Practice 21-12**

''The REALTOR®, acting as the agent of the buyer, shall disclose that relationship to the seller's agent at first contact. (Cross-reference Article 7.)'' (Approved 5/88)

- **Standard of Practice 21-13**

''On unlisted property, the REALTOR®, acting as the agent of a buyer, shall disclose that relationship to the seller at first contact. (Cross-reference Article 7.)'' (Approved 5/88)

- **Standard of Practice 21-14**

''The REALTOR®, acting as agent of the seller or as subagent of the listing broker, shall disclose that relationship to buyers as soon as practicable.'' (Approved 5/88)

ARTICLE 22

In the sale of property which is exclusively listed with a REALTOR®, the REALTOR® shall utilize the services of other brokers upon mutually agreed upon terms when it is in the best interests of the client.

Negotiations concerning property which is listed exclusively shall be carried on with the listing broker, not with the owner, except with the consent of the listing broker.

- **Standard of Practice 22-1**

''It is the obligation of the selling broker as subagent of the listing broker to disclose immediately all pertinent facts to the listing broker prior to as well as after the contract is executed.''

- **Standard of Practice 22-2**

''The REALTOR®, when submitting offers to the seller, shall present each in an objective and unbiased manner.''

- **Standard of Practice 22-3**

''The REALTOR® shall disclose the existence of an accepted offer to any broker seeking cooperation.''

- **Standard of Practice 22-4**

''The REALTOR®, acting as exclusive agent of the seller, establishes the terms and conditions of offers to cooperate. Unless expressly indicated in offers to cooperate made through MLS or otherwise, a cooperating broker may not assume that the offer of cooperation includes an offer of compensation. Entitlement to compensation in a cooperative transaction must be agreed upon between a listing and cooperating broker prior to the time an offer to purchase the property is produced.'' (Adopted 11/88)

ARTICLE 23

The REALTOR® shall not publicly disparage the business practice of a competitor nor volunteer an opinion of a competitor's transaction. If his opinion is sought and if the REALTOR® deems it appropriate to respond, such opinion shall be rendered with strict professional integrity and courtesy.

The Code of Ethics was adopted in 1913. Amended at the Annual Convention in 1924, 1928, 1950, 1951, 1952, 1955, 1956, 1961, 1962, 1974, 1982, 1986, and 1987.

EXPLANATORY NOTES (Revised 11/88)

The reader should be aware of the following policies which have been approved by the Board of Directors of the National Association:

''In filing a charge of an alleged violation of the Code of Ethics by a REALTOR®, the charge shall read as an alleged violation of one or more Articles of the Code. A Standard of Practice may only be cited in support of the charge.''

The Standards of Practice are not an integral part of the Code but rather serve to clarify the ethical obligations imposed by the various Articles. The Standards of Practice supplement, and do not substitute for, the Case Interpretations in *Interpretations of the Code of Ethics.*

Modifications to existing Standards of Practice and additional new Standards of Practice are approved from time to time. The reader is cautioned to ensure that the most recent publications are utilized.

Articles 1 through 5 are aspirational and establish ideals that a REALTOR® should strive to attain. Recognizing their subjective nature, these Articles shall not be used as the bases for charges of alleged unethical conduct or as the bases for disciplinary action.

2. Members, individually and collectively, in performing their agency functions, have no right or responsibility to volunteer information regarding the racial, creedal or ethnic composition of any neighborhood or any part thereof.

3. Members shall not engage in any activity that has the purpose of inducing panic selling.

4. Members shall not print, display or circulate any statement or advertisement with respect to the sale or rental of a dwelling that indicates any preference, limitations, or discrimination based on race, color, religion, sex or ethnic background.

5. Members who violate the spirit or any provision of this Code of Equal Opportunity shall be subject to disciplinary action.

The Code of Ethics and the Code for Equal Opportunity are two segments of the NAR's overall equal opportunity program, which is designed to ensure that no person is denied equal professional real estate services. The National Association of REALTORS® has also entered into the *Voluntary Affirmative Marketing Agreement* with HUD in 1976, which was revised and renewed in May 1987. This agreement is a commitment to further the cause of fair housing by creating brokerage practices among signatories of the agreement consistent with the federal laws to protect the rights of all persons in an open housing market, to be conspicuous in their services to the minority population and to encourage their participation in the real estate industry.

Summary

The federal regulations regarding equal opportunity in housing are principally contained in two laws. The *Civil Rights Act of 1866* prohibits all racial discrimination and the *Federal Fair Housing Act* (Title VIII of the Civil Rights Act of 1968), as amended by the Housing and Community Development Act of 1974 and the *Fair Housing Amendments Act* of 1988, prohibits discrimination on the basis of race, color, religion, sex, handicap, familial status or national origin in the sale, rental or financing of residential property. Discriminatory actions include refusing to deal with an individual or a specific group, changing any terms of a real estate or loan transaction, changing the services offered for any individual or group, making statements or advertisements that indicate discriminatory restrictions or otherwise attempting to make a dwelling unavailable to any person or group because of race, color, religion, sex, handicap, familial status or national origin.

Complaints under the Federal Fair Housing Act may be reported to and investigated by the *Department of Housing and Urban Development*. Such complaints may also be taken directly to a U.S. district court. In states and localities that have enacted fair housing legislation that is "substantially equivalent to the federal law," complaints are handled by state and local agencies and state courts. Complaints under the Civil Rights Act of 1866 must be taken to a federal court.

The Pennsylvania Human Relations Act has been ruled "substantially equivalent" to the Federal Fair Housing Act. For this reason, complaints under both federal law and Pennsylvania law are handled by state and local agencies and state courts. In addition, many localities in Pennsylvania have enacted their own fair housing ordinances, and those of Pittsburgh and Philadelphia have also been ruled "substantially equivalent" to the federal law.

A real estate business is only as good as its reputation. Real estate licensees can maintain good reputations by demonstrating good business ability and adhering to an ethical standard of business practices. Many licensees subscribe to a code of ethics as members of professional real estate organizations. The *Code of Ethics* of the National Association of REALTORS® is reprinted in this chapter. The provisions of this and the *Code for Equal Opportunity* suggest an excellent set of standards for all licensees to follow.

Questions

1. Which of the following acts is permitted under the Federal Fair Housing Act?

   a. advertising property for sale only to a special group

   b. altering the terms of a loan for a member of a minority group

   c. refusing to sell a home to an individual because he or she has a poor credit history

   d. telling an individual that an apartment has been rented when in fact it has not

2. Complaints relating to the Civil Rights Act of 1866:

   a. must be taken directly to a federal court.

   b. are no longer reviewed in the courts.

   c. are handled by HUD.

   d. are handled by state enforcement agencies.

3. In his or her business relations, a broker should:

   I. utilize the services of other brokers when it is in the best interests of his or her clients.

   II. not publicly criticize the business practices of a competitor.

   a. I only   c. both I and II

   b. II only   d. neither I nor II

4. Under the Federal Fair Housing Act, complaints of discrimination in Pennsylvania are:

   a. filed with the Department of Housing and Urban Development.

   b. handled by the local U.S. district court.

   c. filed only if all court actions have been exhausted.

   d. a and b

5. Broker Beth Silverman informs homeowner James Albert of the prospective entry of a minority group into homeowner Albert's neighborhood. Broker Silverman, seeing that Albert is very upset, offers to buy Albert's house at a low price. Silverman is:

   I. guilty of steering.

   II. protecting the best interests of the homeowner.

   a. I only   c. both I and II

   b. II only   d. neither I nor II

6. After broker Harold Gorman takes a sale listing of a residence, the owner specifies that he will not sell his home to a black person. The broker should:

   I. say nothing and show the property to anyone who is interested, including blacks.

   II. explain to the owner that this violates federal law and he cannot do it.

   a. I only   c. both I and II

   b. II only   d. neither I nor II

7. The REALTORS® Code of Ethics suggests a set of standards for all brokers and salespeople to follow. Which of the following provisions is *not* contained in the Code?

   a. A REALTOR® should not engage in the practice of law.

   b. A REALTOR® must protect the public against fraud and unethical practices in the real estate field.

   c. A REALTOR® should not accept compensation from more than one party without the full knowledge of all parties to the transaction.

   d. In the event of a REALTOR®'s controversy with another REALTOR®, the matter should be settled through litigation.

8. Under the Supreme Court decision in the case of *Jones* v. *Alfred H. Mayer Company:*
   a. racial discrimination is prohibited by any party in the sale or rental of real estate.
   b. sales by individual residential homeowners are exempted provided the owner does not employ a broker.
   c. laws against discrimination apply only to federally related transactions.
   d. a and b

9. The act of inducing home seekers to a particular area either to maintain or to change the character of a neighborhood is:
   a. blockbusting.
   b. redlining.
   c. steering.
   d. permitted under the Fair Housing Act of 1968.

10. The EZ-Go Mortgage Co. makes it a practice not to lend money to potential homeowners attempting to purchase property located in predominantly black neighborhoods. This practice is:
    a. blockbusting.
    b. redlining.
    c. illegal.
    d. b and c

11. A REALTOR® is prohibited from discriminating on the basis of race in his or her business practices by the:
    I. Fair Housing Act of 1968.
    II. REALTORS® Code of Ethics.
    a. I only   c. both I and II
    b. II only   d. neither I nor II

12. Joe Jones, a black real estate broker, offers a special discount to black customers. This practice is:
    a. satisfactory   c. legal, but ill-advised.
    b. illegal.   d. not important.

Appendix A: Pennsylvania Real Estate Licensing Examination

Modern Real Estate Practice in Pennsylvania is designed to prepare you for a career in real estate. But before you open a brokerage office or a sales-associate's listing book you have to obtain a license, for which you must pass an examination—a test of what you have already learned about real estate laws, principles and practices.

Why is a prelicensing examination important? A test is a measure of your ability to do something or your knowledge of a particular subject. The Pennsylvania Real Estate Commission requires each license applicant to take an exam, not arbitrarily to keep people out of the real estate business but to ensure that those people who practice real estate sales and brokerage are competent.

Real estate licensing exams vary throughout the country in form and content. They utilize every form of question—from multiple-choice and true-false to essay questions and math problems. But whatever test form is used, each examination reflects the attitudes of the state's real estate licensing agency by stressing the areas of real estate knowledge that its members feel are important.

What to Expect on the Exam

Salesperson license applicants and broker license applicants will be given different exams. The salesperson's exam will be less difficult than the broker's. Questions will be in the form of four-answer, multiple-choice problems like this one:

The State of Pennsylvania requires real estate license applicants to pass a real estate examination prior to licensure. This is to:

a. keep people out of the real estate business.
b. raise revenue from test royalties.
c. protect the public from unqualified persons attempting to practice sales and brokerage.
d. all of the above

The exam consists of two sections, one containing questions on general real estate laws, principles and practices and the other containing questions based on Pennsylvania license law. The general portion of the test comprises 80 questions; the state-specific portion comprises 30 questions for salespersons and 40 questions for brokers. To pass the exam, an applicant must achieve a score of 75 percent or better on each of the two sections. Note that if the applicant fails one (but not both) of the two sections, the applicant will be required to retake only that portion (general or state-specific) he or she failed. (The cost to retake the exam, however, will be the same as if the applicant had to retake the entire exam.)

Broker's examination. The Pennsylvania real estate **broker's exam** (uniform portion) consists of 80 questions designed to test the applicant in greater detail than in the salesperson's exam. The broker's exam lasts approximately four and one-half hours.

Questions for the general section of the broker's exam are drawn from the following areas:

1. Real property and laws relating to ownership—ownership of property, transfer of title, encumbrances, public power over property

2. Valuation of real property—appraisal, competitive market analysis, influences on value

3. Federal income tax laws affecting real estate—owner-occupied residential, investment, other tax considerations

4. Financing of real estate—sources of financing, characteristics of loans, special forms of financing, financing instruments, clauses in financing instruments, foreclosure and redemption, terms and conditions

5. Settlement—evidence of title, reports, settlement procedures

6. Real estate practice—agency relationships and responsibilities, listing of real property, real estate sales contracts, other federal laws, specialty areas

Salesperson's examination. The Pennsylvania real estate **salesperson's exam** consists of 80 multiple-choice questions on the uniform portion of the test. The exam lasts approximately four and one-half hours.

Questions for the general section of the salesperson's exam are drawn from the following areas:

1. Real property and laws relating to ownership—legal concepts of real property, rights of ownership, encumbrances, governmental power affecting property

2. Valuation of real property—methods of estimating property value, factors that may influence value estimates, appraisal process

3. Financing of real estate—sources of financing, forms of financing, methods of repayment, terms and conditions, lender requirements

4. Transfer of property ownership—titles, settlement

5. Real estate brokerage—agency relationship and responsibilities, listing of real property, negotiating real estate sales contracts, federal laws relating to fair practices, specialty areas

Pennsylvania real estate law and other topics. The state-specific portion of the exam for both salespersons and brokers covers the following:

1. Duties and Powers of the Real Estate Commission—general powers, investigations, hearings and appeals, fines and penalties, license suspension and revocation, purposes of the license law

2. Licensing Requirements—activities requiring a license, types of licenses, eligibility for licensing, license renewal, change in license

3. Statutory Requirements Governing the Activities of Licensees—advertising, broker/salesperson relationship, commissions, disclosure/conflict of interest, handling of documents and monies, listings, place of business, record keeping, unfair inducements, unauthorized practice of law, licensee/public responsibility, human relations

4. State Fair Housing Legislation

5. Statutory Requirements Governing Subdivided or Out-of-State Land (questions for brokers only)

Note that only silent, cordless electronic calculators are permitted in the testing center at the time of the exam.

Preparing for the License Examination

We have tried to prepare you for the Pennsylvania real estate licensing examination by including in the text the kinds of items usually found on the test. *Your most important preparation for the test involves studying real estate principles, practices and laws.* Concentrate on learning the material by studying *Modern Real Estate Practice in Pennsylvania* and by working all the tests and exercises, paying particularly close attention to those problems you may have originally missed. Remember, you will be asked to apply your knowledge to situations, combining facts and principles.

Taking the License Examination

For best results you should go through the entire examination first and answer those questions you are certain about, leaving the ones you are in doubt about for last. In this way you will at least avoid running out of time to answer a question you know. After you have answered all the questions you know for certain, return to the remaining questions. Guess, if you are unable to arrive at an answer the second time through. There is no penalty for guessing. The answers to the examination are marked on an answer form that is mechanically graded. Therefore you should be careful to mark only the chosen answer block in order to avoid having the answer graded as incorrect.

An electronic testing device called Keyway, an answer pad similar to a calculator, may be used in place of the paper answer sheets to record answers and information. You may apply on a separate application to take the test using this device. After testing you return the answer pad for immediate scoring and leave the testing center with a score card in hand.

One of the most important techniques in taking an examination is to remain relaxed. If you are nervous, your mind may not function as well as it should and you might have difficulty with the material. If you are prepared and have an adequate knowledge of the subject, there is no reason that you should not be able to complete the examination successfully.

Additional information about the examination, test application, administration and scoring is available from Educational Testing Service in the Pennsylvania Candidate Bulletin.

Appendix B: Real Estate Mathematics Review

Mathematics plays an important role in the real estate business. Math is involved in nearly every aspect of a typical transaction, from the moment a listing agreement is filled out until the final monies are paid out at the closing. Knowledge of and proficiency with mathematical equations are important, both to acquire a real estate license and to operate in the business itself.

This review is designed to familiarize you with some basic mathematical formulas that are most frequently used in the computations required on state licensing examinations. These same computations are also important in day-to-day real estate transactions. Some of this material has been covered in detail in the text. In these cases, reference is made to the appropriate chapter. If you feel you need additional help in working these problems, you may want to order a copy of *Mastering Real Estate Mathematics,* Fifth Edition, by Ventolo, Allaway and Irby.

The math problems are presented in narrative form, what we've come to know as "word problems." This presentation requires two different thought processes: (1) interpreting the events described in the problem and (2) extracting and setting up the data for computation. By taking each step separately the student can correctly solve the problem with the least amount of frustration.

Avoid "working the numbers" until you've determined what you know, what you're solving for and what formulas you need. Remember that the formulas used work only if the data is consistent in quantity. For example, two "knowns" must both be yards or feet, annual amounts or monthly amounts. If necessary, adjust the data. Then, solve the problem. Remember that some questions include extraneous data. Be sure that your solution answers the question.

Percentages

Many real estate computations are based on the calculation of percentages. A percentage expresses a portion of a whole. For example, 50 percent means 50 parts of the possible 100 parts that constitute the whole. Percentages greater than 100 percent contain more than one whole unit. Thus, 163 percent is one whole and 63 parts of another whole. Remember that a whole is always expressed as 100 percent.

In problems involving percentages, *the percentage must be converted to either a decimal or a fraction.* To convert a percentage to a decimal, move the decimal two places to the left and drop the percent sign. Thus,

$$60\% = .6 \quad 7\% = .07 \quad 175\% = 1.75$$

To change a percentage to a fraction, place the percentage over 100. For example:

$$50\% = \frac{50}{100} \quad 115\% = \frac{115}{100}$$

These fractions may then be *reduced* to make it easier to work the problem. To reduce a fraction, determine the lowest number by which both numerator and denominator can be evenly divided and divide each of them by that number. For example:

$$25/100 \ = \ 1/4 \text{ (both numbers divided by 25)}$$
$$49/63 \ = \ 7/9 \text{ (both numbers divided by 7)}$$

Percentage problems contain three elements: *percentage, total* and *part*. To determine a specific percentage of a whole, multiply the percentage by the whole. This is illustrated by the following formula:

$$\text{percent} \times \text{whole} = \text{part}$$
$$5\% \times 200 = \textbf{10}$$

This formula is used in calculating mortgage loan interest, brokers' commissions, loan origination fees, discount points, amount of earnest money deposits and income on capital investments.

For example: A broker is to receive a seven percent commission on the sale of a $100,000 house. What will the broker's commission be?

$$.07 \times \$100,000 = \textbf{\$7,000 broker's commission}$$

A variation, or inversion, of the percentage formula is used to find the total amount when the part and percentage are known:

$$\text{total} \ = \ \frac{\text{part}}{\text{percent}}$$

For example: The Masterson Realty Company received a $4,500 commission for the sale of a house. The broker's commission was 6 percent of the total sales price. What was the total sales price of this house?

$$\frac{\$4,500}{.06} = \textbf{\$75,000 total sales price}$$

This formula is used in computing the total mortgage loan principal still due if the monthly payment and interest rate are known. It is also used to calculate the total sales price when the amount and percentage of commission or earnest money deposit are known; the rent due if the monthly payment and interest rate are known; and the market value of property if the assessed value and the ratio (percentage) of assessed value to market value are known.

To determine the percentage when the amounts of the part and the total are known:

$$\text{percent} \ = \ \frac{\text{part}}{\text{total}}$$

This formula may be used to determine the tax rate when the taxes and assessed value are known or the commission rate if the sales price and commission amount are known.

You can use the following diagram as an aid in remembering the three formulas just discussed:

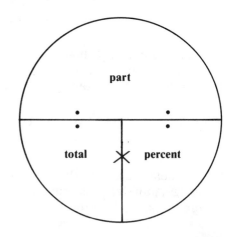

Rates

Property taxes, transfer taxes and insurance premiums are usually expressed as rates. A *rate* is the cost, expressed as the amount of cost per unit. For example, tax might be computed at the rate of $5 per $100 of assessed value in a certain county. The formula for computing rates is:

$$\text{value} \times \text{rate} = \text{total}$$

For example: A house has been assessed at $90,000 and is taxed at an annual rate of $2.50 per $100 assessed valuation. What is the yearly tax?

$$\$90,000 \times \frac{\$2.50}{\$100} = \text{total annual tax}$$

$$\overset{900}{\cancel{\$90,000}} \times \frac{\$2.50}{\underset{1}{\cancel{\$100}}} = \text{total annual tax}$$

$$900 \times \$2.50 = \textbf{\$2,250 total annual tax}$$

See Chapter 11, "Real Estate Taxes and Other Liens," for a further discussion of tax computations.

Areas and Volumes

People in the real estate profession must know how to compute the area of a parcel of land or figure the amount of living area in a house. To compute the area of a square or rectangular parcel, use the formula:

$$\text{length} \times \text{width} = \text{area}$$

Thus, the area of a rectangular lot that measures 200 feet long by 100 feet wide would be:

$$200' \times 100' = \textbf{20,000 square feet}$$

Area is always expressed in square units. To compute the amount of surface in a triangular area, use the formula:

$$\text{area} = \tfrac{1}{2} (\text{base} \times \text{height})$$

The base of a triangle is the bottom, the side on which the triangle rests. The height is an imaginary straight line extending from the point of the uppermost angle straight down to the base:

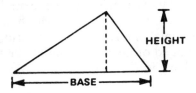

For example: A triangle has a base of 50 feet and a height of 30 feet. What is its area?

$$\tfrac{1}{2} (50' \times 30') = \text{area in square feet}$$
$$\tfrac{1}{2} (1{,}500 \text{ square feet}) = \textbf{750 square feet}$$

To compute the area of an irregular room or parcel of land, divide the shape into regular rectangles, squares or triangles. Next, compute the area of each regular figure and add the areas together to obtain the total area.

Example: Compute the area of the hallway shown below:

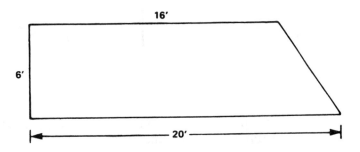

First make a rectangle and a triangle by drawing a single line through the figure as shown here:

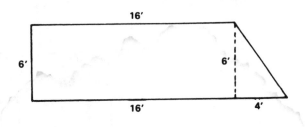

Compute the area of the rectangle:

$$\text{area} = \text{length} \times \text{width} \qquad 16' \times 6' = 96 \text{ sq. ft.}$$

Compute the area of the triangle:

area $= \frac{1}{2}$ (base $\times$ height) $\frac{1}{2}$ (4$'$ $\times$ 6$'$) $= \frac{1}{2}$ (24 sq. ft.) $= 12$ sq. ft.

Total the two areas:

96 + 12 = 108 square feet in total area

The cubic capacity of an enclosed space is expressed as volume. Volume is used to describe the amount of space in any three-dimensional area. It would be used, for example, in measuring the interior airspace of a room to determine the capacity required of the heating unit. The formula for computing cubic or rectangular volume is:

volume $=$ length $\times$ width $\times$ height

Volume is always expressed in cubic units.

For example: The bedroom of a house is 12 feet long, eight feet wide and has a ceiling height of eight feet. How many cubic feet does the room enclose?

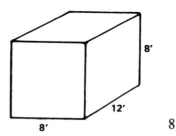

8$'$ $\times$ 12$'$ $\times$ 8$'$ $=$ **768 cubic feet**

To compute the volume of a triangular space, such as the airspace in an A-frame house, use the formula:

volume $= \frac{1}{2}$ (base $\times$ height $\times$ width)

For example: What is the volume of airspace in the house shown below?

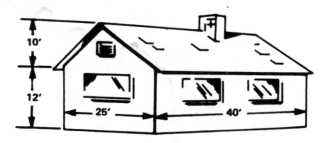

First, divide the house into two shapes, rectangular and triangular, as shown:

Find the volume of T:

$$\text{volume} = \tfrac{1}{2}\,(\text{base} \times \text{height} \times \text{width})$$
$$\tfrac{1}{2}\,(25' \times 10' \times 40') = \tfrac{1}{2}\,(10{,}000 \text{ cu. ft.}) = 5{,}000 \text{ cu. ft.}$$

Find the volume of R:

$$25' \times 40' \times 12' = 12{,}000 \text{ cubic feet}$$

Total volumes T and R:

$$5{,}000 + 12{,}000 = \textbf{17,000 cubic feet of airspace in the house}$$

Cubic measurements of volume are used to compute the construction costs per cubic foot of a building, the amount of airspace being sold in a condominium unit or the heating and cooling requirements for a building.

Remember that when either area or volume is computed, *all dimensions used must be given in the same unit of measure.* For example, you may not multiply 2 feet by 6 inches to get the area; you have to multiply 2 feet by ½ foot.

Prorations

As discussed in Chapter 21, the proration of taxes and other items is customary when a real estate transaction is closed.

When an item is to be prorated, the charge must first be broken down into yearly, monthly and daily amounts, depending on the type of charge. These smaller amounts are then multiplied by the number of years, months and days in the pro-rated time period to determine the accrued or unearned amount to be credited or debited at the closing. Depending on local custom, prorations may be made on the basis of a standard 30-day month (360-day year), 365-day year or the actual number of days in the month of closing.

Questions

1. Broker Sally Smith of Happy Valley Realty recently sold Jack and Jill Hawkins' home for $79,500. Smith charged the Hawkinses a 6.5 percent commission and will pay 30 percent of that amount to the listing salesperson and 25 percent to the selling salesperson. What amount of commission will the listing salesperson receive from the Hawkins sale?

   a. $5,167.50   c. $3,617.25
   b. $1,550.25   d. $1,291.87

2. Susan Silber signed an agreement to purchase a condominium apartment from Perry and Marie Morris. The contract stipulated that the Morrises replace the damaged bedroom carpet. The carpet Silber has chosen costs $16.95 per square yard plus $2.50 per square yard for installation. If the bedroom dimensions are as illustrated, how much will the Morrises have to pay for the job?

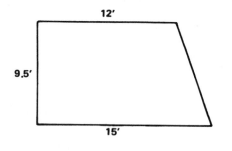

   a. $241.54   c. $277.16
   b. $189.20   d. $2,494.46

3. Hal, Olive, Ron and Marvin decided to pool their savings and purchase a small apartment building for $125,000. If Hal invested $30,000 and Olive and Ron each contributed $35,000, what percentage of ownership was left for Marvin?

   a. 20 percent   c. 28 percent
   b. 24 percent   d. 30 percent

4. Harold Barlow is curious to know how much money his son and daughter-in-law still owe on their mortgage loan. Barlow knows that the interest portion of their last monthly payment was $391.42. If the Barlows are paying interest at the rate of 11½ percent, what was the outstanding balance of their loan before that last payment was made?

   a. $43,713.00   c. $36,427.50
   b. $40,843.83   d. $34,284.70

5. Nick and Olga Stravinski bought their home on Sabre Lane a year ago for $98,500. Property in their neighborhood is said to be increasing in value at a rate of 5 percent annually. If this is true, what is the current market value of the Stravinskis' real estate?

   a. $103,425
   b. $93,575
   c. $104,410
   d. none of the above is within $50

6. The DeHavilands' home on Dove Street is valued at $95,000. Property in their area is assessed at 60 percent of its value, and the local tax rate is $2.85 per hundred. What is the amount of the DeHavilands' annual taxes?

   a. $2,451.00   c. $135.38
   b. $1,470.60   d. $1,624.50

7. The Fitzpatricks are planning to construct a patio in their backyard. An illustration of the surface area to be paved appears here. If the cement is to be poured as a six-inch slab, how many cubic feet of cement will be poured into this patio?

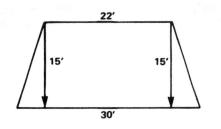

a. 660 cubic feet   c. 330 cubic feet
b. 450 cubic feet   d. 195 cubic feet

8. Happy Morgan receives a monthly salary of $1,000 plus 3 percent commission on all of his listings that sell and 2.5 percent on all his sales. None of the listings that Morgan took sold last month, but he received $4,175 in salary and commission. What was the value of the property Morgan sold?

a. $147,000   c. $122,500
b. $127,000   d. $105,833

9. The Salvatinis' residence has proved difficult to sell. Salesperson Martha Kelley suggests it might sell faster if they enclose a portion of the backyard with a privacy fence. If the area to be enclosed is as illustrated, how much would the fence cost at $6.95 per linear foot?

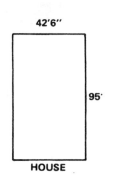

a. $1,911.25   c. $1,615.88
b. $1,654.10   d. $955.63

10. Andrew McTavish leases the 12 apartments in the Overton Arms for a total monthly rental of $4,500. If this figure represents an 8 percent annual return on McTavish's investment, what was the original cost of the property?

a. $675,000   c. $54,000
b. $450,000   d. $56,250

For the following questions regarding closing statement prorations, base your calculations on a 30-day month. Carry all computations to three decimal places until the final solution.

11. A sale is to be closed on March 15, 1986. Real estate taxes for the current year have not been paid; taxes for 1985 amounted to $1,340. What is the amount of the real estate tax proration to be credited to the buyer?

a. $1,060.84   c. $223.33
b. $279.16   d. $1,116.60

12. The buyers are assuming an outstanding mortgage, which had an unpaid balance of $58,200 after the last payment on August 1. Interest at 12 percent per annum is paid in advance each month; the sale is to be closed on August 11. What is the amount of mortgage interest proration to be credited to the seller at the closing?

a. $698.40   c. $213.40
b. $582.00   d. $368.60

13. In a sale of residential property, real estate taxes for the current year amounted to $975 and have already been paid by the seller. The sale is to be closed on October 26; what is the amount of real estate tax proration to be credited the seller?

a. $173.33   c. $798.96
b. $162.50   d. $83.96

14. The buyer is assuming the seller's mortgage. The unpaid balance after the most recent payment (the first of the month) was $61,550. Interest is paid in arrears each month at 13 percent per annum. The sale is to be closed on September 22; what is the amount of mortgage interest proration to be credited to the buyer at the closing?

    a. $666.97   c. $177.82
    b. $488.97   d. $689.01

15. A 100-acre farm is divided into house lots. The streets require one-eighth of the whole farm, and there are 140 lots. How many square feet are there in each lot?

    a. 35,004   c. 27,225
    b. 31,114   d. 43,560

16. Riley's commission on a sale was $14,100, which was 6 percent of the sales price. What was the sales price?

    a. $235,000   c. $846,000
    b. $154,255.31   d. $234,500

Appendix C: Residential Construction Appendix

The illustrations included in this appendix are designed to introduce the reader to basic residential construction techniques and terminology. Specifically, diagrams depicting various architectural styles, roof designs, roof framing systems, exterior structural walls and framing and a cutaway view of a typical house—illustrating all major components—are featured.

For a more detailed treatment of these and other important construction techniques and terminology, consult the book *Residential Construction* by William L. Ventolo, Jr., also available from Real Estate Education Company. If this book is not available at your local bookstore, you may order it directly from the publisher. An order form is included at the back of this text.

Figure 1
Architectural Styles

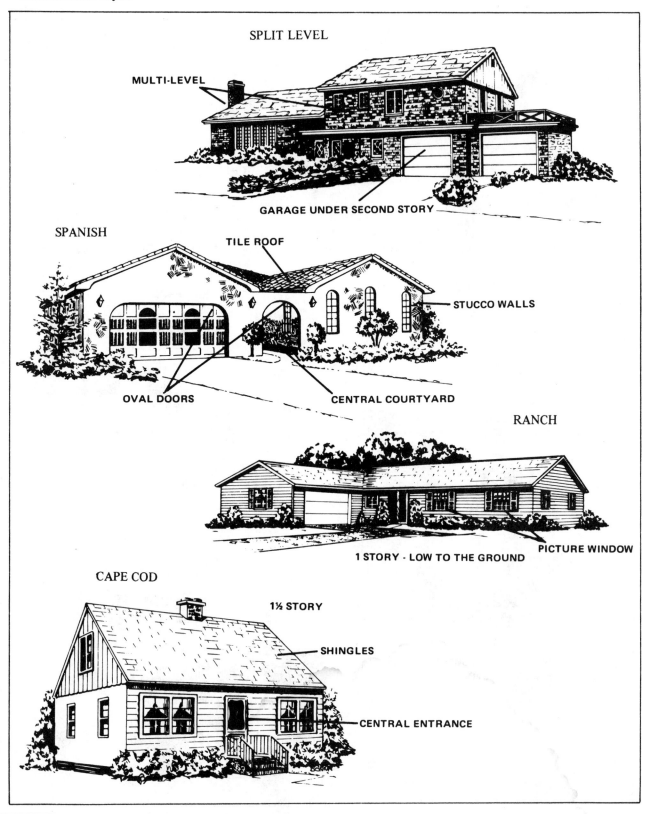

**Figure 1
Architectural Styles
(Continued)**

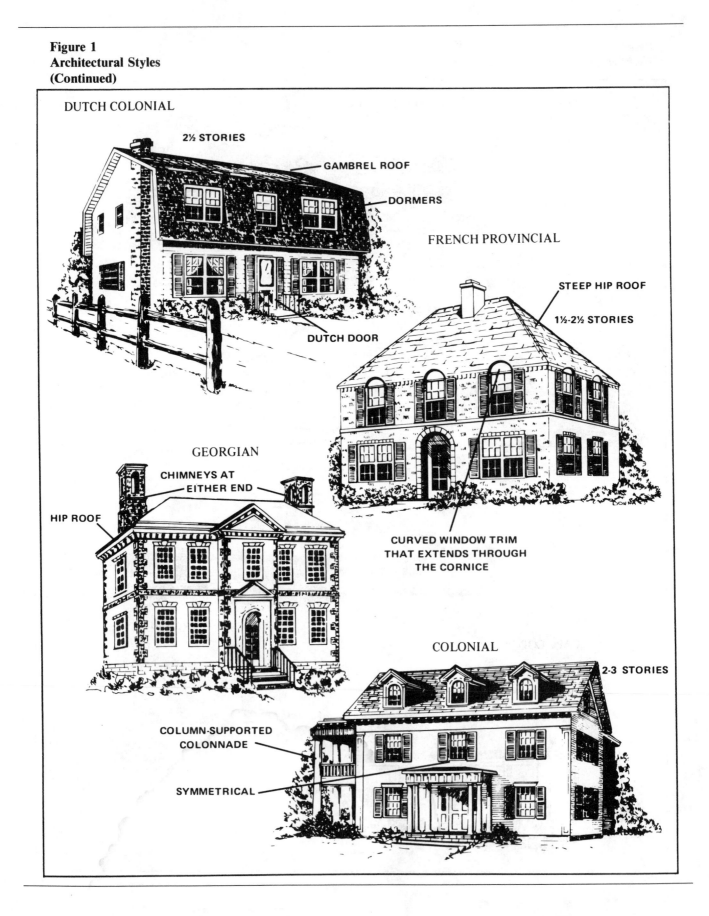

**Figure 2
Roof Designs**

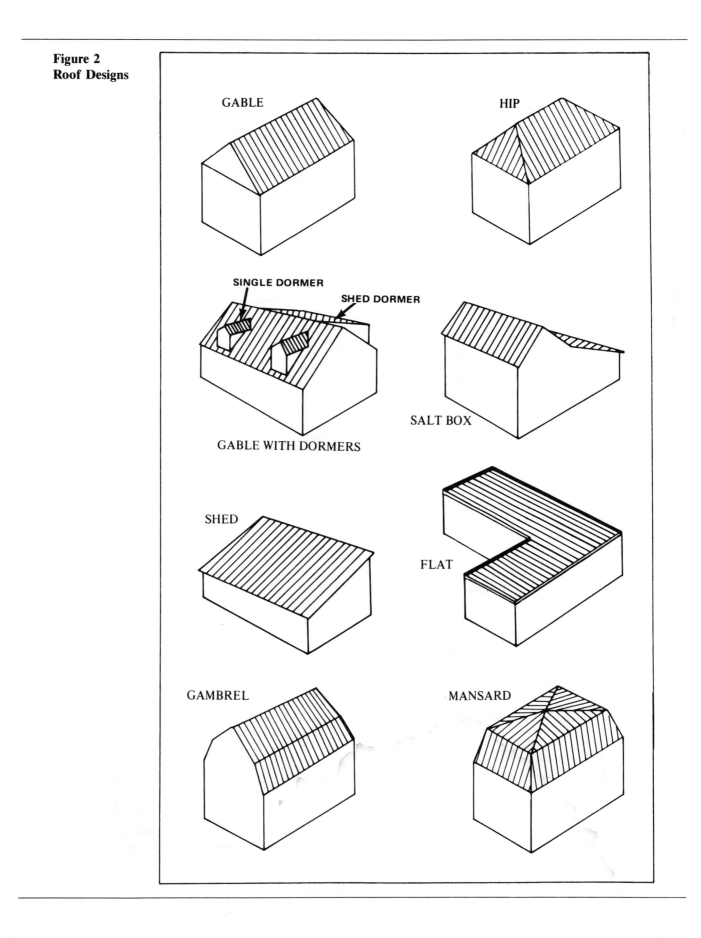

**Figure 3
Roof Framing Systems**

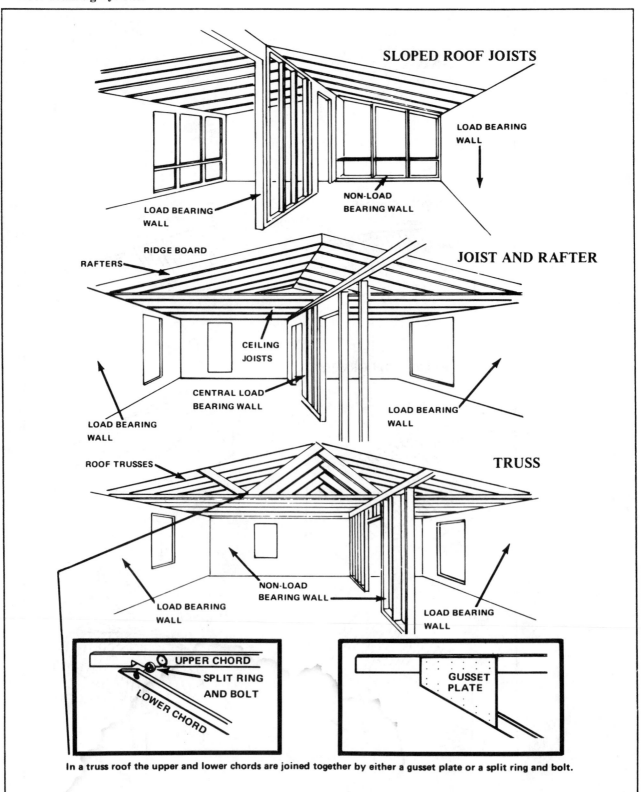

SLOPED ROOF JOISTS

LOAD BEARING WALL

LOAD BEARING WALL

NON-LOAD BEARING WALL

JOIST AND RAFTER

RIDGE BOARD

RAFTERS

CEILING JOISTS

CENTRAL LOAD BEARING WALL

LOAD BEARING WALL

LOAD BEARING WALL

TRUSS

ROOF TRUSSES

NON-LOAD BEARING WALL

LOAD BEARING WALL

LOAD BEARING WALL

UPPER CHORD

SPLIT RING AND BOLT

LOWER CHORD

GUSSET PLATE

In a truss roof the upper and lower chords are joined together by either a gusset plate or a split ring and bolt.

**Figure 4
Exterior Structural
Walls and Framing**

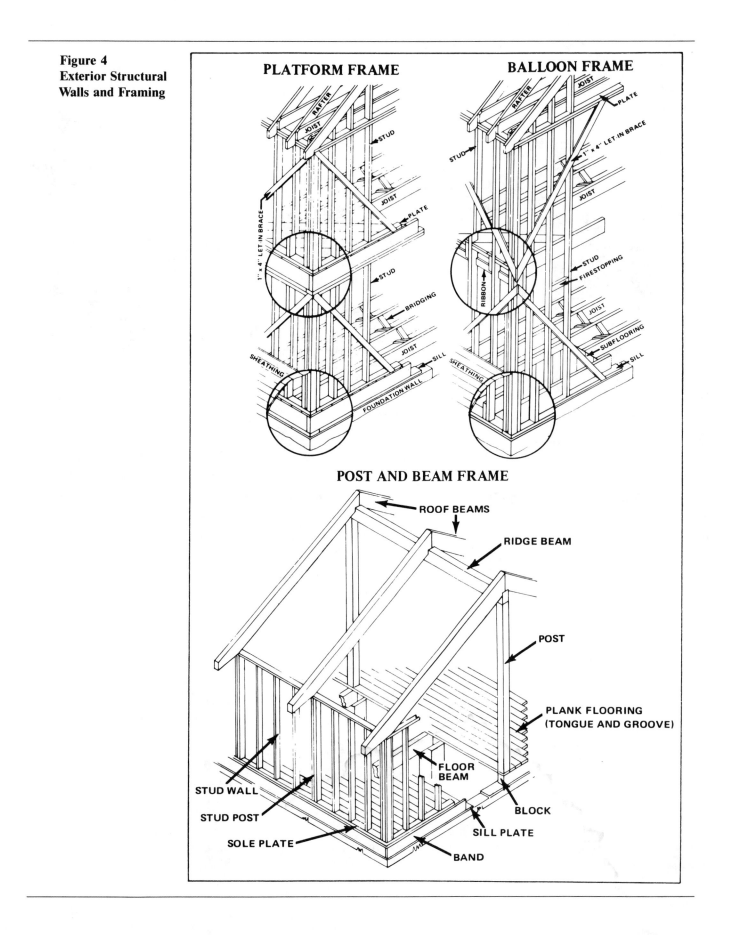

PLATFORM FRAME

BALLOON FRAME

POST AND BEAM FRAME

Figure 4
Exterior Structural
Walls and Framing
(Continued)

HOUSE DIAGRAM

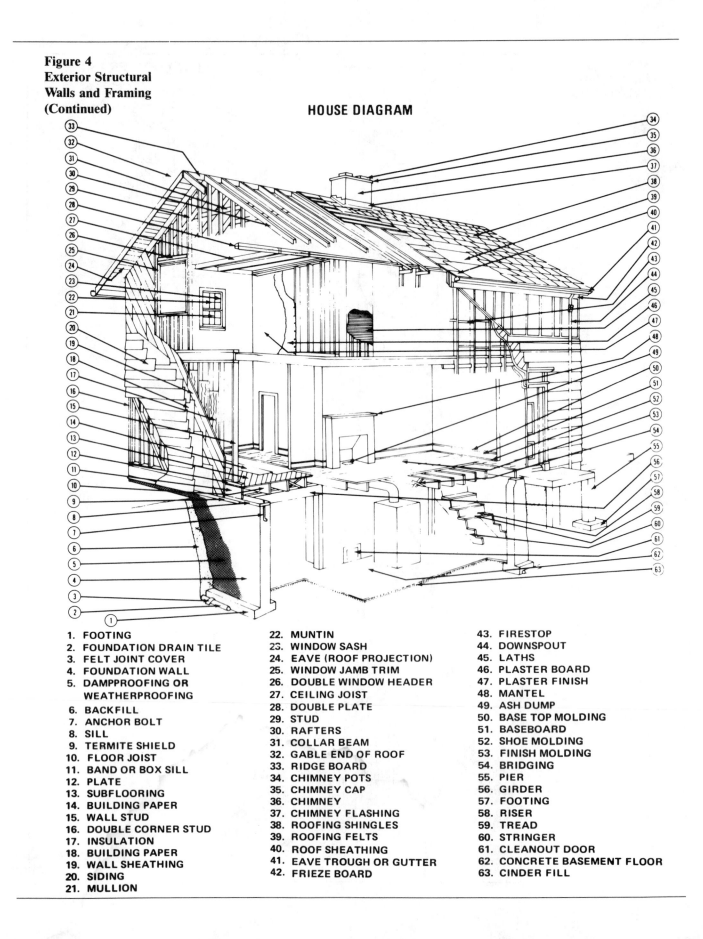

1. FOOTING	22. MUNTIN	43. FIRESTOP
2. FOUNDATION DRAIN TILE	23. WINDOW SASH	44. DOWNSPOUT
3. FELT JOINT COVER	24. EAVE (ROOF PROJECTION)	45. LATHS
4. FOUNDATION WALL	25. WINDOW JAMB TRIM	46. PLASTER BOARD
5. DAMPPROOFING OR WEATHERPROOFING	26. DOUBLE WINDOW HEADER	47. PLASTER FINISH
	27. CEILING JOIST	48. MANTEL
6. BACKFILL	28. DOUBLE PLATE	49. ASH DUMP
7. ANCHOR BOLT	29. STUD	50. BASE TOP MOLDING
8. SILL	30. RAFTERS	51. BASEBOARD
9. TERMITE SHIELD	31. COLLAR BEAM	52. SHOE MOLDING
10. FLOOR JOIST	32. GABLE END OF ROOF	53. FINISH MOLDING
11. BAND OR BOX SILL	33. RIDGE BOARD	54. BRIDGING
12. PLATE	34. CHIMNEY POTS	55. PIER
13. SUBFLOORING	35. CHIMNEY CAP	56. GIRDER
14. BUILDING PAPER	36. CHIMNEY	57. FOOTING
15. WALL STUD	37. CHIMNEY FLASHING	58. RISER
16. DOUBLE CORNER STUD	38. ROOFING SHINGLES	59. TREAD
17. INSULATION	39. ROOFING FELTS	60. STRINGER
18. BUILDING PAPER	40. ROOF SHEATHING	61. CLEANOUT DOOR
19. WALL SHEATHING	41. EAVE TROUGH OR GUTTER	62. CONCRETE BASEMENT FLOOR
20. SIDING	42. FRIEZE BOARD	63. CINDER FILL
21. MULLION		

REAL ESTATE LICENSING AND REGISTRATION ACT

STATE REAL ESTATE COMMISSION

COMMONWEALTH OF PENNSYLVANIA

"REAL ESTATE LICENSING & REGISTRATION ACT"
Act of 1980, P.L. 15, No. 9

AN ACT

Establishing the State Real Estate Commission and providing for the licensing of real estate brokers and salesmen.

The General Assembly fo the Commonwealth of Pennsylvania hereby enacts as follows:

TABLE OF CONTENTS

CHAPTER 1
GENERAL PROVISIONS

Section 101. Short title.

This act shall be known and may be cited as the "Real Estate Licensing and Registration Act."

(101 amended Mar. 7, 1982, P.L. 158, No. 50)

CHAPTER 2
DEFINITIONS

Section 201. Definitions.

The following words and phrases when used in this act shall have, unless the context clearly indicates otherwise, the meanings given to them in this section:

"Associate broker." A broker employed by another broker.

"Broker." Any person who, for another and for a fee, commission or other valuable consideration:

(1) negotiates with or aids any person in locating or obtaining for purchase, lease or acquisition of interest in any real estate;

(2) negotiates the listing, sale, purchase, exchange, lease, time share and similarly designated interests, financing or option for any real estate;

(3) manages or appraises any real estate;

(4) represents himself as a real estate consultant, counsellor, house finder;

(5) undertakes to promote the sale, exchange, purchase or rental of real estate: Provided, however, That this provision shall not include any person whose main business is that of advertising, promotion or public relations; or

(6) attempts to perform any of the above acts.

"Builder-owner salesperson." Any person who is a full-time employee of a builder-owner of single and multifamily dwellings located within the Commonwealth and as such employee shall be authorized and empowered to list for sale, sell or offer for sale, or to negotiate the sale or exchange of real estate, or to lease or rent, or offer to lease, rent or place for rent, any real estate owned by his builder-owner employer, or collect or offer, or attempt to collect, rent for the use of real estate owned by his builder-owner employer, for and on behalf of such builder-owner employer. The term does not include any person employed by an owner of real estate for the purpose of managing or maintaining multifamily residential property: Provided, however, That such person is not authorized or empowered by such owner to enter into leases on behalf of the owner, to negotiate terms or conditions of occupancy with current or prospective tenants, or to hold money belonging to tenants other than on behalf of the owner. The term "negotiate," as used in this definition does not mean the transmission of information between the owner and current or prospective tenants, such as rental amounts, building rules and regulations or leasing determinations, so long as the owner retains the authority to make all such decisions.

"Cemetery." A place for the disposal or burial of deceased human beings, by cremation or in a grave, mausoleum, vault, columbarium or other receptacle, but the term does not include a private family cemetery.

"Cemetery company." Any person who offers or sells to the public the ownership, or the right to use, any cemetery lot.

"Commission." The State Real Estate Commission.

"Commissioner." Commissioner of Professional and Occupational Affairs.

"Department." The Department of State acting throught the Commissioner of Professional and Occupational Affairs.

"Employ, employed, employee, employment." The use of the words employ, employed, employee, or employment in this act shall apply to the relationship of independent contractor as well as to the relationship of employment, except as applied to builder-owner salespersons.

"Limited broker." Any person engaging in or carrying on the business or act in the capacity of a broker within the Commonwealth exclusively within the limited field or branch of business which applies to cemetery lots, plots and mausoleum spaces or openings.

"Limited salesperson." Any person employed by a broker or limited broker to perform duties as defined herein under "limited broker". No person employed by a broker to perform duties other than those activities as defined herein under "limited broker" shall be required to be licensed as a limited salesperson.

"Person." Any individual, corporation, partnership, association or other entity foreign or domestic.

"Real estate." Any interest or estate in land, whether corporeal, incorporeal, freehold or nonfreehold, whether the land is situated in this Commonwealth or elsewhere including leasehold interest and time share and similarly designated interests. A sale of a mobile home shall be deemed to be a transfer of an interest in real estate if accompanied by the assignment of the lease or sale of the land on which the mobile home is situated.

"Rental listing referral agent." Any person who owns or manages a business which collects rental information for the purpose of referring prospective tenants to rental units or locations of such units. The term "rental listing referral agent" shall not include any employee or official of any public housing authority created pursuant to State or Federal law.

"Salesperson." Any person employed by a licensed real estate broker to list for sale, sell or offer for sale, to buy or offer to buy or to negotiate the purchase or sale or exchange of real estate or to negotiate a loan on real estate or to lease or rent or offer to lease, rent or place for rent any real estate or collect or offer or attempt to collect rent for the use of real estate for or in behalf of such real estate broker. No person employed by a broker to perform duties other than those activities as defined herein under "broker" shall be required to be licensed as a salesperson.

"School." Any person who conducts classes in real estate subjects but is not a college, university or institute of higher learning duly accredited by the Middle States Association of Colleges and Secondary Schools or equivalent accreditation.

"Time share." The right, however evidenced, to use or occupy a dwelling unit held in fee simple or by lease according to an arrangement allocating use and occupancy rights between other similar users.

(201 amended Mar. 29, 1984, P.L. 162, No. 32)

Section 202. State Real Estate Commission.

(a) The State Real Estate Commission is hereby created and shall consist of the Commissioner of Professional and Occupational Affairs; the Director of the Bureau of Consumer Protection, or his designee; three members who shall be persons representing the public at large; five other persons, each of whom shall at the time of his appointment be a licensed and qualified real estate broker under the existing law of this Commonwealth, and shall have been engaged in the real estate business in this Commonwealth for a period of not less than ten years immediately prior to his appointment; and one other person who shall have been licensed as a real estate broker, or limited real estate broker, for a period of at least five years and shall have been engaged in selling cemetery lots for at least ten years immediately prior to his appointment. Each of said members of the commission shall be appointed by the Governor.

(b) The term of office of each of said members shall be five years from his appointment, or until his successor has been appointed and qualified but not longer than six months beyond the five-year period. In the event that any of said members shall die or resign during his term of office, his successor shall be appointed in the same way and with the same qualifications as above set forth and shall hold office for the unexpired term.

(c) Six members of the commission shall constitute a quorum. The commission shall elect a secretary from among its members. A commission member who fails to attend three consecutive meetings shall forfeit his seat unless the Commissioner of Professional and Occupational Affairs, upon written request from the member, finds that the member should be excused from a meeting because of illness or the death of a family member.

(d) Each member of the commission other than the Commissioner of Professional and Occupational Affairs shall receive reimbursement for reasonable expenses in accordance with Commonwealth regulations and per diem compensation at the rate of $60 per day for the time actually devoted to the business of the commission.

(e) In addition to regularly scheduled meetings of the commission, there shall be at least one public meeting each year in Pittsburgh, one public meeting each year in Philadelphia and one public meeting each year in Harrisburg. At least 15 days prior to the holding of any public meeting pursuant to this subsection, the Commission shall give public notice of the meeting in a newspaper of general circulation in each of the areas where the public meeting is to be held. The purpose of these special meetings shall be to solicit from members of the public suggestions, comments and objections about real estate practice in this Commonwealth.

(202 added Mar. 29, 1984, P.L. 162, No.32)

CHAPTER 3
APPLICATION OF THE ACT AND PENALTIES

Section 301. Unlawful to conduct business without license or registration certificate.

It shall be unlawful for any person, directly or indirectly to engage in or conduct, or to advertise or hold himself out as engaging in or conducting the business, or acting in the capacity of a broker or salesperson, limited broker, limited salesperson, builder-owner salesperson, rental listing referral agent or cemetery company within this Commonwealth without first being licensed or registered as provided in this act, unless he is exempted from obtaining a license or registration certificate under the provisions of section 304.

(301 amended Mar. 29. 1984, P.L. 162, No. 32)

Section 302. Civil suits.

No action or suit shall be instituted, nor recovery be had in any court of this Commonwealth by any person for compensation for any act done or service rendered, the doing or rendering of which is prohibited under the provisions of this act by a person other than a licensed broker, salesperson, limited broker, limited salesperson, builder-owner salesperson or rental listing referral agent, unless such person was duly licensed and registered hereunder as broker or salesperson at the time of offering to perform any such act or service or procuring any promise or contract for the payment of compensation for any such contemplated act or service.

Any person who shall engage in or carry on the business, or act in the capacity of a broker, salesperson, limited broker, limited salesperson, builder-owner salesperson, rental listing referral agent or cemetery company, within this Commonwealth, without a license or registration certificate, or shall carry on or continue business after the suspension or revocation of any such license or registration certificate issued to him, or shall employ any person as a salesperson or limited salesperson to whom a license has not been issued, or whose license or registration certificate as such shall have been revoked or suspended, shall be guilty of a summary offense and upon conviction thereof for a first offense shall be sentenced to pay a fine not exceeding $500 or suffer imprisonment, not exceeding three months, or both and for a second or subsequent offense shall be guilty of a felony of the third degree and upon conviction thereof, shall be sentenced to pay a fine of not less than $2,000 but not more than $5,000 or to imprisonment for not less than one year but not more than two years, or both.

(303 amended Mar. 29, 1984, P.L. 162, No.32)

Section 304. Exclusions.

Except as otherwise provided in this act, the provisions of this act shall not apply to the following:

(1) An owner of real estate with respect to property owned or leased by such owner. In the case of a partnership or corporation, this exclusion shall not extend to more than five of its partners or officers, respectively, nor to other partnership or corporation personnel or employees.

(2) The employees of a public utility acting in the ordinary course of utility related business under the provisions of Title 66 of the Pennsylvania Consolidated Statutes (relating to public utilities), with respect to negotiating the purchase, sale or lease of property.

(3) The officers or employees of a partnership or corporation whose principal business is the discovery, extraction, distribution or transmission of energy or mineral resources, provided that the purchase, sale or lease of real estate is a common and necessary transaction in the conduct of such principal business.

(4) The services rendered by an attorney-in-fact under an executed and recorded power of attorney from the owner or lessor (provided such power of attorney is not utilized to circumvent the intent of this act) or by an attorney at law.

(5) A person acting as trustee in bankruptcy, administrator, executor, trustee or guardian while acting under a court order or under the authority of a will or of a trust instrument.

(6) The elected officer of any banking institution or trust company operating under Federal or State banking laws where only the real estate of the banking institution or trust company is involved.

(7) Any officer or employee of a cemetery company who, as incidental to his principal duties and without remuneration therefor, shows lots in such company's cemetery to persons for their use as a family burial lot and who accepts deposits on such lots for the representatives of the cemetery company legally authorized to sell the same.

(8) Cemetery companies and cemeteries owned or controlled by a bona fide church or religious congregation or fraternal organization or by any association created by a bona fide church or religious organization or by a fraternal organization.

(9) An auctioneer licensed under the act of September 29, 1961 (P.L. 1745, No. 708), known as "The Auctioneers' License Act," while performing authorized duties at any bona fide auction.

(304 amended Mar. 29, 1984, P.L. 162. No. 32)

Section 305. Civil penalty.

In addition to any other civil remedy or criminal penalty provided for in this act, the commission, by a vote of the majority of the maximum number of the authorized membership of the commission as provided by law, or by a vote of the majority of the duly qualified and confirmed membership or a minimum of five members, whichever is greater, may levy a civil penalty of up to $1,000 on any current licensee who violates any provision of this act or on any person who practices real estate without being properly licensed to do so under this act. The commission shall levy this penalty only after affording the accused party the opportunity for a hearing, as provided in Title 2 of the Pennsylvania Consolidated Statutes (relating to administrative law and procedure).

(305 added Mar. 29, 1984, P.L. 162, No. 32)

CHAPTER 4
POWERS AND DUTIES OF THE STATE REAL ESTATE COMMISSION — GENERAL

Section 401. Duty to issue licenses and registration certificates.

It shall be the duty of the department to issue licenses and registration certificates to any person who shall comply with the provisions of this act.

(401 amended Mar. 29, 1984, P.L. 162, No. 32)

Section 402. Approval of schools.

Any school which shall offer or conduct any course or courses of study in real estate shall first obtain approval from, and thereafter abide by the rules and regulations of the commission covering such schools.

Section 403. Authority to examine applicants.

The commission is empowered to prescribe the subjects to be tested. The department shall arrange for the services of professional testing services to write and administer examinations on behalf of the commission in accordance with commission guidance and approval.

Section 404. Power to promulgate regulations.

The commission shall have the power to promulgate rules or regulations in order to administer and effectuate the purposes of this act. All existing rules or regulations shall remain in full force and effect until modified by the commission.

(404 amended Mar. 29, 1984, P.L. 162, No. 32)

Section 405. Duty to keep records confidential.

(405 repealed Mar. 29, 1984, P.L. 162, N.32)

Section 406. Administration and enforcement.

The commission shall have the power and its duty shall be to administer and enforce the laws of the Commonwealth relating to:

(1) Those activities involving real estate for which licensing is required under this act and to instruct and require its agents to bring prosecutions for unauthorized and unlawful practice.

(2) Those activities involving cemeteries and cemetery companies for which registration is required under this act and to instruct and require its agents to bring prosecutions for unauthorized or unlawful activities.

(406 amended Mar. 7, 1982, P.L. 158, No. 50)

Section 407. Fees.

(a) All fees required under this act shall be fixed by the commission, by regulation and shall be subject to review in accordance with the act of June 25, 1982 (P.L. 633, No. 181), known as the "Regulatory Review Act." If the projected revenues to be generated by fees, fines and civil penalties imposed in accordance with the provisions of this act are not sufficient to match expenditures over a two-year period, the commission shall increase those fees by regulation, subject to review in accordance with the "Regulatory Review Act," such that the projected revenue will meet or exceed projected expenditures.

(b) If the Bureau of Professional and Occupational Affairs determine that the fees established by the commission are inadequate to meet the minimum enforcement efforts required, then the bureau, after consultation with the commission, shall increase the fees by regulation, subject to review in accordance with the "Regulatory Review Act," so that adequate revenue is raised to meet the required enforcement effort.

(407 added Mar. 29, 1984, P.L. 162, No. 32)

Section 408. Reports to legislative committees.

(a) The commission shall submit annually a report to the Professional Licensure Committee of the House of Representatives and to the Consumer Protection and Professional

Licensure Committee of the Senate a description of the types of complaints received, status of cases, board action which has been taken and the length of time from the initital complaint to final board resolution.

(b) The commission shall also submit annually to the House of Representatives and the Senate Appropriations Committee, 15 days after the Governor has submitted his budget to the General Assembly, a copy of the budget request for the upcoming fiscal year which the commission previously submitted to the department.

(408 added Mar. 29, 1984, P.L. 162, No. 32)

CHAPTER 5
QUALIFICATIONS AND APPLICATIONS FOR LICENSES AND REGISTRATION CERTIFICATES
(Hdg. amended Mar. 7, 1982, P.L. 158, No. 50)

SUBCHAPTER A
GENERAL

Section 501. Reputation; inactive licensee; revoked license.

(a) Licenses shall be granted only to and renewed only for persons who bear a good reputation for honesty, trustworthiness, integrity and competence to transact the business of broker, salesperson, limited broker, limited salesperson, builder-owner salesperson or rental listing referral agent, in such manner as to safeguard the interest of the public, and only after satisfactory proof of such qualifications has been presented to the commission as it shall by regulation require.

(b) Any person who remains inactive for a period of five years without renewing his license shall, prior to having a license reissued to him, submit to and pass the examination pertinent to the license for which the person is reapplying.

(c) Unless ordered to do so by Commonwealth Court, the commission shall not reinstate the license, within five years of the date of revocation, of any person whose license has been revoked under this act. Any person whose license has been revoked may reapply for a license at the end of the five-year period but must meet all of the licensing qualifications of this act for the license applied for, to include the examination requirement.

(501 amended Mar. 29, 1984, P.L. 162, No. 32)

SUBCHAPTER B
BROKER'S LICENSE

Section 511. Qualifications for license.

The applicant for a broker's license, shall as a condition precedent to obtaining a license, take the broker's license examination and score a passing grade. Prior to taking the examination:

(1)   The applicant shall be at least 21 years of age.
(2)   The applicant shall be a high school graduate or shall produce proof satisfactory to the commission of an education equivalent thereto.
(3)   The applicant shall have completed 240 hours in real estate instruction in areas of study require instruction in the areas of fair housing and professional ethics.

(4)   The applicant shall have been engaged as a licensed real estate salesperson for at least three years or possess educational or experience qualifications which the commission deems to be the equivalent thereof.

(511 amended Mar. 29, 1984, P.L. 162, No.32)

Section 512. Application for license.

(a) An application for a license as a real estate broker shall be made in writing to the department, upon a form provided for the purpose by the department and shall contain such information as to the applicant as the commission shall require.

(b) The application shall state the place of business for which such license is desired.

(c) The application shall be received by the commission within three years of the date upon which the applicant took the examination.

(512) amended Mar. 29, 1984, P.L. 162, No. 32)

Section 513. Corporations, partnerships and associations.

If the applicant for a broker's license is a corporation, partnership or association, then the provisions of sections 511 and 512 shall apply to the individual designated as a broker of record. The employees of said corporation, partnership or association actually engaging in or intending to engage in the real estate business shall meet the provisions of sections 521 and 522.

SUBCHAPTER C
SALESPERSON'S LICENSE

Section 521. Qualifications for license.

Each applicant shall as a condition precedent to obtaining a license, take the salesperson license examination and score a passing grade. Prior to taking the examination:

(1)   The applicant shall be at least 18 years of age.
(2)   The applicant shall have completed 60 hours in real estate instruction in areas of study prescribed by the rules of the commission, which rules shall require instruction in the areas of fair housing and professional ethics.

(521 amended Mar. 29, 1984, P.L. 162, No.32)

Section 522. Application for license.

(a) An application for a license as salesperson shall be made, in writing to the department, upon a form provided for the purpose by the department, and shall contain such information as to the applicant, as the commission shall require.

(b) The applicant shall submit a sworn statement by the broker with whom he desires to be affiliated certifying that the broker will actively supervise and train the applicant.

(c) The application shall be received by the commission within three years of the date upon which the applicant took the examination.

SUBCHAPTER D
LIMITED BROKER'S LICENSE

Section 531. Qualifications for license.

Each applicant for a limited broker's license shall as a condition to obtaining a license take the limited broker's license examination and score a passing grade. Prior to taking the examinations:

(1) The applicant shall be at least 21 years of age.

(2) The applicant shall have been engaged full time as a salesperson or limited salesperson for at least three years or possess educational or experience qualifications which the commission deems to be the equivalent thereof.

Section 532. Application for license.

(a) An application for a license as a limited broker shall be made, in writing, to the department, upon a form provided for the purpose by the department and shall contain such information as to the applicant, as the commission shall require.

(b) The applicant shall have completed 60 hours in real estate instruction in areas of study prescribed by the rules of the commission, which rules shall require instruction in the areas of professional ethics.

(c) The application shall be received by the commission within three years of the date upon which the applicant took the examination.

(532 amended Mar. 29, 1984, P.L. 162, No. 32)

Section 533. Corporations, partnerships, associations or other entities.

If the applicant for a limited broker's license is a corporation, partnership, association, or other entity, foreign or domestic, then the provisions of sections 531 and 532 shall apply to the individual designated as broker of record, as well as those members actually engaging in or intending to engage in the real estate business.

SUBCHAPTER E
LIMITED SALESPERSON'S LICENSE

Section 541. Qualifications for license.

The applicant for a limited salesperson's license shall be at least 18 years of age.

Section 542. Application for license.

(a) An application for a license as a limited salesperson shall be made, in writing, to the department, upon a form provided for the purpose by the department, and shall contain such information as to the applicant, as the commission shall require.

(b) The applicant for a license shall submit a sworn affidavit by the broker or limited broker with whom he desires to be affiliated certifying that the broker will actively supervise and train the applicant and certifying the truth and accuracy of the certification of the applicant.

SUBCHAPTER F
BUILDER-OWNER SALESPERSON'S LICENSE

Section 551. Qualifications for license.

Each applicant for a builder-owner salesperson's license, shall as a condition precedent to obtaining a license, take the standard real estate salesperson's license examination and score a passing grade. Prior to taking the examination:

(1) The applicant shall be 18 years of age.

(2) The applicant shall be employed by a builder-owner processing those qualifications as contained in section 501.

Section 552. Application for license.

(a) An application for a license as a builder-owner salesperson shall be made, in writing to the department, upon a form provided for the purpose by the department, and shall contain such information as to the applicant as the commission shall require.

(b) The applicant shall submit a sworn statement by the builder-owner by whom he is employed certifying to such employment.

(c) The application shall be received by the commission within three years of the date upon which the applicant took the examination.

SUBCHAPTER G
RENTAL LISTING REFERRAL AGENT'S LICENSE

Section 561. Qualifications for license.

The qualification for licensure as a rental listing referral agent shall be the same as those set forth in sections 521 and 522 except that the applicant need not be affiliated with a broker.

SUBCHAPTER H
CEMETERY COMPANY REGISTRATION
CERTIFICATE
(Hdg. added Mar. 7, 1982, P.L. 158, No. 50)

Section 571. Application and fee for registration certificate.

An application for a registration certificate for a cemetery company to operate a cemetery shall be made, in writing to the department, upon a form provided for the purpose by the department, and shall contain such information as to the applicant as the commission shall require.

(571 amended Mar. 29, 1984, P.L. 162, No. 32)

CHAPTER 6
DUTIES OF LICENSEES

Section 601. Duty of brokers and limited brokers to maintain office.

(a) Each resident licensed broker (which term in this section shall include limited broker) shall maintain a fixed office within this Commonwealth. The current license of a broker and of each licensee employed by such broker shall be prominently displayed in an office of the broker. The address of the office shall be designated on the current license. In case of removal of a broker's office from the designated location, all licensees registered at that location shall make application to the commission before such removal or within ten days thereafter, designating the new location of the office, and shall pay the required fees, whereupon the commission shall issue a current license at the new location for the unexpired period, if the new location complies with the terms of this act. Each licensed broker shall maintain a sign on the outside of his office indicating the proper licensed brokerage name.

(b) If the applicant for a broker's license intends to maintain more than one place of business within the Commonwealth, he shall apply for and obtain an additional license in his name at each office. Every such application shall state the location of such office. Effective 24 months after the effective date of this act, each office shall be under the direction and supervision of a manager who is either the broker or an associate broker: Provided, however, That such broker or an associate broker may direct and supervise more than one office.

(601 amended Mar. 29, 1984, P.L. 162, No. 32)

Section 602. Nonresident licensees.

Any nonresident of this Commonwealth who meets the equivalent experience requirements and other standards and qualifications, as the commission shall by rule provide, shall qualify for a license under this act.

(602 amended Mar. 29, 1984, P.L. 162, No. 32)

Section 603. Employment of associate brokers, salesperson.

No associate broker or salesperson (which term in this section shall include limited salesperson) shall be employed by any other broker than is designated upon the current license issued to said associate broker or said salesperson. Whenever a licensed salesperson or associate broker desires to change his employment from one licensed broker to another, he shall notify the commission in writing no later than ten days after the intended date of change, pay the required fee, and return his current license. The commission, shall, upon receipt of acknowledgement from the new broker of the change of employment issue a new license. In the interim at such time as the change in affiliation of the salesperson or associate broker occurs, he shall maintain a copy of the notification sent to the commission as his temporary license pending receipt of his new current license. It shall be the duty of the applicant to notify the commission if a new license or other pertinent communication is not received from the commission within 30 days.

(603 amended Mar. 29, 1984, P.L. 162, No. 32)

Section 604. Prohibited acts.

(a) The commission may upon its own motion, and shall promptly upon the verified complaint in writing of any person setting forth a complaint under this section, ascertain the facts and, if warranted, hold a hearing for the suspension or revocation of a license or registration certificate or for the imposition of fines not exceeding $1,000, or both. The commission shall have power to refuse a license or registration certificate for cause or to suspend or revoke a license or registration certificate or to levy fines up to $1,000, or both where the said license has been obtained by false representation, or by fraudulent act or conduct, or where a licensee or registrant, in performing or attempting to perform any of the acts mentioned herein, is found guilty of:

(1) Making any substantial misrepresentation.
(2) Making any false promise of a character likely to influence, persuade or induce any person to enter into any contract or agreement when he could not or did not intend to keep such promise.
(3) Pursuing a continued and flagrant course of misrepresentation or making of false promises through salesperson, associate broker, other persons, or any medium of advertising, or otherwise.

(4) Any misleading or untruthful advertising, or using any other trade name or insignia or membership in any real estate association or organization, of which the licensee is not a member.
(5) Failure to comply with the following requirements:
(i) all deposits or other moneys accepted by every person, holding a real estate broker license under the provisions of this act, shall be retained by such real estate broker pending consummation or termination of the transaction involved, and shall be accounted for in the full amount thereof at the time of the consummation or termination:
(ii) every salesperson and associate broker promptly on receipt by him of a deposit or other moneys on any transaction in which he is engaged on behalf of his broker-employer, shall pay over the deposit to the broker:
(iii) a broker shall not commingle the money or other property of his principal with his own:
(iv) every broker shall immediately deposit such moneys, of whatever kind of nature, belonging to others, in a separate custodial or trust fund account maintained by the broker with some bank or recognized depository until the transaction involved is consummated or terminated, at which time the broker shall account for the full amount received. Under no circumstances shall a broker permit any advance payment of funds belonging to others to be deposited in the broker's business or personal account, or to be commingled with any funds he may have on deposit; or
(v) every broker shall keep records of all funds deposited therein, which records shall indicate clearly the date and from whom he recieved money, the date deposited, the dates of withdrawals, and other pertinent information concerning the transaction, and shall show clearly for whose account the money is deposited and to whom the money belongs. All such records and funds shall be subject to inspection by the commission. Such separate custodial or trust fund account shall designate the broker, as trustee, and such account must provide for withdrawal of funds without previous notice. All such records shall be available to the commission, or its representatives, immediately after proper demand or after written notice given, or upon notice given to the depository.
(6) Failing to preserve for three years following its consummation records relating to any real estate transaction.
(7) Acting for more than one party in a transaction without the knowledge and consent in writing of all parties for whom he acts.

(8) Placing a "for sale" or "for rent" sign on any property without the written consent of the owner, or his authorized agent.

(9) Failing to voluntarily furnish a copy of any listing, sale, lease, or other contract relevant to a real estate transaction to all signatories thereof at the time of execution.

(10) Failing to specify a definite termination date that is not subject to prior notice, in any listing contract.

(11) Inducing any party to a contract, sale or lease to break such contract for the purpose of substitution in lieu thereof of a new contract, where such substitution is motivated by the personal gain of the licensee.

(12) Accepting a commission or any valuable consideration by a salesperson or associate broker for the performance of any acts specified in this act, from any person, except the licensed real estate broker, with whom he is affiliated.

(13) Failing to disclose to an owner in writing his intention or true position if he directly or indirectly through a third party, purchased for himself or acquires or intends to acquire any interest in or any option to purchase property which has been listed with his office to sell or lease.

(14) Being convicted in a court of competent jurisdiction in this or any other state, or Federal court, of forgery, embezzlement, obtaining money under false pretenses, bribery, larceny, extortion, conspiracy to defraud, or any similar offense or offenses, or any felony or pleading guilty or nolo contendere to any such offense or offenses.

(15) Violating any rule or regulation promulgated by the commission in the interest of the public and consistent with the provisions of this act.

(16) In the case of a broker licensee, failing to exercise adequate supervision over the activities of his licensed salespersons or associate brokers within the scope of this act.

(17) Failing, within a reasonable time as defined by the commission, to provide information requested by the commission as the result of a formal or informal complaint to the commission, which would indicate a violation of this act.

(18) Soliciting, selling or offering for sale real property by offering free lots, or conducting lotteries or contests or offering prizes for the purpose of influencing by deceptive conduct any purchaser or prospective purchaser of real property. The commission shall promulgate necessary rules and regulations to provide standards for the nondeception conduct under this paragraph. Any offering by mail or by telephone of any prize in relation to the offering of sale of real property, including time sharing, shall be accompanied by a statement of the fair market value, not suggested retail price, of all prizes offered, plus a statement of the odds of receiving any such prize. If the offering is by mail the statement of value and odds shall be printed in the same size type as the prize description and shall appear immediately adja-

cent to said description.

(19) Paying or accepting, giving or charging any undisclosed commission, rebate, compensation or profit or expenditures for a principal, or in violation of this act.

(20) Any conduct in a real estate transaction which demonstrates bad faith, dishonesty, untrustworthiness, or incompetency.

(21) Performing any act for which an appropriate real estate license is required and is not currently in effect.

(22) Violating any provision of the act of October 27, 1955 (P.L. 744, No. 222), known as the "Pennsylvania Human Relations Act," or any order or consent decree of the Pennsylvania Human Relations Commission issued pursuant to such act if such order or consent decree resulted from a complaint of discrimination in the area of activities authorized by virtue of this act.

(i) Such activities include but are not limited to:

(A) Accepting listings on the understanding that illegal discrimination in the sale or rental of housing is to be practiced due to race, color, religious creed, sex, ancestry, national origin, physical handicap, disability or use of a guide dog because of blindness of user of a prospective lessee or purchaser.

(B) Giving false information for purposes of discrimination in the rental or sale of housing due to race, color, religious creed, sex, ancestry, national origin, physical handicap, disability or use of a guide dog because of blindness of user of a prospective lessee or purchaser.

(C) Making distinctions in location of housing or dates of availability of housing for purposes of discrimination in the rental or sale of such housing due to race, color, religious creed, sex, ancestry national origin, physical handicap, disability or use of a guide dog because of blindness of user of the prospective lessee or purchaser.

(ii) Nothing contained in this paragraph is intended to preclude the State Real Estate Commission from conducting its own investigation and maintaining its own file on any complaint of discrimination. The intent hereunder is to allow the Pennsylvania Human Relations Commission a reasonable period of time to conduct its own investigations, hold hearings, render its decisions and inform the State Real Estate Commission of its findings prior to the State Real Estate Commission taking action against any broker, salesperson or sales associate charged with a violation of this paragraph.

(iii) If in the event the Pennsylvania Human Relations Commission does not act on a discrimination complaint within 90 days after it is filed with the Pennsylvania Human Relations Commission then the State Real Estate Commission may proceed with action against such license.

(iv) The 90-day waiting period delaying State Real Estate Commission action against licensee accused of discrimination applies only in initial complaints against such licensee, second or subsequent complaints may be brought by individuals or the Pennsylvania Human Relations Commission directly to the State Real Estate Commission.

(v) The Pennsylvania Human Relations Commission shall notify the State Real Estate Commission of findings of violations by the Human Relations Commission against licensees under this act concerning the sale, purchase or lease of real estate in violation of the "Pennsylvania Human Relations Act."

(23) In the case of a cemetery company registrant, violating any provisions of Title 9 of the Pennsylvania Consolidated Statutes (relating to burial grounds).

(24) In the case of a cemetery company registrant, violating any provisions of the act of August 14, 1963 (P.L. 1059, No., 459), entitled "An act prohibiting future need sales of cemetery merchandise and services, funeral merchandise and services, except under certain conditions; requiring the establishment of and deposit into a merchandise trust fund of certain amount of the proceeds of any such sale; providing for the administration of suchtrust funds and the payment of money there from: conferring powers and imposing duties on orphans's courts, and prescribing penalties."

(25) Violating section 606 or 607.

(b) All fines and civil penalties imposed in accordance with section 305 and this section shall be paid into the Professional Licensure Augmentation Account.

(604 amended Mar. 29, 1984, P.L. 162, No 32)

Section 605. Promotional land sales; approval

(a) Any person who proposes to engage in real estate transctions of a promotional nature in this Commonwealth for a property located inside or outside of this Commonwealth, shall first register with the commission for its approval before so doing, and shall comply with such restrictions and conditions pertaining thereto as the commission may impose by rule or regulation. Registration shall not be required for property located within or outside of this Commonwealth which is subject to a statutory exemption under the Federal Interstate Land Sales Full Disclosure Act (Public Law 90-448, 82 Stat. 590, 15 U.S.C. § 1702).

(b) As used in this section the term "promotional real estate" means an interest in property as defined in this act which is a part of a common promotional plan undertaken by a single developer or group of developers acting together to offer interest in real estate for sale or lease through advertising by mail, newspaper or periodical, by radio, television, telephone or other electronic means which is contiguous, known, designated or advertised as a common unit or by a common name: Provided, however, That the term shall not mean real estate interest involving less than 50 lots or shares, cemetery lots and land involving less than 25 acres.

(c) A person may apply to the commission for registration of promotional land sales by filing a statement of record and meeting the requirements of this section. Each registration shall be renewed annually. In lieu of registration or renewal, the commission shall accept registrations, property reports or similar disclosure documents filed in other states or with the Federal Government: Provided, That the commission may suspend or revoke the registration when the Federal Government or a registering state suspends or revokes a regulation. The commission shall, by rule and regulation, cooperate with similar jurisdictions in other states to establish uniform filing procedures and forms, public offering statements and similar forms. The commission shall charge an application fee as determined by regulation to cover costs associated with processing applications for registrations and renewals.

(d) Unless prior approval has been granted by the commission or the promotional plan is currently registered with the Department of Housing and Urban Development pursuant to the Federal Interstate Land Sales Full Disclosure Act or pursuant to State law, the statement of record shall contain the information and be accompanied by documents specified as follows:

(1) The name and address of each person having an interest in the property to be covered by the statement of record and the extent of such interest, except that in the case of a corporation the statement shall list all officers and all holders of 10% or more of the subscribed or issued stock of the corporations.

(2) A legal description of, and a statement of the total area included in the property and a statement of the topography thereof, together with a map showing the division proposed and the dimensions of the property to be covered by the statement of record and their relation to existing streets and roads.

(3) A statement of the condition of the title to the land comprising the property including all encumbrances, mortgages, judgments, liens or unpaid taxes and deed restrictions and covenants applicable thereto.

(4) A statement of the general terms and conditions, including the range of selling prices or rents at which it is proposed to dispense of the property.

(5) A statement of the present condition of access to the property, the existence of any unusual conditions relating to safety which are known to the developer, completed improvements including, but not limited to, streets, sidewalks, sewage disposal facilities and other public utilities, the proximity in miles of the subdivision to nearby municipalities and the nature of any improvements to be installed by the developer and his estimated schedule for completion.

(6) A statement of any encumbrance, a statement of the consequences for the purchaser of a failure by the person or persons bound to fulfill obligations under any instrument or instruments creating such encum-

brance and the steps, if any, taken to protect the purchaser in such eventuality.

(7) A copy of the articles of incorporation with all amendments thereto, if the developer is a corporation, copies of all instruments by which a deed of trust is created or declared, if the developer is a trust, copies of articles of partnership or association and all other papers pertaining to its organization if the developer is a partnership, unincorporated association, joint stock company or other form of organization and if the purported holder of legal title is a person other than the developer, copies of the above documents for such person.

(8) Copies of the deed or other instrument establishing title to the property in the developer or other person and copies of any instrument creating a lien or encumbrance upon the title of the developer or other person or copies of the opinion or opinions of counsel in respect to the title to the subdivision in the developer or other person or copies of the title insurance policy guaranteeing such title.

(9) Copies of all forms of conveyance to be used in selling or leasing lots to purchasers.

(10) Copies of instruments creating easements or other restrictions.

(11) Certified financial statements of the developer or an uncertified financial statement if a certified statement is not available as may be required by the commission.

(12) Such other information and such other documents and certifications as the commission may require as being reasonably necessary or appropriate to assure that prospective purchasers have access to truthful and accurate information concerning the offering.

(13) Consent to submit to the jurisdiction of the Commonwealth Court with respect to any action arising under this section.

(e) If at any time subsequent to the date of filing of a statement of record with the commission, a change shall occur affecting any material facts required to be contained in the statement, the developer shall promptly file an amendment thereto.

(f) If it appears to the commission that the statement of record or any amendment thereto, is on its face incomplete or inaccurate in any material respect, the commission shall so advise the developer within a reasonable time after the filing of the statement or amendment. Failure of the developer to provide the information requested by the commission within 90 days shall result in an automatic denial of an application or a suspension of registration.

(g) If it appears to the commission that a statement of record includes any untrue statement of material facts or omits to state any material fact required to be stated therein or necessary to make the statements therein not misleading, the commission may reject such application. The commission shall make an investigation of all consumer complaints concerning real estate promotions in the absence of a reciprocal agreement to handle on-site inspections. Under no circumstances shall a member or an employee of the commission perform an on-site inspection. If the commission determines that a violation of this section has occured, the commission may:

(1) suspend or revoke any registration;

(2) refer the complaint to the Consumer Protection Bureau of the Office of Attorney General; or

(3) seek an injunction or temporary restraining order to prohibit the complained of activity in the Commonwealth Court.

(h) Upon rejection of an application or amendment, the applicant may within 20 days after such notice request a hearing before the commission. Prior to, and in conjunction with such hearing, the commission, or its designee, shall have access to and may demand the production of any books and papers of, and may examine the developer, any agents or any other person, in respect of any matter relevant to the application. If the developer or any agents fail to cooperate or obstruct or refuse to permit the making of an investigation, such conduct shall be grounds for the denial of the application.

(605 amended Mar. 29, 1984, P.L. 162, No. 32)

Section 606. Broker's disclosure to seller.

In any listing agreement or contract of agency, the broker shall make the following disclosures to any seller of real property:

(1) A statement that the broker's commission and the time period of the listing are negotiable.

(2) A statement describing the purpose of the Real Estate Recovery Fund established under section 801 and the telephone number of the commission at which the seller can receive further information about the fund.

(606 added Mar. 29, 1984, P.L. 162, No. 32)

Compiler's Note: The act of Mar. 29, 1984, P.L. 162, No. 32, which added this section, provided for an effective date of Mar. 29, 1985.

Section 607. Broker's disclosure to buyer.

In any sales agreement or sales contract, a broker shall make the following disclosures to any prospective buyer of real property:

(1) A statement that the broker is the agent of the seller, not the buyer.

(2) A statement describing the purpose of the Real Estate Recovery Fund established under section 801 and the telephone number of the commission at which the purchaser can receive further information about the fund.

(3) A statement of the zoning classification of the property except for single family dwellings. Failure of any sales agreement or sales contract to contain a statement of the zoning classification of the property shall render the sales agreement or sales contract null and void and any deposits tendered by the buyer shall be returned to the buyer without any requirement for any court action.

(607 added Mar. 29, 1984, P.L. 162, No. 32)

Compiler's Note: The act of Mar. 29, 1984, P.L. 162, No. 32, which added this section, provided for an effective date of Mar. 29, 1985.

Section 608. Information to be given at initial interview.

The commission shall establish rules or regulations which shall set forth the manner and method of disclosure of information to the prospective buyer or seller during the initial interview. Such disclosure shall include, but shall not be limited to:

(1) A statement that the broker is the agent of the seller.

(2) The purpose of the Real Estate Recovery Fund and the telephone number of the commission at which further information about the fund may be obtained.

(3) A statement that the duration of the listing agreement or contract and the broker's commission are negotiable.

(4) A statement that any sales agreement must contain the zoning classification of a property.

(608 added Mar. 29, 1984, P.L. 162, No. 32)

CHAPTER 7
PROCEEDINGS BEFORE THE COMMISSION

Section 701. Hearings held by commission.

(a) The said hearings may be held by the commission or any members thereof, or by any of its duly authorized representatives, or by any other person duly authorized by the commission for such purpose in any particular case.

(b) The commission may adopt the findings in the report or may, with or without additional testimony, either return the matter to the representative for such further consideration as the commission deems necessary or make additional or other findings of fact on the basis of all the legally probative evidence in the record and enter its conclusions of law and order in accordance with the requirements for the issuance of an adjudication under Title 2 of the Pennsylvania Consolidated Statutes (relating to administrative law and procedure).

(c) Proceedings before the commission shall be conducted in accordance with Title 1, Part 2 of the Pennsylvania Code.

Section 702. Imputed knowledge, limitations.

(a) No violation of any of the provisions of this act on the part of any salesperson, associate broker, or other employee of any licensed broker, shall be grounds for the revocation or suspension of the license of the employer of such salesperson, association broker, or employee, unless it shall appear upon the hearings held, that such employer had actual knowledge of such violation.

(b) No violation of any of the provisions of this act on the part of any limited broker or limited salesperson or other employee of any registered cemetery company, shall be grounds for the revocation or suspension of the registration certificate of the cemetery company, unless it shall appear that such cemetery company had actual knowledge of such violation.

(c) A course of dealing shown to have been followed by such employee shall constitute prima facie evidence of such knowledge upon the part of his employer.

(702 amended Mar. 7, 1982, P.L. 158, No. 50)

CHAPTER 8
REAL ESTATE RECOVERY FUND

Section 801. Establishment of the fund.

There is hereby established the Real Estate Recovery Fund for the purposes hereinafter set forth in this act.

Section 802. Funding of the fund.

Each licensee entitled to renew his license on or after February 28, 1980, shall, when so renewing his license pay in addition to the applicable license fee a further fee of $10, which shall be paid and credited to the Real Estate Recovery Fund, thereafter any person upon receiving his initial real estate license or cemetery company registration certificate, shall, in addition to all fees, pay into the Real Estate Recovery Fund a sum of $10. If at the commencement of any biennial renewal period beginning in 1982 and thereafter, the balance of the fund is less than $300,000, the commission may assess an additional fee, in addition to the renewal fee, against each licensee and registrant in an amount not to exceed $10 which will yield revenues sufficient to bring the balance of the fund to $500,000. All said fees shall be paid into the State Treasury and credited to the Real Estate Recovery Fund, and said deposits shall be allocated solely for the purposes of the fund as provided in this act. The fund shall be invested and interest/dividends shall accrue to the fund.

(802 amended Mar. 7, 1982, P.L. 158, No. 50)

Section 803. Application for recovery from fund.

(a) When any aggrieved person obtains a final judgment in any court of competent jurisdiction against any person licensed under this act, upon grounds of fraud, misrepresentation or deceit with reference to any transaction for which a license or registration certificate is required under this act (including with respect to cemetery companies any violation of 9 Pa. C.S. § 308(b) (relating to accounts of qualified trustee)) and which cause of action occurred on or after the effective date of this act, the aggrieved person may, upon termination of all proceedings, including reviews and appeals, file an application in the court in which the judgment was entered for an order directing payment out of the Real Estate Recovery Fund of the amount unpaid upon the judgment.

(b) The aggrieved person shall be required to show:

(1) That he is not a spouse of the debtor, or the personal representative of said spouse.

(2) That he has obtained a final judgment as set out in this section.

(3) That all reasonable personal acts, rights of discovery and such other remedies at law and in equity as exist have been exhausted in the collection thereof.

(4) That he is making said application no more than one year after the termination of the proceedings, including reviews and appeals in connection with the judgment.

(c) The commission shall have the right to answer actions provided for under this section, and subject to court approval, it may compromise a claim based upon the application of the aggrieved party.

(d) When there is an order of the court to make payment or a claim is otherwise to be levied against the fund, such amount shall be paid to the claimant in accordance with the limitations contained in this section. Notwithstanding any other provisions of this section, the liability of that portion of the fund allocated for the purpose of this act shall not exceed $20,000 for any one claim and shall not exceed $100,000 per licensee. If the $100,000 liability of the Real Estate Recovery Fund as provided herein is insufficient to pay in full claims adjudicated valid of all aggrieved persons against any one licensee or registrant, such $100,000 shall be distributed among them in such ratio that the respective claims of the aggrieved applicants bear to the aggregate of such claims held valid. If, at any time, the money deposited in the Real Estate Recovery Fund is insufficient to satisfy any duly authorized claim or portion thereof, the commission shall, when sufficient money has been deposited in the fund, satisfy such unpaid claims or portions thereof, in the order that such claims or portions thereof were originally filed, plus accumulated interest at the rate of 6% a year.

(e) Upon petition of the commission the court may require all claimants and prospective claimants against one licensee or registrant to be joined in one action, to the end that the respective rights of all such claimants to the Real Estate Recovery Fund may be equitably adjudicated and settled.

(f) Should the commission pay from the Real Estate Recovery Fund any amount in settlement of a claim as provided for in this act against a licensee, the license of that person shall automatically suspend upon the effective date of the payment thereof by the commission. No such licensee shall be granted reinstatement until he has repaid in full plus interest at the rate of 10% a year, the amount paid from the Real Estate Recovery Fund.

(g) Should the commission pay from the Real Estate Recovery Fund any amount in settlement of a claim as provided for in this act against a registrant the registrant shall automatically be denied the right to sell cemetery lots upon the effective date of the payment thereof by the commission. No such registrant shall be granted the right to sell cemetery lots until he has repaid in full plus interest at the rate of 10% a year, the amount paid from the Real Estate Recovery fund. (803 amended Mar. 29, 1984, P.L. 162, No. 32)

CHAPTER 9
REPEALER AND EFFECTIVE DATE

Section 901. Repealer.

The act of May 1, 1929 (P.L. 1216, No. 427), known as the "Real Estate Brokers License Act of one thousand nine hundred and twenty-nine," is repealed to the following conditions:

(1) All valid licenses issued prior to the effective date of this act under the provisions of said 1929 act shall continue with full force and validity during the period for which issued. For the subsequent license period, and each license period thereafter, the commission shall renew such licenses without requiring any license examination to be taken: Provided, however, That applicants for renewal or holders of such licenses shall be subject to all other provisions of this act.

(2) All proceedings in progress on the effective date shall continue to proceed under the terms of the act under which they were brought.

(3) All offenses alleged to have occurred prior to the effective date of this act shall be processed under the act of May 1, 1929 (P.L. 1216, No. 427).

Section 902. Effective date.

Section 561 shall take effect September 1, 1980 and the remaining provisions of this act shall take effect immediately.

Glossary of Real Estate Terms

Abstract of title The condensed history of a title to a particular parcel of real estate, consisting of a summary of the original grant and all subsequent conveyances and encumbrances affecting the property and a certification by the abstractor that the history is complete and accurate.

Abstract of title with lawyer's opinion An abstract of title a lawyer has examined and certified to be, in his or her opinion, an accurate statement of fact.

Acceleration clause The clause in a mortgage or trust deed that can be enforced to make the entire debt due immediately if the mortgagor defaults on an installment payment or other covenant.

Accession Acquiring title to additions or improvements to real property as a result of the annexation of fixtures or the accretion of alluvial deposits along the banks of streams.

Accretion The increase or addition of land by the deposit of sand or soil washed up naturally from a river, lake, or sea.

Accrued items On a closing statement, expense items that are incurred but not yet payable, such as interest on a mortgage loan or taxes on real property.

Acknowledgment A formal declaration made before a duly authorized officer, usually a notary public, by a person who has signed a document.

Acre A measure of land equal to 43,560 square feet, 4,840 square yards, 4,047 square meters, 160 square rods, or 0.4047 hectares.

Actual eviction The result of legal action, originated by a lessor, whereby a defaulted tenant is physically ousted from the rented property pursuant to a court order. (*See also* Eviction.)

Actual notice Express information or fact; that which is known; direct knowledge.

Adjusted basis *See* Basis.

Ad valorem tax A tax levied according to value; generally used to refer to real estate tax. Also called the *general tax*.

Adverse possession The actual, visible, hostile, notorious, exclusive and continuous possession of another's land under a claim of title. Possession for a statutory period may be a means of acquiring title.

Agency coupled with an interest An agency relationship in which the agent is given an estate or interest in the subject of the agency (the property).

Agent One who acts or has the power to act for another. A fiduciary relationship is created under the *law of agency* when a property owner, as the principal, executes a listing agreement or management contract authorizing a licensed real estate broker to be his or her agent.

Air lot A designated airspace over a piece of land. An air lot, just as surface property, may be transferred.

Air rights The right to use the open space above a property, generally allowing the surface to be used for another purpose.

Alienation The act of transferring property to another. Alienation may be voluntary, such as by gift or sale, or involuntary, such as through eminent domain or adverse possession.

Alienation clause The clause in a mortgage or trust deed that states that the balance of the secured debt becomes immediately due and payable at the mortgagee's option if the property is sold by the mortgagor. In effect, this clause prevents the mortgagor from assigning the debt without the mortgagee's approval.

Allodial system A system of land ownership in which land is held free and clear of any rent or service due to the government; commonly contrasted to the feudal system. Land is held under the allodial system in the United States.

Amortized loan A loan in which the principal as well as the interest is payable in monthly or other periodic installments over the term of the loan.

Antitrust laws Laws designed to preserve the free enterprise of the open marketplace by making illegal certain private conspiracies and combinations formed to minimize competition. Violations of antitrust laws in the real estate business generally involve either *price fixing* (brokers conspiring to set fixed compensation rates) or *allocation of customers or markets* (brokers agreeing to limit their areas of trade or dealing to certain areas or properties).

Apportionment clause Clause in an insurance policy providing that, if the insured is covered by more than one policy, any payments will be apportioned according to the amount of coverage.

Appraisal An estimate of the quantity, quality, or value of something. The process through which conclusions of property value are obtained; also refers to the report that sets forth the process of estimation and conclusion of value.

Appreciation An increase in the worth or value of a property due to economic or related causes, which may prove to be either temporary or permanent; opposite of depreciation.

Assemblage The combining of two or more adjoining lots into one larger tract in order to increase their total value.

Assessment The imposition of a tax, charge or levy, usually according to established rates.

Assignment The transfer in writing of interest in a bond, mortgage, lease or other instrument.

Associate broker A person licensed as a real estate broker who chooses to work under the supervision of another broker.

Assumption of mortgage Acquiring title to property on which there is an existing mortgage and agreeing to be personally liable for the terms and conditions of the mortgage, including payments.

Attachment The act of taking a person's property into legal custody by writ or other judicial order in order to hold it available for application to that person's debt to a creditor.

Automatic extension A clause in a listing agreement that states that the agreement will continue automatically for a certain period of time after its expiration date. In many states, use of this clause is discouraged; in Pennsylvania it is prohibited.

Avulsion The sudden tearing away of land, as by earthquake, flood, volcanic action or the sudden change in the course of a stream.

Balloon payment A final payment of a mortgage loan that is considerably larger than the required periodic payments because the loan amount was not fully amortized.

Bargain and sale deed A deed that carries with it no warranties against liens or other encumbrances but that does imply that the grantor has the right to convey title. The grantor may add warranties to the deed at his or her discretion.

Base line One of a set of imaginary lines running east and west and crossing a principal meridian at a definite point, used by surveyors for reference in locating and describing land under the rectangular survey (or government survey) system of property description.

Basis The financial interest that the Internal Revenue Service attributes to an owner of an investment property for the purpose of determining annual depreciation and gain or loss on the sale of the asset. If a property was acquired by purchase, the owner's basis is the cost of the property plus the value of any capital expenditures for improvements to the property, minus any depreciation allowable or actually taken. This new basis is called the *adjusted basis.*

Benchmark A permanent reference mark or point established for use by surveyors in measuring differences in elevation.

Beneficiary 1. The person for whom a trust operates or in whose behalf the income from a trust estate is drawn. 2. A lender who lends money on real estate and takes back a note and trust deed from the borrower.

Bilateral contract *See* Contract.

Binder An agreement that may accompany an earnest money deposit for the purchase of real property as evidence of the purchaser's good faith and intent to complete the transaction.

Blanket mortgage A mortgage covering more than one parcel of real estate, providing for each parcel's partial release from the mortgage lien upon repayment of a definite portion of the debt.

Blockbusting The illegal practice of inducing homeowners to sell their properties by making representations regarding the entry or prospective entry of minority persons into the neighborhood.

Blue-sky laws Common name for those state and federal laws that regulate the registration and sale of investment securities.

Boot Money or property given to make up any difference in value or equity between two properties in an *exchange.*

Branch office A secondary place of business apart from the principal or main office from which real estate business is conducted. A branch office generally must be run by a licensed real estate broker working on behalf of the broker who operates the principal office.

Breach of contract Violation of any terms or conditions in a contract without legal excuse; for example, failure to make a payment when it is due.

Broker One who buys and sells for another for a commission. *See also* Real estate broker.

Brokerage The business of bringing together parties interested in making a real estate transaction for a fee or commission.

Building code An ordinance that specifies minimum standards of construction for buildings in order to protect public safety and health.

Bulk transfer *See* Uniform Commercial Code.

Bundle of legal rights The concept of land ownership that means *ownership of all legal rights to the land*—for example, possession, control within the law, and enjoyment—rather than ownership of the land itself.

Capital gain Profit earned from the sale of an asset.

Capitalization A mathematical process for estimating the value of a property using a proper rate of return on the investment and the annual net income expected to be produced by the property. The formula is expressed:

$$\frac{Income}{Rate} = Value$$

Capitalization rate The rate of return a property will produce on the owner's investment.

Cash flow The net spendable income from an investment, determined by deducting all operating and fixed expenses from the gross income. If expenses exceed income, a *negative cash flow* is the result.

Casualty insurance A type of insurance policy that protects a property owner or other person from loss or injury sustained as a result of theft, vandalism or similar occurrences.

Caveat emptor A Latin phrase meaning "Let the buyer beware."

Certificate of sale The document generally given to the purchaser at a tax foreclosure sale. A certificate of sale does not convey title; generally it is an instrument certifying that the holder received title to the property after the redemption period had passed and that the holder paid the property taxes for that interim period.

Certificate of title A statement of opinion on the status of the title to a parcel of real property based on an examination of specified public records.

Chain of title The succession of conveyances, from some accepted starting point, whereby the present holder of real property derives his or her title.

Chattel *See* Personal property.

Closing statement A detailed cash accounting of a real estate transaction showing all cash received, all charges and credits made and all cash paid out in the transaction.

Cloud on the title Any document, claim, unreleased lien or encumbrance that may impair the title to real property or make the title doubtful; usually revealed by a title search and removed by either a quitclaim deed or suit to quiet title.

Clustering The grouping of homesites within a subdivision on smaller lots than normal, with the remaining land used as common areas.

Codicil A supplement or addition to a will, executed with the same formalities as a will, that normally does not revoke the entire will.

Cognovit *See* Confession of judgment clause.

Coinsurance clause A clause in insurance policies covering real property that requires the policyholder to maintain fire insurance coverage generally equal to at least 80 percent of the property's actual replacement cost.

Commingling The illegal act of a real estate broker who mixes the money of other people with his or her own money. By law, brokers are required to maintain a separate trust account for other parties' funds held temporarily by the broker.

Commission Payment to a broker for services rendered, such as in the sale or purchase of real property; usually a percentage of the selling price of the property.

Common elements Parts of a property that are necessary or convenient to the existence, maintenance and safety of a condominium or are normally in common use by all of the condominium residents. Each condominium owner has an undivided ownership interest in the common elements.

Common law The body of law based on custom, usage and court decisions.

Community property A system of property ownership based on the theory that each spouse has an equal interest in the property acquired by the efforts of either spouse during marriage. This system stemmed from Germanic tribes and, through Spain, came to the Spanish colonies of North and South America. The system was unknown under English common law.

Comparables Properties listed in an appraisal report that are substantially equivalent to the subject property.

Competent parties People who are recognized by law as being able to contract with others; usually those of legal age and sound mind.

Competitive market analysis A comparison of the prices of recently sold homes that are similar to a listing seller's home in terms of location, style, size, condition, age and amenities. Based on this analysis, a broker or salesperson can help the seller determine a listing price.

Condemnation A judicial or administrative proceeding to exercise the right of eminent domain through which a government agency takes private property for public use and compensates the owner.

Condition A contingency, qualification or occurrence upon which an estate or property right is gained or lost.

Condominium The absolute ownership of an apartment or a unit (generally in a multiunit building) based on a legal description of the airspace the unit actually occupies plus an undivided interest in the ownership of the common elements, which are owned jointly with the other condominium unit owners. The entire tract of real estate included in a condominium development is called a *parcel* or *development parcel*. One apartment or space in a condominium building, or a part of a property intended for independent use and having lawful access to a public way, is called a *unit*. Ownership of one unit includes a definite undivided interest in the common elements.

Confession of judgment clause A provision that may be included in notes, leases and contracts by which the debtor, lessee or obligor authorizes any attorney to go into court to confess a judgment against him or her for a default in payment. Also called a *cognovit*.

Consideration 1. That which is received by the grantor in exchange for his or her deed. 2. Something of value that induces a person to enter into a contract. Consideration may be "valuable" (money) or "good" (love and affection).

Construction loan *See* Interim financing.

Constructive eviction 1. Actions of the landlord that so materially disturb or impair the tenant's enjoyment of the leased premises that the tenant is effectively forced to move out and terminate the lease without liability for any further rent. 2. A purchaser's inability to obtain clear title.

Constructive notice Notice given to the world by recorded documents. All people are charged with knowledge of such documents and their contents, whether or not they have actually examined them. Possession of property is also considered constructive notice that the person in possession has an interest in the property.

Consummate right The status of the dower or curtesy right when, upon the death of the owning spouse, this right becomes complete or may be completed to become an interest in the real estate.

Contract A legally enforceable promise or set of promises that must be performed and for which, if a breach of the promise occurs, the law provides a remedy. A contract may be either *unilateral,* where only one party is bound to act, or *bilateral,* where all parties to the instrument are legally bound to act as prescribed.

Contract for deed A contract for the sale of real estate wherein the purchase price is paid in periodic installments by the purchaser, who is in possession of the property even though title is retained by the seller until final payment. Also called an *installment contract* or *articles of agreement for warranty deed*.

Conventional loan A loan that is not insured or guaranteed by a government or private source.

Cooperative A residential multiunit building whose title is held by a trust or corporation that is owned by and operated for the benefit of persons living within the building, who are the beneficial owners of the trust or stockholders of the corporation, each possessing a proprietary lease.

Corporation An entity or organization created by operation of law whose rights of doing business are essentially the same as those of an individual. The entity has continuous existence until it is dissolved according to legal procedures.

Correction lines Provisions in the rectangular survey (government survey) system made to compensate for the curvature of the earth's surface. Every fourth township line (at 24-mile intervals) is used as a correction line on which the intervals between the north and south range lines are remeasured and corrected to a full six miles.

Cost approach The process of estimating the value of a property by adding to the estimated land value the appraiser's estimate of the reproduction or replacement cost of the building, less depreciation.

Cost recovery An Internal Revenue Service term for *depreciation*.

Counseling The business of providing people with expert advice on a subject, based on the counselor's extensive, expert knowledge of the subject.

Counteroffer A new offer made as a reply to an offer received. It has the effect of rejecting the original offer, which cannot be accepted thereafter unless revived by the offeror's repeating it.

Covenant A written agreement between two or more parties in which a party or parties pledges to perform or not perform specified acts with regard to property; usually found in such real estate documents as deeds, mortgages, leases and contracts for deed.

Credit On a closing statement, an amount entered in a person's favor—either an amount the party has paid or an amount for which the party must be reimbursed.

Cul-de-sac Circular street having only one entrance and exit.

Curtesy A life estate, usually a fractional interest, given by some states to the surviving husband in real estate owned by his deceased wife. Most states have abolished curtesy.

Datum A horizontal plane from which heights and depths are measured.

Debit On a closing statement, an amount charged; that is, an amount that the debited party must pay.

Decedent A person who has died.

Dedication The voluntary transfer of private property by its owner to the public for some public use, such as for streets or schools.

Deed A written instrument that, when executed and delivered, conveys title to or an interest in real estate.

Deed in trust An instrument that grants a trustee full powers to sell, mortgage and subdivide a parcel of real estate. The beneficiary controls the trustee's use of these powers under the provisions of the trust agreement.

Deed of trust *See* Trust deed.

Deed restrictions Clauses in a deed limiting the future uses of the property. Deed restrictions may impose a vast variety of limitations and conditions—for example, they may limit the density of buildings, dictate the types of structures that can be erected or prevent buildings from being used for specific purposes or even from being used at all.

Default The nonperformance of a duty, whether arising under a contract or otherwise; failure to meet an obligation when due.

Defeasance clause A clause used in leases and mortgages that cancels a specified right upon the occurrence of a certain condition, such as cancellation of a mortgage upon repayment of the mortgage loan.

Defeasible fee estate An estate in which the holder has a fee simple title that may be divested upon the occurrence or nonoccurrence of a specified event. There are two categories of defeasible fee estates: fee simple determinable and fee simple subject to a condition subsequent.

Deficiency judgment A personal judgment levied against the mortgagor when a foreclosure sale does not produce sufficient funds to pay the mortgage debt in full.

Delinquent taxes Unpaid taxes that are past due.

Demand The amount of goods people are willing and able to buy at a given price; often coupled with *supply*.

Density zoning Zoning ordinances that restrict the average maximum number of houses per acre that may be built within a particular area, generally a subdivision.

Depreciation 1. In appraisal, a loss of value in property due to any cause, including *physical deterioration*, *functional obsolescence* and *external depreciation*. 2. In real estate investment, an expense deduction for tax purposes taken over the period of ownership of income property.

Descent Acquisition of an estate by inheritance in which an heir succeeds to the property by operation of law.

Determinable fee estate A fee simple estate in which the property automatically reverts to the grantor upon the occurrence of a specified event or condition.

Developer One who constructs buildings on lots and sells them.

Devise A gift of real property by will. The donor is the devisor and the recipient is the devisee.

Direct sales comparison approach The process of estimating the value of a property by examining and comparing actual sales of comparable properties.

Discount points An added loan fee charged by a lender to make the yield on a lower-than-market-value loan competitive with higher-interest loans.

Dominant tenement A property that includes in its ownership the appurtenant right to use an easement over another person's property for a specific purpose.

Dower The legal right or interest, recognized in some states, that a wife acquires in the property her husband held or acquired during their marriage. During the husband's lifetime, the right is only a possibility of an interest; upon his death it can become an interest in land. Dower rights have been modified by law in most states. *See also* Consummate right, Inchoate right.

Dual agency Representing both parties to a transaction. This is unethical unless both parties agree to it, and it is illegal in many states.

Duress Unlawful constraint or action exercised upon a person whereby the person is forced to perform an act against his or her will. A contract entered into under duress is considered voidable.

Earnest money deposit Money deposited by a buyer under the terms of a contract, that is to be forfeited if the buyer defaults but applied on the purchase price if the sale is closed.

Easement A right to use the land of another for a specific purpose, such as for a right-of-way or utilities; an incorporeal interest in land. An *easement appurtenant* passes with the land when conveyed.

Easement by necessity An easement allowed by law as necessary for the full enjoyment of a parcel of real estate; for example, a right of ingress and egress over a grantor's land.

Easement by prescription An easement acquired by continuous, open, uninterrupted, exclusive and adverse use of the property for the period of time prescribed by state law.

Easement in gross An easement that is not created for the benefit of any *land* owned by the owner of the easement but that attaches *personally to the easement owner.* For example, a right granted by Eleanor Franks to Joe Fish to use a portion of her property for the rest of his life would be an easement in gross. Utility easements are also examples.

Emblements Growing crops, such as grapes and corn, that are produced annually through labor and industry; also called *fructus industriales.*

Eminent domain The right of a government or municipal quasi-public body to acquire property for public use through a court action called *condemnation,* in which the court decides that the use is a public use and determines the price or compensation to be paid to the owner.

Employee Someone who works as a direct employee of an employer and has employee status. The employer is obligated to withhold income taxes and social security taxes from the compensation of his or her employees. *See also* Independent contractor.

Employment contract A document evidencing formal employment between employer and employee or between principal and agent. In the real estate business, this generally takes the form of a listing agreement or management agreement.

Enabling acts State legislation that confers zoning powers on municipal governments.

Encroachment A building or some portion of it—a wall or fence, for instance—that extends beyond the land of the owner and illegally intrudes upon some land of an adjoining owner or a street or alley.

Encumbrance Anything—such as a mortgage, tax, or judgment lien, an easement, a restriction on the use of the land, or an outstanding dower right—that may diminish the rights of property ownership.

Equalization The raising or lowering of assessed values for tax purposes in a particular county or taxing district to make them equal to assessments in other counties or districts.

Equalization factor A factor (number) by which the assessed value of a property is multiplied to arrive at a value for the property that is in line with state-wide tax assessments. The *ad valorem tax* would be based upon this adjusted value.

Equitable lien *See* Statutory lien.

Equitable title The interest held by a vendee under a contract for deed or an installment contract; the equitable right to obtain absolute ownership to property when legal title is held in another's name.

Equity The interest or value that an owner has in the property over and above any mortgage indebtedness.

Erosion The gradual wearing away of land by water, wind, and general weather conditions; the diminishing of property caused by the elements.

Escheat The reversion of property to the state or county, as provided by state law, in cases where a decedent dies intestate without heirs capable of inheriting or when the property is abandoned.

Escrow The closing of a transaction through a third party called an *escrow agent,* or *escrowee,* who receives certain funds and documents to be delivered upon the performance of certain conditions outlined in the escrow agreement.

Escrow agreement A contract that sets forth the duties of the escrow agent, as well as the requirements and obligations of the parties to the transaction, when a transaction is closed through an escrow.

Estate at sufferance The tenancy of a lessee who lawfully comes into possession of a landlord's real estate but who continues to occupy the premises improperly after his or her lease rights have expired.

Estate (Tenancy) for years An interest for a certain, exact period of time in property leased for a specified consideration.

Estate (Tenancy) from period to period *See* Periodic estate.

Estate in land The degree, quantity, nature, and extent of interest that a person has in real property.

Estate taxes Federal taxes on a decedent's real and personal property.

Estoppel certificate A document in which a borrower certifies the amount he or she owes on a mortgage loan and the rate of interest.

Eviction A legal process to oust a person from possession of real estate.

Evidence of title Proof of ownership of property; commonly a certificate of title, or a title insurance policy.

Exchange A transaction in which all or part of the consideration is the transfer of *like kind* property (such as real estate for real estate).

Exclusive-agency listing A listing contract under which the owner appoints a real estate broker as the exclusive agent for a designated period of time to sell the property, on the owner's stated terms, for a commission. The owner reserves the right to sell without paying anyone a commission if he or she sells to a prospect who has not been introduced or claimed by the broker.

Exclusive right to sell A listing contract under which the owner appoints a real estate broker as the exclusive agent for a designated period of time to sell the property on the owner's stated terms, and agrees to pay the broker a commission when the property is sold, whether by the broker, the owner, or another broker.

Executed contract A contract in which all parties have fulfilled their promises and thus performed the contract.

Execution The signing and delivery of an instrument. Also, a legal order directing an official to enforce a judgment against the property of a debtor.

Executory contract A contract under which something remains to be done by one or more of the parties.

Expenses Short-term costs, such as minor repairs, regular maintenance, and renting costs, that are deducted from an investment property's income.

Express contract An oral or written contract in which the parties state the contract's terms and express their intentions in words.

External depreciation A loss of value in real property resulting from factors existing outside the property itself. An example of such a factor would be the building of a factory adjacent to an apartment complex.

Fee simple estate The maximum possible estate or right of ownership of real property, continuing forever. Sometimes called a *fee* or *fee simple absolute*.

Feudal system A system of ownership usually associated with precolonial England, in which the king or other sovereign is the source of all rights. The right to possess real property was granted by the sovereign to an individual as a life estate only. Upon the death of the individual, title passed back to the sovereign, not to the decedent's heirs.

FHA loan A loan insured by the Federal Housing Administration and made by an approved lender in accordance with the FHA's regulations.

Fiduciary relationship A relationship of trust and confidence, as between trustee and beneficiary, attorney and client, or principal and agent.

Financing statement *See* Uniform Commercial Code.

Fiscal policy The government's policy in regard to taxation and spending programs. The balance between these two areas determines the amount of money the government will withdraw from or feed into the economy, which can counter economic peaks and slumps.

Fixture An item of personal property that has been converted to real property by being permanently affixed to the realty.

Foreclosure A legal procedure whereby property used as security for a debt is sold to satisfy the debt in the event of default in payment of the mortgage note or default of other terms in the mortgage document. The foreclosure procedure brings the rights of all parties to a conclusion and passes the title in the mortgaged property to either the holder of the mortgage or a third party who may purchase the realty at the foreclosure sale, free of all encumbrances affecting the property subsequent to the mortgage.

Fraud Deception intended to cause a person to give up property or a lawful right.

Freehold estate An estate in land in which ownership is for an indeterminate length of time, in contrast to a leasehold estate.

Functional obsolescence A loss of value to an improvement to real estate arising from functional problems, often caused by age or poor design.

Future interest A person's present right to an interest in real property that will not result in possession or enjoyment until some time in the future, such as a reversion or right of reentry.

Gap A defect in the chain of title of a particular parcel of real estate; a missing document or conveyance that raises doubt as to the present ownership of the land.

General agent One who is authorized by his or her principal to represent the principal in a specific range of matters.

General contractor A construction specialist who enters into a formal construction contract with a landowner or master lessee to construct a real estate building or project. The general contractor often contracts with several *subcontractors* specializing in various aspects of the building process to perform individual jobs.

General lien The right of a creditor to have all of a debtor's property—both real and personal—sold to satisfy a debt.

General partnership *See* Partnership.

General tax *See* Ad valorem tax.

General warranty deed A deed in which the grantor fully warrants good clear title to the premises. Used in most real estate transfers, a general warranty deed offers the greatest protection of any deed.

Government lot Fractional sections in the rectangular survey (government survey) system that are less than one quarter-section in area.

Government survey system *See* Rectangular survey system.

Grantee A person who receives a conveyance of real property from the grantor.

Granting clause Words in a deed of conveyance that state the grantor's intention to convey the property at the present time. This clause is generally worded as "convey and warrant," "grant," "grant, bargain and sell" or the like.

Grantor The person transferring title to or an interest in real property to a grantee.

Gross lease A lease of property under which a landlord pays all property charges regularly incurred through ownership, such as repairs, taxes, insurance and operating expenses. Most residential leases are gross leases.

Gross rent multiplier A figure used as a multiplier of the gross rental income of a property to produce an estimate of the proeprty's value.

Ground lease A lease of land only, on which the tenant usually owns a building or is required to build his or her own building as specified in the lease. Such leases are usually long-term net leases; the tenant's rights and obligations continue until the lease expires or is terminated through default.

Habendum clause That part of a deed beginning with the words, "to have and to hold," following the granting clause and defining the extent of ownership the grantor is conveying.

Heir One who might inherit or succeed to an interest in land under the state law of descent if the owner dies without leaving a valid will.

Highest and best use That possible use of land that would produce the greatest net income and thereby develop the highest land value.

Holdover tenancy A tenancy whereby a lessee retains possession of leased property after his or her lease has expired and the landlord, by continuing to accept rent, agrees to the tenant's continued occupancy as defined by state law.

Holographic will A will that is written, dated and signed in the testator's handwriting but is not witnessed.

Homeowner's insurance policy A standardized package insurance policy that covers a residential real estate owner against financial loss from fire, theft, public liability and other common risks.

Homestead Land that is owned and occupied as the family home. In many states, a portion of the area or value of this land is protected or exempt from judgments for debts.

Hypothecation The right of a borrower to possess property used as collateral for a loan.

Implied contract A contract under which the agreement of the parties is demonstrated by their acts and conduct.

Improvement 1. An improvement *on* land is any structure, usually privately owned, erected on a site to enhance the value of the property—for example, buildings, fences and driveways. 2. An improvement *to* land is usually a publicly owned structure, such as a curb, sidewalk, street or sewer.

Inchoate right An incomplete right, often a wife's interest in the land of her husband during his life, which upon his death may become a dower interest.

Income approach The process of estimating the value of an income-producing property by capitalization of the annual net income expected to be produced by the property during its remaining useful life.

Incorporeal right A nonpossessory right in real estate; for example, an easement or right-of-way.

Independent contractor Someone who is retained to perform a certain act but who is subject to the control and direction of another only as to the end result and not as to the way in which he or she performs the act. Unlike an employee, an independent contractor pays for all his or her expenses and social security and income taxes and receives no employee benefits. Many real estate salespeople are independent contractors.

Informed consent exception A provision in many state real estate license laws that permits a broker to represent both buyer and seller to a transaction if he or she has their prior mutual consent to do so.

Inheritance taxes State-imposed taxes on a decedent's real and personal property.

Installment contract *See* Contract for deed.

Installment sale A transaction in which the sales price is paid in two or more installments over two or more years. If the sale meets certain requirements, a taxpayer can postpone reporting such income to future years by paying tax each year only on the proceeds received that year.

Interest A charge made by a lender for the use of money.

Interim financing A short-term loan usually made during the construction phase of a building project (in this case, often referred to as a *construction loan*).

Intestate The condition of a property owner who dies without leaving a valid will. Title to the property will pass to his or her heirs as provided in the state law of descent.

Investment Money directed toward the purchase, improvement and development of an asset in expectation of income or profits.

Involuntary alienation *See* Alienation.

Irrevocable consent An agreement filed by an out-of-state broker in the state in which he or she wishes to be licensed, stating that suits and actions may be brought against the broker in that state.

Joint tenancy Ownership of real estate between two or more parties who have been named in one conveyance as joint tenants. If the instrument creating the joint tenancy specifically provides for survivorship, upon the death of a joint tenant his or her interest passes to the surviving joint tenant or tenants by the *right of survivorship*.

Joint venture The joining of two or more people to conduct a specific business enterprise. A joint venture is similar to a partnership in that it must be created by agreement between the parties to share in the losses and profits of the venture. Yet it is unlike a partnership in that the venture is for one specific project only rather than for a continuing business relationship.

Judgment The formal decision of a court upon the respective rights and claims of the parties to an action or suit. After a judgment has been entered and recorded with the county recorder, it usually becomes a general lien on the property of the defendant.

Judicial precedent In law, the requirements established by prior court decisions.

Junior lien An obligation, such as a second mortgage, that is subordinate in right or lien priority to an existing lien on the same realty.

Laches An equitable doctrine used by courts to bar a legal claim or prevent the assertion of a right because of undue delay or failure to assert the claim or right.

Land The earth's surface, extending downward to the center of the earth and upward infinitely into space.

Land contract *See* Contract for deed.

Last will and testament *See* Will.

Law of agency *See* Agent.

Lease A written or oral contract between a landlord (the lessor) and a tenant (the lessee) that transfers the right to exclusive possession and use of the landlord's real property to the lessee for a specified period of time and for a stated consideration (rent). By state law, leases for longer than a certain period of time (generally one year) must be in writing to be enforceable.

Leasehold estate A tenant's right to occupy real estate during the term of a lease; generally considered to be a personal property interest.

Legacy A disposition of money or personal property by will.

Legal description A description of a specific parcel of real estate complete enough for an independent surveyor to locate and identify it.

Lessee *See* Lease.

Lessor *See* Lease.

Leverage The use of borrowed money to finance the bulk of an investment.

Levy To assess; to seize or collect. To levy a tax is to assess a property and set the rate of taxation. To levy an execution is to officially seize the property of a person in order to satisfy an obligation.

License 1. A privilege or right granted to a person by a state to operate as a real estate broker or salesperson. 2. The revocable permission for a temporary use of land—a personal right that cannot be sold.

Lien A right given by law to certain creditors to have their debt paid out of the property of a defaulting debtor, usually by means of a court sale.

Lien theory Some states' interpretation of a mortgage as being purely a lien on real property. The mortgagee thus has no right of possession and must foreclose the lien and sell the property if the mortgagor defaults.

Life estate An interest in real or personal property that is limited in duration to the lifetime of its owner or some other designated person.

Life tenant A person in possession of a life estate.

Limited partnership *See* Partnership.

Liquidity The ability to sell an asset and convert it into cash at a price close to its true value in a short period of time.

Lis pendens A recorded legal document giving constructive notice that an action affecting a particular property has been filed in either a state or a federal court.

Listing agreement A contract between a landowner (as principal) and a licensed real estate broker (as agent) by which the broker is employed as agent to sell real estate on the owner's terms within a given time, for which service the landowner agrees to pay a commission.

Listing broker The broker in a multiple listing situation from whose office a listing agreement is initiated, as opposed to the *selling broker,* from whose office negotiations leading up to a sale are initiated. The listing broker and the selling broker may be the same person. *See also* Multiple listing.

Littoral rights 1. A landowner's claim to use water in large navigable lakes and oceans adjacent to his or her property. 2. The ownership rights to land bordering these bodies of water up to the high-water mark.

Lot-and-block description A description of real property that identifies a parcel of land by reference to lot and block numbers within a subdivision, as specified on a plat of subdivision duly recorded in the county recorder's office.

Management agreement A contract between the owner of income property and a management firm or individual property manager that outlines the scope of the manager's authority.

Market A place where goods can be bought and sold and a price established.

Marketable title Good or clear title reasonably free from the risk of litigation over possible defects.

Market comparison approach See Direct sales comparison approach.

Market price The actual selling price of a property.

Market value The most probable price property would bring in an arm's-length transaction under normal conditions on the open market.

Master plan A comprehensive plan to guide the long-term physical development of a particular area.

Mechanic's lien A statutory lien created in favor of contractors, laborers and materialmen who have performed work or furnished materials in the erection or repair of a building.

Metes-and-bounds description A legal description of a parcel of land that begins at a well-marked point and follows the boundaries, using directions and distances around the tract back to the place of beginning.

Mill One-tenth of one cent. Some states use a mill rate to compute real estate taxes; for example, a rate of 52 mills would be $0.052 tax for each dollar of assessed valuation of a property.

Minor Someone who has not reached the age of majority and therefore does not have legal capacity to transfer title to real property.

Monetary policy Governmental regulation of the amount of money in circulation through such institutions as the Federal Reserve Board.

Money judgment A court judgment ordering payment of money rather than specific performance of a certain action. *See also* Judgment.

Month-to-month tenancy A periodic tenancy under which the tenant rents for one month at a time. In the absence of a rental agreement (oral or written), a tenancy is generally considered to be month to month.

Monument A fixed natural or artificial object used to establish real estate boundaries for a metes-and-bounds description.

Mortgage A conditional transfer or pledge of real estate as security for the payment of a debt. Also the document creating a mortgage lien.

Mortgagee A lender in a mortgage loan transaction.

Mortgage lien A lien or charge on the property of a mortgagor that secures the underlying debt obligations.

Mortgagor A borrower who conveys his or her property as security for a loan.

Multiple listing clause A provision in an exclusive listing for the additional authority and obligation on the part of the listing broker to distribute the listing to other brokers in the multiple listing organization.

Negative cash flow *See* Cash flow.

Negotiable instrument A written instrument that may be transferred by endorsement or delivery. The holder, or payee, may sign the instrument over to another person or, in certain cases, merely deliver it to him or her. The transferee then has the original payee's right to payment.

Net lease A lease requiring the tenant to pay not only rent but also all costs incurred in maintaining the property, including taxes, insurance, utilities and repairs.

Net listing A listing based on the net price the seller will receive if the property is sold. Under a net listing, the broker is free to offer the property for sale at the highest price he or she can get in order to increase the commission.

Nonconforming use A use of property that is permitted to continue after a zoning ordinance prohibiting it has been established for the area.

Nonhomogeneity A lack of uniformity; dissimilarity. Because no two parcels of land are exactly alike, real estate is said to be nonhomogeneous.

Note An instrument of credit given to attest a debt.

Novation Substituting a new obligation for an old one or substituting new parties to an existing obligation, as when the parties to an agreement accept a new debtor in place of an old one.

Nuncupative will An oral will declared by the testator in his or her final illness, made before witnesses and afterwards reduced to writing.

Offer and acceptance Two essential components of a valid contract; a "meeting of the minds."

Open-end mortgage A mortgage loan that is expandable by increments up to a maximum dollar amount, the full loan being secured by the same original mortgage.

Open listing A listing contract under which the broker's commission is contingent upon the broker's producing a ready, willing and able buyer before the property is sold by the seller or another broker.

Option An agreement to keep open for a set period an offer to sell or purchase property.

Ostensible agency A form of implied agency relationship created by the actions of the parties involved rather than by written agreement or document.

Package mortgage A method of financing in which the loan that finances the purchase of a home also finances the purchase of certain items of personal property, such as a washer, dryer, refrigerator, stove and other specified appliances.

Parcel A specific portion of a large tract of real estate; a lot.

Participation financing A mortgage in which the lender participates in the income of the mortgaged venture beyond a fixed return or receives a yield on the loan in addition to the straight interest rate.

Partition The division of cotenants' interests in real property when the parties do not all voluntarily agree to terminate the co-ownership; takes place through court procedures.

Partnership An association of two or more individuals who carry on a continuing business for profit as co-owners. Under the law, a partnership is regarded as a group of individuals rather than as a single entity. A *general partnership* is a typical form of joint venture, in which each general partner shares in the administration, profits, and losses of the operation. A *limited partnership* is a business arrangement whereby the operation is administered by one or more general partner and funded, by and large, by limited or silent partners, who are by law responsible for losses only to the extent of their investments.

Party wall A wall that is located on or at a boundary line between two adjoining parcels of land and is used or is intended to be used by the owners of both properties.

Patent A grant or franchise of land from the U.S. government.

Percentage lease A lease, commonly used for commercial property, whose rental is based on the tenant's gross sales at the premises; it generally stipulates a base monthly rental plus a percentage of any gross sales above a certain amount.

Periodic estate An interest in leased property that continues from period to period—week to week, month to month or year to year.

Personal property Items, called *chattels,* that do not fit into the definition of real property; movable objects.

Physical deterioration A reduction in a property's value resulting from a decline in physical condition; can be caused by action of the elements or by ordinary wear and tear.

Planned unit development A planned combination of diverse land uses, such as housing, recreation and shopping, in one contained development or subdivision.

Plat A map of a town, section or subdivision indicating the location and boundaries of individual properties.

Plottage The increase in value or utility resulting from the consolidation *(assemblage)* of two or more adjacent lots into one larger lot.

Point of beginning In a metes-and-bounds legal description, the starting point of the survey, situated in one corner of the parcel; all metes-and-bounds descriptions must follow the boundaries of the parcel back to the point of beginning.

Point A unit of measurement used for various loan charges; one point equals one percent of the amount of the loan. *See also* Discount points.

Police power The government's right to impose laws, statutes, and ordinances, including zoning ordinances and building codes, to protect the public health, safety and welfare.

Power of attorney A written instrument authorizing a person, the *attorney-in-fact,* to act as agent on behalf of another person to the extent indicated in the instrument.

Precedent In law, the requirements established by prior court decisions.

Prepayment penalty A charge imposed on a borrower who pays off the loan principal early. This penalty compensates the lender for interest and other charges that would otherwise be lost.

Price fixing *See* Antitrust laws.

Primary mortgage market *See* Secondary mortgage market.

Principal 1. A sum lent or employed as a fund or investment, as distinguished from its income or profits. 2. The original amount (as in a loan) of the total due and payable at a certain date. 3. A main party to a transaction—the person for whom the agent works.

Principal meridian One of 35 north and south survey lines established and defined as part of the rectangular survey (government survey) system.

Prior appropriation A concept of water ownership in which the landowner's right to use available water is based on a government-administered permit system.

Priority The order of position or time. The priority of liens is generally determined by the chronological order in which the lien documents are recorded; tax liens, however, have priority even over previously recorded liens.

Probate A legal process by which a court determines who will inherit a decedent's property and what the estate's assets are.

Procuring cause The effort that brings about the desired result. Under an open listing, the broker who is the procuring cause of the sale receives the commission.

Progression An appraisal principle that states that, between dissimilar properties, the value of the lesser-quality property is favorably affected by the presence of the better-quality property.

Property manager Someone who manages real estate for another person for compensation. Duties include collecting rents, maintaining the property, and keeping up all accounting.

Proration Dividing or distributing expenses, either prepaid or paid in arrears, between buyer and seller at the closing.

Puffing Exaggerated or superlative comments or opinions.

Pur autre vie "For the life of another." A life estate pur autre vie is a life estate that is measured by the life of a person other than the grantee.

Purchase-money mortgage A note secured by a mortgage or trust deed given by a buyer, as mortgagor, to a seller, as mortgagee, as part of the purchase price of the real estate.

Quiet title suit *See* Suit to quiet title.

Quitclaim deed A conveyance by which the grantor transfers whatever interest he or she has in the real estate, without warranties or obligations.

Range A strip of land six miles wide, extending north and south and numbered east and west according to its distance from the principal meridian in the rectangular survey (government survey) system of land description.

Ready, willing and able buyer One who is prepared to buy property on the seller's terms and is ready to take positive steps to consummate the transaction.

Real estate Land; a portion of the earth's surface extending downward to the center of the earth and upward into space, including all things permanently attached thereto, whether by nature or by a person; any and every interest in land.

Real estate broker Any person, partnership, association or corporation who sells (or offers to sell), buys (or offers to buy) or negotiates the purchase, sale or exchange of real estate or who leases (or offers to lease) or rents (or offers to rent) any real estate or the improvements thereon for others for a compensation or valuable consideration. A real estate broker may not conduct business without a real estate broker's license.

Real estate investment syndicate *See* Syndicate.

Real estate investment trust (REIT) Trust ownership of real estate by a group of at least 100 individuals who purchase certificates of ownership in the trust, which in turn invests the money in real property and distributes the profits back to the investors free of corporate income tax.

Real estate license law State laws enacted to protect the public from fraud, dishonesty and incompetence in the purchase and sale of real estate.

Real estate mortgage investment conduit (REMIC) A tax entity that issues multiple classes of investor interests (securities) backed by a pool of mortgages.

Real property The earth's surface extending downward to the center of the earth and upward into space, including all things permanently attached to it by nature or by people, as well as the interests, benefits and rights inherent in real estate ownership.

REALTOR® A registered trademark term reserved for the sole use of active members of local REALTOR® boards affiliated with the National Association of REALTORS®.

Reconciliation The final step in the appraisal process, in which the appraiser reconciles the estimates of value received from the market data, cost and income approaches to arrive at a final estimate of market value for the subject property.

Recording The act of entering or recording documents affecting or conveying interests in real estate in the recorder's office established in each county. Until it is recorded, a deed or mortgage generally is not effective against subsequent purchasers or mortgagees.

Recovery fund A fund established in some states from real estate license revenues to cover claims of aggrieved parties who have suffered monetary damage through the actions of a real estate licensee.

Rectangular survey system A system established in 1785 by the federal government, providing for surveying and describing land by reference to principal meridians and base lines.

Redemption The buying back of real estate sold in a tax sale. The defaulted owner is said to have the right of redemption.

Redemption period A period of time established by state law during which a property owner has the right to redeem his or her real estate from a foreclosure or tax sale by paying the sales price, interest and costs. Many states do not have mortgage redemption laws.

Redlining The illegal practice of a lending institution denying loans or restricting their number for certain areas of a community.

Regression An appraisal principle that states that, between dissimilar properties, the value of the better property is adversely affected by the presence of the lesser-quality property.

Regulation Z Implements the Truth-in-Lending Act requiring credit institutions to inform borrowers of the true cost of obtaining credit.

Remainder The remnant of an estate that has been conveyed to take effect and be enjoyed after the termination of a prior estate, such as when an owner conveys a life estate to one party and the remainder to another.

Renegotiable rate mortgage A mortgage loan in which the interest rate may increase or decrease at specified intervals, within certain limits based upon an economic indicator.

Rent A fixed, periodic payment made by a tenant of a property to the owner for possession and use, usually by prior agreement of the parties.

Rent schedule A statement of proposed rental rates, determined by the owner or the property manager or both, based on a building's estimated expenses, market supply and demand, and the owner's long-range goals for the property.

Replacement cost The construction cost at current prices of a property that is not necessarily an exact duplicate of the subject property but serves the same purpose or function as the original.

Reproduction cost The construction cost at current prices of an exact duplicate of the subject property.

Restriction A limitation on the use of real property, generally originated by the owner or subdivider in a deed.

Reversion The remnant of an estate that the grantor holds after he or she has granted a life estate to another person—the estate will return, or revert, to the grantor; also called a *reverter.*

Reversionary interest *See* Reversion.

Reversionary right An owner's right to regain possession of leased property upon termination of the lease agreement.

Right of survivorship *See* Joint tenancy.

Riparian rights An owner's rights in land that borders on or includes a stream, river or lake. These rights include access to and use of the water.

Risk management Evaluation and selection of appropriate property and other insurance.

Sale and leaseback A transaction in which an owner sells his or her improved property and, as part of the same transaction, signs a long-term lease to remain in possession of the premises.

Sales contract A contract containing the complete terms of the agreement between buyer and seller for the sale of a particular parcel or parcels of real estate.

Salesperson A person who performs real estate activities while employed by or associated with a licensed real estate broker.

Satisfaction A document acknowledging the payment of a debt.

Secondary mortgage market A market for the purchase and sale of existing mortgages, designed to provide greater liquidity for mortgagees; also called the *secondary money market*. Mortgages are first originated in the *primary mortgage market*.

Section A portion of a township under the rectangular survey (government survey) system. A township is divided into 36 sections, numbered 1 to 36. A section is a square with mile-long sides and an area of one square mile, or 640 acres.

Security deposit A payment by a tenant, held by the landlord during the lease term and kept (wholly or partially) on default or destruction of the premises by the tenant.

Selling broker *See* Listing broker.

Separate property Under community property law, property owned solely by either spouse before the marriage, acquired by gift or inheritance after the marriage or purchased with separate funds after the marriage.

Servient tenement Land on which an easement exists in favor of an adjacent property (called a dominant estate); also called *servient estate*.

Setback The amount of space local zoning regulations require between a lot line and a building line.

Severalty Ownership of real property by one person only, also called *sole ownership*.

Severance Changing an item of real estate to personal property by detaching it from the land; for example, cutting down a tree.

Shared appreciation mortgage A mortgage loan in which the lender, in exchange for a loan with a favorable interest rate, participates in the profits (if any) the mortgagor receives when the property is eventually sold.

Situs The personal preference of people for one area over another, not necessarily based on objective facts and knowledge.

Sole ownership *See* Severalty.

Special agent One who is authorized by a principal to perform a single act or transaction; a real estate broker is usually a special agent authorized to find a ready, willing and able buyer for a particular property.

Special assessment A tax or levy customarily imposed against only those specific parcels of real estate that will benefit from a proposed public improvement such as a street or sewer.

Special warranty deed A deed in which the grantor warrants, or guarantees, the title only against defects arising during the period of his or her tenure and ownership of the property and not against defects existing before that time, generally using the language, "by, through or under the grantor but not otherwise."

Specific lien A lien affecting or attaching only to a certain, specific parcel of land or piece of property.

Specific performance suit A legal action brought in a court of equity in special cases to compel a party to carry out the terms of a contract. The basis for an equity court's jurisdiction in breach of a real estate contract is the fact that land is unique and therefore mere legal damages would not adequately compensate the buyer for the seller's breach.

Spot zoning A change in a local zoning ordinance to permit a particular use that is inconsistent with the area's zoning classification. Spot zoning is not favored in the law.

Statute of frauds That part of a state law that requires certain instruments, such as deeds, real estate sales contracts and certain leases, to be in writing in order to be legally enforceable.

Statute of limitations That law pertaining to the period of time within which certain actions must be brought to court.

Statutory lien A lien imposed on property by statute—a tax lien, for example—in contrast to an *equitable* lien, which arises out of common law.

Steering The illegal practice of channeling home seekers to particular areas to maintain the homogeneity of an area or to change the character of an area in order to create a speculative situation.

Straight-line method A method of calculating depreciation for tax purposes, computed by dividing the adjusted basis of a property by the estimated number of years of remaining useful life.

Subcontractor *See* General contractor.

Subdivider One who buys undeveloped land, divides it into smaller, usable lots and sells the lots to potential users (often *developers*).

Subdivision A tract of land divided by the owner, known as the *subdivider,* into blocks, building lots and streets according to a recorded subdivision plat, which must comply with local ordinances and regulations.

"Subject to" clause A clause in a deed specifying exceptions and reservations affecting the title.

Subletting The leasing of premises by a lessee to a third party for part of the lessee's remaining term. *See also* Assignment.

Subordination Relegation to a lesser position, usually in respect to a right or security.

Subordination agreement A written agreement between holders of liens on a property that changes the priority of mortgage, judgment and other liens under certain circumstances.

Subrogation The substitution of one creditor for another, with the substituted person succeeding to the legal rights and claims of the original claimant. Subrogation is used by title insurers to acquire from the injured party rights to sue in order to recover any claims they have paid.

Substitution An appraisal principle that states that the maximum value of a property tends to be set by the cost of purchasing an equally desirable and valuable substitute property, assuming that no costly delay is encountered in making the substitution.

Subsurface rights Ownership rights in a parcel of real estate to the water, minerals, gas, oil and so forth that lie beneath the surface of the property.

Suit for possession A court suit initiated by a landlord to evict a tenant from leased premises after the tenant has breached one of the terms of the lease or has held possession of the property after the lease's expiration.

Suit to quiet title A court action intended to establish or settle the title to a particular property, especially when there is a cloud on the title.

Supply The amount of goods available in the market to be sold at a given price. The term is often coupled with *demand*.

Surety bond An agreement by an insurance or bonding company to be responsible for certain possible defaults, debts or obligations contracted for by an insured party; in essence, a policy insuring one's personal and/or financial integrity. In the real estate business, a surety bond is generally used to ensure that a particular project will be completed at a certain date or that a contract will be performed as stated.

Surface rights Ownership rights in a parcel of real estate that are limited to the surface of the property and do not include the air above it (*air rights*) or the minerals below the surface (*subsurface rights*).

Survey The process by which boundaries are measured and land areas are determined; the on-site measurement of lot lines, dimensions and position of a house on a lot, including the determination of any existing encroachments or easements.

Syndicate A combination of people or firms formed to accomplish a business venture of mutual interest by pooling resources. In a *real estate investment syndicate,* the parties own and/or develop property, with the main profit generally arising from the sale of the property.

Tacking Adding or combining successive periods of continuous occupation of real property by adverse possessors. This concept enables someone who has not been in possession for the entire statutory period to establish a claim of adverse possession.

Taxation The process by which a government or municipal quasi-public body raises monies to fund its operation.

Tax deed An instrument, similar to a certificate of sale, given to a purchaser at a tax sale. *See also* Certificate of sale.

Tax lien A charge against property created by operation of law. Tax liens and assessments take priority over all other liens.

Tax levy *See* Levy.

Tax rate The rate at which real property is taxed in a tax district or county. For example, in a certain county, real property may be taxed at a rate of .056 cents per dollar of assessed valuation.

Tax sale A court-ordered sale of real property to raise money to cover delinquent taxes.

Tax shelter A (legal) means by which an investor may reduce or defer payment of part of his or her federal or state income tax.

Tenancy at sufferance The tenancy of a lessee who lawfully comes into possession of a landlord's real estate but who continues to occupy the premises improperly after his or her lease rights have expired.

Tenancy at will An estate that gives the lessee the right to possession until the estate is terminated by either party; the term of this estate is indefinite.

Tenancy by the entirety Under Pennsylvania law, a tenant by the entireties receives nothing upon the death of the other spouse. Each spouse has full ownership of the property; neither one acting alone can convey or encumber the property. There is no legal event that occurs at the death of one spouse because the remaining spouse already owns the property; the ownership of the deceased party is removed.

Tenancy in common A form of co-ownership by which each owner holds an undivided interest in real property as if he or she were sole owner. Each individual owner has the right to partition.

Tenant One who holds or possesses lands or tenements by any kind of right or title.

Testate Having made and left a valid will.

Time is of the essence A phrase in a contract that requires the performance of a certain act within a stated period of time.

Time-share Ownership interest that may include an estate interest in property and which allows use of the property for a fixed or variable time period.

Title 1. The right to or ownership of land. 2. The evidence of ownership of land.

Title insurance A policy insuring the owner or mortgagee against loss by reason of defects in the title to a parcel of real estate, other than encumbrances, defects and matters specifically excluded by the policy.

Title theory Some states' interpretation of a mortgage to mean that the lender is the owner of mortgaged land. Upon full payment of the mortgage debt, the borrower becomes the landowner.

Torrens system A method of evidencing title by registration with the proper public authority, generally called the registrar. Named for its founder, Sir Robert Torrens.

Township The principal unit of the rectangular survey (government survey) system. A township is a square with six-mile sides and an area of 36 square miles.

Township line Lines running at six-mile intervals parallel to the base lines in the rectangular survey (government survey) system.

Trade fixtures Articles installed by a tenant under the terms of a lease and removable by the tenant before the lease expires. These remain personal property and are not true fixtures.

Transfer tax Tax stamps required to be affixed to a deed by state and/or local law.

Trust A fiduciary arrangement whereby property is conveyed to a person or institution, called a *trustee,* to be held and administered on behalf of another person, called a *beneficiary.* The one who conveys the trust is called the *trustor.*

Trust account *See* Commingling.

Trust deed An instrument used to create a mortgage lien by which the mortgagor conveys his or her title to a trustee, who holds it as security for the benefit of the note holder (the lender); also called a *deed of trust.*

Trustee *See* Trust.

Trustee's deed A deed executed by a trustee conveying land held in a trust.

Undivided interest *See* Tenancy in common.

Unenforceable contract A contract that has all the elements of a valid contract yet neither party can sue the other to force performance of it. For example, an unsigned contract is generally unenforceable.

Uniform Commercial Code A codification of commercial law, adopted in most states, that attempts to make uniform all laws relating to commercial transactions, including chattel mortgages and bulk transfers. Security interests in chattels are created by an instrument known as a *security agreement*. To give notice of the security interest, a *financing statement* must be recorded. Article 6 of the code regulates *bulk transfers*—the sale of a business as a whole, including all fixtures, chattels, and merchandise.

Unilateral contract A one-sided contract wherein one party makes a promise in order to induce a second party to do something. The second party is not legally bound to perform; however, if the second party does comply, the first party is obligated to keep the promise.

Unity of ownership The four unities that are traditionally needed to create a joint tenancy—unity of title, time, interest and possession.

Universal agent One who is empowered by a principal to represent him or her in all matters that can be delegated.

Urban renewal The acquisition of run-down city areas for purposes of redevelopment.

Useful life In real estate investment, the number of years a property will be useful to the investors.

Usury Charging interest at a higher rate than the maximum rate established by state law.

Valid contract A contract that complies with all the essentials of a contract and is binding and enforceable on all parties to it.

VA loan A mortgage loan on approved property made to a qualified veteran by an authorized lender and guaranteed by the Veterans Administration in order to limit the lender's possible loss.

Value The power of a good or service to command other goods in exchange for the present worth of future rights to its income or amenities.

Variable rate mortgage A mortgage loan in which the interest rate may increase or decrease at specified intervals within certain limits, based upon an economic indicator.

Variance Permission obtained from zoning authorities to build a structure or conduct a use that is expressly prohibited by the current zoning laws; an exception from the zoning ordinances.

Vendee A buyer.

Vendor A seller.

Voidable contract A contract that seems to be valid on the surface but may be rejected or disaffirmed by one or both of the parties.

Void contract A contract that has no legal force or effect because it does not meet the essential elements of a contract.

Voluntary transfer *See* Alienation.

Waste An improper use or an abuse of a property by a possessor who holds less than fee ownership, such as a tenant, life tenant, mortgagor or vendee. Such waste generally impairs the value of the land or the interest of the person holding the title or the reversionary rights.

Will A written document, properly witnessed, providing for the transfer of title to property owned by the deceased, called the *testator.*

Wraparound mortgage A method of refinancing in which the new mortgage is placed in a secondary, or subordinate, position; the new mortgage includes both the unpaid principal balance of the first mortgage and whatever additional sums are advanced by the lender. In essence, it is an additional mortgage in which another lender refinances a borrower by lending an amount over the existing first mortgage amount without disturbing the existence of the first mortgage.

Year-to-year tenancy A periodic tenancy in which rent is collected yearly.

Zoning ordinance An exercise of police power by a municipality to regulate and control the character and use of property.

Answer Key

Following are the correct answers to the review questions included in each chapter of the text. In parentheses following the correct answers are references to the pages where the question topics are discussed or explained. If you have answered a question incorrectly, be sure to go back to the page or pages noted and restudy the material until you understand the correct answer.

Chapter 1

1. c (5)
2. d (7)
3. c (4)
4. d (5)
5. d (5)
6. d (5)
7. a (5)
8. a (5)
9. b (3)
10. c (3)
11. d (3, 4)
12. c (6)
13. b (5)
14. d (7)
15. b (5)
16. c (5–6)

Chapter 2

1. b (19)
2. d (15–16)
3. b (17)
4. c (15–16)
5. a (18)
6. c (14)
7. b (17)
8. b (14)
9. c (18)
10. d (13)
11. a (17)
12. b (17)
13. c (17)
14. d (14)
15. c (14)
16. a (16)
17. d (18)
18. d (20)
19. d (20–21)
20. c (16, 18)
21. d (21)

Chapter 3

1. a (31)
2. a (28–29)
3. c (29)
4. d (29)
5. b (27)
6. d (31–32)
7. d (28)
8. c (30)
9. c (31–32)
10. d (27–28)
11. b (31–32)
12. d (28–29)
13. a (31)
14. b (27–28)
15. b (29)

Chapter 4

1. b (40)
2. a (37)
3. c (39)
4. b (40)
5. b (41)
6. b (41)
7. d (40)
8. b (44)
9. d (38)
10. d (39–40)
11. c (38)
12. a (41)
13. b (42–43)
14. b (37)
15. a (44)
16. d (39)

Chapter 5

1. b (49)
2. d (56)
3. a (49)
4. b (56)
5. a (54)
6. b (49)
7. c (52)
8. c (49)
9. c (56)
10. d (54)
11. d (58)
12. c (58)
13. c (58)
14. d (58)

Chapter 6

1. d (67)
2. b (63)
3. d (69, 71)
4. c (70)
5. a (64)
6. b (69)
7. b (67)
8. c (66)
9. d (69)
10. b (67)
11. d (70)
12. a (66–67)
13. a (68)
14. a (66)
15. c (71)
16. a (64)
17. c (73–74)
18. c (63)

Chapter 7

1. d (87)
2. d (79–80)
3. c (81–82)
4. c (82-83)
5. b (90)
6. b (79)
7. d (80)
8. c (90)

9. a (84)
10. d (81, 83)
11. b (80)
12. d (86–87)
13. b (86)
14. d (87)
15. d (80)
16. b (88–89)
17. a (84)
18. c (84)
19. a (82–83)
20. b (88)
21. c (82)
22. a (89)
23. a (90)

Chapter 8

1. d (97–98)
2. c (97)
3. c (113)
4. c (112–13)
5. d (111)
6. a (112)
7. c (97)
8. c (113)
9. a (98)
10. c (110)
11. c (108)
12. d (99)
13. d (99, 106)
14. b (111)
15. b (112)
16. a (99)
17. d (110–11)
18. d (111)
19. b (108)
20. b (108)

Chapter 9

1. d (119)
2. b (130)
3. c (120)
4. a (130)
5. d (119–20)
6. d (124)
7. c (121–22)
8. b (123)
9. c (121)
10. b (120)
11. b (121)
12. c (122)

13. a (130)
14. d (133)
15. c (123)
16. d (131)
17. c (123–24)
18. b (125)
19. d (125)
20. d (131)
21. c (132–33)
22. d (133)
23. b (123)

Chapter 10

1. d (141, 150)
2. a (141, 144)
3. d (142)
4. b (145, 150–51)
5. d (153–54)
6. c (143)
7. b (153)
8. a (144)
9. b (144–45)
10. b (155)
11. a (150)
12. d (150–51)
13. c (146)
14. a (154)
15. c (154)
16. d (145)
17. b (146)
18. a (151)
19. c (151)
20. d (151–52)
21. b (153)
22. b (154)
23. d (146)
24. c (150)
25. a (144)

Chapter 11

1. d (161)
2. d (162, 167–68)
3. c (168)
4. b (162)
5. b (166)
6. a (164)
7. c (163)
8. c (165)
9. c (163)
10. c (167)
11. b (161)

12. a (167, 168)
13. c (161)
14. b (162)
15. a (166–67)
16. a (162, 166)
17. b (164)
18. c (161–62)
19. d (169)
20. a (168–69)

Chapter 12

1. d (178)
2. c (179)
3. b (176)
4. a (176)
5. b (177–78)
6. a (178)
7. c (175–76)
8. b (179)
9. c (175)
10. c (178)
11. b (175–76)
12. a (175–76)
13. d (180)
14. a (178)
15. c (178)
16. d (175)
17. c (179)
18. b (180)
19. d (177)
20. a (177)
21. a (177)

Chapter 13

1. c (188–89)
2. a (192–93)
3. b (207)
4. c (206)
5. b (206)
6. c (204)
7. d (206–7)
8. a (195)
9. d (192)
10. a (203)
11. c (193–95)
12. d (202)

Chapter 14

1. a (223)
2. a (226)

3. d (220)
4. c (225)
5. c (224–25)
6. b (223)
7. b (227)
8. b (217)
9. a (216)
10. d (219)
11. c (216)
12. d (221)
13. d (224–25)
14. d (220, 223)
15. d (214–15)
16. b (214)
17. c (215)
18. b (216)
19. a (217)
20. b (219–20)
21. a (215)
22. b (217)
23. c (214–15)
24. c (219, 222)
25. b (225)

Chapter 15

1. d (233–34)
2. a (237–38)
3. a (234)
4. c (238–39)
5. d (236–37)
6. d (236)
7. c (235)
8. d (235)
9. d (235)
10. b (236)
11. d (236)
12. d (235)

Chapter 16

1. d (246–47)
2. d (248)
3. b (247)
4. d (247)
5. d (250–51)
6. a (244)
7. c (245–47)
8. c (247)
9. b (251–52)
10. a (252)
11. c (248)
12. c (250)

13. b (243)
14. d (247)
15. b (247)
16. d (249)
17. c (249)
18. a (248)
19. b (249)
20. d (249)

Chapter 17

1. d (259–60)
2. a (259–60)
3. d (258)
4. b (265)
5. b (265)
6. c (257)
7. b (263)
8. a (258)
9. a (258)
10. b (258)
11. b (257)
12. a (258)
13. c (262)
14. b (258)
15. d (263–64)
16. d (257)
17. c (267–68)
18. a (261)
19. c (262)

Chapter 18

1. b (273)
2. c (273–74)
3. d (276–77)
4. a (273)
5. d (274)
6. c (275)
7. c (276–77)
8. c (275)
9. d (275)
10. a (276)
11. d (277–78)
12. d (275–77)
13. c (276)
14. d (274)
15. d (276–77)

Chapter 19

1. a (290)
2. d (287)
3. b (290)

4. a (287–88)
5. d (290)
6. a (290)
7. d (294)
8. c (297)
9. b (293)
10. d (296)
11. c (295)
12. c (295)
13. a (287)
14. b (295)
15. c (294)
16. b (290–91)
17. d (291)
18. b (296)
19. a (294)
20. c (296)
21. b (294)

Chapter 20

1. d (314)
2. c (307, 314)
3. c (315–16)
4. d (314)
5. d (316)
6. b (310)
7. a (308–9)
8. c (307)
9. c (311)
10. b (317)
11. d (317–18)
12. b (310)
13. d (309)

Chapter 21

1. c (331)
2. d (334–36)
3. a (335)
4. d (333)
5. b (328, 329)
6. d (323)
7. c (331)
8. c (325)
9. a (331)
10. c (335)
11. b (335)
12. b (335)
13. c (333)
14. b (331)
15. c (335)
16. d (335)

17. c (333)
18. c (325)
19. d (325)
20. c (331)

Chapter 22

1. b (353)
2. d (350–51)
3. d (350–51)
4. c (353)
5. c (347)
6. c (351)
7. d (353)
8. d (350)
9. a (349)
10. d (350)
11. c (353)
12. d (351)

13. c (354)
14. c (351–52)

Chapter 23

1. c (362–63)
2. d (366)
3. b (366)
4. d (363–64)
5. a (361)
6. d (368)
7. b (360)
8. a (360)
9. c (361–62)
10. a (363)
11. d (363–64)
12. d (362–63)
13. a (360)
14. b (362)

15. a (362)
16. b (369)

Chapter 24

1. c (376)
2. a (384)
3. c (392–96)
4. d (384)
5. d (378)
6. b (386)
7. d (394)
8. a (377)
9. a (378–80)
10. d (380–81)
11. c (376, 392)
12. b (391)

Mathematics Review Answer Key

1. $79,500 sale price × 6½% commission =
$79,500 × .065 = $5,167.50, Happy Valley's commission
$5,167.50 × 30% or $5,167.50 × .30 = $1,550.25, listing
salesperson's commission

b. $1,550.25

2.

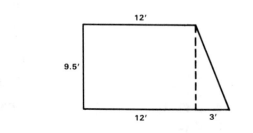

12′ × 9.5′ = 114 square feet, area of rectangle
½ (3′ × 9.5′) = ½ (28.5) = 14.25 square feet, area of triangle
114 + 14.25 = 128.25 square feet
To convert square feet to square yards divide by 9:
128.25 ÷ 9 = 14.25 square yards
$16.95 carpet + $2.50 installation = $19.45 cost per square yard
$19.45 × 14.25 square yards = $277.1625 rounded to $277.16

c. $277.16

3. $30,000 Peters + $35,000 Gamble + $35,000 Clooney = $100,000
$125,000–$100,000 = $25,000, Considine's contribution
$\frac{\text{part}}{\text{total}}$ = percent
$25,000 ÷ $125,000 = .20 or 20%

a. 20%

4. $391.42 × 12 = $4,697.04, annual interest

$$\frac{\text{part}}{\text{percent}} = \text{total}$$

$4,697.04 ÷ 11½% or $4,697.04 ÷ .115 = $40,843.826
rounded to $40,843.83

b. $40,843.83

5. $98,500 × 5% = $98,500 × .05 = $4,925, annual increase in value
$98,500 + $4,925 = $103,425, current market value

a. $103,425

6. $95,000 × 60% = $95,000 × .60 = $57,000, assessed value
Divide by 100 because tax rate is stated per hundred dollars:
$57,000 ÷ 100 = $570
$570 × $2.85 = $1,624.50, annual taxes

d. $1,624.50

7.

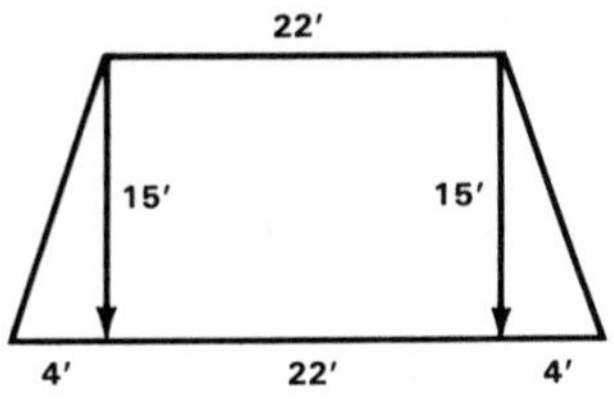

22′ × 15′ = 330 square feet, area of rectangle
½ (4′ × 15′) = ½ (60) = 30 square feet, area of each triangle
30 × 2 = 60 square feet, area of two triangles
330 + 60 = 390 square feet, surface area to be paved
6″ deep = ½ foot
390 × ½ = 195 cubic feet, cement needed for patio

d. 195 cubic feet

8. $4,175–$1,000 salary = $3,175 commission on sales
$3,175 ÷ 2.5% = $3,175 ÷ .025 = $127,000, value of property sold

b. $127,000

9. two sides of 95′ plus one side of 42′6″
95′ × 2 = 190 feet
42′6″ = 42.5 feet
190 + 42.5 = 232.5 linear feet
232.5 × $6.95 = $1,615.875 rounded to $1,615.88

c. $1,615.88

10. $4,500 × 12 = $54,000 annual rental
$54,000 ÷ 8% = $54,000 ÷ .08 = $675,000, original cost of property

a. $675,000

11. $1,340 ÷ 12 months = $111.667/month
    $111.667 ÷ 30 days = $3.722/day
    $111.667 × 2 months = $223.334
    $3.722 × 15 days = $55.83
    $223.334 + $55.83 = $279.164 rounded to $279.16

b. $279.16

12. $58,200 × 12% = $58,200 × .12 = $6,984
    $6,984 ÷ 12 months = $582/month
    $582 ÷ 30 days = $19.40/day
    30-day month–11 days = 19 days
    $19.40 × 19 days = $368.60

d. $368.60

13. $975 ÷ 12 months = $81.25/month
    $81.25 ÷ 30 days = $2.708
    $81.25 × 2 months = $162.500
    $2.708 × 4 days = $10.832
    $162.500 + $10.832 = $173.332 rounded to $173.33

a. $173.33

14. $61,550 × 13% = $61,550 × .13 = $8,001.500
    $8,001.500 ÷ 12 months = $666.792/month
    $666.792 ÷ 30 days = $22.226/day
    $22.226 × 22 days = $488.972 rounded to $488.97

b. $488.97

15. 43,560 sq. ft./acre × 100 acres = 4,356,000 sq. ft.
    4,356,000 total sq. ft. × 1/8 = 544,500 sq. ft. for streets
    4,356,000–544,500 = 3,811,500 sq. ft. for lots
    3,811,500 sq. ft. ÷ 140 lots = 27,225 sq. ft./lot

c. 27,225

16. $14,100 commission ÷ 6% commission rate =
    $14,100 ÷ .06 = $235,000 sales price

a. $235,000

Index

Get the **Performance Advantage** on the job...*in the classroom*

	Order Number	Real Estate Principles and Exam Prep	Qty.	Total Price	Amount
1.	1510-01	Modern Real Estate Practice, 12th edition	_____	$34.95	_____
2.	1510-02	Study Guide for Modern Real Estate Practice, 12th edition	_____	$13.95	_____
3.	1961-01	Language of Real Estate, 3rd edition	_____	$28.95	_____
4.	1610-07	Real Estate Math, 4th edition	_____	$15.95	_____
5.	1512-10	Mastering Real Estate Mathematics, 5th edition	_____	$25.95	_____
6.	1970-04	Questions & Answers To Help You Pass the Real Estate Exam, 3rd edition	_____	$21.95	_____
7.	1970-06	Real Estate Exam Guide: ASI, 2nd edition	_____	$21.95	_____

Advanced Study/Specialty Areas

8.	1560-08	Agency Relationships in Real Estate	_____	$25.95	_____
9.	1978-03	Buyer Agency: Your Competitive Edge in Real Estate	_____	$25.95	_____
10.	1557-10	Essentials of Real Estate Finance, 5th edition	_____	$38.95	_____
11.	1559-01	Essentials of Real Estate Investment, 4th edition	_____	$38.95	_____
12.	5608-50	Fast Start in Property Management	_____	$19.95	_____
13.	1556-10	Fundamentals of Real Estate Appraisal, 5th edition	_____	$38.95	_____
14.	1556-14	How to Use the Uniform Residential Appraisal Report	_____	$24.95	_____
15.	1556-15	Introduction to Income Property Appraisal	_____	$34.95	_____
16.	1556-11	Language of Real Estate Appraisal	_____	$21.95	_____
17.	1557-15	Modern Residential Financing Methods, 2nd edition	_____	$19.95	_____
18.	1556-12	Questions & Answers to Help You Pass the Appraisal Certification Exams	_____	$26.95	_____
19.	1551-10	Property Management, 4th edition	_____	$35.95	_____
20.	4105-10	The Property Manager's Handbook: Business Planning for the Professional	_____	$32.95	_____
21.	1560-01	Real Estate Law, 2nd edition	_____	$38.95	_____

Sales & Marketing/Professional Development

22.	1913-04	Close for Success	_____	$18.95	_____
23.	1927-03	Fast Start in Real Estate	_____	$17.95	_____
24.	1913-01	List for Success	_____	$18.95	_____
25.	1922-06	Negotiating Commercial Real Estate Leases	_____	$34.95	_____
26.	1913-11	Phone Power	_____	$19.95	_____
27.	1926-03	Power Real Estate Letters	_____	$29.95	_____
28.	1907-01	Power Real Estate Listing, 2nd edition	_____	$18.95	_____
29.	1907-04	Power Real Estate Negotiation	_____	$19.95	_____
30.	1907-02	Power Real Estate Selling, 2nd edition	_____	$18.95	_____
31.	1965-01	Real Estate Brokerage: A Success Guide, 2nd edition	_____	$35.95	_____
32.	1913-07	Real Estate Prospecting: Strategies for Farming Your Market	_____	$24.95	_____
33.	1913-13	The Real Estate Sales Survival Kit	_____	$24.95	_____
34.	1978-02	Recruiting Revolution in Real Estate	_____	$34.95	_____
35.	1926-02	Simplified Classifieds, 2nd edition	_____	$29.95	_____
36.	1903-31	Sold! The Professional's Guide to Real Estate Auctions	_____	$32.95	_____
37.	1927-04	Staying on Top in Real Estate	_____	$18.95	_____
38.	2703-11	Time Out: Time Management Strategies for the Real Estate Professional	_____	$19.95	_____
39.	1909-04	Winning in Commercial Real Estate Sales	_____	$24.95	_____

NEW! Audio Tapes

40.	1926-06	Power Real Estate Listing	_____	$19.95	_____
41.	1926-05	Power Real Estate Selling	_____	$19.95	_____
42.	1926-04	Staying on Top in Real Estate	_____	$14.95	_____

Book total _____

Tax _____

Shipping and Handling _____

Less $1.00 off if you fax order _____

Total Amount _____

Shipping/Handling Charges:
$0-24.99 . . . . $4
$25-49.99 . . . . $5
$50-99.99 . . . . $6
$100-249.99 . . . . $8

Orders shipped to the following states must include applicable sales tax:

CA, CO, FL, IL, MI, MN, NY, PA, TX & WI

Prices are subject to change without notice.

810081

Real Estate Education Company

520 North Dearborn Street, Chicago, Illinois 60610-4354

YOUR SATISFACTION IS GUARANTEED!

All books come with a 30 day money-back guarantee. If you are not completely satisfied, simply return your books and your money will be refunded in full.

☐ Please send me the Real Estate Education Company catalog featuring your full list of titles.

Prices are subject to change without notice.
Also available in your local bookstore.

Fill out form and mail today!

Or Save $1.00 when you order by Fax: 312-836-1021.

Name_____

Address_____

City/State/Zip_____

Telephone (_____) _____

Payment must accompany all orders (check one):

☐ Check or money order (payable to Dearborn Financial Publishing, Inc., 520 North Dearborn Street, Chicago, Illinois 60610-4354)

☐ Charge to my credit card:

   ☐ VISA   ☐ MasterCard

Account No. _____ Exp. Date_____

Signature _____

(All charge orders must be signed.)   **8-91**

Return Address:

_____

_____

_____

BUSINESS REPLY MAIL

FIRST CLASS   PERMIT NO. 88176   CHICAGO, IL

POSTAGE WILL BE PAID BY ADDRESSEE:

Real Estate Education Company

Order Department
520 North Dearborn Street
Chicago, Illinois 60610-9857

NO POSTAGE
NECESSARY
IF MAILED
IN THE
UNITED STATES

IMPORTANT · PLEASE FOLD OVER · PLEASE TAPE BEFORE MAILING

NOTE: This page, when folded over and taped, becomes a postage-free envelope, which has been approved by the United States Postal Service. It is provided for your convenience.

IMPORTANT · PLEASE FOLD OVER · PLEASE TAPE BEFORE MAILING